T0142893

IFIP Advances in Information and Communication Technology

618

Editor-in-Chief

Kai Rannenberg, Goethe University Frankfurt, Germany

IFIP – The International Federation for Information Processing

IFIP was founded in 1960 under the auspices of UNESCO, following the first World Computer Congress held in Paris the previous year. A federation for societies working in information processing, IFIP's aim is two-fold: to support information processing in the countries of its members and to encourage technology transfer to developing nations. As its mission statement clearly states:

> *IFIP is the global non-profit federation of societies of ICT professionals that aims at achieving a worldwide professional and socially responsible development and application of information and communication technologies.*

IFIP is a non-profit-making organization, run almost solely by 2500 volunteers. It operates through a number of technical committees and working groups, which organize events and publications. IFIP's events range from large international open conferences to working conferences and local seminars.

The flagship event is the IFIP World Computer Congress, at which both invited and contributed papers are presented. Contributed papers are rigorously refereed and the rejection rate is high.

As with the Congress, participation in the open conferences is open to all and papers may be invited or submitted. Again, submitted papers are stringently refereed.

The working conferences are structured differently. They are usually run by a working group and attendance is generally smaller and occasionally by invitation only. Their purpose is to create an atmosphere conducive to innovation and development. Refereeing is also rigorous and papers are subjected to extensive group discussion.

Publications arising from IFIP events vary. The papers presented at the IFIP World Computer Congress and at open conferences are published as conference proceedings, while the results of the working conferences are often published as collections of selected and edited papers.

IFIP distinguishes three types of institutional membership: Country Representative Members, Members at Large, and Associate Members. The type of organization that can apply for membership is a wide variety and includes national or international societies of individual computer scientists/ICT professionals, associations or federations of such societies, government institutions/government related organizations, national or international research institutes or consortia, universities, academies of sciences, companies, national or international associations or federations of companies.

More information about this series at http://www.springer.com/series/6102

Sujeet K. Sharma · Yogesh K. Dwivedi ·
Bhimaraya Metri · Nripendra P. Rana (Eds.)

Re-imagining Diffusion and Adoption of Information Technology and Systems: A Continuing Conversation

IFIP WG 8.6 International Conference
on Transfer and Diffusion of IT, TDIT 2020
Tiruchirappalli, India, December 18–19, 2020
Proceedings, Part II

Springer

Editors
Sujeet K. Sharma
Indian Institute of Management
Tiruchirappalli
Tiruchirappalli, India

Bhimaraya Metri
Indian Institute of Management Nagpur
Nagpur, India

Yogesh K. Dwivedi
Swansea University
Swansea, UK

Nripendra P. Rana
University of Bradford
Bradford, UK

ISSN 1868-4238   ISSN 1868-422X (electronic)
IFIP Advances in Information and Communication Technology
ISBN 978-3-030-64863-3   ISBN 978-3-030-64861-9 (eBook)
https://doi.org/10.1007/978-3-030-64861-9

This Springer imprint is published by the registered company Springer Nature Switzerland AG
The registered company address is: Gewerbestrasse 11, 6330 Cham, Switzerland

Preface

The IFIP Working Group (WG 8.6) was established in the early '90s "to foster understanding and improve research in practice, methods, and techniques in the transfer and diffusion of information technology within systems that are developed, and in the development process[1]." The 2020 IFIP WG 8.6 conference on the theme "Re-Imagining Diffusion of Information Technology and Systems: A Continuing Conversation" was held at Tiruchirappalli, India, and was hosted by the Indian Institute of Management (IIM) Tiruchirappalli during December 18–19, 2020. We are grateful to IIM Tiruchirappalli for providing all required facilities and the IFIP WG 8.6 for mentoring the successful organization of the conference. The proceedings volumes of this conference focus on the re-imagination of diffusion and adoption of emerging technologies.

Developments in blockchain, artificial intelligence, Internet of Things, social media, mobile computing and applications, agile systems development techniques, cloud computing, and business analytics have become central to the business and the cycle of innovation has sped up, platforms provide quick access to infrastructure, and information spreads on a 24-h cycle. These developments, in turn, have impacted the way both organizations and societies, engage with transfer and diffusion of information technology (IT) systems within and between organizations, in interactions with customers, and society in general. The question is no longer how to adopt and diffuse IT systems, but how to quickly assess and manage those that best serve the broader purposes of businesses and societies. In addition to the idea of adoption and diffusion of IT systems, IT teams in organizations and individuals are also working on how IT systems are contributing to the value creation in both organizations and society.

There is an innate need for understanding the diffusion and adoption of emerging information technologies and systems (i.e., artificial intelligence, blockchain, Fin-Tech applications, Internet of Things, social media), which are expected to have a substantial impact on future economic development of society, organizations, and individuals (Borus et al. 2020; Dwivedi et al. 2019ab; Hughes et al. 2019; Ismagilova et al. 2019; Janssen et al. 2019). A review of the role of information technologies, particularly over the past two decades, clearly shows the vital link between technology adoption and socio-economic development in many economies (Venkatesh et al. 2016; Williams et al. 2015). The Gartner report on "Top Strategic Technology" in 2019[2] lists trends including blockchain, artificial intelligence, autonomous things (robots, vehicles, drones, etc.) among others as the game changers that could revolutionize industries and their strategic models through 2023. These emerging technologies have great potential to contribute to organizational and societal reforms. Thus, in the recent past, the

---

[1] http://ifipwg86.wikidot.com/about-us.

[2] https://www.forbes.com/sites/peterhigh/2019/10/21/breaking-gartner-announces-top-10-strategic-technology-trends-for-2020/#47dbbb940744.

scholarly body is showing an increased interest in the understanding of adoption, usage, impact, and potential of aforementioned technologies mentioned on individuals, societies, and organizations.

This conference brought together scholars and practitioners from interdisciplinary areas for the enrichment of scholarly deliberations on the adoption, usage, impact, and potential of emerging technologies. The conference mainly focused on the papers that addressed questions related to the diffusion and adoption of emerging technologies. Besides, we were also open and committed to the broader theme of the IFIP WG 8.6. We created 15 tracks with 2 or 3 track chairs. We received 247 papers, including 214 through EasyChair account and 33 direct submissions through conference email. All submissions were double-blind reviewed by at least two knowledgeable reviewers. This process resulted in 122 full and short papers. The acceptance rate of the papers in the conference proceedings is about 49.4%. We are grateful to all track chairs who selected reviewers and provided constructive and timely comments to authors to revise and resubmit their manuscripts.

Due to a large number of submissions, the conference proceedings of IFIP WG 8.6 are divided into two volumes. There are seven sections in Volume I and eight sections in Volume II.

Volume one includes sections namely:

- Artificial Intelligence and Autonomous Systems
- Big Data and Analytics
- Blockchain
- Diffusion and Adoption Technology
- Emerging Technologies in e-Governance
- Emerging Technologies in Consumer Decision Making and Choice
- Fin-Tech Applications
- Healthcare Information Technology
- Internet of Things

    Volume two includes:

- Information Technology and Disaster Management
- Adoption of Mobile and Platform-Based Applications
- Smart Cities and Digital Government
- Social Media
- Diffusion of Information Technology and Systems (Conference Theme)

We sincerely thank all authors, reviewers, participants, Program Committee members, track chairs, advisory board, IFIP WG 8.6 officials, and IIM Tiruchirappalli staff who helped in making this conference a grand success.

October 2020

Sujeet K. Sharma
Yogesh K. Dwivedi
Bhimaraya Metri
Nripendra P. Rana

References

Brous, P., Janssen, M., and Herder, P., 2020. The dual effects of the Internet of Things (IoT): A systematic review of the benefits and risks of IoT adoption by organizations. *International Journal of Information Management*, 51, p.101952.

Dwivedi, Y. K., Rana, N. P., Jeyaraj, A., Clement, M., and Williams, M. D. 2019a. "Re-Examining the Unified Theory of Acceptance and Use of Technology (UTAUT): Towards a Revised Theoretical Model," *Information Systems Frontiers* (21:3), Springer New York LLC, pp. 719–734. (https://doi.org/10.1007/s10796-017-9774-y).

Dwivedi, Y.K., Hughes, L., Ismagilova, E., Aarts, G., Coombs, C., Crick, T., Duan, Y., Dwivedi, R., Edwards, J., Eirug, A., and Galanos, V., 2019b. Artificial Intelligence (AI): Multidisciplinary perspectives on emerging challenges, opportunities, and agenda for research, practice and policy. *International Journal of Information Management*, p.101994. DOI: https://doi.org/10.1016/j.ijinfomgt.2019.08.002

Hughes, L., Dwivedi, Y. K., Misra, S. K., Rana, N. P., Raghavan, V., and Akella, V. (2019). Blockchain research, practice and policy: Applications, benefits, limitations, emerging research themes and research agenda. *International Journal of Information Management*, 49, 114-129.

Ismagilova, E., Hughes, L., Dwivedi, Y. K., and Raman, K. R. (2019). Smart cities: Advances in research—An information systems perspective. *International Journal of Information Management*, 47, 88-100.

Janssen, M., Luthra, S., Mangla, S., Rana, N. P., and Dwivedi, Y. K. 2019. "Challenges for Adopting and Implementing IoT in Smart Cities: An Integrated MICMAC-ISM Approach," *Internet Research* (29:6), Emerald Group Publishing Ltd., pp. 1589–1616. (https://doi.org/10.1108/INTR-06-2018-0252).

Venkatesh, V., Thong, J. Y. L., and Xu, X. 2016. "Unified Theory of Acceptance and Use of Technology: A Synthesis and the Road Ahead," *Journal of the Association for Information Systems* (17:5), pp. 328–376. (https://doi.org/10.17705/1jais.00428).

Williams, M. D., Rana, N. P., and Dwivedi, Y. K. 2015. "The Unified Theory of Acceptance and Use of Technology (UTAUT): A Literature Review," *Journal of Enterprise Information Management*, Emerald Group Publishing Ltd., pp. 443–448. (https://doi.org/10.1108/JEIM-09-2014-0088).

Organization

Conference Committee

General Chairs

Viswanath Venkatesh	University of Arkansas, USA
Yogesh K. Dwivedi	Swansea University, UK
Deborah Bunker	The University of Sydney, Australia
Dave Wastell	University of Nottingham, UK

Conference Chairs

Sujeet K. Sharma	IIM Tiruchirappalli, India
Satish S. Maheswarappa	IIM Tiruchirappalli, India
Helle Zinner Henriksen	Copenhagen Business School, Denmark
Santosh K. Misra	CEO and Commissioner of e-Governance, Government of Tamil Nadu, India

Program Chairs

Sujeet K. Sharma	IIM Tiruchirappalli, India
Banita Lal	University of Bedfordshire, UK
Amany Elbanna	Royal Holloway, University of London, UK
Nripendra P. Rana	University of Bradford, UK
Moutusy Maity	IIM Lucknow, India
Jang Bahadur Singh	IIM Tiruchirappalli, India
Saji Mathew	IIT Madras, India

Organizing Chairs

Rajesh Chandwani	IIM Ahmedabad, India
Prashant Gupta	IIM Tiruchirappalli, India
Arpan Kar	DSM, IIT Delhi, India
Sankalp Pratap	IIM Tiruchirappalli, India
Sumeet Gupta	IIM Raipur, India
Sirish Kumar Gouda	IIM Tiruchirappalli, India
Satish Krishnan	IIM Kozhikode, India
G. P. Sahu	MNNIT Allahabad, India

Uthayasankar (Sankar) Sivarajah	University of Bradford, UK
Rajan Yadav	Delhi Technological University, India
Shalini Srivastava	Jaipuria Institute of Management Noida, India
Zahran Al-Salti	Sultan Qaboos University, Oman

Track Chairs

Artificial Intelligence and Autonomous Systems;

Ilias Pappas	University of Agder (UiA), Norway
Amany Elbanna	Royal Holloway, University of London, UK
Kshitij Sharma	Norwegian University of Science & Technology, Norway

Big Data and Analytics;

Patrick Mikalef	NTNU, Norway
Anastasia Griva	National University of Ireland Galway

Blockchain;

Samuel Fosso Wamba	Head of Artificial Intelligence and Business Analytics Cluster, Toulouse Business School, France
Santosh K. Misra	IAS, CEO & Commissioner of e-Governance, Govt of TN, India
Maciel M. Queiroz	Universidade Paulista, Brasil

Diffusion and Adoption of Technology;

Jyoti Choudrie	University of Hertfordshire, Hatfield, UK
Anand Jeyaraj	Wright State University, USA
Harminder Singh	AUT Business School, Auckland University of Technology, New Zealand

Emerging Technologies in e-Governance;

Satish Krishnan	IIM Kozhikode, India
G. P. Sahu	MNNIT, Allahabad, India

Emerging Technologies in Consumer Decision Making and Choice;

Moutusy Maity	IIM Lucknow (IIM-L), India
Sathish S. Maheshwarappa	IIM Tiruchirappalli, India

Fin-Tech Applications;

M. N. Ravishankar	Director of Internationalisation, Loughborough University, UK
Barney Tan	The University of Sydney Business School, Australia

Healthcare Information Technology;

Rajesh Chandwani   IIM Ahmedabad, India
Jang Bahadur Singh   IIM Tiruchirappalli, India

Internet of Things;

Denis Dennehy   National University of Ireland, Galway
Samuel Fosso Wamba   Head of Artificial Intelligence and Business Analytics
                            Cluster, Toulouse Business School, France
Samrat Gupta   IIM Ahmedabad, India

Information Technology and Disaster Management;

Rameshwar Dubey   Montpellier Business School, France
Sirish Kumar Gouda   IIM Tiruchirappalli, India

Adoption of Mobile and Platform-Based Applications;

Parijat Upadhyay   Institute of Management Technology (IMT), Nagpur
R. Raman   Symbiosis Institute of Business Management, Pune
Arpan Kumar Kar   IIT Delhi, New Delhi

Smart Cities and Digital Government;

Vigneswara Ilavarasan   DMS, IIT Delhi, New Delhi
Endrit Kromidha   University of Birmingham, UK

Social Media.

Nripendra P. Rana   University of Bradford, UK
Kuttimani Tamilmani   University of Bradford, UK

Diffusion of Information Technology and Systems (Conference Theme);

Yogesh Dwivedi   Swansea University, UK
Deborah Bunker   University of Sydney, Australia
Sujeet K. Sharma   IIM Tiruchirappalli, India

Contents – Part II

Smart Cities and Digital Government

Social Media

Diffusion of Information Technology and Systems
(Conference Theme)

Contents – Part I

Big Data and Analytics

Blockchain

Diffusion and Adoption Technology

Emerging Technologies in e-Governance

Emerging Technologies in Consumer Decision Making and Choice

Fin-Tech Applications

Healthcare Information Technology

Internet of Things

Information Technology and Disaster Management

ICT Platform-Enabled Socio-Economic Ecosystem in Himalayan Villages of India: The Case of a Forest Protection and Renewable Energy Production Project

Gaurav Dixit[1]([×]), Kapil Kumar Joshi[1,2], and Vinay Sharma[1]

[1] Department of Management Studies, Indian Institute of Technology Roorkee, Roorkee, India
gaurav.dixit@ms.iitr.ac.in
[2] Forest Department of Uttarakhand, Dehradun, India

Abstract. There is a growing focus on developing ICT-based business ecosystems to provide an innovative and socially-embedded solution that is aligned with the UN's sustainable development goals. However, general approaches being used to build the ICT-based business ecosystems face significant challenges in achieving sustainability, participation, and self-organization on their own. In this research, we pursue the new conceptualization of emergent digital designing to understand these challenges and leverage the concepts of multi-sided platforms to design and transform an ICT-based socio-economic ecosystem that enables co-creation of value. Specifically, we use the activity theory perspective to analyze the required features in the development of an ICT-based socio-economic ecosystem for forest protection and renewable energy production. Based on our case analysis, we construct a typology of various features that an ICT-based socio-economic ecosystem should imbibe to facilitate value co-creation by various actors of the ecosystem. This research contributes to the theory of the solution genre by presenting a feature set related to different aspects of the socio-economic ecosystems. We also highlight the needed minimalistic view of ICTs in the digital transformations of societal and environmental initiatives.

Keywords: ICT platform · Platform ecosystem · Activity theory · Forest · Energy · Environment · Sustainability

1 Introduction

Managing forest resources involves dealing with many tough and challenging risks for forest departments in India. It has become even harsher in this age of global warming and climate change. Forest fires, devastating floods, and landslides are few such challenges that are being faced by the Indian forestry in the North-Western Himalayan regions of India and prominently in Uttarakhand (thehindu.com 2013; indianexpress.com 2016). Realizing the history of such disasters and the significance of the Himalayas, the Government of India launched the 'National Mission on Himalayan

© IFIP International Federation for Information Processing 2020
Published by Springer Nature Switzerland AG 2020
S. K. Sharma et al. (Eds.): TDIT 2020, IFIP AICT 618, pp. 3–14, 2020.
https://doi.org/10.1007/978-3-030-64861-9_1

Studies (NMHS)' in 2015 under the Ministry of Environment, Forest, and Climate Change aligned with the UN's sustainable development goals. The mission objectives focused on long-term conservation and sustainable development in the Indian Himalayan region for the ecological security of India (nmhs.org.in 2015). To fulfill its goals, NMHS has set out the call for demand-driven action research and interventions for innovative solutions.

In this research, our focus is on forest fires, which happens in Uttarakhand every year during summers. Forest bio-residue layers created by dry and fallen leaves are one of the primary sources of such a threat due to their highly inflammable nature (Pandey and Dhakal 2013). Pine tree leaves, also called needles, especially are a significant cause of forest fires (Brown et al. 2011). Previous studies have recommended manufacturing bio-briquettes from waste, dry, and fallen pine needles with the involvement of villagers (Joshi and Sharma 2014). Further, Joshi et al. (2015) suggested ways to implement a socio-economic model to manufacture and sell these briquettes as a greener and environment-friendly energy substitute for wood and coal in the open market and thereby fostering social-entrepreneurship (Joshi et al. 2015). Such a socio-economic solution, if successful, will achieve the twin objectives of forest protection and renewable energy production. Past studies have discussed the development of ICT platform-enabled business ecosystems to address societal challenges in rural or remote regions (Li et al. 2019; Jha et al. 2016; Leong et al. 2016). These ecosystems mimicked the e-commerce platforms and proved to be self-sustainable and achieved societal goals of poverty alleviation and digital empowerment in the targeted areas. These studies examined the evolution or development approach of platform ecosystems. However, the main challenge is to understand how and why these e-commerce ecosystems were able to create the necessary and sufficient network effects to self-sustain in the first place. This aspect has not been examined in the studies of ICT platform-based ecosystems for societal challenges, and it is the focus of our study. We address such a research question in a complex phenomenon where the design of the socio-economic ecosystem is entangled with the effort to protect the forest and environment.

We pursued this research question through a case study of an NMHS project, which is running for more than one year in two villages in the Nainital district, a tourism hub in the Uttarakhand state of India. It falls in a mountainous region with extensive and dense coverage of the pine trees forest, one of the leading sources of forest fires in Uttarakhand. Villagers living in the selected villages have limited income opportunities and survive on forest resources to meet part of their daily needs (Joshi et al. 2015; Joshi and Sharma 2014). The villagers who volunteered in the NMHS project were given portable, manually operated briquette machines to produce briquettes, a renewable energy substitute for coal and wood. The produced briquettes had higher calorific content at a substantially lower cost (Joshi et al. 2015). The briquettes were sold to local and nearby hotel owners. The local and national media have covered the NMHS project initiative on pine briquettes through their print and Web channels. Under this project, an ICT platform was developed and used to enable the socio-economic ecosystem comprising of villagers, micro-entrepreneurs, and hotel owners. The ICT platform was considered a key contributor to the success of the project and played an essential role in social and environmental impacts. Unlike the existing approaches of either private enterprise-driven, community-driven, or local government-driven platform ecosystem development, the Nainital case presents a unique experience of a platform ecosystem development driven by a funded research project.

We used the activity theory to guide and implement our research (Engeström, 2015; Karanasios 2014, 2018). We also analyzed the findings of an older case, a public-private partnership, which was tried during 2010–13 (Joshi and Sharma 2014). was also used. The learnings were helpful during the effort conducted through our funded research project. We studied the activity system containing the ICT platform as an artifact. In this research, we document, conceptualize, and analyze the case findings on how this activity system with ICT platform transformed and realized the socio-economic solution envisaged in the older case.

2   Theoretical Background

2.1   Forest Protection and Renewable Energy Production

2016 Uttarakhand forest fires were widely covered in Indian news media because of its severity, administrative failure to tackle the situation in a timely manner, and huge loss of forest resources (indianexpress.com 2016). Ecologists singled out mismanagement of forest floors filled with readily combustible pine leaves for this tragic incident. They also suggested biomass briquette production from the pine needles as the prime solution (tribuneindia.com 2016).

A program by the government in the form of 'public-private partnership' for manufacturing briquettes was started in 2010 in the Nainital district (Joshi and Sharma 2014). This program followed a strict regulatory mechanism. Each actor in the ecosystem was allowed to perform a predefined activity, and rates for each activity were fixed. A local firm Suyas Udyog private limited, was given the responsibility of manufacturing briquettes. Societal actors like villagers, local NGOs, self-help groups, women groups, and van panchayats acted as collectors of pine needles and were financially incentivized. The Forest department levied a fee for issuing a transit permit. This top-down centric regulatory approach constrained the benefits for the stakeholders and eventually led to the failure of the pine needle manufacturing project in 2013 (Joshi and Sharma 2014).

In this public-private partnership model, villagers who were crucial stakeholders of the value chain were involved as labor. The private firm was conceptualized as the value creator and was supposed to sustain the ecosystem. However, the approach of involving a private firm having an industrial approach created significant constraints for the self-sustainability of the business ecosystem due to the geography of the region and the peculiar characteristic of pine needles. Transportation costs were a considerable component in the overall costs because pine needles are lightweight and cannot be carried in high load in trucks. Transportation of pine needles from the collection spots to a distant manufacturing plant in the mountainous terrain was not an economic proposition. Higher transportation costs meant that villagers who were key stakeholders of the ecosystem could not be financially incentivized to keep them in the ecosystem. Therefore, for-profit firms can find it challenging to sustain the business.

The second model conceptualized in the research project considered villagers as the collectors, briquette producers, and micro-entrepreneurs who would sell the produced briquettes in the local market. It was implemented in the project by providing portable, manually operated briquette machines to villagers. However, preparing villagers who lack an understanding of markets, entrepreneurial capability and fall in the backward and lower strata of the society require external intervention (VanSandt and Sud 2012).

2.2   ICT-Based Socio-Economic Ecosystem for Renewable Energy Production

In the last decade, we have seen the emergence of ICT platform-based business (or e-commerce) ecosystems to overcome many societal challenges (Li et al. 2019; Jha et al. 2016; Leong et al. 2016). These studies found beneficial features of the ecosystems, such as self-organization (Li et al. 2019), self-sustainability & evolvability (Jha et al. 2016), digital empowerment (Leong et al. 2016), and emancipatory (Kanungo 2004). Here, by 'ecosystem,' we mean "a community of interacting firms and individuals who co-evolve their capabilities and roles and tend to align themselves with the directions set by one or more central companies (McIntyre and Srinivasan 2017)". There are different types of ecosystems, such as the e-commerce ecosystem (e.g., Alibaba.com, Amazon.com), which typically comprises a network of the ICT platform sponsor, buyers, and sellers (Tan et al. 2015). Next is the platform ecosystem (e.g., Microsoft's Windows, Google's Search Engine), which typically comprises a network of the platform sponsor, its complementors, and users (Tan et al. 2015). However, our focus is on establishing a third type: an ICT platform-enabled socio-economic ecosystem with mostly similar, but few distinct characteristics to an e-commerce ecosystem.

Now, we discuss the existing strategies which have been adopted in the development of e-commerce ecosystems for societal challenges. In a private enterprise-driven approach, the ecosystem governance aspects related to participation, interaction, incentives, concerns, and plans are decided and executed by the private firm. This approach survives on the adequate scope and scale embedded in the potential ecosystem, which can offer commercially accepted profit margins in the local market (Joshi and Sharma 2014). The public-private partnership approach is a constrained version of the private enterprise-driven approach. In a community-driven approach, the actors collaborate and self-organize themselves to create and govern the ecosystem. This approach requires enterprising and risk-taking capacity amongst the actors (Leong et al. 2016). In a local government-driven approach, officers of the local administration make decisions related to all aspects of the ecosystem based on the policies and programs formulated by state or central governments. This approach is mostly dependent on the government. In our study, the situation doesn't suitably fit into these approaches. Renewable energy production by manufacturing briquettes of pine needles using a portable, manually operated machine is a physical labor-based and low-profit margin activity. The initial volume being produced in the NMHS research project was not attractive enough for local entrepreneurs or private enterprises. Therefore, the conceptualization of a novel approach for ecosystem development is required, and it is the focus of our study.

We needed a theoretical lens to develop a holistic view to understand the mechanisms which are being used in the novel ecosystem development approach. The entanglement of forest protection, renewable energy production, and ICT platform development following the emergent digital designing approach increases the complexity to provide a solution. To develop a theory of solution for a societal challenge of forest protection and renewable energy production, we opted for the activity theory perspective as our theoretical lens in all the phases of our research study (Majchrzak et al. 2016).

3 Research Methods

To study the process of ICT-based ecosystem for forest protection and renewable energy production, we followed the qualitative research methodology. We adopted the interpretive case study method based on the following considerations (Walsham 2006). First, past IS studies suggested its usefulness in applying activity theory perspective to a complex phenomenon embedded in the societal context (Sam 2012). Second, interpretive case studies allow us to explore a phenomenon in the richness of its setting, which is essential to study an ICT-based ecosystem with complex social and environmental aspects. Finally, the area of ICT solutions for forest protection and renewable energy production is a scarcely researched area, where theories are yet to be developed. Therefore, it demands more qualitative studies for theorization.

Our case is based on a research project which is part of the National Mission on Himalayan Studies implemented by the Ministry of Environment, Forest & Climate Change, Government of India. The project objectives included socio-economic value creation through forest bio-residue based renewable energy production and development of an ICT platform for value-chain integration and market access (Dixit and Panigrahi 2014; Dixit and Panigrahi 2013). Data collection was conducted between February 2019 and February 2020. Two Himalayan villages of the Uttarakhand state of India were selected as per the project guidelines. Initial visits to the villages were conducted by the first author, shortly after the launch of the research project. An extended study started during March 2019, and three follow-up visits to the field were conducted by the authors during April-May, 2020. Two field visits were conducted during January and February 2020 by the first author to finalize the data collection. Since this was a field-based project, members of the project team regularly visited and stayed in the villages to supervise the project activities on a relatively continuous basis.

Forest Department of Uttarakhand facilitated access to the research sites and introduction with the van panchayats, which are locally elected bodies tasked with the administration of village forests. Van panchayats helped us in discussing the project objectives and employment and earning opportunities in the project with the interested villagers. Villagers were selected to work in the project according to the project guidelines. This type of access eased the project implementation process and provided a cordial atmosphere to interact with the key stakeholders - selected villagers, van panchayats, industries, and the forest department. During our preliminary discussions with them, we were able to create the required comfort and trust among the project participants. A coding scheme was used to differentiate the participants' statements with our thoughts and reflections recorded in the field notes and reports.

Data collection methods included semi-structured interviews, interactions, and focus group discussions with stakeholders. These interviews and discussions were used to acquire a deep understanding of the socio-economic context where the ICT platform was expected to enable the ecosystem for forest protection and renewable energy production. We aimed to gather views of participants and key stakeholders about the process of renewable energy production being used in the project, benefits to participants during and after the project, and the role of the ICT platform in integrating the value-chain and facilitating market access. We incorporated the acquired learnings from the field in subsequent interviews and other aspects of the overall research. The participants were asked to share their experiences of using the ICT platform and changes they could feel in comparison to the paper-based system and existing ways of market access.

We used our observations originating from field visits, discussions, interactions, training sessions as other data collection methods for the development of the ICT platform. These observations, based on the issues raised by the participants and other stakeholders, provided us a mental map of the challenges in the value-chain integration of the renewable energy value system. For example, observations during the interactions with the villagers revealed that some villagers don't use smartphones and depend on some other member in their family when needed. It helped us understand the mobile app design requirement to suit this situation. We also included news articles and research articles on similar ongoing or past initiatives related to pine needles ranging from briquette production to ethanol production. These articles were particularly helpful in understanding the historical, social, political, and successful and failed aspects of similar projects.

It is suggested to use a theoretical lens to guide the iterative process of data collection and data analysis in interpretive case studies (Walsham 2006). As discussed, we use activity theory for this purpose and also for theory development in this research. We followed the four criteria of an activity analysis to guide the framework of our study (Karanasios 2018). The first criterion is about defining the unit of analysis, an activity system that captures the smallest unit encompassing the complexity associated with the activity. The second criterion is that we should be able to analyze the evolution and changes in the activity using the identified activity system. Using the case data, we identified the project team's establishment of an ICT platform-based socio-economic ecosystem for local trade of renewable energy as the activity system. We study the evolution and changes within this activity system. The third criterion is that we should be able to account for the interactions among the subject, community, and other constituents of the activity system. The fourth criterion is that the activity system should allow us to study the mediated activity, related contradictions and their resolutions, and the transformation of the object. Interviews, discussions, and interactions were conducted in Hindi and documented through field notes, digital notes, and video recordings wherever possible.

4 Case Findings

4.1 Socio-Economic Context: Nainital Villages and Pine Forest

The project team selected two villages in the Nainital district for the implementation of the research project according to the NMHS guidelines. Nainital was chosen due to two reasons. First, this district has easy availability of pine needles in the nearby forest area. Second, it is a popular tourist destination of the Uttarakhand state and hosts many hotels. Two villages, Shyamkhet near Bhowali town and Chopra near Jeolikote town, were identified with the help of forest officials as suitable sites. Following NMHS guidelines, we enrolled women and individuals from the disadvantaged sections of the society for this project. Theses villagers come from poor or below poverty line strata of Indian society, and our project presented them an opportunity to earn in the project and gain a long-term earning source and micro-entrepreneurship opportunity. The majority of the enrolled villagers were women. It happened mainly because of their daily routine. They go to the forest for a collection of wood and other forest resources in the morning, then come back for cooking and other household work. Therefore, the project activity of pine needle collection naturally fitted into their schedule. Few of these women were already into pined needle collection required for packing of fruits by local traders. This activity provided them low seasonal income, and scope was limited. Funding from the research project offered them to store pine needles in large amounts and produce briquettes using it throughout the year and sell it to local hotel owners and others. ICT platform would give them not only the market access but also transparency of their collection, production, and sale. The ICT platform-supported ecosystem was a much-needed intervention for the villagers from the previously tried and unsustainable models of public-private partnerships and government programs to overcome forest fires.

4.2 ICT Platform-Based Ecosystem

Activity System and Motivation. The motivations for the ICT-based ecosystem are manifold. The first motivation is the mitigation of forest fires in the Himalayan mountain series. The second motivation is to implement the renewable energy agenda to reduce the reliance on coal as an energy source for some activities in the local industries. The third and most important motivation is creating a long-term local earning source as well as micro-entrepreneurship opportunities for the disadvantaged groups. Documentation of NMHS, the funding agency about its goals, shows compatibility with the motivations of ICT-based ecosystem in the research project.

NMHS envisages to work towards a set of linked and complementary goals to: Foster conservation and sustainable management of natural resources; Enhance supplementary and/or alternative livelihoods and overall economic well-being of the region; Control and prevent pollution in the region; Foster increased/augmented human and institutional capacities and the knowledge and policy environment in the region; and Strengthen, greening, and fostering development of climate-resilient core infrastructure and basic services assets.

The activity system, the ICT platform-based socio-economic ecosystem for local trade of renewable energy, is depicted in Fig. 1. It shows the subject as a collective of individuals and entities has multiple sources of motivation leading it to interact with the community comprising of different stakeholders and jointly acts upon the object to transform it by using several artifacts.

Activity System and Community. The community comprising of villagers, village sarpanches, and hotel owners participated, interacted, and influenced the development and realization of the ICT platform. The village population was witness to instances of forest fires in their area, which caused the loss of life, pollution, and strived them off from collecting forest resources and agricultural work for days. This environmental-historical challenge manifested in many ways, including their desire to control and reduce the forest fire instances. Notably, hotel owners and home-stay owners showed high levels of curiosity in the success of the project before, during, and after the implementation.

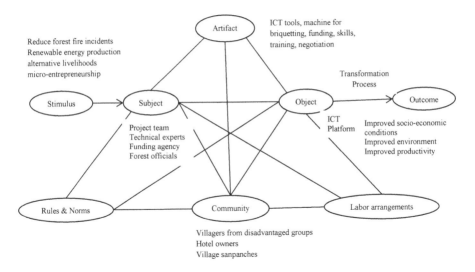

Fig. 1. Activity system

One home-stay owner explained his underlying motivation for the ecosystem: '*my home-stay lies away from the main motorable road. Tourists have to trek the narrow lanes to reach us. Pine needles make these narrow lanes very slippery, especially after rains. But, this new ecosystem will also solve this problem. We would prefer to use briquettes for bonfires instead of forest wood that is very difficult to arrange due to forest restrictions.*' Villagers, particularly women, saw it as a regular, year-long source of income as men typically migrate to nearby metro cities to work for months. We were surprised to find women finding many other ways to mold the briquette into different products for higher-margin sale: '*...after looking at the produced briquette by the machine..., we can make fragranced artifacts from it; those items sell for Rs. 100 or more.*' It was clear that the ICT platform might transform from a two-sided platform into a multi-sided platform in the future. However, the project focus was on establishing the two-sided platform for renewable energy production and sale, which was completed.

Activity System, Object, and Mediation. Several key artifacts or tools were used to mediate the activity. The first artifact is funding to enable the research project as a result of the previous research work of the project team members. Intangible artifacts such as expertize and negotiation were crucial to seek a grant from the funding agency. The second artifact was a technological artifact, the portable, manually operated briquette machine, which was used to mediate the briquette production activity. The machine was designed by the project team members and developed with the help of local manufacturers. The third and most important artifact is the ICT artifact. A mixture of established information technology tools and innovative design expertise was employed to mediate the development of the object. The object, the ICT platform, was created and transformed by the activity system, and consequently, enabled the socio-economic ecosystem. The design of the ICT platform ensured the mediation by the digitization of key activities of the ecosystem, such as the pine needle collection process, briquette production process, and sale process. The socio-economic background of the villagers required us to use the information technology, which has a higher adoption rate among the participants of the ecosystem. We found that mobile technologies can play an essential role in our ecosystem platform, as evident from their success in other ICT-enabled social change initiatives like mobile banking in rural India. The use of mobile technologies has led to an improvement in rural households' savings and also reduced the cost of delivery for banks (Kochar 2018). A mobile app was designed by the first author, which was developed with the help of technical experts. Not all enrolled villagers had smartphones. However, most of them had one smartphone in the family, which was used by them to install the mobile app and become part of the ecosystem. The mobile technologies were not just tools in the project but embodied the accumulation of all the activities of the ecosystem and mechanism to facilitate the knowledge transfer to the community after the project ends. One of the project team member, who was not part of the mobile app development effort, said: '...*after using the mobile app for the first time...it seems simple to use, minimalistic functionality,... just the thing for villagers...they will love it*'. The fourth artifact was training that helped villagers and hotel owners in learning the functionality of the mobile app. Other skilled stakeholders also supported this activity.

Activity System, Rules and Norms, and Labor arrangements. During the establishment of the ecosystem, norms evolved with the involvement of all the stakeholders. For instance, enrolled men took up the field assistant activity. They went to the forest sites and weighed the pine needle collection of each woman. They entered the pine collection data of each woman using the mobile app and took either signature or thump impression in a paper in a standardized format. This paper was uploaded using the mobile app to ensure the transparency and accuracy in the ecosystem. Each field assistant and villager had their own account in the mobile app and could check and verify their details for accuracy. This process is essential to build up the trust in the ecosystem to overcome the historical and cultural baggage of corruption prevailing in the society, where the disadvantaged group is often at the receiving end. A similar process was adopted for the briquette production activity. Field assistants were aspiring micro-entrepreneurs and saw the mobile app as a milestone for their future: *'...after using the mobile app...we can play a role similar to the customer care of companies and can facilitate the women briquette producers in the selling activity in the market'*. For the project work, women were being paid for their pine collections as per the prevailing rate fixed by the forest department. The field assistants were being paid for their work using the allocated funds in the project. The payment process was offline, cash-based for many reasons.

5 Discussion and Case Analysis

Using the activity theory perspective, we highlight the potential of ICT artifact to create an ecosystem out of a low margin economic activity and in a social and environmental initiative. The socio-economic ecosystem established in the research project is similar to an e-commerce ecosystem, but with some different features—first, villagers, one of the participating sides in our ICT platform-based ecosystem, lack self-organization. But if given the direction, they can deliver value, which exhibits the hidden potential in the working capacity of the bottom of the pyramid, which can be realized using ICT. Second, the ecosystem didn't have an IT or e-commerce company to create the ICT platform, and the project team did it. The functionality was developed in the mobile app as the ecosystem evolved. Therefore, it exhibited a minimalistic view of ICT, which is needed to create social value in a developing country like India.

6 Conclusion

In this research article, we embarked upon presenting a case on a socio-environmental project, which led to creating a socio-economic ecosystem for renewable energy production. We contribute to theory by suggesting a new type of ecosystem differing from e-commerce or platform ecosystems. The socio-economic ecosystem has the following characteristics: realizing the working capacity of the bottom of the pyramid and minimalistic view of ICT for creating social value. We also contribute to the activity theory perspective by applying it to a social and environmental case-related activity. Our study has implications for public and private initiatives, interventions, and policy directions for socially weaker sections and ecological issues. The results of our study suggest that livelihood creation and environmental protection can go hand-in-hand. The study has few fruitful research directions such as analyzing the design aspects of the ICT platform, expansion of more sides in a platform, evolution of relationships among platform participants.

Acknowledgment. Funding for this research work was provided by India's National Mission on Himalayan Studies (NMHS) Scheme for a Project titled "Socio-Economic Value Creation through Forest Bio-Residue Based Energy Generation in alignment with the UN's SDGs". Grant no: GBPNI/NMHS-2018-19/MG 3.

References

Brown, P.M., Bhattacharyya, A., Shah, S.K.: Potential for developing fire histories in Chir Pine (Pinus roxburghii) forests in the Himalayan Foothills. Treering Res. **67**(1), 57–62 (2011)

Dixit, G., Panigrahi, P.: Information technology impact and role of firm age and export activity: an emerging economy context. J. Glob. Inf. Technol. Manag. **17**(3), 169–187 (2014)

Dixit, G., Panigrahi, P.: Investigating determinants of information technology investments by indian firms. J. Inf. Technol. Manag. **24**(3), 13 (2013)

Engeström, Y.: Learning by Expanding: An Activity-Theoretical Approach to Developmental Research. Cambridge University Press, New York (2015)

indianexpress.com: Fresh forest fires in Uttarakhand destroy 180 hectares of green cover (2016). https://indianexpress.com/article/india/india-news-india/uttarakhand-forest-fires-180-hectares-green-cover-2806814/

Jha, S.K., Pinsonneault, A., Dubé, L.: The evolution of an ICT platform-enabled ecosystem for poverty alleviation: the case of eKutir. MIS Q. **40**(2), 431–445 (2016)

Joshi, K., Sharma, V.: Challenges in community based forest bio residue resource utilization for bio briquetting in the western Himalayan region of Uttarakhand: a real case study. Commun.-Based For. Manag. SAARC Region 61–69 (2014)

Joshi, K., Sharma, V., Mittal, S.: Social entrepreneurship through forest bioresidue briquetting: an approach to mitigate forest fires in Pine areas of Western Himalaya, India. Renew. Sustain. Energy Rev. **51**, 1338–1344 (2015)

Kanungo, S.: On the emancipatory role of rural information systems. Inf. Technol. People **17**(4), 407–422 (2004)

Karanasios, S.: Framing ICT4D research using activity theory: a match between the ICT4D field and theory? Inf. Technol. Int. Dev. **10**(2), 1–18 (2014)

Karanasios, S.: Toward a unified view of technology and activity. Inf. Technol. People **31**(1), 134–155 (2018)

Kochar, A.: Branchless banking: evaluating the doorstep delivery of financial services in rural India. J. Dev. Econ. **135**, 160–175 (2018)

Leong, C.M.L., Pan, S.L., Newell, S., Cui, L.: The emergence of self-organizing e-commerce ecosystems in remote villages of china: a tale of digital empowerment for rural development. MIS Q. **40**(2), 475–484 (2016)

Li, L., Du, K., Zhang, W., Mao, J.Y.: Poverty alleviation through government-led e-commerce development in rural China: an activity theory perspective. Inf. Syst. J. **29**(4), 914–952 (2019)

Majchrzak, A., Markus, M.L., Wareham, J.: Designing for digital transformation: lessons for information systems from the study of ICT and societal challenges. MIS Q. **40**(2), 267–277 (2016)

McIntyre, D.P., Srinivasan, A.: Networks, platforms, and strategy: emerging views and next steps. Strat. Manag. J. **38**(1), 141–160 (2017)

nmhs.org.in: Mission Document: National Mission on Himalayan Studies (NMHS) (2015). https://nmhs.org.in/pdf/National%20Mission%20on%20Himalayan%20Studies.pdf

Pandey, S., Dhakal, R.P.: Pine needle briquettes: a renewable source of energy. Int. J. Energy Sci. **3**(3), 254–258 (2013)

Sam, C.: Activity theory and qualitative research in digital domains. Theory Pract. **51**(2), 83–90 (2012)

Tan, B., Pan, S.L., Lu, X., Huang, L.: The role of IS capabilities in the development of multi-sided platforms: the digital ecosystem strategy of Alibaba.com. J. Assoc. Inf. Syst. **16**(4), 2 (2015)

thehindu.com: Uttarakhand floods: Over 10,000 rescued amidst misery and devastation (2013). https://www.thehindu.com/news/national/other-states/uttarakhand-floods-over-10000-rescued-amidst-misery-and-devastation/article4843018.ece?homepage=true

tribuneindia.com: Poor mgmt reason for forest fires: Experts (2016). http://www.tribuneindia.com/news/himachal/poor-mgmt-reason-for-forest-fires-experts/230796.html

VanSandt, C.V., Sud, M.: Poverty alleviation through partnerships: a road less travelled for business, governments, and entrepreneurs. J. Bus. Ethics **110**(3), 321–332 (2012)

Walsham, G.: Doing interpretive research. Eur. J. Inf. Syst. **15**(3), 320–330 (2006)

Protective Security by Online Promotions Paired with Mobile Payments: Evidence from Covid-19 Crisis Relief Fund Collection in India

Abhipsa Pal[✉] and Salamah Ansari

Indian Institute of Management Kozhikode, Kozhikode 673 570, India
{abhipsapal,salamah}@iimk.ac.in

Abstract. When developing nations suffer from crises and disasters, it becomes urgent and critical to raise relief funds rapidly with the engagement of a greater number of donors. In this regard, digital technology has repeatedly aided during crises. Two such technologies include online promotions influencing citizens for donations, and mobile payments providing a mechanism for quick transfer of funds. In this paper, we study how online promotions that are notified through mobile payment apps, can be a pair of technology enabling successful and rapid fund transfer, thereby offering protective security during a crisis, along with transparency in transactions (Sen 2001). We examine the role of the two technologies in combination through field interviews amidst the Covid-19 crisis in India and draw implications for relief fund collection mechanisms. Initial results show that the role of online promotions and mobile payments have questionable implications in terms of transparency. The study contributes to both mobile payments and online promotions in crisis literature.

Keywords: IT in crisis · Mobile payments · IT in disaster relief · Online promotions for donations

1 Introduction

In recent times, developing nations were hit by several crises and disasters including civil conflicts, economic crises, natural disasters, and the global Covid-19 pandemic (Saxena 2020; Welborn 2020). This necessitates a quick response from various actors including the state and citizens, in tandem with technology, to facilitate large scale and rapid collection of relief funds (Bennett and Kottasz 2000). This has led researchers to study the positive role of technology concerning the conflicts and disasters that took place in various countries (Harwell 2000; Scott and Batchelor 2013; Troy et al. 2008). The studies bring out the role of technology as a social safety net during crisis providing 'protective security'— one of the freedoms by Sen for empowering individuals, and impacting socioeconomic development (Frediani 2007; Sen 2001). Further, technology has an added advantage of ensuring 'transparency guarantee' as envisaged by Sen. Transparency guarantee is also a freedom that is instrumental in bringing in trust in people, systems, and institutions.

© IFIP International Federation for Information Processing 2020
Published by Springer Nature Switzerland AG 2020
S. K. Sharma et al. (Eds.): TDIT 2020, IFIP AICT 618, pp. 15–23, 2020.
https://doi.org/10.1007/978-3-030-64861-9_2

In this context, we examine the role of two important technological interventions that have been contributory in aiding relief fund collection during crises. First, online promotions for sensitizing and mobilizing the citizens about the urgency of contributing to relief funds (Das 2020; Sharma 2020). Second, convenient online transfer of funds through digital payment mechanisms, like mobile payments (Pollach et al. 2005). Mobile payment mode is highly inclusive because mobile payment has been established as an effective tool for financial inclusion, including the unbanked and marginalized sectors (Donovan 2012). While existing literature engages with these two strands of technology's role in crisis individually, there is a limitation of studies on how the combination of these two can offer a fundraising platform with greater acceptability. Rapid fundraising is particularly crucial for helping the marginalized who are the most critical victims of crises, and fund promotion through payment apps' notification could offer an innovative solution. In this context, this paper makes a normative contribution by analyzing *the combined effect when online promotions are paired with mobile payments.*

This phenomenon is observed in various mobile payment apps in India, as they promote relief fund donations through on-app advertisements and pop-up notifications, that allow users to directly donate by one-click on the promotion text (Dataquest 2020). (See Fig. 1 for the various advertisements by mobile wallets in India). To examine the role of this technological combination, we draw our analysis from the data collected through in-depth field interviews during the Covid-19 crisis in India. The results reveal that although mobile payments are gaining popularity through online promotions, the pre-existent digital divide continues to exclude some sections of the society like the elderly and women. Fund donations are highly sensitive and often online payments carry the fear of fraud transactions (Kundu 2020). Therefore, while the combination of online promotions and payment may appear beneficial, critical investigation of the user perspectives through field data is essential to conclude. The findings contribute not only to the field studying technology in crisis and disaster relief but also to the field of mobile payment as ICT4D.

2 Background and Motivation

Covid-19 is the global pandemic that spread globally across international borders due to its highly contagious nature (Marques et al. 2020). Due to its contagious nature, many nations declared lockdown, shutting down local businesses and travel, to minimize social interactions and curtail the spread of the virus (BBC News 2020). And for India, the lockdown resulted in job losses in tremendous magnitude for the laborers working in the unorganized sectors (Vij 2020). Therefore, as the pandemic rises in the developing nation, the government is in dire need of relief funds to provide both for healthcare facilities in increasing numbers of the growing Covid-19 patients, quarantine facilities for the infected, along with providing food and shelter to the daily wage labors who lost their jobs and were at the verge of starvation. This crisis has been noted as one of the harshest in the history of India (Agrawal 2020). Such a situation calls for the dire need to arrange for funds and donations both quickly and effectively by reaching out to all the citizens and enabling them with the opportunity of easy transfer of money in the lockdown with restricted movement. Online promotions provide awareness to the citizens about the national fund, whereas mobile payments offer a quick transfer from home. This intrigued us to examine the effectiveness of this combination of the two technologies, online promotions on mobile payment apps, in terms of protection and transparency, the two essential freedoms to tackle a crisis in developing nations as prescribed by Sen (2001).

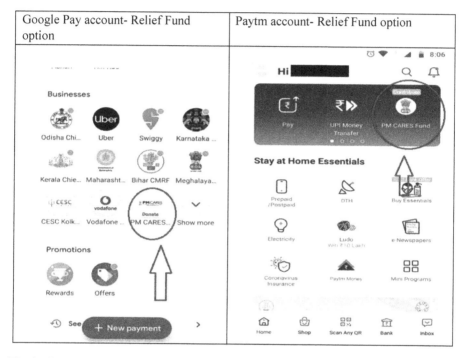

Fig. 1. Screenshots of two leading mobile payment apps in India, Google Pay and Paytm, with Prime Minister's Relief Fund Promotions

3 Literature

This study draws and contributes to two streams of literature on the two technologies in crisis- online promotions and mobile payments.

3.1 Online Promotions and Relief Fund Donation

Online advertisements on mobile phones are often considered highly effective and can be influential in relief fund collection with adequate aesthetics and features (Park et al. 2008; Zhou and Xue 2019). Donation-based promotions are an efficient fund collection mechanism that motivates donors through the act of charity (Winterich and Barone 2011). Ellen et al. (2000) study the structure of marketing promotions in the donation situation, and Mülleret al. (2014) tactical marketing to influence the donation size. While researchers have focused on strategy, message-content, and techniques, to influence donators and donations (e.g., GalánLadero and Galera-Casquet 2013; Grau and Folse 2007), we examine how combining promotions with the payment technology would effectively provide citizens both the motivation and the platform to transfer the donation.

3.2   Mobile Payments During Crises

In crisis and disaster situations where mobility of civilians was restrained, various mobile payment service providers (e.g. Vodafone in Afghanistan, Smart Communication in the Philippines, Safaricom in Kenya, Orange in various countries in Africa) offered swift funds transfer of remittances from migrants to their homes, or relief cash from the government to victims (Aker et al. 2016; Pega et al. 2015; Wachanga 2015). One example is the 2008 post-election civil conflict when many civilians used mPesa to receive money that they needed to escape the threat of ethnic violence (Morawczynski and Pickens 2009). Another such example is the banknote crisis during demonetization in India when mobile payments were one of the key payment channels that enabled the continuity of small-scale businesses in the shortage of hard cash (Firstpost 2016).

4   Theoretical Foundation

Protective security concerns how well the citizens are protected at times of crises (Sen 2001). Ascending from the theoretical framework of protective security are State-specific protective security policies. The framework of these protective security policies articulates directives to government instrumentalities and private sector players to bolster the effective implementation of policy across the arenas of governance, social assurance, and information security et al. The primary objective of enabling protective security is to enable business and economic activity that supports the government's objective of achieving well-being for its citizens.

The basic rationale for adopting protective security policies is that if undertaken promptly, these initiatives increase the probability of protecting citizens from the ill effects of a crisis. In the age of technology, advancement in information technology can be leveraged to this end. Technologies have often served as safety-nets or facilitated more efficient fund transfer during ethnic violence in Kenya or the banknote crisis triggered by demonetization in India, as seen above (Blumenstock et al. 2016; Mirabaud 2009). More importantly, the employment of technology leads to a *transparency guarantee* which is an important contributor towards enhancing capabilities.

Through the transparency guarantee lens provided by Sen, we analyze if the combination of online promotions and mobile payments can be an empowering technology offering protective security to the society in times of need. With the advent of information technology, online promotions, and growth of digital giving has outpaced all other forms of giving. The positive role of online promotions makes it easy for donors to locate the required page and donate. Online promotions leverage existing technological advancements like easy- to- click links, streamlined designs, and steps that allow a donor to make expedited decisions. As one-third of internet traffic is channeled through mobiles, online promotions are easier since a larger group becomes the recipient.

Mobile payments have several advantages over traditional ways of donating like cash and cheques. First, donors can use the same technology that they otherwise use for their routine transactions. Second, the demographics of the donors become relatively redundant as most people across age groups use mobile technologies. Third, by using technology that the donors are already using, we can leverage the trust and reliance that users have on a particular interface. Fourth, not only the collection becomes cost-effective. Sending an acknowledgment receipt is also hassle feel and cost-effective. Fifth, mobile technology is invariably associated with quick and efficient transactions. Sixth, having a transparent system of donation collection increases perceived credibility. All of these factors cumulatively give a boost to the amount of donation collected.

5 Research Methodology

The data for relief fund promotions and collections through mobile payment is collected through field study by interviewing citizens. The interview questions are designed to capture if the pairing of promotions and mobile payments has helped the citizens to easily transfer funds. The study is still in progress, with 8 in-depth interviews collected now, which is preliminary analysis through basic interpretive research methods through the hermeneutic cycle (Klein and Myers 1999). We have followed a semi-structured method for interviews, starting with a set of broad questions, but encouraged a free conversation with the participants. The interviews were transcribed and analyzed for new themes beyond our initial outline based on protective security and transparency guarantees. We transcribed the interviews and analyzed the data following the prescriptions by Klein and Myers (1999), including examining the social and historic background of the field, understanding the interaction between the subjects and researcher, and carefully preserving the theme of the data, with conscious awareness regarding biases of the researcher.

5.1 Research Field and Subjects

The subjects were from the urban locations in the New Capital Region of India including New Delhi, Noida, and Gurgaon. These are infrastructurally advanced cities in the country and the citizens are assumed to be aware of mobile payment technology, as India reports significantly higher digital penetration for urban India (Indian Express 2018). The subjects were both regular mobile payment users, and non-users but with awareness about mobile payments from urban locations with relatively advanced digital infrastructure. This allowed us to understand the concerns of technically aware users related to relief fund transfers through mobile payments. The interviews are held between March and May 2020, amidst the covid-19 global pandemic in India. The critical conditions in India, that needed immediate relief funding, provided a field to study the issues of technology in crisis.

6 Findings

The objective of the study is to analyze the combination of mobile payments with online promotions as a technology that offers protective security and transparency guarantees in times of crisis.

Four respondents mentioned that they have noticed the fund collection notifications, often repeatedly. One user mentioned that he received regular notifications and he has also used mobile payments to make Covid-19 fund donation. He said,

> *"I do get notifications and I would say I get them daily and I've used it couple of times to donate money".*

Similarly, two other respondents noted that they were willing to contribute to the Covid-19 relief fund directly through the mobile wallet promotional ads since it was easier.

A regular user mentioned that she was willing to make the donation through a mobile payment app but her workplace initiated a campaign that deducted amount directly from her salary without the need to transfer personally.

However, an elderly non-user stated her fear of fraudulent transactions through mobile payments, and said, she preferred traditional donation methods through banking channels. She also brought up the fact that she is generally hesitant about using any form of digital transactions since they carry the threat of theft and cybercrimes. This works in reverse of our assumption on transparency guarantees since this subject did that prior developed trust for the mobile payment wallets. She explains,

> *"I will not donate through Paytm [leading mobile wallet in India] because who knows where my money will go. I will rather go to my bank and make the donation if at all I want to donate".*

On a similar note, another user noted that her trust for her bank is much higher and therefore she would choose online banking rather than mobile payments since relief money safety is of utmost concern for her and the people in need.

It can be drawn from the data that pairing promotions with the mobile payments for collection of relief funds have effectively initiated donations. However, pre-existing traditional channels continue to offer a trustworthy donation platform, whereas, mobile payments are trusted by regular users but are questioned by non-users.

Overall, the findings suggest that 'protective security' is established as users note the convenience of transferring relief funds through mobile wallets, but 'transparency guarantees' is questionable with many subjects expressing their trust concerns for the third-party providers of mobile payments.

7 Discussion and Implications

Mobile payments, combined with online promotions for relief funds, provide a technology pair that can provide motivation and mechanisms to citizens for donations. As far as transparency guarantee is concerned, the technology caters to various strata of the society equitably. However, the same cannot be iterated about the protective security parameter. The digital divide, in terms of digital literacy and use of smartphones, can exclude a significant section from the system. Our critical investigation reveals that online promotions, as well as mobile payments, are not truly inclusive processes. Our results are coherent with the assertion made by Sen and Dreze, which states that issues of inequality and participation are particularly crucial in India. These issues tend to accentuate social divisions and are 'pervasive and have tended to take a heavy toll on both economic development and social opportunities' (Drèze and Sen 2002, p. 10).

We also found that the inequality established by the digital divide across online promotions and mobile payments and in the process obstruct participation of the technically incompetent citizens from older generations. Whether this new technology combination provides adequate protective security and transparency guarantee for the people is still in question as non-users have raised questions and expressed their preferences for traditional 'trusted' alternative channels.

To ensure that we as a society can better leverage the advantages unleashed by technological advancement, the State needs to first play a proactive role in enabling equitable access to technology. Both in terms of network coverage as well as access to internet-enabled mobile handsets. Elimination of physical barriers to access is the primary responsibility of the State. Cybersecurity is a major concern that the State ought to keep in mind while initiating any step towards large scale inclusions or before involving private parties in catering to the growing need. Since transparency guarantees leverage on the trust factor, a breach of trust in any manner can cause reputational damages.

8   Conclusion

This paper aimed to examine the role of a combination of two influential technologies – online promotions and mobile payments – during the crisis, particularly focussing on relief fund collection. We understand if this combined technology meets the two important freedoms by Sen, protective security, and transparency guarantees. The preliminary evidence shows us that while protective security is met for most of the subject, transparency guarantee is questioned by some non-users who do not find mobile wallets reliable in comparison to traditional banks of the nation. This needs further investigation.

The future plan for this study includes interviews with subjects infrastructurally diverse cities like tier-2 cities and rural locations, and from diverse backgrounds, with elaborate discussions on their opinions related to promotions and fund transfer through mobile payments. We expect to find more evidence towards the presence or absence of transparency guarantee for mobile payment fund transfer, for which we currently have mixed findings.

References

Saxena, S.: Covid-19 death toll crosses 2.8 lakh worldwide, 80,000 fatalities in US alone: Global tally. Hindustan Times (2020). https://www.hindustantimes.com/world-news/covid-19death-to ll-crosses-2-8-lakh-worldwide-80-000-fatalities-in-us-alone-global-tally/storyFwc6c5LEvNUY ByYssgfRoM.html

Welborn, S.: Servicer response and reaction to natural disasters. DSNews (2020). https://dsnews.com/daily-dose/05-11-2020/response-and-reaction-to-natural-disaster

Bennett, R., Kottasz, R.: Emergency fund-raising for disaster relief. Disast. Prevent. Manag.: Int. J. **9**, 352–360 (2000)

Harwell, E.: Remote sensibilities: discourses of technology and the making of Indonesia's natural disaster. Dev. Change **31**, 307–340 (2000)

Scott, N., Batchelor, S.: Real time monitoring in disasters. IDS Bull. **44**, 122–134 (2013)

Troy, D.A., Carson, A., Vanderbeek, J., Hutton, A.: Enhancing community-based disaster preparedness with information technology. Disasters **32**, 149–165 (2008)

Frediani, A.A.: Amartya Sen, the World Bank, and the redress of urban poverty: a Brazilian case study. J. Hum. Dev. **8**, 133–152 (2007)

Sen, A.: Development as Freedom. OUP Oxford, Oxford (2001)

Das, R.: This artist creates pop art-inspired portraits to raise funds for COVID-19 relief. The Hindu (2020)

Sharma, T.: Coronavirus impact | I-T Dept officials propose 10 main ways to boost tax revenue. Moneycontrol (2020). https://www.moneycontrol.com/news/business/personalfinance/corona virus-pandemic-i-t-dept-officials-propose-10-main-ways-to-boost-tax-revenue-5189941.html

Pollach, I., Treiblmaier, H., Floh, A.: Online fundraising for environmental nonprofit organizations. In: 38th Hawaii International Conference on System Sciences, p. 9 (2005)

Donovan, K.P.: Mobile money, more freedom? The impact of M-PESA's network power on development as freedom. Int. J. Commun. **6**, 23 (2012)

Dataquest: PM CARES fund: all you need to know. DATAQUEST (2020). https://www.dqindia.com/pm-cares-fund-need-know/

Kundu, C.: Fact check: netas push dubious website on social media urging donations for PM CARES. India Today (2020). https://www.indiatoday.in/msn-itt/story/fact-check-netas-push-dubious-website-on-social-media-urging-donations-for-pm-cares-1669119-2020-04-20

Marques, D., McKeever, A., Nowakoski, K.: Coronavirus 101: what you need to know. National Geography (2020). https://www.nationalgeographic.com/science/2020/03/covid-overview-co ronavirus/

BBC News: World must prepare for pandemic, says WHO. BBC News (2020)

Vij, S.: Modi's poorly planned lockdown won't save us from coronavirus, but will kill economy. ThePrint (2020). https://theprint.in/opinion/modis-poorly-planned-lockdown-wont-save-usfro m-coronavirus-but-will-kill-economy/388056/

Agrawal, P.: Is India's COVID-19 Lockdown Biggest & One Of Harshest In World? (2020). https://thelogicalindian.com/story-feed/awareness/india-coronavirus-lockdown-20394

Park, T., Shenoy, R., Salvendy, G.: Effective advertising on mobile phones: a literature review and presentation of results from 53 case studies. Behav. Inf. Technol. **27**, 355–373 (2008)

Zhou, L., Xue, F.: Effects of color in disaster relief advertising and the mediating role of cognitive elaboration. J. Nonprofit Public Sect. Mark. **31**, 403–427 (2019)

Winterich, K.P., Barone, M.J.: Warm glow or cold, hard cash? Social identity effects on consumer choice for donation versus discount promotions. J. Mark. Res. **48**, 855–868 (2011)

Ellen, P.S., Mohr, L.A., Webb, D.J.: Charitable programs and the retailer: do they mix? J. Retail. **76**, 393–406 (2000)

Müller, S.S., Fries, A.J., Gedenk, K.: How much to give?—The effect of donation size on tactical and strategic success in cause-related marketing. Int. J. Res. Mark. **31**, 178–191 (2014)

Galán-Ladero, M.M., Galera-Casquet, C.: Does the donation size influence on attitudes toward cause-related marketing. Responsibility and Sustainability. Socioecon. Polit. Legal Issues **1** (1), 7–19 (2013)

Grau, S.L., Folse, J.A.G.: Cause-related marketing (CRM): the influence of donation proximity and message-framing cues on the less-involved consumer. J. Advert. **36**, 19–33 (2007)

Aker, J.C., Boumnijel, R., McClelland, A., Tierney, N.: Payment mechanisms and antipoverty programs: evidence from a mobile money cash transfer experiment in niger. Econ. Dev. Cult. Change **65**, 1–37 (2016)

Pega, F., Liu, S.Y., Walter, S., Lhachimi, S.K.: Unconditional cash transfers for assistance in humanitarian disasters: effect on use of health services and health outcomes in low-and middle-income countries. Cochrane Database Syst. Rev. (9) (2015)

Wachanga, D.N.: Ethnic differences vs nationhood in times of national crises: the role of social media and communication strategies. J. Afr. Media Stud. **7**, 281–299 (2015)

Morawczynski, O., Pickens, M.: Poor people using mobile financial services: observations on customer usage and impact from M-PESA (2009)

Firstpost. Demonetisation: how 'jugaad' payment systems are helping grocers, small vendors to combat cash crunch - Firstpost (2016). https://www.firstpost.com/india/demonetisation-how jugaad-payment-systems-are-helping-grocers-small-vendors-to-combat-cash-crunch3113006. html

Blumenstock, J.E., Eagle, N., Fafchamps, M.: Airtime transfers and mobile communications: evidence in the aftermath of natural disasters. J. Dev. Econ. **120**, 157–181 (2016)

Mirabaud, N.: Migrants' remittances and mobile transfer in emerging markets. Int. J. Emerg. Mark. Bradford **4**, 108–118 (2009)

Klein, H.K., Myers, M.D.: A set of principles for conducting and evaluating interpretive field studies in information systems. MIS Q. **23**, 67–93 (1999)

Indian Express. Acute urban-rural divide in Internet penetration in India: Report. The New Indian Express (2018). https://www.newindianexpress.com/nation/2018/feb/20/acute-urban-ruraldivi de-in-internet-penetration-in-india-report-1776295.html

Drèze, J., Sen, A.: India: Development and Participation. Oxford University Press, Oxford (2002)

Digital Humanitarianism in a Pandemic Outbreak: An Empirical Study of Antecedents and Consequences

Anup Kumar[1]([✉]) [iD], Niraj K. Vishwakarma[1,2], and Parijat Upadhyay[1]

[1] IMT Nagpur, Nagpur, India
{ankumar, pupadhyay}@imtnag.ac.in, niraj@bhu.ac.in
[2] FMS BHU, Varanasi, India

Abstract. Based on the resource-based view and the thematic analysis of digital humanitarianism, information and Communication Technology (ICT) success, and the potential value of Crowd Sourcing (CS), this study proposes a Digital Humanitarianism Capability (DHC) model. The study extends the above research streams by examining the direct effects of DHC on Disaster Risk Reduction (DRR), as well as the mediating effects of process-oriented dynamic capabilities (PODC) on the relationship between DHC and DRR. To test our proposed research model, we used an online survey to collect data from 150 District Magistrates (DMs) of India who is handling the COVID-19 Pandemic Management. The findings confirm the value of the entanglement conceptualization of the hierarchical DHC model, which has both direct and indirect impacts on DRR. The results also confirm the strong mediating role of PODC in improving insights and enhancing DRR. Finally, implications for practice and research are discussed.

Keywords: Digital humanitarianism · Disaster Risk Reduction · ICT

1 Introduction

Digital Humanitarianism (DH) has been widely regarded as a breakthrough in technological development in academic and business communities. Despite the growing need for digital humanitarianism, there is still limited know-how about the leveraging of such technological concepts into disaster management. The information overflow that occurs in the wake of a disaster can paralyze humanitarian response efforts. Computers, mobile phones, social media, mainstream news, earth-based sensors, humanitarian drones, and orbiting satellites generate vast volumes of data during major disasters. Making sense of this flash flood of information, or Big Data is proving a perplexing challenge for traditional humanitarian organizations. Aid groups are more adept at dealing with information scarcity than overflow. To address this problem many organizations are turning to Digital Humanitarians for help. Digital Humanitarians are volunteers and professionals from all over the world and all walks of life. They share a

Supported by organization IMT Nagpur.

desire to make a difference, and they do by rapidly mobilizing online in collaboration with international humanitarian organizations. In near real-time, they can process Big Data to support relief efforts worldwide. They craft and leverage ingenious crowd-sourcing solutions with trail-blazing insights from artificial intelligence. "Digital Jedis" by sharing their remarkable, real-life stories, highlighting how their humanity coupled with innovative Big Data solutions has changed how humanitarians will respond to disasters. The paper is intended to answer the following questions:

1. How Digital Humanitarian Dynamic Capabilities (DHDC) is measured and its consequences on humanitarian disaster management 2. Whether process oriented dynamic capabilities play a mediator between DHDC and Disaster Risk Reduction.

2 Review of Literature

The 2013 Global Disaster Study refers to the enabling essence of mobile telephones and social media for disaster recovery using the term humanitarian technology. New media innovations are essential to catalyzing a transition in humanitarianism (Madianou 2018).

2.1 Digital Humanitarian During a Pandemic

As per the world health organization report (WHO), there is an ongoing need for humanitarian aid for more than 130 million people due to natural disasters, outbreaks of diseases, and conflicts. Digital health is limited and still in its adolescence, but the sector is developing rapidly (Fernandez-Luque and Imran 2018). Almost every day, new digital studies and capabilities are announced. The standard and conduct of research in the humanitarian environment can be enhanced through the automation of the data custody chain, smart metadata, and other emerging technologies (Perakslis 2018). How digitalization (big data) transforms the face of humanitarian response. Following the Haiti earthquake, a digital map of areas most affected by the earthquake was developed. Hundreds of automated volunteers have labeled crowd-sourced knowledge via social media, allowing U.S. emergency teams to find survivors (Dave 2017; Meier 2015). The study of vast volumes of information generated by various outlets, such as social media material, is increasingly important for humanitarian health crises. They are an important case in which artificial intelligence technologies (AI) are used to assist in the detection and processing of sensitive information. Successful AI systems case studies have been published during a humanitarian crisis (Fernandez-Luque and Imran 2018; Madianou 2019). The technological difficulty is to process vast amounts of data in real-time. Data interoperability is still an obstacle to the convergence of the internet and conventional data sources and is necessary for the exchange of data (Fernandez-Luque and Imran 2018).

2.2 UTAUT2 in Humanetrian Operations Management

Digital Humanitarians are volunteers, students, and professionals from all walks of life. In conjunction with foreign humanitarian organizations, they are mobilizing online. It makes sense to collect vast amounts of social posts, text messages, and photographs from satellites and UAVs to support humanitarian operations. They build and exploit innovative crowdsourcing approaches with relevant artificial intelligence insights (Meier 2015). The information system develops a framework for handling the information while tracking and assessing humanitarian relief operations to enhance the performance of disaster relief operations. The concept of the Unified Theory of Acceptance and Use of Technology (UTAUT) is a method to research and understand better the factors that affect the acceptance and usage of the Information System by potential users (Dwiputranti et al. 2019). Mobile applications also offer ways to boost the efficiency of humanitarian logistics operations. People can regard mobile cash systems as one means of helping refugees. While refugees own cell telephones and have connections to numerous networks, they are people in need, and thousands are unable to live as a result of dangerous travel, harsh weather, medical conditions, and hunger (Abushaikha and Schumann-Bölsche 2016). Another way to provide emergency relief should find last-mile delivery drone applications in humanitarian logistics. Humanitarian organizations are getting increased attention from unmanned aerial vehicles (UAVs). They will help to solve problems of last-mile delivery, i.e., inaccessibility to the cut-off areas (Rabta et al. 2018).

3 Theory Development and Conceptual Framework

The Proposed theoretical model is presented in Fig. 1.

3.1 Constructs and Hypotheses Development

Communicable diseases are a significant cause of death after natural or human made disasters. Controlling an outbreak of an epidemic requires a rapid response. It is of utmost importance to establish and manage an emergency supply chain during the containment effort (Dasaklis et al. 2012).

3.2 DH Dynamic Capabilities

Disasters are increasing, and the assistance received by donors is becoming more and more unpredictable. Humanitarian organizations try effective and reliable solutions (Tomasini and Van Wassenhove 2009). Disaster management brings many organizations together to share resources in crises. The collaboration of different organizations relies heavily on successful activities. The real conditions of the 2013 flood in Acapulco, Mexico, showed that anyone organization had been unable to cope (Rodríguez-Espíndola et al. 2018). The US economy and people have been severely affected by natural disasters. This is important that aid supplies are planed correctly and handled effectively before a disaster begins. Olanrewaju et al. (2020) provide multi-stage

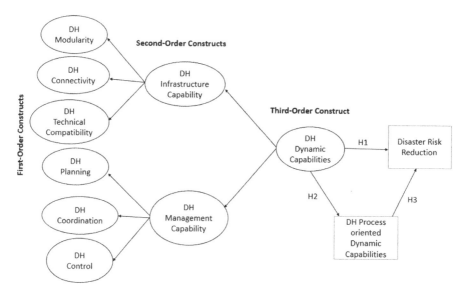

Fig. 1. Proposed model

stochastic programming models for the suppliers in the planning stage of disaster response. It offers relief organizations with information into how the terms of the deal impact the decision to pick a service provider and how to reduce the overall expected contract expense. The models determine whether the chosen suppliers are fulfilling their contractual terms and how much relief the relief agency has bought from suppliers. This model is used to solve the problem for small-scale test cases and also to solve a real word problem (Olanrewaju et al. 2020).

3.3 Process-Oriented Dynamic Capabilities

Logistics is essential for humanitarian relief and disaster response operations (Bastos et al. 2014). Disasters are marked by conflicting, unclear, or data shortages. Disasters like the Asian Tsunami, Hurricane Katrina, and earthquakes in Pakistan have shown the urgent need for powerful technical infrastructure (Tomaszewski et al. 2006). Rapid decisions need to be taken by the humanitarian aid staff. Information availability and consistency expectation are still not met in practice by humanitarian decision support systems (DSS). DSS supports a system for location recognition in the area of disaster relief supply chains to tackle the network architecture. A real-life scenario can then be added to the solution strategy (Timperio et al. 2017). On the other hand, wide complexity reflecting pressures and constraints on the field and accelerated humanitarian logistical forecasting is three main challenges for an operational DSS in support of distribution planning (Rahman et al. 2017). Disasters lead to the collapse of the system of existing ICTs. The ICT failure stops the service from collecting information from disaster-affected areas in real-time last miles. This creates a complex, unpredictable, unstable, and restricting humanitarian relief situation (Nagendra et al. 2020).

3.4 Disaster Risk Reduction

Logistic activity may be described as a socio-technological mechanism by which a human social network organizes a set of technological activities. To understand the functioning of the whole system, all its components must be properly considered (Holguín-Veras et al. 2012). Logistics has gained significant attention from scholars and practitioners in the sense of humanitarian operations. In the next 50 years, the number of both natural and human disasters is expected to increase by five times (Nikbakhsh and Zanjirani Farahani 2011). Disaster recovery is complex and can greatly benefit from careful preparation (Wisetjindawat et al. 2014). Humanitarian relief agencies mobilize billions of dollars annually in support for victims of natural disasters, civil wars, and conflicts (Balcik et al. 2010; Tatham and Houghton 2011; Thomas 2005). Logistics are central to their activities and their strategic tasks. Research shows that environmental factors, such as catastrophe unpredictability and the complexity of the financing, have contributed to highswing logistics activities (Thomas 2005). The 2003 worldwide epidemic of severe acute respiratory syndrome (SARS) has become a wake-up call for healthcare services. Pandemic planning has evolved over the past 15 years, with the introduction of a holistic disease risk management strategy (O'Sullivan and Phillips 2019; Runge et al. 2020). 2020 was the year of COVID-19 managing, World Bank group notes. It calls for the use of the system for controlling the risk of health-emergency disasters to supplement existing responses. It claims that the existing disaster management mechanisms and techniques will strengthen reactions to epidemics or global pandemics such as COVID-19 (Djalante et al. 2020). We, therefore, intended to posit: H1: DH Dynamic Capability has a positive impact on Process-Oriented Dynamic Capabilities H2: DH dynamic capability has a positive impact on Disaster Risk Reduction H3: Process-Oriented Dynamic Capabilities mediates the effect of DH Dynamic Capability on Disaster Risk Reduction.

4 Research Methodology and Data Collection

The questionnaire was designed based on UTAUT2 models, that were developed following an adaptation of the original TAM and TPB to this specific study. The questionnaire was tested using a pilot study before floating it online for pan India respondents. The reliability and internal consistency of the instrument were evaluated by calculating the Cronbach alpha values for each theoretical variable. The construct validity of the model was evaluated using the inter-item correlation analysis. The overall Cronbach alpha was greater than 0.9, and the individual Cronbach alpha for each of the constructs was also greater than 0.9. Although the instrument was conceived from the previous literature, Confirmatory Factor Analysis (CFA) was used to test the adequate item loadings and sampling adequacy, the KMO test results show valid adequacy of the samples while few items were deleted due to cross lodgings and poor loading.

4.1   Data Collection

Data was collected from social media users across pan India in two stages from February 2020 to April 2020 during the COVID-19 lockdown period. A Snowball sampling technique was used. A structured questionnaire was developed using google forms, with a consent form appended to it and shared with the respondents through online mode. The link of the questionnaire was sent through emails, WhatsApp, and other social media to the contacts of the investigator. The participants were encouraged to share the survey with as many people as possible to widen the outreach and increase the sample size. The participants were asked to indicate their responses on the 5-point Likert scale. A total of 150 responses were received through the online survey, 120 were finally considered as they were found to be complete in all the aspects while 7 were found to be incomplete and discarded. The demographic details of the respondents show that there were 53.3% females and 46.69% male participants.

5   Measurement Model

CFA was used to test the fitness of the measurement model. The average factor loading was greater than 0.65 which shows a good model convergent, the average factor lodgings were ¿ AVE and AVE was ¿ the inter-correlation among the constructs. The CFA function was used to validate the measurement model using R studio LAVAAN Package (Barrett 2007; Oberski 2014; Rosseel et al. 2017). The model fit indices like SRMR, TLI, AGFI, GFI, NNFI, and CFI are adequately fit to the specified values.

5.1   Structural Model

The path model represents the linear regressions of the hypothesis and its effect size and p values. The first regression equation represents the independent variable Disaster Risk Reduction regressed with the dependent variables DH Dynamic Capability, and Process-Oriented Dynamic. The second regression equation represents the dependent variable Process-Oriented Dynamic Capabilities regressed with DH Dynamic Capability. It has been seen from the regression that DH Dynamic Capability and Process-Oriented Dynamic are significant predictors of Disaster Risk Reduction with an effect size of 0.528 and 0.36 respectively while Process-Oriented Dynamic Capabilities mediates the effect of DH Dynamic Capability on Disaster Risk Reduction.

5.2   Data Analysis and Results

H1 DH Dynamic Capability has a positive impact on Process-Oriented Dynamic Capabilities Proved H2 DH dynamic capability has a positive impact on Disaster Risk Reduction Proved H3 Process-Oriented Dynamic Capabilities mediates the effect of DH Dynamic Capability on Proved.

6   Practical Implications of the Research

Digital humanitarianism is a new type of shared activism wherein anyone can participate and leverage the Capability of Big data Analytics. Digital Humanitarians are the volunteers from the society with the common goal of rapidly mobilizing online in collaboration with international humanitarian organizations. In virtually real-time, they make sense of vast volumes of social media, SMS and imagery captured from satellites and UAVs to support relief efforts worldwide. The ability to integrate the efforts of the connected volunteers to serve the people during disaster shall be a huge success to reduce the risk of disaster. The government of India has leveraged the use of NGO and civil society workers during the outbreak of COVID-19. The dynamic capability to leverage digital humanitarianism is therefore an important tool for the organizations during the disaster.

7   Limitations and Further Research

The research is based on the survey of the people who are directly or indirectly connected to the relief works during the COVID-19 Outbreak, which might be a potential bias for the research. In the future, the survey may include the other disaster environment.

References

Abushaikha, I., Schumann-Bölsche, D.: Mobile phones: established technologies for innovative humanitarian logistics concepts. Procedia Eng. (2016). https://doi.org/10.1016/j.proeng.2016.08.157

Author, F., Author, S.: Title of a proceedings paper. In: Editor, F., Editor, S. (eds.) Conference 2016. LNCS, vol. 9999, pp. 1–13. Springer, Heidelberg (2016). https://doi.org/10.10007/1234567890

Balcik, B., Beamon, B.M., Krejci, C.C., Muramatsu, K.M., Ramirez, M.: Coordination in humanitarian relief chains: practices, challenges and opportunities. Int. J. Prod. Econ. (2010). https://doi.org/10.1016/j.ijpe.2009.09.008

Barrett, P.: Structural equation modelling: adjudging model fit. Pers. Ind. Differ. **42**(5), 815–824 (2007)

Bastos, M.A.G., Campos, V.B.G., de Mello Bandeira, R.A.: Logistic processes in a post-disaster relief operation. Procedia – Soc. Behav. Sci. (2014). https://doi.org/10.1016/j.sbspro.2014.01.152

Dasaklis, T.K., Pappis, C.P., Rachaniotis, N.P.: Epidemics control and logistics operations: a review. Int. J. Prod. Econ. (2012). https://doi.org/10.1016/j.ijpe.2012.05.023

Dave, A.: Digital humanitarians: how big data is changing the face of humanitarian response. J. Bioeth. Inq. **14**(4), 567–569 (2017). https://doi.org/10.1007/s11673-017-9807-8

Djalante, R., Shaw, R., DeWit, A.: Building resilience against biologicalhazards and pandemics: COVID-19 and its implications for the Sendai Framework. Progress Disaster Sci. (2020). https://doi.org/10.1016/j.pdisas.2020.100080

Dwiputranti, M.I., Oktora, A., Okdinawati, L., Fauzan, M.N.: Acceptance and use of information technology: understanding information systems for Indonesia's humanitarian relief operations. Gadjah Mada Int. J. Bus. (2019). https://doi.org/10.22146/gamaijb.39199

Fernandez-Luque, L., Imran, M.: Humanitarian health computing using artificial intelligence and social media: a narrative literature review. Int. J. Med. Inform. (2018). https://doi.org/10.1016/j.ijmedinf.2018.01.015

Holguín-Veras, J., Jaller, M., Van Wassenhove, L.N., Pérez, N., Wachtendorf, T.: On the unique features of post-disaster humanitarian logistics. J. Oper. Manag. (2012). https://doi.org/10.1016/j.jom.2012.08.003

Madianou, M.: Humanitarianism: myths and realities. AoIR Sel. Pap. Internet Res. **6** (2018). https://journals.uic.edu/ojs/index.php/spir/article/view/8541

Madianou, M.: Technocolonialism: digital innovation and data practices in the humanitarian response to refugee crises. Soc. Media Soc. (2019). https://doi.org/10.1177/2056305119863146

Meier, P.: Digital humanitarians: how big data is changing the face of humanitarian response. In: Digital Humanitarians: How Big Data Is Changing the Face of Humanitarian Response (2015). https://doi.org/10.1201/b18023

Nagendra, N.P., Narayanamurthy, G., Moser, R.: Management of humanitarian relief operations using satellite big data analytics: the case of Kerala floods. Ann. Oper. Res. (2020). https://doi.org/10.1007/s10479-020-03593-w

Nikbakhsh, E., Zanjirani Farahani, R.: Humanitarian logistics planning in disaster relief operations. Logist. Oper. Manag. (2011). https://doi.org/10.1016/B978-0-12-385202-1.00015-3

O'Sullivan, T.L., Phillips, K.P.: From SARS to pandemic influenza: the framing of high-risk populations. Nat. Hazards (2019). https://doi.org/10.1007/s11069019-03584-6

Oberski, D.: lavaan.survey: an R package for complex survey analysis of structural equation models. J. Stat. Softw. **57**(1), 1–27 (2014)

Olanrewaju, O.G., Dong, Z.S., Hu, S.: Supplier selection decision making in disaster response. Comput. Ind. Eng. (2020). https://doi.org/10.1016/j.cie.2020.106412

Perakslis, E.D.: Using digital health to enable ethical health research in conflict and other humanitarian settings Chesmal Siriwardhana and Donal O'mathuna. Conflict Health (2018). https://doi.org/10.1186/s13031-018-0163-z

Rabta, B., Wankmüller, C., Reiner, G.: A drone fleet model for last-mile distribution in disaster relief operations. Int. J. Disaster Risk Reduct. (2018). https://doi.org/10.1016/j.ijdrr.2018.02.020

Rahman, M.T., Comes, T., Majchrzak, T.A.: Understanding decision support in large-scale disasters: challenges in humanitarian logistics distribution. In: Dokas, I.M., Bellamine-Ben Saoud, N., Dugdale, J., Díaz, P. (eds.) ISCRAM-med 2017. LNBIP, vol. 301, pp. 106–121. Springer, Cham (2017). https://doi.org/10.1007/978-3-319-67633-3_9

Rodríguez-Espíndola, O., Albores, P., Brewster, C.: Disaster preparedness in humanitarian logistics: a collaborative approach for resource management in floods. Eur. J. Oper. Res. (2018). https://doi.org/10.1016/j.ejor.2017.01.021

Rosseel, Y., et al.: Package 'lavaan.' (2017). Accessed 17 June 2017

Runge, M.C., et al.: Assessing the risks posed by SARS-CoV-2 in and via North American bats —decision framing and rapid risk assessment. Open-File Rep. (2020). https://doi.org/10.3133/ofr20201060

Tatham, P., Houghton, L.: The wicked problem of humanitarian logistics and disaster relief aid. J. Hum. Logist. Supply Chain Manag. (2011). https://doi.org/10.1108/20426741111122394

Thomas, A.: Humanitarian logistics: enabling disaster response. Fritz Institute (2005)

Timperio, G., Panchal, G.B., Samvedi, A., Goh, M., De Souza, R.: Decision support framework for location selection and disaster relief network design. J. Hum. Logist. Supply Chain Manag. (2017). https://doi.org/10.1108/JHLSCM-11-2016-0040

Tomasini, R.M., Van Wassenhove, L.N.: From preparedness to partnerships: case study research on humanitarian logistics. Int. Trans. Oper. Res. (2009). https://doi.org/10.1111/j.1475-3995.2009.00697.x

Tomaszewski, B.M., MacEachren, A.M., Pezanowski, S., Xiaoyan, L., Turton, I.: Supporting humanitarian relief logistics operations through online geocollaborative knowledge management. In: ACM International Conference Proceeding Series (2006). https://doi.org/10.1145/1146598.1146701

Wisetjindawat, W., Ito, H., Fujita, M., Eizo, H.: Planning disaster relief operations. Procedia – Soc. Behav. Sci. (2014). https://doi.org/10.1016/j.sbspro.2014.01.1484

Information Diffusion for Real Time Resource Planning During Crisis Leveraging Emerging Digital Technologies

Swarnalakshmi Ravi[1,2(✉)], T. J. Kamalanabhan[1],
and Thanga Jawahar[2]

[1] Indian Institute of Technology, Madras, Chennai, India
Swarna.mayu@gmail.com
[2] Tata Consultancy Services, Chennai, India

Abstract. Every day in some corner of this world displacements are happening due to adverse impact of climate change or natural disasters or riots or epidemics and global pandemics. Such displacements could be either internal displacement or cross border displacement. In just last year (2019), nearly 24.9 million people have been displaced due to the above cited reasons as per the report of United Nations Refugee Agency. Warsaw International Mechanism has put forth its effort to address the concern of displacements and support humanity along with United Nations, States, few ad-hoc working groups, civil societies and few supporting countries way back in 2016. On one side while the combined and sincere efforts are being made, on the other side the threats in terms of violence, riots, natural disasters, pandemics keep increasing at an alarming rate. Recent Covid-19 is a classic example which are likely to trigger more displacements to be continued in 2020. This has a spillover effect on demand and supply chain of health care services to the impacted as well as the citizens or locals in a particular region. Our paper aims to bring the combined efficiencies of emerging digital technologies and available data in order to gain insights and use them efficiently at the time of global crisis without causing interruption to health care and humanitarian services to all needy people.

Keywords: Disaster and displacement · Semantics for disaster management · Humanitarian services for the needy · Semantic information system for healthcare · Healthcare service for global crisis

1 Introduction

In today's world, humanity is being overlooked by few sects of people causing violent conflicts and riots while most others understand the need for uninterrupted humanitarian services, health care, education and good standard of living for all beings. Several countries, working committees, ad-hoc groups have joined hands together to provide their best for displaced people through refugee camps or ensuring the rehabilitation for them and so on. Despite these sincere efforts, statistics on global displacement still shows an alarming number across the globe from almost 145 countries several millions of people getting displaced and are homeless. The adverse impact is

© IFIP International Federation for Information Processing 2020
Published by Springer Nature Switzerland AG 2020
S. K. Sharma et al. (Eds.): TDIT 2020, IFIP AICT 618, pp. 33–44, 2020.
https://doi.org/10.1007/978-3-030-64861-9_4

that the major displacements are happening in the top 10 regions where the health risk alert of Covid-19 is high according to UN refugee agency. This is a critical issue that cannot be overlooked for making humanitarian and health care services more efficient at the times of such global crisis. In our study, we aim to bring forth the combined capacities of existing data bases from heterogeneous sources and real time streaming data that could come from any part of the globe and leverage the emerging digital technologies towards dynamic decision making and planning of resources in rescue operations. This proposed system based on the secondary research highlights how the benefits could be taken to various stakeholders such as government authorities, volunteers, media, adhoc working groups, health care professionals and supporting staffs, residents of the impacted areas, new migrants displaced in those areas and the local authorities of those areas. The digital forces such as mobility, cloud computing, analytics, semantics and social media are fast emerging, and the computing resources are available at a much lower costs almost like a commodity (Kalidoss et al. 2016). Therefore, our proposed system is set to bring more efficiency at a reasonable cost for sustenance of such initiatives.

1.1 Compelling Needs for Semantics-Based Information System - Need for System from Integration to Insights

Most publications and recent articles from leading journals, research articles, media channels, governmental data, press news etc. agree that loads of data are available but in isolated manner. This implies the unavailability of insights, even though information of some sort was made available prior. Even though rapid urbanization poses a common problem facing any developed or developing country, the demographics, climate and environmental factors cannot be undermined. Past disaster damages related data and insights should enable urban sensing and drive the future growth plans. All these factors need to be keyed into decision support system for dynamic decision making.

1.2 Need for System that Drives Real Time Actions

In majority of the countries, the federal or central or state government and various departments maintain their respective databases related to the public, officials in that locality and all stakeholders as appropriate. However, information needs more analytics powered by fast growing technologies to facilitate communication dissemination in real time and in seamless manner. Making the heterogenous data work together and making the heterogeneous systems communicate with each other are cumber some tasks unless there is a common language which these information systems can interpret. Semantics is one such technology that serves as a boon to address the interoperability challenge.

This paper is organized as follows. Section 1 gives the context for choosing semantic based system for health care services and disaster management and the perspectives from emerging digital technologies. It also includes the primary causes for severe damages due to disasters and its impact on displacements across the globe. Section 2 includes the literature review related to our study. Section 3 gives the insight into prevailing traditional disaster management system and some of the gaps in the same. Sections 4 and 5 detail out on semantic applications overview and our proposed intelligent communication system that utilizes the available information from various data sources and how they could be aggregated to provide timely alerts to various stakeholders. Section 6 further elaborates on the pilot implementation of the proposed system. It gives insight into various types of databases which handle big data, multiple sources of data flow, and multiple types of data such as text, images, and real-time message streams and so on. Section 7 lists out various potential benefits from the proposed semantic based system. Section 8 provides the summary view of the article and few recommendations for futuristic work to enhance the humanitarian services further.

2 Literature Review

According to UN Refuge agency, in last year alone nearly 2000 disasters have triggered 24.9 million displacements either internally or cross borders put together. The report also indicates that the numbers are expected to increase in 2020 and beyond due to global health crisis prevailing in developed and developing countries. Disaster response and recovery are the most crucial aspects of disaster management whether it is a natural or a man-made disaster. Majority of literature cite the common challenges as lack of coordination, lack of understanding the nature and the impact of disaster, lack of real time inputs, poor urban planning, inadequate infrastructure and resources and so on.

In the research article by Oden et al. (Oden et al. 2012), the authors have determined that the four main challenges to be addressed are coordination among groups involved in the response, communication among these groups, timely information exchange, and effective information technology support for emergency responders in the field. Though this study uses information technologies to connect location dependent desktop system to mobile phone, it does not take into account of multiple data types and multiple data sources from multiple locations and interoperability of such diverse platforms. The study by FAO finds the two main pillars of disaster management and global governance are disaster risk reduction (DRR) and climate change adaptation (CCA). However, integrating these pillars is quite challenging as the rules and laws vary from land to land. The governance structure, constituencies and political stability and several other factors determine the outcome and efficiency of integration. The study further indicates the need for smart disaster risk management system, and this is in line with our proposed system leveraging emerging digital technologies for better health care and humanitarian services to the needy.

The international strategy for disaster reduction indicates set of priorities for disaster management such as early warning, coordinated effort making, utilising available information effectively and innovatively, making information available to relevant stakeholders and strengthen the disaster preparedness. This is in line with our proposed semantic based information system that is capable of providing real time inputs based on context to relevant stakeholders as one version of truth and enables planning and mobilising of resources, food and health care packages to the needy without delays.

The literature work on design science invariably talks about the utility of information systems (IS) design (Bisandu 2016 and Hevner et al. 2004). The applications and the benefits to stakeholders is at the central theme of any IS design. The design science research methodologies emphasize the relevance of utility to creative, cognitive and social behaviour of such stakeholders making use of the IS design implementation. The proposed semantic oriented system aims to enable such cognitive and social behaviour from various stakeholders involved in rescue operations and humanitarian services at the time of crisis by providing contextual inputs in a timely manner. The design science research methodology and framework recommended by Hevner et al. provides seven primary guidelines for IS system development and usage. Though our proposed system is aligned to all the seven guidelines, the primary focus is on guideline 2 of problem relevance that is IT and disaster in today's context and in future, guideline 6 of design as a search process with available information from existing data sources and guideline 7 of design for communication of research to stakeholders both technical and managerial in nature.

3 Existing Disaster Management System and Challenges

The National Institute of Disaster Management (NIDM 2014) report finds that the four main aspects of an early warning system or a disaster management system are knowledge of risk, prediction of the same and monitoring periodically, dissemination of information to all relevant stakeholders and response to the risk in terms of better coordination. It also finds that ICT (Information and Communication Technologies) plays an indispensable role in disaster and risk management. Even though several ICT systems are available, they are either special purpose (like tsunami warning for coastal areas) or lack some enhanced capabilities or suffer from inter system coordination (stand alone and supports only a specific cause).

The United Nations Office for Disaster Risk Reduction (UNISDR) defines warning system as a set of capabilities needed for the timely and meaningful generation and dissemination of alert information to individuals, communities and organizations at risk for optimal preparedness and response and at the appropriate time (UNISDR 2006). At the same time, the Third International Conference on Early Warning also revealed problems and deficiencies of the warning system (EWC III 2006). For instance, some information systems work well with certain format and not with all types and formats of data. The existing Early Warning (EW) system and Disaster Management (DM) system cannot be completely explained in all aspects and the challenges are multi fold and is still an ambition to visualize the processes in real time and take dynamic decisions (Konecny et al. 2010).

4 Semantics Applications for Healthcare and Humanitarian Services During Crisis

As a result of the gaps found from existing information systems for disaster management, this study proposes a semantic oriented system which address interoperability issue and supports multiple sources, multiple types and multiple formats of data.

Semantic based system inherently uses common vocabulary languages such as web ontology (OWL), resource description framework graphs (RDF) and so on which are known for their support in platform independence. Typically, a semantic web can be used for data integration, knowledge synthesis, knowledge representation and management, semantic web services and data interoperability (Mukherjee et al. 2013). The key objective for semantic application in any domain is to have improved usability, completeness of information and its accuracy through knowledge reasoning (Bitar et al. 2014). In our study we focus on semantic based system that can improvise healthcare and humanitarian services to the needy during crisis by addressing the challenges indicated in earlier Sect. 3.

About 11 themes are identified and broadly classified in the healthcare impact during disaster through a study made by Pourhosseini et al. (2015). These themes are related to human resources management, resources management, victims' management transfer, environmental hygiene monitoring, nutrition management, mental health control, inter-agency coordination, training, technology management, information and communication management, and budget management. Most studies from literature also converge at these broad categories of healthcare services impact and emphasize the need to improve the coordination, inter personnel collaboration, planning and execution and so on. Our semantic based approach is aiming to address almost all of these broadly classified challenges. The detailed analysis and illustration of how our proposed system works is being addressed in the next section.

5 Proposed Semantic Oriented System for Healthcare and Humanitarian Services During Crisis

The proposed system components and its high-level architecture for information fusion from multiple data sources has been illustrated in Fig. 1. The working stages of transforming data into actionable insights is shown in the Fig. 2. To bring in more clarity, a scenario analysis has been assumed and explained in Fig. 3 and Fig. 4. The working of semantic information system (SIS) is illustrated in the Fig. 5 with the help of RDF semantic graph.

Let us assume that some part of the nation is affected by a novel disease and the active cases analysis finds that there is no prior availability of treatment details. In our context sensitive system, we propose that the details of the active cases could be aggregated using the available limited data from various private and government databases (Fig. 3).

The data thus obtained could be semantically mapped to real time information coming through a global organization like WHO (World Health Organization) or some alert from authentic sources or recommendations on health care comes as a live stream from a research laboratory based in some other part of the world, the information can be loaded in to a system (decision support system) and further processed with business intelligence tools (ETL- Extract Transform and Load) and fed in to semantic based

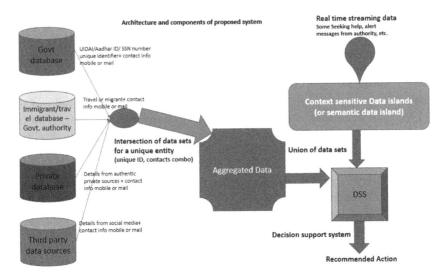

Fig. 1. Architecture and components of our semantic based system

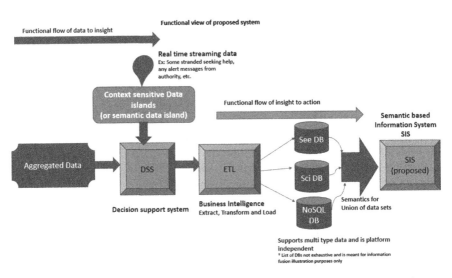

Fig. 2. Functionalities of semantic based system for turning data to insights to actions

information system (proposed) for action plans that are generated automatically (Fig. 4) based on the context and live inputs streaming from different corners of the world.

The proposed system is platform independent (OWL based) and hence overrides the interoperability challenges and semantically aggregates visual data (See DB), geo location maps and coordinates inputs (Sci DB) and other heterogenous inputs (NoSQL DB) to provide set of recommendations to various stakeholders as shown in Fig. 5.

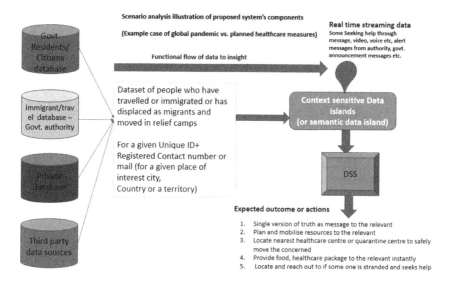

Fig. 3. Scenario analysis architecture for global pandemic using semantic system

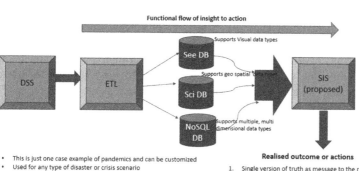

Fig. 4. Scenario analysis functionalities for global pandemic using semantic system

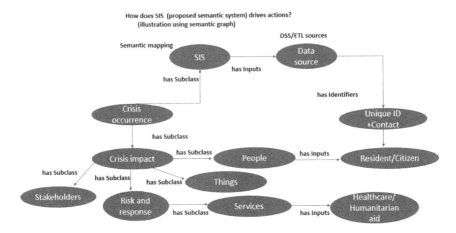

Fig. 5. Context based semantic map for global crisis using RDF graph

6 Pilot Study Implementation and Preliminary Results

A pilot study was conducted to understand the perspectives and challenges from the residents of Chennai during the lockdown period ever since March 2020 owing to Covid-19 global pandemic. The study participants include adults in the age group of 25 to 45 years (50%), senior citizens (30%) and super senior citizens (20%). The study finds that more than 80% of senior and super senior citizens are pensioners in the locality of our study and have access to basic digital technologies like smart phone, email, online surfing etc. We had conducted pilot survey through online and telephonic calls owing to prevailing situation then. We had planned for 50 responses overall through online emails and calls but however we got close to it about 45 responses. The adults group aged between 25 years to 45 years comprised people with working background from IT, ITES, Banking, Colleges and universities, sales and marketing

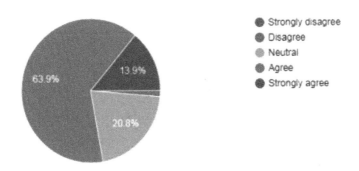

Fig. 6. Participants from pilot study emphasize information integration and diffusion

sectors and are working from home or from respective native locations during the lockdown and unlocking periods.

The overall outcome of the study showed that majority of the participants either agreed or strongly agreed for information as single truth and aggregated one. The pilot study also finds that the information of basic needs such as essentials, medicines, emergency reach out and rescue teams are made available without distortion but with accuracy and reliability. Some participants find other sources of information like special themed apps, information from their peer groups or chat groups are adequate for them to sustain the tough period during crisis (Fig. 6).

Based on the pilot study outcome, we propose to use the context sensitive semantic oriented system which takes into the account the scenario-based implementation. For the context of global pandemic and lockdown scenario, the desired outcome from the semantic system would be to provide single version of current situation in the country (as against more distorted inputs from multiple sources and unreliable sources), provide recommendations on dos and don'ts to every resident of the locality and inputs on some of the basic needs for the residents so as to enable them to sustain through the tough times. Our system is designed to accept inputs in the format of XML, Microsoft Excel or spreadsheet and Web Ontology Language files (OWL). The aggregated data from a business intelligence tool (BI tool/ETL tool) as shown in Fig. 2 can be fed into our SIS semantic information system in any of the formats listed above.

To explain this, the data could be containing a list of health care centres, medical shops, grocery needs, clinics, private ambulance services etc. based on the current location of the person who seeks information or help. The Excel sheet might be available as aggregated secondary data. For creating OWL and XML files, the ontology has to be defined once at least and revised on need basis thereafter. We used Thing-Worx platform by PTC to define the demo ontology as shown in Fig. 7 below. Every entity a living or non- living is considered a thing which is uniquely identifiable.

Fig. 7. Creating disaster response ontology using PTC ThingWorx platform

As a result from pilot study, if we have to populate the list of covid19 or a specialty healthcare centres for a given geo location, then every such centre would be conceptualised as a thing and its meta properties, geo location properties and attributes can be defined using the Thing Worx platform and the details would be populated in to a result set for users to consume the information service.

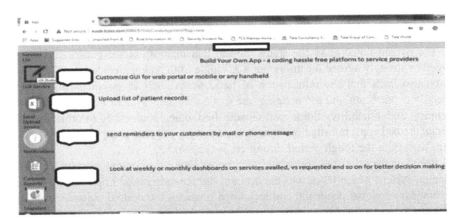

Fig. 8. A simple GUI for viewing of results for a semantic context-oriented search

We then designed a simple user interface using an approach called Build Your Own Application (BYOA) as shown in Fig. 8. The service providers have to subscribe just one time to the master portal of BYOA and they would be provided with unique credentials to login and later customize to build their own application using listed services per se for a specialty clinic or rehabilitation center, it could be the excel upload of patient records, send notifications, dashboard viewing and so on. Thus, having a context driven approach such as semantics is helpful in designing solution which enjoys platform independence and is easy to customize and maintain and is also cost effective and robust.

Another advantage is that neither the citizen nor the service collaborator needs to be aware of underlying technologies or software languages used due to its user friendliness nature in implementation. Even when a person goes offline, technologies like google pins can assist to locate the person at risk through a call or message. The geographic location thus obtained will be pulled by ETL system discussed in Fig. 3 and aggregated for providing humanitarian aids by our proposed semantic based system. One of the classic examples was the rescue operation undertaken during Kerala floods of 2018. Besides all these, the proposed system can also generate some basic reports for governmental units and other authorities like number of cases treated, other third party and private service providers for healthcare who can be reached out for transferring excess number of patients, providing healthcare kits without delays etc.

7The system is in very nascent stage and a lot more to be done in both natural and man-made disaster response front. However, the preliminary results are encouraging and shows by using semantics- oriented information system, we can overcome the interoperability challenge and improve service collaboration during any disaster or crisis.

7   Potential Benefits and Practical Implications

The main and foremost advantage of developing a semantic oriented system is to overcome the challenge of interoperability and hassle-free exchange of information at the hour of need across various IT systems handling various varieties and volumes of data. Our proposed system can work with multiple existing and available data bases that store and retrieve details in different ways using different technologies or platforms. As an initial step, we have come up with the pilot implementation taking into consideration the current global crisis of covid19 and the immediate disaster response of health care and humanitarian services. However, we intend to extend it to other types of disaster scenarios as well like tsunami, forest fire breakout, earthquake and so on. The process of building the holistic response system is time consuming though but largely beneficial to the society if we look at the larger sect and longer period in the future. The proposed system output also avoids distortion of information and at the same time provides needed inputs as reports to authorities, to individuals, to service collaborators and to the information systems administrator for customization. The proposed system can also support when the person at risk goes offline but only if the person is reachable or identifiable through any mobile phone calls or messages and is able to provide geo location inputs in some format so that our system can match relevant records from various sources for the given context and provide timely assistance.

8 Summary and Future Directions

The healthcare and humanitarian services are the most sought after any calamity, be it a man- made such as a riot or a natural disaster such as an earthquake. As the growth redefines itself in terms of communication and computing technologies, most of the hardware and software in today's market is commoditized and can be better utilised to improve any services segment. In our study it is healthcare and humanitarian services segment that is said to enhance with more computing capabilities for dynamic decision making in real time reducing delays in response to crisis. Risk reduction and response improvement during crisis are quite challenging and there is lot of scope for improving communication, coordination and collaboration between various stakeholders. Existing literature indicates that the semantic based disaster management is very limited in scope and capacity and does not take into account every stakeholder concerned (Dirgahayu et al. 2020). Our proposed system in the contrary improves these above specified aspects and in addition takes into consideration, multiple level of individuals (residents/citizens) in the stakeholder chart. The future is set to transform itself with technological advancements for a better world and a safe living for all.

Acknowledgement. The authors thank Indian Institute of Technology Madras (IIT Madras, India) and Tata Consultancy Services (TCS, India) for their encouragement and motivation in writing this paper.

References

UNHCR: COVID-19 Displacement and climate change, June 2020
IDMC: Global report on internal displacement (2020)
UN Secretary General Policy Brief COVID-19 and People on the Move, June 2020

The International Federation of Red Cross and Red Crescent Societies (IFRC), World Disasters Report 2015: Focus on local actors, the key to humanitarian effectiveness, pp. 198–230 (2015)

UNISDR: Global Assessment Report on Disaster Risk Reduction 2015: Making development sustainable: The future of disaster risk management (2015)

Oden, R.V., Militello, L.G., Ross, K.G., Lopez, C.E.: Four key challenges in disaster response. Sage J. **56**(1), 488–492 (2012)

FAO: Governance challenges for disaster risk reduction and climate change adaptation convergence in agriculture: Guidance for analysis., Food and Agriculture Organization of the United Nations, Rome (2019)

International strategy for disaster reduction, Progress and Challenges in Disaster Risk Reduction - A contribution towards the development of policy indicators for the Post-2015 Framework on Disaster Risk Reduction (2014)

NIDM: East Asia Summit-Earthquake reduction center, National Institute of Disaster Management of India retrieved from the website https://nidm.gov.in/easindia2014/err/pdf/themes_issue/technology/early_warnings.pdf. Accessed 25 July 2020

EWC III - Third International Conference on Early Warning - UNISDR. https://www.unisdr.org/2006/ppew/info-resources/ewc3_website/. Accessed 5 Oct 2018

UNISDR: Global Survey of Early Warning Systems An assessment of capacities, gaps and opportunities toward building a comprehensive global early warning system for all-natural hazards (2006). https://www.unisdr.org/we/inform/publications/3612. Accessed 20 July 2018

Konečný, M., Reinhardt, W.: Early warning and disaster management: the importance of geographic information (Part A), pp. 217–220. Taylor & Francis, 20 August 2010

Mukherjee, D., Banerjee, S., Misra, P.: Towards efficient stream reasoning. In: Demey, Y.T., Panetto, H. (eds.) OTM 2013. LNCS, vol. 8186, pp. 735–738. Springer, Heidelberg (2013). https://doi.org/10.1007/978-3-642-41033-8_97

Bitar, I.E., Belouadha, F.-Z., Roudies, O.: Semantic web service discovery approaches: overview and limitations. Int. J. Comput. Sci. Eng. Surv. (IJCSES) **5**(4) (2014)

Pourhosseini, S.S., Ardalan, A., Mehrolhassani, M.H.: Key aspects of providing healthcare services in disaster response stage. Iran J. Public Health **44**(1), 111–118 (2015)

Dirgahayu, T., Setiaji, H.: Semantic web in disaster management: a systematic literature review. In: IOP Conference on Series: Materials Science and Engineering, vol. 803, p. 012043 (2020)

Kalidoss, T.J., Ravi, S.: Disaster management system leveraging the emerging digital technologies. In: 2016 IEEE International Conference on Computational Intelligence and computing Research (ICCIC), pp. 1–7 (2016). https://doi.org/10.1109/iccic.2016.7919518

Hevner, R.A., March, S.T., Park, J., Ram, S.: Design science in information systems research. MIS Q. **28**(1), 75–105 (2004)

Bisandu, D.B.: Design science research methodology in computer science and information systems. Int. J. Inf. Technol. **5**, 55–60 (2016)

From Human Automation Interactions to Social Human Autonomy Machine Teaming in Maritime Transportation

Carine Dominguez-Péry$^{(\boxtimes)}$ and Lakshmi Narasimha Raju Vuddaraju

Univ. Grenoble Alpes, Grenoble INP*, CERAG, 38000 Grenoble, France
carine.dominguez@gmail.com, vamsi.vuddaraju@gmail.com

Abstract. Recent technological advances in the field of Artificial intelligence (AI) and machine learning led to the creation of smart AI-enabled automation systems that are drastically changing maritime transportation. We developed a systematic literature review to understand how automation, based on Information Technologies (IT), has tackled the challenges related to human and machine interactions. We notably discuss the conceptual evolution from Human-Automation Interaction (HAI) to Human Autonomy Teaming (HAT) and present the risks of high levels of automation and the importance of teamwork in safety critical systems. Our results lie on a map of five clusters that highlight the importance of trust in the interactions between humans and machines, the risks related to automation, the human errors that are arising from these interactions, the effects of automation on situational awareness and the social norms in human-computer interactions. This literature show that human-machines interactions have mainly been studied from the computer/information systems' (IS) point of view, hence neglecting the social dimensions of humans. Building on the difference between the concepts of automation and autonomy, we suggest the development of the concept of Social Human Autonomy Machine Teaming (SHAMT) to better consider the social dimensions of humans in these new interactions. Future research should focus on the right equilibrium between social needs, social interactions among humans and with autonomous machines with AI to optimize the global autonomy of the human-machine teammates in a whole ecosystem.

Keywords: Social Human Autonomy Machine Teaming (SHAMT) · Unmanned ship · Artificial intelligence · Maritime transportation · Human automation interactions

1 Introduction

Recent technological advances in the field of Artificial intelligence (AI) and machine learning led to the creation of smart AI-enabled automation systems, that are capable of processing huge amounts of data, evaluate alternatives and execute those decisions [1]. Even though the aviation industry spearheaded the introduction of these automation technologies, the maritime transportation industry is fast catching up in the implementation of these automation technologies [2] leading to increased opportunities to use Information Technologies (IT) and Information Systems (IS) related to lower risk accidents. The major drivers behind the increasing trend of automation are economic benefits or safety [3]. Technological innovations in AI and machine learning create a possibility of autonomous ship operations [4] leading new perspectives on human-machine interactions such as the use of big data and predictive analytics on decision-making and improved social and environmental sustainability related to maritime accidents [5]. The prospects of operationalizing unmanned ships have been gaining traction during the past few years. For instance, the EU funded MUNIN (Maritime Unmanned Navigation through Intelligence in Networks) developed the concept of the unmanned bulk carrier to carry economic, technological, and legal improvements [6]. The project of launching "Yara Birkeland" was the world's first fully autonomous electric-powered container ship that was expected to operate with complete autonomy by 2022 [7]. As of now, most of these unmanned ships are expected to be operated with a high level of supervisory control from the Shore-based Control Centers (SCC) [8]. In the future, most of these ships will be operated with high levels of IT/IS automation with limited human interventions both for operational maneuvers [6] and for super-vision tasks. These evolutions drive several changes in terms of working modes between the crew and automated systems, leading to new challenges and risks. This new configuration of human on boards lead to a reorganization of tasks questioning how humans and autonomous technologies can work together in these safety-critical systems. The task of navigating the ship can be defined as teamwork as it requires coordination and interactions between members of the team [9]. The importance of teamwork and the skills required by the teammates has been highlighted in similar safety-critical environments like nuclear power plant operations [10]. Several research call for further research in order to better understand how humans and machines can act as partners in performing the maritime transportation tasks, the success of such a system depends upon the ability of the system and human operators to understand each other's state and functioning [11]. Even though current concepts have improved our understanding, we argue that too much focus has been paid to machines rather than humans for two main reasons. Firstly, there is still a poor understanding of the importance human social interactions on board, its benefits and the risks generated with the current reduction of crew members. Secondly, little research has been developed to understand how humans on ships should socially interact with IT/IS machines not only with actors on board but also more largely with their ecosystem (notably with the SCC) and hence form a team with increased autonomous machines.

To do so, we suggest to introduce the concept of Social Human Autonomy Machine Teaming (SHAMT) while answering the two following research questions:

RQ1: What are the various concepts that have tackled the interactions between humans and machines in the literature review on maritime transportation industry?
RQ2: What are the future key questions related to this field?

This paper is structured as follows: in Sect. 2, we present a literature review on the different concepts related to the interactions between humans and machines in the maritime transportation industry. In Sect. 3, we present the methodology used for the systematic literature review. In Sect. 4, we present the results structured around the co-citation analysis. Section 5 summarizes the main results, the limits and perspectives for further development.

2 Literature Review

2.1 From Human-Automation Interaction (HAI) to Human Autonomy Teaming (HAT)

The equipment on-board ships became more complex since the 1960s with technological advances and the pace of change has accelerated rapidly from the 1990s with widespread utilization of computers and other navigational technologies like GPS, increasing the trend of automation on ships [2] due to rapid technological advances and economic benefits [12].

Even though historically the term 'autonomy' appeared before the word 'automation', the literature most of the time uses these terms interchangeably [13, 14]. Automation can be defined as "technology that actively selects data, transforms information, makes decisions or controls processes" [15, p. 50]. Automation refers to a system that can only perform tasks for which it was programmed by the designer, without any degree of freedom to adapt itself to the changing dynamic situation at hand [13]. In this paper, we define automation as technology or system that will augment, substitute or replace functions, which human operators were carrying out before. Autonomy is a more refined and well-defined form of automation that can better adapt itself to a wide array of situations [16].

The early work on human-automation interaction was carried by Bainbridge [17]. In his seminal work "Ironies of automation", he shed light into the impact of automation on human cognitive skill degradation and on the role of the human operator in decision making in human-computer collaboration environment [17]. More recently, some research introduced the necessity of forming a team between humans and machines with the concept of Human Autonomy Teaming (HAT), machine as teammates [11], symbiotic teamwork [14] raising questions about "turning automated systems into effective team players" [11, p. 95].

2.2 The Limits of Higher Levels of Automation on HAI and Related Risks

The Level of Automation (LoA) will drastically change human-machine cooperation at various levels [16, 18]. There are multiple taxonomies that explain the levels of automation in complex dynamic systems [13]. These taxonomies fall somewhere between manual operation to fully autonomous systems [18]. There are two development areas in the maritime domain that can be classified as autonomous operations: self-navigating vessels and remotely operated vessels [19]. Both these systems require some sort of human involvement, either from SCCs or human operators on board to take control if needed [8]. For that reason, a fully autonomous vessel without supervision is not going to happen in the near future [20]. Due to the advances in technology, a huge amount of information is siphoned to the human operator, which he needs to process. Hence "information isn't the scarce resource; human time and attention are the scarce resources" [21, p. 5]. The Human-Autonomy teams should act as complimentary in which they should compensate for each other's weakness [22]. Humans have the rare ability to learn and adapt dynamically based on the tasks, environment, situations [1].

Unlike human's, automation systems are trained with data, when the situation emerges out of the limited trained data, the automation systems cannot adopt dynamically, thus human intervention is needed when a system encounters an off-normal situation [11]. Norman et al. stated that the human errors in safety-critical industries were not due to 'over-automation' but rather to "inappropriate feedback and integration" [23]. Too much reliance on the automated system will induce 'automation bias', in which the humans will rely on automated alarms or warning systems without performing any manual checks [24].

Finally, looking at the extreme case of unmanned ships, new risks are appearing that are still understudied [25]. Some risks are related to the lack of social interactions for the reduced crew on board or for those piloting the ships: boredom and related risk of distraction that would lower situation awareness; other risks are related to skill degradation due to overreliance on machines; finally some risks are related to remote operation and monitoring such as diminished ship sense (for instance, no bodily feeling of the ship rocking), information overload (with ships equipped with multiple sensors), latency and cognitive horizon not adapted to the real conditions, mishaps during changeovers and handoffs (when a pilot is managing several ships remotely at the same time).

2.3   The Importance of Teamwork in Safety Critical Systems

A significant portion of operational tasks in safety-critical industries ([14], aerospace or in nuclear disaster [22]) were performed by teams rather than individuals working in isolation [10]. A team can be defined as "a small number of people with complementary skills who are committed to a common purpose, set of performance goals and approach for which they hold themselves mutually accountable" [26, p. 121]. Hutchins described navigation (navigating a vessel) as a collective cognitive process which cannot be accomplished by a single brain and that requires other people, equipment as component [27]. Usually the bridge team in a ship contains a team of individuals having a degree of shared knowledge and experience, each member of the team contributing a distinct part (plotting the course, providing coordination, operating the helm) in successfully maneuvering the vessel [9]. Since navigational decisions and actions are highly time critical, the bridge functions acts as a variant of team-based organization in which tasks and decisions are carried out interactionally [28]. Even though IT/IS improve the performance of the automated systems; yet, humans are still vital for the operation of automation systems for the years to come [12].

"Man-computer symbiosis" is a subset of "man-machine systems", when both the man and the machine are tightly coupled. Symbiosis can be defined as "the living together in more or less intimate association or close union of two dissimilar organisms" [29, p. 4]. It is important to understand how humans and machines work together as a team, especially taking into consideration that the limits of human minds have not been taken into account and may lead to system's failure [21]. The concept of "Human-Autonomy Teams" (HAT) is then valuable because it suggests that both humans and machines may develop autonomy skills to adapt to different contexts with the ability to learn and improve performance [3].

3   Methodology

We used a similar 4-stage systematic review literature review model based on [31], [32]. First, we created a search string ("Human-machine*" or "Man-machine*" or "Human-automation" or "man-automation" or "Human-AI" or "Human-Artificial intelligence" or *machine* or *automation* or AI or *Artificial intelligence* or "Autonomous*") and ("*collaboration" or "*symbiosis" or "*team*" or "interaction*") with the relevant keywords like 'Human-Autonomy Interaction', 'Human-Autonomy collaboration'. We used the Web of Science-core collection, due to its extensive and well curated collection of articles from multiple domains. For the initial search we got around n = 79,191 results. Since our primary motive was understanding Human factors and other ergonomic issues related to the Human and autonomy teaming, we narrowed our research [32] to the Ergonomics domain in Web of Science (WoS) that published most articles related to maritime transportation, knowing that some papers could be included in other categories (for instance Business for research that include cost-arguments in relation to maritime safety) Reading the abstracts, we excluded all the articles that were unrelated to the topic leading to n = 789 results. As the topic of HAT is multidisciplinary in nature, similar to [33], we included all the articles found without considering the journal or discipline they belong to.

In step 2 we downloaded all the records from the WoS portal to conduct a bibliographic analysis and performed a co-citation analysis (CCA) in the VosViewer software, as co-citation analysis provides the theoretical background for the intended topic [32]. "Co- citation is defined as the frequency with which two documents are cited together" [34, p. 269].

Before using the records for creating CCA analysis it is important to ensure that the documents included for conducting the analysis are relevant to our study and match the criteria. First, we looked for any duplicate records in the filtered n = 789 documents and we found two duplicate records and removed them. Second, we looked for false positives, for example the articles might include keywords mentioned in the search string in their titles, abstract and keywords but were not related to the domain [32]. To do so, we checked the abstracts and introductions of the articles to exclude the articles that ware relevant to the study following a protocol that determines the inclusion and exclusion criteria [35]. We found several false positives that we removed from the records: for instance Davis user acceptance model [36]; Mayer et al. model for organizational trust [37] and some articles related to psychology [38] or to human performance under stress and workload [39] engineering psychology and human performance [40]; finally, trust in human relations and some books in behavioral economics [41].

Finally, we created the CCA and adjusted in VosViewer the hyperparameters to 10 minimum citations. 144 documents met the criteria gathered into 5 clusters that are described in details in the following Sect. 4.

4   Results

Figure 1 shows the bibliographic map of five clusters based on CCA. We made the interpretation of these clusters based on the top-five cited articles.

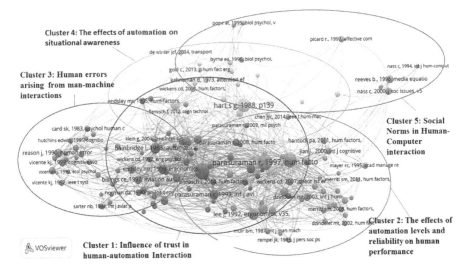

Fig. 1. CCA based on the keywords in VosViewer

4.1   Cluster 1: The Influence of Trust in Human-Automation Interaction

Cluster 1 is the largest with 40 items. It primarily deals with the influence of trust in Human-automation interaction; the trust in automation will determine the use or misuse of automation [15, 42, 43]. Too much or little reliance on the system, would result in automation and complacency bias [44, 45]. This cluster is closed to Cluster 2, as trust in a system with higher level of automation affects the skill of human operators and may result in out of the loop performance [46] Cluster 1 is also closed to the Cluster 3 as there are close associations between trust in automation and potential human errors. This Cluster is located at the center, with linkages to all the other clusters, showing the central role of trust in HAI.

4.2   Cluster 2: The Effects of Automation Levels and Reliability on Human Performance

Cluster 2 has 39 items, most of them presenting classification of automation levels and related taxonomies [47, 48]. Parasuraman classified the automation levels based on four information processing levels [49]. This cluster also includes some papers that emphasize on the importance of functional allocation, describing the functional superiority of humans or machines in performing various tasks [50, 51]. Other papers discuss the issue of complacency at higher automation levels and its effects on performance under different workload conditions [52, 53]. This cluster is in closed to Cluster 1 and Cluster 4 highlighting the effects of higher levels of automation on [54].

4.3   Cluster 3: The Human Errors Arising from Man-Machine Interactions

Cluster 3 has 33 items that mostly deal with human errors that may arise with automation. Human errors are mainly explained according to two different perspectives: firstly, from the cognitive engineering [55, 56] and secondly, from the human factors' perspective [23, 57–60]. Finally, the research of [27, 61] develop the interactions between human and technology in their natural settings. This cluster is in proximity with Cluster 1 and Cluster 4 justifying the links between human performance, trust and situation awareness.

4.4   Cluster 4: The Effects of Automation on Situational Awareness

Cluster 4 has 23 items that deals with increased automation and its effect on situational awareness [17, 62]. When most of the tasks are automated, the human operator is generally restricted to monitoring, a task for which he is not well suited [63]. Cluster 4 is situated at the top of the overall map with links with all other clusters showing that the concept of situational awareness has been central in research related to human errors, levels of automation and performance. It is noticeable that Cluster 4 is the only cluster with connections to Cluster 5, hence considering the social dimension of the situational awareness, notably in case of decision-making within groups.

4.5   Cluster 5: The Social Norms in Human-Computer Interactions

Cluster is the less developed with only 9 items. It is situated at the top right part of the overall map, isolated and widespread compared to the other four clusters. This cluster primarily deals about the perceptions of humans about their machine counterparts, the perceptions of humans on computers as teammates; humans' perceptions about the quality of information provided by computers and finally how humans apply stereotypes of gender to computers [64, 65]. This cluster has strong linkages to Cluster 1 as trust is one of the most important social norms.

The social dimensions related to HAI are still understudied and mainly developed around the perceptions of computers or on their interactions with humans, while neglecting the social human part. Both looking at the literature review and based on the conclusion of the CCA, we call in the next section for further research based on the new concept of "Social Human Autonomy Machine Teaming" (SHAMT).

5   Conclusion: An Agenda for Research Based on the Social Human Autonomy Machine Teaming (SHAMT) Concept

The outcome of the literature review provides a solid foundation on which to build an agenda for future research. Here, we propose the concept of Social Human Autonomy Machine Teaming (SHAMT), which we define as a team consisting of both humans and machines, working together in a complementary way to optimize decision-making, while incorporating the social dimension of humans within the whole ecosystem.

SHAMT will focus researchers' attention on the automation and the social within a sectoral ecosystem.

To date, automation has been mostly considered as a way to fulfill prescribed tasks, with minimal or no human interventions [16] with the ultimate objective of minimizing costs for the ship owner and other stakeholders regardless of the potential economic, human and ecological damage. Advances in automation technology, has led to smart machines that can potentially work with human teams [30], but the literature tends to highlight how increased autonomy of the machine can lead to changing human capabilities and skills in the workplace. For instance, reduced skills, less attention and memory span leading to reduced situational awareness or over reliance on the machine. There is a significant and widening gap in the understanding of how human and autonomous machines can interact with each other and effectively work as part of a team [14]. Humans are better at tasks requiring judgement, whereas machines are better at performing routine and repetitive tasks [2, 10] and if these human and machine skills are combined, they can potentially form a smarter entity, a "Supermind" [66]. If humans combine their unique 'general intelligence' (the capability to achieve different goals effectively in diverse environments) with machine's 'specialized intelligence' and capabilities that humans don't possess, this new combination can mean improved decision-making in certain stress and emergency situations.

Future research should also take into consideration the social aspect from two perspectives. Firstly, the reduction of crew members, as well as the increased number of situations where humans are monitoring or piloting ships alone on board or remotely, raise questions about situations of loneliness. For instance, with different temporalities – such as being alone at the sea in an unmanned ship for long periods of time, or even monitoring several ships at home for months during pandemic or other lockdown periods) - will human behaviors and interactions with machines change? There is still limited research that considers navigation within a whole ecosystem of actors (the ship plus all the information arriving from the outside, notably the SCC) neither does it take into account how these social interactions, both on the ship and with remote actors, may change the way humans acquire and interpret information and how they make decisions.

One of the limitation of this study is the breadth of our search which is based on the Ergonomics domain in Web of Science (WoS) [32]. Broadening the search to include other domains, might bring to light studies that might have not been published in our selected database. Other scholars could develop a bibliographic coupling analysis (BCA) in order to highlight future research trends to cross it with the SHAMT concept.

All in all, our study recommends that future research should focus on all the elements of a maritime ecosystem to optimize the effectiveness of autonomous human-machine teammates incorporating environmental, social and human needs for interactions with autonomous machines and AI. The ideas developed in this research may also be useful in other transportation industries such as aviation [16] space exploration, SAR (Search and Rescue) operations, UAV (Unmanned Aerial Vehicles) UGV (Unmanned Ground Vehicles) enabling both researchers and practitioners to perform tasks in extreme environments and thus improve disaster management without putting human operators at risk [67].

References

1. Dwivedi, Y.K., et al.: Artificial intelligence (AI): multidisciplinary perspectives on emerging challenges, opportunities, and agenda for research, practice and policy. Int. J. Inf. Manage. 101994 (2019). https://doi.org/10.1016/j.ijinfomgt.2019.08.002
2. Grech, M.R., Horberry, T., Smith, A.: human error in maritime operations: analyses of accident reports using the leximancer tool. Proc. Hum. Factors Ergon. Soc. Annu. Meet. **46** (19), 1718–1721 (2002). https://doi.org/10.1177/154193120204601906
3. Pazouki, K., Forbes, N., Norman, R.A., Woodward, M.D.: Investigation on the impact of human-automation interaction in maritime operations. Ocean Eng. **153**, 297–304 (2018). https://doi.org/10.1016/j.oceaneng.2018.01.103
4. Batalden, B.-M., Leikanger, P., Wide, P.: Towards autonomous maritime operations. In: 2017 IEEE International Conference on Computational Intelligence and Virtual Environments for Measurement Systems and Applications (CIVEMSA), Annecy, France, pp. 1–6, June 2017. https://doi.org/10.1109/civemsa.2017.7995339
5. Dubey, R., et al.: Can big data and predictive analytics improve social and environmental sustainability? Technol. Forecast. Soc. Change **144**, 534–545 (2019). https://doi.org/10.1016/j.techfore.2017.06.020
6. Burmeister, H.-C., Bruhn, W., Rødseth, Ø.J., Porathe, T.: Autonomous unmanned merchant vessel and its contribution towards the e-navigation implementation: the MUNIN perspective. Int. J. E-Navig. Marit. Econ. **1**, 1–13 (2014). https://doi.org/10.1016/j.enavi.2014.12.002
7. Yara Birkeland: Autonomous ship project, key facts about YARA Birkeland (2020). https://www.kongsberg.com/maritime/support/themes/autonomous-ship-project-key-facts-about-yara-birkeland/. Accessed 31 July 2020
8. Utne, I.B., Rokseth, B., Sørensen, A.J., Vinnem, J.E.: Towards supervisory risk control of autonomous ships. Reliab. Eng. Syst. Saf. **196**, 106757 (2020). https://doi.org/10.1016/j.ress.2019.106757
9. Bailey, N., Housley, W., Belcher, P.: Navigation, interaction and bridge team work. Sociol. Rev. **54**(2), 342–362 (2006). https://doi.org/10.1111/j.1467-954X.2006.00617.x
10. O'Connor, P., O'Dea, A., Flin, R., Belton, S.: Identifying the team skills required by nuclear power plant operations personnel. Int. J. Ind. Ergon. **38**(11–12), 1028–1037 (2008). https://doi.org/10.1016/j.ergon.2008.01.014
11. Janssen, C.P., Donker, S.F., Brumby, D.P., Kun, A.L.: History and future of human-automation interaction. Int. J. Hum.-Comput. Stud. **131**, 99–107 (2019). https://doi.org/10.1016/j.ijhcs.2019.05.006
12. Parasuraman, R., Wickens, C.D.: Humans: still vital after all these years of automation. Hum. Factors **50**(3), 511–520 (2008). https://doi.org/10.1518/001872008X312198
13. Vagia, M., Transeth, A.A., Fjerdingen, S.A.: A literature review on the levels of automation during the years. What are the different taxonomies that have been proposed? Appl. Ergon. **53**, 190–202 (2016). https://doi.org/10.1016/j.apergo.2015.09.013
14. McNeese, M.D., McNeese, N.J.: Humans interacting with intelligent machines: at the crossroads of symbiotic teamwork. In: Living with Robots, pp. 165–197. Elsevier (2020)
15. Lee, J.D., Moray, N.: Trust, self-confidence, and operators' adaptation to automation. Int. J. Hum.-Comput. Stud. **40**(1), 153–184 (1994). https://doi.org/10.1006/ijhc.1994.1007
16. Endsley, M.R.: From here to autonomy: lessons learned from human-automation research. Hum. Factors J. Hum. Factors Ergon. Soc. **59**(1), 5–27 (2017). https://doi.org/10.1177/0018720816681350

17. Bainbridge, L.: Ironies of automation. Automatica **19**(6), 775–779 (1983). https://doi.org/10.1016/0005-1098(83)90046-8

18. Kaber, D.B., Onal, E., Endsley, M.R.: Design of automation for telerobots and the effect on performance, operator situation awareness, and subjective workload. Hum. Factors Ergon. Manuf. Serv. Ind. **10**(4), 409–430 (2000). https://doi.org/10.1002/1520-6564(200023)10:4%3c409:AID-HFM4%3e3.0.CO;2-V

19. Relling, T., Lützhöft, M., Ostnes, R., Hildre, H.P.: A human perspective on maritime autonomy. In: Schmorrow, D.D., Fidopiastis, C.M. (eds.) AC 2018. LNCS (LNAI), vol. 10916, pp. 350–362. Springer, Cham (2018). https://doi.org/10.1007/978-3-319-91467-1_27

20. Ramos, M.A., Thieme, C.A., Utne, I.B., Mosleh, A.: Human-system concurrent task analysis for maritime autonomous surface ship operation and safety. Reliab. Eng. Syst. Saf. **195**, 106697 (2020). https://doi.org/10.1016/j.ress.2019.106697

21. Simon, H.A.: The future of information systems. Ann. Oper. Res. **71**, 3–14 (1997). https://doi.org/10.1023/A:1018975616482

22. Wynne, K.T., Lyons, J.B.: An integrative model of autonomous agent teammate-likeness. Theor. Issues Ergon. Sci. **19**(3), 353–374 (2018). https://doi.org/10.1080/1463922X.2016.1260181

23. Norman, D.A., Broadbent, D.E., Baddeley, A.D., Reason, J.: The 'problem' with automation: inappropriate feedback and interaction, not 'over-automation'. Philos. Trans. R. Soc. Lond. B Biol. Sci. **327**(1241), 585–593 (1990)

24. Lützhöft, M.H., Dekker, S.W.A.: On your watch: automation on the bridge. J. Navig. **55**(1), 83–96 (2002). https://doi.org/10.1017/S0373463301001588

25. Jalonen, R., Tuominen, R., Wahlström, M.: Safety of unmanned ships - safe shipping with autonomous and remote controlled ships. Aalto University (2017)

26. Sarter, N.B., Woods, D.D.: Team play with a powerful and independent agent: operational experiences and automation surprises on the airbus A-320. Hum. Factors (1997). https://doi.org/10.1518/001872097778667997

27. Hutchins, E.: Cognition in the Wild. MIT Press, Cambridge (1995)

28. Housley, W.: Interaction in multidisciplinary teams (2003)

29. Licklider, J.C.R.: Man-computer symbiosis. IRE Trans. Hum. Factors Electron. **HFE-1**(1), 4–11 (1960). https://doi.org/10.1109/thfe2.1960.4503259

30. McNeese, N.J., Demir, M., Cooke, N.J., Myers, C.: Teaming with a synthetic teammate: insights into human-autonomy teaming. Hum. Factors (2017). https://doi.org/10.1177/0018720817743223

31. Kovács, A., Van Looy, B., Cassiman, B.: Exploring the scope of open innovation: a bibliometric review of a decade of research. Scientometrics **104**(3), 951–983 (2015). https://doi.org/10.1007/s11192-015-1628-0

32. van Oorschot, J.A.W.H., Hofman, E., Halman, J.I.M.: A bibliometric review of the innovation adoption literature. Technol. Forecast. Soc. Change **134**, 1–21 (2018). https://doi.org/10.1016/j.techfore.2018.04.032

33. Guirguis, K.: From big data to big performance – exploring the potential of big data for enhancing public organizations' performance. A systematic literature review. Swiss Yearb. Adm. Sci. **11**(1), 55–65 (2020). https://doi.org/10.5334/ssas.140

34. Small, H.: Co-citation in the scientific literature: a new measure of the relationship between two documents. J. Am. Soc. Inf. Sci. **24**(4), 265–269 (1973). https://doi.org/10.1002/asi.4630240406

35. Brereton, P., Kitchenham, B.A., Budgen, D., Turner, M., Khalil, M.: Lessons from applying the systematic literature review process within the software engineering domain. J. Syst. Softw. **80**(4), 571–583 (2007). https://doi.org/10.1016/j.jss.2006.07.009

36. Davis, F.D.: Perceived usefulness, perceived ease of use, and user acceptance of information technology. MIS Q. (1989). https://doi.org/10.2307/249008

37. Mayer, R.C., Davis, J.H., Schoorman, F.D.: An integrative model of organizational trust. Acad. Manage. Rev. **20**(3), 709–734 (1995). https://doi.org/10.2307/258792

38. Hockey, G.R.J.: Compensatory control in the regulation of human performance under stress and high workload: a cognitive-energetical framework. Biol. Psychol. **45**(1), 73–93 (1997). https://doi.org/10.1016/s0301-0511(96)05223-4

39. Wickens, C.D., Hollands, J.G.: Engineering Psychology and Human Performance. Prentice Hall, Upper Saddle River (2000)

40. Rempel, J.K., Holmes, J.G., Zanna, M.P.: Trust in close relationships. J. Pers. Soc. Psychol. **49**(1), 95–112 (1985). https://doi.org/10.1037/0022-3514.49.1.95

41. Kahneman, D.: Attention and effort. Prentice-Hall, Englewood Cliffs (1973)

42. Lewandowsky, S., Mundy, M., Tan, G.P.: The dynamics of trust: comparing humans to automation. J. Exp. Psychol. Appl. (2000). https://doi.org/10.1037//1076-898x.6.2.104

43. Muir, B.M.: Trust between humans and machines, and the design of decision aids. Int. J. Man-Mach. Stud. **27**(5), 527–539 (1987). https://doi.org/10.1016/S0020-7373(87)80013-5

44. Lee, J.D., See, K.A.: Trust in automation: designing for appropriate reliance. Hum. Factors **46**(1), 50–80 (2004). https://doi.org/10.1518/hfes.46.1.50_30392

45. Dzindolet, M.T., Peterson, S.A., Pomranky, R.A., Pierce, L.G., Beck, H.P.: The role of trust in automation reliance. Int. J. Hum.-Comput. Stud. **58**(6), 697–718 (2003). https://doi.org/10.1016/S1071-5819(03)00038-7

46. Endsley, M.R., Kiris, E.O.: The out-of-the-loop performance problem and level of control in automation. Hum. Factors J. Hum. Factors Ergon. Soc. **37**(2), 381–394 (1995). https://doi.org/10.1518/001872095779064555

47. Sheridan, T.B.: Telerobotics, Automation, and Human Supervisory Control. The MIT Press, Cambridge (1992). pp. xx, 393

48. Endsley, M.R.: Level of automation effects on performance, situation awareness and workload in a dynamic control task. Ergonomics **42**(3), 462–492 (1999). https://doi.org/10.1080/001401399185595

49. Parasuraman, R.: Designing automation for human use: empirical studies and quantitative models. Ergonomics **43**(7), 931–951 (2000). https://doi.org/10.1080/001401300409125

50. Dekker, S.W.A., Woods, D.D.: MABA-MABA or Abracadabra? Progress on human-automation co-ordination. Cogn. Technol. Work **4**(4), 240–244 (2002). https://doi.org/10.1007/s101110200022

51. Fitts, P.M.: Human engineering for an effective air-navigation and traffic-control system. National Research Council (1951)

52. Parasuraman, R., Manzey, D.H.: Complacency and bias in human use of automation: an attentional integration. Hum. Factors **52**, 381–410 (2010). https://doi.org/10.1177/0018720810376055

53. Kaber, D.B., Endsley, M.R.: The effects of level of automation and adaptive automation on human performance, situation awareness and workload in a dynamic control task. Theor. Issues Ergon. Sci. **5**(2), 113–153 (2004). https://doi.org/10.1080/1463922021000054335

54. Onnasch, L., Wickens, C.D., Li, H., Manzey, D.: Human performance consequences of stages and levels of automation: an integrated meta-analysis. Hum. Factors **56**, 476–488 (2013). https://doi.org/10.1177/0018720813501549

55. Hollnagel, E., Woods, D.D.: Cognitive systems engineering: new wine in new bottles. Int. J. Man-Mach. Stud. **18**(6), 583–600 (1983). https://doi.org/10.1016/S0020-7373(83)80034-0

56. Hollnagel, E.: Human Reliability Analysis: Context and Control. Academic Press, Cambridge (1993)

57. Reason, J.: Human Error. Cambridge University Press, Cambridge (1990)

58. Rasmussen, J.: Skills, rules, and knowledge; signals, signs, and symbols, and other distinctions in human performance models. IEEE Trans. Syst. Man Cybern. **SMC-13**(3), 257–266 (1983). https://doi.org/10.1109/tsmc.1983.6313160

59. Rasmussen, J.: Information processing and human-machine interaction: an approach to cognitive engineering. North-Holland (1986)

60. Vicente, K.J., Rasmussen, J.: The ecology of human-machine systems ii: mediating 'direct perception' in complex work domains. Ecol. Psychol. **2**(3), 207–249 (1990). https://doi.org/10.1207/s15326969eco0203_2

61. Hutchins, E.: How a cockpit remembers its speeds. Cogn. Sci. **19**(3), 265–288 (1995). https://doi.org/10.1207/s15516709cog1903_1

62. Endsley, M.R.: Measurement of situation awareness in dynamic systems. Hum. Factors J. Hum. Factors Ergon. Soc. **37**(1), 65–84 (1995). https://doi.org/10.1518/001872095779049499

63. Wickens, C.D.: Situation awareness: review of Mica Endsley's 1995 articles on situation awareness theory and measurement. Hum. Factors (2008). https://doi.org/10.1518/001872008x288420

64. Nass, C., Moon, Y.: Machines and mindlessness: social responses to computers. J. Soc. Issues **56**(1), 81–103 (2000). https://doi.org/10.1111/0022-4537.00153

65. Nass, C., Fogg, B.J., Moon, Y.: Can computers be teammates? Int. J. Hum.-Comput. Stud. **45**(6), 669–678 (1996). https://doi.org/10.1006/ijhc.1996.0073

66. Malone, T.W.: Superminds: The Surprising Power of People and Computers Thinking Together. Little, Brown (2018)

67. Prewett, M.S., Johnson, R.C., Saboe, K.N., Elliott, L.R., Coovert, M.D.: Managing workload in human–robot interaction: a review of empirical studies. Comput. Hum. Behav. **26**(5), 840–856 (2010). https://doi.org/10.1016/j.chb.2010.03.010

Adoption of Mobile and Platform-Based Applications

Effects of MDM Adoption on Employee in the Context of Consumerization of IT

Ashis K. Pani[1], Praveen K. Choudhary[1], Susmi Routray[2(✉)], and Manas Ranjan Pani[3]

[1] XLRI, Jamshedpur, India
[2] IMT, Ghaziabad, India
Sroutray@imt.edu
[3] Seemanta Engineering College, Mayurbhanj, India

Abstract. Enterprises are adopting mobile technologies to increase their operational efficiency. They provide employees with greater access to real-time information that improves responsiveness and competitiveness. The adoption of mobile technologies has given rise to the Consumerization of information technology (CoIT) phenomenon. Consequently, with ubiquity of mobile devices, individuals are concerned about privacy and organization are worried over data security issues. Mobile Device Management (MDM) adoption in organizations is hence, perceived a necessity. However, the effects of mobile technologies, Consumerization, and MDM adoption on employees remains a pertinent question. A review of the literature revealed an apparent gap in the research on the role of MDM adoption in employee engagement and task performance. This paper identifies the possible relationships and interactions between these critical constructs. The results of Partial Least Squares - Structural Equation Modeling (PLS – SEM) indicate some key implications for research. Previously unexplored, CoIT construct has been conceptualized as a 'habit', shows positive influences on MDM adoption, corroborating extant literature. Also, hitherto unreported, MDM adoption positively affects employee engagement and task performance, a potential incentive for organizations to implement MDM solutions. Mediation results show effects of MDM adoption between CoIT and employee engagement apart from corroborating earlier reported relationships between employee engagement and task performance. The managerial implications show the positive role of MDM adoption on employee engagement and task performance in the context of CoIT.

Keywords: MDM adoption · Consumerization of IT · Employee engagement

1 Introduction

Enterprises are adopting mobile technologies to increase their operational efficiency. They provide employees with greater access to real-time information that improves responsiveness and competitiveness. They enable companies to capitalize on the mobile revolution and to meet new customer demands [1]. Mobile technologies have brought about the bring your own device (BYOD) trend. BYOD refers to the increased use of employees' personal devices for professional purposes [2].

© IFIP International Federation for Information Processing 2020
Published by Springer Nature Switzerland AG 2020
S. K. Sharma et al. (Eds.): TDIT 2020, IFIP AICT 618, pp. 59–69, 2020.
https://doi.org/10.1007/978-3-030-64861-9_6

Ortbach, K., Bode, M., and Niehaves, B. [3] defined the CoIT as the dual use of technologies, i.e., the use of private spaces for business purposes. Though advantageous for organizations, the CoIT presents significant security threats. Organizations are under considerable pressure to respond to this challenge, which includes multiple mobile application platforms, form factors, and technologies [1, 4, 5]. As a result, organizations have been implementing mobile device management (MDM) solutions [6].

Moschella, D., Neal, D., Opperman, P., and Taylor, J. [7] termed the phenomenon of personal devices being used for official and personal activities within and outside organizational boundaries as the Consumerization of Information Technology (CoIT). This is the individualization of professional activities using consumer information technology (IT) that is not provided by the enterprise.

In a related stream of literature, Chung et al. [8] stated that the use of the mobile enterprise system positively influences individual perceptions of performance. Other researchers have indicated that mobile device security, especially regarding data, has not received much attention [9].

Effects of mobile technologies on employee performance and creativity have been evaluated in extant research. User perceived value and continued engagement have been addressed earlier [1, 5]. The effects of mobile technologies on employee productivity have also been examined [5, 10]. The CoIT has been found to improve organizational productivity by lowering technology costs [11]. The effects of consumerization on employee workload, autonomy, and stress have also received attention [12].

Many studies have been conducted on the traditional conceptualization of employee engagement. Since Kahn [13, 14] formulated the concept, significant contributions have been made by other researchers, such as Saks [15], Schaufeli et al. [16], and Macey and Schneider [17, 18]. The previous employee engagement literature has shown interaction effects on employee task performance [19]. Employee engagement, regarded as crucial for an organization's success [19], has seen a surge of interest in human resource development (HRD) circles and has been the subject of extensive research in recent years [20–22]. However, the effects of mobility, consumerization, and MDM adoption on employees remains a pertinent question. A review of the literature revealed an apparent gap in the research on the role of MDM adoption in employee performance and engagement [4].

This paper attempts to bridge this research gap by: (1) analyzing the effects of the CoIT on MDM adoption, (2) assessing the effects of MDM adoption on employee engagement from both the job and organization perspectives, and (3) examining the interaction or mediation effects of MDM adoption on employee job engagement and task performance. The remainder of the paper is as follows: The theoretical background and the research questions are presented. The hypothesis is developed, and the research model is discussed. The final sections focus on the research design, including survey administration and construct operationalization, as well as the results and analysis, inferences, conclusions, limitations, and new research opportunities.

2 Theoretical Background

2.1 Consumerization of Information Technology

Moschella, D., Neal, D., Opperman, P. and Taylor, J [7] defined the CoIT as an important trend with significant long-term consequences, including lower costs, improved functionality, and successive generations of ever more technology savvy users, for business. Studies earlier, have identified the critical aspects of the CoIT (e.g., [7, 10, 23]). They include the risks associated with BYOD, "duality of usage of devices", which outlines the fundamental idea behind the CoIT, i.e., the blurring of the boundary between the use of personal and official devices for official and personal purposes.

In addition to privacy and security concerns in the CoIT are the costs of the devices and the related technology [10, 24]. In a review of the literature, Ruch and Gregory [25] discussed the theoretical underpinnings of the CoIT. Kim [26] posited that the memory-based technological usage model identifies four possible mechanisms for the proximal and distal effects of memory-based models. In the proposed framework, habit (i.e., the robustness of the script that is built over repeated usage) is a function of the proximally and distally lagged usage factors. Based on the habit framework used by Kim [42], the present study has articulated the CoIT as a behavioral construct.

2.2 Employee Engagement and Task Performance

Kahn [13, 14], defined personal engagement as the "simultaneous employment and expression of a person's 'preferred self' in task behaviors that promote connections to work and to others, personal presence (physical, cognitive, and emotional), and active, full role performances" (p - 700). He identified the dimensions of the engagement construct as meaningfulness, availability, and safety. Unlike Kahn's definition of personal engagement, which is affected by outside context, the dimensions of the engagement construct incorporate vigor, dedication, and absorption. Gruman and Saks [22] further defined the engagement construct corresponding to the concepts of meaningfulness, availability, and safety based on Kahn [13].

Multiple studies on employee engagement have concluded that employee engagement is a critical element in maintaining the organization's vitality, survivability, and profitability [27]. Turner [28] highlighted that employee engagement may be found higher in an aligned work environment with workplace structures with clear organizational goals, and individual job or role specifications and enabling performance management systems. Murphy et al. [29] defined job performance as the accomplishment of job-related duties and responsibilities. According to Motowidlo et al. [30], "task performance bears a direct relation to the organization's technical core, either executing its technical processes or by maintaining and servicing its technical requirements" (p. 75).

The research on mobile technology has also focused on its effects on individual intellectual capital, roles, and work practices in business organizations [31]. Organizations have been increasingly incorporating these features into their work designs by introducing flexible work schedules [32], open office environments [33], telecommuting arrangements [34], and other recent initiatives. The effects of EMS on employee performance and creativity, as well as mobile users' value perceptions and continued engagement, have been investigated by Stieglitz and Brockmann [5] and Chung et al. [8]. However, the effects of MDM adoption on employee parameters, such as engagement and job performance, have not received much attention.

2.3 Mobile Device Management

This has led to the adoption of MDM and other solutions. MDM refers to the system that performs the critical functions to ensure the security of mobile devices without compromising individual features and privacy. The key features in the implementation of the typical MDM solution include the enrollment and configuration services, distribution, and control of the MDM agent on the device and authentication instructions, device reporting and ensuring security of the device through the provisioning services. MDM solutions also enable the asset management and control of the devices, including reporting about the devices [6, 35].

There is a potential gap in the CoIT literature regarding the effects of CoIT and MDM solution adoption on the employee especially employee engagement and employee task performance. Accordingly, the following research problem was developed: the effects of enterprise MDM solutions on employee engagement and task performance. Thus, the following research questions were posed: RQ1) What is the effect of Consumerization of IT (Mobile devices) on MDM adoption in organization? RQ2) What are the effects of MDM adoption on employee organizational engagement, job engagement and task performance? RQ3) What are the interaction effects of employee engagement and task performance in context of MDM adoption?

3 Hypothesis Development

As was previously mentioned, the CoIT has had a significant effect on organizational perceptions of security threats. Consumerization presents serious security threats and data breach concerns [3, 10, 12]. Therefore, organizations are under pressure to respond to this challenge, given the diversity of mobile application platforms, form factors, and mobile technology variations across the users [1, 4, 5]. Organizations have been responding to this challenge by implementing MDM solutions [6]. There has been a tremendous increase in the number of company- and employee-owned mobile devices in organizations. Comprehensive MDM solutions are needed to accommodate multiple form factors, platforms, and other technologies across many user bases [1, 5]. Thus, the following hypothesis was proposed:

H1: CoIT would positively affect MDM adoption.

Employees have a special relationship with their mobile devices. Organizations have recognized this phenomenon and have attempted to exploit it. Studies have reported that enterprises are adopting mobile technologies to increase operational efficiency, to improve responsiveness and competitiveness, and to cultivate innovativeness [1, 36]. Stieglitz and Brockmann [5] argued that a positive and encouraging institutional climate surrounding the use of mobile technology in the workplace has a positive effect on mobile usage.

Studies have indicated that MDM adoption varies among levels and roles of the employees, and successful implementation is influenced by the perceptions of the fairness of the decisions [4, 8, 37]. Gebauer et al. [38] argued that mobile usage is based ultimately on employee individual preferences and motivations. Therefore, MDM adoption, apart from organizational support for employee adoption, would be expected to exert a significant influence on the characterization of jobs. The following hypotheses were therefore proposed:

H2 a: MDM adoption should positively affect employee job engagement.
H2 b: MDM adoption should positively affect employee organizational engagement.

The effects of mobile computing on employee performance and creativity have also been the focus of recent research [5, 8]. EMSs are being adopted to facilitate employee access to internal IT systems to increase efficiency and, thus, improve organizational competitiveness [39]. EMS implementations have been driven by security concerns and consumerization [2, 40]. Mobility solutions provide opportunities for organizations to explore and to exploit employee capabilities. The effects of mobility in general have been examined. However, it is critical that the influence of MDM implementations on individual performance be assessed. MDM solutions are designed to monitor workflow processes and to manage data and security remotely. Thus, it is argued that higher adoption levels of MDM solutions would lead to higher task performance. The following hypotheses were proposed:

H3: MDM adoption should positively affect employee perception of task performance.
H4: Job engagement should mediate the relationship between MDM adoption and employee perceptions of task performance.

4   Research Design

4.1   Survey Administration and Construct Operationalization

The questionnaire was distributed to more than 400 possible respondents who were mobile phone users in four large organizations in the metropolitan National Capital Region (NCR) of Delhi. The firms to which the questionnaire was sent were selected by convenience sampling. The data from 300 valid respondents (43% female, 57% male) aged 22 to 50 years were used. The data quality review was performed after the questionnaires with too many missing values or the same answer to all the questions were omitted. The survey session lasted approximately 25 min. The survey response rate was 63.8%. The sample was controlled for the following key parameters: firm size, geographic location(s), employee mobility experience, company origin (Indian or non-Indian), and industry type (IT or non-IT). The model was controlled for the above parameters because of their possible influence on MDM implementations and the possible variations in MDM policies across organizations. The sample distributions of the first and second respondent groups were compared through the Kolmogorov–Smirnov test. No non-response bias was found [41]. Common method bias was analyzed through Harman's one-factor test [42]. No single factor emerged to account for most of the covariance among the measurement items.

The CoIT construct was operationalized as CoIT behavior. For this study, the consumerization behavior construct was operationalized based on the adoption literature [43]. Zhou et al. [43] examined mobile usage in the context of mobile banking, and the model that was used in that study was adapted for the CoIT construct. MDM adoption is considered an outcome construct in this study. MDM adoption was conceptualized as the dependent variable, based on the adoption literature on mobile banking [43]. Kahn's [13] definition of job engagement was adopted for the present study as earlier utilized by [15, 44]. Work role was a construct, and Saks' [15] scale was adapted for this study. Task performance was measured in accordance with Chung et al. [8]. The items were pretested in a draft survey instrument. The feedback informed the revisions that ensured the appropriateness of the design and the quality of the presentation. The draft questionnaire was then tested with a group of five MDM experts. Based on their feedback, the design and instructions were finalized.

4.2   Measurement Model and Outcomes

The reliability and validity of the instrument were tested in accordance with the two-step approach recommended by Gerbing and Anderson [45]. First, a Confirmatory Factor Analysis(CFA) was performed to assess reliability and validity, including convergent and discriminant validity. The Heterotrait–Monotrait (HTMT) criterion, were found to be well below 0.85 for all the constructs. This indicated good discriminant validity, as per Henseler et al. [46]. The AVE, CR, and alpha values exceeded or were close to the recommended threshold values of 0.5, 0.7, and 0.65, respectively [47, 48]. The results showed good convergent validity and reliability. Discriminant validity indicates whether two factors are statistically different [46, 47]. Partial least squares (PLS) regression was performed in SmartPLS 3 [49]. PLS regression was appropriate for testing the structural model because a multi-path research model was used, the mediation and moderation effects could be assessed, and the data contained non-normal data. It was also appropriate for testing for mediation effects [50]. The normality of the sampling distribution was assessed in SmartPLS 3 through the Kolmogorov–Smirnov and Shapiro–Wilk tests with sample size of 300 in accordance with Hair et al. [51], with bootstrapping of 5,000.

5   Analysis and Results

The analysis aims to answer the three research questions stated at the beginning of this paper. Table 1 shows the results of the PLS-SEM model run over the bootstrapped samples. The actual values of the other fit indices were better than the recommended values. This indicated that there was a good fit between the model and the data [47]. The t-statistic for each path model was greater than 1.96, with a path coefficient greater than 0.2 at p values below 0.05 [47].

Table 1. T Statistics of hypothesized path model. *at 95% confidence interval, ** at 99.5% confidence interval

Path	Original sample-path coefficients	T Statistics	P-value
COIT -> MDM Adoption	0.261	5.259	*0.000
MDM Adoption - > Job Engagement	0.437	9.406	**0.000
MDM Adoption -> Org. Engagement	0.347	7.072	**0.000
Job Engagement -> Task Performance	0.376	2.309	*0.000
MDM Adoption -> Task Performance	0.137	6.851	*0.020

Given the limitations of PLS-SEM on the calculation of model fit indices, the following key fitness measures were achieved: SRMR – 0.085 GOF – 0.303 Goodness Of Fit (GOF) = SQRT [(Average AVE) * (Average R2)]; GOF small = 0.1, GOF medium = 0.25, GOF high = 0.36. These may serve as baseline values for validating the PLS model globally [100]. The cross-loadings matrix for the measurement model was above the acceptable range of above 0.60 in each case.

In the following sub section of this results, tests of mediations conducted are reported. The two mediation tests conducted on the relationships included (a) Employee job engagement as a mediator of MDM adoption and employee Task performance and (b) MDM adoption as a mediator of the relationship between CoIT and job engagement The Sobel test statistics were found to be 3.79 and 2.78, with one-tailed probabilities of 0.001832 and 0.001763 and two-tailed probabilities of 0.00372 and 0.00564 for these two mediation tests. The relationship between MDM adoption and task performance was found to be significant when job engagement was introduced into the model as a mediator. It is therefore suggested that job engagement partially mediates the relationship between MDM adoption and task performance. In addition, MDM adoption was also found to partially mediate the relationship between CoIT and job engagement. In terms of the proposed path model, all the paths were found to be statistically significant in the hypothesized direction.

6   Findings and Contributions of This Study

Several key findings can be found from this study. Following outcomes can be inferred; CoIT has positive effects on MDM adoption in the organization. MDM adoption positively effects the employee's job and organization and task performance. Finally, there are positive interaction effects observed between MDM adoption, job engagement and task performance and Consumerization, MDM adoption and employee engagement. In summary, the results from the study addressed all the research questions that were initiated.

The insights of Ortbach et al. [3] regarding the new relationships between the CoIT behavior and MDM adoption constructs were confirmed. The results obtained in this study, indicate that given the MDM solution's recent emergence, employees might display a range of behaviors towards its adoption. The employees are often led to use their mobile devices to check for unpredictable work developments during on- and off-job hours. The off-time usage due to Consumerization, corroborates the adoption and usage of MDM solution in the organization.

The results found in this study with respect to organizational engagement confirm those of ter Hoeven et al. [52] regarding the positive effects of reduced burnout and higher employee engagement. Task performance has also been found to be positively affected by employee engagement [13, 14]. This is consistent with the JD-R model, which posits that Resources are better than Demands at predicting motivational work outcomes. The outcomes of the study are also congruent with findings of Doargajudhur and Dell [53] with respect to BYOD and JD-R model.

The results of the present study provide an interesting counter-intuitive insight. MDM adoption was considered driven mainly due to security concerns and possibly thwarted due to privacy issues. However, our findings indicate that consumerization as an individual habit might positively influence MDM adoption. This study contributes to the research on literature stream related to the construct of 'habit' by giving greater credence to the counterargument that individual decisions affect adoption behavior.

Our study confirms that employee tend to be engaged more, when using mobile devices with adoption of MDM solution since that enables the necessary flexibility to operate. The present study contributes to the stream of literature related to supporting the assertion of ter Hoeven et al. [52] related to work engagement and usage of communication technologies. Also, our results provide an additional insight to the findings of Vrontis et al. [39] who contended that the business process changes driven by evolving requirements provide the needed flexibility for employees to use mobile applications to complete the work at hand. Thus far, EMS implementations have been driven by the security concerns related to consumerization by Niehaves et al. [12].

This study has limitations. First, the implications of specific features or sub - dimensions of MDM solutions, e.g., OTA and remote access management or wiping, were not addressed. Such dimensions could have varied effects on employee behavior and engagement. Future studies should explore the impact of MDM dimensions like OTA features or remote wiping on employee engagement and task performance. These studies could also focus on the higher order services and functions such as unified endpoint management (UEM).

References

1. Unhelkar, B., Murugesan, S.: The enterprise mobile applications development framework. IT Prof. **12**(3), 33–39 (2010)
2. Meske, C., Stieglitz, S., Brockmann, T., Ross, B.: Impact of mobile IT consumerization on organizations – an empirical study on the adoption of BYOD practices. In: Nah, F.F.-H., Tan, C.-H. (eds.) HCIBGO 2017. LNCS, vol. 10294, pp. 349–363. Springer, Cham (2017). https://doi.org/10.1007/978-3-319-58484-3_27

3. Ortbach, K., Köffer, S., Bode, M., Niehaves, B.: Individualization of information systems— analyzing antecedents of IT consumerization behavior. In: Proceedings of the International Conference on Information Systems (ICIS), Milano, ITA, pp. 1–18(2013)
4. Ortbach, K., Brockmann, T., Stieglitz S.: Drives for the adoption of mobile device management in the organization. In: Proceedings of the Twenty-Second European conference on Information Systems, Tel Aviv, Israel, 9–14 July 2014, pp. 1–18. AISeL (2014)
5. Stieglitz, S., Brockmann, T.: Increasing organizational performance by transforming into a mobile enterprise. MIS Q. Execut. **11**(4), 189–204 (2012)
6. Harris, A.M., Patten, K.P.: Mobile device security considerations for small- and medium-sized enterprise business mobility. Inf. Manag. Comput. Secur. **22**(1), 97–114 (2014)
7. Moschella, D., Neal, D., Opperman, P., Taylor, J.: The "consumerization" of information technology. In: The Leading-Edge Forum, El Segundo, CA, USA (2004)
8. Chung, S., Lee, K.Y., Choi, J.: Exploring digital creativity in the workspace: the role of enterprise mobile applications on perceived job performance and creativity. Comput. Hum. Behav. **42**, 93–109 (2015)
9. Van Cleeff, A.: Future consumer mobile phone security: a case study using the data-centric security model. Inf. Secur. Tech. Rep. **13**(3), 112–117 (2008)
10. Niehaves, B., Köffer, S., Ortbach, K.: The effect of private IT use on work performance— towards an IT consumerization theory. In: Proceedings of the 18th Americas conference on information systems (AMSIS), paper 18, Seattle, Washington, USA (2012)
11. Köffer, S., Ortbach, K., Niehaves, B.: Exploring the relationship between IT consumerization and job performance: a theoretical framework for future research. Commun. Assoc. Inf. Syst. **35**(1), 261–283 (2014)
12. Niehaves, B., Köffer, S., Ortbach, K., Reimler, S.: Boon and bane of IT consumerization: the burnout–engagement continuum. In: Proceedings of the Nineteenth Americas Conference on Information Systems (AMSIS), Chicago, Illinois, pp. 1–9 (2013)
13. Kahn, W.A.: Psychological conditions of personal engagement and disengagement at work. Acad. Manag. J. **33**, 692–724 (1990)
14. Kahn, W.A.: To be full there: psychological presence at work. Hum. Relat. **45**, 321–349 (1992)
15. Saks, A.M.: Antecedents and consequences of employee engagement. J. Manag. Psychol. **21**, 600–619 (2006)
16. Schaufeli, W.B., Salanova, M.: Enhancing work engagement through the management of human resources. In: Näswall, K., Hellgren, J., Sverke, M. (eds.) The Individual in the Changing Working Life, pp. 380–402. Cambridge University Press, New York (2008)
17. Macey, W.H., Schneider, B.: The meaning of employee engagement. Ind. Organ. Psychol. **1**, 3–30 (2008)
18. Macey, W.H., Schneider, B., Barbera, K.M., Young, S.A.: Employee Engagement: Tools for Analysis, Practice, And Competitive Advantage. Wiley-Blackwell, Malden (2009)
19. Rich, B.L., Lepine, J.A., Crawford, E.R.: Job engagement: antecedents and effects on job performance. Acad. Manag. J. **53**(3), 617–635 (2010)
20. O'Connor, E.P., Crowley-Henry, M.: Exploring the relationship between exclusive talent management, perceived organizational JUSTICE and employee engagement: bridging the literature. J. Bus. Ethics **156**(4), 903–917 (2019)
21. Roof, R.A.: The association of individual spirituality on employee engagement: the spirit at work. J. Bus. Ethics **130**(3), 585–599 (2015)
22. Gruman, J.A., Saks, A.M.: Performance management and employee engagement. Hum. Resour. Manag. Rev. **21**(2), 123–136 (2011)

23. Weber, L., Rudman, R.J.: Addressing the incremental risks associated with adopting bring your own device. J. Econ. Financ. Sci. **11**(1), 169–182 (2018)
24. Dernbecher, S., Beck, R., Weber, S.: Switch to your own to work with the known: an empirical study on consumerization of IT. In: Proceedings of the nineteenth Americas conference on information systems, Chicago, pp. 1–10 (2013)
25. Ruch, T.J., Gregory, R.W.: Consumerization of IT—where is the theory? In: PACIS 2014 proceedings, Chengdu, China, pp. 139–144 (2014)
26. Kim, S.S.: The integrative framework of technology use: an extension and test. MIS Q. **33** (3), 513–537 (2009)
27. Albercht, S.L., Bakker, A.B., Gruman, J.A., Macey, W.H., Saks, A.M.: Employee engagement, human resource management practices and competitive advantage: an integrated approach. J. Organ. Effect.: People Perform. **2**, 7–35 (2015)
28. Turner P.: The organisation of work and employee engagement. In: Employee Engagement in Contemporary Organizations. Palgrave Macmillan, Cham (2020)
29. Murphy, K.R., De Shon, R.: Interrater correlations do not estimate the reliability of job performance ratings. Pers. Psychol. **53**, 873–900 (2000)
30. Motowidlo, S.J., Borman, W.C., Schmit, M.J.: A theory of individual differences in task and contextual performance. Hum. Perform. **10**(2), 71–83 (1997)
31. Murray, A., Papa, A., Cuozzo, B., Russo, G.: Evaluating the innovation of the internet of things: empirical evidence from the intellectual capital assessment. Bus. Process Manag. J. **22**(2), 341–356 (2016)
32. Leslie, L.M., Manchester, C.F., Park, T.Y., Mehng, S.A.: Flexible work practices: a source of career premiums or penalties? Acad. Manag. J. **55**(6), 1407–1428 (2012)
33. McElroy, J.C., Morrow, P.C.: Employee reactions to office redesign: a naturally occurring quasi-field experiment in a multi-generational setting. Hum. Relat. **63**(5), 609–636 (2010)
34. Gajendran, R.S., Harrison, D.A., Delaney-Klinger, K.: Are telecommuters remotely good citizens? Unpacking telecommuting's effects on performance via I-deals and job resources. Pers. Psychol. **68**, 353–393 (2015)
35. Rhee, K., Jeon, W., Won, D.: Security requirements of a mobile device management system. Int. J. Secur. Appl. **6**(2), 353–358 (2012)
36. Del Giudice, M.: Discovering the internet of things (IoT): technology and business process management, inside and outside the innovative firms. Bus. Process Manag. J. **22**(2), 263–270 (2016)
37. Kim, Y.H., Kim, D.J., Wachter, K.: A study of mobile user engagement (MoEN): engagement motivations, perceived value, satisfaction, and continued engagement intention. Decis. Support Syst. **56**, 361–370 (2013)
38. Gebauer, J., Shaw, M.J., Gribbins, M.L.: Task–technology fit for mobile information systems. J. Inf. Technol. **25**(3), 259–272 (2010)
39. Vrontis, D., Thrassou, A., Santoro, G., Papa, A.: Ambidexterity, external knowledge and performance in knowledge-intensive firms. J. Technol. Transf. **42**(2), 374–388 (2016). https://doi.org/10.1007/s10961-016-9502-7
40. Choudhary, P., Mital, M., Pani, A.K., Papa, A., Vicentini, F.: Impact of enterprise mobile system implementation on organizational ambidexterity mediated through BPM customizability. Bus. Process Manag. J. **24**(5), 1235–1254 (2018)
41. Ryans, A.B.: Estimating consumer preferences for a new durable brand in an established product class. J. Mark. Res. **11**, 434–443 (1974)
42. Podsakoff, P.M., MacKenzie, S.B., Lee, J.Y., Podsakoff, N.P.: Common method biases in behavioral research: a critical review of the literature and recommended remedies. J. Appl. Psychol. **88**(5), 879–903 (2003)

43. Zhou, T., Lu, Y., Wang, B.: Integrating TTF and UTAUT to explain mobile banking user adoption. Comput. Hum. Behav. **26**(4), 760–767 (2010)
44. Rothbard, N.P.: enriching or depleting? The dynamics of engagement in work and family roles. Adm. Sci. Q. **46**(4), 655–684 (2001)
45. Gerbing, D.W., Anderson, J.C.: An updated paradigm for scale development incorporating uni-dimensionality and its assessment. J. Mark. Res. **25**(2), 186–192 (1988)
46. Henseler, J., Ringle, C.M., Sarstedt, M.: A new criterion for assessing discriminant validity in variance-based structural equation modeling. J. Acad. Mark. Sci. **43**(1), 115–135 (2014). https://doi.org/10.1007/s11747-014-0403-8
47. Campbell, D.T., Fiske, D.W.: Convergent and discriminant validation by the multitrait–multimethod matrix. Psychol. Bull. **56**(2), 81–105 (1959)
48. Bagozzi, R.P., Yi, Y.: On the evaluation of structural equation models. J. Acad. Mark. Sci. **16**(1), 74–94 (1988)
49. Ringle, C.M., Wende, S., Becker, J.-M.: SmartPLS 3. Bönningstedt: SmartPLS (2015). http://www.smartpls.com
50. Chin, W.W., Marcolin, B.L., Newsted, P.R.: A partial least squares latent variable modeling approach for measuring interaction effects: results from a Monte-Carlo simulation study and an electronic-mail motion/adoption study. Inf. Syst. Res. **14**(2), 189–217 (2003)
51. Hair, J.F., Ringle, C.M., Sarstedt, M.: PLS-SEM: indeed, a silver bullet. J. Mark. Theory Pract. **19**(2), 139–152 (2011)
52. ter Hoeven, C.L., van Zoonen, W., Fonner, K.L.: The practical paradox of technology: the influence of communication technology use on employee burnout and engagement. Commun. Monogr. **83**(2), 239–263 (2016)
53. Doargajudhur, M.S., Dell, P.: Impact of BYOD on organizational commitment: an empirical investigation. Inf. Technol. People (2018). https://doi.org/10.1108/ITP-11-2017-0378

Information Technology Usage and Cognitive Engagement: Understanding Effects on Users' Cognitive Processes

Himanshu Agarwal and Gaurav Dixit[(✉)]

Department of Management Studies, Indian Institute of Technology Roorkee,
Roorkee, India
gaurav.dixit@ms.iitr.ac.in

Abstract. Ubiquitous access to the Internet and digitalization has lead to people completing many of their activities online using a smartphone or other handheld devices such as a tablet. Regular usage of information technology could potentially affect their cognitive processes. In this research, we investigate how different types of online activities influence people's cognitive engagement. Further, we also examine the role of various key mediators such as personal innovativeness, playfulness, and self-efficacy in explaining the effect of information technology use on cognition. Data was collected from 351 Indian users, and the structural equation modeling technique was employed to test and analyze the research model. The results show that online activities associated with content delivery positively affect cognitive engagement, while online activities associated with entertainment negatively affect cognitive engagement. Familiarity with information technology has a positive effect on cognitive engagement. We also find that personal innovativeness, playfulness, and self-efficacy mediate the effect of information technology usage on cognition. The results of the study have both theoretical and practical implications.

Keywords: Cognitive engagement · Information technology usage · Personal innovativeness · Playfulness · Self-efficacy

1 Introduction

The rapid increase in the usage of smartphones and other handheld devices has changed the mindsets of users and their ways to perform many of their routine activities (Agarwal and Dixit 2017). As a consequence, the cognitive processes related to users' perceptions, learning ways, and reasoning mechanisms are potentially changing. Information systems (IS) researchers have studied the issues related to users' cognitive aspects before, such as flow experience, cognitive absorption, and cognitive engagement (Scott and Walczak 2009; Agarwal and Karahanna 2000; Webster and Ahuja 2006; Fan et al. 2017; Koufaris 2002; Zhou and Lu 2011). However, these studies primarily study cognitive aspects in the pre-adoption and usage context of information technology (IT). In this research article, our focus is on examining the effects of the regular and continued usage of IT on cognitive aspects in the post-adoption context.

© IFIP International Federation for Information Processing 2020
Published by Springer Nature Switzerland AG 2020
S. K. Sharma et al. (Eds.): TDIT 2020, IFIP AICT 618, pp. 70–81, 2020.
https://doi.org/10.1007/978-3-030-64861-9_7

Previous studies examining the effect of regular and continued IT usage on cognitive aspects are very scarce. We discuss a few studies which are closer to our research problem. For example, Su et al. (2016) studied flow experience in mobile gaming and found that human-computer interaction can positively affect the perceived enjoyment and attention focus dimensions of flow experience. Leung (2020) studied smartphone usage for the hedonic activities (e.g., watching online videos, playing online games, and sharing pictures or videos online) and eudaemonic activities (e.g., reading news online, seeking information from the Internet or online social media, and using an online dictionary). He found that these activities lead to the flow experience. Both of these studies were concerned with the scenarios and activities related to the utilization of free time. In this research, we focus on the m-commerce scenario and associated activities. IT usage activities in our research are based on the categorization suggested by Mahatanankoon et al. (2005). Specifically, we examine the effect of IT usage related to different types of online activities on cognitive engagement.

IS studies on cognitive aspects have also explored the role of various key mediators such as personal innovativeness, playfulness, and self-efficacy. For example, Agarwal and Karahanna (2000) found personal innovativeness and playfulness to have a significant effect on cognitive absorption. Agarwal et al. (2000) found self-efficacy to affect the perceived cognitive effort associated with IT usage. In this study, we examine the role of personal innovativeness, playfulness, and self-efficacy in understanding the impact of IT usage on cognitive engagement.

We derive the theoretical lens for our study using the prior research on three cognitive variables cognitive engagement, cognitive absorption, and flow experience in the information technology contexts. Theses three variables conceptualize overlapping aspects of the cognitive involvement of users with IT artifacts. We briefly review the relevant past studies to discuss it.

2 Theoretical Background

Cognitive engagement, cognitive absorption, and flow experience have been defined in the existing literature using overlapping or embedded subconstructs, as shown in Table 1. IS researchers have tried to capture the holistic experiences of users with IT artifacts using these constructs.

The first construct of cognitive engagement is a playful state of mind reached by the user during interactions with an IT artifact. It is typically characterized by subconstructs attention focus, curiosity, and intrinsic interest (Webster and Ho 1997). Cognitive absorption seems to be an expanded version of cognitive engagement. It adds two subconstructs control and temporal dissociation. It has been conceptualized as a state of mind reached by the user, which exhibits deep involvement during interactions with an IT artifact (Agarwal and Karahanna 2000). Flow experience seems to be an expanded version of both cognitive engagement and cognitive absorption. It has been conceptualized as an optimal state of mind reached by the user, which exhibits control, mastery, exhilaration, and a deep sense of enjoyment during interactions with an IT artifact (Webster et al. 1993). Therefore, the existing conceptualization of these constructs in the literature measure experiential states where flow experience is a higher-

Table 1. Mapping of Cognitive engagement, cognitive absorption, and flow experience

Cognitive engagement	Cognitive absorption	Flow experience
Attention focus: user narrows himself to a limited stimulus	*Focused immersion:* user ignores other attentional demands	*Total absorption:* nothing else matters for the user
Intrinsic interest: the user is involved for pleasure and enjoyment	*Heightened enjoyment:* a pleasurable experience for the user	*Pleasure and enjoyment:* a deep sense of exhilaration and enjoyment for the user
Curiosity: user experiences arousal of sensory	*Curiosity:* user experiences arousal of sensory	
	Control: the user is in charge of the interaction	*Control:* user feels a sense of being in control
	Temporal dissociation: user inability to register the passage of time	*Transformation of time:* loss of self-consciousness for user

Adapted from Scott and Walczak (2009)

level abstraction of cognitive absorption, which in turn is a higher-level abstraction of cognitive engagement. It is reflected in the hierarchical layers in the conceptualization, inclusion, and removal of subconstructs for these constructs. As we move higher in the cognitive involvement levels from the layer of cognitive engagement to the layer of cognitive absorption, we gain a subconstruct of control and reach higher intensity for other subconstructs. The user seems to move higher from a playful state of mind to a controlled state of mind or from playful interaction to meaningful interaction. Similarly, as we move higher in the cognitive involvement levels from the layer of cognitive absorption to the layer of flow experience, we lose a subconstruct of curiosity and reach higher intensity for other subconstructs. The user seems to move higher from a controlled state of mind to an optimal state of mind or from conscious interaction to subconscious interaction. In this research, we study the cognitive engagement, since it is the lowest layer that can be reached by IT usage. For most of the users, it is the cognitive engagement that can be reliably measured, since higher layers might yet not be in their perceptions.

Prior studies have examined the role of personal innovativeness, playfulness, and self-efficacy on cognitive aspects in IS research since users' capability manifested through these variables can be important in explaining the effects of regular and continued IT usage. Agarwal and Karahanna (2000) defined self-efficacy as an individual characteristic, which reflects a user's confidence in his ability to perform a particular activity. Webster and Martochhio (1995) defined playfulness as the degree of cognitive spontaneity in a user's interactions with IT artifact. Agarwal and Prasad (1998) conceptualized personal innovativeness as an individual trait, which reflects a user's willingness to experiment with a new IT artifact.

In this research, we study the effect of online activities, which users perform in the m-commerce context on cognitive engagement. We consider four types of IT usage activities suggested by Mahatanankoon et al. (2005): content delivery, transaction-based, location-based, and entertainment related. The effect of online activities associated with these different types of IT usage on cognitive engagement is investigated. We also study users' familiarity with IT to determine the impact on cognitive aspects.

3 Hypotheses Development

Online activities associated with content delivery, such as searching for desired information, sending or receiving emails, browsing news, blogs, and social media, require users to spend more time interacting with their smartphones. Users might eventually become more specific in the content activities, narrowing their focus to a limited set of items. Reading important emails marked starred in Gmail, a breaking news story recommended by Google news, and an interesting trend suggested for the user by Twitter are few examples. It is typically followed by the consumption of the content, which might take some time and more interactions. Frequent interactions between users and smartphones for content can be due to pleasurable and sensory experiences. All this can enhance their relevant cognitive abilities, and therefore, the user's state of cognitive engagement will improve. Thus, we posit the following hypothesis:

H1. Online activities associated with content delivery services will positively affect cognitive engagement during interactions with an IT artifact.

Location-based online activities require users to interact with apps such as Google maps to explore routes and places, analyze traffic, and find new or shortest ways. When driving, users might eventually start experimenting with different possible routes and learn by experiences from the Google maps-aided navigation. For example, planning the trip to a place based on the typical traffic information, sharing of the current location or live location with someone through WhatsApp, and sending the link of the location of a meeting or event are few examples. Similarly, Internet platforms such as Justdial.com, Zomato.com, and Swiggy.com also offer location-based services, which require exploration of available choices and interaction with users. Activities on these platforms can enhance the cognitive abilities of users, and therefore, cognitive engagement will improve. Thus, we posit the following hypothesis:

H2. Online activities associated with location-based services will positively affect cognitive engagement during interactions with an IT artifact.

Similarly, transaction-based online activities like finding a suitable train ticket, bus or flight seat, or seat in the best or nearby multiplex require more interaction due to increased choices. Users might spend more time exploring and browsing e-commerce websites such as Amazon.com and Flipkart.com or associated mobile apps, which offer various products for users. These websites offer many features to aid in online shopping, such as the comparison tool and recommendations based on items or user profiling. Therefore, during these types of online activities, users' cognitive engagement with the smartphone might be higher. Thus, we posit the following hypothesis:

H3. Online activities associated with transaction-based services will positively affect cognitive engagement during interactions with an IT artifact.

Websites such as Youtube.com, Netflix.com, Amazon's Primevideo.com, and Hotstar.com and associated mobile apps offer entertainment services such as movies, tv-series, and web series covering different genres and languages. Youtube has a large collection of user-uploaded videos as well. However, once a user selects a particular item for entertainment, further exploratory interaction with the smartphone might not be required for days. The smartphone will be treated as a portable, miniature tv screen, which might lead to a lower level of cognitive engagement. Thus, we posit the following hypothesis:

H4. Online activities associated with entertainment services will negatively affect cognitive engagement during interactions with an IT artifact

User interaction with the smartphones might depend on the familiarity of the user with IT. A higher level of familiarity with IT artifacts might help the user in performing online activities. Many websites and associated mobile apps offer advanced features that can enrich user interactions with smartphones. Therefore, familiarity with IT might affect the ability of users to explore and interact using smartphones. Thus, we posit the following hypothesis:

H5. Familiarity with the use of IT for performing online activities will positively affect cognitive engagement during interactions with an IT artifact.

As users become relatively regular in performing online activities associated with content delivery, location-based, and transaction-based services, their personal innovativeness or willingness to experiment with newer aspects of the IT artifact is expected to improve. However, in the case of entertainment services, chances of experimentations are minimal, rather passively watching videos might lead to a decrease in the personal innovativeness of users. Further, familiarity with IT will help in performing experiments. Thus, we posit the following hypotheses:

H6. Online activities associated with content delivery services will positively affect personal innovativeness during interactions with an IT artifact.
H7. Online activities associated with location-based services will positively affect personal innovativeness during interactions with an IT artifact.
H8. Online activities associated with transaction-based services will positively affect personal innovativeness during interactions with an IT artifact.
H9. Online activities associated with entertainment services will negatively affect personal innovativeness during interactions with an IT artifact.
H10. Familiarity with the use of IT for performing online activities will positively affect personal innovativeness during interactions with an IT artifact.

Improved willingness to experiment during interactions with IT artifacts might lead to increased cognitive spontaneity and confidence. Cognitive spontaneity can also have a direct effect on a user's ability to perform an activity and hence, self-efficacy. Increased confidence can boost cognitive engagement due to more assertive use of IT artifacts. Thus, we posit the following hypotheses:

H11. Personal innovativeness has a positive effect on playfulness during interactions with an IT artifact.

H12. Personal innovativeness has a positive effect on self-efficacy during interactions with an IT artifact.

H13. Playfulness has a positive effect on self-efficacy during interactions with an IT artifact.

H14. Self-efficacy has a positive effect on cognitive engagement during interactions with an IT artifact.

The research model is depicted in Fig. 1.

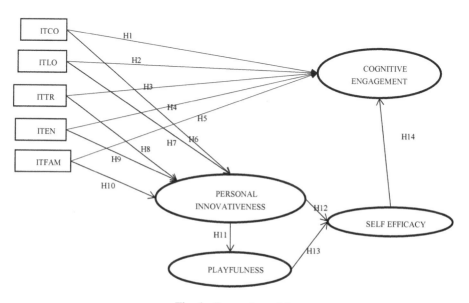

Fig. 1. Research model

4   Methods

We conducted a field study to test the hypothesized relationships depicted in the research model empirically. Data was collected using the survey method, and the mobile app version of the survey was used to expedite the process. We collected data from 351 Indian smartphone users. Survey participants were fairly distributed across gender, mostly from age groups between 20–50. Other important details of the participants, such as their PC experience, Web experience, and work experience, are shown in Table 2.

We measured the established constructs using multi-item scales (refer Appendix). We adopted Webster and Ho's (1997) six-item scale for cognitive engagement. For self-efficacy, we adopted the ten-item scale used by Agarwal and Karahanna (2000). For playfulness, we adopted the seven-item scale used by Webster and Martochhio (1995). We used the four-item scale developed by Agarwal and Prasad (1998) to

Table 2. Profile of respondents

Variable	Scale	Frequency	Percentage
Gender	Male	166	47.3
	Female	185	52.7
Age (years)	20–30	104	29.6
	31–40	132	37.6
	41–50	109	31.1
	50–60	4	1.1
	60–70	2	.6
PC exp (years)	01–05	10	2.8
	06–10	60	17.1
	11–15	108	30.8
	16–20	164	46.7
	21–25	9	2.6
Web exp (years)	01–05	14	4.0
	06–10	82	23.4
	11–15	182	51.9
	16–20	73	20.8
Work exp (years)	01–05	127	36.2
	06–10	37	10.5
	11–15	121	34.5
	16–20	52	14.8
	21–25	8	2.3
	26–30	4	1.1
	31–35	2	.6

Table 3. Pearson correlations

	ITCO	ITTR	ITLO	ITEN	ITFAM	PI	PFS	SE	CE
ITCO	1								
ITTR	.071	1							
ITLO	.156**	.378**	1						
ITEN	.165**	.233**	.289**	1					
ITFAM	−.023	.130*	.324**	.099	1				
PI	.224**	.391**	.480**	.346**	.132*	1			
PFS	.228**	.384**	.477**	.343**	.128*	.997**	1		
SE	.147**	.090	.183**	.118*	.003	.397**	.465**	1	
CE	.152**	.032	.104	-.021	.088	.218**	.251**	.441**	1

**. Correlation is significant at the 0.01 level (2-tailed).
*. Correlation is significant at the 0.05 level (2-tailed).

measure personal innovativeness. Further, we measure the observed variables, such as all IT use variables and control variables using single-item (refer Appendix). IT use variables are IT use of content delivery services, IT use of transaction-based services, IT use of location-based services, IT use of entertainment-related services, and familiarity with IT.

We employed SPSS AMOS to test and analyze the research model using the structural equation modeling (SEM) technique. SEM analysis helped us determine the statistical significance of the model and hypothesized relationships.

5 Results and Discussion

We performed a confirmatory factor analysis to examine the discriminant and convergent validity of the constructs. The average variance extracted (AVE) method was used to determine the discriminant validity.

Table 4 shows the loading and cross-loadings of the constructs used in the research model. Table 3 depicts the correlation among variables in the study.

Table 4. Loadings and cross-loadings

	CE	SE	PFS	PIIT
CEAF1	0.822			
CEAF2	0.866			
CEC1	0.754			
CEC2	0.829			
CEII1	0.89			
CEII2	0.829			
SE1C		0.93		
SE2C		0.783		
SE3C		0.882		
SE4C		0.911		
SE5C		0.85		
SE6C		0.953		
SE7C		0.964		
SE8C		0.909		
SE9C		0.954		
SE10C		0.877		
CPS1			0.697	
CPS2			0.893	
CPS3			0.809	
CPS4			0.724	
CPS5			0.735	
CPS6			0.698	

(continued)

Table 4. (*continued*)

	CE	SE	PFS	PIIT
CPS7			0.744	
PIIT1				0.794
PIIT2				0.772
PIIT3				0.823
PIIT4				0.764

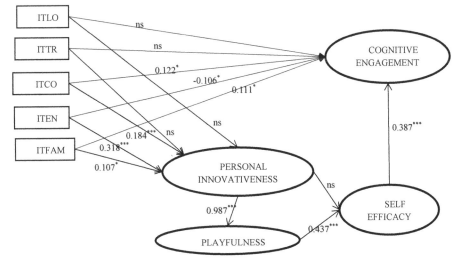

Fig. 2. Results of SEM

All loadings are greater than 0.7 except for two items, where it is almost 0.7. The results of the structural models are shown in Fig. 2.

6   Conclusion

The results show that online activities associated with content delivery positively affect cognitive engagement, while online activities associated with entertainment negatively affect cognitive engagement. Familiarity with information technology has a positive effect on cognitive engagement. We also find that personal innovativeness, playfulness, and self-efficacy mediate the effect of information technology usage on cognition. The results of the study have both theoretical and practical implications.

APPENDIX

Scales and Items

IT Use Variables

ITCO: Extent to which I used mobile or other handheld devices for online content delivery activities

ITTR: Extent to which I used mobile or other handheld devices for performing transactions online

ITLO: Extent to which I used mobile or other handheld devices for online location-based services

ITEN: Extent to which I used mobile or other handheld devices for online entertainment

(1 – Never, 2 – Rarely, in less than 10% of the chances when I could have, 3 – Occasionally, in about 30% of the chances when I could have, 4 – Sometimes, in about 50% of the chances when I could have, 5 – Frequently, in about 70% of the chances when I could have, 6 – Usually, in about 90% of the chances I could have, 7 – Every time)

ITFAM: Extent to which I am familiar with the use of mobile or other handheld devices

(1 – Not at all familiar, 2 – Slightly familiar, 3 – Somewhat familiar, 4 – familiar, 5 – Moderately familiar, 6 – Very familiar, 7 – Extremely familiar).

Cognitive Engagement

CEAF1: Online activity on mobile or other handheld devices keeps me totally absorbed.

CEAF2: Online activity on mobile or other handheld devices holds my attention.

CEC1: Online activity on mobile or other handheld devices excites my curiosity.

CEC2: Online activity on mobile or other handheld devices arouses my imagination.

CEII1: Online activity on mobile or other handheld devices is fun.

CEII2: Online activity on mobile or other handheld devices is intrinsically interesting.

(1 – Strongly disagree, 2 – Disagree, 3 – Somewhat disagree, 4 – Neither agree nor disagree, 5 – Somewhat agree, 6 – Agree, or 7 – Strongly agree).

Self-Efficacy

For each of the conditions, please indicate whether you think you would be able to complete the online activity on a mobile or other handheld device. Circle either "Yes" or "No."

Then, for each condition that you answered "Yes," please rate your confidence about your first judgment, by writing in a number from 1 to 10 (1 – Not at all confident, 2 –, 3 –, 4 –, 5 –, 6 –, 7 –, 8 –, 9 –, or 10 – Totally confident).

S. No.	I could complete the online activity on a mobile or other handheld device…	Yes/No	Confidence (1–10)
SE1	..if there was no one around to tell me what to do as I go	Yes No	
SE2	..if I had never used a mobile or other handheld device like it before	Yes No	
SE3	..if I had only the software manuals for reference	Yes No	
SE4	..if I had seen someone else using it before trying it myself	Yes No	
SE5	..if I could call someone for help if I got stuck	Yes No	
SE6	..if someone else had helped me get started	Yes No	
SE7	..if I had a lot of time to complete the online activity on mobile or other handheld device	Yes No	
SE8	..if I had just the built-in help facility for assistance	Yes No	
SE9	..if someone showed me how to do it first	Yes No	
SE10	…if I had used similar devices like this one before to perform the online activity	Yes No	

Playfulness

CPS1. When using mobile or other handheld devices for online activity, I am Spontaneous.

CPS2. When using mobile or other handheld devices for online activity, I am Imaginative.

CPS3. When using mobile or other handheld devices for online activity, I am Flexible.

CPS4. When using mobile or other handheld devices for online activity, I am Creative.

CPS5. When using mobile or other handheld devices for online activity, I am Playful.

CPS6. When using mobile or other handheld devices for online activity, I am Original.

CPS7. When using mobile or other handheld devices for online activity, I am Inventive.

(1 – Strongly disagree, 2 – Disagree, 3 – Somewhat disagree, 4 – Neither agree or disagree, 5 – Somewhat agree, 6 – Agree, or 7 – Strongly agree).

Personal Innovativeness

PIIT1. If I heard about new information technology, I would look for ways to experiment with it.

PIIT2. In general, I am hesitant to try out new information technologies.

PIIT3. Among my peers, I am usually the first to try out new information technologies.

PIIT4. I like to experiment with new information technologies.

(1 – Strongly disagree, 2 – Disagree, 3 – Somewhat disagree, 4 – Neither agree nor disagree, 5 – Somewhat agree, 6 – Agree, or 7 – Strongly agree).

References

Agarwal, H., Dixit, G.: M-commerce in smart cities: changing mindsets of individuals, organizations, and society. In: Advances in Smart Cities, pp. 167–180. Chapman and Hall/CRC (2017)

Agarwal, R., Karahanna, E.: Time flies when you're having fun: Cognitive absorption and beliefs about information technology usage. MIS Q. **24**(4), 665–694 (2000)

Agarwal, R., Prasad, J.: A conceptual and operational definition of personal innovativeness in the domain of information technology. Inf. Syst. Res. **9**(2), 204–215 (1998)

Agarwal, R., Sambamurthy, V., Stair, R.M.: The evolving relationship between general and specific computer self-efficacy—an empirical assessment. Inf. Syst. Res. **11**(4), 418–430 (2000)

Fan, L., Liu, X., Wang, B., Wang, L.: Interactivity, engagement, and technology dependence: understanding users' technology utilisation behaviour. Behav. Inf. Technol. **36**(2), 113–124 (2017)

Koufaris, M.: Applying the technology acceptance model and flow theory to online consumer behavior. Inf. Syst. Res. **13**(2), 205–223 (2002)

Leung, L.: Exploring the relationship between smartphone activities, flow experience, and boredom in free time. Comput. Hum. Behav. **103**, 130–139 (2020)

Mahatanankoon, P., Wen, H.J., Lim, B.: Consumer-based m-commerce: exploring consumer perception of mobile applications. Comput. Stand. Interfaces **27**(4), 347–357 (2005)

Scott, J.E., Walczak, S.: Cognitive engagement with a multimedia ERP training tool: assessing computer self-efficacy and technology acceptance. Inf. Manag. **46**(4), 221–232 (2009)

Su, Y.S., Chiang, W.L., Lee, C.T.J., Chang, H.C.: The effect of flow experience on player loyalty in mobile game application. Comput. Hum. Behav. **63**, 240–248 (2016)

Webster, J., Ahuja, J.S.: Enhancing the design of web navigation systems: the influence of user disorientation on engagement and performance. Mis Q. **30**(3), 661–678 (2006)

Webster, J., Ho, H.: Audience engagement in multimedia presentations. ACM SIGMIS Database: DATABASE for Adv. Inf. Syst. **28**(2), 63–77 (1997)

Webster, J., Martocchio, J.J.: The differential effects of software training previews on training outcomes. J. Manag. **21**(4), 757–787 (1995)

Webster, J., Trevino, L.K., Ryan, L.: The dimensionality and correlates of flow in human-computer interactions. Comput. Hum. Behav. **9**(4), 411–426 (1993)

Zhou, T., Lu, Y.: Examining mobile instant messaging user loyalty from the perspectives of network externalities and flow experience. Comput. Hum. Behav. **27**(2), 883–889 (2011)

Mobile Wallet Continuance Adoption Intention: An Empirical Study in Cameroon

Samuel Fosso Wamba[1](✉) 🄳 and Maciel M. Queiroz[2](✉) 🄳

[1] TBS Business School, 31068 Toulouse, France
s.fosso-wamba@tbs-education.fr
[2] Paulista University (UNIP), São Paulo 04026002, Brazil
maciel.queiroz@docente.unip.br

Abstract. The mobile payment literature has grown significantly in recent years. It has the power to improve transaction agility, as it also provides financial inclusion of the people, especially in emerging economies. One of the primary modality is the mobile wallet (m-wallet). The literature concerning m-wallet is in its initial stage; most of the studies are concerning the adoption stage. In this study, we investigated the behavior intention of the users in continuance intention in Cameroon. We proposed a model in which satisfaction and perceived trust are antecedents of the continuance intention. We used the Partial Least Squares Structural Equation Modeling (PLS-SEM) to analyze the proposed model. The results showed that the satisfaction exerts a strong influence on continuance intention, and perceived trust performs a mediation effect in the relationship between satisfaction and continuance intention.

Keywords: Mobile wallet · Adoption · Cameroon · Trust · Continuance intention

1 Introduction

Recently, electronic payment modalities increased considerably [1–3]. One of the primary justification for this considerable advance is regarding the proliferation of mobile devices (smartphones, tablets, wearables, among others). It can be seen that the different approach that enables payments and other transactions, like mobile payments, digital wallets, and mobile wallets, can improve the financial inclusion of the users, especially in emerging economies [4]. In this regard, a mobile wallet is a modality that the users can utilize their devices to perform payments and other transactions [5–7].

In this context, several studies approached the initial stage of the user's behavior intention to adopt a mobile wallet [6, 8–13]. However, the literature examining the continuance intention to use mobile wallets is scarce [14]. Few studies explored this related-subject, for instance, in mobile payment [15]. This study proposes to fill this knowledge gap in the literature by investigating the mobile wallet continuance intention to use in an emerging representative economy, namely Cameroon. In this study, we examine more precisely to research questions: 1) How is the influence of the satisfaction on mobile wallet continuance intention? 2) How can perceived trust impact the mobile wallet continuance intention? To answer these questions, we developed a

© IFIP International Federation for Information Processing 2020
Published by Springer Nature Switzerland AG 2020
S. K. Sharma et al. (Eds.): TDIT 2020, IFIP AICT 618, pp. 82–90, 2020.
https://doi.org/10.1007/978-3-030-64861-9_8

conceptual model supported by previous studies on technology acceptance models, mobile wallets, and payment literature. We used the Partial Least Squares Structural Equation Modeling (PLS-SEM) to analyze the proposed model. The results showed that satisfaction exerts a strong influence on both perceived trust and continuance intention. Besides, perceived trust showed a significant impact on continuance intention, as well as a mediation effect in the relationship between satisfaction and continuance intention.

This paper is organized as follows. In Sect. 2, we present the theoretical background and research model. Section 3 provides the methodology approach, followed by the results and discussion in Sect. 4. Finally, Sect. 5 highlights the conclusions, implications, and future research directions.

2 Theoretical Background and Research Model

Mobile wallet (m-wallet) refers basically to a transaction modality in which the users can utilize their devices to perform the payments and other transactions [5–7]. Also, simply, a mobile wallet is a digital wallet, in that a preload of money can be used to perform transactions by using different channels [10]. That is, not only smartphones can be used, but also other devices like wearables. According to Türkmen and Değerli (2015), "*Mobile wallets are digital wallets which are accessed through mobile devices, in that sense m-wallet app has the ability to communicate with the bank and retailer system, based on hardware and software infrastructures enabling secure storage, processing and communication of the data provided by the wallet holder, the wallet issuer and the application/service providers*" [16, p. 380].

The literature concerning m-wallet has gained momentum in recent years [6, 8, 13, 17]. With m-wallet, the users can perform different types of payments and transactions [16], using mainly Near Field Communications (NFC) and other technologies [7, 18, 19]. Also, the mobile payment forms [20–22] can leverage the financial inclusion, especially in emerging economies [8, 10, 13, 15, 19, 23]. However, one of the main constraints in the m-wallet continuance intention worldwide can be explained by the user's satisfaction and trust. Continuance intention refers to the users maintaining the intention of the actual usage of a particular technology [24]. In other words, continuance intention refers to the post-stage adoption of technology and its intention to continue using it [25].

The literature dealing with the m-wallet diffusion stages has been explored mainly in the stage of the intention to adopt [6–10, 12, 13]. The continuance intention stage was examined in mobile technologies [15, 25], mainly to perform payments. In our study, we argue that the satisfaction of the users with m-wallet predicts continuance intention and perceived trust, which in turn predicts continuance intention. Satisfaction construct refers to users previously use of technology in terms of the impact and impressions [24]; Perceived trust is defined as "a psychological state comprising the intention to accept vulnerability based on positive expectations of the intentions or behaviours of another" [26, p. 395].

Regarding satisfaction, a study about the use of mobile payment in South Africa found that satisfaction and trust exerted a substantial effect on continuance intention

[15]. Also, a recent work provided evidence that satisfaction was positively correlated with continuance intention in mobile phone context [25]. Moreover, the literature already highlighted that satisfaction influences mobile wallet adoption and recommendation in the Indian market positively [13].

Also, prior studies found that perceived trust positively influences behavioral intention in mobile wallet adoption [8]. Besides, recently, [10] also showed the positive effect of trust on mobile wallet adoption in India. In this vein, [7] reported that beyond trust exerts a positive influence on mobile wallet intention to use in a developed country, trust mediates the informal learning on the intention to use. Besides, it could be seen that trust represents a reliable driver towards mobile wallet adoption [9].

Moreover, [12] revealed that perceived trust mediates the relationship between perceived usefulness and intention to use a mobile wallet. More recently, the literature on mobile payments found that in the Indian context, the satisfaction on mobile payments usage could be enhanced by factors related to trust, usefulness, credibility, cost, among others [27]. Also, it is interesting to note that the mood is an influential variable towards mobile payment adoption [28]. Besides, the quality perception, as well as customer relationship and trust, represents critical dimensions of mobile payment service [22]. Regarding the continuance intention on mobile wallet adoption, both satisfaction and trust were highlighted as good predictors of continuance intention in the Indian context [14]. Therefore, we point out the following hypotheses, highlighted in Fig. 1.

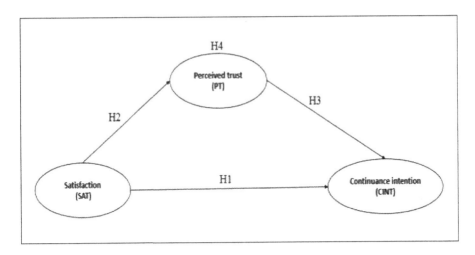

Fig. 1. Research model

H1: *Satisfaction (SAT) has a positive effect on continuance intention to use (CINT).*
H2: *Satisfaction (SAT) has a positive effect on perceived trust (PT).*
H3: *Perceived trust (PT) has a positive effect on continuance intention to use (CINT).*
H4: *Perceived trust (PT) mediates the effect of Satisfaction (SAT) on continuance intention to use (CINT).*

3 Methodology

In this study, we used a survey web-based questionnaire [29, 30] applied in Cameroon. The questionnaire was developed using constructs from previous validated literature. Continuance intention was adapted from Amoroso and Lim (2017) [25]; Wang (2012) [31]. Perceived trust from Kalinic et al. (2019) [32]; Qasim and Abu-Shanab (2016) [33]; Singh and Sinha (2020) [12]. Finally, satisfaction was adapted from Amoroso and Lim (2017) [25]; Singh et al. (2020) [13]. We measured the items of the constructs by using a 7-point Likert scale, ranging from Strongly Disagree (1) to Strongly Agree (7) [8, 32, 34]. Table 1 shows the demographic profile of the respondents, and Table 2 highlights the descriptive statistics.

Table 1. Demographic profile.

Gender/Age	n = 621	%
Gender		
Male	407	65.5
Female	214	34.5
Age		
18–25	383	61.7
26–33	154	24.8
34–41	46	7.4
42–49	21	3.4
50+	17	2.7

Table 2. Descriptive statistics (n = 621).

Items	Mean	Median	Min	Max	SD
PT1	4.652	5.000	1.000	7.000	1.727
PT2	4.643	5.000	1.000	7.000	1.674
PT3	4.704	5.000	1.000	7.000	1.695
PT4	4.631	5.000	1.000	7.000	1.760
CINT1	5.422	6.000	1.000	7.000	1.552
CINT2	5.155	6.000	1.000	7.000	1.585
CINT3	5.306	6.000	1.000	7.000	1.554
SAT1	5.167	6.000	1.000	7.000	1.519
SAT2	5.122	6.000	1.000	7.000	1.524
SAT3	4.963	5.000	1.000	7.000	1.623

4   Results and Discussion

4.1   Measurement Model

We measured our model using PLS-SEM, more specifically, SmartPLS 3.0 [35]. PLS-SEM approach has been used successfully in vast technology adoption literature [10, 36, 37]. We assess the reliability and validity of the model by employing the Cronbach's Alpha, Composite Reliability, Average Variance Extracted (AVE), and the loadings (Table 3). All results were in line with the literature threshold; that is, Cronbach's Alpha and Composite Reliability were higher than the 0.70 [38, 39], ensuring the reliability of the questionnaire. Also, the convergent validity results were assessed by the loadings, which were higher than 0.70 thresholds [38, 40], and by the Average Variance Extracted (AVE), in which the results outperformed the cut-off 0.50 [40]. Besides, we evaluated the discriminant validity by employing the Fornell-Larcker criterion. It means that we ascertain if the constructs differ from each other. By utilizing the correlation considering the inter-construct, in Table 4, we point out the results of the discriminant validity of the model. Due to the values in the diagonal (bold) outperformed the others, it indicates the discriminant validity.

Table 3. Constructs reliability and validity.

Construct Items		Loadings	CA	CR	AVE
Continuance intention (CINT)	CINT1	0.917	0.911	0.944	0.849
	CINT2	0.914			
	CINT3	0.933			
Perceived trust (PT)	PT1	0.899	0.942	0.958	0.851
	PT2	0.935			
	PT3	0.937			
	PT4	0.919			
Satisfaction (SAT)	SAT1	0.919	0.900	0.937	0.833
	SAT2	0.910			
	SAT3	0.908			

Note: CA = Cronbach's Alpha; CR = Composite Reliability; AVE = Average Variance Extracted.

4.2   Hypotheses Testing Results and Structural Model

The hypotheses of the model were measured using SmartPLS 3 [35]. Table 5 highlights the results of the hypotheses. Regarding hypothesis 1, the results of the path ($\beta = 0.591, p = 0.000$) strongly support the positive effect that satisfaction produces on mobile wallet continuance intention. Also, the results of the H2 ($\beta = 0.620, p = 0.000$) confirm the strong positive impact of the satisfaction on perceived trust. Moreover, the H3 showed a significant positive effect ($\beta = 0.215, p = 0.000$) of the perceived trust on mobile wallet continuance intention. Thus, these results (H1 and H3) were in line with

Table 4. Discriminant validity.

	CINT	PT	SAT
CINT	**0.921**		
PT	0.580	**0.923**	
SAT	0.723	0.618	**0.913**

Table 5. Path coefficients.

Hypothesis	Path	β coefficient	SD	t statistics	p values
H1	SAT -> CINT	0.591	0.048	12.272	0.000
H2	SAT -> PT	0.620	0.030	20.432	0.000
H3	PT -> CINT	0.215	0.049	4.427	0.000

previous studies regarding continuance intention behavior [14, 15, 25]. It is also interesting to note that while the literature reported trust as a predictor of satisfaction [14, 41], we identified and confirmed that satisfaction predicts perceived trust (H2). Moreover, Table 6 points out the mediation effect that perceived trust exerts on the relationship between satisfaction and continuance intention (H4). Finally, Table 7 displays the R square results. That is, the results of the model presented good prediction, in which it explains 55.0% of the variation in mobile wallet continuance intention between Cameroonian users. Also, the satisfaction explained 38.1% in the variance of perceived trust.

Table 6. Path coefficients for the mediation.

Hypothesis	Path	β coefficient	SD	t statistics	p values
H4	SAT -> PT -> CINT	0.110	0.043	2.596	0.010

Table 7. R square results.

Construct	R square	R square adjusted
CINT	0.551	0.550
PT	0.382	0.381

Our results align with the extent of the related-literature on the technology continuance intention approach [14]. For instance, we found a strong positive effect of the satisfaction of the mobile wallet, with continuance adoption intention. Our study confirms that satisfaction predicts m-wallet continuance intention in the context of Cameroon. Besides, it is essential to note that in our study, we found that trust predicts the continuance intention of m-wallet and mediates the relationship between satisfaction and continuance intention to use.

5 Conclusion, Implications, and Future Research Directions

In this work, we investigated the continuance intention behavior of mobile wallet users in Cameroon. It can be seen that the mobile wallet can improve financial inclusion, especially in emerging economies. We proposed a conceptual model, in which satisfaction was the antecedent variable of the perceived trust and continuance intention. Also, we investigate a mediation effect of the perceived trust on the relationship between satisfaction and continuance intention. Our study makes several significant implications and contributions. Since the literature regarding mobile wallet continuance intention is scarce [14], we provided advances to the literature of information systems, and, more specifically, in the research dedicated to technology adoption models. Thus, we found that satisfaction exerts a strong positive effect on both perceived trust and continuance intention. Besides, we found that the relationship between satisfaction and continuance intention to m-wallet usage can be mediated by perceived trust. Future studies can use our model as a start point to investigate the mobile wallet continuance intention in other countries. Besides, our results emphasize that managers need to pay attention to the features that impact on user's satisfaction, as also offer mechanisms to ensure the trust in the transactions. As future studies, as highlighted previously, our model can be expanded to a robust model. Also, studies that can compare the mobile wallet continuance intention in developed and emerging economies seems an influential agenda. Furthermore, studies relating to other cutting-edge technologies like blockchain to investigate the perceived trust in continuance intention also is a persuasive topic. As the main limitation, we report that because the literature is in the infancy stage, the comparison of the results was limited, as also, the survey has been applied in only one country.

References

1. Liébana-Cabanillas, F., Muñoz-Leiva, F., Sánchez-Fernández, J.: A global approach to the analysis of user behavior in mobile payment systems in the new electronic environment. Serv. Bus. **12**(1), 25–64 (2017). https://doi.org/10.1007/s11628-017-0336-7
2. Ondrus, J., Pigneur, Y.: Near field communication: an assessment for future payment systems. Inf. Syst. E-Bus. Manag. **7**(3), 347–361 (2009)
3. Fan, J., Shao, M., Li, Y., Huang, X.: Understanding users' attitude toward mobile payment use: a comparative study between China and the USA. Ind. Manag. Data Syst. **118**(3), 524–540 (2018)
4. Singh, S., Rana, R.: Study of consumer perception of digital payment mode. J. Internet Bank. Commer. **22**(3), 1–14 (2017)
5. Sharma, S.K., Mangla, S.K., Luthra, S., Al-Salti, Z.: Mobile wallet inhibitors: developing a comprehensive theory using an integrated model. J. Retail. Consum. Serv. **45**(June), 52–63 (2018)
6. Shin, D.H.: Towards an understanding of the consumer acceptance of mobile wallet. Comput. Hum. Behav. **25**(6), 1343–1354 (2009)
7. Shaw, N.: The mediating influence of trust in the adoption of the mobile wallet. J. Retail. Consum. Serv. **21**(4), 449–459 (2014)

8. Madan, K., Yadav, R.: Behavioural intention to adopt mobile wallet: a developing country perspective. J. Indian Bus. Res. **8**(3), 227–244 (2016)
9. Eappen, N.J.: Mobile wallet adoption in India: impact of trust and information sharing. South Asian J. Manag. **26**(1), 32–49 (2019)
10. Chawla, D., Joshi, H.: Consumer attitude and intention to adopt mobile wallet in India – an empirical study. Int. J. Bank Mark. **37**(7), 1590–1618 (2019)
11. Reddy, R.S., et al.: Factors affecting consumers choice to use mobile wallet to access m-commerce industry in India. Int. J. Cust. Relat. **5**(1), 14 (2017)
12. Singh, N., Sinha, N.: How perceived trust mediates merchant's intention to use a mobile wallet technology. J. Retail. Consum. Serv. **52**(March 2019), 101894 (2020)
13. Singh, N., Sinha, N., Liébana-Cabanillas, F.J.: Determining factors in the adoption and recommendation of mobile wallet services in India: analysis of the effect of innovativeness, stress to use and social influence. Int. J. Inf. Manag. **50**(May 2019), 191–205 (2020)
14. Kumar, A., Adlakaha, A., Mukherjee, K.: The effect of perceived security and grievance redressal on continuance intention to use M-wallets in a developing country. Int. J. Bank Mark. **36**(7), 1170–1189 (2018)
15. Dlodlo, N.: The use of M-payment services in South Africa: a value based perceptions approach. Int. Bus. Econ. Res. J. **14**(1), 159 (2014)
16. Türkmen, C., Değerli, A.: Transformation of consumption perceptions: a survey on innovative trends in banking. Procedia - Soc. Behav. Sci. **195**, 376–382 (2015)
17. Mei, Y.C., Aun, N.B.: Factors influencing consumers' perceived usefulness of M-wallet in Klang Valley, Malaysia. Rev. Integr. Bus. Econ. Res. **8**(4), 1–23 (2019)
18. Madureira, A.: Factors that hinder the success of SIM-based mobile NFC service deployments. Telemat. Inform. **34**(1), 133–150 (2017)
19. Miao, M., Jayakar, K.: Mobile payments in Japan, South Korea and China: cross-border convergence or divergence of business models? Telecomm. Policy **40**(2–3), 182–196 (2016)
20. Farah, M.F., Hasni, M.J.S., Abbas, A.K.: Mobile-banking adoption: empirical evidence from the banking sector in Pakistan. Int. J. Bank Mark. **36**(7), 1386–1413 (2018)
21. Mishra, V., Singh Bisht, S.: Mobile banking in a developing economy: a customer-centric model for policy formulation. Telecomm. Policy **37**(6–7), 503–514 (2013)
22. Singh, B.P., Grover, P., Kar, A.K.: Quality in mobile payment service in India. In: Kar, A. K., et al. (eds.) I3E 2017. LNCS, vol. 10595, pp. 183–193. Springer, Cham (2017). https://doi.org/10.1007/978-3-319-68557-1_17
23. Cruz, P., Neto, L.B.F., Muñoz-Gallego, P., Laukkanen, T.: Mobile banking rollout in emerging markets: evidence from Brazil. Int. J. Bank Mark. **28**(5), 342–371 (2010)
24. Bhattacherjee, A.: Understanding information systems continuance: an expectation-confirmation model. Inf. Syst. Contin. MIS Q. **25**(3), 351–370 (2001)
25. Amoroso, D., Lim, R.: The mediating effects of habit on continuance intention. Int. J. Inf. Manag. **37**(6), 693–702 (2017)
26. Rousseau, D.M., Sitkin, S.B., Burt, R.S., Camerer, C.: Not so different after all: a cross-discipline view of trust. Acad. Manag. Rev. **23**(3), 393–404 (1998)
27. Kar, A.K.: What affects usage satisfaction in mobile payments? Modelling user generated content to develop the 'digital service usage satisfaction model.' Inf. Syst. Front., 1–21 (2020)
28. Karimi, S., Liu, Y.L.: The differential impact of 'mood' on consumers' decisions, a case of mobile payment adoption. Comput. Hum. Behav. **102**, 132–143 (2020)
29. Madan, K., Yadav, R.: Understanding and predicting antecedents of mobile shopping adoption: a developing country perspective. Asia Pacific J. Mark. Logist. **30**(1), 139–162 (2018)

30. Ozturk, A.B., Bilgihan, A., Salehi-Esfahani, S., Hua, N.: Understanding the mobile payment technology acceptance based on valence theory: a case of restaurant transactions. Int. J. Contemp. Hosp. Manag. **29**(8), 2027–2049 (2017)
31. Wang, M.C.H.: Determinants and consequences of consumer satisfaction with self-service technology in a retail setting. Manag. Serv. Qual. **22**(2), 128–144 (2012)
32. Kalinic, Z., Marinkovic, V., Molinillo, S., Liébana-Cabanillas, F.: A multianalytical approach to peer-to-peer mobile payment acceptance prediction. J. Retail. Consum. Serv. **49** (March), 143–153 (2019)
33. Qasim, H., Abu-Shanab, E.: Drivers of mobile payment acceptance: the impact of network externalities. Inf. Syst. Front. **18**(5), 1021–1034 (2016)
34. Liébana-Cabanillas, F.J., Sánchez-Fernández, J., Muñoz-Leiva, F.: Role of gender on acceptance of mobile payment. Ind. Manag. Data Syst. **114**(2), 220–240 (2014)
35. Ringle, C.M., Wende, S., Becker, J.M.: SmartPLS 3. Bönningstedt: SmartPLS (2015)
36. Queiroz, M.M., Fosso Wamba, S.: Blockchain adoption challenges in supply chain: an empirical investigation of the main drivers in India and the USA. Int. J. Inf. Manag. **46**, 70–82 (2019)
37. Gong, X., Zhang, K.Z.K., Chen, C., Cheung, C.M.K., Lee, M.K.O.: Transition from web to mobile payment services: the triple effects of status quo inertia. Int. J. Inf. Manag. **50** (November 2018), 310–324 (2020)
38. Hair, J.F., Hult, G.T.M., Ringle, C.M., Sarstedt, M.: A Primer on Partial Least Squares Structural Equation Modeling (PLS-SEM), 2nd edn. Sage, Thousand Oaks
39. Nunnally, J.C.: Psychometric Theory, 2nd edn. New York (1978)
40. Fornell, C., Larcker, D.F.: Evaluating structural equation models with unobservable variables and measurement error. J. Mark. Res. **18**(1), 39–50 (1981)
41. Cao, X., Yu, L., Liu, Z., Gong, M., Adeel, L.: Understanding mobile payment users' continuance intention: a trust transfer perspective. Internet Res. **28**(2), 456–476 (2018)

An Extended Tam Model to Explain the Adoption of Payment Banks in India

Somya Gupta[✉]⑩ and G. P. Sahu[✉]

Motilal Nehru National Institute of Technology Allahabad, Prayagraj, India
{somya, gsahu}@mnnit.ac.in

Abstract. In the present context banking is all about innovation for survival. With the emergence and complete acceptance of digital KYC and mobile banking model, India has flown to next stage technical banking innovation i.e. Payment Banks. Introduction of Payment banking is one of the most strategic change in Indian banking platform implemented by the Indian government to promote financial inclusion among the Indian economy. Thus, the purpose of this study is to investigate the factors that influence the adoption of Payment Banking by current customers. Through, various dimensions and theories of adoption a comprehensive research model of the current study is established with seven factors i.e. Social Influence, Facilitating Conditions, Trust, Perceived Ease of Use, Perceived Usefulness, Behavioural Intension and Adoption. Data was collected by field survey questionnaire from various customers using Payment Banks services. The results mainly showed that intension to adopt Payment Banks services is significantly and positively influenced by Perceived Usefulness and Trust whereas facilitating conditions found to have effect on perceived ease of use. Social influence construct of UTAUT, used as external variable to TAM model in current study, positively effects both Perceived Usefulness and Trust. This Study has both theoretical and managerial contribution in area of adoption of IT/IS studies and Payment Banks.

Keywords: Payment bank · Adoption · TAM · Trust · Social influence · Facilitating conditions

1 Introduction

The international economy has expanded and advanced both towards institutional and market prowess, as the banking industry has gone through various innovative phases [30]. Information technology and the internet has played a significant role in the development of financial service deliberation for the economic growth of the country. With technology financial services are now available at the fingertips of people, and they are much efficient, trustworthy and secure with the passage of time.

In India, significant semi-urban and rural population remain deprived of the formal financial system; most of them do not actively use their bank accounts. Payments banks were set up with the motive of financial inclusion, so they can extend financial services to non-urban areas with increased quality and reduced cost, which has enhanced financial infrastructure in developing country like India [26, 39]. As like other

S. K. Sharma et al. (Eds.): TDIT 2020, IFIP AICT 618, pp. 91–102, 2020.
https://doi.org/10.1007/978-3-030-64861-9_9

commercial banks, payment banks also provide offers on e-commerce websites for their advertising and adoption and increase customer base.

Many researchers have explored the concept of mobile banking and internet banking. Nevertheless, still, the literature lacks noble research in the area of payments banks though they have a significant role in financial inclusion and expansion of digital payments model in India. So, this study aims to identify the customer's adoptions of payment banks through Technology Acceptance Model (TAM) and constraints of the Unified Theory of Acceptance and Use of Technology (UTAUT) with Trust (TR) as literature has already discussed the framework of payment banks and their motive of implementation in Indian economy [18, 37].

After serving demonetization crises in 2016 and corona pandemic in 2020, payment banks literature is in its nascent stage in India, but still few studies have been carried out in adoption framework of the payment banks [18]. Even though this study has analyzed few predictors of payment banks, but still relevant predictor Perceived Ease of use (PEOU) and Perceived Usefulness (PU) could explain payment banks. TAM and UTAUT variables were considered for the quantitative model of this study, which are widely applied in studies of adoption of Information systems [3, 4, 22, 25].

2 Literature Review

Through the last decade, India has gone through various technological advancement i.e. ATM, mobile banking, internet banking and still fintech are working towards development of payment system day by day. With the implementation of information technology in financial services, they have become quite dynamic and can be accessed anytime from anywhere as compared to traditional financial services that were place and time centric.

Payment Banks consist of the features of both mobile banking and internet banking, as the operations are widely conducted on mobiles or computer screen by the use of the internet. As the literature support, there are various theories which have been studied to ascertain the various factors that lead to the Adoption of mobile banking [10, 28, 37, 38] or internet banking [26, 27, 36] technology by the customers. Therefore, theoretical base for this study is being acquired from various classic theories and models formulated in Information System/Information Technology (IS/IT) areas related to banking. Theory of Reasoned Action (TRA) [1] a psychological theory in which behavioural is directly determined by intension further intension to adopt is predicted by both attitude and subjective norms. Theory of Planned Behaviour (TPB) [2] which is an extension of TRA theory [6], Innovation Diffusion Theory (IDT) [35], the Technology Acceptance Model (TAM) [13], Unified Theory of Acceptance and Use of Technology (UTAUT) [42]. These theories were mostly proposed to study the organizational culture and assess behavioural intension of people.

TAM model is widely considered as the one of the strongest, parsimonious [4], robust and highly accepted model [13], from last two decades. Designed on the base of Theory of Reasoned Action (TRA) [14]. In TAM model as per Davis [13] adoption of technology is directly influenced by Behavioural Intension (BI) to use that technology and Behavioural Intension is further influenced by Attitude and two beliefs: PU and

PEOU. However, through previous studies, it has been concluded that attitude does not mediate the effect of PU and PEOU on BI [39, 45] and Davis [13] in his original study also found weak relation of attitude and BI in comparison of effect of PU on BI. Therefore, attitude has been excluded from the model [32, 42].

Even though TAM being most identified model, but as literature supports TAM alone has not been able to predict and explain properly BI to use any technology [11, 32]. TAM has extended in various studies to improve the predictive power of the model. Al-Somali [6] has extended TAM by including Trust, Social Influence (SI), self- efficacy and quality of internet connection as control variables. TAM was combined with Theory of Planned behaviour. Gefen [16] in his study proposed extended tam model by including trust, lifestyle, FC and compatibility as an additional construct. Gu [17] has incorporated the TAM model with the UTAUT model to predict consumer intension and attitude to adopt mobile wallet in India. To study student intension to adopt mobile banking, Nikou [31] has explained and extended TAM with constructs from the UTAUT model.

2.1 Conceptual Model and Hypothesis

The study aims to examine the BI towards Adoption of payment banks, which is quite a complex process as it involves various personal, utilitarian and behavioural aspects. Constructs of TAM, i.e. PEOU and PU were considered for the study, but theses constructs alone were not sufficient to explain BI and Adoption. Therefore, TAM model has been extended and modified by including Trust [5, 11], as Trust has already been the crucial construct predicting BI to adopt any technology [3].

Even though PEOU and PU as the key constructs to predict BI in the TAM model, Davis [13] mentioned both PEOU and PU could be affected by external variables. So, in the current study, SI [6, 36] and FC [17, 31] are considered as external variables which will affect both PEOU and PU respectively.

Perceived Usefulness (PU). In the TAM model, PU is considered as the significant predictor of BI to adopt any technology. PU has been defined as "the extent to which a consumer believes that using Payment banking services would enhance his or her banking performance" [13]. Many Information Systems (IS) researchers have proven that BI to use any technology is positively influenced by PU [13, 41]. Over and above PEOU, PU is also affected by various external factors.

H1. Perceived Usefulness (PU) will positively influence customers Behavioural Intension (BI) to Adopt Payment Banks services.

Perceived Ease of Use (PEOU). PEOU can be defined as "the degree to which a person believes that using a particular system would be free of effort" [13]. Technology is found to be at ease when a customer finds technology user-friendly, more accessible and effortless to operate. As more comfortable the technology to use, the useful and accepted it becomes for customers [12].

As observed in few studies, PU is also affected by PEOU, as the easy the technology to use, the more useful and accepted it becomes for customers. Studies in various context [33, 44] has pointed that PEOU has a significant and positive effect on PU.

H2. Perceived Ease of Use (PEOU) will positively influence customers Behavioural Intension (BI) to adopt Payment Bank services.

H3. Perceived Ease of Use (PEOU) will positively influence Perceived Usefulness (PU) associated with Adoption of payment banks.

Social Influence (SI). SI was earlier documented in Theory of Reasoned Action (TRA) as "subjective norm" [1, 14], later it emerged as one of the constructs in UTAUT model [42]. SI is defined as "the extent to which an individual perceives that important others believe he or she should apply the new system" [42]. Encouragements and information's provided from peers such as friends, family, reference groups and leaders can deliver awareness and build a sense of trust which inspires to use any technology more effectively. In various studies, SI has successfully been incorporated into the TAM model and found that SI affects both BI and PU [31].

Venkatesh [41] in their study also found SI positively and significantly affect PU.

There are several studies which have demonstrated that Trust is effected by SI especially while operating through online banking as it involves uncertainty about the transaction's outcome [20, 29]. Moreover, when customers find any difficulty while operating through online banking, they try to find a solution by interacting with their social network [29].

H4. Social Influence (SI) will positively influence Perceived Usefulness (PU) to use the payment bank.

H5. Social Influence (SI) will positively influence Trust (TR) associated with the Adoption of the Payment Banks.

Facilitating Conditions (FC). FC can be characterized as "the degree to which an individual believes that an organizational and technical infrastructure exists to support the use of the system" [42]. FC comprises of proper technical infrastructure and convenient availability of technical suggestions to facilitate the use of any technology. In starting people could not use technical services adequately, but they will feel connected to any technology if they realize that various environmental conditions will support them to learn that technology [17]. Gu [17] in his study has found a significant and positive impact of FC on PEOU.

H6. Facilitating Conditions (FC) will positively influence Perceived Ease of Use (PEOU).

Trust (TR). Trust is often defined in three dimensions [8] first ability: ability means technology provider has enough awareness and understanding to complete their task. Second is integrity means that technology service provider keeps their promises with their customers, last but not the least is benevolence with states that technology service providers will work according to the customer needs rather than imposing their own interest. As per the previous literature, their exist a positive relationship between TR and BI. [4, 23]. Luo [23] has shown a positive and significant effect on both BI and performance expectancy.

H7. Trust (TR) will positively influence customers Behavioural Intention (BI) to adopt Payment Banks services.

Behavioural Intention (BI). Consumer willingness and intension are considered as the essential requirement to study the real behaviour of adopting any new technology. As per the previous studies of IS/IT, BI has a significant relationship with Actual Adoption (AD) of any technology [41, 42]. Venkatesh [42] has empirically tested BI as the valid predictor of Adoption. The relationship of BI and AD has largely been proven in various mobile and internet banking studies [4, 24].

H8. Behavioural Intension (BI) will positively influence Actual Adoption (AD) of Payment Banks services.

3 Methodology

Items were measured using a five-point Likert scale where '1' for strongly disagree, '3' for neutral point and '5' for strongly agree. Respondents of the questionnaire were mostly from Allahabad, Auraiya, Kanpur, Delhi-NCR, Pune regions. The questionnaire consisted of two sections, part one consists of demographic questions and part two consist of items (questions based on variables). Thirty scales items have been used in the present study to evaluate the constructs of the conceptual model [13, 16, 40–43]. Four constructs from TAM (PE, PEOU, BI and AD) and two external constructs influences are also included from UTAUT (SI and FC), they are being measured by same items as used in original TAM and UTAUT model by Davis [13] and Venkatesh [42]. Perceived Trust has also been widely enumerated as a significant predictor of BI. In the current study, Perceived Trust is being measured by six items taken from Gefen [16].

Data is collected from both industry professionals and students, as in the field of information systems responses from college students are being criticized as they may not be similar to the target population [25]. However, students often have convenient access to the internet and the basic computer skills required for conducting various online activities. Whereas they also possess necessary technology infrastructure to conduct mobile banking and internet banking. [23, 25].

4 Results

4.1 Respondents' Profile and Characteristics

Two hundred and Forty-Three (243) valid questionnaire of payment banking were completed by current payment banking customers. 63.79% of the respondents were male compared to 36.21% of the respondents were female. Relating to the respondents age, it was noticed that the age group of 21–30 captured the largest part of the total valid sample (74.48%) i.e. 181. With reference to the annual income level, the vast majority of respondents have less than 3,00,000 as their annual income followed by income group of 5,00,000–10,00,000 with (85) 34.98% and (71) 29.22% respectively.

4.2 Normality

To test univariate normality of each variable, the skewness-kurtosis approach has been adopted [9, 21]. The values of skewness and kurtosis are found to be within their respective levels when tested using AMOS 23.0. all the values of skewness and kurtosis are below the cut-off point of '3' and '8' respectively [21].

4.3 Structural Equation Modelling Analysis

Collected data is further being analyzed through Structural Equation Modelling (SEM).

4.4 Measurement Model: Confirmatory Factor Analysis

Model Fitness. To evaluate model fitness all main indices are being tested. The model fitness yields of the initial model of Payment Banks are as follows: CMIN/DF(Normed Chi-Square) = 1.521, GFI (Goodness-of-Fit Index) = 0.875, AGFI(Adjusted Goodness-of-Fit Index) = 0.845, NFI(Normed-Fit Index) = 0.888, CFI(Comparative Fit Index) = 0.958 and RMSEA(Root Mean Square Error of Approximation) = 0.046. As some of these values could not reach the minimum cut-off point as required [19]. So, to increase the goodness of fit of Payment Bank model problematic items were dropped, excluded items involve items with factor loadings less than 0.50 [19] or those which had higher residual value (Anderson et al., 1995).

Items (FC4) from FC, one item (TR4) from the TR, one item of PEOU (PEOU4) and lastly (PU3) from PU were observed to have under their cut-off value and thus removed. The revised model was again tested, after dropping all problematic items and as anticipated model fitness improved significantly (CMIN/DF = 1.223, GFI = 0.914, AGFI = 0.888, NFI = 0.921, CFI = 0.984 and RMSEA = 0.030 [19].

Construct Reliability. Composite Reliability CR), Average Variance Extracted (AVE) and Cronbach's alpha (α) values are being considered to measure adequate level of scale reliability of all constructs. Cronbach's alpha (α) value for all constructs are above cut-off point of 0.70 whereas all value of α range between .788 for SI to .873 for both BI and Trust (Nunnally, 1978). Composite Reliability (CR) for all constructs are above the minimum cut-off point of 0.70 [15]. 0.874 being the highest value for BI while the lowest was for the SI (0.788). as all indexes are above the cutoff point, While Average Variance Extracted (AVE) for all the construct are above 0.50 and as per data its ranges 0.554 Social Influence to 0.661 Perceived Usefulness.

Construct Validity. To measure construct validity both convergent and discriminant validity were observed. As Items of all constructs has significant standardized regression weight (factor loadings) above cut-off point of 0.50 and factor loading of all items are all found to be significant as p value is less than 0.0001 [15, 19]. As the square root of AVE for all constructs is higher than their inter-correlation values with all other constructs. As observed all values are above the cut-off point, which indicates that data has no issue of convergent validity.

Common Method Bias (CMB). For assessing CMB, Harman's single factor test [34] was done with all unremoved items of 7 construct (PU, SI, FC, TR, PEOU, BI, AD). Items of all constructs were entered into exploratory factor analysis, but fixed number of factors were set to 1. With unrotated factor analysis, results showed that first factor explains 44.228% which is less than cut-off value of 50% [34] of variance and no single factor was able to arise as good as first factor.

4.5 Structural Model

All statistical results of measurement model as indicated above are found to be satisfactory. Statistical results of various path coefficients are summarised in Table 1. As recommended by Hair [19], various values of model fit (CFI, IFI and TLI) should be greater than 0.90 and RMSEA value should be less than 0.08 for good fit of model. Various statistical fit indices of the structural model are as follows: Chi-Square/df = 2.005; CFI = 0.926; TLI = 0.915; IFI = 927, and RMSEA = 0.064.

Table 1. Assessment of reliability and discriminant validity

	CA	AVE	CR	PU	SI	FC	TR	PEOU	AD	BI
PU	.854	0.661	0.854	**0.813**						
SI	.791	0.557	0.790	0.629	**0.746**					
FC	.831	0.621	0.830	0.750	0.608	**0.788**				
TR	.873	0.580	0.873	0.691	0.592	0.630	**0.761**			
PEOU	.844	0.706	0.878	0.668	0.594	0.535	0.669	**0.840**		
AD	.835	0.632	0.837	0.673	0.589	0.602	0.716	0.556	**0.795**	
BI	.873	0.635	0.874	0.623	0.743	0.612	0.552	0.507	0.683	**0.797**

Various factors of extended TAM were found to be significant with Behavioural Intension to use Payment Bank services except PEOU. External variables also found to have significant effect on PEOU and PU: SI has positive and significant impact (b = 0.631, p < 0.000) on PU and (b = 737, p < 0.000) on Trust whereas, FC has also significantly impacted PEOU (b = 0.630, p < 0.000). The main path coefficient begin with PU, PEOU and TR and ends on BI: PU (b = 0.501, p < 0.000), Trust (b = 0.268, p < 0.000) were found to have significant impact on BI whereas Ease of Use (b = 0.042, p < 0.577) not proved to have any statistical relation with BI.

Whereas in support of literature, statistical results also proved to have a significant impact of PEOU on PU. Further impact of Behavioural Intension on use of Payment Banks services on adoption was analysed. It reported to positive and significant (b = 0.725, p < 0.000) impact. Therefore, all the hypothesis H1 and H3-H9 except H2 are supported. The value of (R2) for endogenous factors, extracted from dependent variables i.e. 40% for PEOU, 69% for PU, 54% for TR, 54% for BI and 53% for adoption (Fig. 1 and Table 2).

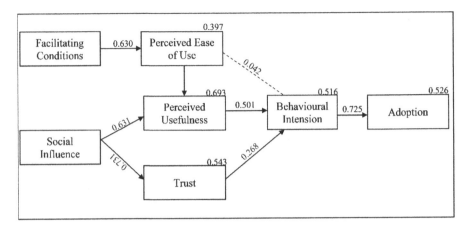

Fig. 1. Validated research model

Table 2. Results of quantitative test between path coefficients and their p-values

	Hypotheses	Estimate	p-value	Result
H1	PU → BI	0.501	***	Supported
H2	PEOU → BI	0.042	.577	Not Supported
H3	PEOU → PU	0.308	***	Supported
H4	SI → PU	0.631	***	Supported
H5	SI → TR	0.737	***	Supported
H6	FC → PEOU	0.630	***	Supported
H7	TR → BI	0.268	***	Supported
H8	BI → AD	0.725	***	Supported

5   Discussion and Implications

This study is performed with the motive to better understand the factors that affect intension and adoption of Payment Banks services among its customers. As per the results shown above, it has been examined that the model has reached the accepted level, as the measurement model validity, reliability and model fitness has achieved their cut-off standard. Whereas in the structural model values for all endogenous factors, i.e. for PEOU is 40%, PU is 69%, TR is 54%, BI is 54% and for AD 53% is attained successfully. Such values of R^2 are far close to other IS studies that have used TAM [41].

From the statistical results shown above, it is clear that PU has a significant relationship with BI [11, 31] with the weight of 0.50. This states that customers are more attracted towards the payments banking if they perceive that payment banking services are more useful, productive and efficient in their day to day life. Hence Payment Banks should try to demonstrate the usefulness and benefits of using their services, whereas Payment Banks should analyse the current customer base and investigate the features which customers find useful. Alike this study, PU is found to have a better impact on Behavioural Intension in the context of mobile and internet banking also.

In the path coefficient analysis Trust is also found to have a positive and significant impact on BI [5, 7, 11, 17] with the weight of 0.27. This implies that Trust is shaping the customer's intension to adopt Payment Banks services. With the increase in the cybercrimes mainly in online banking, Payment Banks should use latest and innovative technology to make their system more secure and trustworthy [8, 16, 20, 23].

Empirical results have also proved a positive and significant relationship between SI and Trust (TR) [20, 25] with a regression weight of 0.74. This implies that users of mobile banking are most impacted by their friends, family and colleagues to trust online platform of Payment Banks. As per the Sociolinguistic Theory, men are interested in task-specific information, whereas women put more focus on exchanging social support and trust that information. So payment banks should use proper marketing channels with secure user interface.

Statistical results also found to have a significant and positive relation of SI and PU. Similar results have been achieved in previous studies as well where SI is found to be a significant predictor of PU [6, 31, 36]. It implies that if customers social groups such as friends, family or colleagues use Payment Banks and find it useful, then they would also find it useful to transact through Payment Banks.

As per the statistical results achieved FC has a positive effect on PEOU. Similar results have also been attainted where FC have a significant and positive relation with PEOU [17, 31]. Payment Banks have been launched in several languages with the friendly interface as due to the diversity of Indian culture, so this will made payment easier and accessible to use for common people.

Quantitative results approved above have considerable influence of PEOU on PU, whereas it has a positive and insignificant effect on BI with regression weight of 0.31 and 0.042 respectively. Consistent with the previous research on TAM, PEOU affects indirectly BI through PU [11, 17]. Research suggests that Payment Banks need to make services easily accessible as local peoples should easily access it by sitting at their doorstep. PEOU states to have an insignificant relationship with BI [7], it implies that the bank can promote its internet services by communicating its usefulness. In contrast, they should make their user-interface friendly with the customers so that customers do not feel difficulty in operating their interface.

6   Conclusion, Limitations and Future Recommendation

This research was in response to the call for customer-oriented research in Payment Banking. As in this study external variables (SI & FC) constructs of UTAUT were found to have impact on TAM Variables, this research contributes to the theoretical framework of technology adoption and Extension of TAM model. As various private and government institutions are involved in payment banking services for financial inclusion, so it is very important people use it for better banking connectivity.

Even through this study contributes in the area of adoption and Payment Banks services research with produces Prolific results, it is limited with certain limitations. Data of the study has been collected using convenience sampling from Five cities, which in turn effect generalisability of the results across other parts of the country. Sample of the study were collected in selected duration, so it raises question about applicability of study in long term as with the passage of the time users' opinion, familiarity with technology may change.

As future research scope, this study can also be considered for longitudinal study, to measure the effect of various factors over time. as the proposed model is conceptually and statistically validated in the current study, so this model can be tested in other information systems adoption study.

References

1. Ajzen, I., Fishbein, M.: Understanding Attitudes and Predicting Social Behavior. Prentice-Hall, Englewood Cliffs (1980)
2. Ajzen, I.: The theory of planned behavior. Organ. Behav. Hum. Decis. Process. **50**(2), 179–211 (1991)
3. Alalwan, A.A., Dwivedi, Y.K., Rana, N.P., Williams, M.D.: Consumer adoption of mobile banking in Jordan Examining the role of usefulness, ease of use, perceived risk and self-efficacy. J. Enterp. Inf. Manag. **20**(2), 145–157 (2016)
4. Alalwan, A.A., Dwivedi, Y.K., Rana, N.P.: Factors influencing adoption of mobile banking by Jordanian bank customers: extending UTAUT2 with trust. Int. J. Inf. Manage. **37**(3), 99–110 (2017)
5. Alalwan, A.A., Baabdullah, A.M., Rana, N.P., Tamilmani, K., Dwivedi, Y.K.: Examining adoption of mobile internet in Saudi Arabia: extending TAM with perceived enjoyment, innovativeness and trust. Technol. Soc. **55**, 100–110 (2018)
6. Al-Somali, S.A., Gholami, R., Clegg, B.: An investigation into the acceptance of online banking in Saudi Arabia. Technovation **29**(2), 130–141 (2009)
7. Bashir, I., Madhavaiah, C.: Determinants of young consumers' intention to use Internet banking services in India. Vision **18**(3), 153–163 (2014)
8. Benamati, J.S., Serva, M.A., Fuller, M.A.: The productive tension of trust and distrust: the coexistence and relative role of trust and distrust in online banking. J. Organ. Comput. Electron. Commer. **20**(4), 328–346 (2010)
9. Byrne, B.M.: Structural Equation Modeling with AMOS: Basic Concepts, Applications, and Programming (Multivariate Applications Series), vol. 396, p. 7384. Taylor & Francis Group, New York (2010)
10. Chawla, D., Joshi, H.: Consumer perspectives about mobile banking adoption in India–a cluster analysis. Int. J. Bank Mark. **35**(4), 616–636 (2017)
11. Chawla, D., Joshi, H.: Scale development and validation for measuring the adoption of mobile banking services. Glob. Bus. Rev. **20**(2), 434–457 (2019)
12. Choudrie, J., Junior, C.O., McKenna, B., Richter, S.: Understanding and conceptualising the adoption, use and diffusion of mobile banking in older adults: a research agenda and conceptual framework. J. Bus. Res. **88**, 449–465 (2018)
13. Davis, F.D., Bagozzi, R.P., Warshaw, P.R.: User acceptance of computer technology: a comparison of two theoretical models. Manag. Sci. **35**(8), 982–1003 (1989)
14. Fishbein, M., Ajzen, I.: Belief, Attitude, Intention and Behavior: An Introduction to Theory and Research. Addison Wesley (1975)
15. Fornell, C., Larcker, D.F.: Structural equation models with unobservable variables and measurement error: algebra and statistics (1981)

16. Gefen, D., Karahanna, E., Straub, D.W.: Trust and TAM in online shopping: an integrated model. MIS Q. **27**(1), 51–90 (2003)
17. Gu, J.C., Lee, S.C., Suh, Y.H.: Determinants of behavioral intention to mobile banking. Expert Syst. Appl. **36**(9), 11605–11616 (2009)
18. Gupta, K.P., Manrai, R., Goel, U.: Factors influencing adoption of payments banks by Indian customers: extending UTAUT with perceived credibility. J. Asia Bus. Stud. **13**(2), 173–195 (2019)
19. Hair Jr., J.F., Black, W.C., Babin, B.J., Anderson, R.E.: Multivariate Data Analysis: A Global Perspective, 7th edn. Pearson Education International (2010)
20. Kline, R.B.: Principles and Practice of Structural Equation Modelling. The Guilford Press, New York (2005)
21. Luarn, P., Lin, H.H.: Toward an understanding of the behavioral intention to use mobile banking. Comput. Hum. Behav. **21**(6), 873–891 (2005)
22. Luo, X., Li, H., Zhang, J., Shim, J.P.: Examining multi-dimensional trust and multi-faceted risk in initial acceptance of emerging technologies: an empirical study of mobile banking services. Decis. Support Syst. **49**(2), 222–234 (2010)
23. Makanyeza, C.: Determinants of consumers' intention to adopt mobile banking services in Zimbabwe. Int. J. Bank Mark. **35**(6), 997–1017 (2017)
24. Malaquias, R.F., Hwang, Y.: Mobile banking use: a comparative study with Brazilian and US participants. Int. J. Inf. Manag. **44**, 132–140 (2019)
25. Malhotra, P., Singh, B.: Determinants of internet banking adoption by banks in India. Internet Res. **17**(3), 323–339 (2007)
26. Malhotra, P., Singh, B.: An analysis of Internet banking offerings and its determinants in India. Internet Res. Electron. Netw. Appl. Policy **20**(1), 87–106 (2010)
27. Mishra, V., Bisht, S.S.: Mobile banking in a developing economy: a customercentric model for policy formulation. Telecommun. Policy **37**(6–7), 503–514 (2013)
28. Montazemi, A.R., Qahri-Saremi, H.: Factors affecting adoption of online banking: a meta-analytic structural equation modeling study. Inf. Manag. **52**(2), 210–226 (2015)
29. Munoz-Leiva, F., Climent-Climent, S., Liébana-Cabanillas, F.: Determinants of intention to use the mobile banking apps: an extension of the classic TAM model. Span. J. Mark.-ESIC **21**(1), 25–38 (2017)
30. Nikou, S.A., Economides, A.A.: Mobile-based assessment: investigating the factors that influence behavioral intention to use. Comput. Educ. **109**, 56–73 (2017)
31. Nunnally, J.C.: Psychometric Theory, 2nd edn. McGraw-Hill (1978)
32. Phillips, L.A., Calantone, R., Lee, M.T.: International technology adoption: behavior structure, demand certainty and culture. J. Bus. Ind. Mark. **9**(2), 16–28 (1994)
33. Podsakoff, P.M., MacKenzie, S.B., Lee, J.Y., Podsakoff, N.P.: Common method biases in behavioral research: a critical review of the literature and recommended remedies. J. Appl. Psychol. **88**(5), 879 (2003)
34. Rogers, E.M.: Diffusion of Innovations, 5th edn. Free Press, New York (2003)
35. Roy, S.K., Kesharwani, A., Bisht, S.S.: The impact of trust and perceived risk on internet banking adoption in India. Int. J. Bank Mark. **30**(4), 303–322 (2012)
36. Sahu, G.P., Singh, N.K.: Paradigm shift of indian cash-based economy to cash-less economy: a study on Allahabad city. In: Kar, A.K., et al. (eds.) I3E 2017. LNCS, vol. 10595, pp. 453–461. Springer, Cham (2017). https://doi.org/10.1007/978-3-319-68557-1_40
37. Sikdar, P., Kumar, A.: Payment bank: a catalyst for financial inclusion. AsiaPacific J. Manag. Res. Innov. **12**(3–4), 226–231 (2016)
38. Singh, S., Srivastava, R.K.: Predicting the intention to use mobile banking in India. Int. J. Bank Mark. **36**(2), 357–378 (2018)

39. Venkatesh, V.: Creation of favorable user perceptions: exploring the role of intrinsic motivation. MIS Q. **22**(2), 239–260 (1999)
40. Venkatesh, V.: Determinants of perceived ease of use: integrating control, intrinsic motivation, and emotion into the technology acceptance model. Inf. Syst. Res. **11**(4), 342–365 (2000)
41. Venkatesh, V., Davis, F.D.: A theoretical extension of the technology acceptance model: four longitudinal field studies. Manag. Sci. **46**(2), 186–204 (2000)
42. Venkatesh, V., Morris, M.G., Davis, G.B., Davis, F.D.: User acceptance of information technology: toward a unified view. MIS Q. **27**(3), 425–478 (2003)
43. Venkatesh, V., Thong, J.Y., Xu, X.: Consumer acceptance and use of information technology: extending the unified theory of acceptance and use of technology. MIS Q. **36**(1), 157–178 (2012)
44. Wang, Y.S., Wang, Y.M., Lin, H.H., Tang, T.I.: Determinants of user acceptance of Internet banking: an empirical study. Int. J. Serv. Ind. Manag. **14**(5), 501–519 (2003)
45. Yi, M.Y., Hwang, Y.: Predicting the use of web-based information systems: self efficacy, enjoyment, learning goal orientation and the technology acceptance model. Int. J. Hum.-Comput. Stud. **59**(4), 431–449 (2003)

Assessing Challenges to Mobile Wallet Usage in India: An Interpretive Structural Modeling Approach

Nripendra P. Rana[1(✉)], Sunil Luthra[2], and H. R. Rao[3]

[1] International Business, Marketing and Branding Research Centre, School of Management, University of Bradford, Richmond Road, Bradford BD7 1DP, UK
nrananp@gmail.com
[2] Department of Mechanical Engineering, Ch. Ranbir Singh State Institute of Engineering and Technology, Jhajjar 124103, Haryana, India
sunilluthra1977@gmail.com
[3] Department of ISCS, COB, University of Texas at San Antonio, San Antonio, TX, USA
hr.rao@utsa.edu

Abstract. India is paving its way towards a cashless society, from physical wallets to virtual (mobile) wallets. Mobile wallets are a fast growing payment method but in developing counties, like India, consumers are still using cash in their daily transactions. This paper identifies and evaluates key challenges to mobile wallet usage in India. Eleven possible challenges to mobile wallets are identified through extensive review and validated from experts' inputs. Further, the Interpretive Structural Modeling (ISM) technique is utilized for constructing a structural framework of the identified challenges. Classification of these challenges has been done using MICMAC analysis. "Lack of adequate infrastructure (Ch4)", "Poor Internet penetration (Ch5)", "Highly fragmented economy (Ch9)" and "Lack of goal oriented and clearly defined mobile wallet strategy (Ch11)" have been found to be four key challenges that inhibit mobile wallet usage in India. This paper may help policymakers, regulatory bodies and banking managers in achieving effective mobile wallet usage in India.

Keywords: Challenges · Mobile wallet usage · Interpretive structural modeling · MICMAC analysis · India

1 Introduction

Smartphone and electronic commerce are an integral part of the modern customer nowadays. Increased use of technology and online shopping has forced the customer to adopt or shift from cash payments to e-wallet or digital wallets for the payment mode for services availed through e-commerce web portals or mobile applications [1]. In a developing country like India, the mobile wallet is becoming popular. There are many reasons behind it. For example, the Indian government is focusing on the cashless initiative and Indian banking sector is taking several initiatives in this direction. The

S. K. Sharma et al. (Eds.): TDIT 2020, IFIP AICT 618, pp. 103–113, 2020.
https://doi.org/10.1007/978-3-030-64861-9_10

consumers know that going cashless is more secure [2, 3]. They know there are various advantages for use of mobile wallets including security [4].

As per recent data, it is predicted that in India, the mobile wallet market will grow to $184 billion by 2024. Consumers are also aware about benefits of cashless economy. Net penetration of Internet is increasing very fast in India as compared to other counties. As per GlobalData (leading data and analytics company), India is one of the top markets in mobile payment adoption and surpasses the US, the UK, China and Denmark. There is no doubt that mobile wallets are a fast-growing payment method but in developing countries, consumers are still using cash in their daily transactions [5]. As per deloitte.com research, in India, although about 10% of accounting transaction volume is through this technology, the consumers are still less aware about mobile wallets and are doing relatively less transactions using it. There are several challenges for mobile wallet use in India and therefore it is important to comprehend the structural framework to overcome these challenges effectively. Realising this, the current research has the following objectives:

1. To systematically identify challenges to mobile wallet in India.
2. To develop a structural framework to overcome these challenges effectively.

This paper aims to recognize and investigate challenges to mobile wallet use in India. An integrated Interpretive Structural Modeling (ISM) and MICMAC methodology is used to develop a structural framework of these challenges. The paper is organized as follows: We review the literature in Sect. 2, literature analysis in Sect. 3, and conclusion, limitations and future work in Sect. 4.

2 Literature Review

The presence of challenges offers a retarding effect, thereby decelerating the development of continuous improvement. Thus, it is crucial to understand key challenges to mobile wallet use in India. In order to identify the challenges, prior literature was explored. Various keywords such as "Key Challenges/Hurdles/Hindrances/ Inhibitors + Mobile wallet usage or mobile wallet usage in India" were searched on Google and Google Scholar. 11 key challenges to mobile wallets usage in India were identified from a detailed review and are presented in Table 1 below.

Table 1. Challenges to mobile wallet in India

SN	Challenges	Brief description	References
1	Risk of security breaches and fraud (Ch1)	Risks of online fraud, leakage of confidential information, cyber-crimes and virus attacks etc. have been rising. This is a big concern to deal with, in order to popularize mobile wallet usage	[6, 7]
2	Privacy concerns (Ch2)	This challenge is related to the privacy concern of consumers about mobile wallet	[8, 9]
3	Low trust in mobile wallets (Ch3)	In a developing country like India, the consumers are showing less trust of mobile wallets as compared to cash	[10–12]
4	Lack of adequate infrastructure (Ch4)	The lack of adequate infrastructure is a major challenge in India because of this challenge, consumers still use cash	[13–15]
5	Poor Internet penetration (Ch5)	No doubt, India is growing very fast but as compared to country population, internet penetration is low, this is also a main challenge	[16, 17]
6	Perception of customers regarding the value of using mobile wallets (Ch6)	For any initiative, customer awareness and perception play an important role but still in India perception of customers are not strong regarding use of mobile wallet. Most of the customers feel comfortable without mobile wallet and feel that there is not much value to use	[18–20]
7	Low digital literacy (Ch7)	Digital literacy is just 10% in India. People in rural areas (more than 50% of the country population) still don't know about using and applications of smart phone in the context of electronic money	[21–23]
8	Language issues (Ch8)	The message received on mobiles regarding transactions is in English, which is problematic for people who have trouble communicating in English language	[24, 25]

(continued)

Table 1. (*continued*)

SN	Challenges	Brief description	References
9	Highly fragmented economy (Ch9)	Digital payments have reached out to only 10% of Indian users so far. In fact, while India has over 30 million retail outlets, only one million of them possess the required wherewithal for digital payments. There is no doubt that India is a growing economy and there is huge potential for digital payments. But still not growing as per predicted for instance as per Google and KGMP report, 68% of Indian SMEs have remained completely offline	[9, 12, 26]
10	Psychological factors (Ch10)	This challenge is related to the consumer's perceptions about mobile wallet. They feel more comfortable using cash in their transactions	[10, 27]
11	Lack of goal oriented and clearly defined mobile wallet strategy (Ch11)	Mobile wallet companies must develop a goaloriented and clearly defined strategy but, most service providers have failed to develop proper strategies to grab the market	[28, 29]

3   Results and Data Analysis

An integrated ISM-MICMAC methodology is used in this study. Warfield first proposed the ISM in 1974. ISM helps in the modeling of the variables by allowing development of interrelationships between them [30]. ISM uses practical awareness and practices of decisions makers to construct a logical hierarchical based modeling of the variables based on the driving and depending power this can done by using cross-impact matrix multiplication applied to classification, known as MICMAC analysis, which helps in developing the binary type of relationships among the considered variables [31]. In this work, ISM-MICMAC methodology is applied through different steps as below [32–41]:

i. Distinguish the variables associated with the research problem. In this research, we selected key challenges regarding the inhibition of mobile wallet usage in India.
ii. Construct Structural Self-Interaction Matrix (SSIM) to assess contextual relationships of selected mobile wallet usage related challenges.
iii. Transform the SSIM into Initial Reachability Matrix (RMi). Next, we developed the Final Reachability Matrix (RMf) from RMi. This transformation of RMi into RMf involves considering the transitivity relations among selected challenges.

iv. Determine the dependency and driving power of each challenge. Use summation of rows and columns of values in RMf to determine dependency and driving power of each challenge.

v. Draw various levels from RMf. Develop the reachability and antecedent set. Reachability and Antecedent set include the challenge itself and the other challenges influenced by it and influence the particular inhibitor. Next, a common set is produced by means of reachability and antecedent set.

vi. Transform the RMf into a digraph that illustrates the real image of challenges and their interrelationships. Transform the digraph into ISM based structural model, which is comprised of various levels (as obtained in Step v) of selected challenges. vii. Form a graph of selected challenges using MICMAC.

To analyse key challenges that prevent successful mobile wallets in India, initially, twenty experts related to banking systems were contacted by phone and direct visit. Twelve out of the twenty experts agreed to participate in this research. All the selected experts had experience of more than 10 years. Further, validation of identified challenges from literature review and identification of the contextual interrelationships between the challenges was established by discussions with the selected experts, for developing SSIM matrix (see Table 2). The following four denotation symbols have been used for indicating the type of relation between identified challenges in the (i, j) form:

V-Variable i helps achieve or has influence on Variable j;
A-Variable j helps achieve or has influence on Variable i; X-Variables i and j help achieve or influence each other; O-Variables i and j are not related to each other.

The initial reachability matrix (RMi) is developed from SSIM. The RMi consists of binary numbers (0 and 1) and formed using several rules [20], given as:

Table 2. SSIM matrix of challenges to mobile wallets

SN	Contextual relationships									
	Ch11	Ch10	Ch9	Ch8	Ch7	Ch6	Ch5	Ch4	Ch3	Ch2
Ch1	A	V	A	V	V	V	A	A	V	X
Ch2	A	V	A	V	V	V	A	A	V	
Ch3	A	A	A	A	A	V	A	A		
Ch4	X	V	X	V	V	V	X			
Ch5	X	V	X	V	V	V				
Ch6	A	A	A	A	A					
Ch7	A	X	A	X						
CH8	A	X	A							
Ch9	X	V								
Ch10	A									

If SSIM contains V in the SSIM, then RMi should replace with entry 1 for (i, j) and 0 for (j, i);

If SSIM contains A in the SSIM, then RMi should replace with entry 0 for (i, j) and 1 for (j, i);

If SSIM contains X in the SSIM, then RMi should replace with entry 1 for both (i, j) and (j, i);

If SSIM contains O in the SSIM, then RMi should replace with entry 0 for both (i, j) and (j, i).

Then, the final reachability matrix (RMf) was developed from the RMi using transitivity rule (for more details see step iii and iv of methodology) as depicted in Table 3.

If the reachability set and the intersection set (for more details see step V of methodology) for any challenge was the same, then that challenge was assigned as level 1st (highest place in the ISM model). Once the level was assigned to the chal-

Table 3. Final reachability matrix of challenges to mobile wallets

SN	Ch1	Ch2	Ch3	Ch4	Ch5	Ch6	Ch7	Ch8	Ch9	Ch10	Ch11	DR
Ch1	1	1	1	0	0	1	1	1	0	1	0	07
Ch2	1	1	1	0	0	1	1	1	0	1	0	07
Ch3	0	0	1	0	0	1	0	0	0	0	0	02
Ch4	1	1	1	1	1	1	1	1	1	1	1	11
Ch5	1	1	1	1	1	1	1	1	1	1	1	11
Ch6	0	0	0	0	0	1	0	0	0	0	0	01
Ch7	0	0	1	0	0	1	1	1	0	1	0	05
CH8	0	0	1	0	0	1	1	1	0	1	0	05
Ch9	1	1	1	1	1	1	1	1	1	1	1	11
Ch10	0	0	1	0	0	1	1	1	0	1	0	05
Ch11	1	1	1	1	1	1	1	1	1	1	1	11
DP	06	06	10	04	04	11	09	09	04	09	04	76

Note: DR = Driving Power; DP = Dependence Power

lenge, then that challenge was eliminated. This procedure was repeated to assign at most one level to each challenge. Final levels for the challenges are depicted in Table 4.

From the RMf (see Table 3) and final developed six levels of the challenges (Table 4), a hierarchical structural model regarding the challenges that retard mobile wallet usage in India was developed and is shown in Fig. 1.

Table 4. Final level of challenges to mobile wallets in India

Level	Challenges to mobile wallets in India
1st	• Perception of customers about the value of using mobile wallets (Ch6)
2nd	• Low trust in mobile wallets (Ch3)
3rd	• Low digital literacy (Ch7) • Language issues (Ch8) • Psychological factors (Ch10)
4th	• Risk of security breaches and fraud (Ch1) • Privacy concerns (Ch2)
5th	• Lack of adequate infrastructure (Ch4) • Poor Internet penetration (Ch5) • Highly fragmented economy (Ch9) • Lack of goal oriented and clearly defined mobile wallet strategy (Ch11)

It is clear from Fig. 1 that 'Lack of adequate infrastructure (Ch4)', 'Poor internet penetration (Ch5)', 'Highly fragmented economy (Ch9)' and 'Lack of goal oriented and clearly defined mobile wallet strategy (Ch11)' are foundational challenges in the

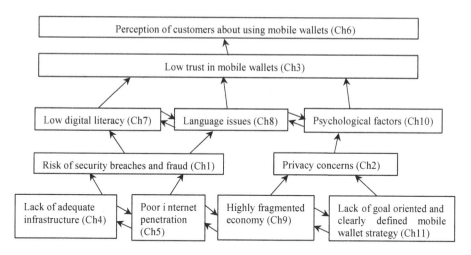

Fig. 1. ISM based structural model of identified challenges

ISM hierarchical model i.e. cluster of independent challenges, thus these are most critical hurdles that prevent mobile wallets in India. 'Perception of customers (Ch6)' is found the top hierarchical level in the ISM model.

In the MICMAC analysis [31], the dependence power and driving power of challenges that prevent mobile wallets in India were analysed and plotted in Fig. 2 as four different clusters.

All identified eleven challenges have an influence in implementing mobile wallets in India and are in the four clusters that are shown in Fig. 2.

Autonomous region: Nil

This cluster of challenges has low driving and dependence power. These challenges fall near origin in Fig. 2 and are almost disconnected from other challenges. These

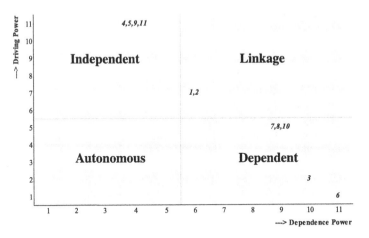

Fig. 2. MICMAC analysis of identified challenges

challenges are not affected by the system. In this research, no challenge is found in this cluster.

Dependent region: Ch7, Ch8, Ch10, Ch3 and Ch6

This region of challenges has high dependence and less driving power values. These challenges come under the top position of the structural model given by the ISM. They are strongly dependent on the independent and linkage region challenges to diminish the effect of these challenges in implementing mobile wallets in India.

Linkage region: Ch1 and Ch2

This cluster of challenges has high driving and dependence power values. These challenges are not stable in behaviour and any changes can affect the entire model and produce some feedback also. These challenges are positioned at the center of the structural model given by ISM.

Independent region: Ch4, Ch5, Ch9 and Ch11

This cluster of challenges has less dependence and high driving power values. They are also termed as key challenges. These challenges are positioned at the bottom of the structural model given by ISM.

4   Conclusion, Limitations and Future Work

This paper aims to identify and scrutinise challenges that prevent successful mobile wallet usage in India. A total of eleven challenges that may prevent successful implementation of mobile wallets usage have been identified through literature survey and decision makers' knowledge and experience. This paper has illustrated contextual interrelationships among the identified challenges and has constructed a hierarchy of challenges that need to be overcome to have successful mobile wallet usage in Indian contexts.

ISM modelling combined with MICMAC has been used to fulfil the aims of this work. The challenges 'Lack of adequate infrastructure (Ch4)', 'Poor internet penetration (Ch5)', 'Highly fragmented economy (Ch9)' and 'Lack of goal oriented and clearly defined mobile wallet strategy (Ch11)' have been found to be independent challenges that prevent mobile wallet usage in India. These challenges are powerful and influential i.e. all other challenges are highly dependent on these challenges in effectively implementing mobile wallets. The findings of the present research may be important for policy makers, regulatory bodies and banking managers/practitioners in better understanding of these identified challenges removal towards effective implementation of mobile wallets system in India.

This work has presented a combined ISM-MICMAC framework that has been constructed using eleven mobile wallets usage challenges identified through literature and experts' inputs. In future research, this work may be extended with identifying more challenges and by using a larger dataset. The developed structural model has used a small number of experts' opinions, so we need to examine more experts' opinions. In future works, the identified challenges may be quantified using graph theory or any other appropriate Multi Criteria Decision Making (MCDM) tools. In future research, ISM model can be extended by applying Total Interpretive Structural Modelling (TISM) in developing a knowledge base of the interpretive logic of all the interactions among and within challenges for interpreting the structure model entirely.

References

1. Shankar, K.G., Raju, P.: A study on opportunities and challenges of adopting digital wallet in India. Our Heritage **67**(2), 127–136 (2019)
2. Sen, S.: Surge in cashless transactions will push digital economy, m-wallets will gain (2016). www.hindustantimes.com/business-news/surge-in-cashless-transactionswillpush-digital-economy-m-wallets-will-gain/storyo6Gc8qndqGA4kbY09KafBI.html. Accessed 17 Feb 2020
3. Bagla, R.K., Sancheti, V.: Gaps in customer satisfaction with digital wallets: challenge for sustainability. J. Manag. Dev. **37**(6), 442–451 (2018)
4. Ramya, N., Sivasakthi, D., Nandhini, M.: Cashless transaction: modes, advantages and disadvantages. Int. J. Appl. Res. **3**(1), 122–125 (2017)
5. Kang, J.: Mobile payment in fintech environment: trends, security challenges, and services. Hum.-Centric Comput. Inf. Sci. **8**(1), 32 (2018)
6. Peters, G.W., Chapelle, A., Panayi, E.: Opening discussion on banking sector risk exposures and vulnerabilities from virtual currencies: an operational risk perspective. J. Banking Regul. **17**(4), 239–272 (2016)
7. Le, D.N., Kumar, R., Mishra, B.K., Chatterjee, J.M., Khari, M. (eds.): Cyber Security in Parallel and Distributed Computing: Concepts, Techniques, Applications and Case Studies. Wiley (2019)
8. Chandrasekhar, C.P., Ghosh, J.: The financialization of finance? Demonetization and the dubious push to cashlessness in India. Dev. Change **49**(2), 420–436 (2018)

9. Sinha, M., Majra, H., Hutchins, J., Saxena, R.: Mobile payments in India: the privacy factor. Int. J. Bank Mark. **37**(1), 192–209 (2019)

10. Madan, K., Yadav, R.: Behavioural intention to adopt mobile wallet: a developing country perspective. J. Indian Bus. Res. **8**(3), 227–244 (2016)

11. Routray, S., Khurana, R., Payal, R., Gupta, R.: A move towards cashless economy: a case of continuous usage of mobile wallets in India. Theor. Econ. Lett. **9**(4), 1152–1166 (2019)

12. Singh, N., Sinha, N.: How perceived trust mediates merchant's intention to use a mobile wallet technology. J. Retail. Consum. Serv. **52**, 101894 (2020)

13. Kumar, N.: Growth drivers and trends of E-wallets in India. MANTHAN: J. Commer. Manag. **3**(1), 65–72 (2016)

14. Bubna, R., Raveendran, J., Kumar, S., Duggirala, M., Malik, M.: A partially grounded agent based model on demonetisation outcomes in India. In: Sokolowski, J., Durak, U., Mustafee, N., Tolk, A. (eds.) Summer of Simulation. SFMA, pp. 247–275. Springer, Cham (2019). https://doi.org/10.1007/978-3-030-17164-3_12

15. Sobti, N.: Impact of demonetization on diffusion of mobile payment service in India. J. Adv. Manag. Res. **16**(4), 472–497 (2019)

16. Goyal, A.: Conditions for inclusive innovation with application to telecom and mobile banking. Innov. Dev. **7**(2), 227–248 (2017)

17. Goswami, K.C., Sinha, S.: Cashless economy and strategic impact on bank marketing. Sumedha J. Manag. **8**(1), 131–142 (2019)

18. Singh, S., Rana, R.: Study of consumer perception of digital payment mode. J. Internet Banking Commer. **22**(3), 1–14 (2017)

19. Singh, N., Srivastava, S., Sinha, N.: Consumer preference and satisfaction of M-wallets: a study on North Indian consumers. Int. J. Bank Mark. **35**(6), 944–965 (2017)

20. Singh, S., Srivastava, R.K.: Understanding the intention to use mobile banking by existing online banking customers: an empirical study. J. Finan. Serv. Mark. **25**, 86–96 (2020)

21. Baptista, G., Oliveira, T.: A weight and a meta-analysis on mobile banking acceptance research. Comput. Hum. Behav. **63**, 480–489 (2016)

22. Priya, S.S.: Digital interventions for economic growth. South Asian J. Manag. **26**(1), 174–177 (2019)

23. Singh, R., Malik, G.: Impact of digitalization on indian rural banking customer: with reference to payment systems. Emerg. Econ. Stud. **5**(1), 31–41 (2019)

24. Reaves, B., et al.: Mo (bile) money, Mo (bile) problems: analysis of branchless banking applications. ACM Trans. Priv. Secur. (TOPS) **20**(3), 1–31 (2017)

25. Iyer, L.: Adoption of digital wallets by petty vendors post demonetisation in India: a prediction approach. Asian J. Res. Soc. Sci. Hum. **8**(6), 117–130 (2018)

26. Bansal, S.: Cashless economy: opportunities and challenges in India. Worldwide J. Multidiscip. Res. Dev. **3**(9), 10–12 (2017)

27. Gupta, K., Arora, N.: Investigating consumer intention to accept mobile payment systems through unified theory of acceptance model. South Asian J. Bus. Stud. **9**(1), 88–114 (2019)

28. Shahid, Q., Razaq, L.: Demonetisation for changing payment behaviour and building platforms. J. Payments Strategy Syst. **11**(2), 158–167 (2017)

29. Iman, N.: Is mobile payment still relevant in the fintech era? Electron. Commer. Res. Appl. **30**, 72–82 (2018)

30. Warfield, J.N.: Developing interconnection matrices in structural modeling. IEEE Trans. Syst. Man Cybern. **1**(1), 81–87 (1974)

31. Luthra, S., Kumar, V., Kumar, S., Haleem, A.: Barriers to implement green supply chain management in automobile industry using interpretive structural modeling technique: an Indian perspective. J. Ind. Eng. Manag. **4**(2), 231–257 (2011)

32. Al-Muftah, H., Weerakkody, V., Rana, N.P., Sivarajah, U., Irani, Z.: E-diplomacy implementation: exploring causal relationships using interpretive structural modelling. Gov. Inf. Q. **35**(3), 502–514 (2018)
33. Dwivedi, Y.K., et al.: Driving innovation through Big Open Linked Data (BOLD): exploring antecedents using interpretive structural modelling. Inf. Syst. Front. **19**(2), 197–212 (2017)
34. Janssen, M., Mangla, S., Luthra, S., Rana, N.P., Dwivedi, Y.K.: Challenges for implementing the Internet of Things (IoT) in smart cities: an integrated MICMAC Interpretive Structural Modeling (ISM) approach. Internet Res. **29**(6), 1589–1616 (2019)
35. Janssen, M., Rana, N.P., Slade, E., Dwivedi, Y.K.: Trustworthiness of digital government services: deriving a comprehensive theory through interpretive structural modelling. Publ. Manag. Rev. **20**(5), 647–671 (2018)
36. Hughes, D.L., Dwivedi, Y.K., Rana, N.P., Simintiras, A.C.: Information systems project failure – analysis of causal links using interpretive structural modelling. Prod. Plan. Control **27**(16), 1313–1333 (2016)
37. Mangla, S.K., Rich, N., Luthra, S., Kumar, D., Rana, N.P., Dwivedi, Y.K.: A combined ISM-Fuzzy DEMATEL based framework for implementing sustainable initiatives in agri-food supply chains. Int. J. Prod. Econ. **203**, 379–393 (2018)
38. Mishra, N., Singh, A., Rana, N.P., Dwivedi, Y.K.: Interpretive structural modelling and fuzzy MICMAC approaches for customer centric beef supply chain: application of a big data technique. Prod. Plan. Control **28**(11–12), 945–963 (2017)
39. Rana, N.P., Luthra, S., Rao, H.R.: Key challenges to digital financial services in emerging economies: the Indian context. Inf. Technol. People **33**(1), 198–229 (2020)
40. Rana, N.P., Barnard, D., Baabdullah, A., Rees, D., Roderick, S.: Exploring barriers of M-commerce adoption in SMEs in the UK: developing a framework using ISM. Int. J. Inf. Manag. **44**, 141–153 (2019)
41. Rana, N.P., Luthra, S., Rao, H.R.: The challenges of Digital Financial Services (DFS) in India: deriving a framework using Interpretive Structural Modeling (ISM). In: PACIS 2018, Yokohama, Japan (2018)

Factors Driving the Adoption of Mobile Banking App: An Empirical Assessment in the Less Digitalized Economy

Alex Ntsiful[(⊠)] [iD], Michael Adu Kwarteng [iD],
Abdul Bashiru Jibril [iD], Boris Popesko [iD], and Michal Pilik [iD]

Faculty of Management and Economics, Tomas Bata University in Zlin,
Mostni 5139, 76001 Zlin, Czech Republic
{Ntsiful,Kwarteng,Jibril,Popesko,Pilik}@utb.cz

Abstract. Financial institutions remain one of the key industries making use of information and communication technologies to transform their products and services and their business in general. As the Internet becomes pervasive, most banks, in addition to their traditional mobile banking, have introduced mobile banking apps, which ride on smart devices and the Internet to offer banking services remotely to customers. However, given some contextual factors such as unstable Internet, adoption of this innovation may be a challenge in an emerging economy. Thus, the study sought to find out the factors, which could affect the adoption of mobile banking app in a less digitalized environment. To this end, data was sourced via the intercept approach on a sample of the entire population in Ghana for the analysis. By using the partial least square structural equation modelling (PLS-SEM) technique, the study found that performance expectancy and hedonic motivation were the key factors that influence mobile banking app adoption. Contrary to our expectation, effort expectancy, perceived transaction cost, and privacy and information concerns were found to have no effect on consumers' intention to adopt mobile banking app. Implications for further research and practice are presented and discussed.

Keywords: Mobile banking app · Mobile banking · Privacy concern · Transaction cost

1 Introduction

Financial institutions remain one of the key industries making use of information and communication technologies, such as the Internet and wireless technologies to transform their products and services and their business in general. With and through mobile technologies, banks can meet customers' expectations by offering them different services (Singh and Srivastava 2018). The banks started with the introduction of mobile banking, which according to Barnes and Corbitt (2003) can be defined as the channel allowing customers to use their digital devices to interact with the bank. As the Internet becomes more pervasive, the banks have now developed their applications to augment the mobile banking service. Unlike mobile banking which can be done without smartphone and Internet, services offered by the bank on mobile banking app can only

© IFIP International Federation for Information Processing 2020
Published by Springer Nature Switzerland AG 2020
S. K. Sharma et al. (Eds.): TDIT 2020, IFIP AICT 618, pp. 114–125, 2020.
https://doi.org/10.1007/978-3-030-64861-9_11

be accessed by smartphones with the Internet. To this end, the mobile banking app is less useful in developing economies where the Internet is a challenge. For instance, research shows that in rural India where there is less access to the Internet, mobile banking is easily accessed, and remains the preferred channel of banking services (Singh and Srivastava 2018). Whilst studies on mobile banking abound (see Chhonker et al. 2018; Grover and Kar 2020; Singh et al. 2017) research on mobile banking apps remain scant. Moreover, the few studies we have on mobile banking apps have also been conducted in Internet-endowed economies (e.g. Munoz-Leiva *et al.* 2017; Wijland *et al.* 2016); with few in developing economies such as Ghana (e.g. Ansong and Synaepa-Addision 2019).

In studying the adoption of the predecessor of mobile banking apps, Owusu *et al.* (2020) note that although there is a high rate of mobile device penetration in Africa (ITU 2007), the diffusion of mobile banking technologies is far below expectation. We thus argue that there are myriad of factors in developing economies, which make direct applications of the previous findings contextually irrelevant in those economies. For instance, in a less digitized environment such as Ghana where consistent pervasive stable Internet is a dream and even in the capital city, Accra, where one expects to have a stable Internet in place, is also not the case. Thus, we argue that an introduction of a mobile banking app to attract a massive adoption may be a mirage. We also contend beyond downloading of the mobile banking app, customers in such growing economies would have other issues such as privacy/cybersecurity or perceived transaction cost, as the modalities and how the Internet of things work are not popular in these environments. In other words, the study argues that the issues on mobile banking apps are not well researched and empirically tested. As these apps are at their infancy stage, there is the need to examine thoroughly to know which issues could influence customers' adoption behaviour. Following these arguments, the key objective of the present study is to address the factors or issues, which could affect customers' adoption of mobile banking app in Ghana. To achieve this objective, the study uses the modified version of the unified theory of acceptance and use of technology (UTAUT2) (Venkatesh *et al.* 2012). Specifically, we examine the relationships between performance expectancy, effort expectancy, and hedonic motivation (UTAUT2), and intention to use mobile banking apps. Further, the study also adds perceived transaction cost and privacy and information concern to the constructs of the said theories in examining the relationships. We make significant contributions to literature with this paper. First, we extend UTAUT2 with two additional constructs to help understand the issues customers may have in adopting mobile banking apps. Second, contextually, we add to the scanty of research output on mobile banking app adoption in a less Internet-penetrated territory. These, we believe, would offer insights to managers and policymakers in organizations especially those in the financial sector as a guide in the development and introduction of their banking apps on the markets.

We organize the rest of the paper as follows: While the next Sect. 2 presents the theoretical background and hypotheses development, Sect. 3 explains our empirical study. This is followed by Sects. 4, which presents the discussion and conclusion of the study.

2 Theory and Hypotheses Development

2.1 Unified Theory of Acceptance and Use of Technology

The theory from which our study takes inspiration is the modified version of the unified theory of acceptance and use of technology (UTAUT2) by Venkatesh (2012). As the name suggests, UTAUT is an integration of eight information system theories and models. The first four of these theories and models include the theory of reasoned action-TRA (Fishbein and Ajzen 1975), social cognitive theory-SCT (Bandra 1986), technology acceptance model-TAM (Davis 1989), and theory of planned behaviourTPB (Ajzen 1991). The other four theories/models include the model of PC utilization (MPCU-(Thomsposn *et al.* 1991)), the motivational model-MM (Davis *et al.* 1992), the decomposed theory of planned behaviour-DTPB (Taylor and Todd 1995) and the innovation diffusion theory-IDT (Rogers 1995). Thus, the first UTAUT (Venkatesh *et al.* 2003) posits that for factors such as performance expectancy (PE), effort expectancy (EE), social influence (SI), and facilitating conditions (FC) are the key determinants of a person's intention to adopt a technology. This means for a person to use a certain technology, the technology should meet performance expectations, and should not require excessive effort to use. The theory also acknowledges that social norms or influence from other people the individual value and also certain conditions such as technical and human support can affect the person's intention to use the technology. Thus, PE, EE, SI, and FC were the key four constructs of UTAUT. In his study, Venkatesh moderated these variables with age, experience, gender, and voluntariness of use.

However, in 2012, Venkatesh and his colleagues modified the UTAUT to UTAUT2 by including new constructs: price value, habit, and hedonic motivation, and dropped the voluntariness of use as a moderator and concluded that UTAUT2 better explain consumer intention. We also design our present study in line with the UTAUT2 but specifically adopt only the performance expectation (PE), effort expectancy (EE), and hedonic motivation (HM). We also extend the UTAUT2 with perceived transaction cost (PTC), and privacy and information concern (PIC). We argue that in an environment such as Ghana, as mobile banking apps use the Internet, customers may have problem Internet and transaction costs. We further contend that in such an environment where technology acceptance is at infancy, customers could be more sceptical over cybersecurity issues regarding personal information if they should use the mobile banking app, which uses the Internet. To this end, we explain performance expectation, effort expectancy, hedonic motivation, perceived transaction cost, and privacy and information concern, as well as our dependent variable, intention to adopt mobile banking app in details as follows: We summarize previous works on our study's constructs in Table 1 below:

Table 1. Definitions & summary of previous works using UTAUT2/PTC & PIC

Construct	Definition	Some findings
Performance expectancy (PE)	PE measures the extent to which a new technology assists users to get what they need in a more useful and convenient manner (Venkatesh *et al.* 2003)	Extant studies have found that PE affects users behavioural intention to adopt new technology (see Shareef *et al.* 2018; Alalwan *et al.* 2017; Venkatesh *et al.* 2003). For instance, Alalwan *et al.* 2017 found that performance expectancy has a positive impact on customers behaviour intention to mobile food ordering apps in Jordan
Effort expectancy (EE)	EE is the degree to which users of a technology perceive it to be easy to use. Thus, in this study, we define effort expectancy as the extent to which consumers perceive mobile banking apps to easy to use (Venkatesh *et al.* (2012)	Several studies have confirmed the relationship between EE and customers' intention to adopt new technology (Thusi and Maduku 2020; Albashrawi *et al.* 2017; Alalwan *et al.* 2017). For example, Albashrawi *et al.* (2017) noted that EE influence customers intention in using mobile banking app in US banks
Hedonic motivation (HM)	HM refers to the pleasure gained from using an innovation (Venkatesh *et al.* 2012)	HM has been found as a good predictor of behavioural intention to use innovation (Thusi and Maduku 2020; Okumus *et al.* 2018; Yeo *et al.* 2017). For instance, Okumus *et al.* (2018) found that HM positively affects customers' intention to adopt smartphone diet apps to order food at restaurants
Perceived transaction cost (PTC)	Perceived transaction cost refers to the perception that customers hold that using innovation or new technology will attract financial charges. Mobile banking app costs may include initial purchase price, transaction cost, subscription charges (Singh and Srivastava 2018)	Overall, PTC is a major obstacle to the adoption of mobile technology (Lubua and Pretorius 2018; Hanafizadeh *et al.* 2014)

(continued)

Table 1. (*continued*)

Construct	Definition	Some findings
Privacy and information concern (PIC)	PIC denotes the extent to which a user of technology feels sceptical about personal data	Prior studies have found that PIC negatively affects technology adoption (Hayikader, *et al.* 2016; Tang and Liu 2015; Alkhater *et al.* 2014; Gupta *et al.* 2013)
Intention to use a mobile banking app	An intention is defined as the plan of action to engage in a certain behaviour (Armitage and Christian 2003). In this study, the intention to use is conceptualized as a dependent variable and is influenced by PE, EE, HN, PTC, and PIC	

Following the theoretical review and the previous empirical works summarized in Table 1 above, we argue that the three constructs of UTAUT2(performance expectancy, effort expectancy, hedonic motivation) plus perceived transaction cost, and privacy and information concern will directly influence usage intention to use the mobile app (our dependent variable) and are therefore conceptualized as independent variables. Accordingly, we derive the following hypotheses:

H1: Performance expectancy positively affects the adoption of Mobile Banking App
H2: Effort expectancy positively affects the adoption of Mobile Banking App
H3: Hedonic motivation positively affects the adoption of Mobile Banking App
H4: Perceived transaction cost negatively affects the adoption of Mobile Banking App
H5: Privacy and information concern negatively affect the adoption of Mobile Banking App

The methodology used to test the proposed model is outlined in the following section.

3   Empirical Study

3.1   Survey Data and Method

The study made use of both probability and non-probability sampling techniques for data collection. In effect, the non- probability sampling technique was adopted to select the target banks (unit of our analysis) comprising universal, rural, investment management firms/banks. On the other hand, the probability sampling technique (random sampling- which we consider to be most practical in this case) was then adopted via the intercept approach to gathering data for our analysis. Initially, we aimed to recruit 600 participants for the study. However, the influx of the COVID-19 pandemic did not allow us, therefore we ended up getting 327 respondents of which 291 was used for our analysis, after cleaning the data. We must emphasize that the first author was on the ground for data collection and recruited research assistants from his previous

University to help gather the entire data (A token of reward from the funds of our research project was given to these research assistants). Data collection was undertaken in the months between November 2019 and January 2020. On average, the questionnaire took seven minutes to fill.

The mainstream of sampled respondents was male (65%), aged between 21–35 (39.6%), and a bachelor's degree (63.2%). In this study, statistical analyses were performed using both IBM SPSS and ADANCO 2.0 version (Henseler et al. 2014). Lastly, the research constructs – except for demographic variables - were measured using a five-point scale (ranging from completely disagree to completely agree). Besides, our work is consistent with most of the views expressed in Podskaoff et al. (2003) regarding the minimization of common method bias.

3.2   Measurement Model Analysis

By way of improving the face and construct validity, we curled the study's constructs from the existing literature. Specifically, the measures for Performance Expectancy (PE), Effort Expectancy (EE), Hedonic Motivation (HM) and Intention to adopt mobile banking app (INT) were adapted from Farah et al. (2018), while the measures, Perceived transaction cost (PTC) and Privacy/information concern (PIC) were modified from Hanafizadeh et al. (2014) and Albashrawi and Motiwalla (2019) respectively. Moreover, the research hypotheses were tested by using the PLS-path modelling technique and precisely using mode A algorithm for path analysis while mode B was used to measure control variables on the dependent variable. The inspected composite reliability scores pertaining to the reflective measurement model were recorded as follows: 0.85 (EE), 0.84 (PE), 0.80 (HM), 0.71 (INT), 0.85(PTC), 0.68(PIC). Moreover, the lower bound estimate of the reliability of sum scores of the reflective model (Cronbach's alpha-although not recorded here exceeded the minimum threshold of 0.6). Furthermore, all indicator loadings and weights were statistically significant at $p < 0.05$. Besides all the indicator loadings exceeded the 0.6 scores required for this kind of exploratory work. Likewise, in terms of convergent validity, average variance extracted (AVE) scores range from 0.843 (EE), 0.849 (PE), 0.880 (HM), 0.923 (INT), 0.676 (PTC.), 0.791 (PC). While not reported here, following Fornell and Larcker (1981), discriminant validity was documented for the constructs.

3.3   Model Fit Analysis

Model fit and quality criteria were assessed based on Standardized Root Mean Squared Residual (SRMR). We obtained 0.0562 (SRMR value and thus acceptable since it is less than 0.1) (Henseler et al. 2014). The SRMR is calculated as the square root of the sum of the squared differences between the model-implied correlation matrix and the empirical correlation matrix, i.e. the Euclidean distance between the two matrices. Hence, the lower the SRMR, the better the theoretical model's fit. As a rule of thumb, a value of 0 for the SRMR indicates a perfect fit, and, mostly, an SRMR value less than 0.05 indicates an acceptable fit (Byrne 2013). However, a recent replication study shows that even totally correctly specified models can yield SRMR values of 0.06 and higher (Henseler et al. 2014). Therefore, a baseline value of 0.0562, as proposed by Hu and Bentler (1999), appears to be better for variance-based SEM in our case depicting a model fit.

Table 2. Structural Model statistics

Hypothesis	β (t-ratios)	p-values	Remarks
H1: PERFORM-EXPT -> INTENT-ADOPT	0.2422	0.0012	Significant
H2: EFFORT-EXPT -> INTENT-ADOPT	0.0720	0.1855	Not significant
H3: HEDONIC-MOTIV -> INTENT	0.5112	0.0000	Significant
H4: PRIV-INFO-CONCERN -> INTENTADOPT	−0.0308	0.6758	Not significant
H5: TRANS-COST -> INTENT-ADOPT	0.1322	0.2981	Not significant
Control Variables			
Gender	−0.1419	0.0091	Significant
Age	0.1246	0.0411	Significant
Past Experience	0.0385	0.3552	Not significant
Coefficient of determination (R^2)	R^2	*Adjusted R^2*	
INTENT-ADOPT	0.5939	0.5810	Acceptable

NB: *Model/path is significant at P < 0.05*

3.4 Structural Model Evaluation

Table 2 shows an empirical analysis of the proposed model of this study. We performed a structural path analysis using a statistical software: ADANCO 2.0 version as earlier disclosed. Reflecting on the recommendation of pioneer scholars (Hair et al. 2014; Henseler et al. 2016), the summary of our PLS-SEM (see Table 2) indicates direct path analysis with control variables as well as the estimated coefficient of determination (R^2). Concerning the hypothesis testing, we found that hypotheses: (HI and H3) proved significant at p-value < 0.05 whilst the remaining direct hypotheses; (H2, H4, H5) were insignificant. Again, in testing the control variables: gender, age, and experience of the study's respondents, it was found that 'Gender' and 'Age' of respondents played a significant control variable regarding the use of the e-banking app. Further, the value of the coefficient of determination (R^2) (see Table 2) indicates that our endogenous variables (e.g. Performance expectancy, hedonic motivation etc.) explain significant variance in the exogenous variable (intent to adopt banking app). This suggests that the model satisfied beyond the appreciable threshold of 50% (see Table 2 and Fig. 1).

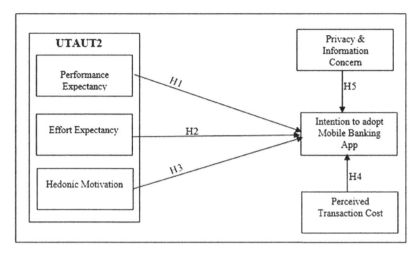

Fig. 1. Empirical model

4 Short Discussion and Conclusion

We took inspiration from the modified version of the unified theory of acceptance and use of technology (UTAUT2) by Venkatesh (2012) to investigate thoroughly and to know which issues could influence customers' adoption behaviour of the use of mobile banking app in a less digitized country as earlier unveiled. Hence, the key objective of the present study was to address the factors or issues, which could affect the customer's adoption of the mobile banking app in Ghana. The research model based on the UTAUT2 was tested with a sample of the population in Ghana using an intercept approach via a cross-sectional study. The measurement and structural models recorded good model fit metrics, and the study measures possessed sufficient validity and reliability.

RQ1 investigated which issues could influence customers' adoption of mobile banking app in Ghana. For this research question, it is worth noting that the research results revealed that potential users (or users) of the mobile banking app within the preview of the less digital economy are much more passionate about the performance expectancy (PE) and the hedonic motivation (HM) attached to the use of the mobile banking app. This assertion further corroborates with the recent works of Abdul-Hamid *et al.* (2019) and Boateng *et al.* (2016) who examined the adoption of mobile money apps, and Internet banking adoption in a developing country respectively. Similarly, it is important to note that the current empirical findings revealed 'age and gender' variations as key control variables, which significantly predict the user's intention to adopt the banking app.

RQ2 examined the relationship between UTAUT2 factors and the intentions to continue using the mobile banking app in Ghana. In answering this question, the current analysis confirmed PE and HM but not EE as the two major UTAUT2 factors that have a positive influence towards the intention to adopt the said app amongst potential users in the less digitalized economy (Alalwan *et al.* 2017). Again, in evaluating the impact of Privacy/information concern (PIC) on the intent to adopt the banking app, the former showed an inverse relation towards the latter (Jibril *et al.* 2020; Owusu *et al.* 2020). Perceived transaction cost (PTC) has no significant impact per the responses evaluated. This further suggests that any additional charges that may arise in an attempt to use the said app would not deter the potential users from using the service (i.e. mobile banking app). Hence the result is consistent with the research of (Oliveira *et al.* 2014; Owusu *et al.* 2020).

Theoretically, the study's findings advance the literature on UTUAT in two ways: First, we utilized an abreast version of the technology adoption model to examine the influence of UTUAT2 on the intentions to adopt mobile banking app, while introducing additional two constructs to measure the intention and adoption of the app. This enabled a valued contribution to the evolving literature on the relationship between adoption/intentions, which has remained underexplored thus far. This is in line with the consistent recommendation of recent literature that has called for urgent steps to be taken to recognize the factors driving the adoption of online banking transactions in the developing world (Jibril *et al.* 2020; Nwaiwu *et al.* 2020). Second, this research further informs scholars on the need to re-consider an extensive exploration of technology studies geared toward technology adoption/resistance in the less digitalized economies so far as digital divide continues to perpetuate between developed and developing worlds.

Practically, this study has two significant implications for stakeholders and shareholders in the financial sector in the developing country. First, the study findings could be of particular relevance to those emerging banks or lesser banks, which are yet to transition to the online banking system. Second, the study offers relevant information and knowledge to bank customers on the need to make use of banking technologies (apps) since the latter performs several functions to the user including enhancing service delivery, quick bank transaction, ability to use the app at the comfort of your home, and among others.

The present study has some limitations, which need to be kept in mind. First, the study participants were selected from a single country, namely Ghana. Therefore, the study could not have been generalised to reflect the entire economies that are described as less digitalized economies. However, despite these limitations, the study makes notable contributions to the existing literature. Hence, we recommend the following possible future directions for future studies. First, scholars could use our model to study customer behaviour in other contexts because the mobile banking app has come to stay. Lastly, scholars should explore the causal relationships of different theory as explained earlier with the adoption or resistance intention through longitudinal investigations.

Acknowledgement. This work was supported by the research project NPU I no. MSMT-7778/2019 RVO - Digital Transformation and its Impact on Customer Behaviour and Business Processes in Traditional and Online markets, and IGA/FAME/2020/002 and IGA/FAME/2019/008 of Tomas Bata University in Zlin.

Appendix

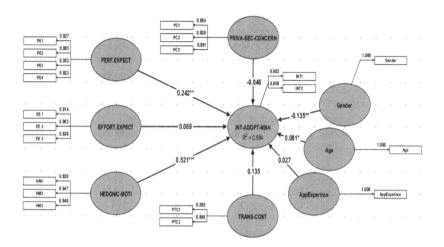

References

Abdul-Hamid, I.K., Shaikh, A.A., Boateng, H., Hinson, R.E.: Customers' perceived risk and trust in using mobile money services—an empirical study of Ghana. Int. J. E-Bus. Res. (IJEBR) **15** (1), 1–9 (2019)

Ajzen, I.: The theory of planned behavior. Organ. Behav. Hum. Decis. Process. **50**(2), 179–211 (1991)

Alalwan, A.A., Dwivedi, Y.K., Rana, N.P.: Factors influencing adoption of mobile banking by Jordanian bank customers: extending UTAUT2 with trust. Int. J. Inf. Manag. **3**(37), 99–110 (2017)

Albashrawi, M., Motiwalla, L.: Privacy and personalization in continued usage intention of mobile banking: an integrative perspective. Inf. Syst. Front. **21**(5), 1031–1043 (2019)

Albashrawi, M., Kartal, H., Oztekin, A., Motiwalla, L.: The impact of subjective and objective experience on mobile banking usage: an analytical approach. In: Proceedings of the 50th Hawaii International Conference on System Sciences, January 2017

Alkhater, N., Wills, G., Walters, R.: Factors influencing an organisation's intention to adopt Cloud computing in Saudi Arabia. In: IEEE 6th International Conference on Cloud Computing Technology and Science (CloudCom), 15–18 December 2014, pp. 1040–1044 (2014)

Ansong, E.D., Synaepa-Addison, T.Q.: A comparative study of user data security and privacy in native and cross platform Android mobile banking applications. In: 2019 International Conference on Cyber Security and Internet of Things (ICSIoT), pp. 5–10. IEEE, May 2019

Armitage, C.J., Christian, J.: From attitudes to behaviour: basic and applied research on the theory of planned behaviour. Curr. Psychol. **22**(3), 187195 (2003)

Bandura, A.: Social Foundations of Thought and Action, pp. 23–28. Englewood Cliffs (1986)

Barnes, S.J., Corbitt, B.: Mobile banking: concept and potential. Int. J. Mobile Commun. **1**(3), 273–288 (2003)

Boateng, H., Adam, D.R., Okoe, A.F., Anning-Dorson, T.: Assessing the determinants of Internet banking adoption intentions: a social cognitive theory perspective. Comput. Hum. Behav. **65**, 468–478 (2016)

Byrne, B.M.: Structural Equation Modeling with LISREL, PRELIS, and SIMPLIS: Basic Concepts, Applications, and Programming. Psychology Press (2013)

Chhonker, M.S., Verma, D., Kar, A.K., Grover, P.: m-commerce technology adoption. The Bottom Line (2018)

Davis, F.D.: Perceived usefulness, perceived ease of use, and user acceptance of information technology. MIS Q. **13**(3), 319–340 (1989)

Davis, F.D., Bagozzi, R.P., Warshaw, P.R.: Extrinsic and intrinsic motivation to use computers in the workplace 1. J. Appl. Soc. Psychol. **22**(14), 1111–1132 (1992)

Hair Jr., J.F., Sarstedt, M., Hopkins, L., Kuppelwieser, V.G.: Partial least squares structural equation modeling (PLS-SEM) an emerging tool in business research. Eur. Bus. Rev. **26**(2), 106–121 (2014)

Farah, M.F., Hasni, M.J.S., Abbas, A.K.: Mobile-banking adoption: empirical evidence from the banking sector in Pakistan. Int. J. Bank Mark. **36**(7), 1386–1413 (2018)

Fishbein, M., Ajzen, I.: Belief, Attitude, Intention, and Behavior, pp. 913–927. Addison-Wesley, Reading (1975)

Fornell, C., Larcker, D.F.: Evaluating structural equation models with unobservable variables and measurement error. J. Mark. Res. **18**(1), 39–50 (1981)

Grover, P., Kar, A.K.: User engagement for mobile payment service providers–introducing the social media engagement model. J. Retail. Consum. Serv. **53**, 1–13 (2020)

Gupta, P., Seetharaman, A., Raj, J.R.: The usage and adoption of cloud computing by small and medium businesses. Int. J. Inf. Manag. **33**(5), 861–874 (2013)

Hanafizadeh, P., Behboudi, M., Koshksaray, A.A., Tabar, M.J.S.: Mobile-banking adoption by Iranian bank clients. Telemat. Inform. **31**(1), 62–78 (2014)

Hayikader, S., Hadi, F.N., Ibrahim, J.: Issues and security measures of mobile banking Apps. Int. J. Sci. Res. Publ. **6**(1), 36–41 (2016)

Henseler, J., Hubona, G., Ray, P.A.: Using PLS path modeling in new technology research: updated guidelines. Ind. Manag. Data Syst. **116**(1), 2–20 (2016)

Henseler, J., Ringle, C.M., Sarstedt, M.: A new criterion for assessing discriminant validity in variance-based structural equation modeling. J. Acad. Mark. Sci. **43**(1), 115–135 (2014). https://doi.org/10.1007/s11747-014-0403-8

Hu, L.T., Bentler, P.M.: Cutoff criteria for fit indexes in covariance structure analysis: conventional criteria versus new alternatives. Struct. Eq. Model. Multidiscip. J. **6**(1), 1–55 (1999)

ITU. Telecommunication/ICT market trends in Africa 2007 (2007). http://www.itu.int/ITUD/ict/statistics/material/af_report07.pdf

Jibril, A.B., Kwarteng, M.A., Chovancova, M., Denanyoh, R.: Customers' perception of cybersecurity threats toward e-banking adoption and retention: a conceptual study. In: ICCWS 2020, 15th International Conference on Cyber Warfare and Security, 12 March 2020, p. 270. Academic Conferences and Publishing Limited (2020)

Lubua Dr, E.W., Pretorius, P.: The role of the transaction assurance, perceived cost and the perceived innovation in the decision to continue using mobile money services among small business owners. Afr. J. Inf. Syst. **10**(2), 3 (2018)

Munoz-Leiva, F., Climent-Climent, S., Liébana-Cabanillas, F.: Determinants of intention to use the mobile banking apps: an extension of the classic TAM model. Span. J. Mark.-ESIC **21**(1), 25–38 (2017)

Nwaiwu, F., Kwarteng, M.A., Jibril, A.B., Buřita, L., Pilik, M.: Impact of security and trust as factors that influence the adoption and use of digital technologies that generate, collect and transmit user data. In: ICCWS 2020, 15th International Conference on Cyber Warfare and Security, 12 March 2020, p. 363. Academic Conferences and Publishing Limited (2020)

Okumus, B., Ali, F., Bilgihan, A., Ozturk, A.B.: Psychological factors influencing customers' acceptance of smartphone diet apps when ordering food at restaurants. Int. J. Hosp. Manag. **72**, 67–77 (2018)

Oliveira, T., Faria, M., Thomas, M.A., Popovič, A.: Extending the understanding of mobile banking adoption: when UTAUT meets TTF and ITM. Int. J. Inf. Manag. **34**(5), 689–703 (2014)

Owusu, G.M.Y., Bekoe, R.A., Addo-Yobo, A.A., Otieku, J.: Mobile banking adoption among the Ghanaian youth. J. Afr. Bus. 1–22 (2020)

Podsakoff, P.M., MacKenzie, S.B., Lee, J.Y., Podsakoff, N.P.: Common method biases in behavioral research: a critical review of the literature and recommended remedies. J. Appl. Psychol. **88**(5), 879 (2003)

Rogers, E.M.: Diffusion of Innovations, 4th edn. Free Press, New York (1995)

Shareef, M.A., Baabdullah, A., Dutta, S., Kumar, V., Dwivedi, Y.K.: Consumer adoption of mobile banking services: an empirical examination of factors according to adoption stages. J. Retail. Consum. Serv. **43**, 54–67 (2018)

Singh, B.P., Grover, P., Kar, A.K.: Quality in mobile payment service in India. In: Kar, A.K., et al. (eds.) I3E 2017. LNCS, vol. 10595, pp. 183–193. Springer, Cham (2017). https://doi.org/10.1007/978-3-319-68557-1_17

Singh, S., Srivastava, R.K.: Predicting the intention to use mobile banking in India. Int. J. Bank Mark. **36**(2), 357–378 (2018)

Tang, C., Liu, J.: Selecting a trusted cloud service provider for your SaaS program. Comput. Secur. **50**(1), 60–73 (2015)

Taylor, S., Todd, P.A.: Understanding information technology usage: a test of competing models. Inf. Syst. Res. **6**(2), 144–176 (1995)

Thompson, R.L., Higgins, C.A., Howell, J.M.: Personal computing: toward a conceptual model of utilization. MIS Q. **15**(1), 125–143 (1991)

Thusi, P., Maduku, D.K.: South African millennials' acceptance and use of retail mobile banking apps: an integrated perspective. Comput. Hum. Behav. **111**, 106405 (2020)

Venkatesh, V., Morris, M.G., Davis, G.B., Davis, F.D.: User acceptance of information technology: toward a unified view. MIS Q. **27**(3), 425–478 (2003)

Venkatesh, V., Thong, J.Y., Xu, X.: Consumer acceptance and use of information technology: extending the unified theory of acceptance and use of technology. MIS Q. **36**(1), 157–178 (2012)

Wijland, R., Hansen, P., Gardezi, F.: Mobile nudging: youth engagement with banking apps. J. Finan. Serv. Mark. **21**(1), 51–63 (2016)

Yeo, V.C., Goh, S.K., Rezaei, S.: Consumer experiences, attitude and behavioral intention toward online food delivery (OFD) services. J. Retail. Consum. Serv. **35**, 150–162 (2017)

Antecedents of Digital Platform Organising Visions

Fábio Neves da Rocha$^{(\boxtimes)}$ and Neil Pollock

University of Edinburgh Business School, Edinburgh EH8 9JS, UK
fabio.rocha@ed.ac.uk

Abstract. Organising vision theory has been increasingly used in Information Systems (IS) scholarship to study how IT innovations are adopted, used, and diffused. Although providing comprehensive social cognitive account on the phenomena, organising vision theory is less adequate to explicate how visions emerge. Bringing in scholarship from Science and Technology Studies (STS) together with IS, our examination of a case study involving the organising vision emergence of an ERP digital platform technology unearthed details of its origin and management. Our findings suggest that organising visions originate from repurposing of other structured frameworks. This research contributes to the organising vision theory by providing a more nuanced comprehension of vision's antecedents, which more broadly may help better understand digital innovation adoption.

Keywords: Organising vision · Adoption · Diffusion · Digital platform · Enterprise system · ERP

1 Introduction

Information Systems (IS) scholars have a long concern to understand the reasons that drive a wide diffusion of some digital innovations while others fail [1–4]. Several writers have followed the rational-economic perspective [5], paying attention to how organisations assess properties and performance of technologies to understand digital innovation diffusion and its relation to value generation. While predominant in the IS innovation research, the rational-economic perspective is not alone in the field, and other ways to theorise digital innovation diffusion are increasingly gaining relevance. Organising vision is a good exemplar of an alternative explanation [6].

The organising vision theory [7, 8] draws attention to the environment beyond the organisational borders, recognising the work of a wider focal community as consequential to innovation diffusion. The organising vision is a collective sense-making of digital innovations' application and use. It consists of discourses that emerge as 'buzzwords,' terminologies that aim at synthetising digital innovations that acquire a variety of understandings and interpretations when passing through the hands of, among others, technology vendors, prospective customers, consulting firms, and academics. The buzzword ambiguity is seen as the compelling reason that attracts actors to find together a common meaning for the organising vision [7].

S. K. Sharma et al. (Eds.): TDIT 2020, IFIP AICT 618, pp. 126–137, 2020.
https://doi.org/10.1007/978-3-030-64861-9_12

We find useful the organising vision formulation that sheds light to the wide range of constituencies involved in the shaping of the market and the consequent interpretive flexibility that usually surrounds emerging digital innovations. However, the way the origin of organising visions is formulated seems less adequate. Pollock and Williams [9] highlighted the diminishing ambiguity around technology terminologies due to a better establishment of institutional frameworks that currently surround them (e.g., [10–12]). Therefore, if not compelled by the ambiguity of buzzwords, how do organising visions emerge? How are they performed? A deeper investigation on the antecedents of organising visions is required [6], and this chapter develops towards this call.

Vendors are particularly relevant actors in the organising vision construction as major contributors [6] creating terminologies [11], providing subsidies to the collective interpretation and legitimation of digital innovations [13], and mobilising resources to create and promote new digital technologies [7]. In search for the organising visions' antecedents, we draw on a study of the emergence of an organising vision of a large enterprise resource planning (ERP) digital platform. Bringing in scholarship from Science and Technology Studies (STS) together with IS, our examination of semi-structured interviews and a rich archive of interviews, webinars, public presentations, and a varied sort of documents shows that organising visions are born within platform leaders' organisations. We posit organising visions originate from repurposing other structured frameworks and grow as 'in-house' organising visions that are performed by platform leaders' internal community before going public.

Our study contributes to the organising vision theory [7, 8] by giving socio-material and geographical accounts of organising vision genesis, advancing our underdeveloped knowledge of organising visions' antecedents and emergence [6]. Moreover, as most diffusion studies in IS literature can be classified as adopter studies [14, p. 309], we hope our research would also contribute to digital innovation diffusion literature, depicting the prelude of innovation adoption.

2 Organising Visions: Making Sense of Organisational Futures

Digital innovation diffusion is of great interest in the IS scholarship [1–4, 14, 15]. Scholars seek to understand why and how some innovations are widely adopted, while others do not succeed. The literature has largely advanced under a rational-economic 'paradigm' [5], assuming "the properties and performance of technologies can be assessed in technical or financial terms, and their selection and implementation can, therefore, be guided to optimise economic and business outcomes" [16, p. 56]. Under this perspective, rationally assessed effectiveness and efficiency determine which digital innovations will eventually diffuse [2, 17]. Although this literature has sharpened our understanding of how potential users can effectively evaluate and assimilate digital innovations, the focus has been restricted to the inherent technological value of digital innovation and the characteristics of these prospective customers [3]. Moreover, this literature does not appropriately account for the social processes intrinsic to innovation diffusion [16, 18].

Our focus is on the notion of organising vision as it is a native IS theory [6], offering perhaps "the most comprehensive account of this phenomenon in the IT application sector" [9]. There is a lot of work for organisations to make sense of a digital innovation in relation to their own reality, history, needs and capabilities. It is not the work of a single actor but rather a result of communal processes [7] – through socialisation, interaction and negotiation – that develop over time [8]. Swanson and Ramiller [7, p. 460] called these processes collectively as organising vision, defined as "a focal community idea for the application of information technology in organizations." A broader business concerns related to planning, decision-making, and action are the core ingredients for organisations to start forming visions – expectations about their future in which perceived uncertainty can be possibly remedied by some kind of innovation.

Swanson and Ramiller [7] explained the dynamic of organising visions. For instance, from a certain core technology such as a new entrepreneurial product or a novel experiment-in-practice, sketchy discourses are created in an initial attempt to frame that core technology as a response to a business problematic. These discourses are enveloped by a label, which serves as a hoisted standard, eventually turning into a 'buzzword' [7, 19] – i.e., a label that causes confusion – as soon as it is promoted, for example, at conferences, trade expositions, and sales presentations. An organising vision comes into being when the community rallies around its buzzword in interpretative communication, followed by legitimation and further by mobilisation. In other words, buzzwords spark the emergence of organising visions. Although illuminating, the formulation of organising visions seems less appropriate. It is argued that there is a diminishing ambiguity around technology terminologies [9] due to a better establishment of institutional frameworks surrounding these technologies (e.g., [10–12]).

A key aspect of organising vision is it has a 'career' [7, 8, 20], that is, it evolves as the community engages in its shaping, having adopters gaining experience with innovation and refining their understanding of it [9, 13, 21]. Swanson and Ramiller [7, p. 468] posited all organising visions "vary over the course of their careers in their visibility, prominence and influence," rising and falling and drifting along any number of complex paths. Importantly, not all visions are successful. Some may expand to a point to get their boundaries tattered and frayed, losing distinctiveness and fading away (ibid). Others may face competition [3, 7] and fail to triumph. However, some do succeed. ERP is a good example of innovation that has had cycles of diffusion after its visions successfully widespread. In this chapter, we hope to illuminate the antecedents of one exemplar of the emerging ERP organising visions that are still being formed, in which the combination of previous capabilities with emergent technologies such as data analytics, blockchain, Internet of things (IoT), artificial intelligence (AI) and machine learning will lead to a different, more intense human-machine relationship.

3 Methodological Considerations

A large ERP digital platform vendor with global presence and influential position in its market (ERPCo) was the company selected for our research, credentials that make the firm a distinctive exemplar of an organising vision development actor [7]. We are looking for organising vision antecedents, an important topic that remains unclear despite all advancements in the literature [6]. Therefore, we designed this research as a single instrumental case study [22, 23], which is recommended for in-depth investigation when there is a lack of clarity and scant literature [24].

The body of data is composed of 23 semi-structured, digitally recorded interviews (55 min in average) involving 24 key actors of 13 organisations (platform leader, complementors, customers, industry analysts, trade associations, consulting, and education) in nine countries (Brazil, France, Germany, India, Italy, Spain, Switzerland, UK, USA). In addition, we have 34 archival interviews involving 30 respondents from six firms (platform leader, customers, and industry analysts) in eight countries (Brazil, Bulgaria, Germany, India, Slovenia, South Africa, UK, USA), and we have attended four video recorded webinars. Moreover, we had access to ERPCo's internal webinars and documents, along with public material from the Internet.

After interview transcriptions, we analysed the data inductively [25] using constant comparison techniques [26]. The analytical process was initiated in the course of data gathering during which we coded the data based on in vivo inputs using NVivo 12 after multiple readings of interview transcriptions, field notes, and documentation. As we gradually proceeded with theoretical sampling [27], we consolidated the sampling adequacy. The recurrent phrases, terms, and labels were clustered and subsequently compared to make sense of the variation within the clusters and to clarify emerging links and interrelations. This allowed us to trim it down into a set of first-order categories that mostly express the similarities in our informants' own explanations of their actions.

The process then followed grounded theory [26] and resulted in a set of second order categories, subcategories, and entries therein. We proceeded with a further comparison among the entries in each category and literature, which allowed us to collapse the categories into induced themes at a more abstract level, such as 'fine-tuning the vision,' 'aligning with business goals,' combating competing visions,' 'creating artefacts,' 'customising artefacts,' 'employing artefacts,' 'managing feedbacks,' 'managing roll-out,' 'mobilising champions,' 'mobilising communication,' 'providing hands-on experience,' and 'transferring knowledge.' These second-order categories showed different practices performed. New comparisons among the categories and literature finally gave us the insights onto the whole performance of the organising vision evolvement.

4   Findings

4.1   The Vision: Intelligent Enterprise

ERPCo is a company well known for the successful diffusion of its ERP digital platform. This technology is still at the core of the platform leader's innovation portfolio, but over the years ERPCo has acquired and developed a large number of other emergent digital innovations to complement its ERP platform, such as data analytics, blockchain, IoT, AI and machine learning. For ERPCo, the exploitation of its technologies by organisations can lead them to a digital transformation, becoming what the platform leader describes as 'Intelligent Enterprises.' Despite all novelties brought by these emergent technologies, the Intelligent Enterprise vision is not new. We find it instructive to briefly review the history of this term. We, thus, discuss previous related visions before showing how ERPCo came up with its own.

4.2   Older Intelligent Enterprise Visions

The intelligent enterprise term was coined by Quinn [28] in the 1990s. He defined it as "a highly disaggregated, knowledge and service based enterprise concentrated around a core set of knowledge or service skills" [28, p. 373]. Although considering the role of digital technologies as subsidiary – since the concept is managerial rather than technological – Quinn acknowledged the importance of digital technologies in supporting organisations to "handle a much wider array of data, output functions, or customers" [28, p. 25]. Instead of intuition, the understanding of what customers want should be based on data [28, p. 338].

While keeping the same ethos, the term in the further decade was used slightly differently, giving higher importance to machine intelligence. In the 2000s, the Intelligent Enterprise vision was associated with AI, which would give organisations the ability to morph into new forms and create new businesses [29]. Knowledge management was central in its envisioned organisational architecture, surrounded by different technologies that work in tandem, self-regulating and self-optimising them in order to provide an adaptation to the short-term, changing business environment.

Later in the 2010s, Intelligent Enterprise became associated with data analytics, presented as the powerhouse for innovation, thus a major source for competitive advantage [30, 31]. In the 'New Intelligent Enterprise,' analytics plays a pivotal role in allowing company-wide continuous improvement and experimentation that eventually leads to innovation, outperforming competitors and serving customers better.

More recently, AI returned to the conversation accompanied by machine learning [32], bringing the idea that these intelligences would not only support organisations' decision-making process, but also be a key move towards completing the digital transformation journey.

For ERPCo, Intelligent Enterprise vision indeed encompasses a whole set of emergent digital technologies, as we commented earlier. However according to the company, technology is not where the emphasis should be. While retaining all the technological content found in other Intelligent Enterprise visions produced more recently, ERPCo's vision established its focus explicitly on customer satisfaction that would be achieved through organisational learning and change, based on data. It resonates with the direction given originally by Quinn [28]. It is unclear whether platform leader's vision was specifically based on Quinn's work, but the Global VP Marketing from ERPCo acknowledged possible connections between the two.

4.3   The Vision Emergence

Intelligent Enterprise is a vision of digital transformation of organisations. It came from platform leader's vision about innovation, developed by strategy and innovation areas. We will start showing how ERPCo's innovation vision was formed, presenting the construction of the Intelligent Enterprise after that.

The Roots: Innovation Vision

ERPCo has a temporally segmented approach to its innovation vision – it has a time span of 10 years, divided into three sequential time windows, or what the vendor calls 'horizons,' having current and future innovations distributed across them. Horizon 1 has a window time of two years from now; horizon 2 involves the following four years; and horizon 3 has the remaining four years. Horizon 1 encompasses current business issues and respective technologies that are addressing them. Horizon 3 accounts for innovation concepts and prototypes. In between is the horizon 2, which is formed by a forecast (from horizon 1) of incremental innovation needed to fulfil the gaps of current products, along with a 'backcast' from horizon 3 of some of the innovation concepts allocated there – those that are more likely to be adopted in the horizon 2's time frame. The outcome of the horizons exercise is a complex innovation vision, predicting machine and human interplay, having machines as protagonists in some organisational areas and assuming a more supportive role in others. The vision includes an autonomous ERP; an ability to create instant virtual enterprises that can dynamically assemble and disassemble value chains; personal digital assistants helping in decision making; and process malleability that allows redefinition of business models and even markets.

ERPCo's innovation vision is quite comprehensive, although very complex. It proved to be very difficult for customers in general to imagine themselves in the vision and how to get there. The vendor, then, converted it into a form hopefully easier to grasp. ERPCo found the composition of words 'intelligent' plus 'enterprise' a tagline that could express adequately in a nutshell what they want to entail in their vision, meaning companies that are able to learn, think, and change to provide better experiences to their customers. Initially involving a small number of executives of vendor's organisation (mainly from strategy, R&D and marketing) in this translation from a product-centric vision to a market-driven vision, it gradually got more participants in its shaping until having the entire organisation engaged. Following we show how ERPCo created an organising vision mobilising the entire company.

Intelligent Enterprise Vision, from Creation to Roll-Out

There are three stages in the development of ERPCo's organising vision. In the beginning, only a handful of people (primarily those that were involved in its conception) are familiar with the vision, which is in an immature format and open for improvements. The vision gets support (and amendments) over time, being consolidated and embraced by the entire organisation before reaching the market.

Step 1: socialise and engage

The first step is about creating vision awareness in key areas of the organisation. It is mostly made in an unstructured, informal way, in which primarily top executives from customer-facing areas are involved and invited to help in the vision shaping. Although predominantly internal, curiously 'beta customers' – those engaged in programmes of early product development – also participate. ERPCo attributes great value to the contributions coming from beta customers not just for the feedback that they can provide to directly improve the vision, but also for the insights gotten from the experiences beta customers had with vendor's emerging technologies. These experiences are monitored and analysed by 'value engineers,' a kind of management consultants within ERPCo's organisation, eventually producing knowledge artefacts (e.g., business cases, reports on financial and operational efficiency) that in this step are fundamental in helping the engagement of 'right people' (the customer-facing executives). These assets will also provide subsidies for supporting the vision in further stages as well. As soon as a number of key people are convinced about the vision potential, the second stage starts.

Step 2: buy-in

This step is structured and formal. After getting buy-in from the right people in order to crystallise what the vision's message should be, it is assembled a core team composed of delegates from each customer-facing area, responsible for the messages that go out and the development of a core set of assets. These messages – discourses – and core set of assets, such as website content and customer-facing material, are parsimoniously negotiated among the core team members under the coordination of a crosscompany marketing unit. This unit acts as the guardian of the vision's consistency, having, for instance, to get everybody to agree on the common set of words to going to a brochure. The coordination is fundamental because the core team is not only giving the vision a corporative shape but it is also creating versions of the vision.

Versioning the Vision

Although claiming their innovations would virtually look after all possible operations a company may have, ERPCo was aware that customers may not use these innovations in the same way. For example, the use of IoT that a railway operator can make (e.g., to understand the maintenance renewal schedule on their trains) can be completely different from how a city council use it (e.g., to better manage traffic routing during peak hours). Due to several factors that make one company different from others, such as industry sector it is in, its business model, its organisational culture, just to name a few, customers would probably enact the Intelligent Enterprise vision differently. Being sensible to this, vendor's core team created different *versions* of the vision. We examined exemplars of core assets produced by them. We noticed that there are several 'The-Intelligent-Enterprise-for...' versions. For example, 'The Intelligent Enterprise for Telecommunications' and 'The Intelligent Enterprise for Professional Services' both describe ideal intelligent organisations as able to serve their customers better while achieving stronger financial results. Nonetheless each of them enacts the vision distinctively, using the same technology differently and different sets of technologies.

Step 3: keep alive

In this stage, the vendor mobilises its entire organisation around the Intelligent Enterprise vision and its versions, both internally and towards the market. All areas that have customer-facing responsibilities are called to recast the vision (version) into each one's business-related activities. For instance, the area responsible for business partnerships should create programmes and additional assets for helping partners' sales force to sell the set of technologies behind the vision (version), along with certification programmes for their technicians to deliver implementation services. The academic partnerships area should create programmes, curricula and set technology environments to be made available in the campi of academic partners. The analyst relations area has to create assets to be shared with industry analyst firms, and influencer relations has to do the same to share with digital influencers. As each area finalises their production, they should start to deliver them to the market. These deliveries do not make this stage to an end; the core team's mission of improving and updating the vision and versions is continuous until ERPCo decides to replace its vision.

The Intelligent Enterprise vision is not alone. When it comes to the market it meets many other competing visions [14]. Few are similar, some are complementary, and others are antagonistic. But all are battling to engage the same audiences. We do not know yet whether the Intelligent Enterprise vision will eventually materialise, whether customers will be willing and able to become that kind of organisation the vision proposes, or even whether the vision will thrive on the competition against, for instance, Gartner's 'Composable Enterprise' [33]. The Intelligent Enterprise vision was still rolling out when we finished the data collection.

5   Discussion: How Organising Visions Emerge

The platform leader's organising vision derived from its innovation vision. This vision is a result of a multi-temporal analysis of platform leader's technology in relation to its market, crafted to describe an image of an ideal (customer) organisation that makes the most usage of all current and near-future technologies. However, the innovation vision could not be used as an organising vision as is. In the innovation vision, the driving force is technology, which made it difficult for prospective customers to imagine how their organisations would benefit from which technologies out of that complex image. To (potentially) become a successful organising vision, the innovation vision needed to be *repurposed* in a way that any prospective customer would "find it possible to engage in discourse about the organising vision" [7, p. 462]. We use repurpose here similarly to Ribes and Polk's [34] concept where elements of visions (e.g., concepts, definitions) can be reassembled without changing their structure. In this sense, innovation vision's repurposing does not change its technology frameworks, but it rather reassigns vision's orientation from technology-driven to business problematic [7] direction. Moreover, repurposing involved not just the innovation vision but also elements from other visions. Using the concept of vision career [7, 8, 20], we traced back ERPCo's Intelligent Enterprise vision to older ones. Repurposing gathering elements from a management vision (Quinn's [28] Intelligent Enterprise) and from IS visions (the Intelligent Enterprise based on AI [29] and the New Intelligent Enterprise based on data analytics [30, 31]). Repurposing is led by a restricted group of people, usually related to strategy office and/or marketing, and the vision resulting from repurposing is what we call 'in-house' organising vision. We see the whole process from sourcing elements to repurposing to generate the in-house organising vision as the *seeding* of organising vision. Figure 1 shows the elements from other visions repurposed in the in-house organising vision.

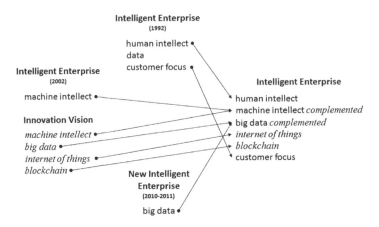

Fig. 1. Organising vision seeding.

We identified in the platform leader's in-house vision the human intellect left the sole protagonism as found in Quinn's [28] vision to be accompanied by the machine intellect suggested by Delic and Dayal [29] in their vision, which is complemented by specific details coming from platform leader's innovation vision (shown in *italics* in Fig. 1). Quinn's idea of data-driven decision-making is also present, but more associated with big data, precisely the core idea in Hopkins and colleagues' [30] and Kruschwitz and Shockley's [31] work. Similar to the case of machine intellect, Hopkins and colleagues' [30] and Kruschwitz and Shockley's [31] big data also got idiosyncratic complements from platform leader's innovation vision. We did not find IoT and blockchain clearly associated with the intellect (intelligent, knowledge, learning) or other early concepts, so it seems these pieces came directly from platform leader's innovation vision. The way these key elements mentioned were oriented – toward providing a better customer experience – is different from Delic and Dayal's [29] focus on firms adaptation to markets, and from Hopkins and colleagues' [30] and Kruschwitz and Shockley's [31] concern on firms' competitive advantage, but resemble quite well the customercentric idea of Quinn [28].

At the highest abstract, general level, the question to be answered by the in-house organising vision is: How does an organisation that has solved all major current and near future business issues look like? The identified most important characteristics of this envisioned organisation (e.g., intelligent) are purposefully linked to platform leader's current or near-future technologies (e.g., machine learning), those that the platform leader intends to be adopted in the short- to medium-term. Meaning and language drawn from other visions should be familiar to the communities the in-house organising vision targets as an attempt to create desirable intelligibility [7], which implies that these visions are likely to relate to the IS and management cultural collection. In other words, these external visions (or their elements) are not randomly picked from the crowd but rather have specific characteristics that make them suitable for repurposing.

The in-house organising vision is articulated inside the platform leader organisation. The result of this articulation is an organised vision that is shared across the organisation, shaped to accommodate (often different) voices of key organisation leaders. In the case of large companies with a vast portfolio of technologies aimed at a large number of industry segments, it is possible to have several *versions* of the organising vision, each one targeting different communities with proposals closer to their business idiosyncrasies. These versions either enact common technologies in specific, unique way, or are backed by a different set of technologies. Figure 2 below shows the whole process of the organising vision genesis.

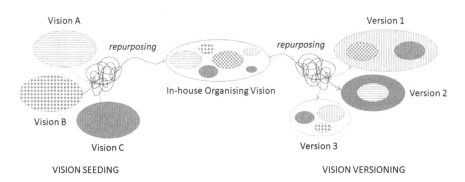

Fig. 2. The genesis of an Organising Vision.

6   Conclusion

Gorgeon and Swanson [20], Ramiller and Swanson [8], and Swanson and Ramiller [7] claimed organised visions emerge during the innovation's earliest diffusion from buzzwords, highly flexible labels that make it difficult to grasp as to what it is actually being referred to, but even though provide "a portal into the community discourse that builds the organising vision" [7, p. 463]. We see it differently. We do support the idea that organising visions are communally co-developed with market actors [7, 8], but we argue that organising visions do *not* emerge from buzzwords. Rather, organising visions derive from *repurposing* [34] other structured frameworks – especially when they come from the practitioner subculture [7, 11] – eventually reducing their ambiguity [9] and tending to engage communities by its intelligibility, which contrasts to the idea of engagement derived from high flexibility and confusion.

Repurposing suggests an additional consequence. It defines an earlier point in time when organising visions emerge, revealing new characteristics of their evolvement. We consider organising visions as developed *within* platform leaders' organisations before reaching an external, wider community. In other words, they do not become organising visions only when they start to engage (external) market actors; they were shaped early on by different communities inside platform leaders' organisations. Therefore, platform leaders do not present to the market "a sketch of uncertain form – a modest, localized, interpretive swirl" [7, p. 462], but rather an organising vision with already a certain degree of maturity.

References

1. Huff, S.L., Munro, M.C.: Information technology assessment and adoption: a field study. MIS Q. **9**(4), 327–338 (1985)
2. Rogers, E.M.: Diffusion of Innovations, 5th edn. Free Press, New York (2003)
3. Barrett, M., Heracleous, L., Walsham, G.: A rhetorical approach to IT diffusion: reconceptualizing the ideology-framing relationship in computerization movements. MIS Q. **37**(1), 201–220 (2013)
4. Zamani, E.D., Pouloudi, N., Giaglis, G.M., Wareham, J.: Appropriating information technology artefacts through trial and error: the case of the tablet. Inf. Syst. Front. 1–23 (2020)
5. Fichman, R.G.: Going beyond the dominant paradigm for information technology innovation research: emerging concepts and methods. J. Assoc. Inf. Syst. **5**(8), 314–355 (2004)
6. Kim, I., Miranda, S.M.: 20 years old but still a teenager? A review of organizing vision theory and suggested directions. In: Proceedings of the Pacific Asia Conference on Information Systems (PACIS 2018), pp. 1–14 (2018)
7. Swanson, E.B., Ramiller, N.C.: The organizing vision in information systems innovation. Organ. Sci. **8**(5), 458–474 (1997)
8. Ramiller, N.C., Swanson, E.B.: Organizing visions for information technology and the information systems executive response. J. Manag. Inf. Syst. **20**(1), 13–50 (2003)
9. Pollock, N., Williams, R.: Who decides the shape of product markets? The knowledge institutions that name and categorise new technologies. Inf. Organ. **21**(4), 194–217 (2011)
10. Swanson, E.B.: Consultancies and capabilities in innovating with IT. J. Strateg. Inf. Syst. **19**(1), 17–27 (2010)
11. Wang, P., Swanson, E.B.: Launching professional services automation: institutional entrepreneurship for information technology innovations. Inf. Organ. **17**(2), 59–88 (2007)
12. Wang, P., Swanson, E.B.: Customer relationship management as advertised: exploiting and sustaining technological momentum. Inf. Technol. People **21**(4), 323–349 (2008)
13. Wang, P., Ramiller, N.C.: Community learning in information technology innovation. MIS Q. **33**(4), 709–734 (2009)
14. Cavusoglu, H., Hu, N., Li, Y., Ma, D.: Information technology diffusion with influentials, imitators, and opponents. J. Manag. Inf. Syst. **27**(2), 305–334 (2010)
15. Fichman, R.G.: The diffusion and assimilation of information technology innovations. In: Zmud, R.W. (ed.) Framing the Domains of IT Management: Projecting the Future Through the Past, pp. 105–127. Pinnaflex Educational Resources, Cincinnati (2000)
16. Pollock, N., Williams, R.: Software and Organisations: The Biography of the Enterprise-Wide System or How SAP Conquered the World. Routledge, London (2008)
17. Jiang, Z., Sarkar, S.: Speed matters: the role of free software offer in software diffusion. J. Manag. Inf. Syst. **26**(3), 207–240 (2009)
18. Robertson, M., Swan, J., Newell, S.: The role of networks in the diffusion of innovation. J. Manag. Stud. **33**(3), 333–359 (1996)
19. Swanson, E.B.: Talking the is innovation walk. In: Wynn, E.H., Whitley, E.A., Myers, M.D., DeGross, J.I. (eds.) Global and Organizational Discourse about Information Technology. ITIFIP, vol. 110, pp. 15–31. Springer, Boston (2003). https://doi.org/10.1007/978-0-387-35634-1_2
20. Gorgeon, A., Swanson, E.B.: Web 2.0 according to wikipedia: capturing an organizing vision. J. Am. Soc. Inf. Sci. Technol. **62**(10), 1916–1932 (2011)

21. Davidson, E.J., Østerlund, C.S., Flaherty, M.G.: Drift and shift in the organizing vision career for personal health records: an investigation of innovation discourse dynamics. Inf. Organ. **25**(4), 191–221 (2015)
22. Yin, R.K.: Case Study Research, 2nd edn. SAGE Publications, Thousand Oaks (1994)
23. Stake, R.E.: The Art of Case Study Research. SAGE Publications, Thousand Oaks (1995)
24. Bryman, A., Bell, E.: Business Research Methods, 4th edn. Oxford University Press, Oxford (2015)
25. Eisenhardt, K.M.: Building theories from case study research. Acad. Manag. **14**(4), 532–550 (1989)
26. Glaser, B.G., Strauss, A.L.: The Discovery of Grounded Theory: Strategies for Qualitative Research. Aldine, New York (1967)
27. Strauss, A.L., Corbin, J.M.: Basics of Qualitative Research: Techniques and Procedures for Developing Grounded Theory, 2nd edn. SAGE Publications, Thousand Oaks (1998)
28. Quinn, J.B.: Intelligent Enterprise - A Knowledge and Service Based Paradigm for Industry. Free Press, New York (1992)
29. Delic, K.A., Dayal, U.: The rise of the intelligent enterprise. Ubiquity **2002**(December), 1–8 (2002)
30. Hopkins, M.S., LaValle, S., Balboni, F.: The new intelligent enterprise survey on winning with data and analytics at work 10 insights: a first look at the new intelligent enterprise survey. MIT Sloan Manag. Rev. **52**(1), 22–31 (2010)
31. Kruschwitz, N., Shockley, R.: First look: the second annual new intelligent enterprise survey. MIT Sloan Manag. Rev. **52**(4), 87–89 (2011)
32. Gartner: 2019 CIO Survey: CIOs Have Awoken to the Importance of AI. Stamford (2019)
33. Gartner: Future of Applications: Delivering the Composable Enterprise. Stamford (2020)
34. Ribes, D., Polk, J.B.: Organizing for ontological change: the kernel of an AIDS research infrastructure. Soc. Stud. Sci. **45**(2), 214–241 (2015)

Are Video Resumes Preferred by Job Applicants? Information Technology in Recruitment

Apoorva Goel[1](✉) and Richa Awasthy[2]

[1] Indian Institute of Technology, Madras, Chennai 600036, Tamil Nadu, India
`ms19d039@smail.iitm.ac.in`
[2] Ambedkar University Delhi, Lothian Road, Kashmere Gate,
Delhi 110006, India

Abstract. In this work, we have analyzed the perceptions of Master of Business Administration (MBA) enrolled job-seekers towards video resumes along with determining the reasons for preference and non-preference for it. We administered 210 semi-structured self-designed questionnaires among MBA enrolled candidates looking for internships or final year placements of various Indian Universities. They were asked to use a video resume platform followed by filling up a semi-structured questionnaire focussed on gathering viewpoints about the perceived interface features, fairness, validity, privacy. Qualitative data analysis was also done to determine the reasons affecting user's adoption of platform driven services. Video resumes hosted on video-sharing platforms offer a unique opportunity to both the sides concerned i.e. the job applicant as well as the recruiter. Research on determining video resumes from job applicants' viewpoints is scarce and this study will add to the paucity of research pool on this topic. Moreover, this is the first study to highlight the issue of security and privacy of video resume platforms and, provide technical recommendations to these platforms from the applicants' perspective. With this study we hope to reach out to recruiters (practitioners), job-seekers, researchers and information system application developers for better acceptability of the product.

Keywords: Privacy · Recruitment · Video resume

1 Introduction

The COVID-19 pandemic has brought about many significant and unexpected changes in all realms of life. The entire global economy is going through major complications and transformations. Those who are in search of their first jobs may face difficulties in finding one. Even though the concept of a resume is familiar to everyone in the job market, the preparation of an up-to-date resume in this pandemic situation is all the more significant. While imposing great challenges, COVID-19 makes us learn new ways of surviving and succeeding and that includes a new approach to resumes as well, which attracts the attention of the recruiter and helps one stand out of the great number of other job-seekers. The social distancing and quarantine make the technological part of a resume extremely important, together with the visual element. In a time where in-

S. K. Sharma et al. (Eds.): TDIT 2020, IFIP AICT 618, pp. 138–149, 2020.
https://doi.org/10.1007/978-3-030-64861-9_13

person interviews can barely be conducted, video resumes can help in the initial screening. No matter how much video resumes are perceived to be important or useful, their acceptance by the job applicants is of prime importance for its widespread usage and is much unexplored in research. Some questions which need to be answered are, "Do job applicants prefer to use a video resume?", "What encourages or discourages them to use it?", "What future remedies are available to make it more acceptable?".

A video resume can be defined as a short video-recorded message where job applicants present themselves to potential employers [17]. In comparison to the traditional paper resumes, video resumes reveal a lot about the person beyond just the educational background and work experience [17]. Also, they offer the person the flexibility to highlight their skills, learnings, potential, personality, communication abilities, and the reasons why they are better than the rest for a particular job or company [8, 30]. The recent technological developments and its widespread availability present new opportunities for the study of video resumes. A literature search in Web of Science and Scopus on video resume shows that there has been limited research done on it. The majority of it has been done in the last few years, indicating recent research attention to video resumes. However, this growth in research is still limited and disproportionate when compared to the use of video resumes in practice. This urges more research in this area. Even though some studies have highlighted the importance of applicants' perspectives in the adoption of this new technology in selection [25], however less is known in detail about their perspectives when compared to the traditional hiring tools. Despite the numerous benefits and the latest technological infrastructure available for video resume, the previous studies have not been able to study the views and perceptions of job-seekers who are the users of this new recruiting tool.

The main contributions of this work are the following: First, this study related to examining video resumes from a job applicant's viewpoint will add to the paucity of research on this topic. Second, this study constitutes the first attempt to infer perspectives related to validity, fairness, discrimination, and impression towards video resumes, qualitatively. Third, this study highlights the element of the 'privacy' of video resumes, which is much unexplored. Fourth, this is the first study to provide recommendations based on responses gathered, to the video resume platforms to incorporate changes to cater to the various challenges faced by the users. Last but not the least, we have collected data from a diverse set of MBA candidates spread across various universities in India, geographically to gather diverse viewpoints.

This paper is structured as follows. Next, we discuss the Literature review. We then explain the method used for data collection and analysis. Later, we present the results and findings. In the next section, we arrive at the inferences. Consequently, we discuss the recommendations, limitations, scope of future research and, theoretical and practical implications. We finally conclude in the last section.

2   Literature Review

Despite the rise of video resumes and video interviewing platforms as a new mechanism for workforce recruitment, scholarly publications on this subject are still rare. The digital advancements are changing the landscape of workforce recruitment [27, 29].

Until recently, paper resumes were among the most utilized instrument for the screening of job candidates in the workforce selection process. With the increased emergence of inexpensive sensors (webcams, microphones) and the success of online video resume platforms have empowered the introduction of another sort of resume, the video resume [15]. These platforms bridge the gap between job applicants and prospective employers. Videos recorded by the users become a part of their profile which can be shared, accessed by others and are not available to any company in particular.

The following parameters are being considered in this study to assess the perceptions of the respondents towards video resumes. These are:

2.1   Validity

Validity refers to the accuracy and value attached to video resumes in comparison to the other methods of recruitment [9, 26]. The validity being referred here is the predictive validity, which measures whether the job applicants believe that this tool (video resume) will help them attain the expected outcome (job) [20]. The predictive validity of video resumes may be increased by greater consistency of the types of questions answered and their responses [19].

2.2   Impression

The medium (video vs paper) influences the type of impression formation and hiring decision making. The same individual may leave a positive impression on the recruiter in a video resume at the same time leaving a negative impression in case of a traditional paper resume and vice-versa [17]. Job applicants are concerned with the fact that their video resumes may create a positive or negative impression on the recruiter based on their vocal cues such as voice pitch [12], recruiter's language attitude and accent understandability, which can ultimately alter the hiring decision.

2.3   Preference

Preference is based on the influence of the format (e.g., a highly structured, predefined format with content requirements vs. an unstructured format in which the content is determined by the applicant), the medium (paper vs. video vs. interview), and, individual differences (e.g., educational level, ethnicity, personality) on applicant's and recruiter's perceptions [17]. Technological developments have made possible the creation and sharing of video resumes. Such facilities are available and accessible to most applicants. Hence, they find it more convenient, up-to-date to use a video resume, and may prefer it more over the traditional resumes [17].

2.4   Discrimination

New selection techniques such as video resumes may be regarded more positively by applicants as compared to the traditional paper-and-pencil versions in terms of overall fairness [7, 24]. Therefore, these innovative tools for selection can be said to not necessarily leading to a negative applicant perception [3] and can even lead to a more favorable perception [24]. Research shows that paper resumes are prone to ethnic discrimination [4]. Hence, ethnic minorities are likely to welcome video resumes more due to a more personalized and competency-based approach [23]. On the other hand, empirical evidence also states that e-recruitment practices are perceived to be unfair and may lead to negative applicant reactions due to a tendency to 'self-select out' [1]. They may discriminate against a person based on the stigmas such as religious attire, disability, and disfigurements [21].

3   Methodology

3.1   Research Design

The research adopts both exploratory and descriptive research designs. The exploratory research design was used to focus on the discovery of more insights related to the subject. Since the problem is relatively new hence exploratory research method was used to incorporate some of the fresh viewpoints and achieve a better understanding of the topic [5]. To find answers to questions like what, how and why, grounded theory approach was applied. The descriptive research was used to define opinion, attitude, and behavior of the respondents towards video resumes. It was also done to describe video resume perspectives in more detail, filling in the missing parts and expanding the understanding. Secondary research and survey technique were made use of to study trends, opinions and behavior of future job applicants with respect to video resumes in their job-related process.

3.2   Data Collection

Participants were contacted through telephonic calls and electronic mails (e-mail) to participate in the study which aimed to determine their perceptions regarding the emerging concept of video resumes. They were further instructed to use a video resume platform which they could either find over the internet or choose any from the three links (randomly chosen) of video resume platforms provided to them in the e-mail, for their convenience. After using a platform, they were then required to complete the self-designed semi-structured questionnaire [6], provided in the e-mail. The questionnaire had two parts: close and open-ended questions. The closed-ended questions were aimed to gather facts about video resumes on dimensions of validity, preference, impression, and discrimination [17]. The open-ended question was used to gather any thoughts they had regarding video resumes. Quantitative data analysis was used to analyze data on percentage of responses which are in-favour or against or neutral on each of the pre-decided dimensions. A content analysis which is used to make valid inferences by interpreting and coding textual material [18] was used for qualitative data obtained from open-ended responses to determine the reasons of favourability and unfavoura- bility towards video resumes. Recommendations were then suggested from the responses obtained to the existing video resume platforms using primary and secondary research.

3.3   Participants

Participation in this study was solicited from MBA students either in the first year or the second year of the course enrolled in various Indian Universities. Convenience sampling [22] technique was deployed. A total of 210 individuals participated in the study. This sample size is based on the number of different Universities and the available target respondents in each University. An effort was made to obtain an approximately equal number of responses from each University to avoid skewness and ensure diversity. Of the 210 participants who completed the survey, 4 responses were eliminated due to incomplete information. Therefore, the participation rate was 98.1%. Of the 206 usable responses, 48% were from females and 52% from males. Addi- tionally, 32% of participants had at least one year of work experience.

4   Data Analysis

Data analysis is drawn on the coding paradigm of Grounded Theory [10], including the phases of open, axial, and selective coding. The coding was done mainly by the first author and then discussed and verified by the second author to eliminate any biases and improve reliability and validity of qualitative data [2]. The codes were comprehen- sively reviewed and scrutinized by asking whether they are relevant and represent the interpretations of encouraging or discouraging the use of video resumes.

In the phase of open coding, we broke down the data so obtained into character- istics related to video resumes. The resulting codes were then aggregated into themes, categories, and theoretical dimensions for each case. We found many overlapping sentences hence; we merged and eliminated the rest. In the phase of axial coding, we looked more closely for statements encouraging or discouraging the use of video resumes. This was utilized for establishing connections between categories and dimensions inducted in the first phase. In the final phase of selective coding, we reduced the data into the most important categories which could explain why applicants are encouraged or discouraged to adopt the usage of video resumes. Figure 1 illustrates the resulting data structure. Here, resume format refers to characteristics including the communication code (verbal vs. nonverbal), the administration duration, the number of actors involved, the direction of communication (one-way vs. two-way) the degree of surveillance. Goal and content refer to the type of information that is exchanged. Ease of use refers to user convenience. Fairness refers to non-judgmental outcomes. Privacy refers to the security of personal information.

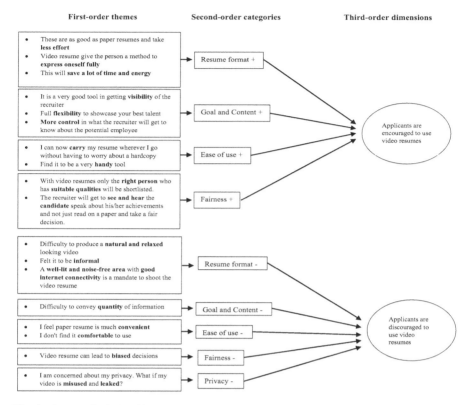

First-order themes

- These are as good as paper resumes and take **less effort**
- Video resume give the person a method to **express oneself fully**
- This will **save a lot of time and energy**

- It is a very good tool in getting **visibility** of the recruiter
- Full **flexibility** to showcase your best talent
- **More control** in what the recruiter will get to know about the potential employee

- I can now **carry** my resume wherever I go without having to worry about a hardcopy
- Find it to be a very **handy** tool

- With video resumes only the **right person** who has **suitable qualities** will be shortlisted.
- The recruiter will get to **see and hear** the **candidate** speak about his/her achievements and not just read on a paper and take a fair decision.

- Difficulty to produce a **natural and relaxed** looking video
- Felt it to be **informal**
- A **well-lit and noise-free area** with **good internet connectivity** is a mandate to shoot the video resume

- Difficulty to convey **quantity** of information

- I feel paper resume is much **convenient**
- I don't find it **comfortable** to use

- Video resume can lead to **biased** decisions

- I am concerned about my privacy. What if my video is **misused** and **leaked**?

Second-order categories

Resume format +

Goal and Content +

Ease of use +

Fairness +

Resume format -

Goal and Content -

Ease of use -

Fairness -

Privacy -

Third-order dimensions

Applicants are encouraged to use video resumes

Applicants are discouraged to use video resumes

Fig. 1. Proposed relationship model (where '+' signifies in favor and '−' signifies not in favor)

5 Findings

The following section on findings presents the statistics of responses obtained from the close-ended questions in our survey based on the dimensions of validity, impression, preference, and discrimination. We also explain the reasons behind their encouragement or discouragement to use video resumes based on close and open-ended responses.

5.1 Validity

Validity refers to the accuracy in hiring decisions. Regarding the validity of the video resume, 76.7% (majority) of respondents consider it to be valid for a job applicant and solves its purpose of creation while 23.3% oppose this view. Video resume offer a short and precise platform for applicants to portray themselves to the recruiter. Some of them may consider it very useful for their purpose of securing a job and some may not, questioning its validity.

5.2   Impression

Impression refers to the opinion formed about someone based on some evidence. For this dimension, 72.3% (majority) of respondents hold the view that video resumes lead to a positive impression of the applicant on the recruiter whereas 17% are against this. Moreover, 9.7% of respondents say it won't create any impression. These impression views are more inclined to each applicant's personal reasons such as personality.

5.3   Preference

Preference refers to a greater liking for one alternative over another. Around 54% (majority) of respondents prefer video resumes equally as paper resumes whereas 27.2% prefer video resumes less and 18.8% prefer video resumes more. Some applicants may prefer a video resume above, equal or below a paper resume due to reasons personal and unique to each.

5.4   Discrimination

Discrimination refers to the unjust treatment of different categories of people based on different grounds. From the data collected, the order of discrimination in hiring due to video resumes is derived to be as follows: (Where '>' signifies followed by) Attractiveness> Disfigurements> Personality> Disability> Gender> Age.

Majority of the respondents are of the opinion that attractiveness of the person can create the maximum halo effect [14] on the recruiter, which means that the recruiter will only notice the good qualities in a person while disregarding any flaws and disfigurements no matter how small they may be, can create the maximum horn effect [28] on the recruiter, which means that the recruiter will only notice the flaws in a person while disregarding any good qualities.

Applicants are Encouraged to Use Video Resume Platforms

The above data reveals that a major proportion of respondents are in favor of video resumes which encourages them to make use of it for their job hunt process. Several varied reasons play an instrumental role in this perceived usefulness. According to Daft and Lengel's [11] media richness theory, types of media differ from one another in terms of 'information richness' based on four factors. These factors are capacity for immediate feedback, several cues (text, sound, and image) which can be transmitted through the medium, personalization (ability to convey with personal focus), and language variety (simple vs complex). These respondents perceive video resumes in a much broader sense which allows them to demonstrate their knowledge, skills, abilities, and other characteristics, such as career objectives and motivation. Video resumes provide a platform to present themselves in a tailor-made way to highlight as well as explain their interests and achievements which suit the requirements of a particular job. This grants them an opportunity to present themselves more flexibly than just a paper resume which has a rigid format and deters them to express freely, making video resumes score higher in information richness. Video resumes are also considered by them as a handy tool. The videos can be taped in their smartphones and sent across to the recruiters anytime and anywhere.

Applicants are Discouraged to Use Video Resume Platforms

Our data also conveys that some of the respondents, who are a part of the job applicant pool are apprehensive of using video resumes for obtaining jobs or internships. This can be explained with the help of the realistic accuracy model [13]. This says that applicants consider information to become more salient in information-rich video platforms such as their look and appearance. Our respondents also worry that according to them, the recruiters are more likely to pay more attention to the applicants who are perceived to be more attractive. The perceived physical attractiveness by the recruiters will lead to biased job-related outcomes. This perceived attractiveness also impacts the validity (accuracy) of the purpose of video resumes and also its reliability for the applicants. The other major inhibiting factor for the adoption of video resumes by some of the applicants is the hardware requirements necessary to support its format. Video resumes require a well-lit and noise-free area for effective recording. Even though this isn't a mandate but is much required to eliminate any background flaws in the video. Also, the requirement of good internet connectivity to shoot a video and send it across to the targeted recruiters is a drawback for the applicants residing in areas where internet connectivity is slow or even absent. Data from open-ended questions led to the identification of an unexplored category which is 'Privacy'. Westin [31] defined privacy as, the claim of individuals, groups, or institutions to determine for themselves when, how, and to what extent information about themselves is communicated to others. It is one of the reasons for the unfavorability of video resumes due to the apprehension of the video going viral and may getting misused for unforeseen reasons. This can be inferred from one of the respondents who says, "what if my video is misused and leaked?". This element is one of the major roadblocks for the acceptability of video resumes and hence we have tried to suggest recommendations for the same.

Summarizing the findings of both sets of data collected with the help of open and close-ended questionnaire [16], we see that the overall dimensions influencing the adoption of video resumes are validity, impression, discrimination, resume format, goal and content, fairness and privacy. In Fig. 2, we thus outline relevant contextual characteristics and their influence on dis/encouraging using video resume platforms. We identified resume format, goal and content, ease of use, fairness, and privacy as five relevant contextual factors either facilitating or restricting video resume usage. These first-order themes act as a feedback loop to the video resume platforms for their modifications.

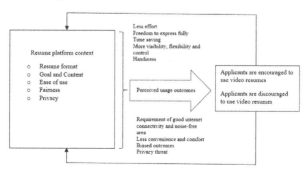

Fig. 2. Contextual characteristics and their influence on encouraging or discouraging video resume usage.

6 Discussion

The purpose of this paper was two-fold. Regarding our first research goal, results have shown that the majority of the respondents are in favor of this newly emerging recruitment tool but they along with those not in favor of it have some common concerns which when taken care of can result in wider acceptability. Focussing on the second major goal of this study, we have suggested some recommendations in the platforms based on the open-ended responses of the participants. We have taken the utmost caution to address each of their concerns.

6.1 Recommendations

The following are the recommendations for video resume applications (apps)/platforms, based on the responses gathered:

Uniformity of Background: There must be a provision in the form of a technical feature that can remove the existing background of the candidate and replaces it with a pre-selected one out of the specified background themes available for uniformity and better visual quality of videos. This will help in removing any distractions due to the background where the video is being shot. This, in turn, will ensure that the job applicant is not being judged or unfavoured due to the unavoidable background distraction(s).

Noise Cancellation: Noise cancellation feature in a video resume platform will allow for minimal background noise and hence a better audio quality of the video. This can be achieved by filtering the noise signals from the candidates' end before reaching the employers' side. Otherwise, in the case where there is too much unavoidable noise from the applicant's side, the recruiter (viewer) may just stop and move on to the next video. This may seem to be unfair for the applicant and the recruiter may even lose a potential candidate.

Ability to Shoot Video on the Platform Even Without Internet Connectivity: Ability to keep recording the video even if internet connectivity goes off temporarily. This is an effective solution especially for areas where high-speed connectivity is still not available and also for cases where internet connection may disappear momentarily due to unavoidable reasons. In such an adverse situation, the candidate will not have to re-shoot the video, instead, it can continue shooting and upload when the internet connection is regained.

Eye Detection Feature: Eye detection feature to enable the candidate to maintain eye contact with the viewer (Employer). In the case of there is no eye contact, the entire purpose of a video resume is meaningless due to a lack of effective delivery of content. It is a very important feature and can be made possible with the help of the iris detection feature available in almost all smartphones.

Development of a Mobile Application (App): In a time where a majority of the people use their mobile phones for every task, providing a seamless candidate experience in the form of an app (independently or in addition to a website) is the need of the hour. This will attract more job applicants towards the platform.

Handling of Privacy Issue: It may happen that a recruiter who receives the video resume of a candidate may not find him fit for a job role in his/her organization but may want to recommend it to someone known and he/she is will forward the link of the video. In this process, there is a possibility that the video is misused or leaked. Hence, a solution for this is to make the video resume link of a candidate his/her property which can be forwarded only by requesting permission from the concerned person for forwarding so that the person can keep a track where the video is being forwarded and who else is viewing it.

6.2   Research Limitations

Our study was done with a limited number of students enrolled in the MBA course in India. Hence, the findings of this study cannot be generalized to the entire job applicant population. Our participants were unemployed job seekers, who may welcome video resumes more than other (employed) applicants because of their inexperience and low understanding of the labor market. Also, the fairness and procedural justice perceptions of video resumes may be related to participants' ethnic backgrounds, knowledge, skills (language proficiency, education), and attitude (ethnic identity) than to actual career outcomes. Hence, different respondents may have different perceptions relating to it.

6.3   Future Research

There is a scope of research in this field related to the fairness of video résumés for a broader array of subgroups such as disabled applicants, different vocal characteristics, different educational and ethnic backgrounds, job roles, and from different countries to have a cross-cultural perspective. Future research may also focus on privacy issues in video résumé screening since there is apprehension in the users of video resumes regarding the inappropriate use of their videos when circulated. An extraverted and outspoken person may likely prefer video resumes more than that of a person of the opposite personality type. Hence, future studies may attempt to correlate the personality type and gender of an individual with their tendency to be in-favor or not in favor of video resumes. We have limited our examination to limited contextual factors, future studies could study additional factors such as types of jobs and industries for the suitability of a video resume over a paper resume.

References

1. Anderson, N.: Perceived job discrimination: toward a model of applicant propensity to case initiation in selection. Int. J. Sel. Assess. **19**, 229–244 (2011)
2. Bachiochi, P.D., Weiner, S.: Qualitative data collection and analysis. In: Rogelberg, S.G. (ed.) Handbook of Research Methods in Industrial and Organizational Psychology, pp. 161–183. Blackwell Publishers, Malden (2004)

3. Bauer, T.N., Truxillo, D.M., Paronto, M.E., Weekley, J.A., Campion, M.A.: Applicant reactions to different selection technology: face-to-face, interactive voice response, and computer-assisted telephone screening interviews. Int. J. Sel. Assess. **12**, 135–148 (2004)

4. Bertrand, M., Mullainathan, S.: Are Emily and Greg more employable than Lakisha and Jamal? A field experiment on labor market discrimination. Am. Econ. Rev. **94**, 991–1013 (2004). https://doi.org/10.1257/0002828042002561

5. Bowman, A., Wyman, J.F., Peters, J.: The operations manual: a mechanism for improving the research process. Nurs. Res. **51**(2), 134–138 (2002)

6. Bryman, A.: Social Research Methods, 5th edn. Oxford University Press, London (2016)

7. Chan, D., Schmitt, N.: Video-based versus paper-and-pencil method of assessment in situational judgment tests: subgroup differences in test performance and face validity perceptions. J. Appl. Psychol. **82**, 143–159 (1997). https://doi.org/10.1037/0021-9010.82.1.143

8. Cole, M.S., Rubin, R.S., Field, H.S., Giles, W.F.: Recruiters' perceptions and use of applicant résumé information: screening the recent graduate. Appl. Psychol. Int. Rev. **56**, 319–343 (2007). https://doi.org/10.1111/j.1464-0597.2007.00288.x

9. Cole, M.S., Field, H.S., Giles, W.F., Harris, S.G.: Recruiters' inferences of applicant personality based on résumé screening: do paper people have a personality? J. Bus. Psychol. **24**, 5–18 (2009). https://doi.org/10.1007/s10869-008-9086-9

10. Corbin, J., Strauss, A.: Grounded theory research: procedures, canons, and evaluative criteria. Qual. Sociol. **13**(1), 3–21 (1990)

11. Daft, R.L., Lengel, R.H.: Organizational information requirements, media richness and structural design. Manag. Sci. **32**(5), 554–571 (1986). https://doi.org/10.1287//mnsc.32.5.554

12. DeGroot, T., Motowidlo, S.J.: Why visual and vocal interview cues can affect interviewers' judgments and predict job performance. J. Appl. Psychol. **84**, 986–993 (1999). https://doi.org/10.1037/0021-9010.84.6.986

13. Funder, D.C.: On the accuracy of personality judgment: a realistic approach. Psychol. Rev. **102**(4), 652–670 (1995). https://doi.org/10.1037/0033-295X.102.4.652

14. Gerald, L., William, E., Helmreich, R.: The strength of the halo effect in physical attractiveness research. J. Psychol. **107**, 69–75 (1981)

15. Gissel, A.L., Thompson, L.F., Pond, S.B.: A theory-driven investigation of prospective applicants' intentions to submit video résumés. J. Appl. Soc. Psychol. **43**(12), 2449–2461 (2013). https://doi.org/10.1111/jasp.12191

16. Heale, R., Forbes, D.: Understanding triangulation in research. Evid.-Based Nurs. **16**(98), 98 (2013)

17. Hiemstra, A.M.F.: Fairness in paper and video resume screening. Ph.D. thesis, Erasmus University Rotterdam, Netherlands (2013)

18. Hsieh, H.F., Shannon, S.: Three approaches to qualitative content analysis. Qual. Health Res. **15**(9), 1277–2005 (2016)

19. Huffcutt, A.I., Conway, J., Roth, P.L., Stone, N.J.: Identification and meta-analytic assessment of psychological constructs measured in employment interviews. J. Appl. Psychol. **86**(5), 897–913 (2001)

20. Lin, W.L., Yao, G.: Predictive validity. In: Michalos, A.C. (ed.) Encyclopedia of Quality of Life and Well-Being Research. Springer, Dordrecht (2014). https://doi.org/10.1007/978-94-007-0753-5_2241

21. Madera, J.M., Hebl, M.R.: Discrimination against facially stigmatized applicants in interviews: an eye-tracking and face-to-face investigation. J. Appl. Psychol. **97**, 317–330 (2012). https://doi.org/10.1037/a0025799

22. Palinkas, L.A., Horwitz, S.M., Green, C.A., Wisdom, J.P., Duan, N., Hoagwood, K.: Purposeful sampling for qualitative data collection and analysis in mixed method implementation research. Adm. Policy Ment. Health Ment. Health Serv. Res. **42**(5), 533–544 (2013). https://doi.org/10.1007/s10488-013-0528-y
23. Quinn, K.A., Mason, M.F., Macrae, C.N.: Familiarity and person construal: individuating knowledge moderates the automaticity of category activation. Eur. J. Soc. Psychol. **39**, 852–861 (2009). https://doi.org/10.1002/ejsp.596
24. Richman, W., Olson, J., Drasgow, F.: Examining the impact of administration medium on examinee perceptions and attitudes. J. Appl. Psychol. **85**, 880–887 (2000). https://doi.org/10.1037//0021-9010.85.6.880
25. Ryan, A.M., Ployhart, R.E.: Applicants' perceptions of selection procedures and decisions: a critical review and agenda for the future. J. Manag. **26**, 565–606 (2000). https://doi.org/10.1177/014920630002600308
26. Schmidt, F.L., Hunter, J.E.: The validity and utility of selection methods in personnel psychology: practical and theoretical implications of 85 years of research findings. Psychol. Bull. **124**, 262–274 (1998). https://doi.org/10.1037/0033-2909.124.2.262
27. Stoughton, J.W., Thompson, L.F., Meade, A.W.: Examining applicant reactions to the use of social networking websites in pre-employment screening. J. Bus. Psychol. **30**(1), 73–88 (2013). https://doi.org/10.1007/s10869-013-9333-6
28. Sundar, A., Kardes, F., Noseworthy, T.: Inferences on Negative Labels and the Horns Effect. Association for Consumer Research (2014)
29. Sylva, H., Mol, S.T.: E-recruitment: a study into applicant perceptions of an online application system. Int. J. Sel. Assess. **17**, 311–323 (2009). https://doi.org/10.1111/j.14682389.2009.00473.x
30. Waung, M., Hymes, R.W., Beatty, J.E.: The effects of video and paper resumes on assessments of personality, applied social skills, mental capability, and resume outcomes. Basic Appl. Soc. Psychol. **36**(3), 238–251 (2014)
31. Westin, A.F.: Privacy and Freedom. Atheneum Books, New York (1967)

Virtual Platforms for Government Services in COVID-19 and Beyond: A Sociomaterial Case Study of Passport Service in Ghana

John Effah[(✉)]

Department of Operations and Management Information Systems,
University of Ghana Business School, Accra, Ghana
jeffah@ug.edu.gh

Abstract. In the COVID-19 era, the use of virtual platforms to meet social and physical distancing requirements has become more important across the world. Before COVID-19, information systems research on virtual platforms had focused on born-digital organizations and virtual platformization of pre-digital organizations in the private sector. Not much research therefore exists on virtual platformization of government services, especially from the developing world. This study therefore investigates a virtual platformization initiative for passport service in Ghana and its performance under the COVID-19 lockdown and beyond. The findings show that the service could not be fully platformized to meet physical distancing requirements due to activities related to physical materials such as signature, stamps, and documents as well as non-platformized systems of collaborating institutions. The paper discusses these constraints and how they can be addressed to enable end-to-end virtual platformization of government services in COVID-19 and beyond.

Keywords: Virtual platform · Platformization · Sociomateriality · Case study · Government service · Ghana

1 Introduction

The COVID-19 era has made virtual platforms important for online interactions in place of physical, face-to-face contacts [1–3]. Virtual or digital platforms are ICT infrastructure that enables online interactions between different actor groups [4, 5]. In terms of architecture, a virtual platform comprises a core module, standardized interfaces, and complementary applications [6, 7]. The standardized interfaces such as APIs and web services are boundary resources that connect the core module to various web client and mobile complementary applications [8, 9].

Virtual platforms contrast physical platforms that require co-located spaces such as traditional offices in buildings for direct and face-to-face contacts [10]. Over the years, virtual platforms have been used by born-digital organizations such as Amazon, Airbnb, and eBay to create values for their customers. In recent years, pre-digital or traditional organizations without virtual platforms have begun to adopt them for digital services. The process by which pre-digital organizations migrate their activities from

© IFIP International Federation for Information Processing 2020
Published by Springer Nature Switzerland AG 2020
S. K. Sharma et al. (Eds.): TDIT 2020, IFIP AICT 618, pp. 150–161, 2020.
https://doi.org/10.1007/978-3-030-64861-9_14

physical or offline onto online platforms is termed virtual platformization [11–13]. Generally, virtual platformization seeks to replace face-to-face, physical contacts with digital interactions [14].

The use of virtual platforms has become important for pre-digital organizations during and after the COVID-19 lockdowns, as social and physical distancing have become a requirement rather than a choice [2, 15]. As a result, virtual platforms for service delivery in some sectors, including education, shopping, and healthcare have begun to attract information systems (IS) research [e.g. 3, 16, 17]. However not much is known about government services involving physical materials such as passports, especially in a developing country context where digital infrastructure remains limited.

Following this gap, this study seeks to explain how virtual platformization of government services in a developing country context can enable online interactions to meet physical distancing requirements during and after COVID-19. The accompanying research question is: *how can government services involving physical materials be virtually platformized for COVID-19 and beyond.* To address the question, this study employs qualitative interpretive case study methodology [18] and sociomateriality theory [19] to investigate Ghana's passport service platformization before and during the COVID-19 pandemic.

The rest of this paper is organized as follows. Section 2 reviews literature on virtual platformization and COVID-19. Section 3 presents sociomateriality as the theoretical foundation. Section 4 presents the methodology. Section 5 reports on the empirical findings. Section 6 provides sociomaterial analysis of the empirical findings. Section 7 discusses the research findings, while Sect. 8 concludes the paper with its contribution.

2   Virtual Platformization and COVID-19

The term platformization generates platform as a hub for interactions among people and objects [20]. Platformization becomes virtual when the process involves digital technologies. Generally, the term platform refers to any space or location that enables interactions among different actors [10]. While a physical platform brings people into co-located environments for face-to-face interactions [10], a virtual platform brings them together for online interactions [6, 7, 21]. Thus virtual platforms function as hubs for online services without the need for physical contacts [12].

Over the years, born-digital organizations have been using virtual platforms for service delivery [22] while pre-digital organizations have been operating from physical locations such as buildings and office spaces. Thus, virtual platformization offers them the opportunity to migrate onto virtual platforms. Doing so enables them to integrate their silo systems and replace physical face-to-face contacts with virtual interactions for improved service delivery [21, 23].

As virtual platforms are mostly enabled by the Internet and mobile technologies [24, 25], they offer benefits such as customer self-service instead of employee service [25]. They also promote mobile connectivity for anywhere anytime transactions including online and mobile payments. Virtual platforms also support working from home without the need for a dedicated physical office [16].

Although virtual platformization was increasingly becoming the norm for pre-digital organizations seeking to migrate online, COVID-19 has made it more of a need than a choice for such organizations [15, 26]. Thus pre-digital organizations are expected to promote working from home to sustain service provision to customers [16]. While material objects such as food and drinks could not be virtualized during the lockdown, their online purchase and home delivery became important for organizations and their customers [3]. Generally, information objects such as books and educational services can be digitalized for online delivery. Yet, physical materials such as passport booklets cannot be easily virtualized and delivered online due to legal and international requirements. Hence, the need exists for a study into digital platformization of government services involving such materials during and after the COVID-19 lockdown.

3   Theoretical Foundation: Sociomateriality

The theoretical foundation for this study is the relational perspective of sociomateriality [19], which was developed to explain entanglement between social and material entities in practice. The core concepts are social, material, and sociomaterial practice. The term social refers to interactions between people as shaped by social structures, including rules, norms, and traditions; material refers to "stuff" the world is made up of [27 p. 86], see also [28, 29]. Moreover, a material can be physical (e.g., hardware) or digital (e.g., software and online data) [29, 30]. Sociomaterial practices are activities that are performed by entangled social and material components [19].

From the relational perspective, the key principles of sociomateriality are entanglement, relationality, and performativity [19, 31]. First, entanglement refers to inextricable constitution of the social and material in action [19]. Barad [31] refers to actions taking place within entanglement as intra-action rather than interactions. Second, relationality is ontological and refers to how an entity's existence or function is related to other entities. This shows that no entity (social, material, or practice) is independent in action. Therefore, sociomaterial analysis does not look for dependent and independent variables. Finally, performativity, which is also ontological, is the notion that sociomaterial practices produce outcomes or bring realities (social, material, or their combination) into being [31].

In recent years, sociomateriality has increasingly become a paradigm in IS research with its own ontology, epistemology, and methodology [32]. However, its application in the digital or virtual platform literature remains limited. Given that virtual platform development and use involve people, social structures, and material objects, sociomateriality can be a useful theoretical lens for studying such a phenomenon. Therefore, this study seeks to use it to analyze the virtual platformization phenomenon.

4   Methodological Approach

The setting for the study is Ghana, a developing country in Africa. The case phenomenon is the national passport service in Ghana and related activities from the perspective of both service providers and consumers. This study follows a qualitative methodology with case study as the research method [18]. Qualitative case study was chosen to enable detailed analysis of activities and processes of the research phenomenon within its real-life context. The underlying research paradigm is sociomaterial ontology and epistemology [19], which together view the social and the material as entangled, relational, and performative. In recent years, the sociomaterial paradigm has recently emerged in IS research as an alternative to positivism and interpretivism [32].

Qualitative data collection for the study occurred over one-year from June 2019 to June 2020 and came from multiple sources, namely interviews, participant observations, and documents. In line with the relational view of sociomateriality [19], data collection focused on tracing activities of relational practices and their changes over time [28, 33]. The intention was to track entanglements, relationality, and performativity of the phenomenon.

Participants for the study included employees of the Passport Office, their collaborating institutions, citizens who had been applicants and/or witnesses. The researcher also drew on his own observation and experience of going through the process as an applicant. Additional data came from online and offline documents on the case.

Data analysis was based on sociomateriality analysis involving mapping the concepts of entanglement, relationality, and performativity as practiced in the research phenomenon. This was followed by breaking the practice into specific activities (intra-actions) and their sociomaterial components. The output of the sociomaterial analysis is presented in Sect. 6.

5   Empirical Findings

In Ghana, the Passport Office is the agency of the Ministry of Foreign Affairs responsible for issuing national passports to citizens. The passport service activities include form filling, witnessing, submission and vetting, background checks as well as printing and issuing. Before 2016, these activities were physical. However, from 2014, a digitalization process was initiated to platformize them.

5.1   Activities Before Platformization

Before the platformization initiative, the physical and paper-based activities were as follows:

Form Filling: Involved acquiring and completing a physical form from any post-office. Filling involved using a pen to inscribe personal details onto the form and signing or thumbprinting the relevant portions.

Witnessing: Involved getting a person with high status to endorse contents of the completed form and passport pictures of the applicant with stamps and signatures. Possible witnesses included: the clergy, army and police officers, heads of institutions, and qualified professionals such as doctors, lawyers, and accountants.

Submission and Vetting: Involved physical submission of witnessed application forms with original identity documents, namely birth certificate for fresh passport application, previous passport for renewal, and police report for a replacement of missing passports. Vetting at the passport office involved checking the documents for accuracy and completeness. Applicant's biometric data and passport pictures were then captured and added to the application dossier. The details were subsequently keyed into a passport processing software.

Background Checks: Involving given copies of the application dossier to officers from collaborating agencies such as the Birth and Death Registry (BDR) to check and verify the birth certificate and government security agencies to check criminal records on the applicant, if any. If all went well, the dossier was sent to management for approval.

Printing and Issuing: Involved sending relevant details of the applicant to a printing company to print the passport booklet and return it to the passport office for issuing to the applicant.

The physical process before the platformization was fraught with some challenges. One applicant complained as follows:

> ...*passport process is full of bureaucracy, document losses, delays and corruption. We know some officers team up with illegal intermediaries called "Goro Boys" to collect bribes to speed up the process for some applications.*

An officer at the passport office also commented on data entry errors:

> *sometimes data entry clerks introduce errors when keying application details into the processing software.*

5.2   Platformizing the Service

In 2014, the Ministry of Foreign Affairs engaged the National Information Technology Agency (NITA) to help digitalize and platformize the passport service. The main goals were to (1) streamline the constituent activities for an efficient process, (2) promote collaboration among the BDR and collaborating security agencies for criminal and background checking (3) reduce actual and perceived corruption, and (4) remove data entry errors.

NITA subsequently analyzed the existing system and developed a requirement specifications document for the virtual platform project. The ministry accepted the specifications and worked with NITA to engage a software company, which re-developed the existing application into a core platform module as well as interfaced and online complementary applications for applicants and the printing organization.

Core Platform: The core platform was set up as an intranet for processing and connected to computers at the physical passport office. Therefore, employees of the passport office can only use the platform from their physical offices. They are unable to access from home or outside the office. The core platform enabled online vetting and prompting of applicants for any corrections. It also had functionalities for capturing biometrics data and pictures of applicants during submission.

Complementary Applications: The applicant facing software was internet-based and therefore accessible online via PCs and smartphones. Its functionalities included online form filling, document uploads, and printing of physical documents for witnessing and physical submission. It also had functionalities for mobile and online payments. The printing company's interfaced online application enables remote printing of passport booklets after management approval. However, no supplementary applications were developed for the BDR and the security agencies for criminal background checking. On this, an immigration officer complained as follows:

> *The core platform is not connected to our system. It is very frustrating for us to use printed documents and travel between our officers and the passport office. If they integrate the various systems, we can do work from our offices without the need to physically come here.*

5.3 After the Platformization (Before and During COVID-19)

From 2016, the passport service platform came into use with both online and offline activities as follows:

Form Filling: The platform enabled online form filling, uploading of supporting documents, and paying for the service through online banking and mobile money platforms. It also enabled online submission of completed forms to the passport office for processing.

Witnessing: In the absence of an online complementary application, witnessing continued to be physical with stamps and signatures. The process remained as offline interaction between the applicant and the witness.

Submission: Two types of submission emerged. Virtual submission through the online platform and physical submission of the printed and witnessed copy. In addition to uploading copies of supporting documents, applicants were still required to submit original physical copies to the passport office for background checks.

Vetting and Processing: Vetting and processing occurred in the passport office as combined digital and physical activities. The core platform was used to vet the online documents while the printed form and supported documents were vetted and process offline. In addition, applicants need to be physically present for their biometrics and picture capturing.

Background Checking: In the absence of an online complementary application, background checking continued to be physical from the passport office. Birth registry and security personnel need to be physically present and use physical documents for the background checks.

Printing and Collection: With the online printing company application, an applicant's data for passport booklet are electronically submitted for printing. However, in line with international conventions, passport booklets need to be physically printed and issued. After printing, applicants are informed through the online platform for collection. Although applicants could opt for home delivery through courier services, the high costs and lack of trust for postal services discourage them. Therefore, most applicants go to the office physically to collect their passport booklet.

During Covid-19: From March 2020, the Government of Ghana announced a lockdown to the restrict movement of people to reduce the spread of the disease. Notwithstanding the virtual platformization effort made by the passport office, the organization closed down and stopped providing services to citizens. Even when the lockdown was lifted in April 2020, the passport office continues to operate under the same combined online and physical interactions as before the lockdown.

One question that some applicants and IT professionals in the country keep asking is why the passport office has not migrated online during and after the lockdown. The next section provides a sociomaterial analysis of the situation.

6 Sociomaterial Analysis

This section employs sociomateriality principles as an analytical lens for the passport service platformization and outcome. The analysis focuses on activities of the service in relation to sociomaterial entanglement, relationality, and performativity as shown in Table 1.

Online Form Filling, Payment, and Submission: Before the platformization, form filling, payment, and submission were purely physical and paper-based. With the virtual platform, these activities have become digital. As shown in Table 1, the sociomaterial entanglement within which the virtual activities occur as intra-actions comprise the applicant, officers, application data and documents, virtual platform, guidelines, scanners, and payment platform. The relationalities of elements within the entanglement include the use of guidelines for form filling, scanner for digitizing documents for upload, payment platform form for online and mobile payments. The performative outcome is the completed and online submitted form.

Witnessing and Physical Submission: Previously, form witnessing was physical. After the platformization, it remains physical. The sociomaterial entanglement comprises the applicant, the witness, the printed form, rubber stamp, pens, and signature. For relationality, the printed form is for the applicant, pens, and rubber stamps are for witnessing while witness's signature and stamps are for endorsing the documents. The performative output is the witnessed form ready for physical submission to the passport office.

Vetting and Processing: Before the platformization, vetting and processing were also physical. Following the platformization, vetting and processing have become partly digital and partly physical. The digital part involves accessing and checking applicant's details and documents on the virtual platform. The physical part involves checking and processing printed and witnessed documents for signature and stamps. The physical part also includes e-capturing of applicant's biometric and picture while the digital part is uploading them onto the core platform. The performative outcome is combined digital and physical application document processing.

Background Checking: Before the platformization, background checking was physical and remained so after. The entanglement and relationalities include birth registry and security officers, applicant details, passport office location and silo systems of the

Table 1. Sociomaterial analysis of the passport service platform performance

Activities	Entanglement	Relationality	Performativity
Online form filling, payment, and online submission	Applicant, officers, application data and documents, virtual platform, guidelines, scanner, and payment platform	Form is for applicant's data, guidelines for form filling; scanner for digitizing documents for upload; payment platform for online and mobile payments	Completed and submitted online application form
Witnessing and physical submission	Applicant, witness, printed form, stamp signature	Applicant's printed form for witness' stamp and signature	Witnessed form ready for physical submission
Vetting and processing	Applicant, passport officers, online form, printed form, original copies of supporting documents, platform, biometric devices and digital camera, office location	Applicant's printed form and supporting documents are for vetting and processing by officers; applicant provides biometric data and takes a picture; officers access online forms for vetting and processing	Digital and physical application document processing
Background checking	Collaborating agents, printed documents, document stands, background records	Printed documents, quality standards, applicant's background records are for confirming citizenship and critical records (if any) of applicants	Application dossier cleared for approval and printing
Approval, printing, and issuing	Director, passed application, applicant, passport, printing organization, international convention, applicants	Passed application is for management approval and booklet printing. Printed booklets are for issuing and collection	Printed passport booklet ready for collection

collaborating agencies. The performative outcome constitutes application dossier cleared for approval and printing.

Approval, printing, and Issuing: Following the platformization, approval for printing and issuing have also become partly digital and partly physical. Management depends on both online content and physical trails of documents from processing and background checks to approve application documents for printing. Through the extranet system, the printing organization accesses applicant details to print passport booklet, after which applicants are electronically informed through the platform to for collection. Thus, the performativity is the printed passport booklet ready for collection.

7 Discussion

This study's research question focused on how government services involving physical materials and activities can be virtually platformized for physical distancing under COVID-19 and beyond. Overall the findings show how Ghana's passport service platformization was partial and therefore could not be delivered online during and after COVID lockdown. Thus, the service could not meet the necessary physical distancing requirements under COVID-19 [2, 15]. Among the reasons are the nature of the virtual platform's sociomaterial entanglement, continuation of physical practices, silo systems operations and unreliable postal services.

First, the virtual platform's sociomaterial entanglement was partly digital in nature. The digital part includes the online application. The physical materiality includes signatures and stamps as well as printed passport booklets. As a result, practices such as witnessing, vetting, and background checks could not be online but required physical interaction in the passport office space. Since these activities form significant part of the passport process, the service could not be completely virtualized during and after the lockdown. Given that digitization is a requirement for virtual process and service platformization [34]. Thus, to enable fullly virtual platformization, it is important to consider not only data content but also digitization of physical objects such as stamps and signature and how to use their digital equivalent to avoid the need for physical contact.

Also, the infrastructure and the necessary preparations had not been made for working from home. Per the working culture, employees work with physical applications with signature and stamps by witnesses. Despite the attempt to virtually platformize the passport process, the focus had been on just the applicant's part while other participants were ignored. As a result, the form filling part could be completed from home but other activities including witnessing, vetting and background checks could not be done without physical contact. This finding calls for relationality in virtual platformization to ensure that all participants can have online interactions. Thus, in line with the relationality principle of sociomateriality, form filling should be related to witnessing, vetting, and background checks. Hence, platformizing some activities and leaving others does not provide the needed maximum benefits.

Another reason for the partial platformization was the failure to connect the core platform to the information systems of collaborating institutions involved in the background checks, including the birth registry and the security agencies. Consequently, their officers had to be physically present at the passport office to check original documents. Since silo systems should be the starting point for digital platformization [13], it is important that the passport office platformize the collaborating institutions to avoid face-to-face contacts.

Another factor that required physical presence of applicants was the need to collect the printed passport. In line with international convention, the office needed to print the booklet as a physical product and issue it as such. To avoid physical contact, the need exists to post the booklets. Again, this calls for trusted postal and reliable home addresses.

8 Conclusion

This study began with the aim of explaining how government services involving physical materials can be virtually platformized to meet physical distancing requirements in COVID-19 and beyond. The findings show that the virtual platformization of Ghana's passport services was not able to migrate all activities online to meet the social and physical distancing requirements during and after the lockdown. The failure was due to lack of telecommuting infrastructure, non-platformization of collaborating agencies, and unreliable postal systems. The discussion section offers implications for how such constraints can be addressed.

The study contributes to research, theory, and practice. For research, it extends the extant literature on virtual (digital) platformization into government service domain involving physical materials. It demonstrates how sociomaterial entanglements of virtual platforms can shape physical and digital activities for online and offline service provision for lockdowns and physical distancing requirements during pandemics.

The paper also contributes to sociomateriality theory by using entanglement, relationality, and performativity for activity analysis as intra-actions [31] of practices. By this, the study shows how sociomaterial practices can be broken down into constituent activities for more detailed analysis. Given that specific guidelines for sociomaterial methodology and analysis are still emergent [28], the approach used here can serve as a framework for analysis between practice and activity levels.

For practice, the findings provide an insight into how a particular configuration of virtual platform can enable or constrain virtualization of services from offline to online environment to avoid physical interactions. Thus, the findings can serve as a framework for IS and service practitioners on how to configure virtual platforms to support online service delivery during and after COVID-19.

The paper's limitation stems from its focus on a single case within a developing country context and use of evolving methodological and theoretical approaches that are yet to be stabilized. Future research can evaluate the novel approaches used in this study.

References

1. Kodama, M.: Digitally transforming work styles in an era of infectious disease. Int. J. Inf. Manag. (2020, in press). https://doi.org/10.1016/j.ijinfomgt.2020.102172
2. Richter, A.: Locked-down digital work. Int. J. Inf. Manag. (2020, in press). https://doi.org/10.1016/j.ijinfomgt.2020.102157
3. Barnes, S.J.: Information management research and practice in the post-COVID-19 world. Int. J. Inf. Manag. (2020, in press). https://doi.org/10.1016/j.ijinfomgt.2020.102175
4. Lee, H.: Virtual vs physical platform : organizational capacity and slack, strategic decision and fi rm performance. J. Bus. Ind. Mark. (2020, in press). https://doi.org/10.1108/jbim-07-2019-0341
5. Schultze, U., Hiltz, S.R., Nardi, B.: Using synthetic worlds for work and learning. Commun. Assoc. Inf. Syst. **22**, 351–370 (2007)

6. Kannan, V., Mathew, S., Lehner, F.: Sociomaterial perspective of digital platforms. In: Proceedings of the 27th European Conference on Information Systems (ECIS), Stockholm & Uppsala, Sweden, 8–14 June 2019 (2019)
7. Tiwana, A.: Evolutionary competition in platform ecosystems. Inf. Syst. Res. **26**, 266–281 (2015). https://doi.org/10.1287/isre.2015.0573
8. Ghazawneh, A., Henfridsson, O.: Balancing platform control and external contribution in third-party development: the boundary resources model. Inf. Syst. J. **23**, 173–192 (2013). https://doi.org/10.1111/j.1365-2575.2012.00406.x
9. Constantinides, P., Henfridsson, O., Parker, G.G.: Introduction - platforms and infrastructures in the digital age - semantic scholar. Inf. Syst. Res. **29**, 381–400 (2018). https://doi.org/10.1287/isre.2018.0794
10. Schultze, U., Orlikowski, W.: Metaphors of virtuality: shaping an emergent reality. Inf. Organ. **11**, 45–77 (2001). https://doi.org/10.1016/S1471-7727(00)00003-8
11. Tormer, R.L.: Internal digital platforms and generative mechanisms of digital innovation. In: Thirty Ninth International Conference on Information Systems, San Francisco, CA, pp. 1–17 (2018)
12. Kazan, E., et al.: Disentangling digital platform competition: the case of UK mobile payment platforms. J. Manag. Inf. Syst. **35**, 180–219 (2018). https://doi.org/10.1080/07421222.2018.1440772
13. Bygstad, B., Hanseth, O.: Transforming digital infrastructures through platformization. In: Twenty-Sixth European Conference on Information Systems (ECIS 2018), Portsmouth, UK, 23–28 June (2018)
14. Overby, E.: Process virtualization theory and the impact of information technology. Organ. Sci. **19**, 277–291 (2008)
15. De, R., Pandey, N., Pal, A.: Impact of digital surge during Covid-19 pandemic: a viewpoint on research and practice. Int. J. Inf. Manag. (2020, in press). https://doi.org/10.1016/j.ijinfomgt.2020.102171
16. Fletcher, G., Griffiths, M.: Digital transformation during a lockdown. Int. J. Inf. Manage. (2020, in press). https://doi.org/10.1016/j.ijinfomgt.2020.102185
17. Doyle, R., Conboy, K.: The role of IS in the covid-19 pandemic: a liquid-modern perspective. Int. J. Inf. Manage. 102184 (2020). https://doi.org/10.1016/j.ijinfomgt.2020.102184
18. Myers, M.: Qualitative Research in Business & Management. SAGE Publications, London (2013)
19. Orlikowski, W., Scott, S.: Sociomateriality: challenging the separation of technology. Work Organ. Acad. Manag. Ann. **2**, 433–474 (2008). https://doi.org/10.1080/19416520802211644
20. Tormer, R.L., Henningsson, S.: Platformization and Internationalization in the LEGO Group. In: Hawaii International Conference on System Sciences, pp. 5779–5788 (2020)
21. Overby, E., Slaughter, S.A., Konsynski, B.: Research commentary—the design, use, and consequences of virtual processes. Inf. Syst. Res. **21**, 700–710 (2010)
22. Tumbas, S., Berente, N., Vom Brocke, J.: Born digital: growth trajectories of entrepreneurial organizations spanning institutional fields. In: Thirty Eighth International Conference on Information Systems, South Korea 2017, Seoul, South Korea, 10–13 December (2017)
23. Overby, E.: Migrating processes from physical to virtual environments: process virtualization theory. In: Dwivedi, Y.K., Wade, M., Schineberger, S. (eds.) Information Systems Theory: Explaining and Predicting Our Digital Society. Integrated Series in Information Systems, vol. 28, pp. 107–124. Springer, New York (2012). https://doi.org/10.1007/978-1-4419-6108-2_6
24. Saarikko, T.: Digital platform development: a service-oriented perspective. Eur. Conf. Inf. Syst. 0–16 (2015). https://doi.org/10.18151/7217454

25. De Reuver, M., Sørensen, C., Basole, R.C.: The digital platform : a research agenda. J. Inf. Technol. **33**, 124–135 (2018). https://doi.org/10.1057/s41265-016-0033-3
26. Carroll, N., Conboy, K.: Normalising the "new normal": changing tech-driven work practices under pandemic time pressure. Int. J. Inf. Manag. (2020, in press). https://doi.org/10.1016/j.ijinfomgt.2020.102186
27. Østerlie, T., Almklov, P.G., Hepsø, V.: Dual materiality and knowing in petroleum production. Inf. Organ. **22**, 85–105 (2012). https://doi.org/10.1016/j.infoandorg.2012.01.001
28. Cecez-Kecmanovic, D., Galliers, R., Henfridsson, O., Newell, S., Vidgen, R.: The sociomateriality of information systems: current status. Fut. Direct. MIS Q. **38**, 809–830 (2014). https://doi.org/10.1016/j.infoandorg.2013.02.001
29. Jones, M.: A matter of life and death: exploring Conceptualizations of sociomateriality in the context of critical care. MIS Q. **38**, 200–201 (2014)
30. Leonardi, P.: Digital materiality? How artifacts without matter, matter. First Monday, **15** (2010)
31. Barad, K.: Posthumanist performativity: toward an understanding of how matter comes to matter. Signs (Chic). **28**, 801–831 (2003)
32. Schultze, U., Heuvel, G. Van Den, Niemimaa, M.: Enacting accountability in is research after the sociomaterial turn (ing). J. Assoc. Inf. Syst. **21**, 811–835 (2020, in press). https://doi.org/10.17705/1jais.00620
33. Hultin, L.: On becoming a sociomaterial researcher: exploring epistemological practices grounded in a relational, performative ontology. Inf. Organ. **29**, 91–104 (2019). https://doi.org/10.1016/j.infoandorg.2019.04.004
34. Mihailescu, M., Mihailescu, D.: The emergence of digitalisation in the context of health care. In: Proceedings of the 51st Hawaii International Conference on System Sciences, Hawai, 3–6 January 2018 (2018)

Consumer Resistance to Mobile Banking Services: Do Gender Differences Exist?

Kayode A. Odusanya[1]([✉]) [iD], Olu Aluko[2], and Ayodeji Ajibade[3]

[1] School of Business and Economics, Loughborough University,
Loughborough, UK
k.odusanya@lboro.ac.uk
[2] Nottingham Business School, Nottingham Trent University, Nottingham, UK
[3] Department of Accounting, Babcock University, Ikenne, Nigeria

Abstract. Consumers still experience significant challenges that hinder the adoption of technological innovations. In this study, we draw on three theory-driven barriers to investigate variation in consumer resistance to mobile banking services. Data was collected from 252 consumers in Nigeria. Preliminary findings from the independent t-test suggest that no significant gender differences exist across usage, risk, and image barriers for our sample. We contribute to academic literature by exploring which barriers contribute to the gender gap that has been observed in mobile banking adoption.

Keywords: Barriers · Mobile banking · Gender gap · Innovation resistance theory

1 Introduction

Mobile banking services (MBs) are vital in promoting access to financial services. For instance, financial institutions such as banks encourage existing customers to access mobile platforms whereby, they can complete banking transactions and access other services without the need to travel to brick-and-mortar branch locations. Also, MBs can promote financial inclusion by providing an alternative platform for unbanked segments of the population to access otherwise out-of-reach financial services without having a bank account (Demirgüç-Kunt et al. 2018). Yet there are growing concerns that consumers exhibit resistance to the adoption of MBs and only a few studies (e.g. Laukkanen 2016) have attempted to shed insight into the differences in barriers exhibited across gender. Thus, this study aims to answer explore gender differences in consumer resistance to mobile banking services. We draw on three theory-driven barriers anchored on the innovation resistance theory (IRT). The next section summarizes previous research that has adopted IRT while Sects. 3 and 4 present the method and analysis, respectively. Section 5 concludes with concluding remarks and next steps.

© IFIP International Federation for Information Processing 2020
Published by Springer Nature Switzerland AG 2020
S. K. Sharma et al. (Eds.): TDIT 2020, IFIP AICT 618, pp. 162–169, 2020.
https://doi.org/10.1007/978-3-030-64861-9_15

2 Related Literature

There is a growing body of literature exploring consumer resistance as the cause of innovation failure. Numerous studies drawn on the innovation resistance (Ram 1987) as a theoretical lens to investigate consumer resistance to innovation-induced change. Ram's (1987) initial work was further developed by Ram and Sheth (1989) who argued that consumer resistance can be conceptualized into functional (that is, usage, value, and risk) and psychological (tradition and image) barriers. In this section, we preview relevant literature that have drawn on the innovation resistance theory. An illustration of these studies can be found in Table 1 from which two observations are made. The first observation from the literature is that the range of innovation contexts has mostly been explored in developed country contexts. While these studies have offered valuable insights, more studies are needed from developing country contexts. Such studies, we would argue, will provide a more rounded understanding of consumer resistance for the academic literature. Second, most studies have focused on service innovations within the banking sector such as mobile wallet, internet banking (e.g. Laukkanen et al. 2009) and mobile wallet (Leong et al. 2020), mobile payment solutions (Kaur et al. 2020) and mobile banking (Chaouali and Souiden 2019). As seen from Table 1, the literature on consumer resistance is growing and more research is needed to explicate demographic differences given these attributes affect the adoption of technological innovations.

For example, Laukkanen (2016) found that men are nearly twice as likely as women to adopt MBs, pointing to a gender gap in mobile banking adoption. Consequently, studies explaining the nature of barriers contributing to this gap may well provide valuable insight into the existing literature. In this research-in-progress paper, we present preliminary findings resulting from an examination of gender differences using the five theory-driven barriers based on the innovation resistance perspective. While studies have offered valuable insights on consumer resistance, the lack of research focusing on African countries is a gap in the literature given that financial exclusion remains a problem in Africa (Demirgüç-Kunt et al. 2018). Our study seeks to fill this gap by providing insights from the Sub-Saharan context. Consequently, the potential contribution offered by this study occurs at the intersection of research gaps observed in the consumer resistance literature based on the summary of existing studies.

3 Method

To examine gender differences in consumer resistance to mobile banking adoption, we chose a positivist approach using a questionnaire survey to collect data. The feedback received was used to improve the clarity of the survey questions. All questions in the first section were measured using a seven-point Likert scale, ranging from "strongly disagree" to "strongly agree". We also collected demographic details of gender, age, education level. The survey link was sent out to 366 respondents. In response, 252 completed the survey indicating a 69% response rate. With regard to demographic characteristics, 56% of respondents were male while 44% were female.

Table 1. Related literature

Citation	Objective	Country and innovation context	Main findings
Laukkanen (2016)	To investigate predictors of consumer adoption/rejection decisions in internet and mobile banking services	Finland, mobile and internet banking services	Value barrier is the strongest inhibitor of innovation adoption and usage intention for mobile and Internet banking services. The usage barrier is not an issue influencing consumer adoption/rejection decisions in the Internet and mobile banking
Chen and Kuo (2017).	To enhance effective management of enterprise social media platforms by exploring the nature and source of user resistance toward enterprise social media	Taiwan, enterprise social media platforms	The study identifies the functional and psychological barriers affecting knowledge sharing on enterprise social media and how they might be overcome
Talwar et al. (2020)	Study examines the barriers to positive purchase intentions toward online travel agencies (OTA)	India, online travel agencies	The value barrier is the strongest inhibitor of purchase intentions. Risk barriers on the other hand, positively predict purchase intentions towards OTAs. Young and old OTA users differ in the association between barriers and purchase intentions
Laukkanen et al. (2009)	To investigate how customers experiencing different kinds of resistance to Internet banking perceive the information and guidance offered by the service provider	Finland, internet banking services	Customers reporting both functional and psychological resistance to Internet banking are more dissatisfied with the information and guidance offered by the service provider compared to those with only psychological resistance or no resistance to the innovation
Kaur et al. (2020)	To study the different consumer barriers toward the intentions to use and	India, mobile payment solutions	Usage, value, and risk barriers negatively associated with user intentions. Tradition and

(continued)

Table 1. (*continued*)

Citation	Objective	Country and innovation context	Main findings
	recommend mobile payment systems		image barriers not significantly associated with user intentions. Risk, tradition, and image barriers not associated with intentions to recommend
Leong et al. (2020)	Examines the inhibitors of m-wallet innovation adoption	Malaysia, mobile wallet	Usage, risk, value & tradition barriers have positive effects on m-wallet resistance
Ma and Lee (2019)	Investigates the barriers underlying the adoption of MOOCs in the context of a developing country	China, Massive Open Online Courses, focus groups	The main barriers to the adoption of MOOCs are usage barriers, value barriers, and tradition barriers
Lian and Yen (2014)	To provide a better understanding of the drivers and barriers affecting older consumers' intention to shop online	Taiwan, Online shopping among older adults	The major factors driving older adults toward online shopping are performance expectation and social influence. The major barriers that keep older adults away from shopping online include value and tradition
Lian and Yen (2013)	The study attempts to understand why consumers rarely shop online for experience goods. Experience goods as a product or service with quality information that cannot be easily observed and determined before its purchase and use	Taiwan, online shopping	Major barriers for people who refuse to shop 'experience goods' online include value and tradition. Rejecters have the highest barriers, followed by opponents and then postponers
Laukkanen et al. (2007)	To investigate innovation resistance among mature consumers in the mobile banking context	Finland, mobile banking services	Value barrier is the most intense barrier to mobile banking adoption among both mature and younger consumers. Aging appears to be related especially to the risk and image barriers

(*continued*)

Table 1. (*continued*)

Citation	Objective	Country and innovation context	Main findings
Chaouali and Souiden (2019)	Study investigates mobile banking resistance among elder individuals	France, mobile banking services	Tradition and image barriers affect usage, value, and risk barriers. In turn, all barriers influence resistance behavior. Furthermore, cognitive age was found to moderate these relationships
Laukkanen et al. (2008)	To identify and understand innovation resistance among three groups of internet banking non-adopters	Finland, internet banking services	Significant differences were identified between the groups explored. The resistance of the rejectors is much more intense and diverse than that of the opponents, while the postponers show only slight resistance

4   Analysis and Results

The data was analyzed using IBM SPSS 24 software. As a research-in-progress paper, we report only preliminary findings based on the factor analysis and the independent samples t-test. Based on exploratory factor analysis using the principal component method with varimax rotation, three variables (usage, image, and risk barriers) from the original variable list were fitted into the factor model after five rotations. The other two (tradition and value barriers) both had very low Cronbach Alphas, and were thus dropped from the further analysis. Table 2 shows the factor loadings and Cronbach Alphas of the survey items and variables, respectively.

Table 2. Measurement items of study

Variables	Items	Factor loadings	α - value	Source(s)
Usage barrier[*]	UB 1 - In my opinion, mobile banking services are easy to use	0.872	0.856	Laukkanen (2016)
	UB2 - In my opinion, the use of mobile banking services is convenient	0.849		
	UB 3 - In my opinion, mobile banking services are fast to use	0.867		

(*continued*)

Table 2. (*continued*)

Variables	Items	Factor loadings	α - value	Source(s)
	UB 4 - In my opinion, progress in mobile banking services is clear	0.886		
	UB 5 - The use of changing PIN codes in mobile banking services is convenient	0.544		
Risk barrier	RB1 - I fear that while I am using mobile banking services, the connection will be lost.	0.780	0.744	
	RB2 - I fear that while I am using a mobile banking service, I might tap out the information of the bill wrongly	0.861		
	RB3 - I fear that the list of Pin codes may be lost and end up in the wrong hands.	0.781		
Image barrier	IB1 - In my opinion, new technology is often too complicated to be useful.	0.896	0.752	
	IB2 - I have such an image that mobile banking services are difficult to use.	0.857		

Note: *Items were reversed before analysis | IB: image barriers; RB: risk barriers; UB: usage barriers

As seen from the table, the Cronbach Alphas as vary between 0.744 and 0.951, indicating acceptable reliability levels (Hair et al. 2016). The Kaiser-Meyer-Olkin (KMO) measure of sampling adequacy (KMO = 0.840) and Bartlett's test of sphericity ($p < 0.001$) confirmed that the factor analysis was appropriate. The factors identified represent 72.1% of the variance of the variables. Next, we examine if there are gender differences to usage, risk, and image barriers. The results are shown in Table 3.

Table 3. Results of independent sample t-test

Items	Mean (SD)		Total	F-value	Sig.
	Male	Female			
UB 1 - In my opinion, mobile banking services are easy to use	5.89 (1.27)	5.84 (1.21)	5.87 (1.23)	0.302	0.750
UB2 - In my opinion, the use of mobile banking services is convenient	5.96 (1.24)	5.64 (1.04)	5.95 (1.13)	1.922	0.881
UB 3 - In my opinion, mobile banking services are fast to use	5.86 (1.30)	5.79 (1.27)	5.82 (1.28)	0.272	0.693
UB 4 - In my opinion, progress in mobile banking services is clear	5.88 (1.15)	5.79 (1.24)	5.83 (1.20)	0.373	0.556
UB 5 - The use of changing PIN codes in mobile banking services is convenient	5.18 (1.54)	5.20 (1.38)	5.19 (1.45)	0.263	0.908

(*continued*)

Table 3. (*continued*)

Items	Mean (SD)		Total	F-value	Sig.
	Male	Female			
RB1 - I fear that while I am using mobile banking services, the connection will be lost	5.21 (1.62)	5.23 (1.62)	5.22 (1.62)	0.007	0.945
RB2 - I fear that while I am using a mobile banking service, I might tap out the information of the bill wrongly	5.01 (1.56)	5.34 (1.60)	5.19 (1.59)	0.451	0.105
RB3 - I fear that the list of Pin codes may be lost and end up in the wrong hands	4.77 (1.76)	5.04 (1.63)	4.92 (1.69)	1.753	0.212
IB1 - In my opinion, new technology is often too complicated to be useful	3.18 (1.80)	3.14 (1.72)	3.15 (1.76)	0.671	0.848
IB2 - I have such an image that mobile banking services are difficult to use	2.71 (1.76)	2.58 (1.50)	2.64 (1.62)	3.761	0.510

Note: IB: image barriers; RB: risk barriers; UB: usage barriers

As seen from Table 3, the results indicate that usage barriers received the highest mean compared to risk and image barriers. This means that users were most concerned by the complexity of the use of mobile banking services. The t-test results also show no statistically significant difference between men and women across survey items.

5 Concluding Remarks and Next Steps

The gender gap in the adoption of mobile banking services has been observed in previous studies (Laukkanen 2016). This paper aims to build on the work of Laukkanen (2016) by exploring which barriers explains the gender gap in mobile banking adoption. Preliminary t-test results based on our sample suggests that usage, image, and risk barriers do not contribute to gender differences observed in consumer resistance to mobile banking services. One possible explanation may however lie in the relatively young demographic of our sample - 92% less than 40 years and 80% between 18–35 years old. It is likely that our finding could be assigned to a distinct prior experience with technology that has been ascribed to younger users in extant technology adoption research (Kaba and Touré 2014). Hence, we do not entirely eliminate the possibility that gender differences may exist among older users of mobile banking services. Going forward, further analysis will be conducted to explore the demographic differences. We are also planning to expand our analysis to include more variables – both moderating and dependent variables.

References

Chaouali, W., Souiden, N.: The role of cognitive age in explaining mobile banking resistance among elderly people. J. Retail. Consum. Serv. **50**, 342–350 (2019)

Chen, P.T., Kuo, S.C.: Innovation resistance and strategic implications of enterprise social media websites in Taiwan through knowledge sharing perspective. Technol. Forecast. Soc. Chang. **118**, 55–69 (2017)

Demirguc-Kunt, A., Klapper, L., Singer, D., Ansar, S., Hess, J.: The Global Findex Database 2017: Measuring Financial Inclusion and the Fintech Revolution. World Bank, Washington, DC (2018)

Hair Jr., J.F., Hult, G.T.M., Ringle, C., Sarstedt, M.: A Primer on Partial Least Squares Structural Equation Modeling (PLS-SEM). Sage Publications, Thousand Oaks (2016)

Kaba, B., Touré, B.: Understanding information and communication technology behavioral intention to use: applying the UTAUT model to social networking site adoption by young people in a least developed country. J. Assoc. Inf. Sci. Technol. **65**(8), 1662–1674 (2014)

Kaur, P., Dhir, A., Singh, N., Sahu, G., Almotairi, M.: An innovation resistance theory perspective on mobile payment solutions. J. Retail. Consum. Serv. **55**, 102059 (2020)

Laukkanen, T.: Consumer adoption versus rejection decisions in seemingly similar service innovations: the case of the internet and mobile banking. J. Bus. Res. **69**(7), 2432–2439 (2016)

Laukkanen, T., Sinkkonen, S., Kivijärvi, M., Laukkanen, P.: Innovation resistance among mature consumers. J. Consum. Mark. **24**(7), 419–427 (2007). https://doi.org/10.1108/07363760710834834

Laukkanen, P., Sinkkonen, S., Laukkanen, T.: Consumer resistance to internet banking: postponers, opponents, and rejectors. Int. J. Bank Mark. **26**(6), 440–455 (2008). https://doi.org/10.1108/02652320810902451

Laukkanen, T., Sinkkonen, S., Laukkanen, P.: Communication strategies to overcome functional and psychological resistance to internet banking. Int. J. Inf. Manag. **29**(2), 111–118 (2009)

Leong, L.Y., Hew, T.S., Ooi, K.B., Wei, J.: Predicting mobile wallet resistance: a two-staged structural equation modeling-artificial neural network approach. Int. J. Inf. Manag. **51**, 102047 (2020)

Lian, J.W., Yen, D.C.: To buy or not to buy experience goods online: Perspective of innovation adoption barriers. Comput. Hum. Behav. **29**(3), 665–672 (2013)

Lian, J.W., Yen, D.C.: Online shopping drivers and barriers for older adults: age and gender differences. Comput. Hum. Behav. **37**, 133–143 (2014)

Ma, L., Lee, C.S.: Understanding the barriers to the use of MOOCs in a developing country: an innovation resistance perspective. J. Educ. Comput. Res. **57**(3), 571–590 (2019)

Ram, S.: A model of innovation resistance. Adv. Consum. Res. **14**(1), 208–212 (1987)

Ram, S., Sheth, J.N.: Consumer resistance to innovations: the marketing problem and its solutions. J. Consum. Mark. **6**(2), 5–14 (1989)

Talwar, S., Dhir, A., Kaur, P., Mäntymäki, M.: Barriers toward purchasing from online travel agencies. Int. J. Hosp. Manag. **89**, 102593 (2020)

Harnessing the Potentials of Mobile Phone for Adoption and Promotion of Organic Farming Practices in Nigeria

A. Kayode Adesemowo[3(✉)] [iD], Adebayo Abayomi-Alli[1] [iD],
O. Oluwayomi Olabanjo[1], Modupe O. Odusami[2] [iD],
Oluwasefunmi T. Arogundade[1] [iD], and Tope Elizabeth Abioye[1] [iD]

[1] Federal University of Agriculture, Abeokuta, Nigeria
{abayomiallia, arogundadeot}@funaab.edu.ng,
yomibanjo24@gmail.com, elizatope_2005@yahoo.com
[2] Covenant University, Ota, Nigeria
modupe.odusami@convenantuniversity.edu.ng
[3] Nelson Mandela University, Port Elizabeth, South Africa
Kadesemowo@soams.co.za, kayode@mandela.ac.za

Abstract. The goal of organic agriculture is to show the interrelationship between farm biota, its production, and the overall environment. In cooperation with various Organic Farming unions, a system called the organic farming mobile agricultural extension services (OrgFarMob) was developed to provide farmers with instant information to problems with organic crop cultivation. Hence, this project provides organic farmers with crop lifecycle support system, leading to effective management and sustainable economic development in organic agriculture. The system powered by Azure cloud platform, was developed using Model-View-Architecture and programmed with AngularJS and Ionic. The design followed the computer research framework with incorporate users' requirement elucidation and validation. The system was designed and evaluated using data obtained through the collection of materials from professionals in the field of organic agriculture. The results showed that the system can be used in real-time and foster organic agriculture cultivation.

Keywords: Agriculture · Mobile application · Organic agriculture · Organic farming · Mobile phone · OrgFarMob

1 Introduction

Agriculture has been a subject of quite extreme importance. Its origin can be traced back to the origin of man. It is a core basis of existence to mankind and several forms of life in the area of feeding, atmospheric oxygen-carbon dioxide exchange, anti-erosion and raw materials for key industries including clothing and textiles (cotton), bio-energy which is gradually replacing conventional energy, defense (corn starch in the production of bombs) and several others [1]. As the demand for food has become increasingly high, the transition to chemical agriculture has become alarmingly high. We, therefore, find ourselves in a situation where harmful chemical fertilizers, pesticides, and herbicides are

© IFIP International Federation for Information Processing 2020
Published by Springer Nature Switzerland AG 2020
S. K. Sharma et al. (Eds.): TDIT 2020, IFIP AICT 618, pp. 170–181, 2020.
https://doi.org/10.1007/978-3-030-64861-9_16

gaining alarming acceptance among farmers practicing agriculture on a commercial scale and more recently subsistent farmers [2]. This has led to the contamination of the environment, habitual ruinous, and threat to human health and welfare.

Also, commercial agriculture land practices have led to the destruction of the physical structure of land and biodiversity leading to erosion and climate change [3–5]. A solution to these negative impacts is organic agriculture. The goal of organic agriculture is to show the deep interrelationship between farm biota, its production, and the general environment. In basic terms, this means organic agriculture is not just concerned with the production of crops, but also the conservation of the true nature of the environment and the production of crops that are biochemically helpful to man and animals and not the other way round. One key area in organic agriculture is the production of crops. Cereals such as rice and millet are excellent sources of carbohydrate and energy while legumes such as beans and soya beans are excellent sources of protein [6]. An interesting fact here is that cereals are the largest suppliers of carbohydrates while legumes are the largest suppliers of protein feeding the global population. The resource for Organic agriculture's emanates from using technologies assigned to sites, scales, and also recycles natural resources. The best means to facilitate this, is through mobile application technology due to the ubiquitous nature of smart mobile phones and hand-held devices. The infiltration of mobile and handheld devices, which is increasing exponentially daily, bring entirely different world of innovation through, enabling in-situ information search, activities and actions [7]. Yet, despite its usage for personal use, mobile phone based agricultural extension for real-time, organic farming has not diffused through.

This study is motivated by the problem of real-time access to information and resources that will enable organic farmers to cultivate their crops and strategize better. A mobile application for farmers and key stakeholders practicing organic agriculture focusing on the cultivation of crops is developed in this research work. The main contribution of this study is the provision of a mobile application for organic agriculture extension services that helps organic farmers to solve the problem of access to information on organic best practices thereby fostering the development of the organic agriculture industry.

The rest of this paper is sectioned as follows: Sect. 2 discusses the adoption of information and communication technology in agriculture. Section 3 reviews related works. Section 4 designs and develops the proposed system. Section 4.1 implements the system, with results presented in Sect. 5. Section 6 concludes this study.

2 Information and Communication Technology in Agriculture

One of the challenging issues facing Researchers and inventors of new technologies in agriculture is how to promote the uptake of these new innovations. [8] showed the dynamism in the adoption of new technologies. In [9] research, the adoption of mobile phone helped in saving farmers' energy and time thereby increasing farmers' income. Reporting on mobile phone usage in agricultural extension in India, [10] indicated higher market participation and high value crops through diversification among farmers, thus leading to increase profit margin and reduction in crops wastage in farming activities. [11] reported that easy accessibility to market information and financial transaction of farm produce were the most accessed information among farmers on mobile phone. Yet, investigation by [12] showed traditional typical mobile phone use for calling and sending SMS with a mere 5% use for agricultural information. With the disparity calls are made for awareness among farmers on the need and benefit of proper usage of mobile phone, and farmers knowing that mobile interventions are for agricultural extension services and increase in their income.

There is a growing usage of Information and communication technology (ICT) in rural Africa in the last three to four years [13]. The growth in ICT creates avenues for African farmers to upgrade their knowledge and livelihoods [14, 15]. According to the work carried out by [16], the level of usage of mobile phone, its usefulness and challenges was examined among the farmers in some rural part of Africa: At the end of this study, it was found out that 40% of farmers' phone bills were spent on farm activities while 17. 32% were spent on gaining more knowledge and marketing farm produce. In Mali and Burkina Faso, ICT usage for an agricultural extension has been resolved historically been from the top-down. [17]. Recently mobile phones have become an important tool for communications in rural Africa.

3   Related Works

Mobile gadgets provided an avenue for real-time interaction between several systems and people or other mobile devices. This interaction guarantees an efficient and timely manner of rendering and getting information; a major condition in an effective Mobile-Agriculture application. Several solutions have been deployed by several authors through the use of mobile phones. Abishek et al. [18] developed a mobile and web application that conveyed farm produces from the location to the final destination. The application enables farmers and consumers to do transaction on the farm products without middlemen. They revealed that the application will boost farmers' morale to be more committed to farming. Chen et al. [19] further developed a system that is portable and able to handle agricultural information with a high degree of versatility using mobile GIS. Their research outcome showed that the system can process information promptly and can capture the GPS coordinate of the farmland. Marimuthu et al. [20] introduced a persuasive technology method to orientate farmers about the advantages of technology-supported farming. The developed method consists of a website part and a mobile app part. The mobile app is connected to the website with enough facts on marketing and farming subsidiaries such as dairy, organic products, and farm machinery. Farmers were able to learn about crops, how to market their crops, how to market their products and by-products, and how to get support from field operations. Shirsath et al. [21] suggested a decision support system based on a smartphone app and data mining. The system enabled farmers to identify the best matching crop in farming hence, increasing the productivity of their fields and also increase the gross domestic product. Venkatesan et al. [22] on the other hand, proposed a framework for efficient organic farming using a mobile phone application with an in-built mobile module for automatic application of pesticide. While Castro et al. [23] focused on mobile application implementation that enables farmers to plant crops. A time-series moving average algorithm was used and assessed by agriculture professional, IT professionals, and the right consumers through the usage of ISO/IEC 9126 software engineering standard. Assessment outcome revealed that the model accomplished the major goals. Kerns and Lee [24] designed automatic software based on the Internet of Things technology that will help farmers with the increasing productivity in farming. The system consisted of a mobile application, a service platform, and IoT devices with sensors. [25] further developed an Android-based mobile application for the production and management of organic manures based on Intelligent Computer-Aided Instruction. The proposed system helps small and medium-scale farmers. Shikalgar [26] presented an advisory, information, and financial system deployed on a mobile platform for farmers. The system helped farmers to be aware of necessary pieces of information as regard government schemes and strategies. The system helped farmers to have access to timely advice and alerts on crops, and most recent and up-to-date information on government plans and strategies that have to do with agricultural domain were also accessible. In [27], a market space for marketing organic farm products was introduced leveraging automated geo-location services.

Considering the outcome of the related study, the mobile platform has shown a remarkable increase in its usage towards agriculture. This study thereby leverages on existing advantages in its mobile applications for organic farming, OrgFarMob, an extensions logical framework solution to agricultural extension farmers.

4 Design Methodology

The purpose of developing mobile app for agricultural extension services is to render applicable answers and outcome which is supported by pragmatic philosophy regarding its functionalities [28]. This has to do with a serial step of build and process method coined from design research aspect [29, 30] as opposed to design science research methodology strategy. The main focus of this research is on organic farming mobile. The process is initiated with inductive method to a clearer understanding of the nature of difficulty within the scope of agricultural extension services and a guide in collecting requirement [28, 30].

Before going into comprehensive narration of the proposed methodology, the steps taken in the build and process approach will be stated first. The building process was founded on the aspect of framework for computing research methods which is in accordance with the functional approach used in Holz et al. [30]. The area that is needed and relevant to this study is used. Consideration is given to the following:

4.1 Computing Research Framework

- What are things we stand to accomplish?

  a. (To seek for more knowledge) - the authors seek to gain more understanding in the aspect of adoption and application of ICT mobile development in organic farming in Nigeria and the whole world at large.

b. (Implement functional IT app) - the authors will start the development of a mobile app, orgfarMob, to provide information and resources on the cultivation of crops for organic farmers.

- What are sources of data needed?

c. (Study) - the authors will search literatures on organic farming and the adoption of ICT in agriculture.

d. (Pay attention to details, interview) - the authors will interact with organic farming practitioners Nigeria to seek for their view and equally gain more information from them.

e. (Design and Model) - the authors will develop the system using Model-View-controller architecture which will be integrated with cloud infrastructure while UML will be used to model the activities of the OrgFarMob actors using Use case diagram.

f. (Collection location) - the authors will source for and gather right information and design data from the field and conceptual analysis.

- What is the data collected use for?

g. (To discover old and new trends) - the researchers tend to use the gathered information for more understanding in organic farming and the adoption of ICT in organic farming.

h. (Create framework, prototype) - the authors will firstly design a logical architectural framework for orgfarmob extensions. After which, in iterative manner, the orgfarmob extensions application will be prototyped.

- Is the objective/goal of this study realized?

i. (Result evaluation, infer conclusion) - the authors, who by now, have better understanding of organic farming extension services and implemented functioning prototype, will be able to assess and iteratively modify the design and build (mobile app implementation).

j. (Fish-out limitations) - the writers will infer from the design and development method the limitations and/or how existing work can be extended or criticized.

Based on the guideline contained in the framework for computing research approach, this research work was executed using information gathered from organic farmers associations, and one-on-one interaction with the organic farmers.

The Unified Modelling Language (UML), Meta-model features are set up diagrammatically. Many diagrams can be used for a specific objective depending on the way one is looking at the system. The diverse ways of visualizing are referred to as "architectural views". These architectural views help in the organization of knowledge, and diagrams permit the communication of knowledge. Invariably, knowledge is embedded in the model or set of models which is concentrated on the problem and solution. Figure 1 showcase the architectural view of the study. The development model is mainly subdivided into two major divisions which are the mobile user platform and the remote infrastructure.

The remainder of this section gives a comprehensive detail of how the study was carried out. It involves six subsections namely data collection, architectural framework, Flow Chart of the Graphical User Interface, Sequential Logic of the Developed System, Use Case Diagram, and Logical Framework of Proposed System;

4.2 Data Collection

The data was obtained through the collection of materials from professionals in the field of organic agriculture, a review of organic farming practitioners in Nigeria and around the globe using the internet and one-on-one interaction with organic farming practitioners. Interview was conducted with the president of NOAN who lavishly supplied information on currently practiced organic farming practices in Nigeria. The information gathered from him actually form the basis and focus of this research. The mobile application developed was limited to the organic practices that are being adopted presently in Nigeria because the aim was to ensure wide adoption of the practiced organic principles. We also interacted with OAPTIN (Organic Agricultural Practitioner in Tertiary Institution in Nigeria,) to gather information from their experiences in the field. Each of their members specializes in production of one or two crops which they have been doing over the years. Sharing their experiences also helped us in realizing the goal of this research.

4.3 Architectural Framework

For optimum performance and the best user experience, the adopted architecture for the given mobile application is the Model-View-Controller architecture which was integrated with cloud infrastructure. This was modified to fit into standard mobile application framework. The proposed model is made up of two major subdivision namely the mobile user platform and the remote infrastructure.

The mobile user platform is made up of three sections namely the Presentation, Business, Data, and Data storage. The mobile user platform takes into account the configuration, security, and communications aspects which is the bedrock of the robustness of the mobile application. The presentation layers comprise of the user interface and the logic layer which is the tool for moving around the user interface m. This tier displays information related to best practices in the organic cultivation of the given crop and the e-extension forum interface majorly. It communicates with the other tiers by sending human gesture input and receiving data output from the other layers. The business logic layer is solely used for exchange of information between the user interface and project database. The concern of the structure of the mobile application is heavily placed here. It works out the inference of the user input involved with the application. The final stack of the three-layered architecture is the data access layer that is solely made up of database servers. The information update takes place here and the server communication concern also lies here.

4.4   Flowchart of the Graphical User Interface Citations

The GUI consists of three modules namely the Tutorials Module, E-Extension Module, and About Module. Users can learn about the organic cultivation of organic crops by querying the database. The overall system flowchart is shown in Fig. 1.

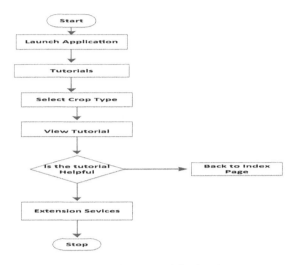

Fig. 1. Flowchart of Orgfamob

4.5   Sequential Logic of the Developed System

The sequential logic of the system developed shows the interaction between the users which are the organic farmers, the application, and the cloud infrastructure as depicted in Fig. 2. This shows the core features of the application which is mainly information dissemination and real-time connection with the professional extension service agents.

4.6   Use Case Diagram

Two main actors were identified in the organic agriculture extension services mobile application software. The actors are the user and the administrator. The use case model diagram indicates the functions of the actors identified as shown in Fig. 3.

System User
Application Interface
Cloud
Login
Select
Tutorials
Extensions
E
Extension
Sevices

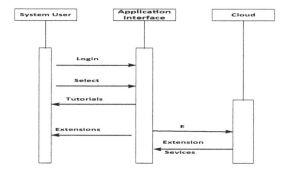

Fig. 2. Orgfamob sequence diagram

Sign up
Login/ Logout
Manage Profile
Tutorials
Extension Services
Update Tutorials

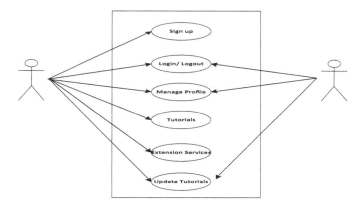

Fig. 3. Orgfamob use case diagram

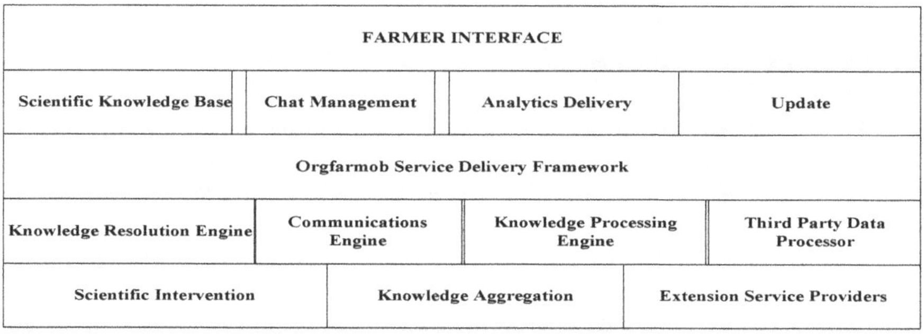

FARMER INTERFACE
Scientific Knowledge Base
Chat Management
Analytics Delivery
Update
Orgfarmob Service Delivery Framework
Knowledge Resolution Engine
Communications Engine
Knowledge Processing Engine
Third Party Data Processor
Scientific Intervention
Knowledge Aggregation
Extension Service Providers

Fig. 4. OrgFarMob extensions logical framework

4.7   Logical Framework and Infrastructure

The OrgFarMob extensions service delivery system is built over a multi-tier service delivery framework that provides stakeholders with the flexibility to scale up the services if required. This framework offers organic farmers a collaborative environment where they can access a wide range of services. The logical framework shown in Fig. 4, offers organic farmers a collaborative environment where they can access a wide range of services. The orgfarmob extensions service delivery system is built over a multi-tier service delivery framework that provides stakeholders with the flexibility to scale up the services when required. The programming language used for project work is AngularJS, NodeJS, and PHP. The database used is the MySqlLite which is the standard SQL engine for mobile devices. The cloud platform used is the azure engine. It is a very powerful and flexible platform that is robust. It is also a very secure platform which allows for privacy and confidentiality of message that is passed through this platform. The mobile-based application for organic agriculture extension services can run on android mobile phones.

5   Results and Discussion

The result of the stages involved in developing the mobile application are depicted in Fig. 5, 6, 7, 8 and 9. The index screen of the OrgFarMob E-extension is depicted in Fig. 5(a) and Fig. 6(b), and this indicates the user side which is the tutorials and the admin side of the e-extension services as elucidated from organic farmers and the association engaged.

Fig. 5. (a): Index screen

Fig. 6. (b): Lower part of the index screen

Fig. 7. Selection screen

From security and users experience (UX) viewpoint, all users must register to obtain their unique username and password, allowing for future predictive services and analytics. Figure 7 depicts the spinner which consists of the list of organic products where the user can select from based on their interest. Field run indicates that users were able to select from the spinner and Orgfamob generated results based on the chosen products as shown in Fig. 8 and 9; for Beans and for Cabbage.

Fig. 8. One of the tutorials page (for beans)   **Fig. 9.** A tutorials page (for cabbage)

The organic farmers were excited to discover that they can have an application that can serve as reminder of the practices they have learnt. The idea was applauded by OAPTIN and they promised to give support for publicity and visibility of the application. Already, we were invited to give talks on the mobile applications at farmers workshops; many were excited and continued to keep in touch.

6 Conclusion and Future Work

An organic farming mobile agricultural extension services (OrgFarMob) is presented here. The organic agriculture sector is of considerable economic importance, as well as providing a valuable and nutritious food source. However, many farmers interested in organic agriculture have little or no access to information regarding best practices. This leads to low performance of this agricultural sector which hinders the establishment of medium to large scale production especially in rural areas. With the introduction of the organic agriculture extensions services mobile application, farmers are now able to fully understand and produce organically certified crops in a sustained environment. This study has examined the feasibility of the mobile digitization of organic extension services and would help in the faster fostering of the transience of agriculture from harmful chemical-based farming to a healthier and more efficient organic-based farming scheme. For future recommendations, we intend to extend the service to all organic farmers in local languages.

Acknowledgments. The authors acknowledge the release of organic practices documents received from OAPTIN (Organic Agricultural Practitioner in Tertiary Institution in Nigeria). We appreciate the reviewers for their insightful feedback.

References

1. De Janvry, A.: 8 annex: agriculture for development–implications for agro-industries. In: Agro-industries for Development, pp. 252–270 (2009)
2. Perry, A.S., Yamamoto, I., Ishaaya, I., Perry, R.Y.: Insecticides in Agriculture and Environment: Retrospects and Prospects. Springer, Heidelberg (2013)
3. Backlund, P.: Effects of Climate Change on Agriculture, Land Resources, Water Resources, and Biodiversity in the United States. Diane Publishing, Darby (2009)
4. Günal, H., Korucu, T., Birkas, M., Özgöz, E., Halbac-Cotoara-Zamfir, R.: Threats to sustainability of soil functions in Central and Southeast Europe. Sustainability 7(2), 2161–2188 (2015)
5. Kanianska, R.: Agriculture and its impact on land-use, environment, and ecosystem services. In: Landscape Ecology-The Influences of Land Use and Anthropogenic Impacts of Landscape Creation, pp. 1–26 (2016)
6. Macauley, H., Ramadjita, T.: Cereal crops: rice, maize, millet, sorghum, wheat. Feeding Africa, p. 36 (2015)
7. Chhonker, S.M., Verma, D., Kumar Kar, A., Grover, P.: m-commerce technology adoption: thematic and citation analysis of scholarly research during (2008-2017). Bottom Line. 31, 208–233 (2018)
8. Mwangi, M., Kariuki, S.: Factors determining adoption of new agricultural technology by smallholder farmers in developing countries. J. Econ. Sustain. Dev. 6(5), 208–216 (2015)
9. Chhachhar, A.R., Hassan, Md.S.: The use of mobile phone among farmers for agriculture development. Int. J. Sci. Res. 2(6), 95–98 (2013)
10. Mittal, S., Mehar, M.: How mobile phones contribute to growth of small farmers? Evidence from India. Q. J. Int. Agric. 51(3), 227–244 (2012)
11. Khan, N.A., Qijie, G., Ali, S., Shahbaz, B., Shah, A.A.: Farmers' use of mobile phone for accessing agricultural information in Pakistan: a case of Punjab province. Ciência Rural, Santa Maria 49(10), 1–12 (2019)
12. Chhachhar, A.R., Qureshi, B., Khushk, G.M., Maher, Z.A.: Use of mobile phone among farmers for agriculture information. Eur. J. Sci. Res. 119(2), 265–271 (2014)
13. Sousa, F., Gian, N., Home, R.: Information technologies as a tool for agricultural extension and farmer-to-farmer exchange: mobile-phone video use in Mali. Int. J. Educ. Dev. Inf. Commun. Technol. 12(3), 19–36 (2016)
14. Mtega, W.P., Msungu, A.C.: Using information and communication technologies for enhancing the accessibility of agricultural information for improved agricultural production in Tanzania. EJISDC 56(1), 1–14 (2013)
15. Moyo, J.M., Bah, E.H.M., Verdier-Chouchane, A.: Transforming Africa's agriculture to improve competitiveness. The Africa Competitiveness Report, p. 37 (2015)
16. Ogbeide, O.A., Ele, I.: An analysis of mobile phone use in Nigeria agricultural development. Int. J. ICT Res. Africa Middle East 6(2), 1358–1377 (2017). https://doi.org/10.4018/978-1-5225-9621-9.ch061
17. Sousa, F., Nicolay, G., Home, R.: Video on mobile phones as an effective way to promote sustainable practices by facilitating innovation uptake in Mali. Int. J. Sustain. Dev. Res. 5(1), 1–8 (2019)

18. Abishek, A.G., Bharathwaj, M., Bhagyalakshmi, L.: Agriculture marketing using web and mobile based technologies. In: 2016 IEEE Technological Innovations in ICT for Agriculture and Rural Development (TIAR), pp. 41–44. IEEE (2016)

19. Chen, X., Zhao, J., Bi, J., Li, L.: Research of real-time agriculture information collection system base on mobile GIS. In: 2012 First International Conference on Agro-Geoinformatics (Agro-Geoinformatics), pp. 1–4. IEEE (2012)

20. Marimuthu, R., Alamelu, M., Suresh, A., Kanagaraj, S.: Design and development of a persuasive technology method to encourage smart farming. In: 2017 IEEE Region 10 Humanitarian Technology Conference (R10-HTC), pp. 165–169. IEEE (2017)

21. Shirsath, R., Khadke, N., More, D., Patil, P., Patil, H.: Agriculture decision support system using data mining. In: 2017 International Conference on Intelligent Computing and Control (I2C2), pp. 1–5. IEEE (2017)

22. Venkatesan, R., Kathrine, G.J.W., Ramalakshmi, K.: Internet of things based pest management using natural pesticides for small scale organic gardens. J. Comput. Theor. Nanosci. 15(9–10), 2742–2747 (2018)

23. Castro, P.J.M., Caliwag, J.A., Pagaduan, R.A., Arpia, J.M., Delmita, G.I.: A mobile application for organic farming assistance techniques using time-series algorithm. In: 2019 2nd International Conference on Information Science and Systems (2019)

24. Kerns, S.C., Lee, J.L.: Automated aeroponics system using IoT for smart farming. In: 8th International Scientific Forum, ISF, pp. 7–8 (2017)

25. Arogundade, O.T., Abayomi-Alli, A., Fatoye, I., Adejuyigbe, C.O., Olowe, V.I.O.: Development of an Android based mobile application for the production and management of organic manure (MoAPOM). J. Organ. Agric. Environ. 6 (2018)

26. Shikalgar, S., Kolhe, M., Bhalerao, N., Pansare, S., Laddha, S.: A cross platform mobile expert system for agriculture task scheduling. In: 2016 International Conference on Computing, Communication and Automation (ICCCA), pp. 835–840. IEEE (2016)

27. Arogundade, O.T., Abayomi-Alli, A., Adesemowo, K., Bamigbade, T., Odusami, M., Olowe, V.: An Intelligent Marketspace Mobile Application for Marketing Organic Products. In: Hattingh, M., Matthee, M., Smuts, H., Pappas, I., Dwivedi, Y.K., Mäntymäki, M. (eds.) I3E 2020. LNCS, vol. 12066, pp. 276–287. Springer, Cham (2020). https://doi.org/10.1007/978-3-030-44999-5_23

28. Saunders, M.N.K., Lewis, P., Thornhill, A.: Understanding research philosophy and approaches to theory development. In: Research Methods for Business Students, pp. 128–170. Pearson, Harlow (2019)

29. Amaral, J.N., et al.: About Computing Science Research Methodology, Edmonton (2011)

30. Holz, H.J., Applin, A., Haberman, B., Joyce, D., Purchase, H., Reed, C.: Research methods in computing. In: Working Group Reports on ITiCSE on Innovation & Technology in Computer Science Education - ITiCSE-WGR, p. 96. ACM Press, New York (2006)

The Impact of Personality Traits Towards the Intention to Adopt Mobile Learning

Nesa Nabipour Sanjebad[1]([✉]), Anup Shrestha[2], and Pezhman Shahid[1]

[1] University Technology Malaysia, Johour Bahru, Malaysia
nesanabipour@gmail.com
[2] University of Southern Queensland, Toowoomba, Australia

Abstract. Mobile devices have become increasingly more common in the digitally connected world. Mobile learning as a model of e-learning refers to the acquisition of knowledge & skills utilizing mobile technologies. The aim of this study is to identify the extrinsic influential factors for the adoption of mobile learning. This study proposes the use of an extended technology acceptance model (TAM) theory that includes variables of personality traits such as perceived enjoyment and computer self-efficiency. The participants of this study were 351 students at University Technology Malaysia who had experiences in e-learning. The study found that perceived usefulness as an extrinsic factor has the highest influence on students' intention to adopt mobile learning through an investigation of technology acceptance toward mobile learning. Personality traits such as perceived enjoyment and self-efficacy have impact on behavior intention to adopt mobile learning.

Keywords: Mobile learning · Adoption · Personality traits · e-learning · Perceived enjoyment · Self-efficacy

1 Introduction

Mobile devices have spread at an unprecedented rate in the past decade and 95% of the global population live in an area covered by a mobile-cellular network [1]. Mobile learning (m-learning) can be used to support students' learning in higher education settings [2], particularly significant in cases such as the COVID-19 pandemic. The integration of mobile technology into higher education has gained considerable attention [3]. Mobile devices, especially smart phones, are the most frequently used technological devices for daily routines. Reflecting this, they are being integrated into teaching [4]. M-learning as a dynamic learning environment makes use of the wireless mobile devices such as mobile phones, personal digital assistants (PDAs), iPads, and smart phones [5]. M-learning allows students to access course materials as well as learning activities at any location and in real time and to share ideas with others, and participate actively in a collaborative environment [6], thus overcoming the deficiencies of e-learning such as lack of human interaction and enthusiasm [7].

In order to engage digital generation in the learning process, interactive learning as part of m-learning is recommended in the higher education classroom [8]. However, the success or failure of m-learning implementation depends on learners' readiness to

© IFIP International Federation for Information Processing 2020
Published by Springer Nature Switzerland AG 2020
S. K. Sharma et al. (Eds.): TDIT 2020, IFIP AICT 618, pp. 182–193, 2020.
https://doi.org/10.1007/978-3-030-64861-9_17

embrace technology in their education [9]. To enrich studies on the m-learning discipline, the objective of this study is to identify the highest influential extrinsic factor that influence the m-learning adoption.

According to the Ambient Insight Comprehensive Report (2015), in Asia, Malaysia is ranked fifth highest for predicted m-learning growth rates for 2014 to 2019. In spite of this, m-learning in Malaysia is still in an emerging stage [10]. Most projects or studies continue to emphasize the notion of establishing foundational understanding of m-learning, and activities sustained by mobile technology [11, 12].

This study identifies factors that influence m-learning adoption based on technology acceptance model. An individual's intention to adopt m-learning may vary according to the perceived benefits and costs, but the factors that affect this adoption may also vary according to the usage behavior of technologies. Technology Acceptance Model (TAM) is one of the most widely used theories in studying the adoption of IT innovation and new information systems [13], thereby identifying extrinsic and intrinsic motivations on the individual's acceptance of different information technologies. Perceived enjoyment as an external variable can affect the adoption of a new technology phenomena like m-learning. Moreover, we determine the impact of personality traits such as self-efficacy on the intention to adopt m-learning. Specifically, the present study poses a research question: *What is the effect of personality traits on adoption of m-learning?*

2   Literature Review

2.1   Technology Acceptance Model (TAM)

Users' acceptance and adoption of technology has captured the attention of various scholars and became a principal field of study over the past few decades [14]. The need to explain the usage behavior of technologies and their determinants has prompted the development of a number of theoretical frameworks. A number of theories have been used in existing literature, and "adoption" is one of the more popular research areas in the Information Systems discipline [15]. Dominant theories in the technology adoption literature are Theory of Reasoned Action (TRA), Technology Acceptance Model (TAM), Theory of Planned Behavior (TPB), and Unified Theory of Acceptance and Use of Technology (UTAUT). Several studies have attempted to add more constructs to better explain adoption behavior over the years.

The findings from various research areas such as mobile commerce studies show that usage of TAM and UTAUT is the first priority of researchers to research on the understanding of user intentions [16]. Moreover, the associations between certain constructs such as ease of use, usefulness, attitude, and intention were found as the strongest determinants to identify user intentions. Likewise, the UTAUT model includes the individual dimension but it investigates the individual in term of experience, age, and gender. Personalities of students and lecturers are very different and there are many indicators for these behaviors. Therefore, personality traits can provide critical factors to explain the process of adoption. Figure 1 describes the utilization of technology adoption theories in the m-commerce literature. TAM has been used in the majority of studies (n = 87) in comparison with hybrid models or other theories in the literature [16].

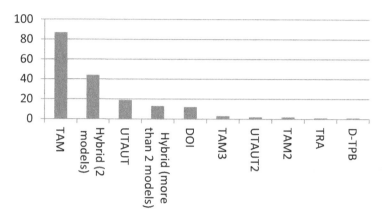

Fig. 1. Dominant theories in mobile commerce adoption [16]

The TAM explains how users come to accept and use technology. Noticeably the TAM has been adopted and expanded by including many factors of mobile internet or similar mobile systems (i.e. mobile commerce, mobile payment, mobile shopping). For example, in mobile payments, the service adoption, perceived usefulness, social influence, mobility and reachability are the key factors that affect adoption. TAM was adopted to analyze user satisfaction and intention to continually use m-wallets [17]. According to data collected from young users in India, perceived usefulness and perceived ease of use significantly affect user satisfaction [18]. Likewise, in order to validate the customers' adoption of mobile payments services in India [15], expanded TAM includes other external factors: perceived usefulness, trust, cost, and social-influence are used. Their statistical results largely approved the role of both perceived usefulness and ease of use in predicting customers' intention to adopt mobile internet commerce.

Another review study conducted on mobile commerce suggested TAM as the most popular technology acceptance frameworks used in research. This study reviewed 201 articles and adopted a systematic literature review to analyze and highlight the usage of technology adoption theories in mobile commerce [19].

The constructs of TAM: Perceived Ease of Use (PEOU) and Perceived Usefulness (PU) of the technology, are the two major outcomes of TAM. TAM with these variables can realize the benefits of positive adoption of the technology innovation. The degree to which a user thinks a new technology improves their performance called Perceived Usefulness. The degree to which a user thinks selecting a technology is simple and user-friendly is Perceived Ease of Use. The true behavioral intention to use findings affect real usage. Moreover, other constructs like perceived risk, perceived enjoyment, personal innovativeness, self-efficacy, trust, security, and perceived cost have been increasingly investigated. Hence this research has adopted the TAM model as one of the most widely used theories in studying the adoption of IT innovations.

Customers' personality characteristics attracted some attention from mobile internet studies as well. For example, self-efficacy as a personal trait was mentioned by a number of studies as a key predictor of the customer's perception and intention towards use of different kinds of mobile technology [13, 20].

2.1.1   Behavioral Intention

Behavioral Intention evaluates the strength of a user's commitment to perform a specific behavior and shows the intensity of an individual's intention to adopt a specific behavior. This factor has been widely used as an antecedent of user acceptance in various technology acceptance theories [3]. Extant studies on m-learning, like e-learning [21], and social networking sites [22] have integrated this factor to evaluate adoption and implementation of technology. Thus, this factor is regarded as a prime determinant in this research.

2.1.2   Perceived Usefulness

Perceived usefulness could be addressed as the functional and extrinsic benefits that are realized by using technologies [23]. Benefits could be related to the extent to which student perceive using mobile internet as being a more productive way of doing things, saving their time and effort in using services rather than employing traditional tools to access the same kind of services [3].

2.1.3   Perceived Ease of Use

The extent to which students perceive using a new system as being simple and not requiring too much effort usually shapes their willingness to adopt such a system [24]. Indeed, mobile internet could be considered as a new low-cost technology that will require that student have a certain level of experience and knowledge to use it both safely and efficiently. In the prior literature of mobile technology, there are a good number of studies that have approved the impact of the role of perceived ease of use on the student intention to adopt such technology [25].

2.2   Perceived Enjoyment

Perceived enjoyment is defined as the "degree to which the activity of using technology is perceived to be enjoyable in its own right apart from any performance consequences that may be anticipated". Prior studies have proposed that intrinsic motivators, such as perceived enjoyment [23]; can explain the Behavioral Intention to use information systems. The Perceived Usefulness has a significant effect on the intention for technology adoption and its influence was complemented by enjoyment. Therefore, "enjoyment" as an external variable can affect the adoption of a new technology as in m-learning.

2.3 Self-efficacy

Self-efficacy is an individual's belief in their ability to successfully perform the behaviors required to produce certain outcomes [26]. Self-efficacy as an index may measure an individual's self-confidence in utilizing innovation, and it is an important factor that affects high technology adoption [27]. Self-efficacy in a learning environment may positively affect learner's motivation, concentration, and learning effectiveness. Students with a higher level of self-efficacy tend to have more confidence in learning situations [20]. Moreover, self-efficacy has been found to have a positive effect on the intention to use web-based learning, and instructors with a high level of self-efficacy related to technology tend to prefer teaching that uses technology [20].

3 Hypotheses Development

This study focuses on the relationship between TAM and the two external factors related to personality traits. Therefore, we posit the following hypotheses:

Self-efficacy is the thought of a human being around their capacity for using and managing several actions that require designed types of performance. In this condition, the users that show higher intention to use mobile tools in educational processes are the users that have previously used mobile devices and have good experience about that [13].

H1: Self-efficacy has a Positive Effect on Perceived Ease of Use.

Extrinsic motivation is an example of Perceived Usefulness in the TAM model [28] One of the effective factors of usage behavior and intention in the TAM model is Perceived Usefulness.

H2: Perceived Ease of Use of m-learning has a Positive Effect on Perceived Usefulness.

M-learning systems are useful because of context-aware support that provides useful data to users all the time and from anywhere. Furthermore, these tools can develop and foster the relationship among students and lecturers.

H3: Perceived Usefulness of m-learning has a Positive Impact on Behavioral Intention to Use.

Perceived enjoyment based on the prior researches has a significant influence on behavioral intention to use computer systems [29]. It is predictable that perceived enjoyment can have a salient effect on behavioral intention. Personality traits might have a significant influence on perceived enjoyment and behavioral intentions.

H4: Perceived enjoyment is positively related to behavioral intention to use.

4   Research Methodology

4.1   Measurement

A survey questionnaire was designed as part of the quantitative research methodology. The questions were designed on a five-point Likert scale to evaluate the explanation coverage of each item. The scale included 1 to 5, where 1 = strongly disagree, 2 = disagree, 3 = neutral, 4 = agree and 5 = strongly agree. A major consideration in the survey tool design was to maintain its brevity with a focus on obtaining a sufficient response rate.

4.2   Data Collection and Sample Characteristics

This study collected data from undergraduate and postgraduate students of two faculties in University Technology Malaysia that used e-learning previously. Data were collected through structured questionnaires. According to Krejeie and Morgan [30] list method, 351 questionnaires were disseminated to the respondents.

We used descriptive statistics for assessing the demographic data of the respondents. Table 1 shows the general characteristics of the sample.

Table 1. General characteristics of the sample

Measure	Items (coding)	Ratio %
Gender	Male (1)	39%
	Female (2)	61%
Age	>25	28%
	25–34	57%
	<35	15%
Education level	Undergraduate	49%
	Postgraduate	51%
Faculty	Faculty of Health Science	68%
	Faculty of Biomedical engineering	32%
Type of devices	Smart phone	89%
	Tablet	11%

4.3   Data Analysis

The collected data were entered in SPSS V21 for data analysis. Different analyses were done in SPSS, such as descriptive analysis to demonstrate the respondents' attributes and properties, and regression analysis to obtain the relationship between relevant variables.

5 Results

5.1 Reliability and Validity

The reliability coefficient demonstrated whether the test designer was correct in expecting a certain collection of items to yield interpretable statements about individual differences [31]. The general agreed-upon lower limit for Cronbach's α is 0.70 [32]. Table 2 shows the correlations between total scores.

Table 2. Correlations between total scores

Scale items	No. of items	Corrected item-total Correlation
Perceived ease of use	4	0.636
Perceived usefulness	4	0.699
Behavior intention	4	0.522
Perceived enjoyment	3	0.521
Computer self-efficacy	4	0.673

For analyzing the basic structure for questions on the research survey and separately categorizing them into their respective scales, a principal component analysis with a varimax rotation method was performed. Table 3 shows factor loading for the rotated adoption factors.

Table 3. Factor loading for the rotated adoption factors

Factor	Scale item	Item loading	% of Variance explained	Cumulative percentages
Perceived enjoyment	PE1	0.854	57.048	57.048
	PE2	0.884		
	PE3	0.862		
Perceived ease of use	PEU1	0.902	16.114	73.162
	PEU2	0.90		
	PEU3	0.856		
	PEU4	0.625		
Perceived usefulness	PU1	0.769	12.016	85.178
	PU2	0.765		
	PU3	0.834		
	PU4	0.796		
Self-efficacy	SE1	0.904	8.666	93.844
	SE2	0.929		
	SE3	0.915		

(*continued*)

Table 3. (*continued*)

Factor	Scale item	Item loading	% of Variance explained	Cumulative percentages
	SE4	0.903		
Behavior intention	BI1	0.879	6.156	100.0
	BI2	0.891		
	BI3	0.890		
	BI4	0.889		

5.2 Regression Analysis

Linear regression was applied to calculate the values of the relationships between two variables. The linear regression matrix has built four parameters and R^2 as the coefficient of the correlation. The significance of the relationship was shown by the p-values, which should be equal or less than 0.05 for a significant relationship. The slope and the direction of the relationship are shown by the Beta (β) value. Table 4 shows the regression results of the hypotheses.

Table 4. Regression results of hypotheses

Construct	β	t	p	R^2	Result
PEU→PU	0.330	7.049	0.00	0.353	*H2* is supported
PU→BI	0.636	12.373	0.00	0.553	*H3* is supported
CS→PEU	0.414	12.373	0.00	0.365	*H1* is supported
PE→BI	0.402	6.739	0.00	0.340	*H4* is supported

From Table 4, we can determine that Perceived Ease of Use impacts Perceived Usefulness towards m-learning adoption. The highest value of R^2 shows that the relationship is strong. We found the Perceived Usefulness is the most influential factor, towards Behavior Intention to use m-learning. The hypothesis 2 (H2) was accepted because the relation between the variables are strongly sufficient. In this case hypothesis 3 (H3) was accepted because P = 0.000 and R^2 = 0.365 and β has a positive value (0.404) showing that the relationship is positive as it describes the direction. As can be seen that Self-Efficacy and Perceived Ease of Use are positively related. Hypothesis (H4) is accepted because the result shows a strong relationship between Perceived Enjoyment and Behavior Intention. Consequently, it can be resulted that Perceived Enjoyment is related to Behavior Intention in the m-learning adoption. Based on the accepted hypotheses, the research model has been presented in Fig. 2.

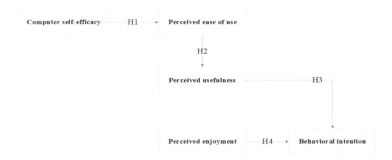

Fig. 2. Research model

6 Discussion and Implications

We empirically analyzed the effectiveness of personality traits factors in m-learning adoption in an educational context. M-learning adoption aims to help students to access course materials at any location and any time, which is highly relevant in the digital world, especially as the world is forced to undertake most tasks online during the Covid-19 pandemic. Secondly, we propose an extended TAM, which considers the inclusion of relevant additional variables from personality traits such as perceived enjoyment and self-efficacy. The results supporting the TAM [23] in the context of adoption, reinforce the critical role that perceived ease of use and usefulness have in creating students' acceptance of m-learning as a new technology [33]. Therefore, when the purpose of m-learning adoption is beyond the intrinsic motivation of simply "having fun", it appears that the impact of easiness and usefulness in users' attitudes should be considered. Although the literature recognizes that personality attracted some attention from mobile studies [13], to our knowledge, there is no research that simultaneously considers the personality trait variables of self-efficacy and perceived enjoyment, to better understand the individuals' level of adoption of m-learning. Third, the study suggests that the students' self-efficacy and perception of enjoyment revealed a strong positive influence on perceived ease of use on students' adoption of internet-based learning systems such as m-learning.

The empirical results provide noteworthy evidence for teachers wishing to adopt m-learning in their classrooms. The results of the study demonstrate how enjoyment, perceived ease of use and usefulness positively influence students' intention towards m-learning. Besides, the results indicate that the more exciting the m-learning can be for the students; the more likely it is that they will use it for effective learning. Although it is generally accepted that in mixed utilitarian–hedonic systems "time flies when you are having fun", instructors should be aware that students' time could also be spent significantly as they experience states of anxiety [30]. Therefore, enjoyment should be considered to include a level of learning challenge that is appropriate, i.e. the learning activities are not discouragingly hard or boringly easy. This is important since the student population of digital natives may be more heterogeneous than expected. Students may have different ability and capabilities to use computer and mobile for learning.

The obtained results suggest that the design of the m-learning platforms should consider not only the students' learning outcomes, but also the enjoyment component and self-efficacy that refer their ability must have a primordial role in these pedagogical endeavors for learning.

Our results also indicate that Self-Efficacy refers to the judgment of individuals about their capabilities to use information systems in diverse situations [33]. The result of analysis in this research shows a relationship between ability of students and Perceived Ease of Use. In addition, according to [34], Self-Efficacy revealed a strong positive influence on Perceived Ease of Use. On the other hand, most of the new University students (Gen Z students) have capability of using information technology so they will not be afraid easily and they show enormous persistence in the use of their mobile devices for majority of activities. In this regard, transition of learning on their mobile devices is expected to be more natural to new students rather than a transition from face-to-face learning.

Finally, it should be highlighted that instructors should pay attention to the students' personality in their education. Specifically, the results show that personality traits have impact on behavior intention. Two variables, perceived enjoyment and self-efficacy are extrinsic motivations that have an impact on behavior intention. In other words, through improving hedonic elements of the system, teachers can make significant impact on adoption m-learning. In addition, m-learning is found useful in the learning mode for individuals due to its learning flexibility. These findings support that perceptions of the usefulness of m-learning and that the perceived usefulness as an extrinsic factor has the highest influence on students' intention to adopt mobile. These results provide valuable insights for educators to formulate and design interesting interface and enjoyable content for m-learning environments. We conclude with a note that the design of future m-learning should encompass features which can deliver higher levels of satisfaction to the learners, as affirmed by the results of this research.

7   Limitations and Conclusion

This research is prone to several limitations. First, the actual use of m-learning was not incorporated in the proposed research model. Second, the causality among the constructs may not be readily inferred owing to the study's cross-sectional nature. Third, the investigation was based on the respondents' self-reported intention to use m-learning. Lastly, since the sampling locations were confined to two faculties of one university only, the findings could not be generalized across all University students and around the world. There could be situational factors such as education policies, learning culture and specific university procedures that may impact the adoption of m-learning. Nevertheless, we argue that there will be some impact of student personality traits on the adoption of m-learning, albeit the degree of impact may vary across different geographical areas.

Apart from considering behavioral intention, future scholars are encouraged to integrate the actual use of technology in the proposed model and adopt a longitudinal study to validate the cause-effect relationships. Furthermore, instead of relying on self-reported intention to use, actual usage of m-learning is recommended to be tracked and recorded to deliver insightful information on students' m-learning progress. Further studies are encouraged to broaden the sample size and involve an extensive range of public and private tertiary education institutions across the world.

References

1. Itu, L., Rapaka, S., Passerini, T., Georgescu, B., Schwemmer, C., Schoebinger, M., et al.: A machine-learning approach for computation of fractional flow reserve from coronary computed tomography. J. Appl. Physiol. **121**(1), 42–52 (2016)
2. Tzeng, N.-S., Chang, C.-W., Hsu, J.-Y., Chou, Y.-C., Chang, H.-A., Kao, Y.-C.: Caregiver burden for patients with dementia with or without hiring foreign health aides: a cross-sectional study in a northern taiwan memory clinic. J. Med. Sci. **35**(6), 239 (2015)
3. Almaiah, M.A., Jalil, M.A., Man, M.: Extending the TAM to examine the effects of quality features on mobile learning acceptance. J. Comput. Educ. **3**(4), 453–485 (2016). https://doi.org/10.1007/s40692-016-0074-1
4. Yurdagül, C., Öz, S.: Attitude towards mobile learning in english language education. Educ. Sci. **8**(3), 142 (2018)
5. Keengwe, J., Bhargava, M.: Mobile learning and integration of mobile technologies in education. Educ. Inf. Technol. **19**(4), 737–746 (2013). https://doi.org/10.1007/s10639-013-9250-3
6. Wicaksono, A.H.: The influence of mobile learning toward 10th graders' test score. In: ICLI 2018, p. 5 (2019)
7. Sabah, N.M.: Exploring students' awareness and perceptions: influencing factors and individual differences driving m-learning adoption. Comput. Hum. Behav. **65**, 522–533 (2016)
8. Watty, K., McKay, J., Ngo, L.: Innovators or inhibitors? Accounting faculty resistance to new educational technologies in higher education. J. Account. Educ. **36**, 1–15 (2016)
9. Mortby, M.E., Black, S.E., Gauthier, S., Miller, D., Porsteinsson, A., Smith, E.E., et al.: Dementia clinical trial implications of mild behavioral impairment. Int. Psychogeriatr. **30**(2), 171–175 (2018)
10. Ismail, I., Azizan, S.N., Gunasegaran, T.: Mobile learning in malaysian universities: are students ready? Int. J. Interact. Mob. Technol. (iJIM) **10**(3), 17–23 (2016)
11. Hussin, S., Manap, M.R., Amir, Z., Krish, P.: Mobile learning readiness among Malaysian students at higher learning institutes. Asian Soc. Sci. **8**(12), 276–283 (2012)
12. Curum, B., Khedo, K.K., (eds.): Improving user cognitive processes in mobile learning platforms through context-awareness. In: 2015 International Conference on Computing, Communication and Security (ICCCS). IEEE (2015)
13. Liu, H., Roeder, K., Wasserman, L., (eds.): Stability approach to regularization selection (stars) for high dimensional graphical models. In: Advances in Neural Information Processing Systems (2010)
14. Bayraktarov, E., Saunders, M.I., Abdullah, S., Mills, M., Beher, J., Possingham, H.P., et al.: The cost and feasibility of marine coastal restoration. Ecol. Appl. **26**(4), 1055–1074 (2016)
15. Kar, A.K.: What affects usage satisfaction in mobile payments? Modelling user generated content to develop the "digital service usage satisfaction model". Inf. Syst. Front. 1–21 (2020). https://doi.org/10.1007/s10796-020-10045-0
16. Chhonker, M.S., Verma, D., Kar, A.K., Grover, P.: m-commerce technology adoption. The Bottom Line (2018)

17. Grover, P., Kar, A.K.: User engagement for mobile payment service providers–introducing the social media engagement model. J. Retail. Consum. Serv. **53** (2020)
18. Kumar, A., Adlakaha, A., Mukherjee, K.: The effect of perceived security and grievance redressal on continuance intention to use M-wallets in a developing country. Int. J. Bank Mark. (2018)
19. Chhonker, M.S., Verma, D., Kar, A.K.: Review of technology adoption frameworks in mobile commerce. Procedia Comput. Sci. **122**, 888–895 (2017)
20. Chen, Y.-C., Kao, T.-H., Tseng, C.-Y., Chang, W.-T., Hsu, C.-L.: Methanolic extract of black garlic ameliorates diet-induced obesity via regulating adipogenesis, adipokine biosynthesis, and lipolysis. J. Funct. Foods **9**, 98–108 (2014)
21. Chang, C.-T., Hajiyev, J., Su, C.-R.: Examining the students' behavioral intention to use e-learning in Azerbaijan? The general extended technology acceptance model for e-learning approach. Comput. Educ. **111**, 128–143 (2017)
22. Chou, C.-H., Chang, N.-W., Shrestha, S., Hsu, S.-D., Lin, Y.-L., Lee, W.-H., et al.: miRTarBase 2016: updates to the experimentally validated miRNA-target interactions database. Nucleic Acids Res. **44**(D1), D239–D47 (2016)
23. Davis, S.G.: Parades and Power: Street Theatre in Nineteenth-Century Philadelphia. Temple University Press, Philadelphia (1986)
24. Shen, C., Ho, J., Kuo, T.-C., Luong, T.H., (eds.): Behavioral intention of using virtual reality in learning. In: Proceedings of the 26th International Conference on World Wide Web Companion (2017)
25. Luarn, P., Lin, H.-H.: Toward an understanding of the behavioral intention to use mobile banking. Comput. Hum. Behav. **21**(6), 873–891 (2005)
26. Furneaux, B., Wade, M.R.: An exploration of organizational level information systems discontinuance intentions. MIS Q. 573–598 (2011)
27. Kulviwat, S., Bruner, II G.C., Neelankavil, J.P.: Self-efficacy as an antecedent of cognition and affect in technology acceptance. J. Consum. Mark. (2014)
28. Asin, K.E., Davis, J.D., Bednarz, L.: Differential effects of serotonergic and catecholaminergic drugs on ingestive behavior. Psychopharmacology **109**(4), 415–421 (1992). https://doi.org/10.1007/BF02247717
29. Park, J.-S., Mo, Y.-G., Jeong, J.-K., Jeong, J.-H., Shin, H.-S., Lee, H.-J.: Thin film transistor and organic light-emitting display device having the thin film transistor. Google Patents (2008)
30. Van der Heijden, H., Verhagen, T., Creemers, M.: Understanding online purchase intentions: contributions from technology and trust perspectives. Eur. J. Inf. Syst. **12**(1), 41–48 (2003)
31. Klopfer, B., Kelley, D.M.: The Rorschach technique (1942)
32. Tippins, M.J., Sohi, R.S.: IT competency and firm performance: is organizational learning a missing link? Strateg. Manag. J. **24**(8), 745–761 (2003)
33. Hsu, C.-Y., Liang, J.-C., Chai, C.-S., Tsai, C.-C.: Exploring preschool teachers' technological pedagogical content knowledge of educational games. J. Educ. Comput. Res. **49**(4), 461–479 (2013)
34. Rana, K., Meshcheriakova, O., Kübler, J., Ernst, B., Karel, J., Hillebrand, R., et al.: Observation of topological Hall effect in Mn2RhSn films. New J. Phys. **18**(8), 085007 (2016)

Smart Cities and Digital Government

Impact of Disruptive Technologies on Smart Cities: Challenges and Benefits

Balasubramaniam Krishnan[1]([✉]) ⓘ, Seetharaman Arumugam[2] ⓘ, and Koilakuntla Maddulety[3] ⓘ

[1] SP Jain School of Global Management, Sydney Olympia Park, NSW 2127, Australia
balasubramaniam.dbl804005@spjain.org
[2] SP Jain School of Global Management, Hort Park, Singapore, Singapore
[3] SP Jain School of Global Management, Lower Parel, Mumbai, India

Abstract. The growing importance of leveraging disruptive technologies is gaining prominence, while digitalizing smart cities. This paper is grounded in theory of disruptive technologies and seeks to develop and empirically test a comprehensive framework to leverage key disruptive technologies namely Internet of Things (IoT), Autonomous Vehicles (AV), Artificial General Intelligence (AGI) and 5G Networks (5G) for smart cities. Further, it not only identifies key disruptive technologies and the challenges while implementing them but also the benefits that the smart cities could attain by leveraging these disruptive technologies. With systematic literature review of 700 articles and using Structural Equation modelling (SEM) technique, to analyse the data collected from a sample of 575 industry practitioners and scholars, the results provide an appropriate model to leverage identified the disruptive technologies for smart cities. This article further provides implications for researchers, theories that govern smart cities and industry practitioners, while leveraging disruptive technologies of smart cities.

Keywords: Disruptive technologies · Smart cities · Internet of Things · Artificial general intelligence · Autonomous vehicles · 5G networks

1 Introduction to Disruptive Technologies and Smart Cities

There is radical change in smart cities due to impact of disruptive technologies [28]. Further, the authors described that International organization for standardization (ISO) and the International Electrotechnical Commission (IEC) had recognized smart and sustainable city as the one which is able to meet the social, economic and environmental requirements; also help improve the efficiency of urban operations and quality of life. The importance of disruptive technologies have been underscored by stating contributions to plan the policy of smart cities [4]. Disruptive technology is defined as the one that has capability to change lives of the human, industry trends and other factors like communication and transportation [1]. Smart cities are defined as those that use digital technologies cohesively drive economic growth, to provide information, enhance welfare of the public and improve services of government. [14].

© IFIP International Federation for Information Processing 2020
Published by Springer Nature Switzerland AG 2020
S. K. Sharma et al. (Eds.): TDIT 2020, IFIP AICT 618, pp. 197–208, 2020.
https://doi.org/10.1007/978-3-030-64861-9_18

This definition by Gil-Garcia after researching over 200 scholarly publications is a benchmark definition of smart cities arrived at exhaustive study of literature and is adopted as the definition of smart cities for this research study.

2 Theories for Smart Cities and Disruptive Technologies

Leveraging disruptive technologies in smart cities, as we digitalise them so that urban planners, strategists, digital consultants, regulatory bodies and stakeholders incorporate them and leverage the opportunities to achieve holistic objectives of smart cities is essential. Many theories that govern smart cities namely theory of connecting networks and theory of urban systems, indicate the importance of enabling micro-instrumentation for smart cities to advance the theories governing smart cities and studying disruptive technologies that can enable this micro-instrumentation of the smart cities. In this study, theory of disruptive technologies defined by Prof. Clayton Christensen has been chosen as the theory, as it aims to explain establishment of disruptive technologies.

3 Literature Review Approach

The databases that were used for the literature review include EBSCO host Business Source Complete, ProQuest Business complete collection, Directory of Open Access Journals and Google Scholar, as they are considered to be the most wide-ranging databases for scholarly study in this field. Articles were selected only from peer-reviewed journals and conferences and date between 2014 and 2020 to ensure that we have considered the latest work, trends and technologies in this field. It is not only clear from [8] who mentioned that IoT, AV, AGI and 5G networks would function in an integrated fashion in the context of smart cities, but it can also be inferred from [34] that AV, IOT and AGI need 5G technologies' support to provide highly efficient services to smart cities. The scope of the study also included the success factors that affect the digitalization and disruptive technologies of smart cities, namely, sustainability, digital citizens and ecosystems to make it comprehensive. The following table (Table 1) provides details on systematic literature review conducted for the study.

Table 1. Nine phases of the systematic literature review

Stage wise representation of literature review
Step 1: Scanning for the literature through a search using keywords 'disruptive technologies' and 'smart cities' in the databases. Around 750 publications were identified (20.03.2020)
Step 2: Leveraging limiter texts in multiple fields like title, keyword and abstract, in order to ensure the relevance of articles. This reduced the number to 700 publications (25.03.2020)

(continued)

Table 1. (*continued*)

Stage wise representation of literature review
Step 3: Elimination of duplicates and non-English language papers
Step 4: Scanning of the abstracts of the remaining publications for selected independent constructs IoT, AV, AGI and 5G Networks disruptive technologies in development of smart cities
Step 5: Complete review of publications for selected independent variables of smart cities
Step 6: Screening of references of shortlisted publications to identify further publications on digitalisation of smart cities leveraging the selected disruptive technologies
Step 7: Inclusion of additional publications and books of researchers from the field of smart cities and disruptive technologies
Step 8: Identification of key findings and research gaps in articles short-listed for smart cities and disruptive technologies
Step 9: Identification of key findings and research gaps in disruptive technologies impacting smart cities

4   Internet of Things

IoT is considered as most important disruptive technology since it can augment life-style of humans and drastically alter the way in which digital citizen interact and consume the digital information [27]. The importance of Internet of things is re-iterated as one of the most promising disruptive technology [25]. Also in existing literature, factors affecting deployment of IoT technologies in smart cities is scarce.

4.1   Sub-variables of IoT

The literature review also focused on sub variables of disruptive technology IoT while studying challenges of its deployment and its impact on smart cities and are coded as IO1 to IO5. Interoperability (IO1): It is important to develop a software standard so that newly developed products across manufacturers will be connectable [22]. Collaborative IoT Architecture (IO2): Collaborative Internet of Things (IoT) architecture is required to test new data analysis methods [7]. Performance (IO3): Performance of the OAuth 2.0 protocol for authorization, in large IoT deployments should be evaluated [6]. Government IO4: Governments will need to collaborate closely with IoT providers to understand security risks [21]. Smart Engineering (IO5): It is important to model a smart engineering methodology that enables development of digital services [7]. Thus it needs to be investigated the impact of IoT on smart cities to enhance its policies, while it is leveraged as a disruptive technology leading to hypothesis (H1).

H1: Internet of Things (IoT), as a disruptive technology impact smart cities, leading to better policies.

5   Autonomous Vehicles

With autonomous vehicles, the smart cities are set to be revolutionized by autonomous vehicles and would replace current human driving activity for over a century [30]. The potential of autonomous vehicles as one of key disruptive technologies of smart cities and discusses about its tremendous opportunities and challenges [42].

5.1   Sub-variables of AV

The literature review also focused on sub variables of disruptive technology Autonomous vehicles, while studying challenges of its deployment and its impact on smart cities and are coded as AV1 to AV7. V2Control Networks (AV1): Communication between autonomous Vehicles to control Networks is important for content distribution of information [32]. Connected Cars (AV2): Adaptive solutions involving user preferences is required for content distribution in connected cars [9]. Protocols (AV3): Cross Layer approach involving infrastructure aspects is important to improve information-centric protocols in connected car applications [9]. Orchestration (AV4): It is important to further investigate orchestration of distributed autonomous systems [35]. Automotive OEMs (AV5): Automotive Original Equipment Manufacturers (OEMs) need to embrace identity as service providers [43]. Security (AV6): Autonomous vehicles and their mapping software need to be alert to the possibility of hacking [12]. High Reliable Network (AV7): High Reliable network provides opportunities for operating services and control functions for autonomous vehicles [29]. Therefore, it needs to be investigated, if Autonomous vehicles has significant impact on smart cities to reshape its mobility, while it is leveraged as a disruptive technology leading to hypothesis (H2).

H2: Autonomous Vehicles (AV) as a disruptive technology impact smart city, to reshape its mobility.

6   Artificial General Intelligence (AGI)

Artificial general intelligence as a disruptive technology that will help systems to operate independently on a specific problem domain and these guidelines would be used to integrate various systems that are able to perform it in an intellectual way similar to how human being is capable of executing a task and even beyond that [41].

6.1 Sub-variables of AGI

The literature review also focused on sub variables of disruptive technology AGI while studying challenges of its deployment and its impact on smart cities and are coded as AG1 to AG6. Robotic Systems (AG1): Robotic systems will be the main drivers of the digital transformation of the economy [40]. Human Effects – Methods (AG2) need to be developed to assess the human effects of Artificial intelligence (AI) [31]. Businesses (AG3) - Future development of AI will affect competition among businesses [26]. Learning engine (AG4) - Reliable data analytics process to explore properties of the available data is required to design the learning engine of Artificial General Intelligence systems [41]. Smart Environment (AG5): Technologies involved in the creation of smart environment (Space which can communicate digital data) requires attention [38]. Metasystem transition (AG6): Transition of metasystems (systems that monitor, model and process data from other systems) will lead to Artificial General Intelligence [33]. Thus it needs to be investigated if Artificial General Intelligence has a significant impact on smart cities, to enhance their economic opportunities, while it is leveraged as a disruptive technology leading to hypothesis (H3).

H3: Artificial General Intelligence (AGI), as a disruptive technology impacts smart cities, to enhance economic opportunities in smart cities.

7 5G Networks

5G has capability to create significant impact in multiple industries and how it will deliver AI based services; how it will spawn technology, business and operations based innovations for all sections of society [34]. However, the vision of 5G will not become a reality without robust security measures in context of smart cities [23].

7.1 Sub-variables of 5G

The literature review also focused on sub variables of disruptive technology 5G Networks while studying challenges of its deployment and its impact on smart cities and are coded as FG1 to FG8. Scalability (FG1): Scalable business models that can be adapted to business is important for 5G. Traffic Dynamicity (FG2): Predicting traffic dynamicity will enable 5G Network to increase resource utilization. Co-ordinated Multipoint (FG3): Co-ordinated Multipoint Access amongst multiple heterogeneous base stations is yet to be explored in 5G [5]. Energy Harvesting (FG4): Energy harvesting techniques exploiting green energy resources is yet to be explored in 5G [5]. Interference cancellation (FG5): Optimization of Interference Cancellation amongst cells in 5G is yet to be achieved [5]. Trust (FG6): Architectures to improve trust of the user is required in 5G networks. Commercial Implementation (FG7) - It is important to commercialize implementation of 5G Networks [17]. Security (FG8): Security measures are required to protect the privacy concerns of users in 5G network. [23]. Thus, it needs to be investigated if 5G networks has significant impact on smart cities to cater to the real time needs of society, while it is leveraged as a disruptive technology leading to hypothesis (H4).

H4: 5G networks (FG) as a disruptive technology impacts smart cities, to cater to their real time needs.

8 Benefits to Smart Cities

The literature review on benefits that the smart cities that are expected to gain by leveraging the identified disruptive technologies are listed below as outcome measures BE1 to BE7. Improving Quality of Life of Citizens (BE1) - Optimizing digital ecosystems can improve the quality of citizens' life in Smart Cities [2]. Enhancing Sustainability of Cities BE2: Seamless amalgamation of their core enabling technologies will help facilitate smart sustainable cities [39]. Participation of Digital Citizen (BE3): Digital citizens will have the opportunity to be involved in development of Smart cities [36]. Enhance policies (BE4): Open Innovation model will bridge the gap between IoT push and Smart Cities' policy pull leading to sustainable development [37]. Optimizing Urban Mobility (BE5): Autonomous vehicles shape urban mobility such that it contributes to sustainable smart cities [16]. Address Real time capability needs (BE6): Deployment of 5G communication networks will address real-time capability needs of smart cities [24]. Better Economic Opportunities (BE7): Digitalization of Smart Cities with disruptive technologies will lead to optimal positioning of businesses within the ecosystem to benefit from economic opportunities [20].

9 Research Methodology

We have chosen questionnaire survey as a research method using web-based data collection instruments using likert scale. Qualitative research is leveraged as a method of exploratory research to arrive at quantitative research hypotheses later [11].

9.1 Qualitative Research

We have used qualitative research for mining the existing literature and research gaps, as the research is about Impact of disruptive technologies on smart cities and it is a socio-technical subject. The literature review of 700 articles helped to understand the key independent variables that identify impact of disruptive technologies without attempting to look at inter-relationship. The research gaps identified were further verified and pilot tested with R-square value of 0.711 involving 12 industry experts, validating the questionnaire and research hypothesis. The pilot study provided insights to fine tune the questionnaire and received appreciations. The responses were obtained with informed consent to manage privacy and anonymity of the data collected in compliance with ethical considerations.

9.2 Quantitative Research

Quantitative research is leveraged to test the hypothesis arrived at from the theory and able to deduce the size of phenomenon of interest. It uses mathematics and statistics to report findings of research. In the study, the Structural equation modelling (SEM) is used to study structural relationships. It is used in our study to analyse the structural relationship between latent constructs and measured variables of smart cities. The strategy of using SEM permits various measures to be associated with one latent construct. SEM is also ideal when testing theories that include latent variables.

Survey strategy was used through questionnaires to address various research gaps in the study. The research questionnaire was administered to 575 participants using convenience sampling. In this study, the stakeholders of smart cities were selected as respondents as respondents were either users, industry practitioners or research scholars involved in digitalization (or) smart cities (or) disruptive technologies. The role of the respondents in smart city was categorized as a) User b) Touch base with Smart City service flow c) Observer d) Implementer e) Developing software/hardware for smart city development. 60% of the respondents were from top and senior management, 28% of respondents were from middle management, while junior management and others contributed 10% of respondents. In terms of demography, around 59% respondents were from Asia Pacific region, 18% of responses were from Americas, around 15% UK & Europe geographies and around 8% of respondents were from Africa and Middle East. The data obtained through survey strategy was analysed using structural equation modelling. The conceptual framework of the research framework is given below in Fig. 1.

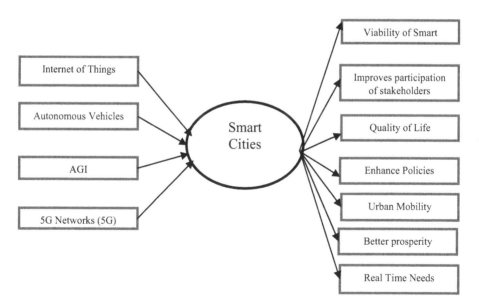

Fig. 1. Conceptual model of research framework

10 Results and Analyses

The results were analyzed using ADANCO 2.0.1 software and the highlights of results are provided below. Examining the reliability of the constructs and discriminant validity of the construct is the first step to represent each construct [3]. These results are shown in Table 2.

10.1 Construct Reliability

The reliability of scale can assessed by Cronbach's alpha and Jöreskog's rho. In Structural Equation Modelling (SEM) Jöreskog's rho is a better reliability measure than Cronbach's alpha, since Jöreskog's rho is calculated on the loadings rather than the correlations between the observed variables [10]. Jöreskog's rho required for validity of construct is greater than 0.7 [13]. In our model, value of Jöreskog's rho of all constructs are above 0.84 which demonstrates the validity of constructs. The minimum threshold value of Cronbach's alpha is also 0.7 and we observe that all our constructs are above 0.7. The reliability coefficient Dijkstra-Henseler's rho (ρA) need to be above 0.70 in case of exploratory research and above 0.80 for more advanced stages of research [15]. The constructs identified in the study satisfy Dijkstra-Henseler's rho's values as well [18].

10.2 Discriminant Validity

The factor of discriminant validity is evaluated in two steps using Fornell and Larcker criterion. It is leveraged to validate if the square root of construct's Average variance Extracted (AVE) is higher than correlations between any other construct within the model and itself. Secondly, the factor loading of an item on its associated construct should be greater than the loading of another non-construct item [19]. The measurement model in the study displayed good discriminant validity and the Fornell and Larcker criterion is met.

10.3 Goodness of Fit and Convergent Validity

The model established SRMR (Standardized Root Mean Square Residual) values of 0.0518 (saturated model) and 0.0796 (estimated model). A value of less than 0.08 for SRMR values is recommended and hence the model has good fitness of fit. The convergent validity is measured by Average Variance Extracted (AVE). The independent variables of the model have indicated a score of more than 0.5 indicating convergent validity and uni-dimensionality.

10.4 Multi-collinearity

The model has also displayed lower degree of multi-collinearity amongst all sub variables and is measured through variance inflation factor (VIF) as per ADANCO user manual. All the sub-variables of model have VIF values of less than 2.2386 which is well below value of 10 and proves lower degree of multi-collinearity. The summary of hypothesis results arrived at through literature review are provided below:

H1: Internet of Things (IoT) as disruptive technology impact smart cities, leading to better policies.

H2: Autonomous Vehicles (AV) as a disruptive technology impact smart city, to reshape its mobility.

H3: Artificial General Intelligence (AGI), as a disruptive technology impacts smart cities, to enhance economic opportunities in smart cities.

H4: 5G networks (5G) as a disruptive technology impacts smart cities, to cater to their real time needs.

Table 2. Results of hypotheses from SEM technique

Hypotheses	Representation of relationships	Path loadings	t-value	p-value (2-sided)	Results
H1	IO -> BE	0.4076	7.7381	0.0000	Accepted
H2	AV -> BE	0.3098	6.6928	0.0000	Accepted
H3	AG -> BE	0.4036	8.8371	0.0000	Accepted
H4	FG -> BE	0.1685	3.7633	0.0002	Accepted

From total effect perspective, all hypothesis have been proven such that all the dependant variables identified from literature review, have significant impact while digitalizing Smart Cities leveraging disruptive technologies as we have seen higher t-values to the associated hypothesis. Further we see that all p-values on the above Table 2 have a value of lesser than 0.02 and all our hypotheses are accepted. The Co-efficient of determination (R-Square Value) of the model is 0.6736 proving the structural validity of the model. Hence, we can conclude as follows for each of the hypothesis after analysis.

- Internet of Things (IoT), as a disruptive technology very significantly impacts smart cities leading to better policies.
- Autonomous Vehicles (AV), as a disruptive technology very significantly impacts smart cities, to reshape its mobility.
- Artificial General Intelligence (AGI), as a disruptive technology very significantly impacts smart cities to enhance economic opportunities in smart cities.
- 5G networks (5G), as a disruptive technology very significantly impacts smart cities to cater to their real time needs.

From the analysis of results, the values of loadings of outcome variables for Smart Cities (BE) are above 0.69. The values of loadings of all sub variables for AV are above 0.67. The values of loadings of all sub variables for AG, IoT and 5G are above 0.69.

11   Conclusion

The total effects from the study indicate that it is more important to focus on disruptive technologies IoT (0.4076) and Artificial General Intelligence (0.4036) amongst the set of chosen four disruptive technologies, as they seem to have higher impact on smart cities and help to achieve its objectives. It is to be highlighted that IoT is well positioned as a disruptive technology and that it is set to become ubiquitous and its key characteristic is that it helps merge the digital and physical world [44]. They are followed by Autonomous Vehicles (0.3098) and 5G networks (0.1685) in this study. It is also clear that while disruptive technologies like IoT, AGI, AV and 5G Networks can be utilized for smart cities to enable micro instrumentation, it is required to consider the factors of leveraging ecosystems, digital citizen and sustainability. These initiatives can have a broader transdisciplinary impact to truly impact on smart cities and thus it contributes to theory of disruptive technologies as the study identifies disruptive technologies in the context of smart cites. From theoretical perspective, it is clear that it also contributes to theory of connecting networks, theory of urban systems and evolving urban systems in terms of suggestion of deployment of combination of disruptive technologies that are to be targeted for smart cities as this enables micro instrumentation needed for smart cities. The limitation of this research is that it has focused on identified four disruptive technologies. The study also provided some insights to practitioners of technology of smart cities such as IoT practitioners to consider inter-operability with both IoT systems under open connectivity foundations and those that are not under open connectivity.

References

1. Ab Rahman, A., Hamid, U.Z.A., Chin, T.A.: Emerging technologies with disruptive effects: a review. Perintis e-J. **7**(2), 111–128 (2017)
2. Abella, A., Ortiz-De-Urbina-Criado, M., De-Pablos-Heredero, C.: A model for the analysis of data-driven innovation and value generation in smart cities' ecosystems. Cities **64**, 47–53 (2017)
3. Agag, G., El-Masry, A.A.: Understanding consumer intention to participate in online travel community and effects on consumer intention to purchase travel online and WOM: an integration of innovation diffusion theory and TAM with trust". Comput. Hum. Behav. **60**, 97–111 (2016)
4. Ahmadian, E., Byrd, H., Sodagar, B., Matthewman, S., Kenney, C., Mills, G.: Energy and the form of cities: the counterintuitive impact of disruptive technologies. Archit. Sci. Rev. **62**(2), 145–151 (2019)
5. Alnoman, A., Anpalagan, A.: Towards the fulfilment of 5G network requirements: technologies and challenges. Telecommun. Syst. **65**(1), 101–116 (2017). https://doi.org/10.1007/s11235-016-0216-9
6. Alonso, A., Fernandez, F., Marco, L. and Salvachúa, J. IAACaaS: IoT application-scoped access control as a service, Future Internet, **9**(4), 64, 322–324 (2017)
7. Belkacem, I., Nait-Bahloul, S., Sauveron, D.: Enhancing dependability through profiling in the collaborative internet of things. Multimed. Tools Appl. **78**(3), 2983–3007 (2017). https://doi.org/10.1007/s11042-017-5431-1
8. Clark, J.: From theory to practice: what policies can prepare regions for the challenges and opportunities associated with disruptive technologies? In: Background Paper for an OECD/EC Workshop on, vol. 22 (2018)
9. Coutinho, R.W., Boukerche, A., Loureiro, A.A.: Design guidelines for information-centric connected and autonomous vehicles. IEEE Commun. Mag. **56**(10), 85–91 (2018)

10. Demo, G., Neiva, E.R., Nunes, I., Rozzett, K.: Human resources management policies and practices scale (HRMPPS): exploratory and confirmatory factor analysis. BAR-Braz. Adm. Rev. **9**(4), 395–420 (2012)
11. Djari, A.J.: The relationship between marketing mix towards consumer purchasing decision of pro plan (A case study at pekayon petshop Bekasi), Doctoral dissertation. President University, Indonesia (2011)
12. Edwards, C.: Digitizing the world. Commun. ACM **60**(4), 15–16 (2017)
13. Ghouri, A.M., Kin, T.M., bin Yeop Yunus, N.K., Akhtar, P.: The dataset for validation of customer inspiration construct in Malaysian context. Data in Brief, **25**, 104131 (2019)
14. Gil-Garcia, J.R., Pardo, T.A., Nam, T.: What makes a city smart? Identifying core components and proposing an integrative and comprehensive conceptualization. Inf. Pol. **20** (1), 61–87 (2015)
15. Hair, J.F., Ringle, C.M., Sarstedt, M.: PLS-SEM: indeed a silver bullet. J. Mark. Theory Pract. **19**(2), 139–152 (2011)
16. Hand, A.Z.: Redefining urban mobility: four ways shared autonomous vehicles will reshape our cities. Real Estate Issues, 49–52 (2017)
17. Hemilä, J., Salmelin, J.: Business model innovations for 5g deployment in smart cities. In: ISPIM Conference Proceedings. The International Society for Professional Innovation Management (ISPIM), pp. 1–7 (2017)
18. Henseler, J., Dijikstra, T.K.: Adanco 2.0, p. 28. Composite Modeling GmbH & Co., Kleve (2015)
19. Human, G., Naudé, P.: Heterogeneity in the quality–satisfaction–loyalty framework. Ind. Mark. Manag. **43**(6), 920–928 (2014)
20. Iivari, M.M., Ahokangas, P., Komi, M., Tihinen, M., Valtanen, K.: Toward ecosystemic business models in the context of industrial internet. J. Bus. Models **4**(2), 42–59 (2016)
21. Jadhav, V., Kumar, K.N., Alias Rana, P.D., Seetharaman, A., Kalia, S., Maddulety, K.: Understanding the correlation among factors of cyber system's security for internet of things (IoT) in smart cities. J. Account. Bus. Manag. **24**(2), 1–15 (2017)
22. Jesús Mario, V.C., Papinniemi, J., Hannola, L., Donoghue, I.: Developing smart services by internet of things in manufacturing business. LogForum **14**(1), 59–71 (2018)
23. Latif, S., Qadir, J., Farooq, S., Muhammad, A.I.: How 5G wireless (and concomitant technologies) will revolutionize healthcare. Future Internet **9**(4), 93–117 (2017)
24. Lea, R.J.: Smart cities: an overview of the technology trends driving smart cities (2017)
25. Lopes, N.V., Dhaou, S.B.: Public service delivery framework: case of Canada, China and Estonia. In: Proceedings of the 11th International Conference on Theory and Practice of Electronic Governance, pp. 101–110 (2018)
26. Makridakis, S.: Forecasting the impact of artificial intelligence (AI), Part 2 of 4: examining four scenarios of possibility. Foresight: Int. J. Appl. Forecast. **48**, 7–12 (2018)
27. Minovski, D.: Research challenges in connecting internet of things for pervasive and mobile computing. Study Report, Luleå University of Technology (2017)
28. Moustaka, V., Vakali, A., Anthopoulos, L.: A systematic review for smart city data analytics. ACM Comput. Surv. **51**(5), 1–41 (2019)
29. Normann, O.S.: Importance of human influence in systems engineering-implications for autonomous vehicles. Master's thesis, NTNU (2018)
30. Nikitas, A., Kougias, I., Alyavina, E., Njoya Tchouamou, E.: How can autonomous and connected vehicles, electromobility, BRT, hyperloop, shared use mobility and mobility-as-a-service shape transport futures for the context of smart cities? Urban Sci. **1**(4), 36, 1–21 (2017)
31. Oliveira, E.: Beneficial AI: the next battlefield. J. Innov. Manag. **5**(4), 6–17 (2017)

32. Pakusch, C., Stevens, G., Bossauer, P.: Shared autonomous vehicles: potentials for a sustainable mobility and risks of unintended effects. In: ICT4S2018, 5th International Conference on Information and Communication Technology for Sustainability (2018)

33. Potapov, A.: Technological singularity: what do we really know? Information, **9**(4), 82, 1–9 (2018)

34. Quinn, L.: The Evolving 5G Landscape. In: McClellan, S. (ed.) Smart Cities in Application, pp. 121–139. Springer, Cham (2020). https://doi.org/10.1007/978-3-030-19396-6_7

35. Schaeffer-filho, A., Lupu, E., Sloman, M.: Federating policy-driven autonomous systems: Interaction specification and management patterns. J. Netw. Syst. Manag. **23**(3), 753–793 (2015). https://doi.org/10.1007/s10922-014-9317-5

36. Scholten, H.: Geocraft as a means to support the development of smart cities, getting the people of the place involved - youth included. Qual. Innov. Prosper. **21**(1), 119–150 (2017)

37. Scuotto, V., Ferraris, A., Bresciani, S.: Internet of things. Bus. Process Manag. J. **22**(2), 357–367 (2016)

38. Sehrawat, D., Gill, N.S.: Emerging trends and future computing technologies: a vision for smart environment. Int. J. Adv. Res. Comput. Sci. **9**(2), 839 (2018)

39. Simon, E.B., Krogstie, J.: The core enabling technologies of big data analytics and context-aware computing for smart sustainable cities: a review and synthesis. J. Big Data **4**(1), 1–50 (2017). https://doi.org/10.1186/s40537-017-0091-6

40. Sokolov, I., Misharin, A., Kupriyanovsky, V., Pokusaev, O., Kupriyanovsky, Y.: Robots, autonomous robotic systems, artificial intelligence and the transformation of the market of transport and logistics services in the digitalisation of the economy. Int. J. Open Inf. Technol. **6**(4), 92–108 (2018)

41. Soviany, C.: The benefits of using artificial intelligence in payment fraud detection: a case study. J. Paym. Strategy Syst. **12**(2), 102–110 (2018)

42. Tan, X., Leon-Garcia, A.: Autonomous mobility and energy service management in future smart cities: an overview. In: 2018 4th International Conference on Universal Village (UV), pp. 1–6. IEEE (2018)

43. Viereckl, R., Ahlemann, D., Koster, A., Jursch, S.: Racing ahead with autonomous cars and digital innovation. Auto Tech Rev. **4**(12), 18–23 (2015). https://doi.org/10.1365/s40112-015-1049-8

44. Zdravković, M., Zdravković, J., Aubry, A., Moalla, N., Guedria, W., Sarraipa, J.: Domain framework for implementation of open IoT ecosystems. Int. J. Prod. Res. **56**(7), 2552–2569 (2018)

Developing Indian Smart Cities: Insights from Social Media

Naganna Chetty[(⊠)] and Sreejith Alathur

National Institute of Technology Karnataka, Surathkal, Mangalore, India
nsc.chetty@gmail.com, sreejith.nitk@gmail.com

Abstract. Smart cities play an important role in overall development of a nation by progressing with economic, environmental and social domains. India has projected to create 100 smart cities in near future. The purpose of the paper is to identify the key influencing components and the social media users' expectations for smart cities development in India. The Twitter social media content of smart cities council and the user posts on smart cities are collected through Twitter application programming interface. The collected tweets are cleaned by pre-processing methods and analyzed for insights. Technology, infrastructure, innovation, transport, mobility and management are the key influencing components for smart cities development in India. The social media users are expecting to emphasize on combating the issues like Covid-19 and use of IoT technology for the success of smart cities project. The integration of different components could increase the success of the project. The analysis of the content shared by the groups (smart cities council and the social media users) which are at different sides of smart cities' development project, increases the novelty of the study.

Keywords: Smart cities · Urbanization · Social media · Twitter · India

1 Introduction

Smart cities try to attain different objectives such as economic, environmental and societal for overall development of the nation. Therefore, countries across the globe are transforming their cities into smart cities. The population in cities exceeds the 50% of the world population (Falconer and Mitchell 2012). With increased population, the administration of the cities for providing necessary services to public could be difficult. The administrative difficulties of the cities can be reduced by adopting information and communications technology (ICT). The cities which uses ICT for public service are referred as smart cities (Bakıcı et al. 2013; Falconer and Mitchell 2012). The usage of ICT may improve the economic, environmental and social conditions of a country. The Internet of things (IoT) can be used to connect different components of a city to provide smart services (Zanella et al. 2014).

The concept behind the smart city is to mitigate the problems of increased urban population (Chourabi et al. 2012). The urban development of a nation is multifaceted and depends on infrastructure (physical capital), knowledge associated with the people (human capital) and societal relations (social capital) (Caragliu et al. 2011).

© IFIP International Federation for Information Processing 2020
Published by Springer Nature Switzerland AG 2020
S. K. Sharma et al. (Eds.): TDIT 2020, IFIP AICT 618, pp. 209–218, 2020.
https://doi.org/10.1007/978-3-030-64861-9_19

Collectively, all these capitals can improve the economic condition of a country. Overall, the smart cities administration should try to meet changing expectations of people.

The Indian government is working towards the creation of 100 smart cities in near future (Chatterjee et al. 2018a). Smart cities council India is a team which keeps updating the developments related to smart cities in India. Indian smart cities working concept is based on three core values such as livability, workability and sustainability. The Kanpur city administration has established a tool based on artificial intelligence to monitor activities in the city during the lockdown (SCC India Staff 2020a). The Europe's infrastructure development company A & M has announced to initiate the activities towards smart cities and low-cost housing in India (SCC India Staff 2020b).

With this information, the study aims to identify the key influencing components and the social media users' expectations for smart cities development in India. The rest of the paper is structured as follows. In Sect. 2, the brief literature review on smart cities is made. Section 3 outlines the methodology adopted in the study. The results of the analysis are presented in Sect. 4. Section 5 interprets and discusses the results. In the end, Sect. 6 concludes the work.

2   Literature Review

Cities do not have sufficient budget for developmental activities and other services. The application of smart city concept increases cost consciousness and competency level of cities while reducing complexity of the functions to be performed (Anttiroiko et al. 2014). Sometimes, to solve a problem, we need to be at higher level than the level in which the problem originated. The limited technology may not solve the problem of urbanisation, so needs to be go beyond and adopt full pledged technology solution (Goodspeed 2015). The city environment condition can be improved by implementing wireless sensor networks at different locations in the city (Jamil et al. 2015). Domain-wise select researches on smart cities are presented in Table 1.

Table 1. Domain-wise research on smart cities

Authors/year	Purpose/development domain	Remarks
Angelidou 2015; Anttiroiko et al. 2014	To improve economic status of smart cities	Smart city development needs smart solutions as well as smart service platforms Smart city development needs four forces such as urban future, innovation economy, technology push and demand pull
Jamil et al. 2015; Mitton et al. 2012	To improve environmental status of smart cities	A system to monitor and control air pollution in the environment A design to provide interaction between the services and the environment
Anttiroiko et al. 2014; Bibri and Krogstie 2017	To improve societal status of smart cities	Smart cities can shape socio-cultural practices in the society

The Indian smart city project is initiated in 2015 with an aim to meet infrastructural requirements of growing population (Wray 2020). Apart from the IT infrastructure, the success of smart city mission depends on multiple factors. The human factors such as skills of IT staff and participation of citizens to use IT services are important to consider for the success of Indian smart cities project (Chatterjee et al. 2018b). Some of the select researches on smart cities in Indian context are summarized in Table 2.

Table 2. Smart cities research in India

Authors/year	Purpose	Methodology	Result
Anand et al. 2017	To identify sustainability indicators for smart cities	Experts' views are collected and analysed with fuzzy, analytical hierarchy process	Economic and energy development policies are important for the growth of a nation
Praharaj et al. 2018	To identify the issues associated with the complex planning for smart cities	A case study is conducted with smart city and local body plans	Lack of integration, conflicts with master plans and neglecting local governance bodies are drawbacks of smart city planning
Chatterjee and Kar 2018	To understand the effects of IT services in smart cities	Data is collected using questionnaire and analysed with statistical tools	There are social/technological effects and security/safety threats
Chatterjee et al. 2018a	To identify factors which influences information system adaptation in Indian smart cities	Data is collected using questionnaire and analysed with statistical tools	The use of IoT is influenced by its benefits and the quality of information being accessed
Jawaid and Khan 2015	To evaluate need of smart city projects	Census data is analysed	There is rapid urbanization but lack of basic services such as infrastructure

The review shows that like the efforts of government, the research is also active towards the smart cities' development in India. To support smart cities project, the researchers are trying to identify the challenges and possible solutions using quantitative as well as qualitative studies.

3   Methodology

Methodology is a three-phase activity. First, the Twitter developer account is created and login credentials are authenticated. The Twitter social media content of smart cities council, India and the user posts on smart cities are collected through Twitter application programming interface. To collect data from smart cities council, the Twitter handle "SmartCitiesIn" is used with the userTimeline function in R. This function returned 464 tweets, which are posted by smart cities council in a timeline from 2017 to 2020. Further, to collect opinions of social media users about smart cities development in India, the Twitter is queried with the keywords set "smart cities". This search/query returned 2,791 tweets for the duration of about a week.

Second, after collecting the tweets, the pre-processing approach is applied to clean both the datasets. Pre-processing is done with the help of functions in R such as tolower (), removePunctuation(), removeNumbers(), stripWhiteSpace() and removeWords(). The outcome of pre-processing is the set of tweets without upper case letters, punctuations, numbers, whitespaces and stop words.

Third, both the data sets are combined together to form a single dataset. This combined dataset is analysed and evaluated for common and dissimilar words. The common words are represented by wordcloud and a pyramid graph and the dissimilar words by a wordcloud. Further, to draw the insights from opinions of social media users, the emphasis is made on users' posts dataset analysis. The users' posts are analysed for association among the words and represented through table and a graph. Finally, the resulted are interpreted for inference.

4   Results

The common similar words which are expressed by smart cities council and the general social media users about the development of smart cities in India are shown as wordcloud in Fig. 1. The words smart, city and cities are used most of the times during the sharing of information about the smart cities' development. Other developmental components such ad technology, infrastructure and transport are highlighted during the discussion over social media.

The most common dissimilar words from both the information sharing groups are shown in Fig. 2. The words expressed by smart cities council are shown with orange colour and the words by social media users are shown with blue colour. Urbanation is a very common and dissimilar word in the tweets shared by smart cities council. Similarly, cities is a common and dissimilar word in the tweets shared by social media users.

Figure 3 shows the common words and their frequency of occurrence in each information sharing group as a pyramid. The most frequent words are located at the bottom of the pyramid. The left-hand side of the Fig. 3 shows the frequency of words in smart cities council's posts and the right-hand side shows the frequency of words in social media users posts.

Fig. 1. Wordcloud of common similar words

Fig. 2. Wordcloud of common dissimilar words

After analyzing the tweets combinedly, the social media users' posts are analyzed for association among the words. The adjacency graph shown in Fig. 4 represents association of words. A node represents a word in Twitter dataset and an edge represents the relation between the words. The distance between the nodes in the graph shows the level of association (frequency of their occurrence together) between those words. The overlapping nodes reveals that they occur mostly together in the tweets.

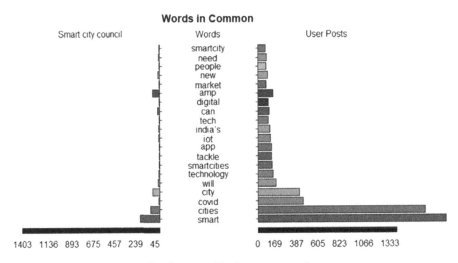

Fig. 3. Pyramid of common words

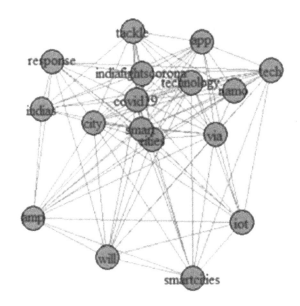

Fig. 4. The adjacency graph for users' posts

5   Discussion

The analysis results are represented in the previous section. In this section will discuss more on the results and the interpretation form the results.

Common Similar Words: As the Fig. 1 shows the common similar words present in the combined tweets, the smart, cities and city are the most frequent words. The frequent occurrence of these words indicates that the discussion taking place on social media is about the smart cities. Some of the select words to discuss from the wordcloud are technology, infrastructure, innovation, transport, mobility and the management. The occurrence of technology in the discussion indicates its necessity for the development of smart cities. The technology may involve IoT, social media and any other ICT tools. For examples, the tweets "ISRO is working on the 100 smart cities. Karnataka has been using remote technology in a big way" and "I invite entrepreneurs in the area of cybersecurity for the police department. We need experts, we need technology" highlights the importance of technology for smart cities development.

Often, the word infrastructure is occurring in the discussion about the smart cities. This indicates that the infrastructure is also an essential component of the smart cities project in India. This statement can be supplemented by the tweets "Government sanctions Rs 15 k cr to boost health infrastructure" and "India is no longer a learner, but now a contributor for infrastructure". Similarly, the innovation component is also important for the smart cities' development. The occurrence of the term innovation during the discussion about the smart cities indicates its importance. The innovation can improve the quality of infrastructure. A tweet "Digital Innovation will be the key to ramp up Healthcare Infrastructure to allow for predictive analysis going hea…" reveals the power of innovation backed infrastructure.

Another important component for smart cities development is public transport. The term transport occurred several times in the discussion. The example tweets "Rapid urbanisation is putting tremendous pressure on our transportation" and "Smart IoT in Transportation and Logistics is the Key Tech to Improve Cities in Motion #Smart-Cities" reveals the importance of transport component for smart cities development in India. Often, the term mobility is also occurred in the discussion and indicates its importance for smart cities development. This is supported by the tweets "#Amravati goes mobility friendly! The city plans the upgradation and development of its roads and walking areas…" and "India has been leveraging #technology to enable #smart mobility in #cities. Supporting #governments in this drive,…".

Finally, the management component is also equally important like other components for smart cities projects. The tweets "Uttarakhand's cleanest city is now fighting with waste management" and "Now, Goa to introduce waste management in school syllabus". In this way, the different components play an important role smart cities development in India.

Common Dissimilar Words: In Fig. 2, the dissimilar words from both the groups are shown in different colours. The smart city council, usually, posts the information on smart cities development in India. Urbanation is the most frequent word used in the discussion and indicates that the smart cities development project is emphasizing on the urbanization of the country and related issues. The urbanation is supported by the tweets "India's Premier Smart City Event - Smart Urbanation 2019 at Hotel Shangri-La, Bengaluru" and "It's an honour to have t-hub as our innovation partner at Smart Urbanation, Convention and Expo 2019".

On the other hand, the social media users' group posts the information on completed and expected tasks towards the development of smart cities projects. Smart and cities are the most frequent words shared by the group. Apart from this, the group emphasizes on the use of IoT for the smart cities project. The tweet "Impact of Covid-19 Internet of Things (IoT) in Smart Cities Market Expected to Witness the Highest Growth 2024" highlights the importance of IoT for smart cities development. The group also shares the information on Covid-19 outbreak and suggests its control as prioritized one. The tweets "Researchers explore effects of COVID-19 on urban mobility | Smart Cities Dive" and "COVID-19 to Accelerate Adoption of Technology-Enabled Smart Cities Resilience Approaches" from the users' posts reveals the influence of Covid-19 outbreak on smart cities development. Some of the other tweets emphasizes on control of Covid-19 to resume the smart cities developmental activities. In entirety, the social media users group expects to combat deadly outbreak Covid-19 and use of IoT for smart cities development in India.

Common Words and Frequency: As mentioned in results section, Fig. 3 shows the common words and their frequency form both the groups. The word smart appeared in both the groups discussions but with varying frequency. With the posts from smart cities council, the term smart occurred around 200 times whereas with the posts from social media groups appeared around 2000 times. This huge difference is not only due to the different tweets size, could be due to social media users' expectations towards smart cities development in India. Similarly, the words city and cities are occurred with varying frequency between the groups.

The term covid is also occurred most frequently with users' posts than the smart cities council posts and indicates that combating of covid-19 is most important for smart cities development to succeed. The increased frequency of occurrence for the term technology with users' posts reveals that technology adoption and upgradation are essential for smart cities projects. The word IoT is used frequently in discussion to indicate its importance for smart cities development. As most of the terms occurred frequently with users' posts, the users' expectations towards smart cities are revealed with higher magnitude.

Association Among Words: As shown in Fig. 4, the association among the words indicates the bonding between the words and their occurrence in the tweets together. In the graph, the nodes with words smart and cities are overlapping each other and indicates that most of the times their occurrence is together (higher association between the words). Similarly, the word technology is associated with most of the terms in the tweets. The nodes with the words Indiafightscorona and covid-19 are very close to each other in the graph as they occurred together most of the times in tweets.

6   Conclusion

India has projected to create 100 smart cities in near future. With this intention, the concerned governance authorities are trying their best for the development of smart cities in India. The smart cities council team is created to update the information on smart cities development for public. This team serves through the web portal and different social media accounts such as Twitter, Facebook and LinkedIn. To analyze the content posted by the council, the Twitter social media is queried with council's Twitter handle. Apart from the smart cities council's posts, the Twitter social media users' posts are also collected and analyzed for information on smart cities development in India.

The observation of the wordcloud for common words and the discussion form the example tweets shows that technology, infrastructure, innovation, transport, mobility and the management are the important components for smart cities development in India. The innovation backed infrastructure development could be sustainable in future. The information shared by smart cities council reveals that the team emphasizes on urbanization of the country and addressing related issues. On the other hand, the information shared by Social media users revealed that the people expecting to combat the covid-19 like outbreaks first for the success of smart cities project. People are also expecting the use of IoT for successful implementation of the smart cities project.

The association among the words reveals that often, working collectively with different components yields success in the smart cities project. Emphasizing on key influencing factors and users' expectations during design of future smart cities solutions, the possibilities of project success can be increased. The study used only smart cities council's timeline tweets and the Twitter content of social media users to analyze smart cities development in India. Therefore, the results reported may lack generalization. In future, the study can be extended to incorporate the posts shared through other social media platforms such as Facebook and LinkedIn by both the groups.

References

Anand, A., Rufuss, D.D.W., Rajkumar, V., Suganthi, L.: Evaluation of sustainability indicators in smart cities for India using MCDM approach. Energy Proc. **141**, 211–215 (2017)

Angelidou, M.: Smart cities: a conjuncture of four forces. Cities **47**, 95–106 (2015)

Anttiroiko, Ari-Veikko, Valkama, Pekka, Bailey, Stephen J.: Smart cities in the new service economy: building platforms for smart services. AI Soc. **29**(3), 323–334 (2014)

Bakıcı, T., Almirall, E., Wareham, J.: A smart city initiative: the case of Barcelona. J. Knowl. Econ. **4**(2), 135–148 (2013)

Bibri, S.E., Krogstie, J.: On the social shaping dimensions of smart sustainable cities: a study in science, technology, and society. Sustain. Cities Soc. **29**, 219–246 (2017)

Caragliu, A., Del Bo, C., Nijkamp, P.: Smart cities in Europe. J. Urban Technol. **18**(2), 65–82 (2011)

Chatterjee, S., Kar, A.K., Gupta, M.P.: Success of IoT in smart cities of India: an empirical analysis. Govern. Inf. Q. **35**(3), 349–361 (2018a)

Chatterjee, S., Kar, A.K., Gupta, M.P.: Alignment of IT authority and citizens of proposed smart cities in India: System security and privacy perspective. Global J. Flexible Syst. Manage. **19**(1), 95–107 (2018b)

Chatterjee, S., Kar, A.K.: Effects of successful adoption of information technology enabled services in proposed smart cities of India. J. Sci. Technol. Policy Manage. **9**(2), 189–209 (2018)

Chourabi, H., et al.: Understanding smart cities: an integrative framework. In: 2012 45th Hawaii International Conference on System Sciences, pp. 2289–2297. IEEE (2012)

Falconer, G., Mitchell, S.: Smart city framework. Cisco Internet Business Solutions Group (IBSG), pp. 1–11 (2012)

Goodspeed, R.: Smart cities: moving beyond urban cybernetics to tackle wicked problems. Cambridge J. Reg. Econ. Soc. **8**(1), 79–92 (2015)

Jamil, M.S., Jamil, M.A., Mazhar, A., Ikram, A., Ahmed, A., Munawar, U.: Smart environment monitoring system by employing wireless sensor networks on vehicles for pollution free smart cities. Proc. Eng. **107**, 480–484 (2015)

Jawaid, M.F., Khan, S.A.: Evaluating the need for smart cities in India. Int. J. Adv. Res. Sci. Eng. IJARSE, 4(1), 991–996 (2015)

Mitton, N., Papavassiliou, S., Puliafito, A., Trivedi, K.S.: Combining cloud and sensors in a smart city environment. J Wirel. Comput. Netw. **2012**, 247 (2012)

Praharaj, S., Han, J.H., Hawken, S.: Urban innovation through policy integration: Critical perspectives from 100 smart cities mission in India. City. Cult. Soc. **12**, 35–43 (2018)

SCC India Staff: UP's largest city ropes in Tech Mahindra to deploy AI tool for administrative work (2020a). https://india.smartcitiescouncil.com/article/ups-largest-city-ropes-tech-mahindra-deploy-ai-tool-administrative-work Accessed 05 May 2020

SCC India Staff: Europe-based company forms Indian consortium to develop smart cities, low-cost housing (2020b). https://india.smartcitiescouncil.com/article/europe-based-company-forms-indian-consortium-develop-smart-cities-low-cost-housing. Accessed 05 May 2020

Wray, S.: India pledges five more smart cities (2020). https://www.smartcitiesworld.net/news/news/india-pledges-five-more-smart-cities-4998. Accessed 07 May 2020

Zanella, A., Bui, N., Castellani, A., Vangelista, L., Zorzi, M.: Internet of things for smart cities. IEEE Internet Things J. **1**(1), 22–32 (2014)

Orchestration of an e-Government Network: Capturing the Dynamics of e-Government Service Delivery Through Theoretical Analysis and Mathematical Forecasting

Sayantan Khanra[1,2]([⊠]) [ID] and Rojers P. Joseph[2] [ID]

[1] Woxsen University, Hyderabad 502345, Telangana, India
[2] Indian Institute of Management Rohtak, Rohtak 124010, Haryana, India
{sayantan.khanra,rojers.joseph}@iimrohtak.ac.in

Abstract. Despite the recent growth in e-Government services, there is a paucity of research dedicated to explaining the dynamism of an e-Government network in the extant literature. The process of an e-Government service delivery is vulnerable to changes in the degree of benefits delivered to the public through the e-Government network. Therefore, we developed a theoretical model which is grounded on the actor-network theory, and formulated a mathematical model following the Bass diffusion model to explain the dynamics of various actors within an e-Government network. We also conducted a meta-ethnography study on e-Government maturity models to understand the key benefits of a mature e-Government network. Furthermore, we proposed a technique based on system dynamics modeling, which could aid appropriate authorities in forecasting network stability and monitoring performance of an e-Government network. The study may also aid future researchers, policymakers, and practitioners in conceptualizing the dynamic processes involved in e-Government service delivery.

Keywords: Actor-network theory · Bass diffusion model · e-government service delivery · Meta-ethnography · Network performance monitoring · System dynamics modeling

1   Introduction

The United Nations is extensively promoting the use of innovative technologies as effective tools to deliver public services more efficiently and promote social inclusion through participatory decision-making [1, 2]. The relationship between technology and society in the context of socio-technical transformations in organizations are explained by two schools of thought [3]. One school of thought focuses on technological determinism, which suggests that technology follows its logic to bring changes in society [4]. Alternatively, the view based on social constructionism argues that society develops the requirement of a technology and determines its role [5]. However, researchers in the field nowadays acknowledge that there is a mid-point between these two schools of thought, which reflects the truer picture, that is, the ability of technology

© IFIP International Federation for Information Processing 2020
Published by Springer Nature Switzerland AG 2020
S. K. Sharma et al. (Eds.): TDIT 2020, IFIP AICT 618, pp. 219–229, 2020.
https://doi.org/10.1007/978-3-030-64861-9_20

to both enable and restrict transformation in the case of service networks [6, 7]. The Actor-Network theory is suitable to explain the dynamics involved in such contexts [6, 7]. The theory proposes that mobilization of resources is the key to sustaining the commitment towards a network, and the actors in the network help do so by enrolling allies [8].

Surveys conducted by the United Nations indicate that the efforts by governments to utilize advanced electronic services are increasing in almost every part of the world [1]. The strategic use of innovative technologies to transform government services are called 'Electronic Government services' (abbreviated as 'e- Government services') and involves the relationships among an arm of government, the citizens it serves, the businesses related to it, and other arms of government [2, 9]. The major advantages of adopting e-Government services over the traditional means are redistribution of power from governments at different levels to the citizens, enhancement of the mechanisms for efficient coordination in policy-making and faster information exchange among various stakeholders, promotion and co-production of public services between government and citizens with real-time data, and measurement of collective sentiments of the citizens for the persuasion of appropriate action [9, 10].

Arguably, the inherent processes involved in e-Government services are most appropriately represented through a network that helps define and improve the crucial connection between a citizen and the Government [7]. However, the conceptualization of interactions among relevant factors of an e-Government network is scarce in the extant literature. The present study addresses this research gap by developing a theoretical model. Based on the extant literature, the actor-network theory is found to be appropriate for providing a conceptual foundation to meet this objective [7]. We base this argument on the premise that for an e-Government network, enrollment rate among the potential users would depend on the perceived benefits of e-Government services by an actual user of the service [10].

We developed a conceptual model with the help of the actor-network theory, to report the interaction among relevant factors of an e-Government network. To complete the model, the key benefits of e-Government services are identified following a meta-ethnography approach proposed by Noblit and Hare [11]. This approach is widely adopted when it is required to translate a concept from one study to its counterpart in another based on the interpretation of findings from multiple studies [3]. Furthermore, a mathematical model is formulated to forecast the dynamism of important factors in the conceptual model with the help of the Bass diffusion model [12], which is widely followed in the literature related to technology forecasting to understand the interaction between the current and potential adopters of a new technology [7]. This model classifies adopters into innovators and imitators based on their timing of adoption and their degree of innovativeness [12, 13].

The rest of the paper is organized as follows. The second section of this paper provides a concise background of the actor-network theory and its application to an e-Government network. A meta-ethnography study of the e-Government maturity models is presented in the third section. Section four is dedicated to discoursing the formulation of a mathematical model that forecasts the dynamism of important factors in an e-Government network. The operating principle of the mathematical model and the possibility to apply the system dynamics modelling technique are discussed in the fifth section. The sixth section presents a brief discussion on the theoretical and practical implications of the study. Finally, the paper is concluded in the seventh section with the suggestions for future research in the domain.

2   Theoretical Background

The actor-network theory conceptualizes that the process of building and changing networks depends on the actors who spread positive or negative words about solutions among their peers [8]. A network of actors observes two phases, namely translation and transformation (see Fig. 1) [14]. Actors in the translation phase translate to actors outside the network the benefits of being inside the network, or otherwise [15]. In other words, actors within a network try to enroll more allies to it and eventually, the more the number of allies enrolled to the network, the more durable and irreversible the network would become [15]. On the other hand, the transformation phase captures the dynamic behavior of a network through stocks and flows [14, 16]. The stocks present the pool of certain resources at a particular time, while flows from one stock to the next one in the network determine the changes in those stocks [16].

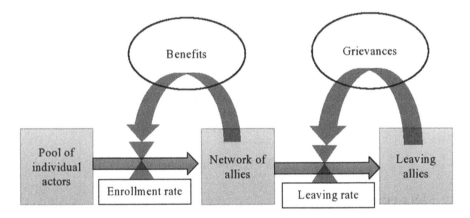

Fig. 1. An Illustration of an Actor-network

E-Government networks are reportedly dynamic and vulnerable to changes following the entry or leaving of an actor and subsequently, some networks turn out to be more stabilized than the others [15]. Here, we have two stocks that represent the potential users and the actual users and the flow from the first stock (potential users) to the second stock (actual users) is controlled by the enrollment rate. The benefits of e-Government perceived by an actual user, who may either stay in the network or leave the same, potentially influence his/her peers' decision to join the network.

Following Kirkwood [17], the enrollment process is conceptualized in Fig. 2. The other part of the network is developed from the service providers' perspective and contains the stocks of offline Government services and e-Government services. The flow from the first stock (offline) to the second stock (e-Government) is controlled by the implementation rate. The implementation process is also presented in Fig. 2. Thus, the benefits of e-Government have impact on both the flows in the network, that is, the enrollment rate and the implementation rate. This warrants further investigation to study the benefits of an e-Government network and identify the key components of the same.

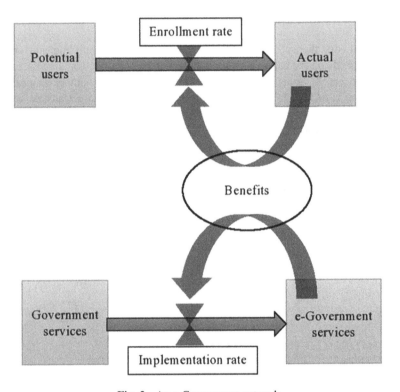

Fig. 2. An e-Government network

3   Meta-ethnography Study

A maturity model provides a structured guide to the development of capabilities in a domain to achieve the required objectives of an organization [3]. The maturity models for e-Government services are scattered among various outlets such as academic journals, annual reports, books, and conference proceedings. To fill this gap, we conducted a meta-ethnography study on the available maturity models for e-Government services to identify the key benefits of a mature e-Government network. Meta-ethnography is a thorough qualitative synthesis method to select, analyze, and interpret studies from the literature related to a focused research objective in order to deliver new insights that complement the extant literature [11, 18].

The rigorous method followed by Khanra et al. [19, 20] in identifying resources is adopted here. A total of 27 maturity models were selected and analyzed in the study. Following this, the key focus areas or constructs in different stages of the maturity models under analysis were interpreted. Then, the constructs of one maturity model are translated into that of another, and vice versa, based on the interpretation of the explanation provided for each of the constructs. From the meta-ethnographic analysis and interpretation, the constructs were assigned to five distinct clusters, as reported in Table 1. It may be noted that the synthesisation process prioritizes the knowledge offered by the constructs over the difference in opinion among the researchers about their appearance. Therefore, different constructs appearing in different stages of different maturity models may belong to the same cluster.

To concisely report our findings, we noted down the definition(s) and explanation (s) provided for each construct within a cluster. Constructs belonging to the same cluster provide similar, if not identical, information about their meaning. Thus, we refined the information by eliminating repetitive points within each cluster. Then, we summarized the filtered information such that it defines or explains the constructs of the five clusters as presented in Table 1.

Table 1. Benefits of e-Government services

Feature	Details
Cluster 1: Online Presence	Static information about Government policies and services is available. The information should be updated regularly and organized efficiently. Downloadable forms may be available for certain e-Government services.
Cluster 2: Facilitating Interaction	A two-way communication channel is established via e-mails and online chat rooms to exchange information between the users and the Government agencies. Advanced services like personalisation options, search options, push notifications, email alerts and uploading documents may be available. The users may provide feedbacks and comments on issues related to a service as well as various rules and regulations concerning the service.
Cluster 3: Integrated Ecosystem	Vertical integration process involves integration of systems at various levels within a department or jurisdiction. Horizontal integration process refers to inter-departmental data sharing. Full integration yields a portal for all e-Government services or a 'one-stop-shop' for joined-up services. Multichannel integration i.e. a blend of online and offline services is also desirable.
Cluster 4: Online Payments	Users should be able to perform complete transactions online which often includes a requirement for payment. Online payment gateways are to be included in the e-Government services so that the users can easily perform financial transactions as per the requirements of those services. There may be a possibility of accepting electronic payments by the users, particularly in the case of e-procurement by the Government.
Cluster 5: Participatory e-Democracy	The users may participate in online discussion within forums that are openly accessible to all. They may take part in anonymous opinion surveys to provide input for policy and legislation proposals. Eligible citizens may cast their votes online.

The clusters are named as 'Online Presence' [B_1], 'Facilitating Interaction' [B_2], 'Integrated Ecosystem' [B_3], 'Online Payments' [B_4], and 'Participatory e-Democracy' [B_5] based on the benefits they offer. Therefore, the benefits of e-Government [B] at a particular time [*t*] may be expressed as the sum total of five dimensions, as shown in Eq. 1. The dimensional benefits [B_i] of an e-Government network are normalized with respect to a reference time when the network was launched [$t = 0$]. Therefore, Bt actually measures the improvements in the benefits provided by an e-Government network over time t.

$$B_t = \sum_{i=1}^{5} B_{\tilde{u}}; \; where B_{\tilde{u}} = (B_{it} - B_{i0})/B_{i0} \; and \; B_{i0} > 0 \tag{1}$$

Upon updating Fig. 2 with the findings from the meta-ethnography study, we get the theoretical model to understand an e-Government network, as exhibited in Fig. 3.

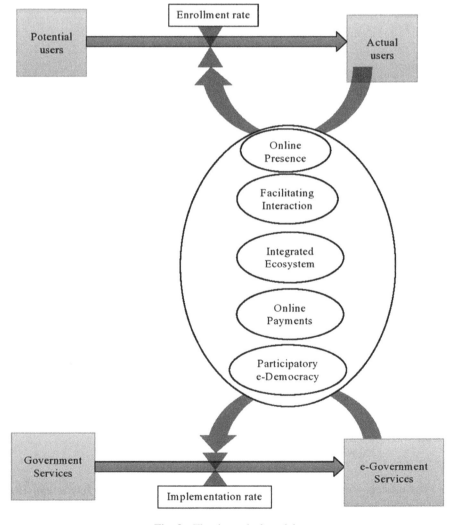

Fig. 3. The theoretical model

4 Mathematical Model Development

An essential property of a dynamic model is that the conditional probability of technology adoption at a certain point [time = T] depends on the cumulative adoption at time T [12, 13]. The Bass diffusion model resonates with the property of actor-network theory by incorporating knowledge about the actors' behavioral process in a dynamic model's parameters [7]. Therefore, the proposed theoretical model may be best complemented by a mathematical model based on the Bass diffusion model [12], where the model parameters include the knowledge about the dynamism of an e-Government network. The Bass diffusion model is defined by a function, F(T), for the total number of adaptors at time T from a likelihood function, f(t), as shown in Eq. 2 [12]. The likelihood of adoption at time T is partly driven by the innovators and partly by the imitators, where p and q (generally q > p; p,q > 0) are the coefficients of innovators and imitators, respectively. Equation 3 defines the rate of change in F(T). The solution to this non-linear differential equation is presented in Eq. 4. Thus, we arrive at the function of f(T) in Eq. 5, from which the maximum value of f(T) can be determined, as reported in Eq. 6.

$$F(T) = \int_0^T f(T); \, where f(T) = [p + qF(T)][1 - F(T)] \, and \, F(0) = 0 \qquad (2)$$

$$\frac{dF(T)}{dT} = p + (q - p)F(T) - q[F(T)]^2 \qquad (3)$$

$$F(T) = 1 - e^{-(p+q)*T} / 1 + \frac{q}{p} e^{-(p+q)*T} \qquad (4)$$

$$f(T) = \frac{(p+q)^2}{p} e^{-(p+q)T} \left[1 + \frac{q}{p} e^{-(p+q)T} \right]^2 \qquad (5)$$

$$f_{max}(T^*) = \frac{(p+q)^2}{4q}; \, T^* = 1/(p+q)\ln\left(\frac{q}{p}\right) \qquad (6)$$

Considering the case of user enrollment, p_{IT} gives the co-efficient of users who join an e-Government network without the influence of others (see Eq. 7) and q_{IT} represents the co-efficient of users who join the network after the actual users translate the benefits of e-Government to them (see Eq. 8), where G_{uT} denotes the historical growth in enrollment and ε_1 denotes the effectiveness of translation phase. Following Eq. 3, the enrollment rate is expressed in Eq. 9. Further, the stock of actual users and the likelihood of enrollment are forecasted in Eqs. 10 and 11, respectively.

$$p_{1T} = G_{uT} * U(T) \qquad (7)$$

$$q_{1T} =_1 *B_T * U(T) \qquad (8)$$

$$\frac{dU(T)}{dT} = p_{1T} + (q_{1T} - p_{1T})U(T) - q_{1T}[U(T)]^2 \qquad (9)$$

$$\widehat{U}(t) = 1 - e^{-(p_{1T} + q_{1T})*t} / 1 + \frac{q_{1T}}{p_{1T}} e^{-(p_{1T} + q_{1T})t} \qquad (10)$$

$$\hat{u}(t) = \frac{(p_{1T} + q_{1T})^2}{p_{1T}} e^{-(p_{1T} + q_{1T})t} \left[1 + \frac{q_{1T}}{p_{1T}} e^{-(p_{1T} + q_{1T})t}\right]^2 \qquad (11)$$

A similar exercise is carried out for the service implementation part of our theoretical network. The stock of e-Government services and the likelihood of implementation may be forecasted following Eqs. 12 and 13, respectively.

$$\hat{S}(t) = 1 - e^{-(p_{2T} + q_{2T})t} / 1 + \frac{q_{2T}}{p_{2T}} e^{-(p_{2T} + q_{2T})t} \qquad (12)$$

$$\hat{s}(t) = \frac{(p_{2T} + q_{2T})^2}{p_{2T}} e^{-(p_{2T} + q_{2T})t} \left[1 + \frac{q_{2T}}{p_{2T}} e^{-(p_{2T} + q_{2T})t}\right]^2 \qquad (13)$$

5 Implementation of Mathematical Model

The equations expressing the enrollment rate and the implementation rate provide an important insight with regard to the growth of stocks. The respective equations indicate that the enrollment rate and the implementation rate slow down as U(T) and S(T) grow. These phenomena may be understood with the help of the system dynamics modeling technique, which primarily refers to the principle of accumulation (Shin, 2007). With the help of this technique, a causal loop diagram consisting of two feedback loops is conceptualized to explain the dynamism of the enrollment rate (Fig. 4). Similarly, the feedback loops for the implementation rate is presented in Fig. 5. The feedback loops contributing to the net positive and net negative effects are known as reinforcing loop (R1 and R2) and balancing loop (B1 and B2), respectively [17]. These two loops stabilize the rate of change, as they interact by exerting opposite effects of the desired intensity in order to achieve equilibrium in a network [17].

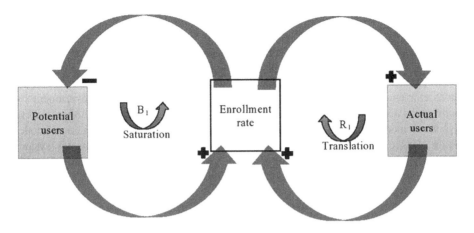

Fig. 4. Causal loop of user enrolment process

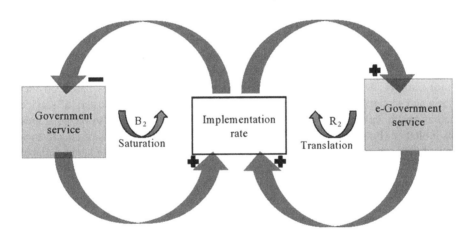

Fig. 5. Causal loop of service implementation process

6 Discussion and Implications

The objective of this paper is to model the dynamics of an e-Government network, which is fulfilled through theoretical and mathematical models. These models are among the earliest ones to analyze and forecast the dynamics of an e-Government network, and hence, this paper yields important theoretical implications on three aspects. First, the theoretical model may contribute towards a better understanding of the dynamism of an e-Government network. Second, the theoretical model is complemented with mathematical equations to forecast the dynamism of important factors in the network. Third, in the process of developing the theoretical and the mathematical models, a meta-ethnography study is conducted, which identified five key dimensions to analyze the benefits provided by a mature e-Government network.

This study extensively discusses how the important attributes of an e-Government network could be forecasted. Since the mathematical model is easy to use once calibrated, this study may appeal to the policymakers and service developers interested in forecasting the important factors in an e-Government network. Thus, the models developed by this study may help the government organizations continue delivering more efficient services and improve the positive social impact of e-Government by better utilization of the network in the long run. Moreover, the provision to use system dynamics modelling technique may make the operation of the mathematical model easier. Hence, continuous assessment of an e-Government network using system dynamics may help the government agencies sustain their operations over time.

7   Conclusion and Future Scope

On critically evaluating the study findings and obtaining expert opinions on the same, four limitations of this study are identified, and consequently, the future scope of this research is suggested. First, the paper only modelled the users' and service providers' perspectives. A future study may incorporate the service developers' perspectives in the theoretical and mathematical models. Second, in our models, we did not classify the pool of users based on different demographic attributes. Also, the purpose of using e-Government may vary among different clusters such as students, entrepreneurs, and senior citizens. Third, we did not differentiate government services based on their nature and scope. Future studies may consider examining specific clusters of services such as health services, educational services, business services, and so on, to address this limitation. Fourth, we considered the estimation of the coefficients of effectiveness beyond the scope of this paper. Interested researchers may explore the latent variables that influence these coefficients using methods such as experimental design and longitudinal study. Despite the aforementioned limitations, this study assumes importance in modelling the dynamics of an e-Government network by using theoretical analysis and mathematical forecasting, thereby making significant contributions to the literature on e-Government services.

References

1. Department of Economic and Social Affairs (United Nations), https://publicadministration. un.org/egovkb/en-us/Resources/E-Government-Survey-in-Media. Accessed 10 Oct 2020
2. Khanra, S., Joseph, R.P.: Adoption and diffusion of e-government services: the impact of demography and service quality. In: Baguma, R., De, R., Janowski T. (eds.) The 10th International Conference on Theory and Practice of Electronic Governance 2017, pp. 602–605. Association for Computing Machinery, New York (2017). https://doi.org/10.1145/3047273.3047301
3. Khanra, S., Joseph, R.P.: E-governance maturity models: a meta-ethnographic study. Int. Technol. Manag. Rev. 8(1), 1–9 (2019). https://doi.org/10.2991/itmr.b.190417.001
4. Winner, L.: Upon opening the black box and finding it empty: social constructivism and the philosophy of technology. Sci. Technol. Hum. Values 18(3), 362–378 (1993). https://doi.org/10.1177/016224399301800306

5. Woolgar, S.: The turn to technology in social studies of science. Sci. Technol. Hum. Values **16**(1), 20–50 (1991). https://doi.org/10.1177/016224399101600102
6. Demirkan, H., Kauffman, R.J., Vayghan, J.A., Fill, H.G., Karagiannis, D., Maglio, P.P.: Service-oriented technology and management: perspectives on research and practice for the coming decade. Electronic Commerce Res. Appl. **7**(4), 356–376 (2009). https://doi.org/10.1016/j.elerap.2008.07.002
7. Khanra, S., Joseph, R.P., Ruparel, N.: Dynamism of an e-government network in delivering public services. In: Academy of Management Global Proceedings Slovenia 2019, p. 376. Academy of Management, New York (2019)
8. Callon, M.: The sociology of an actor-network: the case of the electric vehicle. In: Mapping the Dynamics of Science and Technology, pp. 19–34. Palgrave Macmillan UK (1986)
9. Khanra, S., Joseph, R.P.: Adoption of e-Governance: the mediating role of language proficiency and digital divide in an emerging market context. Transf. Gov.: People Process Policy **13**(2), 122–142 (2019). https://doi.org/10.1108/TG-12-2018-0076
10. Guha, J., Chakrabarti, B.: Making e-government work: adopting the network approach. Gov. Inf. Q. **31**(2), 327–336 (2014). https://doi.org/10.1016/j.giq.2013.11.008
11. Noblit, G.W., Hare, R.D.: A Meta-Ethnographic Approach. Meta-ethnography: Synthesizing Qualitative Studies. Sage, California (1988)
12. Bass, F.M.: A new product growth for model consumer durables. Manag. Sci. **15**(5), 215–227 (1969). https://doi.org/10.1287/mnsc.15.5.215
13. Bass, F.M., Krishnan, T.V., Jain, D.C.: Why the Bass model fits without decision variables. Market. Sci. **13**(3), 203–223 (1994). https://doi.org/10.1287/mksc.13.3.203
14. Law, J.: Notes on the theory of the actor-network: ordering, strategy, and heterogeneity. Syst. Practice Action Res. **5**(4), 379–393 (1992)
15. Bernhard, I., Wihlborg, E.: Policy entrepreneurs in networks: implementation of two Swedish municipal contact centres from an actor perspective. Int. J. Entrepreneurship Small Bus. **21**(3), 288–302 (2014). https://doi.org/10.1504/IJESB.2014.060893
16. Latour, B.: On actor-network theory: a few clarifications. Soziale Welt **47**(4), 369–381 (1996)
17. Kirkwood, C.W.: System dynamics methods. College of Business Arizona State University USA (1998)
18. Khanra, S., Budankayala, M., Doddi, S.T.: Barriers towards the adoption of digital learning platforms. Acad. Market. Stud. J. **24**(4), 317–323. Article in press
19. Khanra, S., Dhir, A., Mäntymäki, M.: Big data analytics and enterprises: a bibliometric synthesis of the literature. Enterprise Inf. Syst. **14**(6), 737–768 (2020). https://doi.org/10.1080/17517575.2020.1734241
20. Khanra, S., Dhir, A., Islam, A.K.M.N., Mäntymäki, M.: Big data analytics in healthcare: a systematic literature review. Enterprise Inf. Syst. Article in press (2020). https://doi.org/10.1080/17517575.2020.1812005

Investigating Emerging Technologies Role in Smart Cities' Solutions

Ali Al-Badi[1], Sujeet Kumar Sharma[2], Vishal Jain[3],
and Asharul Islam Khan[4(✉)]

[1] Academic Affairs and Research, Gulf College, Al Mabaila, Muscat,
Sultanate of Oman
aalbadi@gulfcollege.edu.om
[2] Department of Information System and Analytics,
Indian Institute of Management, Tiruchirappalli,
Tiruchirappalli, Tamil Nadu 620 024, India
sujeet@iimtrichy.ac.in
[3] Department of Business Administration, University of Technology
and Applied Sciences, Ibri, Sultanate of Oman
vishalj.ibr@cas.edu.om
[4] Industry Research Chair, Sultan Qaboos University, Alkhodh,
Muscat, Sultanate of Oman
a.khan@squ.edu.om, ashar.367@gmail.com

Abstract. A smart city is defined as a one that provides solutions to rapid urbanization, exploding population, scarce resources, congested traffic, and energy management through the effective and integrated use of information and communication technology. The conceptualization, integration, and implementation of smart cities have been recognized and seen as a means to optimize the limited resources and improve the quality of human lives. The smart cities planning, designing, and development have been affected due to big data storage, big data governance, Internet of Things (IoT), and artificial intelligence (AI) techniques. The smart cities' solutions cover different themes of varying importance such as smart health, smart education, intelligent transportation, smart energy, smart governance, etc. The emerging technologies are the one which are presently under development or might be developed in the future, and which can have a wide impact on research, business, and social lives. The emerging technologies are the groups of technologies that have been partially explored, continuously evolving, and under development such as, IoT, big data, machine learning (ML), social network, and cloud computing. The emerging technologies have created renewed interest in smart cities' solutions. The smart cities' progress and advancement are the results of the successful exploitation of emerging technologies.

This paper aims to investigate and discuss the success stories of emerging technologies in smart cities' solutions. The emerging technologies included in the study are the IoT, big data, and AI. The paper further summarizes a process of applying tools and techniques for the successful initiative of transforming a traditional city into a smart one using emerging technologies.

Keywords: Smart cities · Smart energy · Smart education · Internet of Things · Big data · Machine learning · Artificial intelligence

© IFIP International Federation for Information Processing 2020
Published by Springer Nature Switzerland AG 2020
S. K. Sharma et al. (Eds.): TDIT 2020, IFIP AICT 618, pp. 230–241, 2020.
https://doi.org/10.1007/978-3-030-64861-9_21

1 Introduction

A smart city aims to optimize resources, minimize wastage, and improves the quality of life. The smart cities implementation is not the one-step solution instead, it incorporates many phases and sub phases such as infrastructure development, stakeholder engagements, cloud computing, edge computing, AI, and collaboration with big companies.

The European Union took the smart cities initiative in 2011, since then several countries have designed their blueprints such as, SMART (China), u-City Smart City (South Korea), i-Japan Smart City, Multimedia Super Corridor-Malaysia, Intelligent Nation iN2015-Singapore, and Intelligent Taiwan- Taiwan. The South Korean government has targeted smart grid/energy solutions [1]. The prominent private companies actively participating in smart cities solutions are Cisco, Hitachi, and IBM. There are a number of smart technologies available for smart cities design, development, and implementation. The fast-evolving emerging technologies are the IoT, big data, and AI. According to McKinsey (2015), the revenue from IoT will increase from \$3.9 in 2015 to \$11.1 trillion by 2025 [2]. The sensors and actuators are major components of the IoT. A sensor converts the physical parameters into human understandable electronic signals while an actuator gives a mechanical response based on an input. The IoT has applications in waste management, disaster management (earthquake (vibration and deformation sensors), floods), understanding crime patterns, and enhancing the security of cities. The smart renewable and non-renewable energy management systems use big data technologies for operational efficiency, cost control, system stability, and reliability. The social networks/media analytics helps in monitoring crime, natural calamity (fires, floods) reporting, and public complaints disposal. Moreover, drones (unmanned aerial vehicles) have applications delivering healthcare and emergency services to remote areas [3]. In the COVID-19 pandemic, countries such as China, Spain, Italy, and Oman among others have used drones for healthcare delivery and crowd control. The study investigates and explores the role of emerging technologies in smart cities solutions. The emerging technologies considered in this study are the IoT, big data, and AI.

This paper includes the following parts: Sect. 2, describes the research method and motivation. Section 3, presents the emerging technologies in smart cities. Section 4, illustrates the smart cities solutions. Section 5, highlights the smart cities initiatives in the Sultanate of Oman. Section 6, discusses the findings. The last section draws the conclusion.

2 Research Method and Research Gap

The study investigates and explores contents on smart cities solutions extracted from academic manuscripts, scientific reports, government reports, and IT companies reports. The "UN Urbanization Perspective 2011 Revision" report says that by 2050, 6.3 Billion people will move to major Metropolitan Cities. This enhanced urbanization will put unimaginable pressure on the already fast depleting earth resources, unless the solutions in the form of smart cities are implemented. The inherent goal of smart cities is to solve the citizens' problems and ease the government in public administration.

There are many articles on smart cities that bring to notice the different aspects. They mostly cover advantages and challenges, but pay little attention to highlight and analyze the role of emerging technologies. The existing emerging technologies in smart cities solutions are the IoT, big data, and AI. The integrated approach of the IoT, big data, and AI are paving the way for personalized services in smart cities. The emerging technologies are the source of successful stories in the design, development, and implementation of smart cities solutions. Therefore, this research article lays down the role of emerging technologies in smart cities solutions.

3   Emerging Technologies in Smart Cities

The present study covers the emerging technologies mainly, IoT, big data, and AI. Each of them has its role and contributions to the smart cities solutions, which are described as follows.

3.1   Internet of Things

IoT is a platform for global connection and integration of sensors, actuators, RFID, Bluetooth, and other digital devices. The IoT consists of integrated components of services, data networks, and sensors. In the IoT, "Things" represent different devices (sensors, actuators, RFID, NFC). The IoT is the key driver of smart cities, facilitating communication and connection of a large number of devices. The IoT through connectivity and interoperability helps in the realization of smart cities around the world [4]. The IoT and its advanced form Industrial IoT integrate smart homes, wearable devices, smart grids, automobiles, smart farming, smart traffic, health applications, retail, security, energy, water management, waste management systems, smart factories, and smart industries [5]. The communication mechanisms between IoT devices can be device-to-device, device-to-cloud, device-to gateway, and backend data sharing. The main concerns of the IoT are security, privacy, confidentiality, and integrity. The cloud server, RFID, Wireless Sensor Network, Bluetooth, ZigBee etc., are the base of smart cities solutions.

In cloud computing, many computers are connected/clustered via real-time communication network for processing the data. The cloud computing has Platform as a Service (PaaS), Software as a Service (SaaS), and Infrastructure as a Service (IaaS) to the IoT devices. The smart cities computing model could be cloud, fog, and edge computing [6]. Radio Frequency Infrared Detection (RFID) is a tag attached to objects for tracking and uniquely identifying them. They are used in hospitals, libraries, and supply chains. The smart reading devices such as smart meters have RFID embedded. Wireless Sensor Network (WSN) are miniature devices attached to the sensors, for communication between different types of sensors (connect various distributed and independent devices). The applications include, smart homes and smart healthcare for monitoring temperature, light, humidity, pressure, etc. Wi-Fi is a wireless protocol that allows users to access the internet when connected to an access point. The Ultrawideband is oriented to high bandwidth is indoor short-range wireless networks over multimedia links. ZigBee is a wireless communication technology designed for short-range communication between devices. Longer battery life is an advantage of ZigBee. In smart cities, it is widely used in a smart home for connecting smart lighting devices. The Bluetooth uses a wireless radio system for short-range communication. It has replaced cable for keyboards, mouse, printer, joysticks, and so on, due to lower power consumption and cost.

The LTE technology describes the 4G wireless network (extension of 3G). The 4G shifts the paradigm from hybrid data and voice networks to a data-only IP network. The 4G uses multiple-input multiple-output (MIMO) and orthogonal frequency division multiplex (OFDM) to acquire more data throughput than 3G. The 5G networks will result in fast and resilient access to the Internet and support for smart cities realization. Many useful applications can be derived for smart cities using Near Field Communication (NFC), mobile communication technology, and cloud architecture. The manufacturer can directly interact with customers when the NFC tag is scanned and data is stored in the cloud.

3.2   Big Data

The healthcare, education, transportation, e-governance, etc. generate a huge volume of heterogeneous data through the sensor devices. The produced data are structured, semi-structured, and unstructured. The big data governance is concerned with managing and identifying meaningful patterns in large data sets (big data) [7]. The big data analysis faces a lot of challenges, such as data compatibility and inconsistency [8]. The big data management, storage, and analysis form the backbone of a smart city design, development, and implementation.

The big data is stored either at the dedicated server of the company or the data centers provided by vendors such as Amazon, Google, Microsoft, and Cloudera. The traditional relational databases such as MySQL, Oracle, etc. are unsuitable since the smart cities data are mostly unstructured, so the NoSQL database management system is used. The NoSQL databases are of three types, Key-Value, Column-Oriented, and Document-Oriented. The different platforms supporting each of them are Redis (KeyValue), Hbase (Column-oriented), and MongoDB (Document-Oriented). The InfluxDB, handles the time-series database. In Hbase the data is stored in tables, which can expand vertically and horizontally as opposed to the traditional SQL databases. The columns are like variables assigned for each row. The Hbase provides real-time read-write access to files stored in the Hadoop Distributed File System (HDFS). The big data analytics help in faster decisions on data. The big data analytic platforms are HDFS, HPCC, and Stratosphere. Big data analytics approaches include YARN (Yet Another Resource Negotiator), Map Reduce, Spark, HBase, Hive, and Kafka. The Hadoop vendors are Cloudera, Hortonworks, IBM, and MapR.

Hadoop (High availability distributed object-oriented platform) is an Open Source platform for data processing on cloud/clusters. There are two primary components:

HDFS and Map Reduce. MapReduce is a batch-based programming model for parallel and distributed processing of data on clusters. The MapReduce breaks tasks into smaller, dispatching to different servers, and then accommodating the results.

The HDFS has two nodes Namenode/Masternode and Datanode/Slavenode. The Datanode executes operations requested by the Namenode. The Apache Hive enables SQL processing and analytical capabilities on the data stored in HDFS. The Apache Spark has replaced the Map Reduce jobs for batch and stream processing. The platforms such as Amazon EC2 and HDFS manage smart cities data from multiple sources. The HDFS provides scalability and fault-tolerance. The analytic part is the key to decision making in smart cities solutions [9]. The backend distributed processing is due to Hadoop and Microsoft Azure. The big data analytic helps in getting valuable insight into big data.

3.3   Artificial Intelligence

The AI uses various algorithms and models to extract useful information from big data. The smart cities have a huge volume of data generated through data sources such as shopping centers, traffic sensors, transit points, police records, etc. AI has applications in counting vehicles, license plate reading, and objects recognition in image and video files [10]. The big data needs advanced algorithms to handle the volume, variety, velocity, and veracity of data. In Changsha (China - smart transportation), AI has been used for processing information generated through surveillance cameras [11]. In Taipei (Taiwan- smart governance, smart transportation, smart health, smart security, smart energy, and smart finance) AI has been used for processing information generated through the IoT [8]. The relationships between the IoT, big data, and AI are shown in Fig. 1.

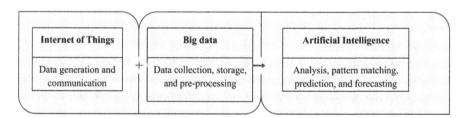

Fig. 1. Relationship between emerging technologies in smart cities solutions

The most common method of performing big data analytics is ML. AI is the superset of ML and deep learning. The ML is supervised, unsupervised, semisupervised, and reinforcement learning. ML has a number of applications in smart cities solutions [12, 13]. The traditional ML approaches are Support Vector Machines (SVM), Decision Tree, and Nearest Neighbor classifier. For example, [14] used Bayesian approach to residential property valuation, [15] used SVM for forecasting of photovoltaic (PV) output for efficient renewable energy systems. Deep learning is a subset of ML. It includes Deep Neural Network (DNN), Convolutional Neural Network (CNN), Recurrent Neural Network (RNN), Long Short Term Memory (LSTM), Auto encoders (AEs), Generative Adversarial Networks (GANs), and Deep Belief Network

(DBNs). They have been studied for smart cities solutions including mobility, safety, energy, healthcare, education, and governance.

4   Smart Cities Solutions and Emerging Technologies

Smart solutions to cities problems are needed for overcoming population growth, and sustainable utilization of natural resources. The realization of a smart city is successful, when it has smart healthcare, smart education, smart home, intelligent transportation, and smart energy. The important smart cities solutions and technologies used are described below.

4.1   Smart Healthcare

In smart healthcare, the IoT (sensors, wearable devices, smart devices) connect health centers, hospitals, patients, doctors, and pharmacists. This eases online appointments, digital record storage, remote home services, and remote patient monitoring. Smart healthcare includes wearable technologies, patient's electronic records, hospitals electronic records, and remote monitoring systems. The big healthcare data upon analysis is useful in monitoring patients' health, epidemics prediction, disease diagnosis, personalized medicine, and maintenance of health records. The patients' data could be used by insurance agencies for managing their businesses.

4.2   Smart Education

The smart education environment uses big educational data for learning analytics. The learning analytics helps in delivering personalized learning content, monitoring the learners' progress, and improving teaching quality. The AI along with the big educational data identifies the learning patterns and generates personalized learning contents [16]. The IoT has been enabling data generation and collection in the educational sector. Adaptive learning content is delivered to learners via web applications and mobile apps [17].

4.3   Intelligent Transportation

An intelligent transportation system monitors vehicle movements, minimizes accidents (understanding accident cause), optimizes supply chain, and enables smart parking. The sensors and actuators record the vehicle movements. AI is implemented on the big data for vehicle route optimization and fleet movement. The traffic is monitored by applying adaptive signal control technology, integrating sensors data, vehicle tracking devices, and cameras for traffic analysis.

4.4   Smart Governance

The smart governance entails integration, collaboration, communication, and data processing. The government and organization can devise policies and implement schemes based on the analyzed results from health, educational, transportation, energy, and social network data. Using ML algorithms entities with a common interest can be identified for smooth governance. The smart governance leads to judicious utilization of natural resources and urban planning. IoT and big data analytics process real-time user data thereby the government can make efficient and accurate decisions. This improves citizens' quality of life.

4.5   Smart Home

The sensors and actuators based smart devices are interconnected inside homes. The smart homes have smart meters, smart light, smart heating, and smart waste management systems. These devices are controlled by applications running on smartphones and tablets. The smart home has benefits of monitoring and controlling home devices at any time and from anywhere [18].

4.6   Smart Energy

Smart energy regulates energy demand and supply. It consists of power grids, solar energy, and wind energy. The smart grids and smart meters in conjunction with communication network records the energy consumptions and power utilization habits of customers, which help in understanding the future demand and developing pricing plans. For instance, on-demand energy supply in passive buildings (i.e., not all the building and houses need power supply/water supply all the times of the day) [19].

4.7   Smart Tourism

Smart tourism uses the IoT and big data for providing optimized packages and information on touristic destinations for attracting the visitors. The data recorded in smart tourism consists of money transactions, capturing photographs/videos, using social networks (Facebook/Twitter/Flicker).

4.8   Smart Environment

The smart environment solution uses IoT, big data, and ML for waste management, water management, air pollution monitoring, and control. The waste management employs smart techniques of waste collection, smart bins, and recycling. Sensors attached to smart bins send messages about the level of waste in the bin for the waste truck collector to come and collect the waste.

4.9   Smart Parking

The smart parking uses sensors and application data (i.e., parking requests through app) for sensing, understanding, and monitoring the available parking space. The smart parking has two parts; sensors that send information about the parking status and mobile application which displays the nearest free parking space. The sensors record the incoming vehicles, outgoing vehicles, free parking slots, and then propagate the information among the citizens via website or mobile application.

4.10   Smart Advertisement

In smart cities, the mobile network-based solutions such as GPS sensors or the Call Detail Record (CDR) data can be effectively used for the position and location-based advertisement. As soon as a consumer passes through a shop, he will get a message about the latest discount and offers.

4.11   Smart Weather Forecasting

Instant and real-time weather information is very useful for travelers. Weather conditions such as humidity, high winds, sandstorms, thunderstorms etc. could help people to visit the areas. They might get warning and advisory messages.

5   Smart City Initiatives in the Sultanate of Oman

The Ministry of Transport, Communication, and Information Technology (MTC) (-formerly, Ministry of Technology and Communication/Information Technology Authority) conducted a workshop on smart cities solutions in 2015. The workshop was focused on smart cities transformation. The Gartner's Research Vice President for Environmental Sustainability, Bettina Tratz-Ryan, discussed different smart cities solutions to logistics, health, and energy [20]. In July 2018, the South Korean Government Authorities and Omani Government signed an agreement for the development of a smart city at Duqm port. A memorandum of understanding was signed between Oman and South Korea for establishing futuristic smart cities in the Sultanate [21]. They plan to replicate success of Duqm in other parts of Oman.

The Sultanate of Oman has set two important initiatives: Oman vision 2040 and eOman 2030 strategy to meet the present and future needs by rapid technology adoption, smart infrastructure development, and creating a competitive economy. The MTC in cooperation with the Public Establishment for Industrial Estate (Madayn) has implemented Smart City Pilot in Knowledge Oasis Muscat (KOM). The project covers 1-Environment dimension (air quality, smart energy management, smart water management, and smart waste management), 2-Quality of life dimension (public transportation, and safety and security), 3-Infrastructure dimension (urban mobility) [22]. In Oman, urbanization, digitization, and adoption of Industry 4.0 technologies are taking place at fast speed, giving rise to realization of smart city solutions.

6   Results and Discussions of the Study

The applicable domain of smart cities includes smart transportation, smart environment (pollution monitoring and control), smart energy, and smart government. The smart cities design, development, and implementation are based on layered structure in the form of 1) data generation layer, 2) data transmission/network layer, 3) data collection layer, 4) data analysis/computing layer, and 5) presentation layer. In the data generation layer, the end-users interact with the digital devices, sensors, and actuators. The data transmission serves as a sender of data generated at the data generation layer. In the data collection layer, cloud and servers store the collected data. The data analysis layer is the place where big data analytics, ML computation is applied on the data. The last layer is presentation, which shows the output in an understandable format such as graphs, charts etc.

The integrated approach of IoT, big data, and AI, help in optimized and orchestrated use of natural and manmade resources. Likewise they are needed in identifying the crime pattern, video surveillance, drones, and cybersecurity. The IoT, big data, and AI must work together to ensure the uniformity, accuracy, consistency and accountability of informed decisions. The heterogeneous data sources are smart sensors, smart meters, social networking platforms, crowdsourcing mobile applications, ERP systems, facility management systems, transportation management, and building management systems. The smart cities services include smart energy, smart management, smart transportation etc. AI and IoT are used in contextdependent recommendations and support systems [23]. The first-wave smart cities relied on smart transportation and security services. The second-wave smart cities have provided comprehensive urban services such as smart energy. The smart cities solutions are mainly in the area of intelligent transportation, smart grid, and smart energy as shown in Fig. 2. The obtained value is the result of quantifying the explored study on emerging technologies and smart cities solutions. The data has been derived from the explored study on emerging technologies and smart cities solutions.

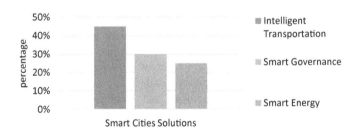

Fig. 2. Smart cities solutions as identified from different studies

The intelligent transportation for real-time traffic patterns analysis and management using GPS navigation, and installed sensors have been implemented in Amsterdam, Barcelona, Taipei, London, Copenhagen, New York, Stockholm, Rio de Janeiro, and Changsha (China). The smart governance for monitoring crimes, sewage treatments, and emergency calls using installed surveillance cameras, sensors, social networks, and web dashboards have been implemented in Amsterdam, Santa Cruz, Songdo City, Paris, London, and New York. The smart energy for energy saving, real-time water requirements using smart meters, installed sensors, have been implemented in Amsterdam, Barcelona, Songdo City, and Taipei. Figure 3 shows successful implementation of smart cities solutions in some of the major cities of the world. The values have been extracted from the multiple studies on emerging technologies and smart cities solutions found in the literature.

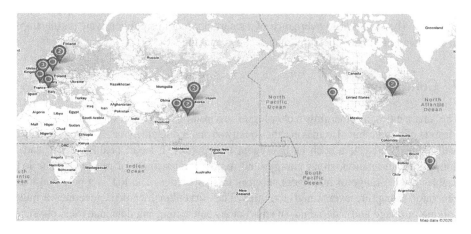

Fig. 3. Smart cities solutions in major world cities

The process used to implement smart cities solutions is shown in Fig. 4. The sensors/connected devices generate data. The JSON/RESTAPI/MQTT converts the generated data into an understandable format. The Cassandra/Apache HBASE stores the data. Apache Spark/Hadoop Map Reduce along with ML model processes the data. The decision makers get outputs in the form of graphs and charts.

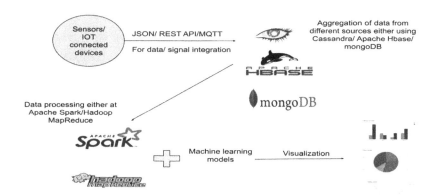

Fig. 4. Tools, technologies, and smart cities solutions process

The AI provides a strong processing capability. ML implementation can help smart cities in computation of thousands of variables. There are a number of challenges that hinder successful integration, such as different data sources and their formats, uncleaned data, security and privacy issues, cost, and speed of data generation. The challenges associated with the IoT are power efficiency, security, data privacy, and interoperability. The challenges with big data are heterogeneity and privacy of data. The data quality in terms of inconsistency, inaccuracy, incompleteness, and irrelevance has been major obstacles affecting the efficiency and effectiveness of smart cities solutions. The successful governance of a smart city requires publicprivate partnerships in co-designing, data collection, and decision-making.

7 Conclusion

The smart cities in emerging technologies environments are not only improving the lifestyle of people but also making the society stronger and cohesive. A smart city has a well-defined ecosystem such as intelligent transportation, smart health, smart education, home automation, smart energy, and remote management of resources. The IoT enables a wide range of intelligent services in smart cities. The IoT is a potential data generator to capture events and activities. The surveillance camera generates a huge volume of image and video data. In smart cities connecting big data analytics, physical infrastructure, the IT infrastructure, the social infrastructure, and the business infrastructure leverages in investigating the residents' behaviors, lifestyles, and opinions. The issues with big data are data security risks, data inconsistency, and data traceability. The study has analyzed and assessed the role of emerging technologies in smart cities solutions. Additionally, the tools, technologies, process, and future prospects have been discussed concerning smart cities solutions. The study concludes that emerging technologies have applications in smart cities for intelligent transportation, smart governance, and smart energy solutions. The future research needs to pay attention towards solutions such as epidemiology, telemedicine, in smart city settings using emerging technologies.

References

1. Lim, Y., Edelenbos, J., Gianoli, A.: Smart energy transition: an evaluation of cities in South Korea. Informatics **6**, 50 (2019)
2. Manyika, J., Chui, M., Bisson, P., Woetzel, J.: The internet of things: mapping the value beyond the hype. McKinsey Global Institute (2015)
3. Khan, A.I., Al-Mulla, Y.: Unmanned aerial vehicle in the machine learning environment. Proc. Comput. Sci. **160**, 46–53 (2019)
4. Jiang, D.: The construction of smart city information system based on the internet of things and cloud computing. Comput. Commun. **150**, 158–166 (2020)
5. Khan, A.I., Al-Badi, A.: Open source machine learning frameworks for industrial internet of things. Proc. Comput. Sci. **170**, 571–577 (2020)
6. Bibri, S.E.: The IoT for smart sustainable cities of the future: an analytical framework for sensor-based big data applications for environmental sustainability. Sustain. Cities Soc. **38**, 230–253 (2018)
7. Al-Badi, A., Tarhini, A., Khan, A.I.: Exploring big data governance frameworks. Proc. Comput. Sci. **141**, 271–277 (2018)

8. Wu, Y.C., Wu, Y.J., Wu, S.M.: An outlook of a future smart city in Taiwan from post – internet of things to artificial intelligence internet of things. In: Smart Cities: Issues and Challenges, pp. 263–282. Elsevier (2019)

9. Lim, C., Kim, K.-J., Maglio, P.P.: Smart cities with big data: reference models, challenges, and considerations. Cities **82**, 86–99 (2018)

10. Khan, A.I., Al-Habsi, S.: Machine learning in computer vision. Proc. Comput. Sci. **167**, 1444–1451 (2019). https://doi.org/10.1016/j.procs.2020.03.355

11. See, S.: Artificial intelligence computing for a smart city. In: Mehmood, R., Bhaduri, B., Katib, I., Chlamtac, I. (eds.) SCITA 2017. LNICST, vol. 224, pp. 6–8. Springer, Cham (2018). https://doi.org/10.1007/978-3-319-94180-6_2

12. Mohammadi, M., Al-Fuqaha, A., Sorour, S., Guizani, M.: Deep learning for IoT big data and streaming analytics: a survey. IEEE Commun. Surv. Tutor. **20**, 2923–2960 (2018)

13. Zaouali, K., Rekik, R., Bouallegue, R.: Deep learning forecasting based on auto-LSTM model for home solar power systems. In: 20th International Conference on High Performance Computing and Communications, Smart City, Data Science and Systems, pp. 235–242. IEEE, Exeter (2018)

14. Liu, Z., et al.: A Bayesian approach to residential property valuation based on built environment and house characteristics. In: International Conference on Big Data, pp. 1455–1464. IEEE, Seattle (2018)

15. Preda, S., Oprea, S.-V., Bâra, A.: PV forecasting using support vector machine learning in a big data analytics context. Symmetry **10**, 748 (2018)

16. Jules, T.D., Salajan, F.D.: The Educational Intelligent Economy: Big Data, Artificial Intelligence, Machine Learning and the Internet of Things in Education. Emerald Group Publishing, Bingley (2019)

17. Sadeh, A., Feniser, C., Dusa, S.I.: Technology education and learning in smart cities. In: Developing Technology Mediation in Learning Environments, pp. 78–95. IGI Global (2020)

18. Fakroon, M., Alshahrani, M., Gebali, F., Traore, I.: Secure remote anonymous user authentication scheme for smart home environment. Internet Things **9**, 100–158 (2020)

19. Navarro, J.L.A., Ruiz, V.R.L., Peña, D.N.: The effect of ICT use and capability on knowledge-based cities. Cities **60**, 272–280 (2017)

20. Muscat Media Group. https://timesofoman.com/article/48874/Oman/Omans-ITA–focuson-smart-cities

21. Conrad, P.: S Korea to support Oman's smart city ambitions. Oman Daily Observer (2018)

22. Al-Mahrooqi, S.: Developing the most significant and suitable smart city indicators for smart city pilot in Knowledge Oasis Muscat (KOM), Sultanate of Oman. United Nations University (2019)

23. Igel, C., Ullrich, C., Kravcik, M.: Using artificial intelligence and the internet of things to enable context-dependent recommendations in the smart city and smart factory. Athens J. Sports **5**, 253–262 (2018)

Trust and e-Government Projects – An Exploratory Study

Ambuj Anand[(⊠)] [iD]

Indian Institute of Management Ranchi, Ranchi 834008, Jharkhand, India
ambuj@iimranchi.ac.in

Abstract. Trust forms an important part of the discourse on e-Government. E-Government adoption involves trust relationships amongst three important entities: government, citizens and the enabling technology, forming a trust triad. An important link in this trust triad that has not been studied much in the literature on e-Government is the role of the trust reposed by the government in the citizens. This relationship has enormous potential to simplify the control mechanisms used in e-Government transactions. This in turn, significantly enhances citizens' perceived usefulness of the system. Hence, trust in citizens by the government is expected to eventually lead to higher adoption of the concerned e-Government system. This paper seeks to explore the issue of government trust in citizens using the case study methodology. We identify potential causes of disruption of the government's trust in citizens and mechanisms of production of trust in the same con-text. We emphasize the role of information processing capability in the production of the government's trust in the citizens. Further, we demonstrate that production of trust results in an opportunity for trust-based governance leading to higher adoption of e-Government projects.

Keywords: Trust, E-Government · Government to citizen · Qualitative research · Case study research

1 Introduction

Trust has been recognized as a critical factor for the success of e-Government projects (Carter and Bélanger 2005). It is regarded as a catalyst for e-Government adoption as it is instrumental in helping citizens overcome perceived risks and making them more comfortable in engaging with the system. The adoption of Government to Citizen (G2C) e-Government projects involves trust relationships amongst three important entities: government, citizens and the enabling technology. We term the combination of these three entities along with the interlinking trust relationship as the "trust triad".

Citizens' trust in government and in enabling technology are together termed as trust in e-Government (Carter and Bélanger 2005). The general experience of citizens in its engagement with the government, apart from the overall responsiveness of government officials and their empathy towards individuals, contributes to the development of citizens' trust in the government (Tan et al. 2008).

© IFIP International Federation for Information Processing 2020
Published by Springer Nature Switzerland AG 2020
S. K. Sharma et al. (Eds.): TDIT 2020, IFIP AICT 618, pp. 242–251, 2020.
https://doi.org/10.1007/978-3-030-64861-9_22

The adoption of technology in government services requires that the government has trust in enabling technologies (Pavlou 2003). Lack of government's trust in enabling technology often results in the project getting aborted.

An important link in the trust triad that has not been studied in adequate detail in the existing literature on trust in e-Government is the role of the trust reposed by the government in citizens (Yang 2005). This relationship has enormous potential to simplify the control mechanisms used in e-Government transactions. The relaxation of control mechanisms would con-tribute to process simplification which, in turn, would significantly reduce citizens' transaction costs and thus enhance their perceived use-fulness of the system. Thus, the trust in citizens is expected to eventually lead to higher adoption of the e-Government system.

This paper seeks to address the issue of the government's trust in citizens. We explore three key aspects of trust. First, we identify the potential sources of disruption of the government's trust in citizens. Second, we explore possible mechanisms for the production of trust in the context of e-Government projects. Finally, we establish the role of trust-based governance in simplifying government processes leading to diffu-sion of e-Government projects.

2   Trust and E-Government

2.1   Definition of Trust

In literature, trust is seen as a multidimensional, multidisciplinary construct, whose definition is often guided by the academic anchoring of the researcher (Lewicki and Bunker 1995). Trust is defined in literature as "a set of expectations shared by all those involved in an exchange" (Zucker 1986), "an attitude which allows for risk-taking decisions" (Luhmann 1988), "the generalized expectancy that the statements of others can be relied on or promises will be fulfilled" (Rotter 1980), "trust is a social lubricant that reduces the friction costs of existing trade and/or serves to increase the scope of trade" (Carson et al. 2003) and so on.

2.2   Role of Trust

According to the technology acceptance model (TAM), the actual use of technology is driven by the perceived usefulness and the perceived ease of use of the technology (Davis et al. 1989). Subsequent researchers have extended this model for different technological environments. In the context of internet-enabled technologies like e-commerce, where uncertainty develops due to reduced or non-existent human inter-action, trust is another driver of acceptance, besides perceived usefulness and perceived ease of use (Pavlou 2003; Gefen 2003). Similarly, trust is an important driver of adoption of e-Government services (Al-Adawi et al. 2005). In a cross-country analysis comprising 140 countries, trust was found to have a major influence on e-Government usage (Das et al. 2009). In this paper, we further explore this role of trust in the context of the usage of G2C e-Government projects. We propose a trust triad to capture the intricacies of the role of trust in this context.

2.3   The Trust Triad

Three entities form the core of G2C based e-Government transactions. These are citizens, technology, and the government, forming a trust triad (see Fig. 1). Literature engages mainly with citizens' trust in e-Government, that is, government and technology. We posit that the implication of trust in the e-Government space is more broad-based. Since user attitude towards acceptance is critical for adoption to occur, the widespread interest of the researcher community in the citizen perspective is understandable. However, the government's trust in technology and in citizens are also important relationships that deserve further research.

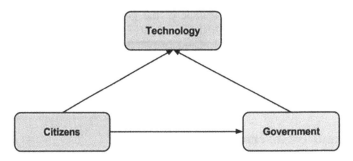

Fig. 1. The trust triad

2.3.1   Citizens' Trust in e-Government

Trust in e-Government literature, for the most part, refers to the citizens' trust in the government and technology. Taking these as two independent dimensions of a two-dimensional trust grid, levels of trust can be classified into one of four quadrants: Adversarial, Competitive, Cooperative, and Collaborative (Srivastava and Teo 2009). Some of the measures that governments can take to move into quadrants with greater trust include soliciting citizen feedback, increasing the nation's IT literacy, demonstrating commitment and support, and building institutional trust (Srivastava and Teo 2009). The presence of trust increases the adoption of e-Government services by making citizens feel comfortable while sharing personal information and performing government transactions over the internet (Alsaghier et al. 2009).

For citizens, the perceived usefulness of e-Government services is high as it makes information access easier and increases the government's accountability, efficiency and cost-effectiveness (Carter and Bélanger 2005). Moreover, ICT has the potential to increase transparency and reduce corruption and hence play a transformative role in governance (Bertot et al. 2010). Due to these possible benefits, successful e-Government initiatives can increase citizens' trust in the government (Parent et al. 2005). Citizens' trust is thus a driver and an outcome of e-government.

However, the level of trust and perceived risk also varies with the type of e-Government service. Perceived risk is higher at the transactional level of e-Government services as compared to the informational level (Horst et al. 2007; Chandler and Emanuels 2002). While the convenience of information access and/or transaction acts as an incentive for the adoption of e-Government services by citizens, privacy concerns act as a deterrent (Cullen and Reilly 2008).

2.3.2 Government's Trust in Technology

The introduction and use of technology in governance affect both the citizens and the government. Hence, technology's impact on the political and bureaucratic adminis- tration is also important and should be considered in managing e-Government projects (Bolgherini 2007). A government that is distrusting of technology will be reluctant to implement e-Government initiatives. In a study comparing the attitudes of citizens and bureaucrats towards e-Government, it was found that public officials in the United States of America were on the whole more positive about the success and impact of e- Government than the citizens, and were keen on a faster pace of implementation of e- Government projects (Moon and Welch 2005). This is because while the governments believed in their ability to provide suitable technological solutions to the citizens' needs, the citizens faced privacy and security concerns and often lacked sufficient awareness regarding e-Government initiatives. They also had general distrust towards the government. Another study found that the proactiveness of American municipal governments towards e-government initiatives was low in terms of strategic planning and expansion of service offerings (Moon 2002). However, among the municipal governments studied, the larger ones were more proactive than their smaller counterparts.

2.3.3 Government's Trust in Citizens

Yang (2005) highlights the importance of trust reposed by public administrators in citizens. In a survey-based analysis, he finds that it is a valid and relevant construct that affects citizen involvement. In more trusting societies, the level of trust between police and citizens has been found to be higher (Kääriäinen and Sirén 2012). Government's trust in citizens shapes its attitudes towards the citizens, and thereby influences citizen participation. "Felt trust", that is, citizen perception of being trusted by the government impacts citizens' trust in e-Government (Dashti et al. 2009). The trust reposed by the government and government institutions in citizens can thus play a large role in the success of e-Government. In this paper, we explore this trust relationship in more details.

3 Research Questions

Government's trust in the citizens plays an important role in governance (Yang 2005). We explore this relationship further in the context of the diffusion of e-Government projects. In this context, we study three broad research questions.

1. What are the possible situations of disruption of the government's trust in citizens in the course of G2C service delivery?
2. What are the mechanisms of production of the government's trust in citizens?
3. What role does the government's trust in citizens play in the diffusion of an e- Government project?

This paper provides empirical evidence for the importance of the role of trust in government to citizen relationship through the case of the Profession Tax Digitization project in West Bengal, India.

4 Method

We adopt a case-based method to seek answers to our research questions. The unit of analysis is the e-Government project – Profession Tax Digitization. This project has been selected based on theoretical sampling (Eisenhardt 1989). Theoretical sampling, in case of a single case study, means that the case is chosen for being usually revelatory, extreme exemplar, or for providing an opportunity for unusual research access (Yin 2009).

The primary mode of data collection was semi-structured interviews and field visits. A total of 13 people participated in the semi-structured interviews conducted over a period of three months. There was a single round of interviews with the end-users and the participants from the Profession Tax unit. The average duration of an interview was one hour. Three rounds of interviews were conducted with the senior leadership of the project, including the head of the State National Informatics Centre (NIC) and the head of the Department of Commercial Taxes. The field visits involved one trip to a Profession Tax unit and three trips to the department headquarters. The secondary sources of data include internal office communications, annual administrative reports, finance commission reports and legal documents describing the Profession Tax Act. Such use of multiple sources of data collection facilitates triangulation of data which ensures the reliability of the study (Yin 2009). In case study research, Yin argues for the adoption of analytical generalization and the use of explanation building for ensuring internal validity of the study. This is done in the analysis and discussion section of this paper.

5 The Profession Tax Project

At the core of a trust-based system is a design that rests on a belief that compliance, and not evasion, is the norm. This allows for significant simplification of the process of compliance and other rules. In keeping with this logic, the processes in the Profession Tax system have been reengineered, and several simplifications have been introduced. The Profession Tax Schedule - the document detailing exact rules to calculate the amount of tax payable for each type of end-users - has been simplified (the number of categories was reduced from 23 to 4). The frequency of filing of returns has been changed from quarterly to annual. The document requirements have been abolished. The process of registration and enrolment is now online and requires no submission of physical documents. The online process requires a valid Permanent Account Number (PAN) but does not require scans of any documents. The PAN data is automatically verified from the National Securities Depository Limited (NSDL) - an agency responsible for issuance of PAN. Payment of taxes is allowed only through Government Receipt Portal System (GRIPS). The GRIPS system, an integrated payment portal for transactions related to government services, facilitates online payment using internet banking, credit card or debit card and counter payment in banks. The existing methods of digitization of processes in Profession Tax project suggest that a paperless system is difficult to implement without trust in end-users and trust in technology. In this project, the department's trust in technology is demonstrated by its willingness to accept automated verification. The use of only digital records for storing and accessing registration, enrolment and payment data is also a manifestation of the department's trust in technology. The taxpayer's preference for the online mode of payment as against the counter-based payment system is a display of their trust in technology.

Most importantly, this application is a demonstration of the department's trust in the end-users (taxpayers). As per the new system, information filled into the enrolment or registration form is accepted at face value. An investigation is initiated only in the case of complaints or for defaulters. There is a future plan to use data analytics extensively for such fraud detection.

6 Analysis and Discussion

For the purpose of our research, we borrow the definition of trust from Zucker (1986). He states that "trust is defined as a set of expectations shared by all those involved in an exchange". In the context of this paper, since we expound on the government's trust in citizens, we focus on the government's expectations from the citizens in G2C transactions. Using the case of the Profession Tax project, we demonstrate that in the context of e-Government, it is possible to create trust in citizens through formal mechanisms. We further argue that it is possible to design more efficient processes based on trust though we agree that trust may not always lead to efficiency maximization (discussed further in Sect. 6.2). The government trusting citizens will not ensure that this trust is not violated. Further, according to Zucker, one's experience of such violations may not always result in distrust. He argues that distrust is a result of the suspicion of generalization of such disruption of expectations to future transactions. The underlying assumption in this argument is that "trust and distrust are not opposite ends of a continuum but rather different constructs altogether" (Zucker 1986). This means that "trust can be disrupted without producing distrust" (Zucker 1986). The remainder of this section is organized as follows. We first discuss four causes of disruption of trust in the context of the Profession Tax project. We identify two mechanisms of "production of trust" in PT. Such production of trust has a positive impact on project performance (Carson et al. 2003). Finally, we revisit the trust triad in the context of G2C e-Government projects.

6.1 Disruption of Trust

In any relationship involving two entities, there could be multiple sources of disruption of trust. Such disruptions may occur multiple times over a long period. At times this may result in the development of distrust. In this section, we identify four sources of disruption of trust in the context of the Profession Tax project. These four types of disruption may also be applicable to most of the other e-Government projects in India.

The first source of disruption of trust is the past experience of government interactions (or lack of it) with citizens. There are several instances of non-compliance of the Profession Tax Act by a large number of taxpayers. Such behaviour of a section of end-users causes disruption of the government's trust in citizens (and also in businesses). The other key implications are loss of tax revenue for the state as a result of a large number of defaulters and increase in the work pressure of government staff as a result of increased litigations and supervision. The second source of disruption of government trust is the behaviour of its own officers. Some officers are known to indulge in corrupt practices. The third source of disruption is the encounter with ghost IDs and fake addresses. In the manual system, when a user was enrolled in the Profession Tax system, (s)he would submit a proof of identity and address. This proof would typically be an attested photocopy of a set of documents. In a typical scenario, the officer-in-charge for approval would not be in a position to authenticate these documents. The department would realize such mishaps during scrutiny of defaults. Finally, there was a concern of generally low levels of trust in India.

6.2   Production of Trust

The relationship between trust and efficiency is widely contested in literature. One perspective is to treat the trust as one of the most efficient mechanisms for governing transactions (Ouchi 1980). Zucker (1986) argues against this perspective. He posits that since the production of trust involves several costs associated with it, it may or may not always lead to efficiency in governance and transactions. In this paper, we identify one such mechanism of trust that can also contribute to enhancing the efficiency of transactions. It has been observed that in the context of interfirm R&D collaboration, information processing capability of the firm positively contributes to the effectiveness of trust-based governance (Carson et al. 2003). E-Government projects also involve transactions between different stakeholders. The information processing capability of the concerned government department contributes to the production of government trust in citizens. Processes redesigned based on such trust would often result in more efficient systems owing to the requirement of less stringent controls.

In the Profession Tax department, the digitization project resulted in developing four distinct information processing capabilities. The first set of capabilities involves the automatic processing of the data in G2C transactions. This has enabled the Profession Tax department to remove human intervention in the process of registration, enrolment, tax payment and issuance of compliance certificate. The job of data entry has now been delegated to the end-users themselves. The automation and delegation of jobs facilitate the department in bypassing corrupt officers to a large extent. The second set of information processing capabilities is in the form of analytics. The department can now generate several reports from the data collected by the transaction processing system. These reports help them in identifying defaulters, potential fraud and in estimating growth in tax collection from various geographies. The third set of information processing capabilities has been achieved by deploying the Profession Tax officers in their new role of processing qualitative information collected from multiple sources in order to identify potential fraud and leakages. This eventually helps in expanding the tax net.

Finally, the Profession Tax department has acquired a more specialized information processing capability through integration with two external systems viz., GRIPS and NSDL. GRIPS facilitates payment of taxes and the automated generation of financial records concerning various types of transactions. It takes care of reconciliation of accounts with various payment gateways and banks. Integration with NSDL helps in the verification of the identity of end-users. Thus, it significantly reduces the concerns of ghost IDs.

These four information processing capabilities have contributed to the production of the government's trust in citizens. The processes of all the G2C services have been further redesigned based on trust in the end-users. In the next section, we discuss the outcome of these changes.

6.3   Outcome of Trust-Based Governance

Lack of trust in citizens contributes to inefficiencies in governance mechanisms. In the Profession Tax Digitization project, trust has played an important role in the reengineering of existing processes. Several controls were removed as an outcome of trust-based re-engineering. These changes, coupled with simplification of tax rules resulted in wider diffusion of government service and an increase in tax collection in general.

The responsibility of maintaining the current level of PT now rests on a small number of officers who are capable of handling a large number of transactions.

This has been made possible only through trust-based governance of G2C transactions. Further, we argue that the information processing capability of the government department acts as a mechanism for the production of trust, leading to efficiency in the government's transactions with various stakeholders, particularly citizens.

7   Conclusion

A large majority of e-Government projects are designed based on the assumption that the government has a lack of trust in the citizens. Yang (2005) highlights the absence of this theme in the e-Government literature. In this paper, we explore three important aspects related to trust in an e-Government project viz., disruption of trust, production of trust and benefits of trust-based governance. Yang's proposition relates to the importance of trust in citizens with respect to policymaking. We extend Yang's argument by proposing that trust in citizens can facilitate simplification of control mechanisms. This would, in turn, enhance the net benefits of digitization, thereby increasing the rate of adoption of e-Government services.

Trust plays an important role in increasing the efficiency of a process (Ouchi 1980). However, early adopters of trust-based mechanisms benefit more than the late adopters (Zucker 1986). The inefficiency creeps into the system through external organizations involved in the production of trust between two independent entities (Zucker 1986). We contribute to this debate about the impact of achievement of trust on the efficiency of a process. We observe that if the production of trust is achieved through building information processing capability of the trusting firm (in this case, the government), then the resultant governance mechanism is more efficient in nature (Carson et al. 2003).

The Profession Tax case has helped us in demonstrating the effectiveness of trust-based governance in G2C e-Government transactions.

Finally, we revisit the trust triad proposed in this paper. The three existing popular trust relationships (as shown in Fig. 2) in the context of G2C e-Government projects are citizens' trust in technology, government's trust in technology and citizens trust in the government. To this, we add a new trust relationship – government's trust in the citizens. We believe that this new trust relationship has the potential to significantly impact existing governance mechanisms by radically simplifying existing processes.

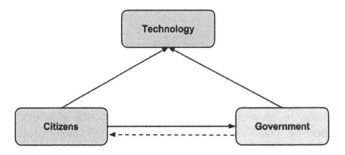

Fig. 2. The revised trust triad

The use of a single case is one of the key limitations of this paper. This has been partly necessitated by the general lack of projects where trust forms the basis of governance mechanisms and limited access to such e-Government projects. Future work in this area can look at other possible mechanisms for the production of trust in government and citizen relationship. Further, it is also possible to extend this theory by incorporating the role of other stakeholders in the trust triad. Some such important stakeholders are private implementation partners, other government departments and businesses.

References

Carter, L., Bélanger, F.: The utilization of e-Government services: Citizen trust, innovation and acceptance factors. Inf. Syst. J. **15**(1), 5–25 (2005)

Tan, C.-W., Benbasat, I., Cenfetelli, R.T.: Building citizen trust towards e-Government services: Do high-quality websites matter? In: Proceedings of the 41st Hawaii International Conference on System Sciences, pp. 217–227. IEEE, Washington, DC (2008)

Pavlou, P.A.: Consumer acceptance of electronic commerce: integrating trust and risk with the technology acceptance model. Int. J. Electr. Commer. **7**(3), 101–134 (2003)

Yang, K.: Public administrators' trust in citizens: a missing link in citizen involvement efforts. Public Adm. Rev. **65**(3), 273–285 (2005)

Lewicki, R.J., Bunker, B.B.: Trust in relationships: a model of development and decline. In: Bunker, B.B., Rubin, J.Z. (eds.) Conflict, Cooperation, and Justice: Essays Inspired by the Work of Morton Deutsch, pp. 133–173. Jossey-Bass, San Francisco (1995)

Zucker, L.G.: Production of trust: Institutional sources of economic structure, 1840-1920. Res. Organ. Behav. **8**, 53–111 (1986)

Luhmann, N.: Familiarity, confidence, trust: problems and alternatives. In: Gambetta, D. (ed.) Trust: Making and Breaking Cooperative Relations, pp. 94–107. Basil Blackwell Ltd., Oxford (1988)

Rotter, J.B.: Interpersonal trust, trustworthiness, and gullibility. Am. Psychol. **35**(1), 1–7 (1980)

Carson, S.J., Madhok, A., Varman, R., John, G.: Information processing moderators of the effectiveness of trust-based governance in interfirm R&D collaboration. Organ. Sci. **14**(1), 45–56 (2003)

Davis, F.D., Bagozzi, R.P., Warshaw, P.R.: User acceptance of computer technology: A comparison of two theoretical models. Manag. Sci. **35**(8), 982–1003 (1989)

Gefen, D.: TAM or just plain habit: a look at experienced online shoppers. J. Organ. End User Comput. **15**(3), 1–13 (2003)

Al-Adawi, Z., Yousafzai, S., Pallister, J.: Conceptual model of citizen adoption of e-government. In: Proceedings of The Second International Conference on Innovations in Information Technology (IIT 2005, Dubai, UAE, pp. 1–10 (2005)

Das, J., DiRienzo, C., Burbridge Jr., J.: Global e-Government and the role of trust: a cross country analysis. Int. J. Electr. Gov. Res. **5**(1), 1–19 (2009)

Srivastava, S.C., Teo, T.S.H.: Citizen trust development for e-Government adoption and usage: insights from young adults in Singapore. Commun. Assoc. Inf. Syst. **25**(1), 359–378 (2009)

Alsaghier, H., Ford, M., Nguyen, A., Hexel, R.: Development of an instrument to measure theoretical constructs of a model of citizens' trust in e-Government. In: Proceedings of the 8th European Conference on Information Warfare and Security, Lisbon, Portugal, p. 65 (2009)

Bertot, J.C., Jaeger, P.T., Grimes, J.M.: Using ICTs to create a culture of transparency: E-Government and social media as openness and anti-corruption tools for societies. Gov. Inf. Q. **27**(3), 264–271 (2010)

Parent, M., Vandebeek, C.A., Gemino, A.C.: Building citizen trust through e-Government. Gov. Inf. Q. **22**(4), 720–736 (2005)

Horst, M., Kuttschreuter, M., Gutteling, J.M.: Perceived usefulness, personal experiences, risk perception and trust as determinants of adoption of e-Government services in the Netherlands. Comput. Hum. Behav. **23**(4), 1838–1852 (2007)

Chandler, S., Emanuels, S.: Transformation not automation. In: Proceedings of 2nd European Conference on E-Government, Oxford, UK, pp. 91–102 (2002)

Cullen, R., Reilly, P.: Information privacy and trust in government: a citizen-based perspective from New Zealand. J. Inf. Technol. Polit. **4**(3), 61–80 (2008)

Bolgherini, S.: The technology trap and the role of political and cultural variables: a critical analysis of the e-Government policies. Rev. Policy Res. **24**(3), 259–275 (2007)

Moon, M.J., Welch, E.W.: Same bed, different dreams? A comparative analysis of citizen and bureaucrat perspectives on e-Government. Rev. Public Pers. Adm. **25**(3), 243–264 (2005)

Moon, M.J.: The evolution of e-Government among municipalities: rhetoric or reality? Public Adm. Rev. **62**(4), 424–433 (2002)

Kääriäinen, J., Sirén, R.: Do the police trust in citizens? European comparisons. Eur. J. Criminol. **9**(3), 276–289 (2012)

Dashti, A., Benbasat, I., Burton-Jones, A.: Developing trust reciprocity in electronic-government: the role of felt trust. In: Proceedings of the European Mediterranean Conference of Information Systems, Izmir, Turkey, pp. 1–13 (2009)

Eisenhardt, K.M.: Building theories from case study research. Acad. Manag. Rev. **14**(4), 532–550 (1989)

Yin, R.K.: Case Study Research: Design and Methods, 4th edn. Sage Publications, Thousands Oaks (2009)

Ouchi, W.G.: Markets, bureaucracies, and clans. Adm. Sci. Q. **25**(1), 129–141 (1980)

Expanding Beyond Technology-Driven Factors: IoT for Smart City Services

Malliga Marimuthu[(⊠)] [iD]

La Trobe Business School, La Trobe University, Melbourne, Australia
m.marimuthu@latrobe.edu.au

Abstract. Understanding the gaps in promoting the communal or societal benefits of the technology will facilitate the planning organization and technology designer to decide how the technology can be diffused into the market to best meet the expectation of the user and the organization. This study argues that the service user-centric technology adoption in smart cities namely online participatory technologies (OPT) should expand beyond technology-driven factors to explore the effect of personality-belief based factors. Individual-level behavior generated from people connectedness with human, society and environment are important to understand the influence of user's social personality belief on technology adoption and continuous usage. This study extends the existing research on technology adoption to reveals the importance of social personality belief fundamentals for the adoption of Internet of Things (IoT) in the interest of creating citizen-centric services in smart cities. Systematic review studies conducted to identify the factors that drive IoT adoption and to reveal the challenges in diffusing the technology in the context of smart cities. We propose a methodological solution to explore structural patterns of the citizen's relationship within the groups, for the organization to create opportunities to exploit the social personality factors for technology adoption and usage purpose.

Keywords: Smart cities · Participatory technologies · Internet of Things · Service user-centric · Societal benefits · Social personality

1 Introduction

The two fundamental aims of the Smart Cities are improving the service they deliver to their citizens for economic efficiency and social effectiveness in meeting the stakeholders' expectations [1]. The attainment of these two goals are not only dependent on government and service providers but it hugely depends on the support provided by the citizens [1]. Knowing this, citizen-centric smart cities have given rise to their efforts of finding ways to incorporate active connection, engagement and intelligence of its citizens via smart technologies for public issues identification and solutions [2]. Accordingly, Smart City Service Technologies have been introduced to enhance life quality in a city and to make the city livable.

Aguilera et al. [1] claimed that the following technologies are important to promote public participation: mobile broadband, smart personal devices, government-sponsored cloud and open-source public databases. The advancement of Internet of Things (IoT),

© IFIP International Federation for Information Processing 2020
Published by Springer Nature Switzerland AG 2020
S. K. Sharma et al. (Eds.): TDIT 2020, IFIP AICT 618, pp. 252–258, 2020.
https://doi.org/10.1007/978-3-030-64861-9_23

Linked and Open Data and Crowd-sourced data and the rise of wireless internet has facilitated the creation of user-centric mobile services that exploit open data and add value by providing user-generated data [1]. The emergence of smartphone-based technologies and user-centric mobile services app to support the functional value of smart cities through monitoring and improving the civil infrastructure systems is rising as the modern smartphones are equipped with various sensing, computing, communication and crowdsourcing capabilities.

The involvement of the citizens in the citizen-centric smart cities services planning is operationalized via the introduction of online participatory technologies (OPT) in which citizens are seen as intelligent sensors. OPT is defined as 'the method or tool that is used for engaging communities and organizations' [3]. In this OPT, citizens function as intellectual sensor via two methods. First, real-time data gathered automatically by the city sensor from the move or interaction generated by citizens. This data is useful to create prevention, implement early action and improve decision making [2]. For example, the data utilize for transportation maintenance (e.g. traffic management) and risk prevention (e.g. COVID-19 control). Second, is referring to the data provided by citizens as crowd-sourced data supplied by citizens. The spread of IoT technologies into Smart Cities allows citizens to obtain knowledge about their surroundings and to contribute with new data captured through their mobile devices. Citizens can also edit the data for example information about the damaged of public facilities, anything broken in the public area, poor public transport services etc.

Citizens are enabled and empowered to participate into the process of Smart City's data consumption and production of their own data for the benefits of the citizens, businesses and governing bodies [4]. Example of a smart city project that aims data gathering, crowdsourcing, collaboration and empowering of citizens are IES Cities [1] and examples of tools utilized in EIS Cities for participatory purpose are FixMyStreet, FixMyTransport, Open City Toolkit, Mind Mixer, ClickFix and Crowdbrite. These tools provide citizens with analytical tools and citizen-centric services to solicit problems, reporting problems and form an online collaboration in city services such as the issues of public infrastructure [2]. The adoption of these tools is technology-driven and citizen-centric [4]. However, in most cases the technology adoption and technology diffusion drivers were explored and understood from technology-driven aspect. Less emphasize give to explore the citizen-centric aspect with respect to the unique nature of the technology implementation purpose and expected outcomes.

2   Research Question

Although the technology-driven factors are crucial for successful implementation of the technology, however recognizing the difference in the functional necessities of the IoT, it is equally important to embrace the influence of other non-technology driven factors. The demand for technology adoption solution varies from IoT to IoT based on various factors such as technology competencies, providers supports, government interventions and user involvements. Expensive infrastructure and advancement of technology are unserviceable without proper end-user adoption. It is a bigger challenge when there is not enough support from the users to use technology or to add value to the data. Hence, to truly streamline the adoption process of a technology that developed for the benefits of the people, it is crucial to understand what exactly the end-users want, whether they are ready to opt a smart solution, what may influence them to adopt and continuously use the technology, and how their needs or experience in using the technology can be prioritized. Hence, in this review article, we explore the following research question:

"What considerations should planning organizations take into account when they are promoting the adoption and use of online participatory tools?" What overlooked? How to fill in the gap?

3 Gaps in Understanding IoT Adoption: Overlooked Challenges

The introduction of technology can hold a number of unique benefits for users. Across the studies, we can see that several factors have been consistently examined and found to be predictive of the decision to adopt IoT in smart cities. Individual factor (personal innovativeness), product factors (relative advantage, cost), interface factors (trust in the government and/or provider of the technology, perceived expectations of others in one's social environment) are the common factors referred for IoT adoption [5–7].

However, studies of IoT adoption in 'smart cities' primarily focus on generic IoT [8] or category of IoT such as mobile application but very few studies focus on the specific function of the IoT. As a result, we have a limited understanding of the unique factor that influence the respective technology or cause barriers to the adoption of the technology. From the literature review, we found that many cities are failing to influence the citizens to adopt the technology while some are struggling to keep the face of the technology usage among the citizens, while technology diffusion is frequently disrupted. One of the key challenges facing the sustainable adoption of IoT is understanding the stimulus that encourages citizens to adopt and continuously support the use of the IoT [4, 8]. Facilitating the technology adoption in smart cities in term of citizens involvement will help the local stake authorities to succeed with the technology adoption and diffusion. Moreover, expanded holistic technology adoption framework should be developed to understand unique IoT adoption in the context of smart cities.

In the context of OPT, the pervasive connectivity of the smart technology for communal benefits is the strength of the technology that should be utilized for stimulating technology adoption and diffusion [9]. Hence, this study proposes the importance to identify the community-based value as a personality effect on technology adoption and feasibility in optimizing this factor should be explored. A thorough mapping of the factors listed in the study of IoT against the literature review conducted in this study brings us to the conclusion that feel of responsibilities towards community are ignored in the IoT studies in smart cities context although these factors form the foundation of the smart cities ecosystem. Moving in this path, this study explores the significance of personality-specific belief that focus on citizen's "sense of community" in technology adoption frame.

3.1 Personality-Specific Belief: Sense of Community

One of the extensively applied concepts to understand the connections of individuals to social groups is a sense of community (feel of responsibility). The development of these psychological elements on oneself lies in their involvement in community activities [10]. A sense of community is usually related to the pride of belonging to a place and can be influenced by the perceived livability. It is associated not only to other citizens but to the commonly shared norms, norms of reciprocity, social order, and, codes of behavior [11]. The citizen with this personality quality adopts into the aggregated civic society concept: participation and civic sociability in organized activities (Putnam, 1993; Dempsey et al. 2011). Macke et al. [11] claimed that "sense of community is fundamental for understanding innovation, institutional dynamics, and value creation" in smart cities context.

Based on the literature studies conducted in this study, we propose that sense of community affects the attitudes of users to act for the harmonies of the community in their area. The stronger the sense of community is, it is predicted that the users will demonstrate higher social responsibility and emotional commitment to protect their surroundings and promote the nature and societal benefits for the better living of the community. Studies proved that people with a higher sense of community are more likely to engage and participate in the development of the city and likely adopt the innovation that supports the development of the surroundings [7, 11]. Wang et al. [7] found that sense of community at the individual level affect the adoption behavior of the developers.

4 Method/Approach

A systematic literature search was conducted to set the direction of the research by identifying the factors that commonly used to study IoT and mapped that against the emerging factors of adoption in smart cities. The contribution of this study is building and integrative framework elaborating technology adoption comprising technology and human-driven factors for participatory based IoT. Further literature analysis on the human-centric factors allows us to understand the human-driven factors based on various classification. This is important to strategies the solution to enhance IoT adoption and diffusion in the context of smart cities.

5 Theory

A number of theories have been used to explain the factors that influence technology acceptance and adoption at the individual level. 'Theory of Reasoned Action' (TRA) (Fishbein and Ajzen 1975) and 'Theory of Planned Behavior' (TPB) (Ajzen, 1991) explain behavior about beliefs for acceptance of technologies. 'Technology Acceptance Model' (TAM) (Davis 1989), the 'Unified Theory of Acceptance and Use of Technology' (UTAUT) (Venkatesh et al. 2003), and its successor (UTAUT2) (Venkatesh et al. 2012) are other technology acceptance theories that dominate IS adoption research. However, in this study, we argue that that the common technology acceptance factors as described in the above technology adoption models are not adequate predictors of service user-centric technology adoption in smart cities. The Rogers diffusion model [12] was also challenged when scholars argued that people are more likely to engage in socially responsible behavior when they derive pleasure and satisfaction from this behavior compared to their obligation [13]. Hence it is important to understand the process behind the technology adoption and diffusion that takes the user through the journey of becoming aware of the technology, accepting the technology after assessing it against various influencing factors, fully utilize the technology and continuously use the technology. Scholars stated that currently, there are still very few studies that explore the adoption of IoT from a multiple theory perspective [14].

In this study, we proposed that technology adoption theory should be married with Social Theory. In the context of this study, motivation theory will be relevant to identify the factors that motivate the citizens to adopt and use the OPT. Studies have found that sense of community have behavioral consequences and these effects are noticed to operate at the individual level [11]. Hence, this study proposes to embed the lens of motivation theory into technology adoption and diffusion model to explore the inspiration for citizens to adopt and continuously use the technology for own benefits, social identity and self-satisfaction derive from helping others within the smart city boundary.

6 Discussion: Solution to the Challenges

We foresee from the literature that the individual-level behavior developed from the communities of interconnected people may serve as stimulation for technology adoption in smart cities. The theoretical connections between social networks and sense of community have been shown in some recent studies by evaluating the sense of belonging and social identify [7, 11, 15]. Therefore, in this study, we suggest exploring the effects of individual-centric factors that developed from their network to speed-up the adoption and to assure sustained usage of the user-centric technology. This study suggests urban planner and social researchers find a method to analyze the social interaction that forms the sense of community. This will be useful to generate a constructive understanding of how the sense of community can be nurtured for innovation adoption, idealization and continuous usage. Thus, the smart city technology developer, designers, government and other stake agents must carefully emphasize with the diverse set of users of their everyday experiences in using the IoT technology. The users' needs or experience should be mapped across various factors including demographic challenges, personal needs, personality beliefs, social needs, social networking and etc. In this study, we also propose the utilization of social networking analysis to identify the structure and pattern of the citizen networking that influence them to adopt and actively use OPT for citizen-centric service design.

7   Conclusion

While the technical capability of the participatory IoT in facilitating the adoption for functional purpose is important, the communal benefits of the technology attraction to the users (citizens) should be considered as well. We propose that the citizens as the city service users must be aware of, and also perceive, the collective benefits of particular smart city services technologies to forcefully participate in customer-centric service design. They must be able to experience the benefits of their participation in accomplishing improvement in their surrounding communities' quality of life that could lift their self-satisfaction. Many scholars claimed that customer-centric smart city service design has great potential to change or uplift societies. However, the success requires active participation of the service users in co-creating the social values for themselves and their community. Hence understanding service users' perceptions about the technology from technology-driven and citizen-centric are equally crucial for adoption and continuous usage of this service user-centric technology. This study reflects on the theoretical expansion in the discussion as well as the future implications of this study on research and practice related to service user-centric IoT adoption.

References

1. Aguilera, U., Peña, O., Belmonte, O., López-de-Ipiña, D.: Citizen-centric data services for smarter cities. Future Gener. Comput. Syst. **76**, 234–247 (2017). http://dx.doi.org/10.1016/j.future.2016.10.031
2. Kopackova, H., Komarkova, J.: Participatory technologies in smart cities: what citizens want and how to ask them. Telemat. Inform. **47**, 101325 (2020). https://doi.org/10.1016/j.tele.2019.101325, (June 2019)
3. Afzalan, N., Sanchez, T.W., Evans-Cowley, J.: Creating smarter cities: considerations for selecting online participatory tools. Cities **67**, 21–30 (2017). http://dx.doi.org/10.1016/j.cities.2017.04.002, (May)
4. Degbelo, A., Granell, C., Trilles, S., Bhattacharya, D., Casteleyn, S., Kray, C.: Opening up smart cities: citizen-centric challenges and opportunities from GIScience. ISPRS Int. J. Geo-Inf. **5**(2), 16 (2016)
5. Abu Salim, T., El Barachi, M., Onyia, O.P., Mathew, S.S.: Effects of smart city service channel- and user-characteristics on user satisfaction and continuance intention. Inf. Technol. People (2020)
6. Sepasgozar, S.M.E., Hawken, S., Sargolzaei, S., Foroozanfa, M.: Implementing citizen centric technology in developing smart cities: a model for predicting the acceptance of urban technologies. Technol. Forecast. Soc. Change. **142**, 105–116 (2019). https://doi.org/10.1016/j.techfore.2018.09.012
7. Wang, W., Zhang, S., Su, Y., Deng, X.: An empirical analysis of the factors affecting the adoption and diffusion of GBTS in the construction market. Sustainability **11**(6), 1795 (2019)
8. Janssen, M., Luthra, S., Mangla, S., Rana, N.P., Dwivedi, Y.K.: Challenges for adopting and implementing IoT in smart cities: an integrated MICMAC-ISM approach. Internet Res. **29**(6), 1589–1616 (2019)
9. Padyab, A., Habibipour, A., Rizk, A., Ståhlbröst, A.: Adoption barriers of IoT in large scale pilots. Information **11**(1), 1–23 (2020)

10. Ramos-Vidal, I.: A relational view of psychological empowerment and sense of community in academic contexts: a preliminary study. Behav. Sci. (Basel). 9(6), 1–19 (2019)
11. Macke, J., Rubim Sarate, J.A., de Atayde Moschen, S.: Smart sustainable cities evaluation and sense of community. J. Clean. Prod. 239, 118103 (2019)
12. Rogers, E.M.: Diffusion of Innovations, 5th edn. Free Press, New York (2003)
13. Girod, B., Mayer, S., Nägele, F.: Economic versus belief-based models: shedding light on the adoption of novel green technologies. Energy Pol. 101, 415–426 (2017). http://dx.doi.org/10.1016/j.enpol.2016.09.065, (September 2016)
14. Mital, M., Chang, V., Choudhary, P., Papa, A., Pani, A.K.: Adoption of Internet of Things in India: a test of competing models using a structured equation modeling approach. Technol. Forecast. Soc. Change 136, 339–46 (2018). https://doi.org/10.1016/j.techfore.2017.03.001
15. Rotta, M.J.R., Sell, D., dos Santos Pacheco, R.C., Yigitcanlar, T.: Digital commons and citizen coproduction in smart cities: assessment of Brazilian municipal e-government platforms. Energies 12(14), 1–18 (2019)

Aspects of Digital Urbanism in India and Abroad

Sriram Rajagopalan and R. Sriram[(⊠)]

Great Lakes Institute of Management, Chennai, India
{Sriram.raj,sriram.r}@greatlakes.edu.in

Abstract. Digital urbanism is described as an emergent understanding of city administration shaped by the influx and pervasiveness of information and communication technologies. This description covers three aspects of Information and Communication Technology, Pervasive Computing and City Administration driven by social organs. This paper has observed the aggregate use of computing technologies linked to social organs of cities through a digital transformation. International cities, have benefitted from the use of such computing technologies in resolving social problems, understanding different models of its implementation. However, for Indian cities where social problems are aplenty, use of such technologies has its intuitive experiences. Further, while past literature on digitally urbanized global cities relies primarily on technology dimensions of radministration, this is found wanting in Indian context. Our paper focuses on bringing out pertinent aspects of computing technologies across India and international cities, observing how these technologies are linked to social organs of city administration.

Keywords: Digital Urbanism · Information Communication Technology (ICT) · Pervasive computing · Social organs · International cities · Dimensions

1 Introduction

An early literature on "Digital Urbanism" has described the concept as "Influence of information and communication technology (ICT) and pervasive computing in City Administration" (Chatterji 2017). Two themes, "ICT" and "Pervasive Computing" evolve from this precise description linking technologies to cities. To study them in detail, relevant literature in the last two decades were reviewed on these themes (from 1999 - until recent). A large number of studies on "ICT" has revealed its significance in social transformation across international cities (Mazihnan 1999; Hollands 2008; Toppeta, 2010; Chourabi et al. 2012; Washburn et al. 2012). In India, the journey of using ICT began much later during the process of digitalizing city administration (Khatoun et al. 2017). Of all measures undertaken for using ICT in India, "E-Governance" was the first (Khatoun et al. 2017). The emergence of a more advanced computing technology in International cities through interconnected systems, allowed ubiquitous networks to access data worldwide (Malhalle and Dhotre 2020). For India, the applicable use of technology in different forms to communicate between users like RFIDs, Smart phones, and Sensors had already ensured an active presence of such

© IFIP International Federation for Information Processing 2020
Published by Springer Nature Switzerland AG 2020
S. K. Sharma et al. (Eds.): TDIT 2020, IFIP AICT 618, pp. 259–273, 2020.
https://doi.org/10.1007/978-3-030-64861-9_24

computing technologies in every organ of Indian city administration (Aggarwal and Mohanty 2015). However, social skeptics on technology placed their critiques in endorsing a planned approach in transforming city administration in India (Datta 2018). As evidenced in research studies quoting International cities, the objective of digital urbanism in India too should focus more in approaches that eradicate social problems, improve efficiency, and optimize resources in administration absorbing technology (Kennedy et al. 2018).

This paper is prepared with this context addressing the objective of bringing out literature on (a) aspects of using ICT in India, (b) the various computing technologies in practice at disposal for communication between devices and users, and (c) the social organs which has utilized this technology to make its effective contribution in society.

2 Background

Developing nations have benefitted from the use of ICT. The ICT has brought-in structuring changes in society and economy for India (De and Bandyopadhyay 2020). For India, the ICT began with "E-governance" as a model oriented towards automation in collection and accounting of any payments, registration and approval of housing plan documents (Ojo 2014). The arguments placed to diffuse an ICT enabled service often required the adaptability of innovation in technology (Khanh 2014). The different models of e-governance vis-à-vis "four" pillar and "six" stage models contemplated an enterprise transformation for departments, municipalities, and government agencies. The social focus of a governance system also encouraged Indian administration to move away from making a "participatory" role in processes (Vinoth Kumar 2015). Further, these developing nations were ambitious to embrace a complete digitalization for enhancing quality of infrastructure, service delivery and citizens' interface in cities (Aijaz and Hoelscher 2015; Hatuka and Zur 2020). During this same period, research organisations like McKinsey identified challenges on availability of internet infrastructure, its cost of access and usage, awareness and literacy among public, and the narrow range of applications available (Vinoth Kumar 2015). International literature on smart cities are also continuously identifying different frameworks and factors contributing to create an informational urbanism (Barth et al. 2017). People in small towns of India too are faced apprehensions within their local bodies stating a lack in technical capacity and knowledge to operate digital structures (Housing and Land Rights Network 2017). At the macro-level, the use of ICT in development plans has promoted for a clean and sustainable livelihood in urban areas. The economic issues in India like deficient development plans, slacks in implementing plans, apportioning land availability, and fund insufficiencies have been a challenge for improving the quality of governance in cities (Kennedy et al. 2018).

The role described of ICT's in literature was as an agent of development to steer enabling environment with (a) Transparent governance systems, (b) Efficient technology infrastructure, (c) People oriented capacity resources and (d) Effective policy measures (UN Habitat and Ericcson 2015). The international cities have adopted them into their urban development plans. In the initial stages, these cities oriented themselves to integrating physical and social infrastructure with technology infrastructure (Hollands 2008; Washburn et al. 2009; Toppeta 2010). The progress of digitalization proved to have an economic transformation with set goals in cities of East Asia, Europe and Americas, illustrating the benefits on using technology for social concerns (Mazihnan 1999; Harrison et al. 2010; Aggarwal et al. 2014; Trivellato 2016; Talari et al. 2017; Zhuhadar et al. 2017). The advantages drawn from his progress resulted in investments for infrastructure by government and private corporates embedding technology with society, citizens' participation for campaigns and policy changes at local/regional/national level (Mazihnan 1999; Beranek et al. 2014; Kar et al. 2019). Literature and secondary sources reveal an amount of Rs.273 lakh crore as outlay in the budget for an extended period to making these investments (Chatterji 2017).

3 Motivation

The motivation for this paper evolves from assessing achievements and failures at micro/macro-scales in bringing development reforms in Indian city administration (Aijaz and Hoelscher 2015). To recap the development plans, each one (1979, 1993, 2005 and 2015) made significant efforts in improving the economy and physical infrastructure of cities, creating urban settlements on agglomeration metrics (Wu 2016). The urban development reforms for International cities were completely based on understanding trivial needs of society gathering information from citizens' participation on technology (Chourabi et al. 2012; Beranek et al. 2014). The active innovation factor used by international cities in tracing down checks for social organs gives a larger substantive evidence of involving technology in administration (Talari et al. 2017; Zhuhadar et al. 2017). The progress of innovation (in last two decades) in cities is explained in the below Fig. 1. This significant difference in development reforms between nations and a promotion for the concept "future cities" in India kindled the interest to analyze various approaches to digitalize administration of cities (Kennedy et al. 2018). The other reason is driven by the fact that penetration levels of ICT has been more than 75% in urban clusters with 18% influenced by Internet usage in India (Chatterji 2017). The information published from media reports observes the process of digitalization to have a major lack in conceptualizing city administration. These reports show nearly 67% of the work pending at desk level with rest in implementation stages (Hindu Business line, dt: December 16, 2018). This clueless situation, a desperate need for planned approach, differences between nations in implementing a full-fledged ICT enablement has motivated the academia to choose digital urbanism and identify functional areas where such enablement can help improve city administration in Indian context.

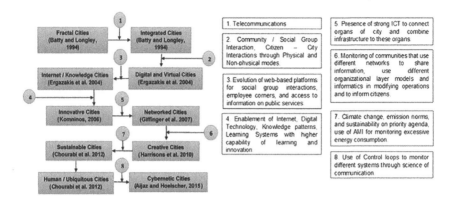

Fig. 1. Innovative progresses categorizing cities

4   Research Questions

The objectives set for the article discloses three important areas of interest. The aspects of using ICT in India, the computing technologies in practice for communication between devices and users, and enumerating the social organs that has utilised the technology for social contribution in India. In line with these three themes, the set of questions answered throughout this article includes

(a) The preparedness or readiness in Indian cities to use ICT enabled technologies,
(b) The approach observed by Indian cities in implementing plans to adopt/extend ICT in city administration,
(c) The salient features available in an advanced technology operated service for adoption in cities,
(d) The measurability of technology infrastructure to social organs like land and other infrastructure.
(e) The outcome of enabling computing technology and its sustainable benefits to society.

5   Information and Communication Technology - India

India has begun its journey in using ICT to digitalize city administration through the e-Governance measures (Khatoun et al. 2017). This ICT has induced a structural change in economy and society through urban centres to the global world (Castells 1996; Thrift 1996; Hall 1998; Sassen 2001). The concept of future cities were built on the premises of using ICT to create technology infrastructure in the international cities (Giffinger et al. 2007). An early literature quoted "E-governance" as one of the mechanisms in extending services to citizens using internet (Mittal and Kauar 2013). In its initial stages for India, the "e-governance" laid a greater emphasis on digitalizing documents in various departments although the key initiative was on merging the divide between urban and rural clusters (Vinoth Kumar 2015). The ICT did not stop only with digitalizing departments but also delivered online services through e-payments, rail ticket bookings, online transactions, and ordering food in India (De and Bandyopadhyay 2020). The core social benefit of an ICT was primarily to build clean sustainable infrastructure and a safe environment that enhances the income for poor and disadvantaged in India (Aijaz and Hoelscher 2015). The measures undertaken by government (state and central) to enable ICT in different states of India are enlisted in the below Table 1.

Table 1. State-wise brief Digital Measures in India (Vinoth Kumar 2015)

State	Digital Programs	Purpose
Andhra Pradesh	Twin Cities Network Service and Integrated Citizen Services Centre	Linking twin cities of Hyderabad and Secunderabad. Helps citizens to access information about state and central governments, pay utility bills, property taxes, purchasing certificates and licenses. Receiving information regarding building permits, property registration, and transport procedures.
Madhya Pradesh	E-Governance	Preparation of payrolls, budgets, official communication, land records, public programmes and relief operations. Uses hindi as an official language for state departments to communicate within.
Karnataka	Centre for E-Governance	Computerisation of Department records and to support vision of creating awareness on use of Information Technology.
Tamil Nadu	E-Governance Tamil Internet Research Centre	Computerisation of Department records, building technical capacity, creating effective citizen centric services.
Kerala	Information Kerala Project Transliteration Technology	Networking district cooperative banks and credit societies through core banking services. Recording tax collection, welfare schemes, government orders.
	Facilitation Booths	Information Kerala is to computerise and connect 1214 local bodies through digital network. The project has adopted the model of e-Governance for three constituent villages under one district panchayat to build information on land holdings, age structure, health and tax payments.
	Dr.SMS	The Facilitation booths help provide internet access to cooperative societies, aids to deliver information relating to agriculture, health and education to people in villages.
	Transport Services	Dr. SMS – To provide comprehensive information on healthcare facilities available within the locality through SMS.
	Utility Services	Transport related services – To provide information on schedule of state transport buses, details on road tax, and vehicle registration.
	Education Services	Utility Services – Kerala State Electricity Board and Kerala Water Authority to provide consumer billing and complaint resolution. Education Services – to provide information on various examinations to students.
Rajasthan	RajSWIFT RajNIDHI	RajSWIFT – Facilitates the use of online data and communications among officials. RajNIDHI – Providing services to citizens in a transparent and responsive manner.
Gujarat	E-Nagar SWAGAT E-Procure E-Jamin m-Governance Self-help Kiosks E-Ward	E-Nagar – Connects all offices complexes and cooperations in the state. SWAGAT – A four tier grievance system to provide state wide attention to grievances using technology. E-Procure – to provide a system for efficient and transparent process for e-tendering. E-Jamin – to provide a system for accessing land records in a transparent way.
Maharashtra	e-Governance	Transforming Mumbai and Pune into IT hubs, developing skills and awareness among employees through training while linking all district level offices through WAN.

6 Moving Ahead from ICT to Computing Technologies

The participation of citizens in society was the focus of the e-governance measure in India. The ICT has encouraged such participation by society through a planned approach (Vinoth Kumar 2015). This approach began with building the vision for a vibrant computing technology (Mitton et al. 2012). It was the power sector in the initial stages to map customer databases through networks using Geographical Information Systems (GIS) for collecting data on energy consumption (MoP 2005). Three years later, the power department established a customer service center to handle grievances (MoP 2008). It was observed that the grievance handling at these customer centres faced challenges of making huge expenditures with lack of capacity for action (Aggarwal et al. 2010). Additionally, the government made policy decisions to bring operational efficiencies in power sector with installation of Automatic Meter Reading (AMR)/Automated Metering Infrastructure (AMI) to assess energy consumption (TERI and NASSCOM 2011). It was further extended with Supervisory Control and Data Acquisition (SCADA) for accounting purposes (Powerline 2012). These strategic decisions yielded the department to lower down its revenue losses and manage peak loading issues at the grid level (Powerline 2013). During this period, the government took efforts in setting up command/control centers to support a data-driven networked model of urbanism (Townsend 2013). Computing technologies were effectively utilised by public services in setting-up a network between a series of user driven essentials like Aadhar (personal information) and banking services; spatial data support systems (SDSS) and GIS (for fund allocation); dashboards to report critical field level information to the command centres (Vinoth Kumar 2015). The spatial data support systems uses its infrastructure (SDI) to help small towns in urban regions identify hotspots for reducing time lapses in offering public services (Sridharan 2015). Computing technologies have been utilised by international cities to procure data and prepare analytical reports for administration to ensure a sustainability of future resources (Bibri 2018). The development of command centres and its cyberspace has brought-in a new digital environment, communicating between devices and users. Technology literatures in computing has observed the performance of innumerable tasks by these command centres in communicating information between devices and users (Haldorai et al. 2019). The four-layer structure in command centres and their design architecture captures data on different aspects for actions by authorities (Sarabeshwar 2020) This design architecture of command center is enlisted in the below Table 2.

Table 2. Design architecture of command control centres (Sarabeshwar 2020)

Four Layers of Command Centres	Details of information available from these layers
Application and Devices Layer (Top)	**Sub Layer 1:** Collects information on audio, video, sound, sensing and crowdsourcing through devices in the secured network.
	Sub Layer 2: Sensors and edge-level devices collect information and make public announcements or actionable information available to citizens.
	Sub Layer 3: Back-end support services like call centers and messaging services supply information using devices and actuators.
Integration Layer (Second)	This layer aggregates the data, interacts with API in different urban centres for processing voluminous information. This layer brings together platforms and data through software development kits / Web services.
Platform and Analytics (Third)	This layer involves the platform in which the command center is created and different analytical approaches created within for handling information. For ex. Data analytics, AI, Video and Predictive Analytics.
Integrated Control Center (Fourth)	This layer involves the physical set-up of infrastructure involving technology like Computer Terminals, Simulation Rooms, and Server Rooms.

7   Digital Urbanism – Linking Social Organs to Computing Technologies

Erstwhile measures on urbanization during 70 s (for cities) had described the presence of sociological characteristics in cities (Goist 1971). These descriptions were reiterated in the recent past when preparing redevelopment plans of cities explaining the compounded sociological challenges prevalent in the present society (Aijaz and Hoelscher 2015). International cities had involved computing technologies to support city administration in resolving the sociological challenges. A detailed list of applications in computing technologies used for administering social organs in international cities are given in the below Table 3.

Table 3. Details of applications in computing technologies administering social organs

Sl no.	Types of technology	Organs of the society	Short particulars of technology adopted in addressing solutions to the organs of society	Research references
1		Theoretical		
2	Radio Frequency Identifier (RFID)	Hangars	Identifying Directions for Vehicle Parking and Permits in Europe	Kosmatos et al. (2011)
		Power and Energy	Transferring data on consumption of energy to other parties. Saving consumption of energy	Jaradat et al. (2015)
		Health Services	Locating Patient/Hopsitals/Ambulatory Services for Treating patients	Kosmatos et al. (2011)
3	Sensors	Hangars	Identifying the correct path for parking vehicles in Europe	Kosmatos et al. (2011)
		Power and Energy	Charging and Discharging Enegy of Batteries in Electric Vehicles	Saber et al. (2011)
		Power and Energy	Integrated with Renewable energy resources to improve his consumption of energy (Fujisawa, Japan) to reduce carbon footprints	Hancke et al. (2012)
		Environment	Monitoring Lighting, circulation, waste and environment in France	Mitchell et al. (2013)
		Environment	Monitoring Air, Noise and Water resources in environment using sensor nodes. (using route choice behaviours)	Zhuhadar et al. (2017)
		Water	Identifying faulty power lines in water pipes in Portugal. Sensors (Vibration, Pressure and Sound types) help improve water distribution	Hancke et al. (2012)
		Health Services	Biosignalling helps in identifying patient information for treatment	Talari et al. (2017)
		Pathway	Using Transponders, receiving information on travellers on road (Electronic Road Pricing) in Singapore	Arun (1999)

(continued)

Table 3. (*continued*)

Sl no.	Types of technology	Organs of the society	Short particulars of technology adopted in addressing solutions to the organs of society	Research references
4	Near Field Communication (NFCs)	Community	Identifying community people through Access Cards/Bank and Personal ID cards	Hancke et al. (2012)
5	Networking Technology	Power and Energy	Automated Meter Reading (AMR) and Advanced Metering Infrastructure (AMI) to acquire data on consumption and loss of energy	Aggarwal et al. (2014)
		Water	Using Siphonic pressure pumps and user scale growth to assess water levels in water bedpan	Jiang (2015)
		Adminsitration	Connecting Universities, Industries, Citizens, and Government using Apps for City and Munipcal Administration. iOBridge and SpeakThing are examples (Busan South Korea)	Talari et al. (2017)
		Pathway	Using Transponders, charging travellers on roads (Electronic Road Pricing) in Singapore	Arun (1999)
6	Wireless Sensor Nodes	Traffic/Transport	Capturing information on flow of Traffic and Transport using coordinator, router and end-devices	Hancke et al. (2012)
		Power and Energy	Connecting to electrical meters for tracing energy consumption. ZigBee is a network layer in this process of transferring information	Hancke et al. (2012)
		Environment	Connecting to understand demographic and weather conditions of a city. ZigBee is a network layer in this process of transferring information	Rathore et al. (2016)
7	Space-Time Mapping	Environment	Use Space-time mapping in capturing Noise pollution in different areas of city through IoT. Data is shared with government for better local administration	Maisonneuve et al. (2009)
8	Map-Layering Technology	Environment	Using CURI (Rest Interfaces) adaptors in locating places with predefined areas of interaction such buildings and facilities. For example - Locating seating arrangements in a stadium	Bhowmick (2012)

(*continued*)

Table 3. (*continued*)

Sl no.	Types of technology	Organs of the society	Short particulars of technology adopted in addressing solutions to the organs of society	Research references
		Housing	Using Trasactive controllers in this technology to dim out lighting in houses and streets saving energy consumption (Netherlands)	Mitchell et al. (2013)
		Power and Energy	Using Smart Meters to dim up lighting to save consumption of energy in Songdo, Korea. This is done with creation of Automated Buildings	Strickland (2011)
		Power and Energy	LED lighting is also used along with Smart Meters in calculating energy consumption (Netherlands)	Talari et al. (2017)
9	MATLAB Programming	Environment	Applications like iOBridge and Speakthing are being used in capturing real-time data for visualising city administration. The MATLAB programming codes are being used	Talari et al. (2017)

The inception of the computing technologies to support urban development evolves from use of pervasive models where-in, the physical aspects of the environment (or social organs) is integrated into a technology system (or computing system) through different models (Haldorai et al. 2019). Category of technology services like Infrastructure-as-a-Service (IaaS), Software-as-a-Service (SaaS), and Platform-as-a-Service (PaaS) has helped city administration identify solutions to the problems of social organs (Vinoth Kumar 2015). The progress of experimenting integration of computing technologies to social organs in these cities continued for more than two decades (research literatures quote references from 1994 till-date). Some of the notable progresses include (1) The concept of measuring landscapes using fractal geometry (Batty and Longley 1994); (2) Behavioral aspects of society like positive intentions and attitude in using technology is measured with interactive models on adoption (Davis et al. 1989; Dabholkar 1994; Dabholkar 1996; Eastlick 1996; Asop 1999; Mosberg 1999); (3) e-Commerce for society to procure products (Hoffman et al. 1999); (4) Technology platforms for social interactions between community groups (Ergazakis et al. 2004); (5) Knowledge platforms and learning systems for innovation (Komninos 2006); (6) Assessment of risks in climate change, extraction of natural resources, floods, blackouts, pollution, inundation of solid wastes, and use of hazardous chemicals (Kitchin et al. 2007); (7) Absorbing public sentiments on different issues to educate society and de-risk society from its problems (Nohara et al. 2008; Cucchiara et al. 2011; Mora Mora et al. 2015); (8) Monitoring urban activities through network, layer models and informatics (Harrisons et al. 2010); (9) Protecting environment from use of obsolete technology products (Morton et al. 2012); (10) Creating virtual proto-types in visualization of landscapes using advanced networks (Morton et al. 2012); (11) Measuring availability of land and natural resources making it effective for use in society using computing technologies (Carli et al. 2013); (12) Different models of pervasive computing uses Urban IoT for finding solutions to social problems (Mitton et al. 2012; Kitchin 2014); (13) Using different applications like 3E Housing and ZigBee (in housing) for measuring scale and capacity of computing technologies to handle large sets of data/information (Gubbi et al. 2013).

In this time-period, a conceptual model "Technology readiness indices (TRI)" measuring the propensity of a readiness in cities for adopting technology having four constructs was prepared covering service industries to test its delivery among customer, company (community for sociology) and environment (Parasuraman 2000). The other literature studies on service industries, measured challenges in a four factor model vis-à-vis ideation plans, web-portals (for recording inquiries), continuous quality in delivery, and recovery of service failures (Bitner et al. 2000; Parasuraman 2000; Batty et al. 2012; Zaslavsky et al. 2013; Kumar 2015). The revised model of TRI had enablers and inhibitors as measuring variables testing the overall change in state of mind among people who use technology resources (Parasuraman and Colby 2015). This readiness to utilize technology helps administration of Indian cities replicate progressive strategies followed by international cities (McLaren and Agyeman 2015).

For urban development and social organs, a progressive growth in research was visible with creation of a strong framework linking dimensions in urban development and computing technologies. The framework prepared by Hollands (2008, 2015) clearly differentiates the purpose of urbanization in cities underlining the strategies of branding them with people-orientation. Chourabi et al. 2012 in their research study on assessing performances of cities brought-out an eight-dimensional framework consisting of Organization, Technology, Policy Context, People, Economy, Built infrastructure and Natural environment as critical factors for observance. This research study observed the use of AMR/AMI in power and energy department to assess consumption. The use of AMR/AMI combats the issues of climate change and emission norms maintaining a sustainable future. Batty et al. 2012 in their research on post-modern urbanization discusses the incubation of intelligent technology infrastructure for assessing social needs. A model framework for linking technology with modern urbanization tracking changes through mobile applications in city was also developed through the concept of Urban IoT (Zanella et al. 2014; Aijaz and Hoelscher 2015).

Ruta et al. 2010 in their research on frequencies of technology, observed the sufficient need for possessing technical skills among users of technology – from low-end to high-end. Modern infrastructure are already set-up for the ambitious use of digital technology in India a decade ago (Gann et al. 2011). The progress observed in such infrastructure is larger than what was found to resolve social problems (Aggarwal et al. 2015; Vinoth Kumar 2015; Talari et al. 2017). Bibri (2018) in their research on ensuring sustainability of information resources for urban centres, discuss the progress of different thematic approaches (Green ICT development, pervasive computing and deep learning) for decision making and countering actions on society to utilize environmental resources. Kennedy et al. (2018), too in his research on outsourcing urban e-governance as a state subject, re-emphasizes the need for making a conscious effort to promote use of ICT in urbanization plans.

Different schools of thought emerge in society for adopting technology during these years of experimentation. These schools of thought – restrictive, reflective, rationalistic, or pragmatic and critical has placed its views on technology vs. anti-technology sentiments (Kummitha et al. 2017). The larger negatives include (1) Unemployment/ underemployment (Hollands 2008), (2) State authored market fundamentalism (Harrisons and Donnelly 2011; Watson 2013; Washburn et al. 2010), (3) Addressing inequalities (Carvalho 2015; Hollands 2015; Caragliu et al. 2011; Leydesdorff and Deakin 2011; Mudler 2014), (4) Privatization of urban space (Hogan et al. 2012; Gibbs et al. 2013; Waart et al. 2015), (5) Vendor push (Komninos et al. 2013; Bunnell 2015; Moser 2015; Datta 2015), (6) Closed planning (Datta 2015), (7) Reduced social capital (Calzada and Cobo 2015), land grabbing (Datta 2015), (8) Land grabbing (Datta 2015), (9) Distant dream (Datta 2015; Jazeel 2015)

In addition, several critiques were placed on use of technology for cities. These include (a) Creating social inequality and income differences among people, their educational and employment standards (Graham 2002; Caragliu et al. 2011; Leydesdorff and Deakin 2011), (b) Use of technology for cities are considered to be increasingly speculative, risky and arcane (Kirkpatrick and Smith 2011), (c) Focus on achieving sustainability than on reality as a strategic vision in enabling technology (Angelidou 2015; Komninos et al. 2013; Wolfram 2012), and (d) The arguments on achieving social order through adoption of ICT given the social realities (Helgason 2002).

A common sentiment too prevailed in India where discussions on urban development were conducted in different forums with the idea of building advanced technology systems with challenges faced by administration (MoUD, GoI, 2015; 2018). Today, the adoption of ICT and pervasive computing goes beyond these critiques and negativities to address social concerns of city administration. Recent literatures on engineering research reveal continuous efforts taken to link social organs to technology. In this approach, the following social organs were tested in engineering for linking them to computing technologies. They are (1) Water/Sewer treatment and Energy Management

(Pampana et al. 2020), (2) Traffic and Transport congestions in roads (Singh and Srivastava 2020), (3) Healthcare and Patient Management (Prabhu et al. 2020), (4) Housing and Security Administration (Govindaraj et al. 2020), (5) Restoring natural resources and environment (Rathore et al. 2016)

8   Benefits and Managerial Implications of Adopting Computing Technologies in Social Organs

The international cities have utilised the pervasive computing systems for social organs largely as described in the previous picture, explaining how different social organs are linked to these computing technologies. This salient technology tools mentioned in the picture table helps the administration in taking decisions towards adopting these computing technologies for Indian cities. The social benefit in utilizing these computing techniques have been the improvements observed in quality of life as the authors (Harrisons et al. 2010; Washburn et al. 2010; Toppeta 2010) describe them in their research papers on technology enabled cities. The two-factor TAM model evolved a decade ago, brought-in the interest of adopting technology measuring it with ease of use and satisfaction of the user (Venkatesh and Bala 2008). Later, the readiness in innovation brought strategies to encourage effective utilization of data and its resources with emerging technology products like dashboards in society for cities (Rosenthal 2010; Morton et al. 2012). This innovation continued in manufacturing to make advancements for identifying alternate use of raw material to make products. For example, the use of bagasse for peppre wood is a real-time illustration (Perera et al. 2014). Further, the sentiments and opinions of people in society on administering cities too, can be measured from the advancements in digital technology (Mora Mora et al. 2015). The efforts to create sustainability in optimizing future resources prospected the digital technology to measure the quantum of de-risking required for administration (Bibri 2018).

For India, where the challenges listed in adoption of ICT and pervasive computing are absorbed from literature review, some of these challenges often point to the methods adopted in handling them (Aggarwal and Mohanty 2015; Aijaz and Hoelscher 2015; Vinoth Kumar 2015; Bhattacharya et al. 2016). The reiterated need for a planned approach required in adopting technology, enlisted as a social skeptic leads the discussion to have an advanced approach in assessing the progress of linking technology to social organs in an Indian context (Datta 2018). This need has encouraged us to analyse factors contributing to digital urbanism that can be measured for observing the degree of enablement, technology has made in administration of social organs for Indian cities. The related constructs and their references are provided in the below Table 4.

Table 4. Proposed dimensions of Digital Urbanism in India

Dimensions	Possible options	Key elements	Representative Work
Conceptual	City Theory	Topography, climate, history, economy, culture, space and time	Gerst, 1971 Ayaz and Hoelscher, 2015
	Definitions	Social organs, Post-modernism, Information communication technology, Community, Urbanisation	Hall et al 2000 Washburn et al 2010 Chourabie et al 2012
	Case Studies	Singapore city - National IT Plan, Intelligent Island, IT2000 report, National Information Infrastructure, Padova city – Urban IoT	Mazibhan, 1999 Zanella et al 2014
	Stakeholders	Swachch Bharat Mission (SBM), Atal Mission for Rural Urban Transformation (AMRUT), Heritage City Development and Augmentation Yojana (HRIDAY)	Ministry of Urban Development, GoI 2015 Gore M. et al 2018
	Experimental	Urbanism, creative industries (Brisbane, Australia), Future city (San Diego), Entrepreneurial city	Hollands et al 2008
City Administration	Policy / Vision	Retrofitting, Redevelopment, Green and Brown field development	Ministry of Urban Development, GoI 2015, Ministry of Housing and Urban Affairs, GoI, 2018
	Organs	Traffic, Transport, Road Network, Power / Energy, Housing, Environment, Water, Healthcare, Community, Security and Administration	Giffinger et al 2007 Toppeta, 2010
	Institutions	NITI Aayoog, TECOM, Dubai, Hitachi, Siemens, CII	Bhattacharya et al 2015
	Agglomeration	Movement of people, Excessive Population, Poverty, Unemployment	Ratti et al 2006 Girardin et al 2008
Infrastructure	Types	RFID, NFC, SCADA, Sensors, Wifi, Wireless Sensor Nodes (WSN), Fibre Optic, Network Effects, Map Layering	Aggarwal et al 2015 Harrison et al 2010 Vinoth Kumar, 2016 Lingli, 2015 Mazibhan, 1999 Ruta et al 2010 Talari et al 2017 Zhuhadar et al 2017
	Levels	Lower end technologies – RFIDs, Sensors, Wireless Sensor Nodes, Wifi High end technologies – SCADA, Cloud, Space Time Mapping, Map layering, Machine Learning Methods	Washburn et al 2010 Gubbi et al 2013
	Application	Electronic Road Pricing (ERP), 3E Housing, ZigBee, Transport, IoT, Internet of Energy (IoE)	Carlo et al 2013 Dodge et al 2007 Kitchin, 2014
	Pervasive Computing	In-vehicle sensors, cloud computing, software abstraction layers	Mitton et al 2012 Kitchin, 2014 Bibri et al 2018
Service Encounter	Categories	Area-based development, Part-based development, Infrastructure as a Service, Platform as a Service, Software as a Service	Batty et al 2012 Vinoth Kumar, 2015
	Customer Interface	Self-service technology, Customer Web Portal, Sensor Data Consumer layer, Expanded Conceptualization	Parasuraman, 2000 Vinoth Kumar, 2015
	Service Delivery	Sensing as Delivery, Sensor Owner Layer, Sensor Publisher Layer	Zaslavsky et al 2013 Perera et al 2014
	Service Quality	Pyramid model, Technical Quality, Functional Quality, Customer loyalty	Bitner et al 2000 Parasuraman, A, 2000
	Service Recovery	Interactive, Internal and External Marketing, Customer Feedback portal, Critical Problems, Feasibility	Batty et al 2012 Perera et al 2014, Parasuraman, A, 2000,
	Continuum of Service	Storing, archiving, processing of data, SFPark, Square kilometer array (SKA), Customization, Spontaneous delight	Parasuraman, A, 2000 Zaslavsky et al 2013
Disruption	Innovativeness	New and Emerging Technologies, Peer learning	Bitner et al 2000 Parasuraman, A, 2000
	Competitiveness	Technology Readiness, Technology paradoxes, Drivers, Inhibitors	Bitner et al 2000 Parasuraman, A, 2000
	Uniqueness	Stability, Loyalty Chain	Bitner et al 2000 Parasuraman, A, 2000
	Relevance	Competitive leverage, Redemption value	Bitner et al 2000 Parasuraman, A, 2000
Physis	Climate Change	Chloro Flouro Carbons, Carbon Emission, Pollution	Kyriazis et al 2013 Rathore et al 2016
	Deluge Protection	Fire, Flooding, Inundation of solid and liquid waste	Bitner et al 2000 Dodge et al 2007
Sustainability	Strategy	Green ICT, Thematic Analysis, Efficiency of Energy systems	Perera et al 2014 Bibri et al 2018
	Mechanism	Inductive analytic approach, Mobile Applications, storing, integration, Processing and	Perera et al 2014 Bibri et al 2018
	Data Utilisation	Big Data, Pattern recognition, Optimizing Resource Utilization, Operational functioning, Mitigate Environmental risks	Perera et al 2014 Bibri et al 2018
	Obsolescence	Technological changes, Electronic Waste, Recycling of Waste, Virtual City Models	Rosenthal 2010 Morton et al 2012
Measurement	Spatial	Mark-up, Availability of Land, natural resources, global positioning	Harrison et al 2010 Carli et al 2013
	Traceability	Intruder Detection, Sophisticated filtering techniques, Transferable belief model	Cucchiara et al 2011 More Mora et al 2015
	Social Interaction / Fear	Human Capital Interaction (HCI), Twitter com, Orkut com,	Nohara et al 2008 Cucchiara et al 2011

9 Limitations and Future Scope of the Study

The present paper is only a literature review of all relevant studies conducted in adoption of ICT and pervasive computing across Indian and International cities. The aspects covered in this paper limits itself only bringing out use of ICT and pervasive computing technologies in social organs of cities where such technologies are either implemented or under-implementation stage evidenced in literature. The study does not include other administrative aspects such as investments and financial outlay undertaken for utilising such technologies. The timelines chosen for the literature review is from post-period of liberalization (in India) to the current period during which continuous technological changes are observed across international cities. The research literatures cited from engineering studies are only to enlist the technical use of the concept and not to elucidate the mechanism involved in its use for social organs. This paper does not make comparative studies on approaches undertaken by Indian and international cities in lieu of adopting computing technologies for their social organs. The reviews given in this paper are a collation of social actions taken by international cities for adopting computing technologies and are not prescriptive to other nations or cities.

The future scope of the present study attempts to understand the factors contributing to digital urbanism in detail for India absorbed from the above table. Hence, the literature pertaining to these factors have been presented lucidly in this paper. A detailed study on each factor is presently under progress for the topic involving a qualitative analysis to aggregate critical sub-factors contributing to the concept.

10 Conclusion

The concept of digital urbanism was described in this article with three important aspects - ICT, pervasive computing and social organs respectively. These aspects were studied in this article providing several relevant literature references from India and international cities. The article also made available relevant literature and concepts covering the research questions mentioned. The summary of this literature elucidates the involvement of computing technologies (from low to high-end) in supporting social organs for administering international cities. Studies on Indian context, had some recent references from technical literature implying the progressive approach adopted by society to transform city administration. News from the Indian digital media had recently claimed that more than 67% of the urban development projects are either partially being implemented or at the desk-level with no forward movement in paper work (The Hindu Business Line, December 16, 2018). This scenario encourages us to study the critical factors contributing to adoption of technology. The literatures referred in this paper and the factors observed in the above table would be studied further not only for understanding the use of computing technologies in India but also how the social organs of city administration are linked to these computing technologies and their social benefits to cities.

References

Adapa, S.: Indian smart cities and cleaner production initiatives–integrated framework and recommendations. J. Clean. Prod. **172**(1), 3351–3366 (2018)

Aijaz, R., Hoelscher, K.: India's smart cities mission: an assessment. ORF Issue Brief **124**(1), 1–12 (2015)

Alderete, M.V.: Exploring the smart city indexes and the role of macro factors for measuring cities smartness. Soc. Indicat. Res. 1–23 (2020). https://doi.org/10.1007/s11205-019-02168-y

Batty, M., et al.: Smart cities of the future. Eur. Phys. J. Spec. Top. **214**(1), 481–518 (2012)

Beranek, P.M., Klein, G., Jiang, J.J.: Building user engagement for successful software projects: meaningfulness, safety, and availability. Pac. Asia J. Assoc. Inf. Syst. **6**(3) (2014). http://aisel.aisnet.org/pajais/vol6/iss3/1

Bibri, S.E.: The IoT for smart sustainable cities of the future: an analytical framework for sensor-based big data applications for environmental sustainability. Sustain. Cities Soc. **38**(1), 230–253 (2018)

Chatterji, T.: Digital urbanism in a transitional economy–a review of India's municipal e-governance policy. J. Asian Public Policy **11**(3), 334–349 (2017)

Chourabi, H., et al.: Understanding smart cities: An integrative framework. In: 45th Hawaii IEEE International Conference on System Science, pp. 2289–2297 (2012)

McLaren, D., Agyeman, J.: Sharing Cities. The MIT Press, Cambridge (2015). ISBN 987-0-262—02972-8

Gann, D.M., Dodgson, M., Bhardwaj, D.: Physical–digital integration in city infrastructure. IBM J. Res. Dev. **55**(1.2), 8–11 (2011)

Giffinger, R., Fertner, C., Kramar, H., Meijers, E.: City-ranking of European medium-sized cities, pp. 1–12. Centre of Regional Service, Vienna University of Technology (2007)

Girardin, F., Calabrese, F., Fiore, F.D., Ratti, C., Blat, J.: Digital footprinting: uncovering tourists with user generated content. Perv. Comput. IEEE **7**(4), 36–43 (2008)

Goist, P.D.: City and community: the urban theory of robert park. Am. Q. **23**(1), 46–59 (1971)

Gore, M., Meenal, A.: 'Swachha Bharat Abhiyan' (clean India campaign): a step towards social accountability. Eur. J. Multidisc. Stud. **7**(2), 60–69 (2018)

Gubbi, J., Buyya, R., Marusic, S., Palaniswami, M.: Internet of things (IoT): a vision, architectural elements, and future directions. Future Gener. Comput. Syst. **29**(7), 1645–1660 (2013)

Hatuka, T., Zur, H.: From smart cities to smart social urbanism: a framework for shaping the socio-technological ecosystems in cities. Telemat. Inf. **55**, 101430 (2020)

Hollands, R.G.: Will the real smart city please stand up? Intelligent, progressive or entrepreneurial? City **12**(3), 303–320 (2008)

Kar, A.K., Gupta, M.P., Ilavarasan, P.V., Dwivedi, Y.K.: Advances in Smart Cities: Smarter People, Governance, and Solutions. CRC Press, Taylor and Francis, New York (2017)

Kennedy, L., Sood, A.: Outsourced urban governance as a state rescaling strategy in Hyderabad, India. Cities **85**, 130–139 (2018)

Kosmatos, E.A., Tselikas, N.D., Boucouvalas, A.C.: Integrating RFIDs and smart objects into a unified internet of things architecture. Adv. Internet Things **1**(1), 5–12 (2011)

Lingli, J.: Smart city, smart transportation: recommendations of the logistics platform construction. In: IEEE International Conference on Intelligent Transportation, Big Data & Smart City (ICITBS), pp. 729–732 (2015)

Madakam, S., Ramaswamy, R.: 100 new smart cities (india's smart vision). In: 5th IEEE National Symposium on Information Technology: Towards New Smart World, pp. 1–6 (2015)

Mahizhnan, A.: Smart cities: the Singapore case. Cities **16**(1), 13–18 (1999)

Citizens' Participation as an Important Element for Smart City Development

Anton Manfreda[✉], Nejc Ekart, Matic Mori, and Aleš Groznik

School of Economics and Business, University of Ljubljana, Ljubljana, Slovenia
{anton.manfreda,ales.groznik}@ef.uni-lj.si,
ekart.nejc@gmail.com, matic.mori@gmail.com

Abstract. It seems that the smart cities concept is confidently becoming one of the highly exposed current challenges. Undoubtedly, it brings a lot of interest and excitement both among academia and professional researchers since it presents a futuristic project with many intriguing features that will influence the quality of life. The technological aspects of smart cities are quite well researched, while an important issue remains with the acceptance of the technology among individuals. Participation in the projects seems to be one possible solution when it comes to the wider acceptance of the services offered within the smart city. Scholars have already examined different aspects of the participation in smart cities, however, no one has explored and quantified the impact participation would have on overcoming the issues and concerns people feel towards smart cities.

Thus, the main focus of our research is not only to highlight the participation as a possible solution in overcoming well-known issues but also to measure and examine to what extent the participation is a viable solution in terms of changing people's perspective and attitude towards smart cities, towards services provided in the smart city and towards smart city development. The purpose of our research is, therefore, to examine the actual impact participation has on the perceived issues that are related to smart cities. Using an online questionnaire, we empirically tested the research topic on more than 500 individuals in different countries.

Keywords: Smart city adoption · Citizens · Participation · Digital transformation

1 Introduction

In the world of unlimited connectivity, knowledge, and data, it seems like the smart cities concept is surely becoming one of the most exposed challenges on the earth. Undoubtedly, it brings a lot of interest and excitement to the table since it presents a futuristic project with many intriguing features that could hypothetically take the quality of life to another level. However, it seems like people have not accepted the concept yet as currently, smart cities tend to go hand in hand with a lot of burning issues due to lack of trust. For this reason, more and more scholars are pointing out the importance of trade-off between tremendously improved services on one hand and challenging issues on the other.

© IFIP International Federation for Information Processing 2020
Published by Springer Nature Switzerland AG 2020
S. K. Sharma et al. (Eds.): TDIT 2020, IFIP AICT 618, pp. 274–284, 2020.
https://doi.org/10.1007/978-3-030-64861-9_25

Participation in relation to smart cities is not a novelty as it has been described by several authors. Among them Habib has described issues related to smart cities and has proposed participation as a solution [7]. Besides, a set up framework for participation in building smart cities together with possible implementations was proposed [20]. Additionally, the urge to turn to participation, the urge to turn to smart citizens instead of smart cities was also claimed [10]. Participation was also connected with a fundamental factor in achieving desired level of quality of life in smart cities [2]. In one of the recent systematic literature reviews [22] show some strong evidence about the importance of participation and engagement but also lists anticipated problems that could come with it. Reviewing the literature, we see that scholars have written about different aspects, implementations, etc. of the participation in smart cities, but no one has explored and quantified the impact participation would have on overcoming the issues and concerns people feel towards smart cities. Thus, our main focus of the research is to not only highlight participation as a possible solution in overcoming those issues, but to actually measure and find out if participation is a viable solution in terms of changing people's perspective towards smart cities.

The goal of our research is to examine the actual impact participation has on the perceived issues that are related to smart cities. We are starting with a literature overview, focusing on participation and perceived issues. We continue with explaining our methodology. After that we focus on the perceived issues, explaining our key findings about them. Our last part of the articles is about the impact of the participation has in solving the issues stated in a chapter before that. We highlight the results from the questionnaire and tie our findings to the literature.

2   Literature Review

2.1   The Definition of Smart Cities

An immense excitement for 'smart city' concept took its research to another level and the number of 'smart city' papers have exploded. However, there is still no universal description, let alone a definition.

The term 'smarty city' is not entirely new since it was already mentioned in the late 1990s by Bollier in his 'smart growth movement'. However, it was not until 2008 that it became globally known as it was used by some big global corporations including IBM, Cisco, and Siemens [18].

Hollands raised doubts about the motive of big corporations in building smart cities. In other words, those descriptions mentioned the importance of people, but were still too 'technocentric'.

While smart city definitions are evolving from day to day a lot of 'new' propositions base on [16] description. They present a smart city as a human concept and therefore implement some sort of socio-institutional dimension. The concept of a smart city means more than just technological city. City upgrades from technological to smart when the increased quality of life and continued sustainability is possible due to adequate investments in ICT and human capital.

By another popular definition [14] smart city is 'a community that systematically promotes the overall wellbeing for all of its members, and is flexible enough to proactively and sustainably become an increasingly better place to live, work and play'. Even though this definition made another big step towards citizen-centric smart cities, it still completely respects dimensions defined by Nam and Pardo. Therefore, we adopted this definition as our basis for the purpose of our research.

2.2   Burning Issues of a 'Smart City' Concept

In our literature overview we have highlighted the most relevant issues based on already existing literature and our own opinion. The expressed issues as such are perceived by individuals and could be nothing but lack of trust. For this reason we think that participation might be a possible solution. We have identified the following issues: 5g, Perceived privacy, Perceived security, Corporate interest and Overwhelmed by technology.

Health and Security Concerns due to 5G
It has been argued [13] that smart cities cannot be built without the implementation of the 5g network. Due to vast amounts of data needed, being able to be transferred only by 5g network, the timing for the first smart cities will be closely related to the timing of building a 5g network [13]. Different authors [1] have recognized the important social factor of implementing the 5G network. With 5G being crucial factor for implementing Smart cities, raising doubts in 5G network are highlighted in our article as an issue. Kumar have also written that there is a strong movement of people not in favor of 5G network being built. They concluded, that the majority of doubts are related by a distrust in the security of the networks. It has been found in the analysis of the social media activity of users writing about the 5G that the most expressed concerns are related to radiation and a threat of cancer, speaking in general that the most of the doubts are related to potential health issues [9].

Can Smart Cities Fulfill Perceived Security?
Every single modern technology or invention brings new issues and challenges. Cerrudo [3] discusses different security problems in smart cities including lack of testing, poor security systems, encryption issues on devices, simple technology bugs, etc. Even though initially it seems like terrorism around the world is reducing, thinking that would be very naïve. It's actually evolving like never before. Individuals with university degrees and very advanced skills are pursuing extremist groups. Since they basically live on the internet, cybercriminals are very well organized and have a lot of resources. Consequently, billions of dollars are lost every year because of many cyber attacks.

Every smart grid or city consists of numerous internet-connected devices. Therefore, a smart city with millions of connected devices over a wide area presents a very tempting target for cyber attackers. In addition, due to a big number of connected nodes attacks like this could be devastating [11].

The attack surface for smart cities is vast and wide open to attacks. The 'smartening' of cities does not increase the number or capability of a threat, but it does increase the vulnerability due to increasing complexity and widening the surface.

Furthermore, it increases possible consequences since it is possible to deal real-world damage by attacking network or data [8].

For this reason, every technology that smart city implements must be security audited throughout to be completely sure about its safe use. If the data in smart cities system is not used with caution, it could be easily exploited. Thus, preventing security problems and hackings is one of the core things that have to be assured in a city for it to become smart instead of just being a 'dumb' city [3].

A Thin Line Between Smart and Surveillance City

Modern smart city technologies and data-driven urban science raise numerous privacy harms [12]. In the concept of smart cities, privacy exceeds its physical definition of not being observed or disturbed since more advanced technologies collect information that goes beyond the physical sense. Instead, 'smart' definition of privacy should be built around modern concepts including IoT and cybersecurity. An important issues is the challenge of privacy in smart cities as the preservation of collected information about an individual's physical characteristics behavior, habits, communication, location, associations and feelings [5]. More datafication means that people are exposed to even higher rate of surveillance. With every improvement or an innovation there is an increase in number of everyday aspects that are collected as data. With an increasing number of connected devices, cameras and unique identifiers (usernames, emails, IDs, etc.) it is becoming impossible to live without leaving so-called digital footprints and shadows [12].

Thus, excessive data collecting and even activity following may make the belonging citizens feel like they are taking part in Big Brother [7]. The importance of understanding several group's preferences has also been pointed out [7]. What's more, it is immensely important to analyze trade-off between city's effectiveness and its security.

Smart Cities as an Opportunity for Corporations

The process in building the smart cities has been so far made in a strictly top down manner and there is a vast corporate interest, due to an emerging new urban market with a potential of high profits [9]. Even more, doubts about corporatization of city governance were raised out, stating that technological corporations see city governance as a potential future market for their products. Those corporate interests can easily lead to a monopoly over the city's technological platforms [12].

As stated, this can result in a path of a dangerous corporate dependency [12]. Different authors are emphasizing the rather importance of the smart citizens, not the smart city being run with the corporate interests [10].

How Much of a New Technology is Too Much?

Open innovation and modern technology can help cities reach so-called knowledge based urbanization which should lead to continued economic development [23]. However, if a city uses advanced technology and connectivity, this does not necessarily mean that it is a smart city. These devices itself do not improve the quality of life or economy [7].

As [15] point out 'smart city services would be better developed following the actual and precise needs of citizens. Otherwise, new implementations can lead to overwhelming technology. Current situation in China represents great example of several problems that show up while developing and integrating smart governments. The synergy between collected information and business is not as great as it is supposed to be. In addition, smart governments with a lot of modern technology result in high operating costs [4]. However, many question the impact of citizen engagement because of the increasing use of technology [7]. Consequently, lack of use could lead to big loss due to previously mentioned high operating costs.

Thus, it is challenging to assure data security in the process of digitalization of cities and integration of new technology [4]. This again leads to the previously mentioned issues of privacy and security which indicates how closely connected identified issues are. Similarly, [21] listed innovation concept, service quality and perceived privacy as a key factors of whether citizens would accept and use smart city services.

2.3 Participation as a Possible Solution

With the rise of the Design Thinking methodology, participation is becoming more widely recognized as a successful method in dealing with 'wicked' problems. Shelton writes about participation as 'happy hypothesis of change through involvement of more people rather than fewer' [19]. Participation is described as a process in which a subject takes a role in the planning and administrative processes of government [20]. Participation has been used as a method in fields that we associate as highly corporate and complex. The usage of participation has described in building hospitals, focusing on the inputs of all the stakeholder, including patients [17].

Several authors have recognized participation as a possible solution to the process of building and implementing smart cities. Extensive explanations and issues arising with smart cities were presented together with participation as a suggested possible solution [7]. Moreover, participation has been emphasized as the only way to keep the process democratic by highlighting the problem of people, who have the interest being unable to express their voice and being far away from the structures of power [19]. Participation has also been recognized as a vital factor in ensuring efficiency and good quality of life in the smart cities. The connection between smart city privacy challenges and people's willingness to participate was also pointed out [2], meaning that is vital that participation is a building block from the very beginning of the process.

There are various possibilities of implementing participation in building the smart cities. Exploring many different possibilities, it is vital that we take into consideration all the important stakeholders [17]. As stated in the article about building the 'world smartest city' Medellin it is important that the focus is shifted from the technological part to the will of the people. In Medellin they have set up elections for people's representatives, who have a direct word in setting up smart cities [6]. Representative group of citizens has been emphasized as a possible solution, not only in Medellin, but in various projects around the globe [20]. Speaking about the possible solutions, there is still much work to be done, many suggestions haven't been tried on the smart cities case and it still uncertain, which options will work.

There are a lot of ideas that are currently being discussed and could save smart city concept from rising issues, but it seems like exactly participation seems like the best one. Scholars are even moving the definitions toward the more citizen-oriented smart cities that definitely involve some kind of participation. Therefore, a lot of discussions and literature analysis have been made in the last few years. However, there is a lack of quantitative analysis on this issues. For his reason, we focus on researching the actual impact participation has on issues related to smart cities and examining whether participation can be a solution in solving individuals' perceived issues towards smart cities'.

3 Methodology

For the purpose of this article we have firstly made an in-depth literature review. After that a web-based questionnaire has been made. A web-based questionnaire has been testing a variety of topics related to smart cities. Among them we have tested issues that are related to the perceived issues by people, and we have tested what effect participation as a possible solution would have. With the questions relevant for our article we have used Likert scale ranging from 1, strongly disagree to 5, strongly agree. As stated a questionnaire has been used to validate our research question. One question has been used to directly determine and analyze each of our five issues, having at least one question focusing on each of the aspects. Important part of the questionnaire is the one where we quantitatively tested participation as a possible solution. We also proposed some potential solutions, which are all based on participation and are related to perceived issues. We are measuring the impact participation would have in solving those solutions. We also measure how different actions would impact the trust people have towards participation, thus further exploring our research question.

Of the 1529 responses collected, more than 500 were retained after removing the noncompleted ones. Data collection process began in May and was completed in August 2020. Table 1 presents the profile of the respondents.

Table 1. Profile of the respondents.

		Percent (%)
Gender	Male	40.9
	Female	59.1
Education	Primary or less	5.2
	Secondary	55.6
	Tertiary	39.2
Type of settlement	Urban settlement	62.2
	Suburban areas	17.3
	Small city	14.7
	Village areas	5.8

The sample was selected from population of people living mostly in Slovenia. The pretest was done by a sample of 10 representative students. The results of the survey were analyzed using quantitative approaches. Participation oriented questions were analyzed and compared based on descriptive statistics. Independent t-test and ANOVA test will also be used for purpose of identifying differences between different groups based on gender and level of education.

4 Data Analysis

In the preliminary data analysis, we identified perceived issues of the participants towards the smart city concept. In order to answer our research question, firstly we wanted to see to which extent some problems identified in the literature are actual concerns of our participants. Participants agreed with listed issues, as 'Implementing 5G networks', with an average of 2.9, is the only one with an average below 3 (neutral).

Furthermore, we can see from the results that the majority of the concerns identified in the literature are actual problems perceived by our participants. With an average answer of 4,0 or above the participants have highlighted 'data privacy', 'security issues' and 'the use of my data and preferences by the third parties' as their biggest concerns. Among them 'data privacy' was identified as the most challenging issue with an average of 4.1. With the concerns being highlighted we have devoted the rest of our analysis in testing participation and its solutions as a possible solution.

Further, we asked participants to give opinion on actual solutions in development of smart cities. We highlighted seven possible solutions, which are related to participation and measured if the participants would trust more in the concept of smart cities. This question is focusing directly on our research question and are measuring how participation could affect the trust people have in smart cities.

Results can be seen in the Table 2 and Table 3. It is definitely positive that mostly it seems like the most attractive measures are also the ones that are fairly easy to implement, e.g. 81% of participants have agreed or strongly agreed that they would trust smart cities more if they would be introduced to potential dangers and corresponding benefits.

We additionally compared results based on gender variable. A T-test analysis has been conducted, calculating if there is a statistical significance in answers among the genders. The results of the analysis can be found in the third column.

The last part of the analysis consists of segmenting the audience based on their finished level of education. We have grouped individuals in four groups: high school, undergraduate programme, graduate programme and doctoral programme. In both tables in the column 4 results of the Anova test can be found.

Table 2. Attitude towards possible participation solutions

Variable I would...	Average	Std. Dev.	Sig. (gen.)	Sig. (edu.)
...trust smart cities more if they were built by local businesses	2.9	0.94	.604	.079
...be willing to participate in building smart cities	3.6	0.91	**.008**	**.000**
...have more confidence in the safety of smart cities if each individual could participate in round tables	3.2	0.97	.207	**.012**
...trust the privacy of smart cities more if I could express my concerns at any point and talk to someone about the problem	3.6	0.92	.635	**.006**
...trust smart cities more if I could make my own suggestions for improvements	3.6	0.88	.090	**.001**
...trust smart cities more if I could elect representatives to represent me in decision-making	3.5	0.93	.225	**.002**
...trust smart cities more if I were introduced to certain potential dangers (without embellishment) and corresponding benefits of smart cities	4.1	0.81	.157	.108

Table 3. Attitude towards possible participation solutions

Variable: I would trust more in smart cities if...	Average	Std. dev.	Sig. (gen.)	Sig. (edu.)
...advantages and potential dangers of each upgrade or novelty would be presented to me before implementation	4.1	0.79	.071	**.008**
...each innovation would be implemented only after a successful trial period	4.2	0.72	.069	.357
...I could test certain functions by myself before implementation	3.9	0.84	.402	.090
...in the case of a negative testing experience, the idea could also be rejected by the users themselves	4.2	0.73	.686	.487

5 Discussion

As seen in our analysis we have determined that there are various problems and concerns identified in the literature, which are actually present among the people. In the beginning of our article we have proposed the research question if participation could be a solution. In the preliminary analysis we have examined participation and, being aware of the sample the size, we would like to express that participation is a viable solution in solving concerns people have towards smart cities.

Our issues were well accepted as every highlighted concern got an average answer of at least 3 with an exception of 5G networks which was very surprising. Due to all the smoke in media we expected that implementation of 5G networks would present a huge concern for participants. As it has also been pointed out [1] that there is an important social factor of building a 5g network. Concluding the analysis, we can state that the social factor of building a 5g network should not be the biggest concern of the stakeholders. It has been stated [13] that there is a 'strong movement' not in favor of the implementation. From our results we can conclude that there may be a movement, but the concern does not irritate the majority of the people.

Perceived security has been highlighted in the literature as being 'one of the most important issues' [11]. Similarly, it is not only an issue in the technological terms, but also in the minds of the people. Perceived security is with an average answer above 4, among the three issues that concern the people the most. It has been argued [12] that it is becoming impossible to live without living digital footprints and shadows. People are deeply aware of that and this reflects in their perceived issues towards the smart cities. 'Data privacy' and 'The use of my data' are among the perceived issues with the biggest average. To some extent we have proved that those issues could be overcame by participation. But, there is a paradox that when you participate, even more data about you is collected and could be potentially misused.

Being a part of a project like building smart cities, can due to ethical concerns regarding the data collection be discouraging for some. In order to participate or to collaborate you have to be even more involved in the "system", thus more of your data is being collected. On one hand we are trying to mitigate the perceived issues, but on the other we are suggesting that people would be even more exposed to it. There is a thin line between participation and too much participation.

In following research we have presented participation as a possible solution. We measured to which extent the people would be willing to participate in building the smart cities. As it has been found [2] in the theoretical framework there is a connection between arising issues and people willing to participate. With an average of 3.6 we can state that people are to some extent willing to participate in the process. This average more or less aligns with the average of the perceived issues towards the smart cities concept.

Furthermore, when measuring the different possibilities for participation, which were already pointed out [20], we found out that the answer that would change the individuals perception the most is the one focusing on explaining the potential benefits and dangers of the project. This is mostly the case with implementing participation. We can see a big impact already in implementing steps that are relatively easy to implement, such as educating the people about the concept and project. Interestingly enough some ideas, which are harder to implement have yielded worse results. For example, the answer 'I would trust smart cities more if they were built by local businesses' has had an average answer of 2.9. Meaning that the average was below neutral. One could argue that moneywise it could be easier to educate people than to solely rely on local companies when building the smart cities.

In general, all of the ideas would greatly affect individual's perceived issues with the average being way above the neutral. We have only focused slightly more on a concept, which is very popular among scholars, trial periods. Trial period has proved in our research to be the idea that would yield the highest result in solving individuals perceived issues towards the smart cities. One question focusing on the topic has an average of 4.1 and the other has an average of 4.2. It is very important that the ideas that have yield the highest results are implemented and tested, when building smart cities.

As mentioned in the analysis we have conducted analysis based on gender and education. Starting with the gender, as it can be seen from the data small differences can be seen. The only question where significant difference has been calculated is the one regarding how willing individuals are to participate in the project of building smart cities. We can see that men would be more willing to participate than women. However, generally no other significant difference has been detected and therefore we can conclude that gender does not play a role in perceiving participation as a viable solution to our research problem.

Lastly, we conducted a segmentation based on education level. A statistical significance has been found in the majority of the questions (6/11), meaning that answers were greatly impacted by the education level of the individuals. In addition, an interesting observation can be made. Individuals with undergraduate and graduate level are found to be more prone to accept participation as a solution in overcoming their perceived problems. We can observe similar patterns among the individuals with the undergraduate (2) and graduate (3) education level and on the other hand there are similar patterns with the individuals who have high school (1) or doctoral (4) level of education. Results conducted in segmentations are very interesting and should be researched furtherly, especially in finding the reason behind those connections between very different groups.

6   Conclusion

We believe that there is a positive answer to our research question and that participation is a solution in solving individuals' perceived issues towards smart cities. Even more, we would like to express that there are some participation solutions and practices, which are easy to implement and would have a significant impact on the trust people have in smart cities. We would like to emphasize that those solutions should be studied and used by innovators, researchers, governments and builders of the smart cities.

Now that we have highlighted and proved that participation is a viable solution, we have only laid the fundamentals. There is a vast space of unknown that can be explored by implementing participation in real case studies and measuring the impact it has on real scenarios. We are looking forward to further researching and discussing this specific topic.

References

1. Alén-Savikko, A.: Network neutrality in the era of 5g–a matter of faith, hope, and design? Inf. Commun. Technol. Law **28**, 115–130 (2019)
2. Braun, T., Fung, B.C., Iqbal, F., Shah, B.: Security and privacy challenges in smart cities. Sustain. Cities Soc. **39**, 499–507 (2018)

3. Cerrudo, C.: An emerging Us (and world) threat: cities wide open to cyber attacks. Secur. Smart Cities **17**, 137–151 (2015)
4. Chen, X.: The development trend and practical innovation of smart cities under the integration of new technologies. Front. Eng. Manag. **6**, 485–502 (2019)
5. Curzon, J., Almehmadi, A., El-Khatib, K.: A survey of privacy enhancing technologies for smart cities. Pervasive Mob. Comput. **55**, 76–95 (2019)
6. Freedman, D.: How Medellín, Colombia, became the world's smartest city. Newsweek Mag. **11**, 2019 (2019)
7. Habib, A., Alsmadi, D., Prybutok, V.R.: Factors that determine residents' acceptance of smart city technologies. Behav. Inf. Technol. **39**, 610–623 (2020)
8. Habibzadeh, H., Nussbaum, B.H., Anjomshoa, F., Kantarci, B., Soyata, T.: A survey on cybersecurity, data privacy, and policy issues in cyber-physical system deployments in smart cities. Sustain. Cities Soc. **50**, 101660 (2019)
9. Herrera-Contreras, A.A., Sánchez-Delacruz, E., Meza-Ruiz, I.V.: Twitter opinion analysis about topic 5g technology. Paper presented at the International Conference on Applied Technologies (2019)
10. Hill, D.: Essay: On the Smart City; or, a 'Manifesto'for Smart Citizens Instead', City of Sound, 1 Feb 2013 (2013)
11. Kimani, K., Oduol, V., Langat, K.: Cyber security challenges for Iot-based smart grid networks. Int. J. Critical Infrastructure Protection **25**, 3649 (2019)
12. Kitchin, R.: The ethics of smart cities and urban science. Philos. Trans. Royal Soc. A: Math. Phys. Eng. Sci. **374**, 20160115 (2016)
13. Kumar, M.J.: Smart Cities with Massive Data Centric Living Are Hard to Build without 5g Networks. Taylor & Francis (2015)
14. Lara, A.P., Da Costa, E.M., Furlani, T.Z., Yigitcanla, T.: Smartness that matters: towards a comprehensive and human-centred characterisation of smart cities. J. Open Innov.: Technol. Market Complexity **2**, 8 (2016)
15. Lee, J., Lee, H.: Developing and validating a citizen-centric typology for smart city services. Gov. Inf. Q. **31**, S93–S105 (2014)
16. Nam, T., Pardo, T.A.: Smart city as urban innovation: focusing on management, policy, and context. Paper presented at the Proceedings of the 5th International Conference on Theory and Practice of Electronic Governance (2011)
17. Pourdehnad, J., Wexler, E.R., Wilson, D.V.: Integrating systems thinking and design thinking. Syst. Thinker **22**, 2–6 (2011)
18. Praharaj, S., Han, H.: Cutting through the clutter of smart city definitions: a reading into the smart city perceptions in India. City Culture Soc. **18**, 100289 (2019)
19. Shelton, T., Lodato, T.: Actually existing smart citizens: expertise and (non) participation in the making of the smart city. City **23**, 35–52 (2019)
20. Simonofski, A., Asensio, E.S., De Smedt, J., Snoeck, M.: Citizen participation in smart cities: evaluation framework proposal. Paper presented at the 2017 IEEE 19th Conference on Business Informatics (CBI) (2017)
21. Yeh, H.: The Effects of successful ICT-based smart city services: from citizens' perspectives. Gov. Inf. Q. **34**, 556–565 (2017)
22. Yigitcanlar, T., Kamruzzaman, M., Foth, M., Sabatini-Marques, J., da Costa, E., Ioppolo, G.: Can cities become smart without being sustainable? A systematic review of the literature. Sustain. Cities Soc. **45**, 34865 (2019)
23. Yun, J.J., Jeong, E., Yang, J.: Open innovation of knowledge cities. J. Open Innov.: Technol. Market Complexity **1**, 16 (2015)

Social Media

There Is Nothing Real! A Study of Nonuse of TikTok in India

Imon Chakraborty[1], Unnati Kapoor[2(✉)],
and P. Vigneswara Ilavarasan[2]

[1] UQ-IITD Academy of Research, Indian Institute of Technology Delhi,
New Delhi, India
[2] Department of Management Studies, Indian Institute of Technology, Delhi,
New Delhi, India
unnatikapoor07@gmail.com

Abstract. Social media platforms are used for both entertainment and information sharing purposes across diverse populations in the world. Though content in all possible formats is shared in these platforms, there is a differential
preference among the users. Despite the phenomenal growth and adherence to
the regulations, TikTok, a video sharing platform, is dissuaded by a few governments and is discontinued by the users. But this platform seems to be preferred by people who are from semi-urban and are digital have-less. The present
paper attempts to understand the non-use of TikTok in India. This paper has
explored the negative perceptions resulting in the nonusage of social media
among individuals by taking the case study of the application TikTok. For that, a
qualitative approach was used, and twenty in-depth semi-structured interviews
were conducted from various regions in India through online and offline mode.
The data were analyzed using a thematic analysis approach. A framework is
provided to understand why people may not use social media platforms.
Suggestions are also given as to how social media platforms can be altered or
redesigned to appeal to a broader set of people. Numerous reasons were identified that resulted in negative perceptions about the platform. The findings
indicate that individuals seem to dislike TikTok mostly because it leads to a
waste of time, does not contribute to knowledge, and includes unrealistic and
unethical content. People appeared to be concerned about the social stigma
attached to it. Specific measures are suggested, for instance, filtering out content,
culture-specific user interface, statutory warnings, safety, and encryption to
address the negative perceptions and to improve the authenticity of the platform.

Keywords: TikTok · Social media platforms · Adoption · Non-use · India ·
Dislike · Entertainment

1 Introduction

Social media platforms such as Whatsapp, LinkedIn, Facebook, Twitter, and Youtube
all have unique structures and acculturations. The users download and utilize these
social media platforms based on their choice and affordance. Multiple businesses are
continuously developing new social media platforms and applications. They are

© IFIP International Federation for Information Processing 2020
Published by Springer Nature Switzerland AG 2020
S. K. Sharma et al. (Eds.): TDIT 2020, IFIP AICT 618, pp. 287–302, 2020.
https://doi.org/10.1007/978-3-030-64861-9_26

focused on creating exciting applications with novel ideas and advanced features to make life easy and engage and connect millions of users. TikTok is one such initiative that has become extremely popular in a short duration of time. It was launched in 2016 in China and finally propelled internationally in 2017 by ByteDance Technology Co Ltd. This video-sharing application provides the facility to create lip-synced or short music videos for 3 to 15 s and 3–60 s for looping videos [1, 2]. This application is gradually getting popular in Asian countries, the US, and the rest of the world [3]. It is available in more than 75 languages over the world. It is one of the fastest-growing social media applications and is also tagged as the most downloaded app in the US, 2018 [4, 5].

Social media platforms encourage millions of users to interact socially and participate in various virtual networking activities on an unprecedented scale. Users' behavior towards the platform changes according to their personal choices and preferences. Previous research has been able to successfully capture the adoption and user behavior of individuals invested in social media platforms [6, 7]. Smartphone users state that their phones have become a necessary part of their self and have both positively and negatively influenced their identity [8]. Research has been able to beautifully capture the impact of social media platforms on the well being of the users. It has also tapped upon the positives and negatives of social media [9].

Social media can fulfill numerous needs and aid in developing and reinforcing social capital [10, 11]. Existing evidence on social media has primarily investigated individuals' motivations behind social media usage and positive experiences. Multiple researchers have also studied the negative experiences and harmful effects of social media on the users' self-image, fear of missing out, feeling of isolation, and hype to physical prosperity [12]. Investigations of negative views of social media users have called for a surge in research that explicitly considers the non-use of social media [13].

There is, however, limited research on the non-use of social media platforms. It is, therefore, crucial to explore why individuals dislike social media platforms. It can also help us provide suggestions as to what drives people away from social media, aid its usage to ensure a better and more significant impact of these platforms on the users.

With this background, this study is aimed to conceptualize the users' behavior towards the reduced usage or non-use of social media platforms. The first section introduces the paper. The second section depicts a brief overview of social media and TikTok. The third section provides the research settings. The fourth section discusses the detailed consumer behavior towards social media. The final section draws the conclusion and recommendations.

2   Background

2.1   Social Media

Social media platforms provide an environment for sharing entertaining content that stimulates live experiences. It is also a medium for virtual networking worldwide. Various social networking platforms facilitate numerous forms of social interactions. Social media platforms include several dimensions focused mainly on communication, community formation, participation in various activities, information sharing, and connectedness [14, 15]. Some of the widely used social networking sites are Facebook, Linkedin, YouTube, Twitter, Whatsapp, and TikTok. The architecture and content of all these platforms play a significant role in influencing its users.

2.2   Tiktok as a Social Platform

TikTok provides the facility to create short videos with background music, that can be modified using multiple filters [16]. Artificial intelligence has been utilized by the platforms to evaluate user preferences by identifying their interests and interactions in order to provide suitable content [17, 18]. In 2018, TikTok downloads surpassed the download rate of other popular social media applications like Whatsapp, Instagram, and YouTube [19].

Towards the end of 2018, TikTok faced multiple challenges. Journalists from several countries have raised their voices against the privacy issues and exposure of children to sexual predators [20]. Several users also raised their voices against cyber-bullying and racism [21]. In July 2018, the Indonesian government banned TikTok in Indonesia due to inappropriate content, pornography, and blasphemy [22, 23]. One week later, TikTok was reintroduced after filtering out harmful content and the formation of new guidelines [24]. Bangladesh's government also blocked access to the application later in 2018 [25].

In February 2019, the ByteDance Technology was fined US 5.78 $ million for violating the Children's online privacy protection act; They were accused for gathering information of minors who were under 13 years of age [26]. Post that, TikTok upgraded its 'kids only' mode that blocks such video upload, direct messaging, and comment on other's videos [27]. In February 2019, several Indian politicians raised their voice to ban TikTok and initiated strict regulations over its sexually explicit content and cyber-bullying cases. In April 2019, Madras high court appealed to the Government of India to ban this application because of the increasing cases of pornography and targeted risk to children who were getting exposed to sexual predators [28, 29].

The company has removed more than 6 million videos from the content that violated their policy and government guidelines. The court refused to reconsider providing the user access to this application [30]. In April 2019, the Indian government lifted the ban over TikTok, but by then, the video streaming application had lost over 2 million users. Multiple users dislike TikTok because of personal social and legal issues. The government also recently included an updated set of guidelines to filter out more content considered inappropriate for the platform. It is crucial to understand the desuetude behavior towards social media platforms and evaluate as to why and how users participate and consume information on social media. Researchers are especially interested in understanding how the design and architecture of such social media platforms impact user engagement.

2.3   Use and Nonuse of Social Media

Social media has become an indispensable section of people's daily lives. People like social media platforms for multiple reasons. From the existing empirical evidence, people engaged in social media for information seeking, entertainment, relaxation, communication, and convenient social interaction [31]. Social media platforms also play a crucial role in the business internationalization and marketing of products and services [32, 33].

Not all individuals, however, share a similar opinion about social media [34]. They deal with social media as an enforced platform to check unsolicited content that is neither appealing nor of their interest [35]. Some individuals dislike social media because of unreal content and experiences, while others consider it as valuable [36]. It has been found that individuals often take a break from social media platforms because it can lead them to mental health issues like anxiety, depression, addiction, and self-doubt, along with other issues like privacy and time management [37].

Existing evidence highlighted the hedonic motivation and utilitarian views regarding consumers' use and non-use of social media platforms [38, 39]. It is quite evident that TikTok is on the hedonic side of motivations; however, it would be intriguing to investigate what types of discomfort drive consumers towards the non-use of the platform.

The case study of TikTok has been considered for this paper because it is among the most downloaded platforms, and its growth is constrained by the growing perception of social undesirability [40–42]. Therefore, it essential to understand what drives individuals away from social media and how these platforms can be altered to ensure the best user experience. To explore this unrevealed phenomenon, the following research question was formulated and addressed in the study:

RQ1: What is the rationale behind the non-use of the social media platform, TikTok?

3   Research Setting

3.1   Methods

In order to address the research question, 20 semi-structured in-depth interviews were conducted who were users of the social media platform "TikTok" in India. At present, they are not using the platform. The interviews were conducted both via online mode (Telephone/Skype) and offline mode (face to face). The interviews included questions about the reason for not using TikTok, the type of content or features disliked by the participants, and the individual perceptions of the platform. Lastly, individual suggestions are also captured to address the challenges and concerns regarding TikTok. Thematic analysis was used to gather insights from the data.

Non-probabilistic convenience sampling was used for the selection of the participants. In this sampling method, 20 participants are selected consecutively in the order of appearance according to their convenient accessibility. To increase reliability, an equal number of participants had chosen from both the genders between the ages of

24–29. The participants were mostly located in urban areas like Delhi, Haryana, Banaras, Kolkata, and Mumbai.

3.2   Data Analysis Process

Data analysis is one of the essential steps in qualitative research. In the current paper, the information of all interviews was analyzed using the process of thematic analysis. A rigorous thematic analysis is a highly flexible approach and can produce trustworthy and insightful findings [43]. It is a well-structured approach and is also useful for summarizing prominent features of large data sets [44]. This analysis process is also the least understood and is extremely challenging when it comes to explanation [45]. Initially, the findings are broadly categorized, and then dimensions are emerged to find aggregated themes.

4   Data Analysis

The process of data analysis is depicted in Table 1. Based on the result, a set of nine themes emerged from the interviews. Each of the themes is elaborately discussed and in the findings.

Table 1.   Data analysis result

Representative Quotes	First order categories	Second order themes/aggregate dimensions
"I don't find it useful. It doesn't help me to improve my personality or my social awareness, like other social media app does"	Not useful. Doesn't contribute to personality growth and social awareness	No contribution to learning
"I don't find it productive in any way"	Non Productive	
"Videos on TikTok don't show any knowledgeable content, and all the users are focused on becoming popular"	Focus on popularity and doesn't contribute to knowledge	
"People do all sorts of stupid things and its such a waste of time because you don't learn anything"	Waste of time and no learning	
"I have seen people wasting hours and hours on this app, trying to shoot illogical videos"	Wastage of time	Wastage of time
"It is time consuming and usually full of nonsense. This app mostly promotes stupid content which is not even funny"	Time consuming and nonsensical content	

(continued)

Table 1. (*continued*)

Representative Quotes	First order categories	Second order themes/aggregate dimensions
"I feel it's not a very good platform for me to waste my time on. I don't find the right type of content and audience there"	Wastage of time	
"It's meant for passing time. There is nothing informative and we are not gaining anything"	Non informative and wastage of time	
"Already instagram and whatsapp consume most of my time so I can't allow TikTok to waste the remaining time left to do productive activities"	Wastage of time	
"Its a waste of time"	Wastage of time	
"Very addictive and a big waste of time"	Addictive and waste of time	
"I think its just a waste of time and should be banned"	Waste of time	
"This is spoiling the youth minds of India who should be focusing on the career or further admission prospectus, than focusing on getting maximum followers on TikTok"	Deviates the youth from their career	Source of distraction
"People should not get publicity out of such stupidity. They should rather be focusing on their talent"	Deviates focus from actual talent	
"I do not like the app because there is nothing real; people only lip-sync the dialogues/music played in the background"	Unreal, away from reality	Away from reality
"It's not real. You have to lips dialogues and its not actual performance. It makes you look good through the effects of the phone and is unreal. But it was initially fun to use with friends, but at home, its a lie to yourself"	Unreal and shows a fake image of self	
"It's a very heavy app and uses a lot of phone storage"	Large in size and impacts storage	Large size
"It floods my phone and uses memory"	Reduced memory	

(*continued*)

Table 1. (*continued*)

Representative Quotes	First order categories	Second order themes/aggregate dimensions
"It is giving a wrong notion regarding time productivity to the youngsters of our country. So the app developers should include a reminder system which keeps on buzzing after every 15 min to remind the users that they have used this app for 15 min"	Include a reminder system or buzz	Filtering or restriction of content
"They should put a check on such unrealistic things and posts"	Put a check on posts	
"It can be meant for entertainment if the activity is restricted"	Should have restricted activity	
"Should be some filter on the spam videos to remove the irrelevant content from users end"	Use of filters In content	
"I think many social messages can be spread through it.There are a lot more topics like Female foeticide, Child labour, Use of sanitary pads, hygiene and cleanliness that can be used to promote awareness because it can reach out to so many people in such less duration of time"	Can be used for creating social awareness	Using Tiktok for awareness and knowledge sharing
"Tiktok users should take an initiative to make something videos on Tiktok in interesting way which is worthy"	Making informative videos	
"They need to have a bigger purpose. I don't understand their mission or what they mean as a brand. Like facebook's purpose is to connect people together globally. I don't know what TikTok stands for as a company"	Should focus on a bigger purpose	

5   Findings

Thematic analysis is one of the most widely used methods in qualitative research. Based on the qualitative interviews and interpretation, several sub-themes are collated, and nine themes have emerged. Firstly, in this section, each of the prominent themes that emerged out of the interviews is discussed in detail to address the research question. Secondly, suggestions are depicted on what measures can be taken to improvise the application to increase the credibility and usage of the platform.

5.1 Wastage of Time and No Contribution to Knowledge

One of the most prominent reasons why individuals dislike the platform that emerged out of the interviews was because they believe that it would result in a wastage of time. The participants stated that the application was time-consuming and would waste most of their time that could otherwise be utilized in productive activity. The application seems to be considered as nonproductive because, as stated by the participants, it does not contribute to knowledge, awareness, and learning and does not lead to any growth. For instance, some of the participants stated:

"I don't find it useful. It doesn't help me to improve my personality or my social awareness, like other social media app does."

"It's meant for passing time. There is nothing informative and we are not gaining anything."

5.2 Questionable Content

From the interviews, it is clear that one of the reasons as to why certain people dislike the platform was because of the quality of content. The content on the platform was labelled as "dirty," "cheap," "Absurd," and "C grade" by the participants. One of the participants also stated that the content was violating the ethical and moral value systems. They also complain that the platform shows nudity and adult content that seemed unacceptable to the participants. For instance, one of the participants stated:

"It has absurd content and cheap content and its not funny at all. They post videos where they show nudity, show off their body and has weird adult content that I don't like. The social media personalities that have emerged from it have a very massy C grade vibe, and everything about it seems more cringy, rather than entertaining."

One of the reasons as to why users dislike the application was because the content was unreal. Users prefer to watch videos that include people displaying real talent rather than lip sing or acting to fake dialogues. It is believed that this was a corrupt means of gaining followers and publicity and is nothing more than a lie because the content is fake. For instance, one of the participants remarked that:

"Its not real. You have to lips dialogues and it's not an actual performance. It makes you look good through effects of the phone and is unreal. But it was initially fun to use with friends but at home its a lie to yourself"

"It drives people beyond their true nature and once you have used it, they start living in it, thats the problem with most social media."

The participants also expressed their concerns regarding the dangers associated with the content posted on the application. People tend to post some videos that can cause severe injuries hard harm to the individual's life. For social fame, they might end up performing stunts that can have disastrous consequences. As stated by one of the participants:

"Ive seen some dangerous videos and heard that people have died during shooting for TikTok because they make videos on trains, platforms on top of buildings that can be very dangerous and cost them their lives."

5.3   Comparison with Other Platforms

In the age of competition, where there are multiple social media platforms available, it becomes imperative for individuals to prefer using specific social media applications over others. The participants compared the application with the other social media platforms like WhatsApp, Facebook, and YouTube. It is found that other platforms are more useful and promising than TikTok. One of the participants believed that because of the shortage of time, she had to choose between various platforms and TikTok would not be one of them. This trade-off between the social media platforms appeared to be a common practice among social media users because of limited time availability. One of the participants described how important it was for her to select specific platforms over the others:

> *"Already Instagram and WhatsApp consume most of my time so I can't allow TikTok to waste the remaining time left to do productive activities."*

> *"I can always log onto youtube and other social media channels that I follow and get my laughter there, I can choose what I want to watch"*

As TikTok allows the sharing of the videos on other social media platforms, most of the participants were also exposed to TikTok without actually downloading the application. However, because the videos were available elsewhere also, some of the participants preferred using the other applications to watch only those videos of TikTok that suited their needs. While TikTok seems to entertain individuals, many other applications like YouTube apart from entertainment also give the viewers the freedom to choose what they want to view.

5.4   Source of Distraction and Unwanted Exposure

It emerged from the interviews that the nonusers of the platform consider it as addictive. They also state that it acts as a source of distraction for the youth. As from literature today, youth are extensively using the app that can impact the amount of time they spend on actual learning and on developing their talent because of easy accessibility and fame through applications like TikTok. It emerged from the interviews that because the content is not adequately filtered, it might lead to exposing children of younger age groups to things that are inappropriate to their age group. Also, young children can be more susceptible because they do not know what is right or wrong for them and can get easily influenced, which can have a detrimental impact on their career and mental health. For instance, the participants stated:

> *"This is spoiling the youth minds of India who should be focusing on the career or further admission prospectus, than focusing on getting maximum followers on TikTok."*

> *"People should not get publicity out of such stupidity. They should rather be focusing on their talent."*

> *"I don't think that's something the young kids should be focusing on at this age... they might be exposed to a lot of content that may not suit their mental age because there are no filters; you get influenced very easily when you are young."*

It also emerged from the interviews that nonusers of the platform believed that experience of sudden fame develops among the users a false sense of self-importance in the name of creativity, increases the urge of novelty, and impacts patience and attention span of regular users.

5.5   Large Size

A few participants also complained that the size of the application was extensive, flooded the phone, and used most of its memory. While only two participants spoke about the large size of the application that took away most of the storage of their phones, multiple other reasons prevented the participants from using the application, as discussed above.

"It's a very heavy app and uses a lot of phone storage"

5.6   Filtering and Knowledge Sharing

Some of the participants gave us suggestions that can help improvise the platform. Most of them stated that restricting uploads and filtering the right content would help improve the quality of content and spread knowledge and awareness. One of the participants suggested that the platform can be utilized to share knowledge and increase awareness about social issues like female feticide and hygiene because of its high accessibility and usage among the youth. Also, focus on having a more meaningful purpose would make the platform more useful. For instance, one of the participants stated:

"I think many social messages can be spread through it. There are a lot more topics like Female foeticide, child labor, use of sanitary pads, hygiene, and cleanliness that can be used to promote awareness because it can reach out to so many people in such less duration of time."

However, the participants raised concerns about the authenticity of the information shared on these platforms.

5.7   Social Stigma

The social stigma associated with the use of TikTok may also prevent individuals from using the application. Based on the interviews, some of the participants stated that they believed that the application is used only by unintelligent and uneducated individuals who belonged to a specific type of strata. This perception can prevent users from utilizing the application because of the social stigma attached to it. As people want to be accepted and viewed in a certain way in society, it can prevent them from using social media platforms like TikTok for social acceptance. For instance, one of the participants stated:

"I think the use of Tiktok depends on the level of education and the state of the society, and I think Tiktok appeals to a larger population that is not very finished."

"In my social circle, no one uses TikTok"

Social identity theory says that individuals define themselves based on social and personal aspects [46]. Individuals intensively engaging in social media platforms formulate their identity using these platforms, which can lead to irrational behaviors and decisions. This perceived identity can also result in symbolic interactionism wherein individuals' idea of self can get distorted based on other's reactions. If being part of a social media platform can be detrimental to their social identity, they can choose to opt-out of it or use it secretly.

5.8   Social Media Domination

With AI and emerging technology, the use of applications, robots, and tools have become an integral part of our lives and have started governing most of our behavior and, as stated by one of our participants, can also direct us to act in specific ways. None of us know what direction AI will take and to what extent the human will become dependent on it. The interview participants have raised their concern for this and believe that most of the information shared on social media platforms like TikTok clouds the ability to form judgments. One of the participants stated:

> *"The availability of so much information impairs my ability to clearly judge about what's happening in the country and the right sources, and I am unable to make the right decisions"*

5.9   Stability and Maturity of Usage

Who should use social media? How is the population defined, and on what basis? One of the themes that emerged out of the interviews communicates the importance of mental stability and maturity to use social media platforms responsibly. Not everyone is aware of what platform to use and for how long, and it is, in these times, very challenging to monitor the right or wrong usage of such platforms.

> *"Unless and until you are very stable that you can clearly see if the platform is making the choices or directing you towards a certain way to act. I do not want to go for it."*

Studies have started exploring the impact of social media usage on the mental well being of individuals belonging to various age groups, especially adolescents. Research has depicted that teenagers who spent the maximum duration of time on electronic platforms (like the internet, social media, messaging and gaming) and gave less time to non-screen activities like outdoor games, exercise, and in-person social interaction had a lower degree of mental upbeat [47]. How should social media content be designed, altered, or managed to ensure optimal usage of the platforms?

6   Discussion

The study contributes to literature by using the case study of TikTok and exploring the factors that lead to the non-usage of the application. The qualitative study findings can help extend existing literature and open up new avenues for research in the non-use of social media platforms. Also, multiple suggestive measures are introduced for the platform that can lead to a better user experience if implemented. These measures can further be extended to other social media applications.

The research findings have identified factors like wastage of time and privacy concerns associated with non-use of social media, evidence of which can also be found in existing research [48]. The findings also show that the non-use of TikTok is mostly due to its low quality of content. The content is not considered very useful because of its lack of contribution to the right knowledge, learning, and social awareness.

Existing literature has highlighted that non-differentiation of specific social media platforms from other platforms can lead to its non-usage [9]. The application's size also plays a vital role in the usage and non-usage of social media platforms, especially when downloading them on mobile devices with limited memory.

Based on the findings, it emerged that TikTok was perceived as a huge source of distraction, especially among teenagers [49]. It was found that two prominent reasons contributed to the negative perception of the platform. Firstly, the perception that TikTok deviates the youth from their focus towards their responsibilities like family and career. Secondly, the perception that Tiktok exposes the users to short term popularity gains based on filters and other technological animations, thus stopping them from developing their actual talents and skills.

It was also found that social stigma related to the usage of TikTok may avert the users from its use. Some of the participants clearly stated that platforms like TikTok are used by uneducated individuals for low level entertainment. These findings suggest that such perceptions can prevent individuals from using the application. However, no such negative perceptions have been identified for platforms like Facebook, Twitter, and LinkedIn [13, 50].

6.1   Implications and Suggestion to Improve the Platform

Human beings have a natural tendency to learn and grow. One of the themes that emerged out of the interviews indicated that individuals prefer using applications that include better quality content in terms of knowledge and authenticity.

TikTok functions on the mission statement "To inspire creativity and bring joy." The content posted on the platform was considered "unreal" by some of the participants in the interviews. They also believed that the experience of sudden fame, develops among the users, a false sense of self-importance in the name of creativity. This false sense of self, in turn, prevents them from working harder, developing their skills, and also prevents them from achieving their actual potential. Measures can be taken to ensure that the right content is uploaded so that the users are inspired and motivated to take their creativity to the next level. It should help them go beyond the fleeting fame that the application seems to provide. The platform can be used to share lessons on various creative activities that can enhance the viewers' knowledge and help them develop their skills. The platform can be successfully used to train individuals on skills like dancing, singing, and other art forms and also help spread awareness regarding important issues like female foeticide, hygiene, and others.

Sharing pranks related to sensitive issues like COVID -19 (like touching other people for entertainment, as shown by some of the TikTok content creators) can negatively impact the users and push them to perform similar pranks on others, and further spread the disease. This behavior can also instill fear and anxiety among the viewers. Other challenges like "Getting naked in front of your boyfriend/family challenge" may not be appropriately received by specific cultures. Consequently, it is crucial to ensure that the platform is culturally sensitive or culture-specific versions of the platform are provided. Sharing stunts related content, as stated by some of the participants, can be extremely dangerous and can have serious consequences. Filtering out potentially dangerous content and providing with statutory warnings can prevent the damage that can be caused to human health and life. It also emerged from the interviews that the participants did not use the platform also because of security reasons. The mistrust in the application about the safety of personal data of users can be addressed to develop trust among the users. Information regarding data safety and encryptions can be included and communicated to enhance transparency. All these measures can help change the social stigma attached to the platform and increase its usage.

7 Conclusion

TikTok is a widely used application, especially in India. Based on the interviews and analysis, it was found that participants dislike the platform because it resulted in a waste of time, included unreal and questionable content, and did not contribute to knowledge, learning, and social awareness. The participants also dislike the platform because they believe that it acts as a source of distraction for the youth and consumes a lot of phone memory. Suggestive measurements are also captured that can help in increasing the usefulness and credibility of the platform like filtering and restricting content and using the broad reach and accessibility for sharing knowledge and creating awareness. Based on the insights from the interviews, some novel points emerged that brought in the picture the social identity aspects that can lead to the nonusage of social media platforms.

7.1 Limitation and Future Research Directions

This study has several limitations that present opportunities for future research. First, most of the participants in this research were from urban areas. A large set of TikTok users are also from rural and suburban areas that were not included in our sample. Consideration of both the populations would help to gather better data. Second, the sample size was based on non-probabilistic convenience sampling. Using a more extensive and random sample would increase the credibility of the research and lead to better results.

The term "Social" in social media clearly emphasizes on the importance of concepts related to multiple social factors like social identity, social influence [51], social capital [52, 53], and many others. It is crucial to identify how social identity can push individuals away from specific social media platforms and reduce their usage. How are these social identities formed? Multiple factors have been identified which prevent individuals from using social media applications in this study. It will be interesting to study the relationship between social media platforms with individual variables (like educational qualification, financial status, gender, personality, culture, and background) of the users and nonusers.

References

1. Top 10 TikTok (Musical.ly) App Tips and Tricks. Guiding Tech
2. TikTok App.Google Play Store.play.google.com (2019)
3. Jenke, T.: TikTok is fast becoming the most popular app in the world. https://theindustryobserver.thebrag.com/tik-tok-most-popular-app/
4. Tik Tok, a Global Music Video Platform and Social Network, Launches in Indonesia. https://en.prnasia.com/releases/apac/Tik_Tok_a_Global_Music_Video_Platform_and_Social_Network_Launches_in_Indonesia-187963.shtml
5. How Douyin became China's top short-video App in 500 days (2018)
6. Davenport, S.W., Bergman, S.M., Bergman, J.Z., Fearrington, M.E.: Twitter versus Facebook: exploring the role of narcissism in the motives and usage of different social media platforms. Comput. Hum. Behav. **32**, 212–220 (2014)
7. Yan, P., Schroeder, R.: Variations in the adoption and use of mobile social apps in everyday lives in urban and rural China. Mob. Media Commun. 205015791988471 (2019)
8. Park, C.S., Kaye, B.K.: Smartphone and self-extension: functionally, anthropomorphically, and ontologically extending self via the smartphone. Mob. Media Commun. **7**, 215–231 (2019)
9. Grandhi, S.A., Plgtnick, L., Hiltz, S.R.: Do I stay or do I go? Motivations and decision making in social media non-use and reversion. Proc. ACM Human-Computer Interact. 3 (2019)
10. Ellison, N., Steinfield, C., Lampe, C.: The benefits of Facebook "friends:" Social capital and college students' use of online social network sites (2007). academic.oup.com
11. Vitak, J., Ellison, N.B.: Users and nonusers: Interactions between levels of Facebook adoption and social capital, pp. 809–819. dl.acm.org (2013)
12. Wohn, D.: Spottswood, E.: Reactions to other-generated face threats on Facebook and their relational consequences. Elsevier (2016)
13. Larsson, A.O., Kalsnes, B.: 'Of course we are on Facebook': use and non-use of social media among Swedish and Norwegian politicians. Eur. J. Commun. **29**, 653–667 (2014)
14. Cui, D.: Beyond "connected presence": multimedia mobile instant messaging in close relationship management. Mob. Media Commun. **4**, 19–36 (2016)
15. Wei, R., Huang, J., Zheng, P.: Use of mobile social apps for public communication in China: gratifications as antecedents of reposting articles from WeChat public accounts. Mob. Media Commun. **6**, 108–126 (2018)
16. Xiao, Y., Jiang, : Research on TikTok APP based on user-centric use the "Insert Citation" button to add citations to this document. Appl. Sci. Innov. Res. **3**, 28–36 (2019)
17. Zhang, J.: China's Kuaishou, TikTok close gap with YouTube among highest-grossing video apps
18. Jonggi, H.: How cutting-edge AI is making China's TikTok the talk of town. https://medium.com/beautytech-jp/how-cutting-edge-ai-is-making-chinas-tiktok-the-talk-of-town-4dd7b250a1a4
19. Chen, Q.: The biggest trend in Chinese social media is dying, and another has already taken its place. https://www.cnbc.com/2018/09/19/short-video-apps-like-douyin-tiktok-are-dominating-chinese-screens.html
20. Soyez, F.: The dangers of Tik Tok for your children and how to protect themselves

21. Zhang, K.: I risked my life, please like!' Mobile app Tik Tok has Hong Kong children craving acceptance – and some are going to dangerous extremes (2018)
22. Indonesia overturns ban on Chinese video app TikTok. The Straits Times
23. Purwaningsih, A.: Indonesia blocks "pornographic" Tik Tok app (2018)
24. Silviana, C., Potkin, F.: Chinese video app Tik Tok to set up Indonesia censor team to Reuters (2018)
25. Islam, A.: Bangladesh 'anti-porn war' bans blogs and Google books. https://www.dw.com/en/bangladesh-anti-porn-war-bans-blogs-and-google-books/a-47684058
26. Lieber, C.: TikTok is the latest social media platform accused of abusing children's privacy - now it's paying up (2019)
27. Lee, D.: TikTok stops young users from uploading videos after FTC settlement. https://www.theverge.com/2019/2/27/18243510/tiktok-age-young-user-videos-ftc-settlement-13-childrens-privacy-law
28. 'It Encourages Pornography': Madras High Court Asks Government to Ban Video App TikTok. https://www.news18.com/news/india/it-encourages-pornography-madras-high-court-asks-government-to-ban-video-app-tiktok-2088337.html
29. Panigrahi, S., Manve, V.: India bans China's TikTok for "degrading culture and encouraging pornography"
30. Chandrashekhar, A.: TikTok no longer available on Google and Apple stores (2019)
31. Whiting, A., Williams, D.: Why people use social media: a uses and gratifications approach. Qual. Mark. Res. An Int. J. **16**, 362–369 (2013)
32. Halawani, F., Soh, P., Global, Y.H.-J.: Social Media Utilisation and Business Performance of Hotels in Lebanon: Exploring the Moderating Effects of Hotel Classification (2020). igi-global.com
33. Rialp-Criado, J., Alarcón-Del-Amo, M. del C., Rialp, A.: Speed of use of social media as an antecedent of speed of business internationalization. J. Glob. Inf. Manag. **28**, 142–166 (2020)
34. Aldarbesti, H., Deng, H., Sutanto, J., Wei, C., David, Phang: Who are more active and influential on Twitter? An investigation of the Ukraine's conflict episode. J. Glob. Inf. Manag. **28**, 66–87 (2020)
35. Zhu, Y.-Q., Chen, H.-G.: Social media and human need satisfaction: implications for social media marketing. Elsevier **58**, 335–345 (2015)
36. Kietzmann, J.H., Hermkens, K., McCarthy, I.P., Silvestre, B.S.: Social media? Get serious! Understanding the functional building blocks of social media. Bus. Horiz. **54**, 241–251 (2011)
37. Smith, B.G.: Socially distributing public relations: Twitter, Haiti, and interactivity in social media. Public Relat. Rev. **36**, 329–335 (2010)
38. Mikalef, P., Giannakos, M., Adamantia, P.: Shopping and word-of-mouth intentions on social media. scielo.conicyt.cl
39. Halpern, D., Gibbs, J.: Social media as a catalyst for online deliberation? Exploring the affordances of Facebook and YouTube for political expression. Comput. Hum. Behav. **29**, 1159–1168 (2013)
40. Fannin, R.: The Strategy Behind TikTok's Global Rise (2019)
41. Inventiva: Demands to ban Tik-Tok raised again, more than 10,000 tweets in 10 hours, Madras High Court had banned it previously. https://www.inventiva.co.in/stories/inventiva/demands-to-ban-tik-tok-raised-again-more-than-10000-tweets-in-10-hours-madras-high-court-had-banned-it-previously/
42. Tech, I.T.: TikTok could be banned in India after July 22: What happened now and everything else you need to know. https://www.indiatoday.in/technology/features/story/tiktok-could-be-banned-in-india-after-july-22-what-happened-now-and-everything-else-you-need-to-know-1570811-2019-07-18

43. Braun, V., Clarke, V.: Using thematic analysis in psychology. Qual. Res. Psychol. **3**, 77–101 (2006)
44. Cassell, C., Symon, G.: Essential guide to qualitative methods in organizational research (2004)
45. Corbin, J.M., Strauss, A.: Grounded theory research: procedures, canons, and evaluative criteria. Qual. Sociol. **13**, 3–21 (1990)
46. Tajfel, H.: Social psychology of intergroup relations (1982)
47. Twenge, J.M., Martin, G.N., Campbell, W.K.: Decreases in Psychological Well-Being Among American Adolescents After 2012 and Links to Screen Time During the Rise of Smartphone Technology (2018). psycnet.apa.org
48. Owen, N., Fox, A., Bird, T.: The development of a small-scale survey instrument of UK teachers to study professional use (and non-use) of and attitudes to social media Journal Item How to cite. Int. J. Res. Method Educ. **39**, 170–193 (2016)
49. Swar, B., Hameed, T.: Fear of missing out, social media engagement, smartphone addiction and distraction moderating role of tracking apps in the youth. pdf. In: International Conference on Health Informatics (2017)
50. Baumer, E.P., Guha, S., Quan, E., Mimno, D., Gay, G.K.: Missing photos, suffering withdrawal, or finding freedom? How experiences of social media non-use influence the likelihood of reversion. 1 (2015). journals.sagepub.com
51. Kelman, H.C.: Compliance, identification, and internalization three processes of attitude change. J. Conflict Resolut. **2**, 51–60 (1958)
52. Chang, H.H., Chuang, S.-S.: Social capital and individual motivations on knowledge sharing: Participant involvement as a moderator. Inf. Manag. **48**, 9–18 (2010)
53. Portes, A.: Social capital: its origins and applications in modern sociology. Annu. Rev. Sociol. **24**, 1–24 (1998)

Mining the Social Discussions Surrounding Circular Economy: Insights from the Collective Intelligence Shared in Twitter

Purva Grover[1]([⊠]) and Arpan Kumar Kar[2]

[1] Information Systems/IT Area, Indian Institute of Management Amritsar, Amritsar, India
groverdpurva@gmail.com
[2] DMS, Indian Institute of Technology, Delhi, Delhi, India

Abstract. Organisations like UNDP, UNEP, CES and many more along with Fortune 500 companies have been sharing support towards the circular economy in order to bring focus towards long term sustainability. The purpose of this study is to explore the collective intelligence towards circular economy which may help in obtaining greater support from different stakeholders. For this objective, three research questions had been explored by analysing Twitter discussions on circular economy through content and network analysis. The insights reveal that users are discussing about all the three elements of circular economy, i.e., economic benefits, environment impacts and resource scarcity. The polarity of sentiments surrounding these elements of circular economy is also established and explained. Insights also indicate that artificial intelligence is strongly being perceived as a solution for resource optimisation, remanufacturing, re-generation of by-products and many more towards achieving circular economy objectives.

Keywords: Circular economy · Collective intelligence · Social media · Twitter analytics · Social media analytics

1 Introduction

Circular economy is an economic model aimed at zero production waste. Circular economy aims to shift resources usage towards regenerative manner [3, 22]. By doing so, it attempts to address social and environmental needs without compromising significantly on the economic profitability for the firm. Successful implementation of circular economy lies on the following principles, whereby waste becomes a resource, focus on reuse, reparation, valorization, eco-design, industrial and territorial ecology. Objectives towards achieving circular economy have been highly supported by organizations like European Union and different national governments [19] Korhonen et al. (2018). Several organizations around the world are also supporting and implementing circular economy concepts in industrial processes. In line with such national and international priorities, academicians are also suggesting frameworks for moving towards a sustainable society by meeting circular economy objectives [5]. One of the popular ways of diffusing circular economy in industrial processes is by integrating

S. K. Sharma et al. (Eds.): TDIT 2020, IFIP AICT 618, pp. 303–314, 2020.
https://doi.org/10.1007/978-3-030-64861-9_27

activities of reverse supply chain into forward supply chain. Lieder and Rashid (2016) had indicated circular economy is the solution for resource scarcity, waste generation and sustaining economic benefit. Kirchherr, Piscicelli, Bour, Kostense-Smit, Muller, Huibrechtse-Truijens and Hekkert (2018) had highlighted that the biggest barrier in the adoption of circular economy is the lack of awareness on circular economy. Circular economy activities requires specific education and training programs among practitioners [8]. However such initiatives are likely to become successful if they get ample support from both the internal and external stakeholders of the firm. In this context, with so much of focused efforts surrounding enhancement of its awareness, there is a need to assess the discussions surrounding circular economy among stakeholders to comprehend the nature and drivers of such support among stakeholders.

As per global digital report 2019, the number of social media users worldwide stands at 3.5 billion [27]. The numbers indicates roughly 50% of world's population is active on social media. Nowadays, organisations are also engaging with users on social media to express their views and interact on different issues in order to spread awareness on their offerings as well as to understand their concerns. Attempts for increasing engagement and awareness among different stakeholders like suppliers and customers are driven by firms on social media to improve business growth [9]. The monthly active users on Twitter grew 9% from third quarter, 2018 to fourth quarter, 2018 and stand at 330 million [24]. Such population are seen to share their perspectives on different areas of interest across themes, and we attempt to mine this collective intelligence for understanding the nature of discussions surrounding circular economy. In such a context, since Twitter being a widely used platform [1, 4] by people of diverse backgrounds and demography as well as organisations [6, 7, 12, 14, 18, 25, 26, 30, 36], it makes Twitter an useful source of analysing views and opinions surrounding circular economy based on user generated content. Assessing progress towards environmental sustainability a systematic and robust knowledge base and buy in from key stake-holders are required. On the basis of this evidence, this study is using social media analytics to understand the major themes of discussion on twitter of the people towards circular economy. Circular economy is about many actors working together to create effective flows of materials and information, in order to move away from linear economy, take make consume throw away approach of resources [10] to recycle, repair and reuse of resources. Therefore to quantify human perspective on circular economy diverse views of users on Twitter had been analysed. Literature indicates diverse perspectives help in making accurate predictions [21]. This study focuses on three interrelated research questions (RQ) surrounding how stakeholders discuss about themes related to circular economy:

RQ1: How do the social media users prioritize among the outcomes of circular economy with respect to economic benefits, environmental impact and resource scarcity?

RQ2: How do the sentiments differ among the social media users regarding these outcome factors, namely, economic benefits, environmental impacts and resource scarcity?

RQ3: How do these factors affecting these outcomes of the circular economy, namely, economic benefits, environmental impact and resource scarcity, associate among each other in social discussions?

Empirical methods had not been used for examining the human perspective on circular economy because circular economy practices involves working of many actors in collaboration. To the best of our knowledge, a single questionnaire cannot capture the perspectives of the different actors. Further geographically dispersed stakeholders cannot share their perspectives through such an approach. Hence to acquire collective intelligence, we attempted to address these questions by analyzing tweets by different actors who were sharing their perspectives on the circular economy surrounding environment impact, resource scarcity and economic benefits (Lieder and Rashid, 2016). The remaining sections have been organized as follows. Section 2 is dedicated to background literature. Section 3 illustrates research question and hypothesis explored in the study. Section 4 presents the research methodology adopted for the study. Section 5 illustrates insights from the social discussions on economic benefits, environmental impact and resource scarcity with context to circular economy. This is followed by the discussion section whereby we share the contributions to literature and the implications of our study for practice. The final section concludes the paper and presents the limitations of the study along with future research directions.

2 Background Literature

Circular economy as a dynamic, multidimensional, integrative approach for promoting transformed socio-technical template for economic development [11]. Korhonen, Honkasalo and Seppälä (2018) had pointed out circular economy is the economy constructed by using cyclical materials flows [34] and cascading energy flows within the societal production consumption systems. Table 1 presents the circular economy activities such as reduce, reuse and recycle for different items and categories.

Table 1. Circular Economy - reduce, reuse and recycle activities for different items and categories

Items & categories	Task - reduce, reuse and recycle	Literature evidence
Rare-earth elements	Recycle material mitigates the supply risk and led to circular economy	[37]
	Recycling Yttrium is profitable rather than extracting	[15]
End-of-life products	Reuse and recycle end-of-life products reduces greenhouse gas emissions while manufacturing and leads to circular economy	[20]
Food waste	Recycling bin for transforming the food waste into usable end product such energy	[38]
Cloth	Textile recycling technologies	[35]

The supply of these resources faces high uncertainty, application of circular economy concept may mitigate the risk of supply of these resources [37]. Reuse and recycling can led to reduction in unused raw material [20]. Circular economy can also improve the sustainable use of critical raw materials such as yttrium [15]. Industrial symbiosis as an effective practice for circular economy [17]. Industrial symbiosis engages different industries in exchange of materials, services and energy. Literature indicates circular economy discussions are at the niche stages [28] and driven because of economic consideration (Masi et al. 2018), therefore there is a need to put in significant efforts for motivating the people towards circular economy practices [28]. Technical and economic factors are hard drivers and barriers in transition towards circular economy whereas institutional and social factors as soft drivers and soft barriers in transition towards circular economy [11]. Institutional factors act as soft drivers when it comes to building environmental legislation, environmental standards and waste management directives. Six challenges of circular economy with respect to environment sustainability [29] these were, (a) thermodynamic limits; (b) spatial and temporal system boundary limitations; (c) limits posed by physical economic growth such as rebound effect, Jevon's paradox and the boomerang effect; (d) limits posed by path dependencies and lock-in; (e) intra-organizational versus inter-organizational strategies and management; and (f) definition of physical flows which varies within social and cultural context.

In this era of digital economy, social media allows people to generate, exchange and share in virtual communities. Online knowledge communities present on Twitter specializes in knowledge seeking and sharing purposes. Such mass media channels are effective for creating awareness on practices. Interaction on Twitter triggers effectual cognitions and more communication on a topic can lead to effectual churn as well [16].

3 Research Question and Hypothesis Development

This study focus on three interrelated questions RQ1, RQ2 and RQ3 on circular economy perspectives. Circular economy revolutionize the existing industrial processes by transforming existing business models by using 3R's, reduce, recycle and reuse, such that resources, materials or goods re-used and continue to remain a part of the cycle and not go out of it. Business models are designed in such a way that products are leased, shared or rented wherever possible. Companies like AirBnb and Zoomcar are prime examples of this concept. In case the goods cannot be rented and have to be sold, incentives are given to ensure that instead of the goods being disposed off at the end of their life, they are returned, which allows reuse of the product or their components [13]. Circular economy brings down production prices, which leads to reduction in selling price, thereby helping the consumer economically as well as socially and environmentally. A comprehensive framework on circular economy which includes three perspectives such as economic benefit, environmental impact and resource scarcity with context to circular economy [31]. Firms and organizations moves towards the circular economy for gaining economic benefits over the competitors. This may require redesigning and restructuring some of the activities related to businesses such as product design, supply chain design, material choices and many more. The three perspectives of circular economy, economic benefits, environmental impact and resource scarcity covers the short-term and long-term objectives of circular economy and are seamlessly linked to each other. Therefore, the comprehensive nature of this framework will enable us to analyze the discussions on circular economy on twitter in a more complete manner. Hypothesis H1 proposes that there is no statistically significant difference among the discussions on three perspectives of circular economy, economic benefits, environmental impact and resource scarcity on Twitter.

H1: All three perspectives of circular economy, economic benefits, environmental impact and resource scarcity had been discussed equally on Twitter.

Resource scarcity takes into account the way scarce critical resources and materials, such as rare-earth elements, use can be reduce, reuse and recycled. Resource depletion speed is reduced in circular economy as compared to linear economy. Literature indicates environment impacts should be avoided and minimized as much as possible. This may include reducing solid waste, landfill and emissions. The solid waste may include food waste, e-waste, waste management and municipal solid waste. Due to competitive pressure on the firms, firms do not consider environment impact over economic benefit. Literature indicates that positive sentiments on themes indicate higher levels of support and user engagement and this becomes critical for the success of the objectives [2]. Thus RQ2 tries to find the sentiments of the people on circular economy with respect to different aspects such as economic benefits, environmental impact and resource scarcity.

RQ2: How do the sentiments differ among the social media users regarding these outcome factors, namely, economic benefits, environmental impacts and resource scarcity?

Economic benefits gained by the firms highly depend on the availability of resources and pricing policies of the resources. Pre-processing of raw materials into products and services directly impacts the environments of the producers and consumers (Lieder and Rashid, 2016). The nation's legislation regulates the impacts of the firms and organizations on environment for economic benefits. Speed of waste generation and speed of resource depletion influences environment.

RQ3: How do these factors affecting these outcomes of the circular economy, namely, economic benefits, environmental impact and resource scarcity, associate among each other in social discussions?

Analyzing these discussions on twitter gives us an idea of the penetration and awareness of circular economy among the people across the world. It also gives us the main themes of discussions and polarity. Compared to offline surveys and interviews, twitter served to be a better source of data as surveys are firstly time-consuming, with different biases coming into the picture and not only this, for issues like circular economy, a concept which is well-spread in India so far, it becomes very difficult to come across people who could share unbiased and useful views on the issue.

4 Research Methodology

To derive insights from Twitter on three perspective of circular economy, economic benefits, environmental impact and resource scarcity of people social media analytics methodology, the CUP framework (Fan and Gordon, 2014) has been applied to the tweets. The CUP framework is a three stage framework. The first stage captures the people generated data from Twitter on circular economy. The second stage tries to understand the data extracted by applying descriptive, content, diagnostic and prescriptive analysis. The third stage presents the insights derived from these analysis. To extract the tweets, a list of synonymous of circular economy had been made by searching through internet and research articles. The list includes the following keywords, "circular economy", "recycling", "reusing", "smart design", "industrial ecology", "war on waste", "zero waste", "adaptive reuse", "upcycle" and "sustainability". These keywords were identified based on the literature which was elaborated earlier in the second section of this article. The extraction of tweets was done using 'Tweepy' library in Python. The extraction of tweets was done for a period of four months from December 2018 to March 2019 and a total of 90,113 tweets were collected.

In stage two, top 100 hashtags had been found in the data. These hashtags through manual coding had been assigned to three perspectives of circular economy, economic benefits, environmental impact and resource scarcity. To better understand the perspective of the users on these sentiment analysis was applied. Sentiment analysis is a part of content analysis and is a technique which analyses underlying sentiment of a tweet. Based on the sentiment, each tweet is categorized as positive, negative or neutral [23, 32]. To find the linkages between economic, environment and resources, the tweets containing top hashtags related to economic, environment and resources hashtags, any two at time were analyzed with the help of the network analysis. The edges in the network diagram represents the linkages among economic, environment and resources. The links between economic benefits and environment impacts may represent value perception or legislation. The links between economic benefits and resource scarcity may represent resource dependency or price volatility. The links between environment impacts and resource scarcity may represent depletion or waste generation. Once the network is formed the community detection algorithm based on greedy optimization of modularity had been applied. To explore the linkages among different economic benefits, environment impacts and resources. The last and third stage of CUP framework the insights of the analysis were discussed in the light of circular economy framework suggested by Lieder and Rashid (2016).

5   Findings

Circular Economy is a concept which is about to become an integral part of our lives, sooner rather than later. In fact, the sharing business models of Zoomcar and AirBnB are prime examples of circular economy in India. The organizations like UNDP, UNEP, TERI, FICCI - Circular Economy Symposium, etc. posting their views on circular economy on twitter and engaging with the users. Various companies were also taking part in discussions related to circular economy on Twitter and had extensively posted their views and vision on circular economy. Figure 1, indicates artificial intelligence (AI) is dominant among economic benefits followed by business and technology hashtags. In environment impact dominant hashtag is on waste and plastic. Within resource scarcity, recycle is the dominant hashtag.

H1: All three perspectives of circular economy, economic benefits, environmental impact and resource scarcity had been discussed equally on Twitter.

Let $\alpha = 0.05$ (assumption), the degree of freedom is $(k - 1, n - k)$, where k is the number of samples (k = 3; economic benefit, environment impact and resource scarcity) and n is the total number of observation (n = 26; say characteristics identified from literature). The degree of freedom for this equal to (2, 25). The decision rule states, if the calculated value of F is greater than table value of F, reject H1. The table value of F at 5% level of significance for degrees of freedom (2, 25) is 3.39. The calculated value of F-statistic on circular economy discussions surrounding economic benefits, environmental impact and resource scarcity is 0.548 which is lesser than the threshold value of 3.39. Therefore, H1 is not rejected. Hence there is no significant difference between means of discussions of economic benefits, environment impact and resource scarcity in context to circular economy. This indicates Twitter had been used equally for discussions related to economic benefits, environmental impact and resource scarcity.

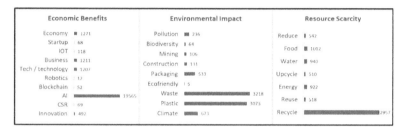

Fig. 1. Occurrence of the hashtags captured related to economic benefits, environmental impact and resource scarcity

Circular economy is a concept that largely draws positive sentiment of the people as presented in Fig. 2. It is see that most of the discussions surrounding economic benefits are having positive sentiments as compared to discussions on environ mental impact and resource scarcity. Discussions related to environmental impact being most negative when compared to economic benefits and resource scarcity.

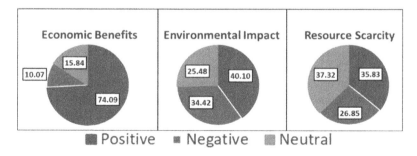

Fig. 2. Sentiment analysis of the three elements of circular economy, economic benefits, environment analysis and resource scarcity

It appears that most of the discussions surrounding circular economy is driven by positive sentiments when it comes to economic benefits. However when such discussions try to address environmental impact and resource scarcity, such discussions invariably become negatively polarized. Figure 3 presents the linkage among three elements of circular economy economic benefits, environmental impact and resource scarcity. The links between economic benefits and environment impacts may represent value perception or legislation, represented with red edges, in Fig. 3. In red edges most of the discussion was on artificial intelligence (AI) from economic benefits to environment impacts in terms of climate, plastic and health.

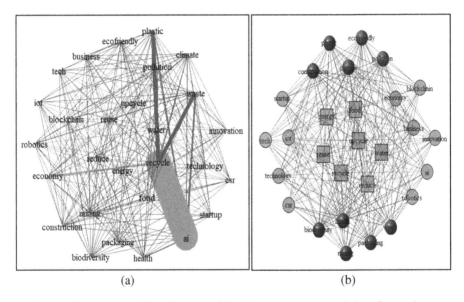

(a)   (b)

Fig. 3. (a) Linkage among three elements of circular economy economic benefits, environmental impact and resource scarcity; (b) Linkages between three elements of circular economy economic benefits, environmental impact and resource scarcity (Color figure online)

The links between economic benefits and resource scarcity may represent resource dependency or price volatility, represented using green edges, in Fig. 3. In green edges most of the discussion was on artificial intelligence (AI) from economic benefits to resource scarcity in resolving measures such as recycle and things such as food, water and energy. Other than these business and technology had been extensively discussed with recycling. The links between environment impacts and resource scarcity may represent depletion or waste generation, represented using blue edges, in Fig. 3. In blue edges most of the discussion was on recycling waste and plastic. Followed by recycling packaging, climate and health. To find grouping among the linkages among three elements of circular economy economic benefits, environmental impact and resource scarcity, the community detection algorithm based on greedy optimization of modularity had been applied. The algorithm resulted in two groups, presented in Fig. 3(b), one demonstrated in grey colour and second group is demonstrated in yellow colour. In each group economic benefits presented using circle, environment impacts presented using sphere and resource scarcity in squares. Group 1 in grey colour, consists of following economic benefits, innovation, CSR, AI, blockchain, technology, business, startup and economy; along with following environment impacts hashtags, waste, packaging, plastic, construction, mining, health and biodiversity; and along with following resource scarcity hashtags, recycle, reuse, upcycle, water and food. Group 2 in yellow colour, consists of following economic benefits, robotics, iot and tech; along with following environment impacts, climate, eco-friendly and pollution; and along with following resource scarcity hashtags, reduce and energy.

6 Discussion

The data extracted for the study indicates circular economy had been extensively discussed by world organizations like UNDP, UNEP, CES, etc. along with Fortune 500 companies, This study had analyzed the circular economy tweets using social media analytics. Linear model has dominated industrial processes as compared to circular economy [29]. The development supported by linear economy had seriously had harm the environment. Social awareness is crucial for a successful transition from a linear economy to circular economy [31]. Figure 1 indicates artificial intelligence (AI) is dominant among economic benefits. Technology is hard driver, when technology facilitates resource optimization, remanufacturing and re-generation of by-products and development of sharing solutions. Technology is hard barrier when inappropriate technology been used in different context. Through this evidence, the authors of the study can suggest if used appropriately artificial intelligence (AI) can be used for resource optimization, remanufacturing, re-generation of by-products and many more. People on Twitter were discussing about waste management and use of the plastic impacting environment. Recycle hashtag had been found as the dominant hashtags. The discussions related economic benefits and resource scarcity have a stronger impact on polarity of discussions as compared to environmental impact.

6.1 Contribution to Theory

The current study contributes to the interface of literature surrounding public opinion, crowd intelligence for achieving multi-stakeholder support towards attaining circular economy objectives. Through hypothesis H1, the study establishes that all the three elements of circular economy, economic benefits, environment impacts and resource scarcity had been equally discussed on Twitter. This is somewhat counterintuitive to existing literature where there are indications that organizations are implementing circular economy practices for economic benefits and in this process environment impact is give less importance [33]. The results of hypothesis H1 is contrasting this evidence, which indicates economic benefits, environment impacts and resource scarcity had been equally discussed on Twitter by the stakeholders. In similar lines, our findings towards RQ2 establishes that people in general have positive sentiments while discussing about the economic benefits of circular economy. However, while discussing about the environ impacts and resource scarcity, often negative sentiments are driving these discussions significantly more. A closer look at the tweets manually reveal that while other stakeholders also support the other two elements of circular economy, the driver for such discussions are predominantly apprehension for the future needs.

RQ3 explores the linkages between the economic benefits, environment impacts and resource scarcity. Artificial intelligence had been strongly linked with climate, plastic and health for linkages between economic benefits and environment impacts. Artificial intelligence had been strongly linked with food, water and energy for linkages between economic benefits and resource scarcity. Recycling waste and recycling plastic had been found to be strongly linked among the links of environment impacts and resource scarcity elements of circular economy.

7   Conclusion and Future Research Directions

Analyzing these discussions on twitter gives us an idea of the penetration and awareness of circular economy among the people across the world. It also gives us the main themes of discussions and polarity. Economic benefits, environment impacts and resource scarcity had been discussed on Twitter equally. However while the discussions on economic benefits mostly have a positive sentiment, the discussions on environmental impact and resource scarcity are often driven by negative sentiments. Further, it is perceived in all such discussions surrounding circular economy, the role of AI is going to be very impactful. Future studies can also explore why these links, highlighted in results and outcomes of RQ3 had been found strong in the discussions on circular economy on Twitter. It would be also interesting to understand the diffusion of such discussions in social media, based on elements, in future research.

References

1. Adams, A., McCorkindale, T.: Dialogue and transparency: A content analysis of how the 2012 presidential candidates used Twitter. Public Relations Rev. **39**(4), 357–359 (2013)
2. Arapakis, I., Lalmas, M., Cambazoglu, B.B., Marcos, M.C., Jose, J.M.: User engagement in online News: under the scope of sentiment, interest, affect, and gaze. J. Assoc. Inf. Sci. Technol. **65**(10), 1988–2005 (2014)
3. Batista, L., Bourlakis, M., Smart, P., Maull, R.: In search of a circular supply chain archetype–a content-analysis-based literature review. Prod. Planning Control **29**(6), 438–451 (2018)
4. Bechmann, A., Lomborg, S.: Mapping actor roles in social media: different per-spectives on value creation in theories of user participation. New Media Soc. **15**(5), 765–781 (2013)
5. Bernon, M., Tjahjono, B., Ripanti, E.F.: Aligning retail reverse logistics practice with circular economy values: an exploratory framework. Production Planning Control **29**(6), 483–497 (2018)
6. Boynton, G.R., Richardson Jr., G.W.: Agenda setting in the twenty-first century. New Media Soc. **18**(9), 1916–1934 (2016)
7. Brabham, D.C.: Crowdsourcing as a model for problem solving: an introduction and cases. Convergence **14**(1), 75–90 (2008)

8. Burger, M., Stavropoulos, S., Ramkumar, S., Dufourmont, J., van Oort, F.: The heterogeneous skill-base of circular economy employment. Res. Policy **48**(1), 248–261 (2019)
9. Chatterjee, S., Kar, A.K.: Why do small and medium enterprises use social media marketing and what is the impact: Empirical insights from India. Int. J. Inf. Manag. **53**, 102013 (2020). https://doi.org/10.1016/j.ijinfomgt.2020.102103
10. De Angelis, R., Howard, M., Miemczyk, J.: Supply chain management and the circular economy: towards the circular supply chain. Prod. Planning Control **29**(6), 425–437 (2018)
11. De Jesus, A., Mendonça, S.: Lost in transition? Drivers and barriers in the eco-innovation road to the circular economy. Ecol. Econ. **145**, 75–89 (2018)
12. Dwivedi, Y.K., Rana, N.P., Slade, E.L., Singh, N., Kizgin, H.: Editorial introduction: advances in theory and practice of digital marketing. J. Retail. Consumer Serv. **53**, 101909 (2020). https://doi.org/10.1016/j.jretconser.2019.101909
13. Ellen MacArthur Foundation and McKinsey & Company. Towards the Circular Economy: Accelerating the scale-up across global supply chains (2014). www3.weforum.org/docs/WEF_ENV_TowardsCircularEconomy_Report_2014.pdf. Accessed 20 Apr 2019
14. Ellison, N.B., Boyd, D.M.: Sociality through social network sites. In: The Oxford Handbook of Internet Studies. https://doi.org/10.1093/oxfordhb/9780199589074.013.0008
15. Favot, M., Massarutto, A.: Rare-earth elements in the circular economy: the case of yttrium. J. Environ. Manag. **240**, 504–510 (2019)
16. Fischer, E., Reuber, A.R.: Social interaction via new social media:(How) can interactions on Twitter affect effectual thinking and behavior? J. Bus. Venturing **26**(1), 1–18 (2011)
17. Fraccascia, L.: The impact of technical and economic disruptions in industrial symbi-osis relationships: an Enterprise Input-Output approach. Int. J. Prod. Econ. **213**, 161–174 (2019)
18. Glenn, J.C.: Collective intelligence systems and an application by The Millennium Project for the Egyptian Academy of Scientific Research and Technology. Technol. Forecasting Soc. Change **97**, 7–14 (2015)
19. Habibi, M.K.K., Battaïa, O., Cung, V.D., Dolgui, A., Tiwari, M.K.: Sample average approximation for multi-vehicle collection–disassembly problem under uncertainty. Int. J. Prod. Res. **57**(8), 2409–2428 (2019)
20. Hasegawa, S., Kinoshita, Y., Yamada, T., Bracke, S.: Life cycle option selection of disassembly parts for material-based CO2 saving rate and recovery cost: analysis of different market value and labor cost for reused parts in German and Japanese cases. Int. J. Prod. Econ. **213**, 229–242 (2019)
21. Hong, L., Page, S.E.: Groups of diverse problem solvers can outperform groups of high-ability problem solvers. Proc. Natl. Acad. Sci. **101**(46), 16385–16389 (2004)
22. Hopkinson, P., Zils, M., Hawkins, P., Roper, S.: Managing a complex global circular economy business model: opportunities and challenges. California Manag. Rev. **60**(3), 71–94 (2018)
23. Hu, M., Liu, B.: Mining and summarizing customer reviews. In: Proceedings of the Tenth ACM SIGKDD International Conference on Knowledge Discovery and Data Mining, pp. 168–177. ACM (2004)
24. Internet live stats. Twitter usage statistics (2018). http://www.internetlivestats.com/twitter-statistics/. Accessed 13 Dec 2018
25. Jarmin, R.S., O'Hara, A.B.: Big data and the transformation of public policy analysis. J. Policy Anal. Manag. **35**(3), 715–721 (2016)
26. Kane, G., Alavi, M., Labianca, G., Borgatti, S.: What's different about social media networks? A framework and research agenda. MIS Q. **38**(1), 275–304 (2014)
27. Kemp, S.: Global Digital Report 2019 (2019). http://hoot-suite.com/pages/digital-in-2019. Accessed 21 Apr 2019

28. Kirchherr, J., et al.: Barriers to the circular economy: evidence from the European Union (EU). Ecol. Econ. **150**, 264–272 (2018)
29. Korhonen, J., Honkasalo, A., Seppälä, J.: Circular economy: the concept and its limitations. Ecol. Econ. **143**, 37–46 (2018)
30. Lawrence, E., Sides, J., Farrell, H.: Self-segregation or deliberation? Blog readership, participation, and polarization in American politics. Perspect. Politics **8**(1), 141 (2010)
31. Lieder, M., Rashid, A.: Towards circular economy implementation: a comprehensive review in context of manufacturing industry. J. Cleaner Production **115**, 36–51 (2016)
32. Liu, B., Hu, M., Cheng, J.: Opinion observer: analyzing and comparing opinions on the web. In: Proceedings of the 14th International Conference on World Wide Web, pp. 342–351. ACM (2005)
33. Masi, D., Kumar, V., Garza-Reyes, J.A., Godsell, J.: Towards a more circular economy: exploring the awareness, practices, and barriers from a focal firm perspective. Production Planning Control **29**(6), 539–550 (2018)
34. Mishra, J.L., Hopkinson, P.G., Tidridge, G.: Value creation from circular economy-led closed loop supply chains: a case study of fast-moving consumer goods. Production Planning Control **29**(6), 509–521 (2018)
35. Norris, L.: Urban prototypes: growing local circular cloth economies. Bus. History **61**(1), 205–224 (2019)
36. Paniagua, J., Sapena, J.: Business performance and social media: love or hate? Bus. Horizons **57**(6), 719–728 (2014)
37. Rogetzer, P., Silbermayr, L., Jammernegg, W.: Sustainable sourcing including capacity reservation for recycled materials: a newsvendor framework with price and demand correlations. Int. J. Production Econ. **214**, 206–219 (2019)
38. Slorach, P.C., Jeswani, H.K., Cuéllar-Franca, R., Azapagic, A.: Environmental sustainability of anaerobic digestion of household food waste. J. Environ. Manag. **236**, 798–814 (2019)

Studying Online Political Behaviours as Rituals: A Study of Social Media Behaviour Regarding the CAA

Amit Kumar Kushwaha, Subhadeep Mandal[(⊠)], Ruchika Pharswan,
Arpan Kumar Kar, and P. Vigneswara Ilavarasan

Department of Management Studies, Indian Institute of Technology Delhi,
New Delhi 110016, India
Kushwaha.amitkumar@gmail.com,
subhadeep.mandal@dms.iitd.ac.in,
ruchi1996pharswan@gmail.com,
arpan_kar@yahoo.co.in, vignes@iitd.ac.in

Abstract. In a world of ever-increasing microblogs, the opinions, preferences, support, frustration, anger and other emotions of people regarding various events and individuals, surface in varied ways on social media. The purpose of this research is to find those hidden patterns in raw data, which can explain meaningful insights about its creation, the groups of people who created them and their sentiments which led to the generation of such data. Sentiment analysis has always been an effective methodology for discovering emotion and bias towards or against a situation, topic, thought or initiative and finding other meaningful insights from unstructured data. In this research, we attempted a type of document clustering wherein we attempted to classify the sentiments of the citizens of India as they micro-blogged their opinions, thoughts, views and ideas during the implication of the Citizenship Amendment Act (CAA) on the social networking site, Twitter. By analyzing the tweets of 13,000 twitter users during a specific timeline during which the discussion regarding the CAA was at its peak, we analyzed the sentiment of those twitter users by clustering their tweets (documents) into four sentiment groups with the help of Latent Dirichlet Allocation (LDA) which is an important tool for topic modelling in the domain of sentiment analysis. Using political ritual theory, the present paper examines the sentiments of people who tweeted during a protest in India. After the classification, our research also maps the online political behaviour of these 13,000 social media participants to the postulates of political ritual theory which is explained by previous research regarding the behaviour of physically co-existing political participants and also justifies this display of various sentiments regarding the CAA in the footsteps of political rituals.

Keywords: Sentiment analysis · LDA · CAA · Twitter · Social media · Politics · Political rituals · Emotional energy

S. K. Sharma et al. (Eds.): TDIT 2020, IFIP AICT 618, pp. 315–326, 2020.
https://doi.org/10.1007/978-3-030-64861-9_28

1 Introduction

The Citizenship Amendment Bill (CAB) created a massive storm of supporters and critics both inside and outside the parliament when it was amended. It was passed in the Loksabha at the stroke of midnight with 311 votes in favour of the bill [1]. The CAB is something which the party of the ruling government has been pushing to implement in the country. The CAB relaxes the eligibility criteria to be considered citizens of India for refugees from three countries, i.e. pakistan, Afghanistan and Bangladesh.

This article involves the research on analyzing the sentiments of people who actively displayed online political behaviour on micro-blogging site, Twitter through tweets when the ruling government of India was focusing on implementing the Citizenship Amendment Act (CAA) through the Citizenship Amendment Bill (CAB). Tweets are micro-blogs or texts whose length is fixed upto 280 characters for all users [2]. Twitter also has the provision of 'retweeting' the tweet of a person which involves the action of sharing a user's previously posted tweet on one's own feed [3]. Social media (like twitter) plays an important role by letting individuals know what other people think about their opinions and thus lets individuals with common beliefs and interests, connect with each other on an online environment [4]. Thus, we considered the importance of both tweets and retweets in our work and extracted the tweets of 13,000 twitter users through the Twitter API. These users tweeted or retweeted content to express their support or protest related to the CAA and NRC. In this work, leaving out all other characteristics of the online behaviour of individuals on social media, we will only be focussing on their political behaviours.

Our analysis would reflect upon the postulates derived by Marx (2019) in the light of Randal Collins' ritual theory and the results would be proved to be in alignment with the philosophies mentioned in the postulates, modelled into the following research questions:

RQ I. Can political conversations be considered as rituals that can succeed or fail in generating positive emotions?

RQ II. Does the intensity or strength of political convictions keep increasing and decreasing over time with the intensity of the political rituals?

RQ III. Are political behaviours inputs to rituals and outcomes of rituals in a feedback loop?

RQ IV. Are political behaviours chosen and adjusted as such that resultant emotional energy is maximized?

2 Prior Literature

The literature review has been mentioned in the light of a brief explanation and understanding of political ritual theory and its components.

2.1   Political Ritual Theory and Its Components

To study how the citizens of a democratic society behaves on social media, it is utmost necessary to understand their variations in political behaviour and the factors affecting them. Thus studying rituals become utmost important, which are particularly vigorous, focussed and coordinated social interactions which has the potential to bring like-minded people together through positive interactions and emotions [5]. This can be explained in depth by *Interaction Ritual chains* [6], which at its core, argues that the move of physical encounters generate emotional energy among individuals which acts as a driving factor for their motivation and such interactions lead to the infusion of positive emotions with belief, interest, identities and norms, which make the latter elements, salient factors in political behaviours [7–9]. Inequality and a political approach that strives to appeal to ordinary people who feel that their concerns are disregarded by established elite groups in political participation have added to a practical desire to better understand subjectivity of citizens of a democracy [10–13] and this subjectivity has constituted to face-to-face encounters or rituals on a large scale [14, 15]. This comes in support through the psychological fact that humans subconsciously automatically align their behaviours in social interactions which comes with increased empathy, affiliation and willingness to cooperate [16–18]. Symbols such as names, slogans, colours, objects, flags etc. are integrative parts of rituals and they are what ties interaction ritual chains together and in which very basic actions are devoid of symbolism [19]. Practically speaking, political values and conviction often compete not only with economic interests but also with other values [20]. Cognitive ability and resonance increase the likelihood of a moral concern to be triggered subconsciously in a situation [21, 22]. Specifically, if experiences that cause an impact are repeated in interaction ritual chains, it is quite possible that unconscious moral intuitions are modelled by past social interactions [23]. Finally and most important, ritual theory can be associated to arguments about the basic role of affect in decision-making and judgement [24–27] and a strong case about how emotions play a prime role in motivated political reasoning [28].

3   Topic Modelling Through LDA

Topic Modelling is a probabilistic approach towards clustering of documents. Going from raw data to topics in the data is called *inference* in the topic model. Latent Dirichlet Allocation (LDA) is a topic model that generates topics based on word frequency from a set of documents. LDA is particularly useful for finding reasonably accurate mixtures of topics within a given document.

In this process, the first objective is to find out 'k' number of topics that best describes our data. A Dirichlet distribution would mean having a distribution over a multinomial distribution. A Dirichlet distribution is represented by the expression:

$$P(p|\alpha m) = \frac{\Gamma(\Sigma_k \alpha m_k)}{\Pi_k \Gamma(\alpha m_k)} \prod_k p_k^{\alpha m_k - 1} \qquad (1)$$

Where α represents variance and m represents the mean.

3.1 Data Collection

We collected the tweets of 13,000 users of the platform who expressed their political views regarding the CAA during a particular timeline when discussions about the CAA was at its peak and also offline events such as protest and support rallies, demonstrations, public addressals by political influencers, riots, violence, clashes with police and mob lynching were soaring throughout the country. These offline events significantly affected the sentiments of the twitter users discussing these events online and their tweets in support and against the CAA reflected their sentiments as they discussed and expressed about the same. The timeline for the collection of these tweets were from Friday, December 20, 2019 till Wednesday, January 15, 2020.

3.2 Topic Modelling Using LDA

Through Topic Modelling, we modelled our data into four sentiment groups by harnessing Latent Dirichlet Allocation (LDA) which is a probabilistic approach of Latent Semantic Analysis (LSA). The positive sentiments, denoted by 'P', denoted individuals (users and influencer) who acted and spoke in favour of CAA and 'N', denoted individuals (users and influencers) who acted and spoke against the CAA. This gave us four sentiment groups, namely: **PP** (Those who were **positive** in the beginning of the discussion & stayed **positive** till the end), **NN** (Those who were **negative** in the beginning of the discussion & stayed **negative** till the end), **PN** (Those who were **positive** in the beginning of the discussion & became **negative** at the end) and **NP** (Those who were **negative** in the beginning of the discussion & became **positive** at the end)

Political Behaviour in Present Timeline

Upon analyzing the present behaviour of the individuals, that is their online political behaviour supporting and opposing the CAA placed the individuals under analysis into 4 distinct sentiment groups. Out of the individuals analyzed, 1000 users were selected in group PP, 316 users in group NN, 394 users in group PN and 455 users in group NP. After the users were assigned to their respective groups through topic modelling, we also extracted 3 influencers by the number of cliques and follower-following difference for each of these groups separately. The distribution of users and influencers in these distinct sentiment groups according to the sentiment or polarity of their tweets are summarized and shown in Table 1.

Table 1. Distribution of users according to sentiments groups.

PP	NN	PN	NP
1000 users	316 users	394 users	455 users
3 influencers	3 influencers	3 influencers	3 influencers

Total users: 13000. Total users showing polarity change: 2165. Rest were neutral.

It is to be noted that out of all the 13,000 users analyzed who participated in the discussion on CAA, not all were expressing through polarity (positive and negative) sentiments. Only 2165 users showed a polarity of sentiments, whereas there was a large number of people who kept their views neutral and expressed themselves as 'free-thinkers', that is either they tweeted in a neutral manner, just expressing their general views on the CAA without supporting or opposing the initiative or they were initially positive and later on became neutral and vice versa or they were initially negative and with due course of time in discussions they became neutral and vice versa. The current work deals with only those cases where a polarity (positive or negative) in the sentiments is noted. A primary and very crucial part of our work involved the division of these citizens into 'users' and 'influencers' which was done by two different approaches. These approaches were the follower-following ratio and determining the number of cliques. Having said that, the 3 influencers identified from each sentiment group are listed in Table 2.

Table 2. Three influencers from each sentiment group.

PP	NN	PN	NP
@_SwarajIndia	@iamnikhilnanda	@ImJaffarHussain	@TheSiasatDaily
@FactCheckIndia	@MRVChennai	@debarati_m	@PBNS_India
@iamakbarowaisi	@GabbarSanghi	@hindupost	@anilkohli54

In our analysis, the tweets were the list of documents which needed to be modelled according to their respective topics.

Political Behaviour in Historical Timeline

After getting the behavioural statistics of the population under analysis, we found out using topic modelling as to how many of these twitter users were maintaining polarities in their conversations and how many were being neutral, was neutral in the beginning or became neutral in the end.

Now the question that arises is that did these people display such positive and negative sentiment polarities only for the discussions regarding the CAA or did they show similar sentimental behaviour in the past too? Does their past behaviour and pattern of sentiment changes dictate their present behaviour in any way?

To find out this relationship, we randomly selected 2000 users from our present corpus of CAA users, went back in their timeline and extracted tweets which were made before discussions regarding CAA even started or discussions had just started off. We focused only on tweets which reflected their political sentiments and opinions regarding a scenario. We identified 200 such tweets for each user and extracted them using Twitter API to build our new corpus of historical data of individuals who also partici-pated in discussions regarding CAA. Our new corpus was having 4,00,000 tweets on which we conducted topic modelling again keeping positive and negative sentiments in polarities. We performed the same procedure and obtained 4 different sentiment groups from these 4,00,000 tweets, the groups being PP, NN, PN, NP, where 'P' and 'N' denoted positive and negative sentiments respectively and PP, NN, PN, NP represented the sentiment changes as mentioned earlier in the article. This new analysis of historical tweets gave us 273 users in the PP group, 831 users in the NN group, 435 users in the PN group and 444 users in the NP group. As before we again identified, 3 influencers each from all of the sentiment groups. The results are tabulated in Table 3. LDA was again performed on these 12 influencers to identify the topics and for validation purposes.

Table 3. Distribution of users in sentiments groups according to tweets in their historical timeline.

PP	NN	PN	NP
273 users	831 users	435 users	444 users
3 influencers	3 influencers	3 influencers	3 influencers

Total users: 2000; Total Tweets: 4,00,000; Total users showing polarity change: 1983. Rest were neutral

The tweets of the 2000 randomly selected users were subjected to LDA and the topics were obtained accordingly.

3.3   Relationship Between Past and Present Behaviour

In order to find the behavioural pattern across the political behaviours exhibited by this selected population, the grouping of sentiments or identification of topics through LDA had to be done on similar parameters. It is not necessary that positive and negative sentiments can be expressed only regarding events such as CAA. If we consider the discussion regarding CAA as a political event, sentiments can be expressed by users of social media regarding any other political discussion irrespective of the timelines in which they occured. Thus our study involved only politically relevant tweets of the users from present and historical timelines to analyze whether the polarities in sentiments that they are displaying in the present discussion, has also been displayed in their past/historic discussions regarding politically relevant events. That is, how does the other sentiment groups (PP/NN/PN/NP) of the present timeline relate to the same sentiment groups (PP/NN/PN/NP) in the past? To understand this behaviour in a simpler manner, the approach is demonstrated by a flowchart in Fig. 1.

The findings of this analysis between the present and past political behaviours of the randomly selected 2000 users suggested that no matter with what sentiment polarity they began a political conversation in the beginning of a timeline in the past, or how many times they had a 'swing' of polarity regarding political sentiments in the past, the final sentiment with which they closed their discussions at the end of the timeline in past, was carried over to start the discussions regarding the CAA, i.e. with the very same sentiment or polarity, they started their political discussion in the present.

If we consider the relationship in grouping the sentiments, we obtain a resultant of 8 sentiment groups which explain the relationship between sentiments in past and present timelines. The results of this relationship are tabulated in Table 4. Although sentiment analysis on the past data returned us 4 sentiment groups and that on the present (CAA) data also returned us the same 4 sentiment groups, but the relationship between them is described by 8 different groups of sentiment relationships i.e. NP $\rightarrow$ PN, PP $\rightarrow$ PN, NP $\rightarrow$ PP, PP $\rightarrow$ PP, NN $\rightarrow$ NP, PN $\rightarrow$ NP, NN $\rightarrow$ NN, PN $\rightarrow$ NN

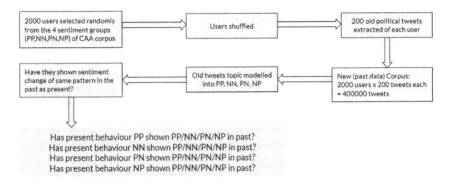

Fig. 1. Flowchart showing the approach followed to relate past political sentiment behaviour with present political sentiment behaviour.

Table 4. The relation of past and present behaviour analysis gave rise to 8 sentiment groups.

GROUPS WITH USERS	PAST BEHAVIOUR CORPUS	PRESENT BEHAVIOUR CORPUS
Group 1 (67 users)	N P	P N
Group 2 (60 users)	P P	
Group 3 (214 users)	N P	P P
Group 4 (130 users)	P P	
Group 5 (174 users)	N N	N P
Group 6 (92 users)	P N	
Group 7 (110 users)	N N	N N
Group 8 (82 users)	P N	

3.4   Tweet Patterns and Hashtags

After the different sentiment groups of users were identified based on our CAA corpus, we analyzed if the tweet patterns and the frequency of tweets of these sentiment groups had any story to convey. Surprisingly not only did the analysis show some clear results but also showed some distinctive differentiation between the tweet patterns of these sentiment groups which also explained a lot about the background, political intellect and political conviction of the users of those groups. The results are displayed in a graphical plot in Fig. 2.

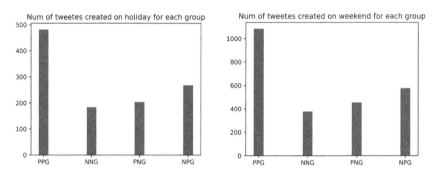

Fig. 2. Different tweet patterns and frequency of the four sentiment groups

The above finding shows that individuals (users and influencers) who were in the PP group i.e. they were positive at the beginning of the political discussion on CAA and stayed positive till the end were the most active regarding posting of tweets and retweeting others tweets on holidays and weekends among all the four sentiment groups. This proves that this group of people were highly determined in their initiative and made proper use of non-working days to spread their word, supporting their cause and successfully generated enough emotional energy which helped them establish significant differentiation with the other groups.

We also studied the hashtags (#) which are used to convey one's view or message regarding support or protest towards a person, event or situation through one or two words. Hashtags help other readers have a rough idea of the message that the tweet carries without even reading the tweet in first place. For example, one of the hashtags found in our context, '#caanrcprotests', helps a reader identify at first glance that the tweet is regarding any of the protest marches and rallies that are being organized to oppose the implementation of CAA. The detailed analysis of the frequency of hashtags for each of the sentiment groups is shown in Fig. 3.

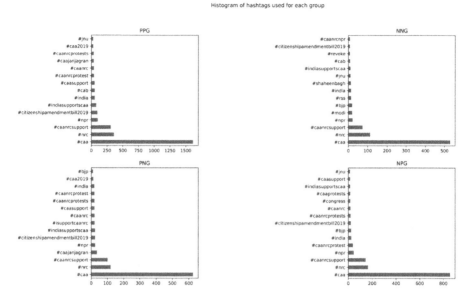

Fig. 3. Use of common and also unique hashtags by the different sentiment groups.

4 Discussion

From our analysis it was clearly observed that people in groups 1, 2, 3, 4 in Table 4 (a total of 471 users [50.7%]), started their positive support for CAA in the present scenario with the same polarity (i.e. positive) with which they ended a political discussion on a historical timeline. I.e.: the person exhibited **PP** or **NP** behaviour in a past discussion, and exhibited either **PP** or **PN** behaviour in present (CAA) discussion.

Same was the case with groups 5, 6, 7, 8 in Table 4 (a total of 458 users [49.3%]), where users ended with a negative sentiment in a past political discussion and also started with a negative sentiment in present (CAA) discussion. This behaviour falls in the light of our RQ I which answers if *political conversations can be considered as rituals that can succeed or fail in generating positive emotions*, because if past political rituals wouldn't have created enough positive emotional energy, the same positive emotional energy wouldn't have been carried over to political rituals in present scenarios.

This past-present relationship of behaviours also answers our RQ II, which asks if *the intensity or strength of political convictions keeps increasing and decreasing over time with the intensity of the political rituals*. The intensity of political convictions dies down after peak moments which are generated through rituals and stay low until reproduced. Such cycles of periodic excitement and boredom are generally exhibited in social movements [29, 30].

The insights obtained in Fig. 3 also answers our RQ I that people prefer discussing politics with like-minded people [31, 32]. It also points out to our RQ III, in the light of which, the online rituals regarding the display of support or protest on CAA, provided the cultural capital on social media and also the opportunity to perform political convictions with confidence and in a skillful way. This further concludes this postulate that *political behaviours are inputs to rituals and outcomes of rituals in a feedback loop.*

According to ritual theory, in the absence of acute needs, material goods are only appealing to the extent that they contribute to emotional energy. It is the case if access to and outcomes of rituals are linked to materialistic benefits such as memberships to expensive clubs, colleges, schools, hospitals etc. or if money making itself becomes an emotionally charged group symbol [33]. But the entire discussion that went online regarding the CAA through tweets, didn't have any personal materialistic gains or monetary benefits associated with it. The sentiment groups 'fought' for establishing their identities, to establish their beliefs and shared ideology that implementation of the CAA will be a good decision by the country and that they support the ruling government and that it should be imposed. In this situation, individuals chose between values, identities and materialistic elements and went for the one with most emotional energy potential. This brings us to answering our RQ IV which answers how *political behaviours are chosen and adjusted as such that resultant emotional energy is maximized.*

5   Conclusion

In terms of influencer-user relationship it can be concluded that there exists a population who gets influenced by an influencer, no matter whatever the event is. Let it be related to the Citizenship Amendment Act or other political discussions in the past, these users always showed strong support and gullible behaviour towards a particular set of influencer(s). The analysis results concludes to the postulates about an online political environment that *political conversations can be considered as rituals that can succeed or fail in generating positive emotions, the intensity or strength of political convictions keeps increasing and decreasing over time with the intensity of the political rituals, political behaviours are inputs to rituals and outcomes of rituals in a feedback loop and political behaviours are chosen and adjusted as such that resultant emotional energy is maximized.*

References

1. The Hindu. Lok Sabha passes Citizenship Bill amidst opposition outcry, 10 December 2019. https://www.thehindu.com/news/national/lok-sabha-passes-citizenship-amendment-bill/article30260415.ece
2. Tech Crunch. Twitter's doubling of character count from 140 to 280 had little impact on length of tweets, 30 October 2018. https://techcrunch.com/2018/10/30/twitters-doubling-of-character-count-from-140-to-280-had-little-impact-on-length-of-tweets/
3. Boyd, D., Golder, S., Lotan, G.: Tweet, tweet, retweet: conversational aspects of retweeting on Twitter. In 2010 43rd Hawaii International Conference on System Sciences, pp. 1–10. IEEE, January 2010

4. Boyd, D., Golder, S., Lotan, G.: Tweet, tweet, retweet: conversational aspects of retweeting on Twitter. In 2010 43rd Hawaii International Conference on System Sciences, pp. 1–10. IEEE, January 2010
5. Marx, P.: Should we study political behaviour as rituals? Towards a general micro theory of politics in everyday life. Rationality Soc. **31**(3), 313–336 (2019)
6. Collins, R.: Interaction Ritual Chains. Princeton University Press (2014)
7. Rossner, M., Meher, M.: Emotions in ritual theories. In: Stets, J.E., Turner, J.H. (eds.) Handbook of the Sociology of Emotions: Volume II. HSSR, pp. 199–220. Springer, Dordrecht (2014). https://doi.org/10.1007/978-94-017-9130-4_10
8. Summers-Effler, E.: Ritual Theory. In: Stets, J.E., Turner, J.H. (eds.) Handbook of the Sociology of Emotions, pp. 135–154. Springer, Boston (2006)
9. Wollschleger, J.: The rite way: Integrating emotion and rationality in religious participation. Rationality Soc. **29**(2), 179–202 (2017)
10. Cramer, K.J.: The Politics of Resentment: Rural Consciousness in Wisconsin and the Rise of Scott Walker. University of Chicago Press (2016)
11. Gest, J.: The New Minority: White Working Class Politics in an Age of Immigration and Inequality. Oxford University Press (2016)
12. Hochschild, A.R.: Strangers in Their Own Land: Anger and Mourning on the American Right. The New Press (2018)
13. Mckenzie, L.: The class politics of prejudice: Brexit and the land of no-hope and glory. Br. J. Sociol. **68**, S265–S280 (2017)
14. Gamson, W.A., Gamson, W.A.G., Gamson, W.A., Gamson, W.A.: Talking Politics. Cambridge University Press, Cambridge (1992)
15. Walsh, K.C., Cramer, K.J.: Talking About Politics: Informal Groups and Social Identity in American Life. University of Chicago Press (2004)
16. Chartrand, T.L., Lakin, J.L.: The antecedents and consequences of human behavioral mimicry. Ann. Rev. Psychol. **64**, 285–308 (2013)
17. Iacoboni, M.: Imitation, empathy, and mirror neurons. Ann. Rev. Psychol. **60**, 653–670 (2009)
18. Launay, J., Tarr, B., Dunbar, R.I.: Synchrony as an adaptive mechanism for large-scale human social bonding. Ethology **122**(10), 779–789 (2016)
19. Zelizer, V.A.: Pricing the Priceless Child: The Changing Social Value of Children. Princeton University Press (1994)
20. Druckman, J.N., Lupia, A.: Preference change in competitive political environments. Ann. Rev. Polit. Sci. **19**, 13–31 (2016)
21. Lodge, M., Taber, C.S.: The Rationalizing Voter. Cambridge University Press (2013)
22. Verplanken, B., Holland, R.W.: Motivated decision making: effects of activation and self-centrality of values on choices and behavior. J. Pers. Soc. Psychol. **82**(3), 434 (2002)
23. Von Scheve, C.: Emotion and Social Structures: The Affective Foundations of Social Order. Routledge (2014)
24. Barrett, L.F.: How emotions are made: The secret life of the brain. Houghton Mifflin Harcourt (2017)
25. Damasio, A.: The Strange Order of Things: Life, Feeling, and the Making of Cultures, p. 32 (2018)
26. Haidt, J.: The righteous mind: Why good people are divided by politics and religion. Vintage (2012)
27. Hatemi, P.K., McDermott, R.: Give me attitudes. Ann. Rev. Polit. Sci. **19**, 331–350 (2016)
28. Lodge, M., Taber, C.S.: The Rationalizing Voter. Cambridge University Press (2013)
29. Jasper, J.M.: The Emotions of Protest. University of Chicago Press (2018)

30. The Hindu. Coronavirus | Shaheen Bagh protest to continue during Janata curfew, 21 March 2020. https://www.thehindu.com/news/cities/Delhi/coronavirus-shaheen-bagh-protest-to-con tinue-during-janata-curfew/article31124975.ece
31. Effler, E.S.: Laughing saints and righteous heroes: Emotional rhythms in social movement groups. University of Chicago Press (2010)
32. Hatemi, P.K., McDermott, R.: Give me attitudes. Ann. Rev. Polit. Sci. **19**, 331–350 (2016)
33. Collins, R.: Emotional energy as the common denominator of rational action. Rationality Soc. **5**(2), 203–230 (1993)

Health Fear Mongering Make People More Sicker: Twitter Analysis in the Context of Corona Virus Infection

Jayan Vasudevan[1]([✉]) [iD] and Sreejith Alathur[2] [iD]

[1] Centre for Development of Advanced Computing (C-DAC),
Thiruvananthapuram 695582, Kerala, India
jayan@cdac.in
[2] National Institute of Technology Karnataka, Surathkal, Mangalore, India
sreejith.nitk@gmail.com

Abstract. The purpose of this study is to assess the fear factor in Social media data in the context of Coronavirus Disease - 2019(COVID-19) across the globe. The fear generated from social media content will adversely affect the mental health of the public.

Design/methodology/approach: The study is followed by a literature survey during the emergence of social media and Internet technologies since the year 2006 where the people commonly started to use the internet across the world. The Twitter data collected on COVID-19 during the infection period and the analysis.

Findings: The social media contents adversely affect the mental health of the common public and also the healthcare programs run by the government organizations to some extent. The findings show that the social media are the major source of fear-mongering information and the people behind the fear-mongering are making use of the disaster situation to set their agenda. The strict enactment of law and the efforts by the social media platforms can reduce the fake news and misinformation.

Research limitations/implications: The research focuses only on the Twitter data for the analysis during the COVID-19 distress. The detailed study needs to be done in similar distress situations across the globe. The data retrieval became limited from different social media platforms because of privacy issues.

Keywords: Fear mongering · Fake news · Misinformation · Coronavirus · Social media

1 Introduction

The Corona Virus infection in China which was reported from Wuhan on December 31, 2019 was a deadly disease which took the lives of about one million people and more than 30 million people infected with the coronavirus as on September 25, 2020. The World Health Organization (WHO) started a link in their website named "Myth Busters" to tackle such issues. Whenever the search for coronavirus comes in a social media platform, the users will get a link to the "Myth Busters" on the WHO official

© IFIP International Federation for Information Processing 2020
Published by Springer Nature Switzerland AG 2020
S. K. Sharma et al. (Eds.): TDIT 2020, IFIP AICT 618, pp. 327–338, 2020.
https://doi.org/10.1007/978-3-030-64861-9_29

website. Self-appointed experts, people work from anecdotes, or making wild claims to get traffic or notoriety [1] during this distress.

The blame game is in full swing between the superpowers like Russia, China and the United States [2]. Mass media are acting as the 'fear-blur' and short circuits the actual events and brings the fear factor at the forefront. COVID-19 was also created a situation where communalism and racism brought in front by masking the actual scenario of the epidemic spread [3, 4]. The tweets in the social media in India utilized to target one particular community rather than the disease. The hash tags appeared as "#CoronaJihad" when many people attended the Tablighi Jamaat function held at New Delhi, India contracted with COVID-19 [6].

The impact of the epidemic may worsen the situation by intensifying the fear and increase in the risk perception. Epidemics are naturally emotion laden and the news report with emotion laden reporting may affect the mental health of the reader and also the people affected [6, 7]. The emotion laden news reporting increases the fear but may not educate about the epidemics [8]. The reporting style depends on the emotion attributed to the risk, i.e. the severity and its portrayal of the health risk in news coverage. The two threat components that influence the risk are perceived severity and the perceived vulnerability. Former is concerned with the seriousness or magnitude and the latter is concerned with the likelihood of the risk impact [9, 10].

The factual reporting itself elicits emotional response and it is not solely attributed to the journalists reporting the news. That is beyond the control of the individual journalist. The audience response is also a subjective matter. The person well aware of the risk may not be affected much compared to the case of an individual naïve to the risk [11]. Sensational news which are evoking sensory and emotional arousal can induce increased risk perception [12]. Exemplification in news stories may strongly influence the audience perception [13]. The examples can be anecdotal evidence in news stories. The emotion evoking health news reporting may be expected to influence the behavioural response to the health contents [14]. The stigmatization and discrimination of victims in treatment may arouse fear among the reader [7].

Studies show that the emotion-laden reporting and the fear depend on the vulnerability also. If the emotion laden reporting of the news is from another far flung country, then the response in an individual is less [15]. Health professionals and scholars have reservations on the boosting hearsay and the misleading medical and scientific information [16]. The fear mongering is also used for political gain by utilizing the capital expenditure. The narrative of fear mongering is escalated in the mind of the public and justifies the implementation cost of the public expenditure for political gain. This may be otherwise done by educating the people and proving awareness to them without much loss to the public money in the long term.

The psychological impact of quarantine among the people affected and suspected to be affected will be huge in some cases. Social media has many versions of the isolation and quarantine. The people feared to be in an isolation ward and expected to spend time in isolation for a specified period may not disclose the disease [17]. The disease like COVID-19 imposes the quarantine for the people identified as the potential carriers of the disease or have contact with the infected individual [18–21].

Fear mongering in media and public health campaigns use scaring tactics to enforce behavioural changes in the user. The fear mongering in the form of warnings and images in food materials, drugs, tobacco, etc. may not work normally. The studies show that the fear mongering along with emotional messages may bring behavioral changes. The fear mongering combined with a message of hope influences the people in behavioral change [22–25].

The noval CoronaVirus (nCoV) that emerged in China has also brought viral misinformation in the social media and other media in cyberspace. The virality of misinformation and the rumors in social media is much faster than the spread of nCoV. The social media filled with the fear mongering posts on discrimination, racism and other hate contents [26].

2 Methodology

With the emergence of the COVID-19 from epidemic to Pandemic, we considered the articles related with corona, fear, epidemics and social media for the study. The social media platform like Twitter and Facebook is considered for the analysis of the data. The twitter data was collected using the R programming. Selected conversations are used to point out the type of discrimination and fake news that are spread through social media. The major contribution of fake news and misinformation that are spreading through the social network groups meant for religion and the political parties. Most often the distress is related with the communal angle in such networking sites.

2.1 Google Trends

Google Trends is a website by Google which analyzes the popular search about various queries across the globe. Normally it assesses the current trending topics in the internet and the user has the option to compare different search keys. Google Trends shows that the search on 'Corona Virus' has the pattern of the virus infection across the globe. There are two peaks in the graph. Initial one is in the fifth week of the emergence when the infection was high in China and it faded for some time. Later it picked up as the infection spread across the globe. People normally are not bothered about when it occurs in China. Other countries did not take advance steps to tackle the situation. The situation became worse when it spread across Europe, Eastern Mediterranean region and region of Americas. Figure 1 shows the trends of search in Google about 'coronavirus' from December 31, 2019 to April 5, 2020.

There were many other trending searches during this period. It includes the "Tablighi Jamaath" conference held in Delhi and the resulting spread of COVID-19 among the participants and the contacts with the participants. This had resulted in the surge of Islamophobia in India. Similarly with the onset of COVID-19 in China and its spread in Europe and America resulted in Sinophobia and the people from China were attacked in different parts of the world. The major search keys related with Sinophobia were "Hatred", "Sinophobia", "Fear" and "Racism" along with the normal keywords like Corona and related queries. Tablighi Jamaath related topics were mainly concentrated on "Hazrat Nizamuddin Aulia Darga", "Spitting", "Zabur", "Muslim", "Mosque" and "Muhammed". The news about the spitting of people gathered for Tablighi Jamaath is not cooperating with the health workers and they even spit over

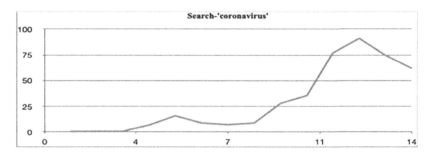

Fig. 1. Google Trends of COVID-19 infection (Source: Data from Google Trends)

them and the surrounding had got much attention. This had created a hate against the Muslims in India [27].

The major queries were on the symptoms and the details about the coronavirus. The breakout query was the corona and its spread in California. "the beer and corona" was another trending query during that period. Some other related queries included the "status of COVID-19 in different countries", "death toll due to corona infection", its "symptoms" and "the map of the corona infection across the globe".

2.2 Twitter Data Analysis

Tweets from Twitter are accessible to the unregistered users also. Other social media platforms like Facebook allow only the registered users to read the messages. So Twitter allows a vast number of users to extract the data of their relevant topic and do research on the data and deduce the socio-economic and behavioural patterns of a particular group based on the analysis. The trending topic in Twitter can be obtained from the Twitter trending hashtags. Twitter has no reciprocated relationship unlike the Facebook relationships. The relationship is either directed or undirected. The life cycle of a particular tweet will be depending on the relevance of the topic at a particular time. Some tweets will be repeated when the similar kinds of the events happen. Twitter data is normally assessed based on the sentiment analysis of a particular topic of consideration using Artificial Intelligence or Natural Language Processing technologies [28–31].

Twitter data related to COVID-19 during January 28, 2020 to March 22, 2020 was collected for the analysis. The initial study of the tweets revealed that many tweets which are becoming viral and creating panic among the public. Normally, the health related information is negative in nature. The news reporting, social media posts, tweets are all contain the negative reports on death, sufferings of people infected and shortage of food, medicine and other essential materials. In addition to that, social media will also flood with the fake news and misinformation. This will impact the mental health of the people already with anxiety, fear and stress. Many factors are behind the emergence of fake news and misinformation spread in social media. The search keys for collecting the Twitter data are given in Table 1. 230000 tweets were collected during this period for the analysis.

The twitter data is processed before subjecting to the sentiment analysis and the word extraction. The tweet extraction and processing is divided into following steps:

i. Extracting tweets using Twitter Application Programming Interface
ii. Cleaning the tweets by removing hyperlinks, special characters, hash tags, converting to lower case letters and numbers
iii. Getting sentiment score for each tweet using the packages available in Comprehensive R Archive Network (CRAN)
iv. Segregating positive and negative tweets for analysis

The keywords were selected based on the trending hashtags in Twitter and also the common slogan followed by different organizations across the globe. The main keywords which are commonly used were the "Social Distancing", "Break the Chain", "Stay Home" and "Flatten the curve". These keywords were commonly used in all the media and some more country specific and virus specific keywords were also used to extract the data.

Table 1. Search Keys for Twitter data collection

Tags used for data mining		
#TogetherApart	#nCoV	#lockdownindia
#socialdistancing	#2019-nCoV	#coronavirusindia
#StayHome	#Betacoronavirus	#CoronavirusLockdown
#FlattenTheCurve	#Wuhan	#21daysLockdown
#lockdownindia	#CoronavirusOutbreak	#CurfewInIndia
#जनता	#CoronaOutbreak	#COVID-19
#JantaCurfew	#BreakTheChain	#coronavirus
	#FightCOVID19	

First, the cleaning of the tweets is done to process further. Normally the tweets are collected and saved as different Comma Separated Files (CSV). They need to merge together for the processing. Initially the tweets are filtered by removing the hyperlinks, symbols like #, @, !, etc., removing the stop words in English, numbers and then converting to lowercase. Now the texts in the tweets are ready for the analysis.

Extraction of Most Frequent Positive and Negative Words
The health domain will be having the negative sentiment words in majority. The classification of positive and negative words is based on the Bing lexicon. Virus being the topic of research and the disease causing element, it is in the top most position and it has occurred more than 20000 times in the collected tweets. Most of the other words coming in the top position are closely related with the virus, its adjectives and the after effects after the viral infection. Most of the negative sentiments are related with fear and sadness. That is causing stress and anxiety among the user who is not well aware of the disease and topic he is dealing with. Figure 2 shows the occurrence of most fifteen frequent negative and positive sentiment words extracted from the tweets collected. Compared to the frequency of negative sentiment words, the positive sentiment word frequency is very less. This can be seen in the Fig. 2. "Trump" is the most frequent

positive word in the tweet and has occurred about 6000 times. The fake news needs to be viral to reach the intended user and the agenda set by one faction will be successful if the news reaches the maximum number of audiences. So they will use maximum negative sentiment in the tweet. As per the human behavior it is natural that he will be more interested in the rumors and spread it across. Thus the viral tweets in virtual world and the word of mouth in real world will have a huge impact. The authorized reports or the justification by the concerned authorities will reach the intended user at a later stage.

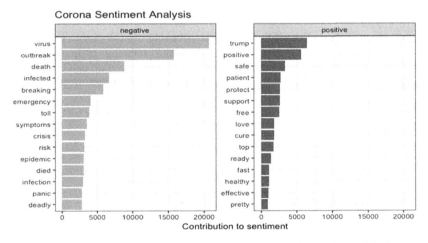

Fig. 2. Positive and negative sentiment words which are most frequently used in the tweets

Sentiment Analysis

The sentiments analysis is done using the "syuzhet" package from CRAN. The "get_nrc_sentiment" package will return the sentiment values for the emotions. Normally the emotions are classified based on the grouping of English words in different emotion categories. The emotion categories are anger, anticipation, disgust, fear, joy, sadness, surprise, trust, negative and positive. Once we run the "get_nrc_sentiment" function, it will return values of different emotions. By assessing those values, we can deduce the type of tweets that are posted during a particular period. Figure 3 shows the sentiment plot for the tweets collected during the COVID-19 incidents. The data is collected till March 22, 2020. The sentiment plot divided into six phases. For each emotion, there will be six values. We divided the period from January 28, 2020 to March 22, 2020 into six phases. This is done to analyze the sentiment of the COVID-19 as it progresses. Normally there will be increased tweets during the onset of an event and it will progress gradually. The agenda setting will be done in the initial phase to get the attention by the audiences. At the later stage government authorities will take necessary actions to prevent the spreading of rumour or fake news. So in the later stage the tweets relating to the agenda or rumour will die down and will be limited in number. We can see that the fear and anger is high in the initial phase and it is decreased in the final phase and in overall the fear got less value compared to trust. The sentiment value is also calculated for each tweet and the overall averaged sentiment value is −0.035. It shows the overall sentiment of the tweets collected during the specified time is negative in nature.

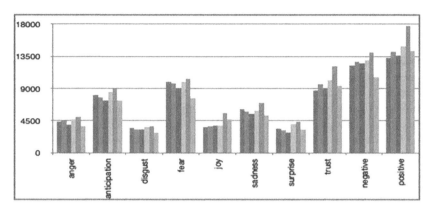

Fig. 3. Sentiment scores during the period specified for data collection during different times

The analysis of sentiment shows that the negative sentiment tweets were decreased in the due course of time. The emotion, fear reduced in the final stages compared to initial stages. Instead of that the positive sentiment and the trust increased. That may be mainly due to the steps taken by the respective governments and the social media platforms in curbing the fake news and the misinformation. The social media groups were continuously alerted by the police department to refrain from posting and sharing un-authentic contents.

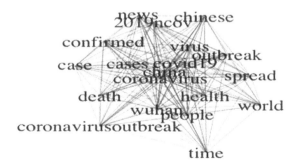

Fig. 4. The Co-occurrence terms in a tweet and the network of tweets shared

There are many words which are related and they are co-occurring throughout the tweets collected. Figure 4 shows such a network with a sparsity of 99 percent. We got around 19 words. All are closely related with virus corona and its impact like death, spread, outbreak, cases, etc. Most of them will generate the fear in the social media user and the patient. Even after the COVID-19 is taken the flattened curve in Wuhan, China, the Wuhan and China remains the most co-occurring even after the infection rate declined there and is prominent in other parts of the world.

3 Discussion

The COVID-19 also resulted in many conspiracies in the cyber world as well as in the physical world. It had resulted in many heated arguments among different world leaders and there were accusations on the spread of the disease and vaccination. But the disease had created a clear damage in the economy of almost all the countries in the world. Most of the countries declared lock-down resulting in many traumas among the citizens of the country. Though the virus is not fatal like MERS and SARS it spread all over the world by killing more than one million people and infecting more than 30 million people across the globe. Along with the disease, the social media spread the rumors and fear mongering messages. Already the people were restricted in their home due to the social distancing. The stress and anxiety in such people is enormous. The people quarantined in hospitals and other relief centres went through a trauma which made many of them to evade from the isolation. The people working away from home are already afraid of the health condition of their in-laws and friends. The physical meeting of the relatives made it impossible for them. The rumours spread among the labourers stranded in different locations were forced to return to their home. That had created havoc in the city like Delhi in India. People gathered in huge numbers that feared to be another disaster if they contracted the disease.

The conspiracy theory is veiled in the time of distress across the world. This has created another ruckus in social media. The media is flooded with lots of fake messages and misinformation to misguide the public and align with some ideologies based on their inclination towards it. Normally the misinformation in social media focuses on race, ethnicity, gender, religion, etc. which are more sensitive in the era of Internet technologies. The COVID-19 is also proved that religious sentiments can set aside when fear of death is inside the minds of people. There was no protest when the government took strict action against the religious gathering. The religious leaders become helpless during this situation. Even different religious leaders came down in the social media and other mass media to refrain from all types of gatherings by the believers.

Any distress happening across the globe will be assessed based on their country of origin, religion, ethnicity, race, etc. Based on that the agenda is set on social media and they will create fake information, misinformation and disinformation. An information to become viral, it should embed with hate and fear or any rumor. This will have an impression on the reader and they will start following such information spreading groups or people. The fear induced in people will be used for promoting some products by the company, attract people towards particular sections of people and sometimes direct them towards hate crimes. The fear mongering fake news is repeatedly spread during all the distress of similar nature. The fake news regarding population control and the vaccine sales agenda has been used during the vaccination campaign, Nipah outbreak and the corona pandemic. Such messages or tweets in social media will create a huge adverse impact on the people already affected. The mainstream media also play a major role in spreading the fake news. They were not verifying the authenticity of the news when it gets viral in the social media. Sinophobia erupted in many European countries during this period. Italy has announced a 'hug Chinese campaign' to curb the corona induced racism. The effects of fear, alienation and discrimination due to the COVID-19 infection are escalated with the restriction of movements, loss of jobs and stereotyping. That led many people to denial, stress and depression. Though the disease can be cured with medicine or other containment methods, the anxiety and fear will last long. They need to get psychological intervention. The healthcare workers, community volunteers, Police officials, relief workers and doctors may also fall into stress and anxiety due to the alienation from their family and relatives. A hope in the minds of the affected people and the people with depression or anxiety will have positive impact. Some messages will have healing impact on the people:

"They are not the hiding patients
They are staying solitude for you"

The message is a hope for both the patient and the listener. There are many initiatives by Police and the volunteers to promote the "stay at home", "Break the chain" and "Social Distancing" campaign through social media. Social media was the only medium to communicate with people directly during the lockdown period. Government has taken strict action to keep the people coming out of the home without any reason. Figure 5 shows a series of the events after occurring a distress and the response in people, government and the media.

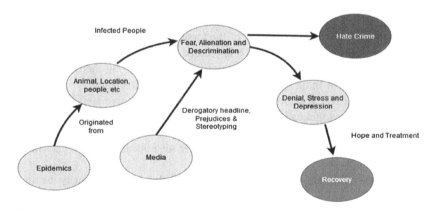

Fig. 5. The occurrence of a distress and the origin of the social media panic and its influences in human being

4   Conclusion

The fear arising from the social media and other mass media can be alleviated using the same media by broadcasting the positive views. That will give hope to the people already affected and others fearing the disease. Following are the findings from the literature review and the practices followed by government and other responsible organizations like WHO. Many governments had enacted the criminal law against spreading the fake news through social media and the government gave a directive to the social media platform to curb the fake news and misinformation. The strict enactment of law can curb the fake news in social media to some extent. It is visible from the analysis of the Twitter data. The study is limited to Twitter data and did not considered other major social media platforms like Facebook and WhatsApp. Similarly, only English texts are used for analysis. The country like India has 22 official languages and other local languages which are used for communication.

5   Suggestions

The fake news and the misinformation in the social media will create fear among the audience especially when it is about the health news. The analysis of COVID-19 Twitter data shows that the sharing of positive news in social media will generate hope in the people with anxiety and stress due to fear. Some of the steps that are followed in the social media that are given hope among the patients and the in-laws are listed below:

- The people coming out after the quarantine were greeted with applause by the healthcare workers and other government authorities. That had created a positive vibe in the public as well as the person put under quarantine for many days.
- Positive news on the epidemics like the recovery rate will reduce the fear among the people affected as well as the in-laws of the affected people. The anxiety and the stress among the patient, doctors, and their in-laws will be reduced in considerable rate.
- Symbolic gestures like the tapping of the utensil and clapping hands as gestures of appreciation of the healthcare workers, doctors, police personnel and volunteers will raise their prestige. That can create a positive energy among them and also in the patients. People in India and Italy showed such an appreciation.
- The "Myth Buster" link on the WHO website is a positive step in handling the misinformation and fake news. This will provide more accurate information and can alleviate the doubts in the minds of people
- Incorporating the appropriate algorithm to filter misinformation by the social media platforms
- Government and other organizations involved should continuously be updated about the infected, cured and the death counts through the social media and the government controlled platforms.
- The recovery from the disease by the patients in the volatile age group was a positive sign. The in-laws living away from the old parents may get more relief from the stress by watching or reading such news from the social media or mass media.
- Creative activities and sharing such arts in the social media platforms will boost the mental health of the people and that will be a kind of psychological intervention to the people living in lock-down condition.
- The platforms like WhatsApp, Telegram are more concentrated on puzzle solving in groups. In addition to that they are also used as crowd sourcing of the relief material and sharing the Do's and Don'ts during the lockdown period.

References

1. Margolis, E.: These self-appointed coronavirus experts really need to pipe down, The Guardian, 10 March 2020. https://www.theguardian.com/commentisfree/2020/mar/10/coronavirus-experts-donald-trump-nigel-farage-twitter. Accessed 13 May 2020
2. Zaman, M.: The Pandemic Blame Game, Magzter, April 2020. https://www.magzter.com/article/News/Northeast-Today/The-Pandemic-Blame-Game. Accessed 13 May 2020
3. Brian, M.: Everywhere you want to be: introduction to fear. In: Brian, M. (ed.) The Politics of Everyday Fear. Minnesota UP, Minneapolis (1993)
4. Nick, M.: Viral terrorism and terrifying viruses: the homological construction of the war on terror and the avian flu pandemic. Int. J. Med. Cult. Polit. **5**(3), 199–216(18) (2009)
5. Akash, B., Sadiq, N.: How Tablighi Jamaat event became India's worst coronavirus vector, Al Jazeera (2020). https://www.aljazeera.com/news/2020/04/tablighi-jamaat-event-india-worst-coronavirus-vector-200407052957511.html. Accessed 11 Apr. 2020
6. Dunwoody, S., Peters, H.P.: Mass media coverage of technological and environmental risks: a survey of research in the United States and Germany. Public Understanding of Science, vol. 1, 199–230 (1992). https://doi.org/10.1088/0963-6625/1/2/004
7. Yusuf, I., Yahaya, S., Qabli, S.: Role of media in portraying Ebola in and outside Africa. J. Trop. Dis. **3**(152), 1–2 (2015). https://doi.org/10.4172/2329-891x.1000152
8. Eagleton Institute of Politics: New Jerseyans concerned about possibility of U.S. Ebola outbreak. http://eagletonpoll.rutgers.edu/rep-ebola-concerns/. Accessed 8 Oct 2014
9. Witte, K., Allen, M.: A meta-analysis of fear appeals: implications for effective public health campaigns. Health Educ. Behav. **27**, 591–615 (2000). https://doi.org/10.1177/109019810002700506
10. Keer, M., Van Den Putte, B., Neijens, P.: The role of affect and cognition in health decision making. Br. J. Soc. Psychol. **49**, 143–153 (2010). https://doi.org/10.1348/014466609x425337
11. Zikmund-Fisher, B.J., Fagerlin, A., Ubel, P.A.: Risky feelings: why a 6% risk of cancer does not always feel like 6%. Patient Educ. Couns. **81**, S87–S93 (2010). https://doi.org/10.1016/j.pec.2010.07.041
12. Grabe, M.E., Lang, A., Zhao, X.: News content and form: Implications for memory and audience evaluations. Commun. Res. **30**, 387–413 (2003). https://doi.org/10.1177/0093650203253368
13. Zillmann, D.: Exemplification effects in the promotion of safety and health. J. Commun. **56**, 221–237 (2006). https://doi.org/10.1111/j.1460-2466.2006.00291.x
14. Smith, S.W., et al.: Using the EPPM to create and evaluate the effectiveness of brochures to increase the use of hearing protection in farmers and landscape workers. J. Appl. Commun. Res. **36**, 200–218 (2008). https://doi.org/10.1080/00909880801922862
15. Celine, K., Tilo, H., Enny, D.: Fear-mongering or fact-driven? Illuminating the interplay of objective risk and emotion-evoking form in the response to epidemic news. Health Commun. **34**(1), 74–83 (2019. https://doi.org/10.1080/10410236.2017.1384429
16. Wilson, K., Keelan, J.: Social media and the empowering of opponents of medical technologies: the case of anti-vaccinationism. J. Med. Internet Res. **15**, e103 (2013)
17. Barry, G.: Narrative techniques of fear mongering. Soc. Res. **71**(4), 819–826 (2004). Fear: its Political Uses & Abuses (Winter 2004)
18. Miles, S.H.: Kaci Hickox: public health and the politics of fear. Am. J. Bioeth. **15**(4), 17–19 (2015). https://doi.org/10.1080/15265161.2015.1010994
19. Jeong, H., et al.: Mental health status of people isolated due to middle east respiratory syndrome. Epidemiol. Health **38**, e2016048 (2016). https://doi.org/10.4178/epih.e2016048

20. Lee, S., Chan, L.Y., Chau, A.M., Kwok, K.P., Kleinman, A.: The experience of SARS-related stigma at Amoy Gardens. Soc. Sci. Med. **61**(9), 2038–2046 (2005)
21. Wester, M., Giesecke, J.: Ebola and healthcare worker stigma. Scand. J. Public Health **47**(2), 99–104 (2019). https://doi.org/10.1177/1403494817753450
22. Dillard, J.P., Li, R., Meczkowski, E., Yang, C., Shen, L.: Fear responses to threat appeals, functional form, methodological considerations, and correspondence between static and dynamic data. Commun. Res. **44**, 997–1018 (2017)
23. Kok, G., Peters, G.-J.Y., Kessels, L.T.E., ten Hoor, G.A., Ruiter, R.A.C.: Ignoring theory and misinterpreting evidence: the false belief in fear appeals. Health Psychol. Rev. **12**(2), 111–125 (2018). https://doi.org/10.1080/17437199.2017.1415767
24. Kok, G., et al.: A taxonomy of behavior change methods; an intervention mapping approach. Health Psychol. Rev. **10**(3), 297–312 (2016). https://doi.org/10.1080/17437199.2015.1077155
25. Nabi, R.L., Myrick, J.G.: Uplifting fear appeals: considering the role of hope in fear-based persuasive messages. Health Commun. **34**(4), 463–474 (2019). https://doi.org/10.1080/10410236.2017.1422847
26. Depoux, A., et al.: The pandemic of social media panic travels faster than the COVID-19 outbreak. J. Travel Medicine, taaa031(2020). https://doi.org/10.1093/jtm/taaa03
27. Shemin J.: Coronavirus: Case against youth connected with Tablighi Jamaat for spitting at doctor in quarantine facility, Deccan Herald (2020). Accessed on 10 April, 2020. https://www.deccanherald.com/national/north-and-central/coronavirus-case-against-youth-connected-with-tablighi-jamaat-for-spitting-at-doctor-in-quarantine-facility-822989.html
28. Tsur, O., Rappoport, A.: What's in a Hashtag? Content based prediction of spread of ideas in microblogging communities. In: Proceedings of the Fifth ACM International Conference on Web Search and Data Mining, pp. 643–652. ACM, New York (2012)
29. Bastos, M.T., Travitzki, R., Puschmann, C.: What sticks with whom? Twitter follower-followee networks and news classification. In: Proceedings of 6th International AAAI Conference on Weblogs and Social Media—Workshop on the Potential of Social Media Tools and Data for Journalists in the News Media Industry (2012)
30. Bruns, A., Stieglitz, S.: Towards more systematic Twitter analysis: metrics for tweeting activities. Int. J. Soc. Res. Methodol. **16**(2), 91–108 (2013)
31. Anber, H., Salah, A., Abd El-Aziz, A.A.: A literature review on Twitter data analysis. J. Comput. **8**(3), 241–249 (2016)

Sentiment Analysis and Topic Modelling of Indian Government's Twitter Handle *#IndiaFightsCorona*

Christina Sanchita Shah[(✉)] and M. P. Sebastian

Indian Institute of Management Kozhikode, Kozhikode, India
{christinasl2fpm,sebasmp}@iimk.ac.in

Abstract. The purpose of this study was to conduct opinion mining on Twitter data containing "#IndiaFightsCorona" to analyse public opinion. This was accomplished using sentiment analysis and topic modelling. First, sentiment analysis was done and positive and negative sentiments were separated. Then, on each sentiment, topic modelling was done to discover hidden topics. Two approaches were used namely Latent Semantic Analysis (LSA) and Latent Dirichlet Allocation (LDA) and then their results were compared. It was found that there were more positive sentiments than negative. For positive sentiments, LDA performed better and for negative sentiments, LSA performed better.

While some topics were common between LSA and LDA for positive sentiments, there was very little overlap for negative comments.

Keywords: Topic modelling · Sentiment analysis · Opinion mining · #IndiaFightsCorona

1 Introduction

India reported its first case of novel coronavirus on 30th January 2020. On 11th February, the World Health Organization (WHO) announced that this coronavirus would be called COVID-19. A month later, on 11th March, WHO declared the COVID-19 outbreak as a pandemic. As of 1st April, there are almost 922,000 confirmed cases of COVID-19 out of which approximately 656,000 cases are active, 193,000 recoveries and 46,000 deaths[1] In India, there were 1,238 confirmed cases with 32 deaths, according to the Ministry of Health and Family Welfare website. On 31st March 2020, the Ministry of Information and Broadcasting set up a dedicated Twitter handle called *@CovidnewsbyMIB* to share news and updates about novel coronavirus COVID-19. The account is named *#IndiaFightsCorona* with the handle @ *CovidnewsbyMIB*. This handle provides information on the latest number of coronavirus

---

[1] https://www.businessinsider.in/slideshows/miscellaneous/a-comprehensive-timeline-of-thenew-coronavirus-pandemic-from-chinas-first-covid-19-case-to-the-present/december-312019-chinese-health-officials-informed-the-world-health-organization-about-a-cluster-of41-patients-with-a-mysterious-pneumonia-most-were-connected-to-the-huanan-seafoodwholesale-market-a-wet-market-in-the-city-of-wuhan-/slideshow/74721165.cms.

© IFIP International Federation for Information Processing 2020
Published by Springer Nature Switzerland AG 2020
S. K. Sharma et al. (Eds.): TDIT 2020, IFIP AICT 618, pp. 339–351, 2020.
https://doi.org/10.1007/978-3-030-64861-9_30

cases in India, and various relief and economic measures[2] While the handle *@CovidnewsbyMIB* was set up by the end of March, hashtag *#IndiaFightsCorona* has been trending even before that as indicated by Twitter data. With the rise of the COVID-19 pandemic, many countries placed restrictions on travel and movement and imposed "lockdowns". The world saw a rise in social distancing initiatives, travel bans, self-quarantines and business closures. As people could no longer access public spaces freely, a significant proportion of the dialogue on the COVID-19 pandemic shifted to online forums and social networking sites such as Twitter [1].

In light of the COVID-19 pandemic and the purpose of this study is to analyse public opinion surrounding hashtag *#IndiaFightsCorona*. Opinion mining, broadly speaking, uses text analytics to understand public sentiment. Twitter is a popular microblogging platform that people use to express themselves in real-time and can be used for opinion mining [2–4]. While there are multiple hashtags for novel coronavirus trending on Twitter, the reason for selecting *#IndiaFightsCorona* was its credibility as it is used by the Ministry of Information and Broadcasting, India. In this research, Twitter data containing *#IndiaFightsCorona* was extracted, and sentiment analysis using Support Vector Machine (SVM) classifier was done to classify data into positive and negative sentiments. The performance of the SVM classifier was measured using the Confusion Matrix. Once the sentiments had been segregated, topic modelling was conducted on each sentiment. Topic modelling discovers hidden topics/themes in each sentiment. Two approaches were used for conducting topic modelling, namely Latent Dirichlet Allocation (LDA) and Latent Semantic Analysis (LSA). Results from each method were then compared and evaluated to decide which method gave the most coherent topics within each positive and negative sentiment data. The preliminary findings of this paper are: (1) It was found that there were more positive sentiments than negative sentiments (2) For positive sentiments, LDA performed better, and for negative sentiments, LSA performed better (3) For negative sentiments, there was minimal overlap between the topics generated by LSA and LDA whereas all other topics were distinct.

1.1   Social Media and Previous Public Health Crises

Research scholars have often used Twitter as a way of understanding trends visible in online social networks [2–5]. More specifically, Twitter offers researchers the opportunity to analyse the role of social media during a public health crisis, such as the latest COVID-19 pandemic [6–9]. This helps researchers investigate the social dimensions of the pandemic. While previous epidemics have demonstrated the relevance of researching social media information, there is a special significance for studying the role of social media during the current COVID-19 pandemic. In today's information age, social media is expected to play a much larger role as compared to previous health crises. For instance, during the Ebola outbreak in February 2014, Twitter comprised of approximately 255 million active users. However, Twitter had 330 million active users

---

[2] https://www.theweek.in/news/india/2020/04/01/govt-launches-twitter-handle-to-smash-falsefacts-on-coronavirus.html.

by 2019 [10]. Thus, a lot of people communicate online and get their news through social media sites like Twitter [11, 12]. Further, compared to past epidemics, there is a much higher risk of incorrect information circulating [10]. Studies have shown that the amount of misinformation available on Twitter regarding medical content is as high as 24% and is being circulated at an alarming rate [10, 13, 14]. Another study developed a multilingual COVID-19 Twitter data set to track misinformation and unverified rumours [1]. Thus, we see that social media sites can be used to spread all kinds of information. However, on the other hand, a positive aspect of the increasing presence of public opinions on social media sites is that policy makers can mine this data to understand popular discourse and develop measures to tackle the pandemic [15].

1.2   Sentiment Analysis

Opinion mining is also known as sentiment analysis which is an analysis of people's opinions, emotions, and sentiments from the written language. With the rapid growth of social media platforms such as Twitter, Facebook, Instagram, the relevance of sentiment analysis and opinion mining has increased. Opinions influence our behaviours and therefore, are essential to almost all human actions. The way we perceive and interpret the world is essentially influenced by our beliefs and interpretations of reality. This is why we always look for the inputs or opinions of others when we have to make a decision. It refers not only to individuals but to businesses as well [16]. Microblogs like Twitter are platforms where users can post their opinions, reactions, feelings, and thoughts in real-time. Some early analyses on Twitter data using sentiment analysis include Bermingham and Smeaton [6], Pak and Paroubek [4], Barbosa et al. [5], Bifet and Frank [6], Davidov et al. [7] and Agarwal et al. [17]. In this study, we use a support vector machine (SVM) classifier for sentiment classification. For the purpose of this study, we have classified sentiments only as being either positive or negative.

1.3   Topic Modelling on Twitter Data

The topic model can be considered as a tool for addressing the enormous amount of data, to find hidden concepts, prominent features or latent variables [9]. It is an unsupervised natural language processing technique that extracts latent topics from a corpus of documents. There are many methods to implement topic modelling. In our study, we use two approaches: (1) Latent Semantic Analysis (LSA) and (2) Latent Dirichlet Allocation (LDA).

Latent Semantic Analysis (LSA). Latent Semantic Analysis is a single value decomposition (SVD) based algebraic process in which a bag-of-words (BoW) model is used to create a document term matrix [9]. LSA is one of the simplest topic models that are easy to understand and implement. More often than not, it gives better results than vector space models. It is also faster.

Latent Dirichlet Allocation (LDA). Latent Dirichlet Allocation learns how words, topics, and documents relate to each other by assuming that documents are generated using a particular probability model [19]. The purpose of LDA is to discover hidden topics based on data [20]. Topic in LDA is defined as "probability distribution over words". It is also a bag-of-words model [13].

Topic Coherence. Topic coherence is a method of evaluating topic models. It measures the degree of semantic similarity between its high scoring words. These measurements help distinguish between topics that are human interpretable and those that are artefacts of statistical inference. Greater coherence scores indicate greater interpretability by humans [21].

2   Research Methodology

This study is divided into several stages. The first stage consists of data collection, followed by the pre-processing of data. Then comes the sentiment analysis stage and segregation of data into positive and negative sentiments. Then topic modelling is done on each sentiment using LSA, and LDA. Finally, both these approaches are evaluated using topic coherence scores. Implementation of each model is done in Python version 3.7.4.

2.1   Data Collection

Twitter data was collected using NodeXL, which is a network analysis software package for Microsoft Excel. Since the aim of the study was opinion mining of novel coronavirus COVID-19 in India, the Twitter database was searched for all tweets containing the hashtag "IndiaFightsCorona" or "indiafightscorona". 33378 tweets in all languages were collected out of which 16665 tweets were in English. For the purpose of this study, we have considered tweets written only in English. The tweets were dated between 16th March to 1st April 2020.

2.2   Data Preparation

The purpose of this pre-processing of the data is to clean it and make it ready for further analysis. At the end of this stage, data is more structured and processed. This was done twice, once before sentiment analysis and once before topic modelling. The preprocessing steps were different before sentiment analysis and different before topic modelling. Combined, all the steps include [18, 21, 22]: *1) Data cleaning.* In this step, data is converted to lowercase, all punctuation and stop words such as "a"," and", "to", "the" and so on and forth, are removed. *2) Tokenization.* A tokenizer splits the document at the word level, and each word is labelled as a token. For our study, we used *word2vec* algorithm. *3) Stemming and Lemmatization.* Stemming and Lemmatization are text normalization techniques in the field of Natural Language Processing that are used to prepare text, words, and documents for further processing. Stemming is the process of reducing inflexion in words to their root forms.

2.3 Sentiment Analysis

To conduct sentiment analysis, SVM classifier was trained and tested. It was then used to predict the sentiment of words using their vector representation. The sentiment score of each word was then calculated. Primarily, there are four steps in training and using the sentiment classifier: (1) Load a pre-trained word embedding. Word embeddings map words in vocabulary to numeric vectors. These embeddings capture semantic details of the words so that similar words have similar vectors. (2) Load an opinion lexicon listing positive and negative words[3] (3) Train the SVM sentiment classifier to classify words into positive and negative categories. (4) Sentiment score of each word is calculated in the text, and the mean score is taken.

2.4 Topic Modelling

Once the corpus of tweets was divided into positive and negative sentiments, topic modelling was run on each sentiment to discover various topics and themes associated with each sentiment. Two approaches to topic modelling were used: Latent Dirichlet Analysis (LDA) and Latent Semantic Analysis (LSA). The results for both approaches were then compared for each sentiment using topic coherence scores to understand which approach gave better topics within each sentiment.

3 Results and Discussion

This study uses tweets containing *"#IndiaFightsCorona"* from 16th March to 1st April 2020. Only English tweets have been considered for this study amounting to 16665 tweets. We first conducted a sentiment analysis on the corpus of tweets, segregating it into positive and neutral tweets. Then topic modelling using LSA and LDA approaches was done on each sub-corpus of the sentiments. Finally, coherence scores of LSA and LDA were computed and compared to see which approach was better.

3.1 Sentiment Analysis

For the purpose of sentiment analysis, support vector machine (SVM) classifier was trained, which classifies word vectors into positive and negative categories. 10% of the corpus was set aside for testing purposes while the rest was used for training. A confusion matrix is a table that is often used to describe the performance of a classification model. Figure 1 shows the classification accuracy in a confusion matrix for SVM sentiment classifier. As can be seen, the classifier is an efficient classifier. Based on this confusion matrix, we found that Precision was 93.26%, Recall was 91.37% and F1 score was 92.30%. Next, the sentiment of all the tweets was calculated to predict the sentiment score of each word in the text. Scores greater than zero were considered as positive sentiments and scores less than zero were considered as negative sentiments. There were 13701 positive sentiments and 2964 negative sentiments.

---

[3] https://www.cs.uic.edu/ ∼ liub/FBS/sentiment-analysis.html.

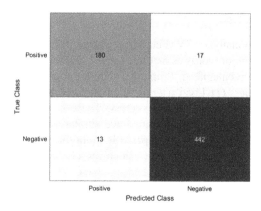

Fig. 1. Confusion matrix of SVM sentiment classifier

3.2 Topic Modelling

After the process of determining the sentiment, then the next step is to find topics within each positive and negative sentiments. Two approaches are used, namely LSA and LDA to find topics, and then their results are compared using coherence scores.

Positive Sentiments. To find the optimal number of topics, we ran the LDA model for a different number of topics' k'. Figure 2 shows the coherence chart in which we see that maximum coherence is achieved at k = 13 with a coherence score of 0.426. We then ran the LDA model with K = 13 and computed individual coherence of each topic. We see in Table 1 that topics 3, 5, 7, 1, 9, 6 and 11 have high coherences while the rest have lower coherence scores. Topic 3 and 5 refer to the positive reception of the news of the nationwide lockdown with many offices, Bollywood celebrities like Kartik Aryan being supportive. Topic 7 praises the lockdown as a response to the pandemic. Topic 1 refers to the State-Trait Anxiety Inventory (STAI), and how people are following the lockdown by working from home. Topic 9 is a favourable reaction to PM Cares fund by Prime Minister Narendra Modi and the measures taken by the government for its citizens. Topic 6 and 11 favour the direction of India's leadership, refer to the people at the forefront of this battle against the pandemic.

Similarly, we compute the coherence score for LSA model. As can be seen from Fig. 3, the optimal number of topics is 12 with a score of 0.428. We then ran the LSA model with K = 12 and then computed individual coherence of each topic. We see in Table 2 that topics 12, 2, 5, 11, 6 and 8 have high coherences while the rest have lower coherence scores.

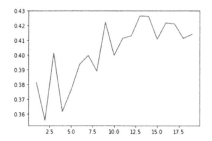

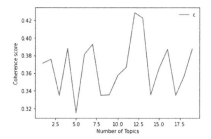

Fig. 2. Coherence chart of LDA model

Fig. 3. Coherence chart of LSA model

Table 1. Topic words and coherence scores from LDA with k = 13

Topic#	Wordlist	Coherence
3	District, given, health, privileg, office, organis, beauti, local, daily, gesture	0.000
5	Celebr, modiji, small, go, bollywood, cycl, aaryan, kartik, acknowledg, virtuous	0.000
7	Good, let, respons, tell, respect, sevasocieti, covid, indiathanksindiafightscorona, india, old	−0.147
1	Stai, safe, inform, home, young, coronaviru, essenti, stayathomesavel, covid, work	−0.154
9	Tax, govt, time, issu, citizen, ordin, pmcare, encourag, rebat, liber	−0.217
6	India, leadership, rise, associ, healthier, welfar, show, compass, coal, occas	−0.219
11	Battl, happi, like, defeat, covid, forefront, hardwork, sportsperson, time, need	−0.240
12	Tata, thank, nation, gestur, servic, indian, group, shri, life, develop	−0.338
13	Covid, stayhom, stayhomestaysaf, coronavirusoutbreak, amp, retweet, stayathomesavel, indiafightscorona, minist, indiafightscoronaviru	−0.471
2	Help, covid, indiafightscorona, coronaoutbreak, donat, swasthabharat, inform, dai, healthforal, fight	−0.507
4	Contribut, care, thank, india, fund, covid, support, fight, pmcare, crore	−0.531
10	Right, thank, covid, precaut, take, matter, proactiv, lead, effort, overcom	−0.545
8	Countri, covid, fight, time, thank, initi, crisi, commun, food, indiafightscorona	−0.721

Table 2. Topic words and coherence scores from LSA with k = 12

Topic#	Wordlist	Coherence
12	Amp, young, ipledgetocontribut, pmnrf, donat, letschaintofightcorona, appeal, food, salari, distribut	−0.445
2	India, show, contribut, leadership, rise, coal, healthier, associ, welfar, occas	−0.446
5	Tax, celebr, modiji, time, govt, issu, ordin, citizen, encourag, rebat	−0.555
11	Fight, amp, care, like, countri, happi, defeat, sportsperson, hardwork, battl	−0.61
6	Tata, celebr, modiji, care, group, servic, nation, commit, indian, gestur	−0.616
8	Inform, stai, help, covid, safe, fund, forefront, battl, contribut, happi	−0.67
3	Contribut, tax, celebr, modiji, pmcare,time, citizen, india, govt, effort	−0.747
10	Safe, thank, help, indiafightscorona, forefront, india, inform, contribut, food, stai	−0.777
7	Amp, covid, support, inform, dai, donat, salari, pmnrf, caus, fund	−0.867
1	Contribut, care, thank, covid, effort, support, right, precaut, proactiv, matter	−0.985
9	Help, covid, care, amp, indiafightscorona, thank, fund, swasthabharat, healthforal, coronaoutbreak	−1.017
4	Covid, amp, indiafightscorona, fight, help, modiji, celebr, effort, inform, contribut	−1.042

Topic 12 talks about the altruistic efforts of people wherein people are donating money and contributing to the Prime Minister's National Relief Fund. Topic 2 looks at the leadership of India and how the measures are taken are for the people's welfare and benefit. Topic 5 and 11 refers to Prime Minister Narendra Modi and his encouragement to the citizens and the hard work of many people in fighting coronavirus. Topic 6 is a reference to Ratan Tata's donation of Rs. 500 crores for this cause. Topic 8 refers to the State-Trait Anxiety Inventory (STAI), people who are at the forefront of this battle against coronavirus and the need for more funds. Topic 3 is a reference to PM Cares fund by Prime Minister Narendra Modi.

In Table 3, we see the comparison of LDA and LSA coherence scores between their most coherent topics. We see that LDA produces greater coherent scores for each topic than LSA demonstrating that LDA performs better than LSA in finding hidden topics.

Table 3. Comparison of coherence scores per topic between LDA and LSA

LDA						
T3	T5	T7	T1	T9	T6	T11
0	0	−0.15	−0.15	−0.22	−0.22	−0.24
LSA						
T12	T2	T5	T11	T6	T8	T3
−0.44	−0.44	−0.55	−0.61	−0.62	−0.67	−0.75

Negative Sentiments. Similar to the process followed for positive sentiments, we ran the LDA model and compute coherence scores to find the optimal number of topics. As can be seen in Fig. 4, the optimal number of topics is 8 with a score of 0.542. We then ran the LDA model with K = 8 and then computed individual coherence of each topic. We see in Table 4 that topics 3, 8, 5 and 2 have high coherences while the rest have lower coherence scores.

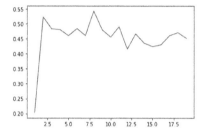

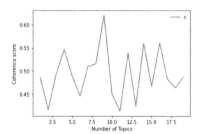

Fig. 4. Coherence chart of LDA model   **Fig. 5.** Coherence chart of LSA model

Topic 3 refers to Tablighi Jamat incident in New Delhi. Topic 8 talks about the lockdown in Kashmir versus lockdown in India due to coronavirus. Topic 5 talks about food availability issues and the impact of workers. Topic 2 talks about the sacrifices made by people during the lockdown period with social life being affected.

Table 4. Topic words and coherence scores from LDA with k = 8

Topic#	Wordlist	Coherence
3	Lakh,right, corona, countri, entir, it', tablighi, fight, crimin, unit	−0.049
8	Socialdistanc, stand, case, make, unit, apart, kashmir, terror, vallei, struck	−0.2
5	Let, crisi, face, covid−, stopcoronaviru, stand, food, worker, amp, packet	−0.316
2	Covid, distanc, mean, social, life, sanitis, dai, sacrific, lock, wrong	−0.358
6	Indiafightscorona, peopl, covid, spread, amp, stayhomestaysaf, urg, awar, actor, tamil	−0.469
7	Pmcare, covid, fight, fund, donat, salari, month, indian, govt, polic	−0.474
1	Covid, infect, person, fight, support, produc, gear, mumbai, minim, step	−0.489
4	Amp, covid, peopl, lockdown, food, distribut, coronaviru, road, needi, time	−0.637

In a similar vein, we compute the coherence score for LSA model to determine optimal number of topics. As can be seen from Fig. 5, optimal number of topics is 9 with a score of 0.62. We then ran the LSA model with K = 9 and then computed individual coherence of each topic. We see in Table 5 that topics 3, 8, 5 and 4 have high coherences while the rest have lower coherence scores. Topic 3 is a reference to the negative perception regarding lockdown and social distancing, lack of availability of sanitizer and how it is affecting people's daily lives. Topic 8 refers to people not following the protocol and staying at their homes. This will result in increased infections spread through cough droplets. There is mention of Software Technology Parks of India (STPI) which refers to IT offices being shut down and people working from home. Topic 5 is about facing coronavirus by staying at home. In some cities of India, police are asking people on the streets to go inside. Topic 4 refers to deaths due to pandemic and the drastic action of nationwide lockdown.

In Table 6, we see the comparison of LDA and LSA coherence scores. We see that LSA produces greater coherent scores for each topic than LDA. This means that LSA performs better than LDA in finding hidden topics here. Thus, we see that while LDA performed better for positive sentiments, LSA performed better for negative sentiments. This is because the corpus size is different for both sentiments. There are 13701 positive sentiments and 2964 negative sentiments. It is a known fact that for bigger data sets, LDA performs better while for smaller datasets, LSA performs betters [18]. This then explains the performance behaviour difference between positive and negative datasets.

Table 5. Topic words and coherence scores from LSA with k = 9

Topic#	Wordlist	Coherence
3	Decis, daily, distanc, social, life, mean, wrong, sanitis, open, lockdown	0.00
8	Person, infect, cough, viru, stpiindia, stayathomesavel, stai, awai, sneez, speak	0.00
5	Let, stand, face, covid, crisi, stopcoronaviru, covid, case, polic, stayhom	−0.073
4	Lakh, right, lockdown, time, india, come, taken, need, death, pandem	−0.108
9	Road, peopl, action, situat, danger, control, kudo, result, team, potenti	−0.195
2	Fight, countri, corona, unit, it', crimin, entir, tablighi, sin, talibani	−0.22
7	Food, distribut, amp, lockdown, coronaviru, poor, indiafightscorona, needi, stayhom, tamil	−0.263
1	Covid, amp, peopl, indiafightscorona, spread, stayhomestaysaf, fight, urg, awar, tamil	−0.613
6	Covid, amp, peopl, fight, support, gear, minim, produc, naval, hazard	−0.64

Table 6. Comparison of coherence scores per topic between LDA and LSA

LDA			
T3	T8	T5	T2
−0.05	−0.2	−0.32	−0.36
LSA			
T3	T8	T5	T4
0	0	−0.07	−0.11

4 Conclusion and Future Work

The purpose of this study was to conduct opinion mining on twitter data containing *"#IndiaFightsCorona"* to analyse public opinion. This was accomplished using sentiment analysis and topic modelling. First, sentiment analysis was done, and positive and negative sentiments were separated. Then, on each sentiment, topic modelling was done to discover hidden topics. Two approaches were used, namely LDA and LSA and then their results were compared. It was found that there were more positive sentiments than negative. For positive sentiments, LDA performed better, and for negative sentiments, LSA performed better. LDA revealed topics within positive sentiments which include positive reception of the news of the nationwide lockdown and praising the measures taken by the government, vocal support of lockdown by Bollywood celebrities like Kartik Aryan, STAI, work from home, PM Cares fund and the people who are at the forefront of the battle against the pandemic. Topics revealed by LSA for positive sentiments include the altruistic efforts of people, money donation, the measures are taken are for the people's welfare and benefit, to Ratan Tata's donation of Rs. 500 crores, STAI, PM Cares fund by Prime Minister Narendra Modi and the hard work of many people in fighting coronavirus. As we can see that while some topics are common between LSA and LDA like STAI, PM Cares fund and the people fighting coronavirus, some topics are distinct such as vocal support of lockdown by celebrities like Kartik Aryan, Ratan Tata's donation of Rs. 500 crores and work from home. For negative sentiments, topics revealed by LDA include Tablighi Jamat incident in New Delhi, the lockdown in Kashmir versus lockdown in India due to coronavirus, food availability issues and its impact of workers and the sacrifices made by people during the lockdown period with social life being affected. Topics revealed for negative sentiments by LSA include a negative perception regarding lockdown and social distancing, lack of availability of sanitizer and how it's affecting people's daily lives, people not following the protocol and leaving their homes, increased infections spread through cough droplets, shut down of IT offices and actions taken by police to make the people follow lockdown protocol. Here, we see very little overlap between the topics generated by LSA and LDA for negative sentiments which include only the negative impact on people's social life. All other topics are distinct. Our findings are echo prior research [1] in which we see that public sentiment is inclined towards positivity.

This study has a few limitations. First, the data was collected only for *#India-FightsCorona*. Future work can include hashtags for broader coverage of public opinion. Second, only one evaluation criteria are used, namely topic coherence. Future work can include other criteria such as log-likelihood and perplexity. Also, other methods of topic modelling can also be used apart from LSA and LDA, and a comparison can be made. Third, the data collected is only a sample of the total Twitter data due to API restrictions. A bigger dataset can, perhaps reveal more insights.

References

1. Chen, E., Lerman, K., Ferrara, E.: Tracking social media discourse about the COVID19 pandemic: development of a public coronavirus Twitter data set. JMIR Public Health Surveill. 6(2), e19273 (2020). https://doi.org/10.2196/19273
2. Lerman, K., Ghosh, R.: Information Contagion: an Empirical Study of the Spread of News on Digg and Twitter Social Networks, ArXiv10032664 Phys., March 2010. http://arxiv.org/abs/1003.2664. Accessed 30 Sept 2020
3. Romero, D.M., Meeder, B., Kleinberg, J.: Differences in the mechanics of information diffusion across topics: idioms, political hashtags, and complex contagion on Twitter. In: Proceedings of the 20th International Conference on World Wide Web - WWW 2011, p. 695, Hyderabad (2011). https://doi.org/10.1145/1963405.1963503
4. Castillo, C., Mendoza, M., Poblete, B.: Information credibility on Twitter. In: Proceedings of the 20th International Conference on World Wide Web - WWW 2011, p. 675, Hyderabad (2011). https://doi.org/10.1145/1963405.1963500
5. Ferrara, E., Varol, O., Davis, C., Menczer, F., Flammini, A.: The rise of social bots. Commun. ACM 59(7), 96–104 (2016). https://doi.org/10.1145/2818717
6. Abd-Alrazaq, A., Alhuwail, D., Househ, M., Hamdi, M., Shah, Z.: Top concerns of tweeters during the COVID-19 pandemic: infoveillance study. J. Med. Internet Res. 22(4), e19016 (2020). https://doi.org/10.2196/19016
7. Chew, C., Eysenbach, G.: Pandemics in the age of Twitter: content analysis of tweets during the 2009 H1N1 Outbreak. PLoS ONE 5(11), e14118 (2010). https://doi.org/10.1371/journal.pone.0014118
8. Liang, H., et al.: How did Ebola information spread on twitter: broadcasting or viral spreading? BMC Public Health 19(1), 438 (2019). https://doi.org/10.1186/s12889-019-67478
9. Park, H.W., Park, S., Chong, M.: Conversations and medical news frames on Twitter: infodemiological study on COVID-19 in South Korea. J. Med. Internet Res. 22(5), e18897 (2020). https://doi.org/10.2196/18897
10. Singh, L., et al.: A first look at COVID-19 information and misinformation sharing on Twitter, ArXiv200313907 Cs, March 2020. http://arxiv.org/abs/2003.13907. Accessed 30 Sept 2020
11. Shearer, E., Matsa, K.: News Use Across Social Media Platforms 2018, Pew Research Center, 10 September 2018
12. Fischer, S.: Social media use spikes during pandemic, AXIOS, 24 April 2020
13. Kouzy, R., et al.: Coronavirus goes viral: quantifying the COVID-19 misinformation epidemic on Twitter. Cureus (2020). https://doi.org/10.7759/cureus.7255
14. Cinelli, M., et al.: The COVID-19 Social Media Infodemic, ArXiv200305004 Nlin Physicsphysics, March 2020. http://arxiv.org/abs/2003.05004. Accessed 30 September 2020
15. Lopez, C.E., Vasu, M., Gallemore, C.: Understanding the perception of COVID-19 policies by mining a multilanguage Twitter dataset, ArXiv200310359 Cs, March 2020. http://arxiv.org/abs/2003.10359. Accessed 30 September 2020

16. Liu, B.: Sentiment analysis and opinion mining. Synth. Lect. Hum. Lang. Technol. **5**(1), 1–167 (2012). https://doi.org/10.2200/S00416ED1V01Y201204HLT016
17. Agarwal, A., Xie, B., Vovsha, I., Rambow, O., Passonneau, R.J.: Sentiment analysis of twitter data. In: Proceedings Workshop on Language in Social Media, pp. 30–38 (2011)
18. Kherwa, P., Bansal, P.: Topic modeling: a comprehensive review. ICST Trans. Scalable Inf. Syst. 159623 (2018). https://doi.org/10.4108/eai.13-7-2018.159623
19. Blei, D.M., Ng, A.Y., Jordon, M.I.: Latent Dirichlet allocation. J. Mach. Learn. Res. **3**, 993–1022 (2003)
20. Onan, A., Serdar, K., Hasan, B.: LDA-based topic modelling in text sentiment classification: an empirical analysis. Int. J. Comput. Linguist. Appl. **7**(1), 101–119 (2016)
21. Stevens, K., Kegelmeyer, P., Andrzejewski, D., Buttler, D.: Exploring topic coherence over many models and many topics. In: Proceedings of the 2012 Joint Conference on Empirical Methods in Natural Language Processing and Computational Natural Language Learning 2012, pp. 952–961, July 2012
22. Aziz, M.N., Firmanto, A., Fajrin, A.M., Hari Ginardi, R.V.: Sentiment analysis and topic modelling for identification of Government service satisfaction. In: 2018 5th International Conference on Information Technology, Computer, and Electrical Engineering (ICITA-CEE), pp. 125–130, Semarang, September 2018. https://doi.org/10.1109/icitacee.2018.8576974

Listen to Your Customers! "A Study About Content Creation on Social Media to Enhance Customer Engagement"

Arjen Doek[✉], Ton AM Spil, and Robin Effing

University of Twente, Enschede, The Netherlands
a.a.m.spil@utwente.nl

Abstract. It is a major challenge for many organisations to create content on social media which leads to customer engagement. The purpose of this research is to develop a framework that contains a strategy for creating content which leads to customer engagement. For developing a framework, a Design Science Research Methodology is applied. Based on the literature and expert-interviews, five elements have emerged that are essential: the goal, target audience, listening, content creation, and evaluation. The element listening, is crucial when creating content. Listening helps to discover the customer's interests, so that an organisation can respond to this. The sub-elements of listening are: listening to influencers, listening to what is said about your brand and competitor, discovering channel preferences, discovering customer motives, and discovering customer interests. Listening allows organisations to determine several content characteristics that influences customer engagement. A case study is used in order to validate the use of the framework. The case study shows that this framework is a useful guide to determine the content for achieving customer engagement. The case study also shows that in practice little attention is paid to listening in relation to content creation.

Keywords: Content marketing · Customer engagement · Social media content · Engaging content strategy

1 Introduction

In 2019, it is impossible to imagine the world without social media. There are around 3.5 billion active users of social media, which is 45% of the total population. On average, people spend 2 h and 16 min a day on social media [20] According to Kapoor et al. [23], people rely on social media for several needs. Examples of these needs are: checking daily news and updates on critical events, entertainment, connecting with family and friends, reviews and recommendations on products/ services and places, the fulfilment of emotional needs, and workplace management. Because so many people make frequent use of social media, this offers opportunities for organisations. Tiago and Verissimo [42] stated that organisations should use social media because many customers are active on social media. For organisations, social media can have several business functions, for instance, marketing and sales, customer support, recruitment and retention, product innovation and strategic communication [43]. Furthermore, with

© IFIP International Federation for Information Processing 2020
Published by Springer Nature Switzerland AG 2020
S. K. Sharma et al. (Eds.): TDIT 2020, IFIP AICT 618, pp. 352–370, 2020.
https://doi.org/10.1007/978-3-030-64861-9_31

the use of social media organisations could create a relationship with the customer or potential customer [39, 42]. This can be achieved by using social media to interact with customers and ensure a two-way of communication between organisation and customer [16, 42]. These activities could strengthen the relationship and lead to customer engagement [42]. This is important for organisations because customer engagement can improve corporate reputation and also enhance customer loyalty [7, 13]. Sashi [39] argues that through customer engagement customers become fans of the brand and that they can play a role as an advocate.

The focus of this study is on social media content. According to Lee, Hosanagar, and Nair [28], content marketing plays an important role in social media and has the aim to develop content to engage targeted users to achieve the goals of the organisation. Several studies pointed out that creating content is a key activity on social media [16, 17, 30, 43]. With content an organisation will develop and maintain relationships. Therefore, the content must be in line with the goals and culture of the organisation [16]. Aladwani [2] argues that when social media content fits the attitudes, preferences, and abilities of the user, this could result in an improved relationship. Both in the business-to-business market and in the business-to-consumer market, it emerges that the biggest challenge is to create engaging content. In the B2C market, 56% of the respondents indicated that producing engaging content is a top challenge, compared to 60% in the B2B market. Also, both the B2C market (73%) and the B2B market (72%) indicate that creating more engagement is a top priority [36, 37].

Furthermore, there is a lack in the literature about content creation that results in customer engagement. For instance, Aldous, An, and Jansen [3] investigated the challenges of creating engaging content for news organisations. They concluded that for content creation, there are no clear guidelines for what would improve engagement. Moreover, Schreiner, Fischer, and Riedl [41] pointed out in their further research agenda that there is a need for development of a communication model for the social media context with the focus on content characteristics that influence engagement. In short, from both a practical and a theoretical point of view, it is relevant to examine how to create content on social media which results in customer engagement. For this reason, the goal of the study is to develop a framework that reduces the gap from the literature and which can be used as hand guide for organisations. When developing the framework, it is important to know which elements should be included in a strategic framework for the process of content creation in order to achieve customer engagement. Therefore the research question is: *What are the key elements in a strategic framework for creating content on social media in order to achieve customer engagement?*

Because this research has the aim of developing a framework for content creation to achieve customer engagement, the paper will follow the structure used in the Design Science Research Methodology of Peffers, Tuunanen, Rothenberger and Chatterjee [33] In the first part the methodology will be described. The second section is about the design and development of the framework. The terms content marketing, social media and customer engagement are defined herein. Thereafter, the framework will be demonstrated in practice. In the fourth part the framework is evaluated through a case study. The last part contains the analysis, conclusion, and discussion and further research.

2 Methodology

For answering the research question, design science will used as method. This methodology is a process by which design sciences can be conducted in a structured manner and describes the different steps from problem to framework and evaluation. Therefore, this method is suitable for this research. A design science study has the aim to develop knowledge for design and establishing artefacts. Design science as method enables researchers to solve construction problems or improving existing entities [1]. For conducting design science, the Design Science Research Methodology (DSRM) [33] is utilized. The objectives for a solution were defined. For the demonstration of the framework, semi structured interviews with experts were carried out to validate the foundations of the framework. As data collection method, semi- structured interviews were used in a face-to-face setting. The purpose of these semi-structured interviews was to investigate how to listen to customers and provide relevant appropriate content on social media. Furthermore, to measure customer engagement in social media. The participants were selected based on their knowledge and experience on the field of social media marketing and content marketing. There were multiple design iterations of the framework based on reflection from both theory and empirical data. The outcomes were deliberately published after careful analysis of the added value to literature. A structured literature search was conducted [46] and the procedural results are shown in appendix B and C. The content analysis is shown in Table 1 as literature results. To formulate an initial version of the framework, a systematic literature review was conducted to select articles that are relevant for this research. The field of research are: Content marketing, Social media and Customer Engagement. For this research, the database of Scopus is used. The reason for using Scopus as appropriate source is that the academic articles in Scopus have certain quality. The articles on Scopus are peer-reviewed by experts. Besides, additional information about the authors will be checked. Determining the search queries is based on the fields of research.

The utilized search queries resulted in a total of 519 articles. Some search queries yielded an enormous amount of results. For this reason, we have chosen to take the top 100 highest cited of every search query. In the 'select' stage several steps are used to refine the sample. Because multiple search terms have been used, the first step is filter out the doubles. This means that 484 articles remained for the next step. Thereafter, the sample were refined based on the title and the abstract of the article, resulting in a remaining number of 98 articles. Based on a quick scan of the full texts, 22 articles were analysed. Moreover, 3 articles were added that were found based on forward and backward citations. This means that the final sample consisted of 25 articles, that were used for the literature review. The fourth stage of Wolfswinkel et al. [46] is about analysing the articles and labelling the articles. Subsequently, in the fifth stage the articles have to be presented. The relevant articles were structured in the way Webster and Watson [45] described.

3 Design and Development

3.1 Defining Customer Engagement

Engagement is crucial in the way it contributes to understand customer outcomes and understanding service performance [7]. Customer engagement has the aim to build long term relationships with trust and commitment. Engagement deals with satisfying the customers and providing superior value to customers [39]. Customer engagement is a complex term that can be interpreted in various ways. For instance, Bowden [7] refers to a psychological process and defined engagement as: *"a psychological process that models the underlying mechanisms by which customer loyalty forms for new customers of a service brand as well as the mechanisms by which loyalty may be maintained for repeat purchase customers of a service brand"*. Other authors argue that the concept engagement can be divided into three dimensions: cognitive, behavioural and emotional [8, 18]. Brodie et al., [8] defined customer engagements as follows: *"Consumer engagement is a multidimensional concept comprising cognitive, emotional, and/ or behavioural dimensions, and plays a central role in the process of relational exchange where other relational concepts are engagement antecedents and/or consequences in iterative engagement processes within the brand community."* The cognitive aspects refer to what extent a customer is interested in the activities of the organisation. Behaviour aspects means to what extent the customer actually participate in the activities of the organisation. Emotional aspects refer to the positive feelings a customer have about the organisation activities [13]. Hollebeek [18] added in her definition of customer engagement that motivational, brand-related and context-dependent the state of mind of the customer is characterised by these dimensions in direct brand interactions, which refers to direct, physical contact-based interactions with a focal brand. Sashi [39] claims that engagement relates to creating experiences and that companies can achieve deeper and meaningful interactions between the company and the customer. Nevertheless, customer engagement should not be confused with involvement. Involvement refers to level of interest and relevance for someone related to a focal object or decision which consist of the values, goals and self-concept of a person [18]. It is seen as an antecedent for customer engagement. This research investigates the role of content in social media in order to achieve customer engagement. Therefore the focus is on the behaviour part which is in line with the definition of Van Doorn et al. [44]: *"Customer engagement behaviours go beyond transactions, and may be specifically defined as a customer's behavioural manifestations that have a brand or firm focus, beyond purchase, resulting from motivational drivers"*. From the above definitions it emerges that engagement is about creating a relationship through interactions based on motivational drivers.

3.2 Engaging Content Strategy

In order to develop a strategy for content creation to achieve customer engagement in the social media environment, it is first necessary to determine which elements a strategy consists of. In addition to knowing how customers engage via social media, it is important to know which forms of social media content provide engagement. Cvijikj and Michahelles [12] studied the engaging content on Facebook pages.

Table 1. Overview of articles that support the framework

Authors and year	Goal and Target Audience	Listening	Creating content	Evaluate
Aydin (2019)			x	
Baltes (2015)	x	x		
Cawsey and Rowley (2016)	x	x		
Cvijikj and Michahelles (2013)		x	x	x
Dolan, Conduit, Fahy, and Goodman (2016)		x		
Jairvinen and Taiminen (2016)		x		
Kaplan and Heinlein (2010)		x		
Kietzman, Hermkes and McCarthy (2011)	x	x		
Kilgour, Sasser and Larke (2015)	x	x		
Muntinga et al. (2011)		x		x
Pentina, Guillox, Micu (2018)				x
Rahman et al. (2016)				x
Schivinski, Christodoulides, and Dabrowski (2016)				x
Schreiner, Fischer, and Riedl (2019)			x	

They argue that one important issue in the engagement plan is to know which content is needed in a social media post for triggering more engagement. Secondly, it is important to know the best moment of posting on social media. According to Baltes [6], a strategy starts with a goal and by determining the target audience. Subsequently, an organisation must discover what content fits the needs of the target audience. This can be achieved by listening to the customers [21]. In addition, Kilgour, Sasser and Larke [27] argued that it is essential to understand the motives and use this knowledge for creating content. Finally, the content must be evaluated. Afterwards, the organisation can act on this based on the effects and outcomes of the social media interactions [27]. Based on literature, a new framework has been developed. In Table 1 an overview is given to show which literature support the several elements. The various elements that have been merged for content creation have never been linked to each other before. Besides, the different steps in the framework have not been shown in this order before. The conceptual framework consists of: a goal, determining the target audience, creating the content, and evaluate. The following sub-sections elaborate on these elements.

Goal and Target Audience.
When offering content on social media, it is necessary to have a certain purpose. Kietzman et al. [26] argue that a strategy must be developed, depending on the functionalities of the social media platform, to achieve goals. Cawsey and Rowley [9] developed a B2B social media strategy framework. In their study they mentioned that organisations should experiment in order to get insights how social media can help to achieve strategic and marketing goals. In addition, this study shows that the goals on social media must be aligned with the overall company goals. Furthermore, Baltes [6] argues that the objectives are an essential element in a content strategy. Examples are: Increasing the brand awareness, building a relationship based on trust with the target, attracting new leads, developing customer loyalty, solving problems, creating a need, or creating an audience [6].

In addition to determine a goal, it must also be determined for whom the content is intended. Several studies highlighted that content must fit the needs of the customer [9, 19, 21, 27]. This indicates that before creating content, the target audience must be determined. According to Kilgour et al. [27], when developing a content strategy, the process starts with the determination of the goals and the target audience. Baltes [6] pointed out that for target analysis is crucial to know who the target group is. Subsequently, the needs of the customer must be determined, for instance, by listening [21]. The following section discusses which aspects are important when listening in order to create social media content.

Listening.

An essential aspect for creating content is to is to determine which content is relevant to achieve customer engagement. According to Kaplan and Heinlein [22], the first step is to listen to your customers. Organisations have to discover what customers like to hear and where they are talking about at the moment. Furthermore, what they find interesting, enjoyable and valuable. The content must be tailored with the customer preferences [22]. Kilgour et al. [27] stated that for social media it is important that organisations understand how users influence, receive, curate and interact. Therefore, it is necessary to obtain knowledge about the customer for the optimization of the content. Analysing customer data and listening to the conversations of the customers will help organisations to determine the customer needs Jarvinen and Taiminen Kilgour et al. [21] [27]. Cawsey and Rowley [9] also mentioned that it is important to determine what customers want to hear before creating content on social media. This is particularly important in the start-up phase. Listening ensures organisations to valuable market research and customer knowledge. Key processes in listening contains intelligent listening to peer to peer conversations, analysing chats on social media to learn about your customer, about where they are talking about, and what do they say about the brand. Furthermore, to investigate who the opinion leaders are. It is challenging to interpret these chat analyses and to understand and predict the perceptions of the customer, related to usefulness relevance, compellingness, and timeliness [9]. Moreover, organisations should track competitors and gauge how they respond [26]. It is also important to know which channel preferences the customer has. Baltes [6] claims that besides the quality of the content, the right channels have influence on the success of the content marketing campaign. According to Kaplan and Heinlein [22], organisations must operate in the same channels as where the customers are present. Therefore, another aspect of listening is to find out the channel preferences of the customer.

Apart from listening what customer's like to hear, it is important to know the customer motives for engagement in social media. Many researchers uses the Uses and Gratifications theory (e.g. [24, 25]), which is an approach to understand the motivations and purposes of the customers for engaging with a certain form of content [12]. Literature based on the Use and Gratifications theory shows that customers use online and social media because they seek for social interaction, entertainment, information, sharing needs, and the desire for rewards or remuneration [14]. Content on social media can be divided into four types: Entertainment, Informative, Relational and Remuneration [12] [14]. According to Muntinga et al. [32], these four types are the motivates for customers to engage with an organisation. Entertainment consists of the sub-motivations: enjoyment, relaxation, and pastime. Information contains sub-motivations, such as: surveillance, knowledge, pre-purchase information, and inspiration. Remuneration refers to prospects of money, job-related benefits, or other rewards. The relational aspect contains the sub-motivations: gaining a sense of belonging, connecting with friends, family and society, seeking support/emotional support, and substituting real-life companionship. However, there are two more motivates: personal identity and empowerment. Personal identity is a motivation that belongs to 'contributing' as an engagement type. Gaining insight into one's self; reinforcing personal values, and identifying with and gaining recognition from peers, are examples of sub-motivations. Empowerment is about influencing other people or companies [32].

Creating Content.
When the listening part has been completed and insights have been gained into which content may be relevant for customer engagement, the next step is to actually create content. It is important to know which characteristics must be determined in order to create content. Aydin [4] investigated the effectiveness of social media posts in the hospitality industry. His research distinguished several factors which affect the popularity of posts, such as the post's vividness, the type content, and the interactivity. According to Aydin [4]: *"Vividness is referred to in marketing communication literature as a means of assessing the level of stimulation expected to be achieved by different message formats"*. The content type also refers to the customer motives, for instance, entertaining content or informational content. Interactivity is concerned with the extent to which parties can act to each other based on the content. Examples of interactivity are sweepstakes, competitions, questions, and polls or links to websites [4]. Cvijikj and Michahelles [12] tested the impact of content characteristics, such as content type, media type and posting time, on customer engagement. Just like Aydin [4], the content type is related to the customer motives. The media type consists of vividness and interactivity. In contrast to Aydin [4], the posting time is also included in this study. The posting time refers to the time when the organisation posts. Schreiner, Fischer, and Riedl [41] reviewed 45 studies to investigate which content characteristics have a positive influence on engagement. In addition to the above content characteristics, Schreiner et al. [41] mentioned four other characteristics which could influence engagement. The first characteristic is the topic of the content. Secondly, the length of the post could have influence on engagement. For instance, too much text or too little text can have a negative effect on engagement. Furthermore, they made a distinction between shared content or created content. As lasts, the position could influence engagement. For instance, a social media post could be pinned to the top of the page. This can have an effect on engagement because this post is seen more often when it is at the top of a page. In this research the focus is on creating content and therefore the characteristics 'shared or original content' and 'position' are not included. To summarize, the content characteristics which must be determined by creating content are: Topic, content type, vividness, interactivity, timing, and length of the post.

Evaluate.
The last part of the engaging content strategy framework consists of evaluating to what extent the content results in customer engagement. Previous research has shown that customer engagement is measured by looking at the number of likes, comments and shares per post. Rahman et al. [38] used likes, comments and shares for analysing several Facebook posts to determine the impact on fan page engagement. Cvijikj and Michahelles [12] tested the impact of content characteristics on engagement by using the likes, comments, shares,and interaction duration, as metrics for engagement. Interaction

duration is the difference between the time of the post and the time of the last interaction. Schivinski, Christodoulides, and Dabrowski [40] established the CEBESC framework which contains consumption, contribution, and creation dimensions, for measuring engagement with social media brand-related content. They have classified different types of engagement on social media in these three dimensions. Consuming consist of watching posts, reading posts, and following the brand. Contribution is about liking, commenting, and sharing the social media posts. Lastly, Creation is about creating content in the way of writing reviews or posting brand-related content. Examples are: uploading videos, music and pictures, or writing weblogs and articles [32]. Pentina, Guillox, Micu [34] identified discrete social media engagement behaviours in the context of Luxury Brands. The social media engagement behaviours can be divided into: Following, commenting, liking, tagging, sharing, and publishing. As mentioned earlier, the purpose of this research is developing an engaging content strategy for creating content. For this reason, only the metrics are included that can result/is measurable from the content of a social media post. Hence, based on literature, engagement on social media posts should be measured by likes, comments shares, quantity read, quantity watched, publishing brand-related content, and interaction duration.

4   Conceptual Framework

As described in the introduction, this research investigates what elements a strategic framework must contain for creating content on social media for achieving customer engagement. The engaging strategy framework starts with determining the goal and the target audience. These elements are not subdivided into sub-elements, because in this research the target and the target group are considered as input for creating content. The goal influences, for instance, what the content should be about. The way in which the content is presented depends on the target audience, because the target audience must ultimately be reached.

The next element in the engaging content strategy framework is listening. Listening can only be performed when the target audience has been determined, otherwise it is not clear who should be listened to. The previous sections have already shown that in several studies it appears that it is important to listen before creating content. By listening, the goal is to identify certain topics which are interesting for the audience. This process consists of analysing customer chats and peer-to-peer conversations. Additionally, the channel preferences should be clear in order to reach the audience. Furthermore, organisations have to know which motives a customer has for engagement. These motives could be divided into entertainment, information, remuneration, relational, personal identity, and empowerment [12, 14, 32]. In addition to listening to the customer, influencers must also be listened to. When the motives are clear and the customer data in the listening part are analysed, the next step is to create relevant content. The listening element plays an essential role because this information provides insight into which content is relevant and what this content should look like in order to ultimately achieve engagement.

Content can be created in many different ways. Thus, by creating content, several characteristics should be determined. In the first place, content can be divided into the content types entertainment, information, remuneration and relational. Another characteristic is the topic of the content. The content should contain the topics which are currently a trend based on the customer data. Furthermore, the additional content characteristics have to be taken into account. These characteristics are: vividness, interactivity, length of the post, source and timing.

The last part of this framework consists of measuring customer engagement in social media. This element has the aim to evaluate whether or not the content has reached customer engagement. As described in the previous section, organisations can learn from this and act accordingly. The metrics used in this research are based on existing literature and are divided into the dimensions: consuming, contributing and creating, based on Muntinga et al. [32] and Schivinski et al. [40]. The consuming metrics are: Quantity read and quantity watched. The contribution metrics contains: Likes, comments, and shares. The creation metric is publishing brand-related content. The interaction duration does not belong to consumption or contribution and is therefore considered as additional metric. Trends in customer data, influencer data in the listening part, and the customers motives could change over time. Therefore, this framework is represented as a process that constantly repeats. The conceptual framework can be found visually in Appendix A without the italics.

5   Demonstration

In this chapter, the results of the interviews will be discussed. In total, five interviews were held with experts in the field of social media and content marketing. The experts have seen a limited version of the framework that only includes listening, social media content, and evaluate. In the first place the experts were asked about the framework in general. It emerged from the interviews that listening is very important for providing content. This is in line with Kaplan and Heinlein [22].

> *"This is just how it works. That is also often the theoretical concept that you often encounter. Start listening, that's right"* (Interviewee 3).

> *"Before you actually start responding, create your own content. So then of course listening is very important"* (Interviewee 2).

Furthermore, from the interviews, it appears that there are two elements that must be added to the limited version of the framework. First, the goal must be added. This is consistent with the theory where it is also indicated that it starts with a certain goal [6, 9, 26].

> *"I think that if you go to work without a goal, then you are by definition wrong"* (Interviewee 4).

> *"You have a plan. And you also post things to achieve something, so it is always part of a larger whole"* (Interviewee 3).

In addition, the experts mentioned that before providing content, it is important that you have a certain goal, so that you can link the content to it. Besides, there is always a reason why you post something.

"It also depends a little on the goal. What do you want to achieve? Is it about them getting to know you? Do you want to score leads?"(Interviewee 4).

"You should also look very closely at the goals you have with social media. And when it comes to lead generation, it is different from when it comes to authority" (Interviewee 2).

In the second place, the target audience must be added. When posting on social media, it is essential to know for whom it is intended. The component 'listening' also depends on it. If the target audience is clear, you know who to listen to. This will result in discovering more specific interests. This too has emerged in the literature [9, 19, 21, 27].

"So that means that everything you communicate must in principle be based on the situation of your target group. So the only way to achieve engagement is to find that connection" (Interviewee 1).

"You have to define very well who do you have in mind as a customer, as a target group. If you make it too wide, you will discover a lot of general interests" (Interviewee 2).

Besides, one expert emphasized that it is a process that starts over and over again and results in better knowledge about your target audience.

"It is a kind of endless loop. Because you keep listening, you keep creating content, and you keep asking questions. So that you always have those loops. So that you actually get to know your target group better and your customer group" (Interviewee 4).

To summarize, the experts noticed that two elements are lacking in the limited framework: The goal and the target audience. This is in line with the theory where it also emerged that the goal and the target audience have to be taken into account before providing content. Additionally, it was also emphasized that it starts with listening before the content has to be provided. Moreover, it was also confirmed that the framework should be presented in a loop because it is a process that starts over and over again.

6   Evaluation

After the demonstration step, the framework will be evaluated to what extent the artefact supports the solution of the problem. This step is about comparing the objectives of the solution and the results of the interviews with the experts. To evaluate whether this framework is useful for creating content that achieves customer engagement, a single case study is used. Babbie [5] stated that: *"a case study is the in-depth examination of a single instance of some social phenomenon, such as village, a family, or a juvenile gang"* (p. 302). The case study is carried out at company V, an organisation that finds funding opportunities. Currently, company Vs has not defined a strategy for creating content, which makes it unclear what the corresponding activities should be and how to create relevant content in order to achieve customer engagement. The company is operating in the financial services sector. They provide assistance to other organisations for obtaining grants. Furthermore, they provide training, support and advice about grants. In the evaluation part, the framework is applied specifically for this company. A focus group has been established for applying the framework. Each part of the framework has been discussed through a discussion between the employees involved. In this case, the focus group consist of: the marketing manager, content marketeer, online marketeer and the director of the organisation.

6.1   Goals

In the first place, the discussion starts with determining the goals of social media. This discussion shows that the company has different goals with social media. These goals are: brand awareness, generating leads, branding & identity, and recruiting staff. They stated that the focus is primarily on brand awareness and generating leads.

6.2   Target Audience

After the goals were discussed, the target audience was determined. The discussion shows that the target group for the company is very broad, because many companies or municipalities can be eligible for grants. In short, the discussion resulted in the following target audiences: innovative SMEs, local municipalities, potential partners, and potential new employees.

6.3   Listening

In this component, the company was inquired about how they would listen to the customer in order to get knowledge about what the customer wants to hear. So that the company can respond to this by offering content that fits the needs of the customer. Five ways of listening emerged from this. First, the company wants to track the search behaviour of the customer. This search behaviour can take place via Google, on the website, social media, but also via the internal database. Secondly, through direct contact with the customer, with preference for questionnaires, by telephone, or an e-mail with a number of questions. Thirdly, the internal database is a source of information for many customers. By measuring and analysing, it enables insights which subjects and regulations are the most popular for customers. Fourth, by obtaining good insights into what customers, competitors, or influencers are talking about. This allows the company to see which topics are most interesting at the moment. Lastly, A/B testing can be a useful way to determine which form of content generates the most customer engagement. When asked what customer motives the customer would have for engagement, it emerged that the customer in particular wants to be informed. Remuneration and entertainment were also mentioned. In addition, some customers also have a trigger to do something if they can take advantage, for example, receive a reward in the form of a discount. Occasionally, the trigger is entertainment, in which the customer is looking for nice news, for example due to pastime or a relaxing "moment".

6.4   Content Characteristics

After the component listening is clarified for the company, the several content characteristics, which could influence customer engagement, were be determined. The Venn diagram was used to fill in which topics can be of interest to customers. The customer is looking for a form of financing for the project. The content sweet spot is therefore mainly in the information about regulations that the company can offer that applies to a customer's project.

6.5 Evaluate

For evaluating the content on customer engagement, the company prefers to use a tool. With the use of a tool, various metrics from different channels can be analysed in one overview. In addition, they would like to use one tool, so this will then have to be combined with listening. Overall, the case shows that the framework is useful to determine how the various elements take shape in order to achieve engaging content.

7 Analysis

The literature has shown that an engaging content strategy starts with determining the goal and the target audience [27]. This is confirmed by the experts, who stated that content is created to achieve a certain goal. Furthermore, they mentioned that the goal influences the content being produced. If your goal is to score leads, the content can be very different than when it comes to brand recognition. Furthermore, the content should fit the needs of the customer [9, 19, 21, 27]. Additionally, the experts stated that the content must fit the needs of the customer. One expert mentioned explicitly that that the content must be based on the situation of your target group, otherwise you will not achieve engagement.

Another element of an engaging content strategy is listening. Once the target audience has been determined, it is also clear who should be listened to. This element is crucial, because the content must be in line with the interest of the customer, which can be achieved through listening [21]. In order to finally reach the customer, the channel preferences of the customer must also be listened to [6, 22]. According to the experts, listening reveals the customer's interests. Furthermore, they stated that listening is essential to find a match between you and your target audience. Finding this match can result in customer engagement. When you know what questions customers have, what they find interesting or where they are talking about, you can respond to this. In addition, the literature and the interviews revealed that listening also means looking at what is being said about the brand, about the competitor, and what influencers are saying. As in the literature [12, 14, 32], the experts also mentioned that the motive plays a role. Customers can look for information but also for entertainment. According to the experts, there are various options for listening. For instance, analysing online behaviour, network meetings, customer sessions, or direct contact. Despite the fact that listening is important, the literature does not say much of it in relation to content creation. The case study also shows that in practice little attention is paid to listening in relation to content creation.

Furthermore, the actual creation of the content is central to the engaging content strategy. By creating the content, several characteristics should be determined. These include: topic, content type, vividness, interactivity, timing, and length of the post [4, 12, 41]. These characteristics can influence the extent to which customer engagement is achieved. The information obtained by listening plays an important role according to the experts. When it is clear what the trends are, the topic can be determined. Furthermore, the content type that fits the customer's motive can have influence on customer engagement. The length of the post can also have an influence, for example, the experts suggested not to make videos too long. Besides, the experts stated that form of content must be determined, which refers to the vividness and interactivity. Additionally, the time could influence customer engagement. Experts mentioned that through testing, you can discover which time leads to higher customer engagement. Moreover, the experts have some additions to the theory. It can make a difference to customer engagement, from whom the content originates, from a company or from an employee. In addition, tone of voice must be used that pleases the customer. Lastly, organisations should have a recognizable design.

The last element of an engaging content strategy contains the evaluation. Ultimately, after the content is created, it should be evaluated to what extent the content is effective and results in customer engagement. Based on the literature, the measurements consist of: quantity read, quantity watched, likes, comments, shares, publishing and interaction duration [12, 32, 34, 38, 40]. The interviews also show that it is important to measure how long people watch a video or to what extent they click through to the website. Just like literature, the experts claim that one form of engagement is more valuable than the other. They stated that it is mainly important to look further than like, shares, and comments.

Lastly, the case study shows that an organisation can use this framework to determine how to listen in order to discover the needs and preferences of the customer, and to see what is currently relevant for creating content on social media. In addition, filling in the various content characteristics provides a good overview of how the organisation can determine the social media content to ensure customer engagement. Furthermore, this framework shows which metrics must be measured to evaluate the content on customer engagement. On the other hand, the framework in this case study is used on an abstract level, which does not directly lead to concrete results. Nevertheless, the case study has ensured that the organisation has become more aware of the various elements of content creation. In the future, the organisation will have to invest in the content creation process in order to ultimately achieve more customer engagement on social media.

8 Conclusion

The aim of this research was to design a framework to create content on social media in order to obtain customer engagement. In this study, the research question was: *What are the key elements in a strategic framework for creating content on social media in order to achieve customer engagement?*

Based on a literature review, a framework has been developed. This framework consists of the elements: The goal, target audience, listening, content creation, and evaluation. These elements were not previously merged and placed in this order. The framework is validated and supplemented with interviews with experts. This has led to a number of conclusions.

It can be concluded that listening is a crucial part for creating content. Listening provides insights into what the current trends are. These insights provide the opportunity to respond to this, which will lead to higher engagement because it better matches the interests of the customer.

When creating content, several characteristics must be taken into account as they can influence customer engagement. According to the experts, three elements must be added in comparison with the literature: source, tone of voice and design. Furthermore, creating engaging content largely depends on the input of listening. The information from the previous element largely determines how the content is created and how the characteristics get substance.

Lastly, this research shows that the elements are in the right order, which can be seen as the first step. Additionally, this framework has the potential to be used by marketeers and could be useful as a guide for organisations to create content in order to achieve customer engagement. The practical value of such a framework is that practitioners can use it as a guideline for creating effective content. Both creative content agencies and digital marketeers can further develop this framework into practical tools for consulting.

9   Discussion and Future Research

In this research, a framework was developed and it thus responded to the need from the literature for a communication model in social media context. Nevertheless, there are a number of limitations of this research. First, the case study shows that it can be a useful guide, but the framework is not actually applied. Therefore, it is not clear whether this framework actually ensures improved customer engagement. And it is also not clear what the impact can be on the content when you listen to the customer. Further research is needed to determine to what extent the impact is on customer engagement when following this framework. Furthermore, the literature does not say much of listening in relation to content creation. Thus, further research is needed into what listening means and how organisations can make optimal use of it. Moreover, this research only uses metrics that can be measured on a specific social media post. There are probably also other forms of engagement that can result from a social media post. In addition, it can also ensure that the customer contacts the organisation through other channels such as telephone or email. It is also possible that customers become advocates as a result of a social media post. Thus, it would be interesting for further research to pay attention to other forms of engagement where the starting point is social media. Furthermore, it could be interesting for further research to investigate other effects that can influence the customer engagement of a social media post. For instance, on many social media channels it is possible to post content in a paid way, so that it appears in someone's timeline. Additionally, when many employees share the content, the reach becomes much larger, which can lead to more customer engagement. Lastly, this framework is established for the social media context, but perhaps it could also work for other channels such as email marketing. Further research is needed to determine to what extent these process steps can be applied for creating content in a different context.

Appendix A – The Framework for Creating Content on Social Media for Achieving Customer Engagement

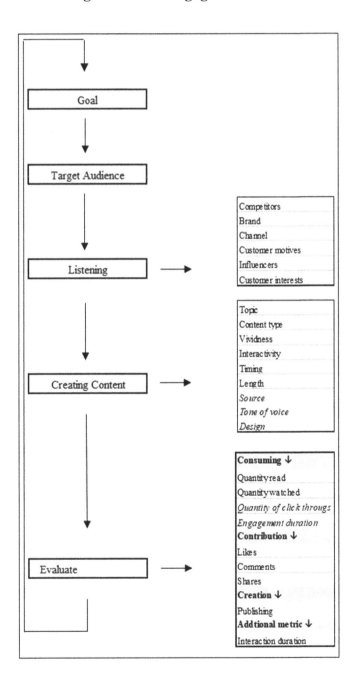

Appendix B – Systematic Research Query

Search query	Amount
"content marketing" AND "social media"	48
"content marketing" *	100
"social media content" *	100
("customer engagement" OR "consumer engagement") AND "marketing" *	100
"social media content" AND "engagement"	83
"social media engagement" AND "content"	88
Total	519

* top 100 highest cited articles

Appendix C – Flowchart Research Query

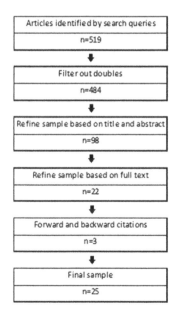

References

1. Aken, J.E.V.: Management research based on the paradigm of the design sciences: the quest for field-tested and grounded technological rules. J. Manag. Stud. **41**(2), 219–246 (2004)
2. Aladwani, A.M.: Compatible quality of social media content: conceptualization, measurement, and affordances. Int. J. Inf. Manag. **37**(6), 576–582 (2017)
3. Aldous, K.K., An, J., Jansen, B.J.: The challenges of creating engaging content: results from a focus group study of a popular news media organization. In: Extended Abstracts of the 2019 CHI Conference on Human Factors in Computing Systems, p. LBW2317. ACM, April 2019
4. Aydin, G.: Social media engagement and organic post effectiveness: a roadmap for increasing the effectiveness of social media use in hospitality industry. J. Hosp. Mark. Manag. **29**(1), 1–21 (2019)
5. Babbie, E.R.: The Practice of Social Research. Cengage Learning (2015)
6. Baltes, L.P.: Content marketing-the fundamental tool of digital marketing. Bull. Trans. Univ. Brasov. Econ. Sci. Ser. **8**(2), 111 (2015)
7. Bowden, J.L.H.: The process of customer engagement: a conceptual framework. J. Mark. Theory Pract. **17**(1), 63–74 (2009)
8. Brodie, R.J., Ilic, A., Juric, B., Hollebeek, L.: Consumer engagement in a virtual brand community: An exploratory analysis. J. Bus. Res. **66**(1), 105–114 (2013)
9. Cawsey, T., Rowley, J.: Social media brand building strategies in B2B companies. Mark. Intell. Plann. **34**(6), 754–776 (2016)
10. Content Marketing Institute: What Is Content Marketing? (2019). https://contentmarketinginstitute.com/what-is-content-marketing/
11. Coursaris, C.K., van Osch, W., Balogh, B.A.: Do Facebook likes lead to shares or sales? exploring the empirical links between social media content, brand equity, purchase intention, and engagement. In: 2016 49th Hawaii International Conference on System Sciences (HICSS), pp. 3546–3555. IEEE, January 2016
12. Pletikosa Cvijikj, I., Michahelles, F.: Online engagement factors on Facebook brand pages. Soc. Netw. Anal. Min. **3**(4), 843–861 (2013). https://doi.org/10.1007/s13278-013-0098-8
13. Dijkmans, C., Kerkhof, P., Beukeboom, C.J.: A stage to engage: Social media use and corporate reputation. Tourism Manag. **47**, 58–67 (2015)
14. Dolan, R., Conduit, J., Fahy, J., Goodman, S.: Social media engagement behaviour: a uses and gratifications perspective. J. Strateg. Mark. **24**(3–4), 261–277 (2016)
15. Effing, R.: The social media participation framework: studying the effects of social media on nonprofit communities. Universiteit, Enschede (2014)
16. Effing, R., Spil, T.A., Both, M.P., Ogbuji, B.: Digital future. MVP2.0 Edition (2013)
17. Goldner, S.: A guide to social media: what tools are worth paying for? EContent **36**(7), 6–7 (2018)
18. Hollebeek, L.D.: Demystifying customer brand engagement: Exploring the loyalty nexus. J. Mark. Manag. **27**(7–8), 785–807 (2011)
19. Holliman, G., Rowley, J.: Business to business digital content marketing: marketers' perceptions of best practice. J. Res. Interact. Mark. **8**(4), 269–293 (2014)
20. Hootsuite: Digital 2019 Global Digital Overview (2019). https://www.slideshare.net/DataReportal/digital-2019-global-digital-overview-january-2019-v01?ref=, https://thenextweb.com/contributors/2019/01/30/digital-trends-2019-every-single-stat-you-need-to-know-about-the-internet/
21. Järvinen, J., Taiminen, H.: Harnessing marketing automation for B2B content marketing. Ind. Mark. Manag. **54**, 164–175 (2016)

22. Kaplan, A.M., Haenlein, M.: Users of the world, unite! the challenges and opportunities of Social Media. Bus. Horiz. **53**(1), 59–68 (2010)
23. Kapoor, K.K., Tamilmani, K., Rana, N.P., Patil, P., Dwivedi, Y.K., Nerur, S.: Advances in social media research: past, present and future. Inf. Syst. Front. **20**(3), 531–558 (2018)
24. Katz, E.: Mass communications research and the study of popular culture: an editorial note on a possible future for this journal. Departmental Papers (ASC), 165 (1959)
25. Katz, E., Foulkes, D.: On the use of the mass media as "escape": clarification of a concept. Public Opin. Q. **26**(3), 377–388 (1962)
26. Kietzmann, J.H., Hermkens, K., McCarthy, I.P., Silvestre, B.S.: Social media? Get serious! Understanding the functional building blocks of social media. Bus. Horiz. **54**(3), 241–251 (2011)
27. Kilgour, M., Sasser, S.L., Larke, R.: The social media transformation process: curating content into strategy. Corp. Commun.: Int. J. **20**(3), 326–343 (2015)
28. Lee, D., Hosanagar, K., Nair, H.S.: Advertising content and consumer engagement on social media: evidence from Facebook. Manag. Sci. **64**(11), 5105–5131 (2018)
29. Macintosh, A.: Characterizing e-participation in policy-making. In: Proceedings of the 37th Annual Hawaii International Conference on System Sciences 2004, p. 10. IEEE (2004)
30. Malthouse, E.C., Haenlein, M., Skiera, B., Wege, E., Zhang, M.: Managing customer relationships in the social media era: introducing the social CRM house. J. Interact. Mark. **27**(4), 270–280 (2013)
31. Mangold, W.G., Faulds, D.J.: Social media: the new hybrid element of the promotion mix. Bus. Horiz. **52**(4), 357–365 (2009)
32. Muntinga, D.G., Moorman, M., Smit, E.G.: Introducing COBRAs: exploring motivations for brand-related social media use. Int. J. Advert. **30**(1), 13–46 (2011)
33. Peffers, K., Tuunanen, T., Rothenberger, M.A., Chatterjee, S.: A design science research methodology for information systems research. J. Manag. Inf. Syst. **24**(3), 45–77 (2007)
34. Pentina, I., Guilloux, V., Micu, A.C.: Exploring social media engagement behaviours in the context of luxury brands. J. Advert. **47**(1), 55–69 (2018)
35. Pulizzi, J.: The rise of storytelling as the new marketing. Publ. Res. Q. **28**(2), 116–123 (2012)
36. Pulizzi, J., Hadley, A.: B2B Content Marketing: 2016 Benchmarks, Budgets and Trends — North America. Washington, D.C.: Content Marketing Institute (2015). https://contentmarketinginstitute.com/2015/09/b2b-content-marketing-research/
37. Pulizzi, J., Hadley, A.: B2C Content Marketing: 2016 Benchmarks, Budgets and Trends — North America. Washington, D.C.: Content Marketing Institute (2015). https://contentmarketinginstitute.com/wp-content/uploads/2015/10/2016_B2C_Research_Final.pdf
38. Rahman, Z., Suberamanian, K., Zanuddin, H., Moghavvemi, S., Nasir, M.H.N.M.: Social media engagement metric analysis-" study on fan page content". J. Telecommun. Electron. Comput. Eng. (JTEC) **8**(8), 71–76 (2016)
39. Sashi, C.M.: Customer engagement, buyer-seller relationships, and social media. Manag. Decis. **50**(2), 253–272 (2012)
40. Schivinski, B., Christodoulides, G., Dabrowski, D.: Measuring consumers' engagement with brand-related social-media content: development and validation of a scale that identifies levels of social-media engagement with brands. J. Advert. Res. **56**(1), 64–80 (2016)
41. Schreiner, M., Fischer, T., Riedl, R.: Impact of content characteristics and emotion on behavioral engagement in social media: literature review and research agenda. Electron. Commer. Res. **19**(3), 1–17 (2019)
42. Tiago, M.T.P.M.B., Veríssimo, J.M.C.: Digital marketing and social media: why bother? Bus. Horiz. **57**(6), 703–708 (2014)

43. Tørning, K., Jaffari, Z., Vatrapu, R.: Current challenges in social media management. In: Proceedings of the 2015 International Conference on Social Media & Society, p. 14. ACM, July 2015
44. Van Doorn, J., Lemon, K.N., Mittal, V., Nass, S., Pick, D., Pirner, P., Verhoef, P.C.: Customer engagement behaviour: theoretical foundations and research directions. J. Serv. Res. **13**(3), 253–266 (2010)
45. Webster, J., Watson, R.T.: Analyzing the past to prepare for the future: writing a literature review. MIS Q. **26**(2), xiii–xxiii (2002)
46. Wolfswinkel, J.F., Furtmueller, E., Wilderom, C.P.: Using grounded theory as a method for rigorously reviewing literature. Eur. J. Inf. Syst. **22**(1), 45–55 (2013)

Social Commerce Constructs and Trust as Influencers of Consumer Decision Making With Reference to Fashion E-Tailing

Sarulatha Neelankandan[1]($\boxtimes$) and Sasirekha Venkatesan[2]($\boxtimes$)

[1] Department of Business Administration, D. G. Vaishnav College, Chennai,
Tamil Nadu, India
sarulatha1811@gmail.com

[2] Sri Sai Ram Institute of Management Studies, Chennai, Tamil Nadu, India
sasirekharamani@gmail.com

Abstract. The disruptive technology of fourth industrial revolution has built new business models. The gaining popularity of social networking sites has facilitated the e-tailers to capitalise the user's conversations. This gave rise to social commerce- ecommerce through social networking sites.

It is significant for marketers to understand the consumer decision making process in the social networking sites. In this framework, the impact of Trust & social commerce constructs - Recommendations & referrals, Forums & communities, Ratings & reviews are studied. Data was collected through structured questionnaire. The study was carried among active social networking site users who purchased fashion products online recently (Less than 6 months). Based on the 581 respondents, regression analysis is carried out to study the impact. The study revealed significant impact of trust and social commerce construct on the consumer decision making. The study provides a guideline for marketers comparing the role of trust & social commerce construct for marketers to strengthen and/or reinforce its usage.

Keywords: Social commerce constructs · Social networking sites · Trust

1 Introduction

India witnesses a significant development in retailing with e-tailing (ET Retail 2017). Increased internet diffusion, smart phone usage, ease of buying & payments, choice of products & services are steering growth in e-tailing. Investments in e-commerce companies are growing up. Also, the government initiatives to promote Digital India and inter-operability systems are facilitating the e-tailing. These scenarios have provided ample opportunities for e-tailers to establish themselves.

With increased internet penetration and popularity of social networking site, e-tailers are bringing out technology steered practices such as Social Commerce.

It originated with Amazon introducing Purchase Circles (Amazon 1999). The term social commerce was introduced by Yahoo as Picklists and Shoposphere (Beach (2005) and Rubel (2006)). Yadav et al. (2013) defined social commerce as "exchange-related activities that occur in, or are influenced by, an individual's social network in

© IFIP International Federation for Information Processing 2020
Published by Springer Nature Switzerland AG 2020
S. K. Sharma et al. (Eds.): TDIT 2020, IFIP AICT 618, pp. 371–383, 2020.
https://doi.org/10.1007/978-3-030-64861-9_32

computer-mediated social environments, where the activities correspond to the need recognition, pre-purchase, purchase and post-purchase changes of a focal exchange." It simple terms it is e-commerce happening in social networking sites.

Web 2.0 has brought new platforms Social commerce constructs such as Recommendations & referrals, Forums & communities, Ratings & reviews in social networking sites. Though technically slightly different, these are primarily content generators to facilitate interactions and promote word of mouth. The economic implication of these constructs is product sales (Forman et al. 2008a, b) in e-tailing which is the ultimate destination for every marketer. Trust is also a very noteworthy factor in e-commerce (Gefen and Straub 2004; Mutz 2005; Pavlou 2003) and also place a very significant role to facilitate social commerce (Hajli 2015). The economic implication of these constructs is product sales (Forman et al. 2008a, b) in e-tailing which is the ultimate destination for every marketer. Understanding the Trust & social commerce construct on consumer decision making is important for marketer to use appropriately and devise strategies accordingly. In this context, the study is carried out to research the impact of trust and social commerce construct across stages of consumer decision making.

2 Literature Review

Aljifri et al. (2003) identified Trust as the key barrier for adopting e-commerce. Senecal and Nantel (2004) studied on consumer choice based on product recommendation. Personal recommendation systems are highly significant among all the online recommendations. Hassanein and Head (2007) researched on impact of online consumer behaviour by individuals representing online environment. Trust has significant positive relationship with perceived social presence and impacts attitude. Park et al. (2007) identified online reviews are informants and recommenders for purchase decision making. Qualitative online reviews build consumers purchase intention. Also the purchase intention increases with increase in online reviews. DEI Worldwide (2008) reported 70% of consumers use social media among other online sources to seek information about a company and it influenced 67% consumers purchase decision. Swamynathan et al. (2008) studied the impact of social networks on e-commerce. Social networks have significant impact on e-commerce and satisfaction level of social network users was high. Lu et al. (2010) studied trust in social networks is high than C2C website. Also, the study revealed consumer intention to get information influences the purchase intention of the consumer. Personal recommendations & Online consumer opinions are the most trusted forms of advertisement among Internet Consumers according to "The Neilsen Global Online Consumer Survey", Nielsen(2009). Hensel and Deis (2010) investigated social media to improve marketing & advertising. Social media facilitates conversations among consumers and also build brand value. Hsiao et al. (2010) studied building trust through product recommendations and relationship between trust and purchase intention for shopping online. The study revealed trust built from product recommendation is comparatively higher than trust built from the product website. Moreover, trust built through product recommendation has a direct impact on purchase intention and indirect impact on intention to buy the product from the website.

Armelini (2011) study revealed direct correlation of sales and number of conversations in social media. Curty and Zhang (2011) traced the evolution of social commerce before Yahoo in 2005 with Amazon & Epinions in August 1999. Amazon used "purchased circles" similar to recommendations & consumer communities. Consumers & visitors of the website are provided with the facility for wishlist and email their friends about products. Epinions provided ratings & reviews, member forums - internal social network and referred to it as "Community of trust." The study focus was on the technology perspective of social commerce. The findings of the study identified two categories of social commerce websites - Direct sales & Referrals.

Anderson et al. (2011) researched social media to be used as a commerce channel. The real- time data collected when customers search, purchase, give ratings, recommend and purchase products aids companies to build strategies influencing consumer behavior. Fijalkowski and Zatoka (2011) proposed a recommender system for e-commerce based on user profiles on Facebook. Rad and Benyoucef (2011) developed a model of social commerce with reference to consumer decision-making process. The model was built on social commerce components (Social shopping, Ratings & Reviews, Recommendations & Referrals, Forums & Communities, Social Media, Social Advertising) and included business. The study related the following social components across stages of consumer decision- making process: 1) Need Recognition Recommender systems. 2) Product brokerage - Trusted reviews. 3) Merchant brokerage - Synchronous shopping, 4) Purchase decision - Recommender system - Product bundling & Group purchase. 5) Purchase - Social Media to post status (Individual purchase/Group purchase) 6) Evaluation- Ratings & reviews. Hoffman (2013) studied social media and consumer behavior. The users review the user-generated content when they want to make a purchase intention or merely to spend time. The content generated by users directly influences the purchase intention. If the users are consuming user-generated information to spend time, it will influence users consequent attitudes and behavior. User-generated information online has several unique features such as popularity, longer carryover effects on consumer behavior especially with users of same group. Wang et al. (2012) analyzed the impact of peer communication on purchase intention. The peer communication about products has a direct (conformity with peers) and indirect (reinforcing product involvement) in purchase decision making. Based on past reviews and social support theory Haji (2013) developed a model for social commerce. The study identified social commerce conceptual elements with social commerce constructs (SCCs) - Ratings & Reviews, Forums & Communities, and Referrals & Recommendations. The social commerce constructs (SCCs) enhances trusts and results in purchase intention. Yadav et al. (2013) carried out a study to leverage social media and sell products. The authors stated the proposition & facilitating the role of social networks for the 4 different stages of decision making viz., Need Recognition, Pre-purchase activities, Purchase decision and post-purchase activities. Maity and Dass (2014) studied the impact of consumer decision making across modern and traditional channels. The findings revealed consumer prefer e-commerce channels for searching product information. Hajli (2014a) studied the impact of social media on consumers. Based on the technology acceptance model (TAM) a social commerce adoption model was developed. The study concludes consumer interactions through online forums, communities, ratings, reviews, and recommendations in social media have given rise to social commerce. Consumers are empowered as content generators which aid in sharing information & experiences in their networks and facilitate social interactions. Consequently, it builds trust and hence users intention to buy. Hajli et al. (2014d) build a trust model for new products & services in the context of social commerce. The study identified the social commerce constructs - Ratings & Reviews, Recommendations & Referrals, Forums & communities and the impact of trust in new products and services. Hajli (2015) built a model for social commerce consumer behaviour with social commerce constructs (Ratings & reviews, Recommendations & referrals, Forums & communities), Trust and Intention to buy. The social commerce constructs (SCCSs) has a direct impact on intention to buy and indirectly on intention to buy through Trust.

3   Conceptual Framework

Based on the above literature Trust and the social commerce constructs have significantly influenced the consumer. The study aims to establish the influence of Trust and social commerce constructs for fashion e-tailing. It also bring out the extent of influence by the social commerce constructs & Trust for fashion e-tailing across stages of consumer decision making viz., Need Recognition, Pre-Purchase, Purchase Decision and Post Purchase. The conceptual framework developed is represented below:

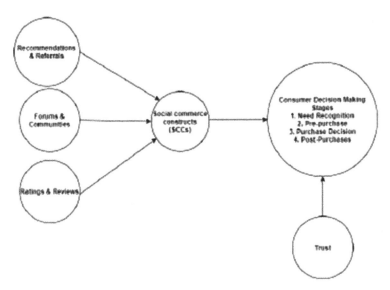

Fig. 1. Relationship of trust & social commerce constructs (SCCs) on consumer decision making stages

4   Research Methodology

The study focussed to identify the impact of Trust & Social commerce construct (SCCs) across four stages of consumer decision making viz., Need Recognition, Pre-purchase, Purchase decision and Post-Purchase for fashion e-tailing. The following objective and the related hypothesis are laid for the study as follows:

Objective 1: To study the impact of Trust on stages of consumer decision making for shopping fashion products in social networking sites.

Hypothesis 1 (H1): There is a significant relationship between trust across stages of consumer decision making for fashion e-tailing.

Objective 2: To study the impact of Social commerce constructs (Recommendations & Referrals, Forums & Communities, Ratings & Reviews) on stages of consumer decision making for shopping fashion products in social networking sites.

Hypothesis 2 (H2): There is a significant relationship between social commerce constructs (Recommendations & referrals, Forums & Communities, Ratings& Reviews) across stages of consumer decision making for fashion e-tailing

The data was collected through structured questionnaire online & offline. The respondents were active social networking site user who purchased fashion products recently (Less than 6 months) based in Chennai. A pilot study was conducted among 42 respondents in Chennai. The reliability test score with Cronbach alpha was 0.81 i.e., 81% reliability. The data collection was carried out during the period Jan 2017 to June 2017.

Convenience sampling, a type of non-probability sampling was used for the study. 600 questionnaires were circulated for data collection. With 3.1% questionnaire rejected, 581 questionnaires were finally used for the study.

The questionnaire consists of statements related to social commerce constructs (Recommendations & referrals, Forums & communities, Ratings & reviews) and Trust. This was measured using the instrument developed initially by Nick Hajli (2015). It consists of 10 items relating to each social commerce construct and trust measured in a five-point Likert type scale. Equal importance was given to all the statements, and the opinion about every social commerce construct and trust was obtained for fashion e-tailing. Also, the questionnire with other set of statements related to the facilitative role of social commerce across stages of consumer decision making was included. This was measured using the instrument developed initially by M.S. Yadav et al. (2013). It comprises of 11 items relating to four stages of consumer decision making namely Need recognition, Pre-purchase, Purchase decision and Post purchase. These are measured in a five-point Likert type scale. All the items were given the same importance, and the respondent's opinion about the facilitative role of social commerce for fashion e-tailing was obtained.

5 Results and Discussion

Regression analysis used to investigate the extent of trust impact and social commerce constructs impact (Recommendations & Referrals, Forums & Communities, Ratings & Reviews) on various stages of consumer decision making (Need Recognition, Pre-purchase, Purchase decision, Post- purchase).

Table 1. Mode Summary for Impact of Trust & Social commerce construct on stages of consumer decision making

Independent Variable	Dependent variable	Multiple R value	R square value	F value	p value
Need Recognition (X_1)	Trust	0.041	0.048	7.257	<0.001**
Pre-purchase (X_2) Purchase decision (X_3)	Recommendation & Referrals	0.095	0.101	16.217	<0.001**
Post purchase (X_4)	Forums & Communities	0.042	0.048	7.288	<0.001**
	Ratings & Reviews	0.103	0.109	17.620	<0.001**

Source: Computed from primary data *denotes significance at 1% level

From Table 1, based on the R square value for the dependent variable trust, recommendations & referrals, forums & communities, ratings & reviews establishes 4.8%, 10.1%, 4.8%, 10.9% variance respectively on the stages of consumer decision making. Also, statistically significant at 1% level i.e., Trust, recommendations & referrals, forums & communities, ratings & reviews is well related with various stages of consumer decision making. This leads to the determination of trust & social commerce constructs impact on each stage of consumer decision making - Need Recognition, Pre-purchase, Purchase decision, Post purchase.

From Table 2, the multiple regression equation is

Table 2. Coefficient table for impact of trust on stages of consumer decision making

Variables	Unstandardized coefficient	SE of B	Standardized coefficient	t value	LOS
Need Recognition (X_1)	−0.261	0.062	−0.248	−4.226	0.000**
Pre-purchase (X_2)	0.054	0.071	0.052	0.770	0.442*
Purchase decision (X_3)	−0.016	0.076	−0.017	−0.211	0.833*
Post purchase (X_4)	0.196	0.064	0.142	3.039	0.002**
Constant	3.389	0.197		17.169	0.000

Source: Computed from primary data
*denotes significance at 1% level and * denotes significance at 5% level

$$Y = 3.389 - 0.261X_1 + 0.054X_2 - 0.016X_3 + 0.196X_4$$

Here the coefficient of X_1 is −0.261 represents the partial effect with Need Recognition on Trust, holding other stages of consumer decision making constant. The estimated negative sign implies that such effect is negative and Trust score would decrease by 0.261 for every unit increase in need recognition. Also, the coefficient value is significant at the 1% level.

The coefficient of X_2 is 0.054 represents the partial effect of Pre-purchase on Trust, holding other stages of consumer decision making constant. The estimated positive sign implies that such effect is positive and Trust score would increase by 0.054 for every unit increase in pre-purchase. Also, the coefficient value is not significant at the 5% level.

The coefficient of X_3 −0.016 represents the partial effect with purchase decision on Trust, holding other stages of consumer decision making constant. The estimated negative sign implies that such effect is adverse and Trust score would decrease by 0.016 for every unit increase in a purchase decision. Also, the coefficient value is not significant at the 5% level.

The coefficient of X_4 is 0.196 represents the partial effect of Post purchase on Trust, holding other stages of consumer decision making constant. The estimated positive sign implies that such effect is positive and Trust score would increase by 0.196 for every unit increase in a purchase decision. Also, the coefficient value is significant at the 1% level.

Table 3. Coefficient table for Impact of Recommendations & Referrals on stages of consumer decision making

Variables	Unstandardized coefficient	SE of B	Standardized coefficient	t value	LOS
Need Recognition (X_1)	−0.296	0.065	−0.260	−4.562	0.000**
Pre-purchase (X_2)	0.238	0.074	0.212	3.213	0.001**
Purchase decision (X_3)	0.021	0.079	0.021	0.270	0.787*
Post purchase (X_4)	−0.313	0.068	−0.210	−4.622	0.000**
Constant	4.200	0.207		20.246	0.000

Source: Computed from primary data
*denotes significance at 1% level and * denotes significance at 5% level

Hence, it is inferred that there is a considerable impact on the Trust in Need Recognition and Post-purchase stage. The impact of Trust in Need recognition stage is high and exhibits inverse relationship compared with Post-purchase stage exhibiting positive relationship

From Table 3, the multiple regression equation is

$$Y = 4.200 - 0.296X_1 + 0.238X_2 + 0.021X_3 - 0.313X_4$$

Here the coefficient of X_1 is −0.296 represents the partial effect with Need Recognition on Recommendations & Referrals, holding other stages of consumer decision making constant. The estimated negative sign implies that such effect is adverse and Recommendations & Referrals score would decrease by 0.296 for every unit increase in need recognition. Also, the coefficient value is significant at the 1% level.

The coefficient of X_2 is 0.238 represents the partial effect of Pre-purchase on Recommendations & Referrals, holding other stages of consumer decision making constant. The estimated positive sign implies that such effect is positive and Recommendations & Referrals score would increase by 0.238 for every unit increase in pre-purchase. Also, the coefficient value is significant at the 1% level.

The coefficient of X_3 0.021 represents the partial effect with purchase decision on Recommendations & Referrals, holding other stages of consumer decision making constant. The estimated positive sign implies that such effect is positive and Recommendations & Referrals score would increase by 0.021 for every unit increase in a purchase decision. However, the coefficient value is not significant at the 5% level.

The coefficient of X_4 is −0.313 represents the partial effect of Post purchase on Recommendations & Referrals, holding other stages of consumer decision making constant. The estimated negative sign implies that such effect is adverse and Recommendations & Referrals score would decrease by 0.313 for every unit increase in a purchase decision. Also, the coefficient value is significant at the 1% level.

Hence, it can be inferred that there is a significant impact of the Recommendations and referrals specfically with the Need recognition; Pre and Postpurchase stages of consumer decision making. The impact of Recommendations & referrals is high with Post purchase followed by Need Recognition and Prepurchase. The impact is negative with Post Purchase & Need Recognition and confidence with the Pre-purchase stage of consumer decision making.

Table 4. Coefficient table for Impact of Forums & Communities on Stages of consumer decision making

Variables	Unstandardized coefficient	SE of B	Standardized coefficient	t value	LOS
Need Recognition (X_1)	0.027	0.076	0.021	0.356	0.722*
Pre-purchase (X_2)	0.354	0.086	0.278	4.097	<0.001**
Purchase decision (X_3)	−0.449	0.093	−0.385	−4.838	<0.001**
Post purchase (X_4)	0.100	0.079	0.059	1.264	0.207*
Constant	2.983	0.242	12.325	<0.001**	

Source: Computed from primary data
*denotes significance at 1% level and * denotes significance at 5% level

The multiple regression equation is

$$Y = 2.983 + 0.027X_1 + 0.354X_2 - 0.449X_3 + 0.100X_4$$

Here the coefficient of X_1 is 0.027 represents the partial effect with Need Recognition on Forums & Communities, holding other stages of consumer decision making constant. The estimated positive sign implies that such effect is positive and Forums & Communities score would increase by 0.027 for every unit increase in Need recognition. However, the coefficient value is not significant at the 5% level.

The coefficient of X_2 is 0.354 represents the partial effect with Pre-purchase on Forums & Communities, holding other stages of consumer decision making constant. The estimated positive sign implies that such effect is positive and Forums & Communities score would increase by 0.354 for every unit increase in pre-purchase. Also, the coefficient value is significant at the 1% level.

The coefficient of X_3 −0.449 represents the partial effect with purchase decision on Forums & Communities, holding other stages of consumer decision making constant. The estimated negative sign implies that such effect is negative and Forums & Communities score would decrease by 0.449 for every unit increase in a purchase decision. Also, the coefficient value is significant at the 1% level.

The coefficient of X_4 is 0.100 represents the partial effect of Post purchase on Forums & Communities, holding other stages of consumer decision making constant. The estimated positive sign implies that such effect is positive and Forums & Communities score would increase by 0.100 for every unit increase in a purchase decision. However, Forums & Communities the coefficient value is not significant at the 5% level.

Hence, it can be inferred that there is a significant impact of Forums & Communities on Pre- and Purchase decision in the study region. The impact is elevated with Purchase decision compared with Pre-purchase. However, Purchase decision exhibits a negative impact and Pre- purchase exhibits a positive relationship with Forums & Communities.

Table 5. Coefficient table for Impact of Ratings & reviews on stages of consumer decision making

Variables	Unstandardized coefficient	SE of B	Standardized coefficient	t value	LOS
Need Recognition (X_1)	0.221	0.054	0.232	4.084	<0.001**
Pre-purchase (X_2)	0.126	0.062	0.133	2.029	0.043*
Purchase decision (X_3)	−0.484	0.066	−0.562	−7.286	<0.001**
Post purchase (X_4)	0.160	0.057	0.128	2.831	0.005*
Constant	3.175	0.173	18.309	<0.001**	

Source: Computed from primary data
*denotes significance at 1% level and * denotes significance at 5% level.

From Table 5, the multiple regression equation is

$$Y = 3.175 + 0.221X_1 + 0.126X_2 - 0.484X_3 + 0.160X_4$$

Here the coefficient of X_1 is 0.221 represents the partial effect with Need Recognition on Ratings & reviews holding other stages of consumer decision making constant. The estimated positive sign implies that such effect is positive and Ratings & reviews score would increase by 0.221 for every unit increase in need recognition. Also, the coefficient value is significant at the 1% level.

The coefficient of X_2 is 0.126 represents the partial effect of Pre-purchase on Ratings & reviews, holding other stages of consumer decision making constant. The estimated positive sign implies that such effect is positive and Ratings & reviews score would increase by 0.126 for every unit increase in pre-purchase. Also, the coefficient value is significant at the 5% level.

The coefficient of X_3 −0.484 represents the partial effect with purchase decision on Ratings & reviews, holding other stages of consumer decision making constant. The estimated negative sign implies that such effect is adverse and Ratings & reviews score would decrease by 0.484 for every unit increase in a purchase decision. Also, the coefficient value is significant at the 1% level.

The coefficient of X_4 is 0.160 represents the partial effect of Post purchase on Ratings & reviews, holding other stages of consumer decision making constant. The estimated positive sign implies that such effect is positive and Ratings & reviews score would increase by 0.160 for every unit increase in the Post-purchase decision. Also, the coefficient value is significant at the 1% level.

Hence, it can be inferred that there is a significant impact of Ratings & reviews on all stages of consumer decision making The various stages of consumer decision making includes need Recognition, Pre-purchase, Purchases decision, and Post purchase. The impact on purchase decision is high with purchase decision followed by need recognition, Post-purchase and low with Pre-purchase. However, the impact of ratings & reviews is negative on purchase decision compared with a positive impact on need recognition stage, Pre-purchase and Post purchase.

Table 6. Summary - Trust & Social commerce construct (SCCs) impact on Stages of consumer decision making

Trust & SCC/consumer decision	Relationship			
	Need	Pre-purchase	Purchase	Post purchase
Making stages	Recognition		Decision	
Trust	Negative	Positive	Negative	Positive
Recommendation & Referrals	Negative	Positive	Positive	Negative
Forums & Communities	Positive	Positive	Negative	Positive
Ratings & Reviews	Positive	Positive	Negative	Positive

From the above results, it is concluded that both Trust & Social commerce construct (SCCs) exhibit significant relationship across all the stages of consumer decision making namely Need Recognition, Pre-purchase, Purchase decision & Post-purchase. Hence, both the hypothesis statement, Hypothesis (H1): There is a significant relationship between trust across stages of consumer decision making for fashion e-tailing and Hypothesis 2 (H2): There is a significant relationship between social commerce constructs (Recommendations & referrals, Forums & Communities, Ratings& Reviews) across stages of consumer decision making for fashion e- tailing is established.

6 Implications of the Study

The study brings out the variations in the extent of impact of trust & social commerce constructs (SCCs) on stages of consumer decision making. Table 6 provides a guideline for the marketers with regard to right usage of social commerce construct & building Trust in accordance with stages of consumer decision making and strategies to build thereon. The results inferred establish significant relationship of Trust & social commerce construct (SCCs) with stages of consumer decision making. However, they are in very inceptive stages. The amplitude of usage of Social commerce construct (SCCs) exhibiting positive relationship has to be strengthened further and those exhibiting negative relationship has to be built upon. The usage of social commerce constructs (SCCs) in Pre-purchase stage can be reinforced further & build Trust thereon. Comparatively, both forums & communities and ratings & reviews have to strengthen to turn out to be constructive social commerce construct (SCCs). Also, Trust in the stages of Need Recognition and Purchase Decision has to be straightened out as positive trend.

7 Limitations and Scope of Further Study

The study was confined to four social networking sites viz., Facebook, Instagram, Google Plus and Twitter. Also, the study was limited to active social networking site users who purchased fashion products online recently (less than 6 months) based in Chennai. The study provides further scope to carry out preferences of social commerce construct(s) & trust factor across fashion product categories. It also provides further scope of research to carry out social networking site specific research.

References

Afrasiabi Rad, A., Benyoucef, M.: A model for understanding social commerce. J. Inf. Syst. Appl. Res. **4**(2), 63 (2011). http://jisar.org/2011-4/N2/JISARv4n2p63.pdf. Accessed 12 Sept 2017

Aljifri, H.A., Pons, A., Collins, D.: Global e-commerce: a framework forunderstanding and overcoming the trust barrier. Inf. Manag. Comput. Secur. **11**(3), 130–138 (2003). http://www.emeraldinsight.com/doi/abs/10.1108/09685220310480417. Accessed 13 Sept 2017

Amazon: Amazon.com Introduces 'Purchase Circles(TM),' Featuring Thousands of Bestseller Lists for Hometowns, Workplaces, Universities, and More [Press Release] (1999). http://phx.corporateir.net/phoenix.zhtml?c=176060&p=irol-newsArticle&ID=502903

Anderson, M., Sims, J., Price, J., Brusa, J.: Turning "Like" to "Buy" social media emerges as a commerce channel. Booz Company Inc. **2**(1), 102–128 (2011). http://boletines.prisadigital.com/LiketoBuy.pdf. Accessed 07 Oct 2017

Armelini, G., Villanueva, J.: The power of word of mouth: adding social media to the marketing mix (2011). https://www.researchgate.net/publication/276137132AddingSocialMediatothe MarketingMixThePowerofWordofMouth. Accessed 20 July 2018

Beach: Yahoo! Shopping Pick Lists & TheShoposphere [Blog post] (2005). http://www.itsbeach.com/blog/2005/11/yahooshopping.html. Accessed 13 Oct 2017

Curty, R.G., Zhang, P.: Social commerce: looking back and forward. In: Proceedings of the Association for Information Science and Technology, **48**(1), 1–10 (2011). http://onlinelibrary. wiley.com/doi/10.1002/meet.2011.14504801096/pdf. Accessed 11 Sept 2017

DEI Worldwide: The impact of social media on purchasing behaviour. Engaging Consumers online. https://themarketingguy.files.wordpress.com/2008/12/dei-study-engagingconsumers-online-summary.pdf. Accessed 19 July 2018

Fijalkowski, D., Zatoka, R.: An architecture of a Web recommender system using social network user profiles for e-commerce. In: 2011 Federated Conference on Computer Science and Information Systems (FedCSIS), pp. 287–290. IEEE (2011). https://pdfs.semanticscholar.org/ 1470/15d51787c8414b0541d04e0e720e83ab8a37.pdf. Accessed 07 Oct 2017

Forman, C., Ghose, A., Wiesenfeld, B.: Examining the relationship between reviewsand sales: the role of reviewer identity disclosure in electronic markets. Inf. Syst. Res. **19**(3), 291–313 (2008)

Gefen, D., Straub, D.W.: Consumer trust in B2C e-Commerce and the importance of social presence: experiments in e-Products and e-Services. Omega **32**(6), 407–424 (2004)

Haji, M.: A research framework for social commerce adoption. Inf. Manag. Comput. Secur. **21** (3), 144–154 (2013). https://www.researchgate.net/profile/NickHajli2/publication/257941706 Aresearcframeworkforsocialcommerceadoption/links/565d7e9f08aeafc2aac7bf65.pdf. Accessed 14 Sept 2017

Hajli, M.N.: A study of the impact of social media on consumers. Int. J. Mark. Res. **56**(3), 387–404 (2014). https://pdfs.semanticscholar.org/b311/27c1dbfc90fe5430d3c57dcf445343614de4.pdf. Accessed 20 July 2018

Hajli, N.: Social commerce constructs and consumer's intention to buy. Int. J. Inf. Manag. **35**(2), 183–191 (2015)

Hassanein, K., Head, M.: Manipulating perceived social presence through the web interface and its impact on attitude towards online shopping. Int. J. Hum.-Comput. Stud. **65**(8), 689–708 (2007). https://www.researchgate.net/profile/KhaledHassanein2/publication/220108449Mani pulatingperceivedsocialpresencethroughthewebinterfaceanditsimpactonattitudetowardsonline shopping/links/541ff6380cf203f155c28e5f/Manipulatingperceived-social-presence-through-the-web-interface-and-its-impact-on-attitudetowards-online-shopping.pdf. Accessed 19 July 2018

Hensel, K., Deis, M.H.: Using social media to increase advertising and improvemarketing. Entrep. Exec. **15**, 87 (2010). http://www.alliedacademies.org/articles/eevol1512010.pdf#pa ge=95. Accessed 07 Oct 2017

Hoffman, D.L., Novak, T.P., Stein, R.: The Digital Consumer, pp. 28–38. Taylor and Francis Group, Routledge (2013). https://www.routledgehandbooks.com/doi/10.4324/97802031053 06.ch3. Accessed 10 Oct 2017

Hsiao, K.L., Lin, C.-C.J., Wang, X.Y., Lu, H.P., Yu, H.: Antecedentsand consequences of trust in online product recommendations: an empirical study in social shopping. Online Inf. Rev. **34**(6), 935–953 (2010)

India replaces China as top retail destination in 2017: Study. https://retail.economictimes. indiatimes.com/news/e-commerce/etailing/india-replaces-china-as-top-retail-destination-in-2017-study/60773884. Accessed 21 Sept 2017

Lu, Y., Zhao, L., Wang, B.: From virtual community members to C2C e- commercebuyers: trust in virtual communities and its effect on consumers' purchase intention. Electron. Commer. Res. Appl. **9**(4), 346–360 (2010)

Maity, M., Dass, M.: Consumer decision-making across modern and traditionalchannels: E-commerce, m-commerce, in-store. Decis. Support Syst. **61**, 34–46 (2014)

Mutz, D.C.: Social trust and e-commerce: experimental evidence for the effects of social trust on individuals' economic behavior. Public Opin. Q. **69**(3), 393–416 (2005)

Nielsen: Nielsen global online consumer survey: trust, value and engagement in advertising. Ad week Media (2009). http://www.nielsen.com/content/dam/corporate/us/en/newswire/uploads/2009/07/prglobal-study07709.pdf. Accessed 08 Oct. 2017

Park, D.H., Lee, J., Han, I.: The effect of on-line consumer reviews on consumerpurchasing intention: the moderating role of involvement. Int. J. Electr. Commer. **11**(4), 125–148 (2007)

Pavlou, P.A.: Consumer acceptance of electronic commerce: integrating trust and risk with the technology acceptance model. Int. J. Electr. Commer. **7**(3), 101–134 (2003)

Rubel, S.: 2006 Trends to Watch Part II: Social Commerce [Blog post] (2005). https://digitalintelligencetoday.com/steve-rubels-original-2005-socialcommerce-post/

Senecal, S., Nantel, J.: The influence of online product recommendations on consumers' online choices. J. Retail. **80**(2), 159–169 (2004)

Swamynathan, G., Wilson, C., Boe, B., Almeroth, K., Zhao, B.Y.: Do social networks improve e-commerce?: a study on social marketplaces. In: Proceedings of the First Workshop on Online Social Networks, pp. 1–6. ACM (2008). http://onemvweb.com/sources/sources/socialmarketplaces.pdf. Accessed 20 Sept 2017

Wang, X., Yu, C., Wei, Y.: Social media peer communication and impacts onpurchase intentions: a consumer socialization framework. J. Interact. Mark. **26**(4), 198–208 (2012)

Yadav, M.S., De Valck, K., Hennig-Thurau, T., Hoffman, D.L., Spann, M.: Socialcommerce: a contingency framework for assessing marketing potential. J. Interact. Mark. **27**(4), 311–323 (2013)

Women's Political Participation on Social Media: The Case of Tanzania

Banita Lal[1], Shrumisha Kwayu[2], and Sajeel Ahmed[3(✉)]

[1] University of Bradford, Richmond Road, Bradford BD7 1DP, UK
[2] Nottingham Trent University, 50 Shakespeare Street,
Nothingham NG1 4FQ, UK
[3] University of Bedfordshire, University Square, Luton,
Bedfordshire LU1 3JU, UK
Sajeel.ahmed@beds.ac.uk

Abstract. This short, developmental paper outlines the rationale and design of a future study relating to women's political participation on social media. The impact of social media upon women's political participation is a topic that has gained some momentum. The affordances of social media now potentially enable women to create, access and distribute content relating to political issues and participate in an online space freely. This article highlights the role that social media can play in enabling more balanced participation and also highlights that despite the potential, there is a lack of IS literature exploring women's use of social media for political participation. This article outlines the aim of the study: to explore what types of platforms women prefer to use for political participation and the factors that influence women's participation in political issues on social media. The research focuses on the case of Tanzania and proposes steps going forward.

Keywords: Women · Political participation social media · Tanzania

1 Introduction

The aim of this paper is to explore women's use of social media, specifically in the context of political participation in Tanzania. This paper aims to provide a brief review of some of the literature pertaining to this topic before advancing onto an outline of the methodology to be adopted in the actual study. For the purpose of this short, developmental paper, data has not been collected yet and we aim to provide a sound base for the proposed empirical study.

As is widely recognised, social media technology is rapidly becoming embedded in society and has been described as 'revolutionary' considering its affordances and rapid levels of adoption by citizens. It has the potential to alter power dynamics in organisations or society (Treem and Leonardi 2012). This is because social media sites have been widely used for the purpose of information sharing and engaging audiences (Osatuyi 2013; Erickson, 2011; Lewis 2010): citizens can now be exposed to – and engage with – information that they may otherwise have not been privy to. Thus, individuals do not need to rely upon information being given to them as they can now

© IFIP International Federation for Information Processing 2020
Published by Springer Nature Switzerland AG 2020
S. K. Sharma et al. (Eds.): TDIT 2020, IFIP AICT 618, pp. 384–390, 2020.
https://doi.org/10.1007/978-3-030-64861-9_33

seek it themselves. Furthermore, the interactive capability of social media has enabled it to transform the web towards user-driven technology (Smith 2009). Web 2.0 is a central driver for this transformation as it enables content and applications to be created and published by users in a collaborative and participatory fashion. This transformation, also known as the social media phenomenon, has made the web highly interactive, enabling individuals to determine the nature, extent and context of information exchanged (Hanna et al. 2011), as well as changing the way people work in terms of how they create and disseminate information (Standing and Kiniti 2011).

It is broadly acknowledged in the literature - and in practice - that Information and Communications Technologies (ICTs) can be a catalyst for wide-ranging social and economic transformation. There is a belief in the direct causal relationship between ICTs and the development of a nation (Brown and Grant 2010). Specifically, social media is viewed as one method by which individuals can become more involved in political participation. 'Political participation' can be defined in different ways: participation in political parties and running for office, signing a petition, political consumerism or donating money, demonstrations or to directly contacting a politician (Coffe and Bolzendahl 2011). Political participation is acknowledged as being good for democracy. However, all democracies are said to be plagued by systematic inequalities in participation and one of the most persistent has been according to gender: less women participate than men (Ocran 2014). Subsequently, a large proportion of the population's interests are less represented (Coffe and Bolzendahl 2011). Thus, the question we aim to explore is: can social media lead to more balanced political participation in relation to gender?

2 Can Social Media Lead to More Balanced Political Participation?

There is agreement amongst scholars that information sharing about a particular topic can influence social behavior (Moussaid et al. 2013). It is acknowledged that social interaction and news-seeking behaviours on social media lead to diverse networks, exposure to non-conforming political opinion and ultimately reconsidering and changing one's political views. Weeks et al. (2017) add that: "individuals are becoming increasingly reliant on others in their online social networks for news recommendations and political information and that their knowledge, opinions, and behaviours are affected by the information stream and social dynamics within these sites" (p.214). The tendency for users to build and maintain friend networks subsequently creates a potential space for political persuasion to take place. According to O'Keefe (2008), 'persuasion', in its most basic form, "involves changing persons' mental states, usually as precursors to behavioural change. Of the various mental states that might be implicated in persuasion, attitude (understood as a person's general evaluation of an object) has been the center of research attention" (p. 32). Attitude change is therefore an important aspect of persuasion: various decisions are subject to changes in attitudes, including which political candidate/party to support.

It is widely stated that there are gender gaps in political participation. One of the key reasons why there are gender gaps is gender norms (Isaksson et al. 2014) and that women's access to the political fora, like their access to resources, is limited which calls into question the notion that women are full citizens (Tamale 2004). Civic education and other mechanisms are needed to encourage more female participation in all aspects of the political process (Amoateng et al. 2014). Overall, there is a very clear need for more women to engage in political participation. Given the rise of social media and the growing use of social media in political movements around the world, this can be regarded as one possible way of encouraging more female engagement in political participation. For instance, much has been written about the Arab Spring in relation to social media and its impact on women. Despite discriminatory behaviours towards women in some Arab countries, it has been stated that there had been considerable gains in terms of women's empowerment due to social media as young women used online platforms to express themselves freely on a global scale; thus, resulting in a personal, social, political and communicative revolution (Radsch and Khamis 2013). Inclusive communities are key not only for the promotion of democracy, but also for a healthy economy and for enhancing equality and equity for all citizens. Social media is a medium to bring both likeminded people and people with opposing views together on one platform. Social media platforms are free and are therefore widely accessible across socioeconomic classes (Joseph 2012). From an Information Systems (IS) perspective, there is a lack of literature focusing on the relationship between IT and women and, specifically, on the impact that social media can have when considering the issue of political participation. Walsham (2017), who has written extensively on the role and impact of technology within developing countries, suggests that the topic of women/gender and ICTs is an area for extensive future research. He asserts that such research should not be relegated to the 'gender studies' category "as if that is a special subject to be studied by women and not part of the mainstream" (p. 26). With regards to the study of social media and women's political participation, this is actually where the majority of the research is currently found – in gender studies. In IS literature, therefore, gender should be regarded as a central issue in developing an understanding of ICTs in developing nations and not, as it currently is at best, another variable.

3 Social Media and Participation

Typically, social media technologies are considered to be Computer Mediated Communication (CMC) technologies which are used to create, share and exchange user-generated content, whilst allowing people to connect with each other (Lewis 2010) and participate in a collaborative fashion (Berthon et al. 2012) without, possibly, ever meeting one another (Grover et al. 2019). In addition, social media is different to traditional Information Technology (IT) because if offers visibility to third parties (Leonardi 2014). Due to such functionalities, the use of social media has soared in a relatively short period of time: today, most of the social media platforms have more than a billion users (Piskorski 2016) and they facilitate a multitude of interactions across the globe. Social media provides individuals with easy access to a multitude of communities and discussion, allowing individuals to participate in discussions which are of interest. According to Leong et al. (2019), social media has the ability to empower individuals and provides the opportunity to give a voice to the powerless and can sometimes become part of a social movement. Further, in relation to politics, Effing et al. (2012) indicated that social media has changed the game both nationally and locally. A relevant example highlighting this is the 2016 US presidential campaign, where communication pathologies presented on various different social media platforms played a major role in how voting decisions were made (Wiggins 2017).

Participation within social media can take many diverse forms. Carpentier (2011) indicated that participation as a concept is a problematic one as it is often rooted within our political realities and is subject to our ideological struggles and power. Furthermore, Jenkins' (2006) views based on convergence culture also recognizes the importance of new media on the changing nature of participation. The changing nature of participation also brings with it many challenges; challenges related to individuals mainly being consumers of content rather than producers of content. Rebillard and Touboul (2010) highlighted the importance of changing the perspectives on content and the importance of encouraging a culture of prosumers. Currently, only a minor group of users contribute to participation in social media posts and discussions (Flew and Wilson 2010). Additionally, the digital divide among users is significant: much of the political participation on social media is from individuals who are more politically interested and the younger the users are, the more they are willing to participant. There a clear need for more political participation on social media.

4   The Context of Tanzania

Tanzania is moving towards general elections in 2020. It is expected, following the trends in other countries and restrictions on physical gathering due to COVID-19, that social media will be increasingly used in Tanzania for campaigning and organizing, for content creation and dissemination by citizens. In Tanzania, with the rising proliferation of mobile phones and access to the internet, people from various classes can potentially all use social media: 81% of the population has access to a phone and 43% have access to the internet. Electoral studies across the world show an increasing use of social media and technology in elections. Social media appears to have enhanced democratic activities: it has increased access to political leaders subsequently making them more accountable, it has facilitated organizing capacity for democratic activists and has provided more access to information and space for political participation. Social media can be regarded as a grassroots form of journalism and a way to shape democracy outside of the conventional party politics (Nardi et al. 2004). Furthermore, it is said to play a pivotal role in impacting the outcomes of national elections (Grover et al. 2019). In Tanzania, political parties have adopted social media.

Tanzania is a low-income country of 54.2 million people with women constituting 27.7 million (51.9%) and men 26.5 million (48.9%). The UNDP 2018 Human Development Report for 2018 ranks Tanzania 154 out of 189 countries in the Human Development Index while gender development index was at 0.928 in 2017. In particular, the 'feminisation of poverty' is a significant challenge in Tanzania where more than half of the female population (60%) live in extreme poverty. Tanzania is still beneath the 50/50 legal representation target of African Union constituents. Due to the lower participation of women, and the social issues that affect females in particular (UN Women, Africa, 2019), the advancement towards women's political supremacy is still a journey. Women in Tanzania are under-represented as voters, candidates and elected representatives. Nevertheless, there are examples of women who have been/are vocal on social media platforms about political issues. These women have a significant number of followers and, despite the government becoming more authoritative, remain active on social media regarding political issues. By engaging with the accounts and the content posted by such women, citizens' interest in politics is increasing and their participation, to some degree, is increasing. As there is currently a lack of empirical data to support this behavior, this study aims to *explore factors that influence women's participation in political issues on social media.*

5 Methodology – Steps Going Forward

The study aims to initially identify individual who are using social media to participate in/engage with political content on social media platforms. This study will adopt an exploratory qualitative approach using semi-structured interviews. The procedure will be as follows: female Tanzanian participants will be identified and recruited using purposive sampling, i.e. a sample of females who actively engage in political discussion on social media platforms. A snowball sampling technique will be used to recruit further participants. Interviews will be conducted via Skype. The participants will be given an information sheet which informs the participants of the research aims. Following this, participants will be asked to provide their consent. Questions for the semi-structured interviews will be based on the general themes developed from the literature and further questioning will be based on prompts during the interview: a more extensive literature review will help to identify key themes. All the interviews will be recorded and transcribed (verbatim). The data will be analysed thematically, following Braun and Clarke's (2006) approach to reflexive thematic analysis. If participants discuss specific posts on their social media account, the researchers will access the source which may be twitter, their online interactions, messages and the impact (in terms of reactions/responses) that they have on the platform. Since social media offers visibility to others beyond one's own network, this provides the potential to analyse the impact of the content that participants share on the wider online community. This will enable us to examine how the participants engage on social media platforms, e.g. sharing/commenting on content particular content, and (iii) the factors that influence their engagement with political issues online. Potential issues that may arise include the recruitment of participants. In order to manage this risk, the researchers plan to utilize their personal network in Tanzania to generate initial participants. The results of this study can contribute in a number of ways. Practically, considering the under-representation of women in politics, this study aims to explore whether the online social media space encourages more women to participate in political discussions; thus, providing women with the platforms to express themselves freely. This is particularly pertinent given that in Tanzania, women are under-represented on the political scene. Theoretically, it is suggested that social media can help to shape democracy and encourage more participation by women; however, there is little empirical data to support this, hence the motivation for this research.

References

Amoateng, A.Y., Kalule-Sabiti, I., Heaton, T.B.: Gender and behavior: gender and changing patterns of political participation in sub-Saharan Africa: evidence from five waves of the Afrobarometer surveys. Gender Behav. **12**(3), 5897–5910 (2014)

Berthon, P.R., Pitt, L.F., Plangger, K., Shapiro, D.: Marketing meets Web 2.0, social media, and creative consumers: Implications for international marketing strategy. Bus. Horiz. **55**(3), 261–271 (2012)

Boyd, D.M., Ellison, N.B.: Social network sites: definition, history, and scholarship. J. Comput.-Mediat. Commun. **13**, 210–230 (2008)

Braun, V., Clarke, V.: Using thematic analysis in psychology. Qual. Res. Psychol. **3**(2), 77–101 (2006)

Brown, A.E., Grant, G.G.: Highlighting the duality of the ICT and development research agenda. Inf. Technol. Dev. **16**(2), 96–111 (2010)

Carpentier, N.: Media and Participation A Site of Ideological-Democratic Struggle. Intellect Books, Bristol (2011)

Coffe, H., Bolzendahl, C.: Gender gaps in political participation across Sub-Saharan African nations. Soc. Indic. Res. **102**(2), 245–264 (2011). https://doi.org/10.1007/s11205-010-9676-6

Erickson, L.B.: Social media, social capital, and seniors: the impact of Facebook on bonding and bridging social capital of individuals over 65. Paper presented at the AMCIS 2011, Detroit, Michigan (2011)

Fischer, E., Reuber, A.R.: Social interaction via new social media: (How) can interactions on Twitter affect effectual thinking and behavior? J. Bus. Ventur. **26**(1), 1–18 (2011)

Gallaugher, J., Ransbotham, S.: Social media and customer dialog management at Starbucks. MIS Q. Exec. **9**(4) (2010)

Grover, P., Kar, A.K., Dwivedi, Y.K., Janssen, M.: Polarization and acculturation in US Election 2016 outcomes – Can twitter analytics predict changes in voting preferences. Technol. Forecast. Soc. Chang. **145**, 438–460 (2019)

Isaksson, A.-S., Kotsadam, A., Nerman, M.: The gender gap in African political participation: testing theories of individual and contextual determinants. J. Dev. Stud. **50**(2), 302–318 (2014)

Jenkins, H.: Convergence Culture: Where Old and New Media Collide. New York University Press, New York (2006)

Leonardi, P.M., Meyer, S.R.: Social media as social lubricant: How ambient awareness eases knowledge transfer. Am. Behav. Sci. **59**(1), 10–34 (2015)

Leonardi, P.M., Treem, J.W.: Knowledge management technology as a stage for strategic self-presentation: implications for knowledge sharing in organizations. Inf. Organ. **22**(1), 37–59 (2012)

Leonardi, P.M.: Social media, knowledge sharing, and innovation: toward a theory of communication visibility. Inf. Syst. Res. **25**(4), 796–816 (2014)

Leonardi, P.M.: Ambient awareness and knowledge acquisition: using social media to learn 'who knows what' and 'who knows whom'. MIS Q. **39**(4), 747–762 (2015)

Lewis, B.K.: Social media and strategic communication: attitudes and perceptions among college students. Public Relat. J. **4**(3), 1–23 (2010)

Moussaid, M., Kammer, J.E., Analytis, P.P., Neth, H.: Social influence and the collective dynamics of opinion formation. PLoS ONE **8**(11), e78433 (2013)

Nardi, B.A., Schiano, D.J., Gumbrecht, M., Swartz, L.: Why we blog. Commun. ACM **47**(12), 41–46 (2004)

Ocran, R.K. Women's political participation: A comparative study on Ghana and Tanzania. *Transition (Sociology)* (2014)

Osatuyi, B.: Information sharing on social media sites. Comput. Hum. Behav. **29**(6), 2622–2631 (2013)

Piskorski, M.J.: A Social Strategy: How We Profit from Social Media. Princeton University Press, Princeton (2016)

Radsch, C.C., Khamis, S.: In their own voice: technologically mediated empowerment and transformation among young Arab women. Feminist Media Stud. **13**(5), 881–890 (2013)

Stromer-Galley, J.: Presidential Campaigning in the Internet Age. Oxford University Press, Oxford (2014)

Tamale, S.: Gender trauma in Africa: enhancing women's links to resources. J. Afr. Law **48**(1), 50–61 (2004)

Walsham, G.: ICT4D research: reflections on history and future research agenda. Inf. Technol. Dev. **23**(1), 18–41 (2017)

Weeks, B.E., Ardevol-Abreu, A., de Zuniga, H.G.: Online influence? Social media use, opinion leadership, and political persuasion. J. Public Opin. Res. **29**(2), 214–239 (2017)

O'Keefe, D.J.: Persuasion. In: The International Encyclopedia of Communication, pp. 31–43 (2008)

Leong, C., Pan, S.L., Bahri, S., Fauzi, A.: Social media empowerment in social movements: power activation and power accrual in digital activism. Eur. J. Inf. Syst. **28**(2), 173–204 (2019)

Effing, R., Hillegersberg, J.V., Huibers, T.W.C.: Measuring the effects of social media participation on political party communities. In: Reddick, C.G., Aikins, S.K. (eds.) Web 2.0 Technologies and Democratic Governance. Public Administration and Information Technology, vol. 1, pp. 201–217. Springer, New York (2012). https://doi.org/10.1007/978-1-4614-1448-3_13

Wiggins, B.E.: Constructing malleable truth: memes from the 2016 U.S. Presidential Campaign. Paper presented at the ECSM 2017, Vilnius, Lithuania (2017)

Flew, T., Wilson, J.: Journalism as social networking: the Australian youdecide project and the 2007 federal election. Journalism **11**, 131–147 (2010)

Rebillard, F., Touboul, A.: Promises unfulfilled? Journalism 2.0, user participation and editorial policy on newspaper websites. Media Cult. Soc. **32**, 323–334 (2010)

What Makes a Social Media Manager? Insights from the Content Analysis of Job Advertisements in India

Ruchika Pharswan[1]([⊠]), P. Vigneswara Ilavarasan[2], and Arpan Kumar Kar[2]

[1] Bharti School of Telecommunication Technology and Management, Indian Institute of Technology, Delhi, New Delhi 110016, India
ruchi1996pharswan@gmail.com
[2] Department of Management Studies, Indian Institute of Technology, Delhi, New Delhi 110016, India
vignes@iitd.ac.in, arpan.kumar.kar@gmail.com

Abstract. With time, advent in technology and a sharp increase in internet penetration in India, there has been a dramatic change in the way we use social media from merely utilizing it for entertainment to businesses. As things currently stand in India, we cannot subvert and ignore the significant role social media is playing in developing and promoting the businesses. Consequently, the organizations either big or small trying to maintain their online presence over the various social media platforms in order to create customer base or communities across the platforms, brand awareness, customer engagement, promotions, and expanding their customer reach hence try to understand the various insights related to customer behaviour. For managing social media profile for an organization, a particular designation is purported as "Social Media Manager". In today's scenario with every company going digital, the requirement for social media managers has spiked in the last half-decade in every sector. As we go deeper, various questions arise then: what skillsets and prerequisite do a Social media manager requires? What specifically Social media manager do? To gain a better insight into current Social media manager status, our study reports on results obtained by performing content analysis over 200 Indian market job advertisements entailed "social media manager" keyword in the job title. Our finding indicates that there is an evolving requirement of Social media managers with great emphasis on Social media analytical skills followed by strategizing and promotional skills. Besides, customer management and content management also seem to be in demand. These findings may be valuable for fine-tuning Social media manager workability and also updating educational courses according to the current market trends.

Keywords: Content analysis · Social media manager job · Skillset · Job advertisements

© IFIP International Federation for Information Processing 2020
Published by Springer Nature Switzerland AG 2020
S. K. Sharma et al. (Eds.): TDIT 2020, IFIP AICT 618, pp. 391–403, 2020.
https://doi.org/10.1007/978-3-030-64861-9_34

1 Introduction

Lately, there is exponential growth in social media (SM) user base, and it has extensively emerged as a primary platform for communication, creating networks, news and information diffusion, endorsing activities and exchanging ideas and opinions for customers as well as businesses [1]. Consequently, the online social networks are currently so well established, and it has become a necessary piece of the way businesses works today. Social media was bound to change the world, and the Indian market is no exception. In India, The number of internet users had expanded throughout the years. As of 2019, there were approximately 560 million Internet users in India. As of now, India has a total population of over 1.36 billion people, and 70% of that or 230 million individuals are social media users [2]. These Statistics indicates the window of opportunities for potential businesses for taking their business to the next level. Presently, social media has become even more critical and innovative business marketing tool for the organization for greater understanding of their customer and eliminating the publicity since it has enabled active customer and company conversation. Apart from customercompany communication, it has a significant impact on the company's reputation hence also increases the brand reputation [3]. It allows an organization to engross, collaborate, promote and interact with the customers in order to gain customer confidence and improve brand loyalty. Because of this fact, social media has entirely embraced by businesses either small firms or large ones, over 92% businesses considered social media having significant importance achieving their business objectives, near about 96% businesses are already into managing their online social portfolio [4]. Thereupon, it is increasingly essential to define the skills and prerequisite and qualities a Social media manager should have for assisting the organization in achieving their business goals.

This study entails content analysis of Social media manager job advertisements across with over 200 job ads for the designation of the social media manager. Referring to the qualitative research study as these job ads can often be reviewed as significantly important information for analyzing the skillset requirement and making hiring decisions [5]. Specifically, 200 job ads are examined that are extracted from job portals like naukari.com, indeed.com, freelancer.com and Google jobs. Data were gathered of various organizations and industry types like IT firms, marketing companies, and manufacturers, clothing brands and hotels and many more. Thus we have analyzed approximately 12000 words out of which 9137 words indicate the skillset and rest were eliminated [6]. We have distributed these 9138 words or can say keywords under eight broad categories depending upon the skills required for a particular theme [7]. So basically complete analysis is compressed into eight broad skills category, and under each of them, there are several subcategory keywords whose frequency is noted. Since this study focuses on Social media manager job ads in various businesses across the Indian market, geographical localization can be a significant factor. Other considerable factors can be the nature of industry posting the job ads or online or offline job boards, size of the firm [8]. This report has been developed without taking these factors into account. The objective of the study is to identify the skills that are presently in demand in the Indian business market for a Social media manager job. Therefore, the outcomes of our study can be relevant and beneficial for business for tabulating its requirement in the advertisement as well education industry for more closely linking their offering education according to the current business requirements. To determine what current Indian market expects from a Social media manager, our report on the skillset can be of great assistance for any business, either big or small. Our study attempts to answer the following questions [9]:

- What is the desired skillset for a Social Media (SM) Manager profile in current Indian businesses?
- Which skills are more significant and in demand for employability?

Numerous studies and reviews have analyzed the job skills that are required in different domains like IT, BPO, Operations. However, there are a limited amount of studies that have explored job like social media manager [10]. Since social media picked up popularity and found to be a potential marketing platform, just a couple of years back. A short while ago, designations like social media manager, assistance social media manager have been paid attention to, and job advertisement analysis is considered to be a great way to get significant bits of insights about the skills, education and years of experience that are required in a particular sector or job [11]. So our study will try to identify the similar significant bits of insights for the newly emerging prominent jobs for social media which will add up value to industry, universities and the individual job aspirant as well. This paper is structured as follows [12]. First, we explore prior literature regarding the content analysis performed over various job advertisements and social media role in businesses. The methodology used by the study follows it. Then the findings are presented. The paper ends with and findings and ending with implications of the study.

2   Prior Literature

Numerous research has been carried out over the past several years to inspect the role and seek the skillset required for various designations like an analyst, librarian, O.R manager and many more. The objective of these studies, more or less, is to examine the skills, prerequisite and knowledge that is required by different job designations varying from analyst to mangers. Prior researches are evidence that there is always a need for keeping the industry either educational or business up-to-date according to the market demands [13]. However, there are a handful of pieces of literature that focus on analyzing the job of Social media manager. Most of this literature perform analysis over the job ads or announcements online or offline. As the social media landscape and social media applications are evolving, the content of the job description of a Social media manager's duties is also changing accordingly. Hence a critical factor of the content analysis is to analyze the currently open job profiles of social media managers and reviewing the changing roles [14]. Content analysis is one of the most often used research approaches that accentuate particular words, concepts or themes within the given data. This data can be verbal as well as written messages comprise of text which is then synthesized by content analysis to gain insights. Authors suggest the intention behind using the content analysis, is to "obtain a compressed and comprehensive description of any event or fact and the result of the content analysis would be various categories or notion expounding that event [15].

Questions like what are the skills and knowledge a business agency expects from a Social media manager? What kind of educational background and years of experience is needed? For what kind of roles organizations are hiring Social media manager? Answers to these questions can be determined by analyzing the job ads from various business agencies as the requirements they mentioned would be those they are willing to pay for [16]. The diffusion of online platforms for various job ads engendered readily available and easily accessible data pool for conducting research. Most of these researches include content analysis either by manually coding the variable and keywords or by using various available software. In our study, we focus on the designation of Social media manager only and attempt to find out the question discussed in this section previously [17]. Thus, aim to determine various skills that are expected from a Social media manager to meet current Indian market demands. Table 1 depicts the extent of prior research that has been conducted over various job ads with the same objective:

Table 1. Conclusion of prior research on job advertisement analysis.

Literatures	Job role, number of ads and duration
Benjamin, Youngseek and Jeffrey [18]	Content analysis on eScience professionals on 200 ads over 6 month time period
Laurel A Clyde [19] Youngok Choi and Edie Rasmussen [20] Karen S. Croneis and Pat Henderson [21] Gail L. Heimer [22]	Librarian, 200 ads over 3 month time period Digital librarian on 363 ads over 9 year time period. Electronic and Digital librarian on 223 ads over 10 year time period Electronic librarian on 78 ads over 10 year time period
Adrian Gardiner, Cheryl Aasheim, Paige Rutner & Susan Williams [23] Peter A. Todd, James D McKeen and R. Brent Gallupe [24] Jung Eun Hong [25] Amit Verma, Kirill M. Yurov, Peggy L. Lane & Yuliya V. Yurova [26]	Big data professionals on 1216 ads over 5 month time period Information System on 1634 ads over 20 year time period Geographic Information System on 946 ads over 7 year time period Business and data analytics on 1235 ads over 3 month time period
M S Sodhi & B-G Son [27]	Operation Research on 1056 ads over 7 year time period
Roger Bennett [28]	Transferable personal skills on 1000 ads over 1 year time period

3   Research Methodology

This section will describe how the content analysis is done over the Social media manager job advertisements. It will include the procedure from data collection to data analysis. After going through prior works of literature, specific steps have been emphasized that are common in almost every literature, but the methods various authors have used can differ. The approach that we have utilized in this study is depicted in Fig. 1.

Fig. 1.   Extracted 200 social media manager jobs advertisement

In content analysis, the primary task would be extraction and accumulation of textual data, and for that, we have explored various job advertisements sites like indeed.com, naukari.com, freelancer, Google jobs and MonsterIndia.com. We have utilized a web scrapping method for extracting the jobs and 200 jobs profiles that include Social media manager as designation are finally extracted [29]. The data we got includes the links from where they are extracted, skills and prerequisite, experience required, salary, locations and industry type depicted in Fig. 1. Our primary motive of extraction is to perform content analysis over these jobs ads and identify the skills that are required to be a Social media manager. Job ads were searched between the period of 3 months and phrases that are used for searching the relevant jobs are like "social media manager", "social media assistance manager", "social media associate manager", "social media lead manager". All these jobs advertisements are limited to various locations of India as we have only considered the Indian market [30]. We have broad categories the list of skills into eight crucial skills that are: designing, customer management, analytics, communication skills, strategy, promotion, content management, management and organization [31]. Content analysis is then performed over these extracted jobs ads, and then the data set is categorized into various subcategory skills keywords under the broad skills categories [32]. In result, we will get a structured form of data having broad and subcategories with the counts depicting the frequency of occurrence of that particular skill in the content. So based on prior studies, the data is classified into broader skills categories manually and further decomposed into keywords that are used within the particular category with the frequency of its occurrence [33].

4 Result and Interpretation

Two hundred jobs advertisements meeting our criteria were extracted from various job portals for 4 months from 18 January to 18 March 2020. These job ads were specific to various locations across India. We examine the skill set that is required for a Social media manager following the current Indian business needs. The Eight most mentioned skills selected and represented in Fig. 2, with the value they hold concerning the required skills [34]. Next, aggregate data is then decomposed into subcategories of skills and includes the keywords with the word count of the frequency of its occurrence depicted in Table 2.

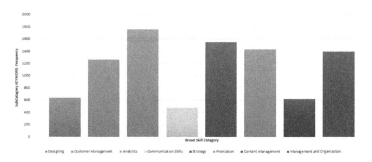

Fig. 2. Eight broad skills categories for social media manager job position

These skills, as mentioned above, are required for a Social media manager to stand in the current Indian market scenario. In conclusion, a Social media manager has to multitask efficiently. We have also observed that Social media manager designation required relevant work experience. One must have skillset as mentioned above and experience in well versed with various social media platforms in India, search engine optimizations of multiple platforms to make the content to reach more number of users in the social media space effectively [35, 36]. From our analysis, we have concluded for a medium, or big organization in Indian market mapped a minimum of 2 years' experience for a social media manager job depicted in Fig. 3. It represents the range of experiences mentioned in the job description of 200 advertisements. It can be seen that very few organization referred to a fresher or 0–1 year of experience. These organization can either be small firms or startups. Most of them prefer 2–3 years of minimum experience, and these can either be medium size or developed firms [37].

We have observed, companies preferring 4–5 years of experience are lesser than those who have referenced 2–3 years of experience. So it is more likely to say as the maturity of organization increases they seek for more experience personals. There is only one firm who mentioned 7 years of experience; it can be quite mature, and big firm [38, 39].

Table 2. Decomposition of broader skill categories into Subcategories

Broader skill category	Subcategory & keywords	Keywords frequency
Designing	Designing	189
	Creativity	21
	Innovative	96
	Page	53
	Video	19
	Logo	87
	Media management	138
Customer management	Customer engagement	158
	CRM	181
	Client support	177
	Consumer insights	132
	Reputation	76
	Social platform	189
	Customer satisfaction	171
Analytics	Analytical skills	169
	Tools	182
	SEO	187
	SMO	158
	Forecasting	91
	Optimization	184
	Reports	179
	Positioning	35
	Research	137
	Google analysis	142
	WebMaster	159
	Social research	135
Communication skills	Communication skills	126
	Writing skills	160
	Interpersonal skills	139
	MS-OFFICE	48
Strategy	Planning	162
	Engagement	178
	Management	181
	Start-ups	122
	Product	117
	Insights	96
	Initiative	67
	Awareness	78
	Networking	53
	Media strategies	157

(*continued*)

Table 2. (*continued*)

Broader skill category	Subcategory & keywords	Keywords frequency
	Channel knowledge	186
Promotion	Online marketing	178
	Commerce awareness	98
	Campaign management	164
	Branding	182
	Social content calendar	187
	Brand engagement	153
	Channel knowledge	174
	Advertising	167
Content management	Content writing	173
	Copy writing	168
	Creative content	151
	Trend savvy	96
	Passionate	33
Management and organization	Team work	130
	Time management	157
	Campaign management	164
	Community management	123
	Multitasking	154
	Decision making	160
	Experience	187

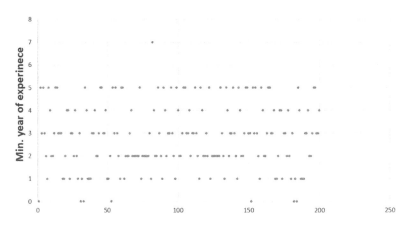

Fig. 3. Range of experiences mentioned in advertisements

5 Implications

No doubt, changes in any job requirements are directly or indirectly reflects on its job advertisements. As being recognized in our analysis of the social media manager's roles and responsibilities, we observe that there can be numerous profile or role a social media manager can play in line with the need of the organizations. There are three-fold implications of our study. First is job aspirants. This report can be beneficial for a job aspirant who is seeking a social media manager or related job as this report has provided a comprehensive view of the current market scenario. Job aspirants can have useful insights and prepare accordingly. Second is educational implication where our study can be helpful to understand better the skills and roles required for social media manager. So various institutions can get better insights into market trends and needs, and they can design, align or modify their courses to comply with the market demands. The third is a business recruitment implication where the outcomes can be valuable for recruiting managers who are looking for a contender for the Social media manager with a suitable skill set. In parallel, by providing a short and well-structured set of required skills, this study has made Social media manager job description more clear as well saved various assets and time for figuring prerequisites and requirements. Every job combines multiple tasks and skills under one umbrella. Similarly, a social media manager need to perform various task like designing, developing strategies, customer management and many more. In our report, we have presented various skillsets and perquisite in line with the current market demand and expectation. We have categorized the skills into eight sections and have shown a clear picture of what are the requirements for each category. We have also spotlighted the experience required for a social media manager to join an organization. Our study can be quite valuable for the social media manager or related job aspirants. They can find the skillset and prepare accordingly to meet the current market expectations and needs. If this study can be modified and performed periodically, it can be an excellent source for the fresher's especially and other job aspirants. Content analysis of current job ads provides a bigger picture of current trends in the marketplace and expectations of recruiters.

In this fast-growing world, everything industry is undergoing rapid changes, and the educational industry is no exception. Universities and training institutes both government and private sector are trying their level best to provide the best educational courses to incorporate with market and hiring. Trends and expectation are likely to change with time and to provide the best, and universities need to adopt these changes by reconfiguring and modifying their courses accordingly. Our study can be one of the useful sources that can provide insights on the latest trends, requirements, experience and skills set to social media manager or related courses. We think that the changing requirements of social media manager professionals can be bright prospects and educational industry expected to produce graduates with more focused skills and excellent knowledge by re-structuring and aligning their programs according to the current market requirements. Nowadays, to find information regarding any job is just one click away, there is numerous job portal where thousands of job have been searched in a single day. One of the aims of an organization is to keep developing and undergo changes according to current market demands and expectation to become a fierce competitor. Many types of research have been performed for analyzing the current market status, trends, expectation and demands, which assists organizations to enhance their job portals accordingly. In light of this, our study also facilitates the convenience of searching the current skill set, roles and experience required in the domain of social media manager position. This study can be valuable for the organization to tailor and modify their job descriptions to hire the best talent and respond to the demands effectively.

6 Conclusion

The key objective to conduct this study is to determine what the desired skillset for a Social Media (SM) Manager profile in current Indian businesses are? And which skills are more significant and in demand for employability of Social media manager position in current Indian businesses? This study has a present comprehensive view of the Social media manager designation concerning with its skills, roles, worker competencies, tasks by analyzing the job advertisements. With most and each business expecting to build up their online presence to participate in today's hyper-connected consumer buying process in India, it is in the organizations' interests benefits to employ the best talent and keep tabs on their continuous development. After all, organizations' online reputation and future deals will rely upon it. The interpretation of the outcomes of our study is exhibited by analyzing the content of the latest job description for Social media manager designation over the period from 15 January to 15 March 2020 in India. To rank the skills mentioned in those job ads, we applied content analysis and find that Social media analytics and strategy development are the two most highly valued skills followed by promotional techniques. Our study has examined eight skills and ranked them depending upon how frequently and commonly they are mentioned in job ads.

There are some potential limitations to our investigation. Recognizing that jobs related to social media are fast evolving its requirements, goals and work expectations simultaneously are also quickly developing. We have to recall that our examination is for a particular period, results and findings may differ if the same analysis would be performed in a different timestamp. In our analysis we have manually categorized the various skills based on prior studies however in the near future we can use machine learning for classifying the job advertisement using supervised learning and can likewise form clusters of various skills under the broad categories that can reduce the redundancy of skills under different categories which is the limitation of manual categorization for the time being. Specifically, an expansion in Social media related jobs is most likely. This study will contribute to designing and modifying, giving knowledge into the more extensive view of the educational courses that are related to jobs includes social media aspects. And also this is valuable for industry or business recruitments to align and tailor their job ads description according to the current Indian business trends. Furthermore, this study can be extended by categorizing the skills sets based on various location of the Indian market, type of industry posting the job ads, size of organizations, type of industry and age of organization.

References

1. Humphreys, L., Wilken, R.: Social media, small businesses, and the control of information. Inf. Commun. Soc. **18**(3), 295–309 (2015). https://doi.org/10.1080/1369118X.2014.989249
2. Smith, K.N.: Chancellor's Honors Program (2011)
3. Hudson, S., Roth, M.S., Madden, T.J., Hudson, R.: The effects of social media on emotions, brand relationship quality, and word of mouth: an empirical study of music festival attendees. Tour. Manag. **47**, 68–76 (2015). https://doi.org/10.1016/j.tourman.2014.09.001
4. P. P. Control P. M. Performance and D. Contexts: Project Portfolio Control and Portfolio. Proj. Manag. J., **39**(October) 28–42 (2008). https://doi.org/10.1002/pmj
5. Melancon, J.P., Dalakas, V.: Consumer social voice in the age of social media: segmentation profiles and relationship marketing strategies. Bus. Horiz. **61**(1), 157–167 (2018). https://doi.org/10.1016/j.bushor.2017.09.015
6. Cortez, M.A., Tu, N.T., Van Anh, D., Ng, B.Z., Vegafria, E.: Fast fashion quadrangle: an analysis. Acad. Mark. Stud. J. **18**(1), 1–18 (2014)
7. Lemish, P., Caringer, K.: The civil society organization media manager as critical communicator. Nord. Rev. **33**(Special-Issue) 189–203 (2013). https://doi.org/10.2478/nor-2013-0035
8. Jones, N., Borgman, R., Ulusoy, E.: Impact of social media on small businesses. J. Small Bus. Enterp. Dev. **22**(4), 611–632 (2015). https://doi.org/10.1108/JSBED-09-2013-0133
9. Chikandiwa, S.T., Contogiannis, E., Jembere, E.: The adoption of social media marketing in South African banks. Eur. Bus. Rev. **25**(4), 365–381 (2013). https://doi.org/10.1108/EBR-02-2013-0013
10. Dawson, N., Rizoiu, M.A., Johnston, B., Williams, M.A.: Adaptively selecting occupations to detect skill shortages from online job ads. In: Proceedings of 2019 IEEE International Conference on Big Data, Big Data 2019, pp. 1637–1643 (2019). https://doi.org/10.1109/bigdata47090.2019.9005967
11. Ward, A., Baruah, B., Gbadebo, A.: How universities and employers specify competence in generic skills findings from an analysis of job advertisements. In: 2017 16th International Conference Information Technology Based High. Educ. Training, ITHET 2017 (2017). https://doi.org/10.1109/ithet.2017.8067829
12. Azahar, D., Manaf, N.A., Dharmarajan, N., Adnan, W.A.W.: Malaysia IT career opportunity analysis based on classified advertisement in the new straits times (2000–2008). In: Proceedings of 2010 International Conference on Information Retrieval & Knowledge Management CAMP 2010, pp. 348–352 (2010). https://doi.org/10.1109/infrkm.2010.5466889
13. Khaouja, I., Rahhal, I., Elouali, M., Mezzour, G., Kassou, I., Carley, K.M.: Analyzing the needs of the offshore sector in Morocco by mining job ads. In: IEEE Global Engineering Education Conference EDUCON, April 2018, pp. 1380–1388 (2018). https://doi.org/10.1109/educon.2018.8363390
14. Zeng, D., Chen, H., Lusch, R., Li, S.H.: Social media analytics and intelligence. IEEE Intell. Syst. **25**(6), 13–16 (2010). https://doi.org/10.1109/MIS.2010.151
15. Baird, C.H., Parasnis, G.: From social media to social customer relationship management. Strateg. Leadersh. **39**(5), 30–37 (2011). https://doi.org/10.1108/10878571111161507
16. Bergström, T., Bäckman, L.: Marketing and PR in social media : how the utilization of instagram builds and maintains customer relationships. Media Commun. 56 (2013)
17. Hays, S., Page, S.J., Buhalis, D.: Social media as a destination marketing tool: its use by national tourism organizations. Curr. Issues Tour. **16**(3), 211–239 (2013). https://doi.org/10.1080/13683500.2012.662215

18. Addom, B.K., Kim, Y., Stanton, J.M.: eScience professional positions in the job market. In: ACM International Conference Proceeding Series, pp. 630–631 (2011). https://doi.org/10.1145/1940761.1940846

19. Clyde, L.A.: An instructional role for librarians: an overview and content analysis of job advertisements. Aust. Acad. Res. Libr. **33**(3), 150–167 (2002). https://doi.org/10.1080/00048623.2002.10755195

20. Choi, Y., Rasmussen, E.: What qualifications and skills are important for digital librarian positions in academic libraries? A job advertisement analysis. J. Acad. Librariansh. **35**(5), 457–467 (2009). https://doi.org/10.1016/j.acalib.2009.06.003

21. Croneis, K.S., Henderson, P.: Electronic and digital librarian positions: a content analysis of announcements from 1990 through 2000. J. Acad. Librariansh. **28**(4), 232–237 (2002). https://doi.org/10.1016/S0099-1333(02)00287-2

22. Heimer, G.L.: Defining electronic librarianship: a content analysis of job advertisements. Public Serv. Q. **1**(1), 27–43 (2002). https://doi.org/10.1300/J295v01n01_05

23. Gardiner, A., Aasheim, C., Rutner, P., Williams, S.: Skill requirements in big data: a content analysis of job advertisements. J. Comput. Inf. Syst. **58**(4), 374–384 (2018). https://doi.org/10.1080/08874417.2017.1289354

24. Todd, P.A., Mckeen, J.D., Gallupe, R.B.: Job skills : a content analysis of is job, vol. 19, no. 1, pp. 1–27 (2016)

25. Hong, J.E.: Identifying skill requirements for GIS positions: a content analysis of job advertisements. J. Geog. **115**(4), 147–158 (2016). https://doi.org/10.1080/00221341.2015.1085588

26. Verma, A., Yurov, K.M., Lane, P.L., Yurova, Y.V.: An investigation of skill requirements for business and data analytics positions: a content analysis of job advertisements. J. Educ. Bus. **94**(4), 243–250 (2019). https://doi.org/10.1080/08832323.2018.1520685

27. Sodhi, M.S., Son, B.-G.: Content analysis of O.R. job advertisements to infer required skills. SSRN Electron. J. (2012). https://doi.org/10.2139/ssrn.1640814

28. Bennett, R.: Employers' demands for personal transferable skills in graduates: a content analysis of 1000 job advertisements and an associated empirical study. J. Vocat. Educ. Train. **54**(4), 457–476 (2002). https://doi.org/10.1080/13636820200200209

29. Kang, Y., Ritzhaupt, A.D.: A job announcement analysis of educational technology professional positions. J. Educ. Technol. Syst. **43**(3), 231–256 (2015). https://doi.org/10.1177/0047239515570572

30. Cho, J., Park, D.J., Ordonez, Z.: Communication-oriented person-organization fit as a key factor of job-seeking behaviors: Millennials' social media use and attitudes toward organizational social media policies. Cyberpsychol. Behav. Soc. Netw. **16**(11), 794–799 (2013). https://doi.org/10.1089/cyber.2012.0528

31. Rahhal, I., Makdoun, I., Mezzour, G., Khaouja, I., Carley, K., Kassou, I.: Analyzing cybersecurity job market needs in Morocco by mining job ads. In: IEEE Global Engineering Education Conference (EDUCON), April 2019, pp. 535–543 (2019). https://doi.org/10.1109/educon.2019.8725033

32. Elo, S., Kyngäs, H.: The qualitative content analysis process. J. Adv. Nurs. **62**(1), 107–115 (2008). https://doi.org/10.1111/j.1365-2648.2007.04569.x

33. Daneva, M., Wang, C., Hoener, P.: What the job market wants from requirements engineers? An empirical analysis of online job ads from the Netherlands. In: International Symposium on Empirical Software Engineering and Measurement (ESEM), 2017 November, pp. 448–453 (2017). https://doi.org/10.1109/esem.2017.60

34. Sodhi, M.S., Son, B.G.: Content analysis of or job advertisements to infer required skills. J. Oper. Res. Soc. **61**(9), 1315–1327 (2010). https://doi.org/10.1057/jors.2009.80

35. Abuhashesh, M.Y.: Integration of social media in businesses. Int. J. Bus. Soc. Sci. **5**(8), 202–204 (2014)
36. Mishra, P., Rajnish, R., Kumar, P.N.: Sentiment analysis of Twitter data: case study on digital India. In: 2016 International Conference on Information Technology InCITe 2016 - Next Generation IT Summit Theme - Internet Things Connect your Worlds, pp. 148–153 (2017). https://doi.org/10.1109/incite.2016.7857607
37. Wright, D.K., Hinson, M.D.: How blogs and social media are changing public relations and the way it is practiced. Public Relat. J. **2**(2), 1–21 (2008)
38. Ramanathan, U., Subramanian, N., Parrott, G.: Role of social media in retail network operations and marketing to enhance customer satisfaction. Int. J. Oper. Prod. Manag. **37**(1), 105–123 (2017). https://doi.org/10.1108/IJOPM-03-2015-0153
39. Thackeray, R., Neiger, B.L., Hanson, C.L., Mckenzie, J.F.: Enhancing promotional strategies within social marketing programs: use of web 2.0 social media. Health Promot. Pract. **9**(4), 338–343 (2008). https://doi.org/10.1177/1524839908325335

A Meta-analysis of Social Commerce Adoption Research

Prianka Sarker[1]([⊠]), Nripendra P. Rana[2], Laurie Hughe[1],
and Yogesh K. Dwivedi[1]

[1] Emerging Markets Research Centre (EMaRC), School of Management,
Swansea University Bay Campus, Swansea SA1 8EN, UK
{937449,d.l.hughes,y.k.dwivedi}@swansea.ac.uk
[2] School of Management, University of Bradford, Richmond Road,
Bradford BD7 1DP, UK
nrananp@gmail.com

Abstract. Social commerce is a subset of e-commerce that utilises social media to facilitate interaction between sellers and consumers. Over the last number of years, the subject of social commerce has attracted significant attention from many researchers as they attempt to understand the factors affecting its adoption by consumers. A review of results from existing studies suggests inconsistent results for many relationships. Hence, this research has conducted a meta-analysis of 65 studies and synthesized the findings from existing studies in order to estimate the cumulative correlation coefficient (β) and significance (p). The investigation found that behavioural intention, trust, perceived usefulness, and social support are frequently examined dependent variables, that are strongly influenced by a number of independent variables. The findings in this study suggests that perceived usefulness, hedonic value, social commerce constructs, subjective norms, informational and emotional support are important for encouraging social commerce adoption. This research highlights various antecedents that have been theoretically examined in different social commerce studies that explore the effect size through meta-analysis.

Keywords: Adoption · Behavioural intention · Meta-analysis · Social commerce · Trust

1 Introduction

Social commerce is considered a form of electronic commerce (e-commerce) that involves social networking applications and facilitates transactional interaction between buyers and sellers [1, 2]. The progress of e-commerce technology merging with social networking sites is one of the key reasons for the development of social commerce [3]. The interactions through online communities has developed the concept of social commerce [4]. There are some key features that have separated social commerce from e-commerce, namely digital profile, search ad privacy, relational tie and network transparency [5]. Consumers are able to interact and support each other throughout the

© IFIP International Federation for Information Processing 2020
Published by Springer Nature Switzerland AG 2020
S. K. Sharma et al. (Eds.): TDIT 2020, IFIP AICT 618, pp. 404–418, 2020.
https://doi.org/10.1007/978-3-030-64861-9_35

purchasing cycle by sharing information and personal experiences of the product and service [6].

In the last decade, social commerce has become a popular topic of research amongst marketing scholars. Different areas of social commerce such as social commerce, feature development, buying behaviour, and adoption have been examined. This has resulted in the application of different theories, theoretical models, and constructs for understanding factors driving or inhibiting the adoption of social commerce. 48.89% of the studies on social commerce have been conducted to examine user behavior [7]. Existing studies have frequently utilised and tested theories/models such as Technology Acceptance Model (TAM), Theory of Planned Behaviour (TPB), and Stimulus-Organism-Response (S-O-R) have introduced different antecedents of behavioural intention for examining consumer involvement and adoption of social commerce. Previously, few attempts have been made to review social commerce research [7–9]. However, the focus of such articles is somewhat limited to reviewing theories and models, research themes, limitations and future research directions [7, 8, 10, 11]. Recently, Sarker et al. [28] assessed the overall weight of various relationships (using weight analysis techniques) examined within social commerce adoption studies. In order to provide a more rigorous analysis for generating cumulative effect size for each pair of relationships, this submission is conducting a meta-analysis-based synthesis of results reported within the existing literature on social commerce adoption and usage. To achieve this overall aim, this research needs to accomplish the following objectives: Firstly, this paper has identified the relevant articles on social commerce and tested various constructs that generated the results related to social commerce adoption. Secondly, this paper has conducted a meta-analysis of existing results of social commerce studies and summarised the coefficient values, total samples and the number of studies.

There are several reasons to choose a meta-analysis approach for this research. For example, meta-analysis is one of the most systemic and reliable methods to conduct a literature review [12]. Meta-analysis offers a better approximation of the relationship amongst two predictors [12] and helps to resolve inconsistencies in research as well as identifying potential moderating or mediating variables [12]. Meta-analysis allows the summarizing of large volumes of literature content into a single data set able to generate relevant conclusions. Also, meta-analysis considers significant and non-significant results to generate overall outcomes [13]. The remaining sections of this paper are structured as follows. Section 2 reports the research method to search and identify relevant articles. Section 3 presents the results from meta-analysis. Section 4 develops the discussion and the study is finally concluded in Sect. 5.

2   Research Method

To find the relevant articles, This study searched through the Scopus database with the following set of keywords: "Social commerce" OR "S-Commerce" OR "F–Commerce" AND title ABS Key "Adoption" OR "Acceptance" OR "Usage" OR "Use Behaviour" OR "Intention" OR "Purchase". Scopus contains a large number of interdisciplinary data related to science and technology. However, there are different databases available such as Web of Science, which search relevant studies. Moreover, Web of Science updates the data weekly while Scopus have daily update frequency, which generates more recent publications. Therefore, this study found updated journal publications though Scopus that are relevant to social commerce. The Scopus search returned 211 articles published between 2006 to 2020, which included 170 journal articles, 41 outputs from various conferences, and newspaper articles. In order to maintain the rigour and avoid duplication, this analysis included only journal articles. A total of 170 journal articles included 44 non-empirical studies and 126 empirical studies. Due to lack of quantitative values required, non-empirical studies (conference papers, literature reviews and editorial papers) have been excluded from this analysis.

This study further screened all 126 selected articles and searched for availability of path coefficient value (β) of different relationships and sample size that were required to conduct the meta-analysis. Through this screening this study found that only 65 studies met the criteria so only these studies were retained for further analysis. To generate the results of all values into a single structure, This study began searching the relationships amongst independent variables and dependent variables of analysed constructs. These values were inputted in the Comprehensive Meta-Analysis (V3) software that was utilised to undertake this analysis.

3   Meta-analysis Result

The study individually gathered coefficient values related to 489 relationships. Amongst the relationships of independent variable (IV) and dependent variable (DV), This study have considered the inclusion of the relationships that had been examined two or more times across 65 studies and eliminated relationships that were only found in just one study, as it is not appropriate to conduct meta-analysis for such relationships. After filtering all the constructs, this study have found the following as most commonly examined dependent variables: behavioural intention, trust, perceived usefulness, social support intention, attitude, relationship quality, urge to buy impulsively, use behaviour, social sharing intention. The outcome of meta-analysis highlighted the key independent and dependent variables, number of studies, total sample size, Average β value, 95% Low β value, 95% High β value, z-Value and p-value (effect size). This paper highlights the cumulative β values along with p-values related to different relationships.

3.1   Behavioural Intention (BI) as a Dependent Variable

Behavioural intention or intention to purchase was examined across several studies of social commerce. Table 1 presents the meta-analysis results related to BI as a DV with various independent variables where This study found two or more studies reporting sample size and the coefficient values for a specific set of relationships. For example, trust is one of the vital independent variables of BI that was tested in 17 studies where one of the studies found negative effects of trust on BI, whilst 16 studies had reported a positive relationship. Within social commerce studies, trust has been used in multidimensional ways. For example, trust towards the community [5, 14] and trust towards members [5, 15]. However, this study consider trust as a single variable that influences BI within social commerce. Additionally, perceived usefulness and perceived ease of use appeared in eight studies. Social commerce constructs such as rating and reviews; forums and communities; recommendation and referral are a critical characteristics of social commerce studies. The social commerce constructs within BI found positive relationships in six studies and negative relationship in one study. Influence of social support, risk and subjective norms on BI have been examined in five social commerce studies. Important antecedents of BI namely attitude, information support, social presence, emotional support, enjoyment, facilitating condition, hedonic value, social influence effort expectancy, performance expectancy, flow, relationship quality and website quality have also been examined in two or more studies (see Table 1).

A total of 65 social commerce studies employed 20 independent variables that influence BI in two and more studies. Table 1 presents the summary of the meta-analysis of 20 average path coefficients between various IVs on BI. The combination of different statistical results constructed more authentic outcomes through meta-analysis. The meta-analysis results of different IVs on BI revealed that attitude is the strongest independent variable that influences BI with average β value = 0.492 (p = 0.002). Additionally, website quality, flow and trust were found to have a strong impact on BI with average β value = 0.434, 0.342 and 0.315 respectively, all with significant p values (p < 0.001). Moreover, subjective norm (β = 0.260), perceived usefulness (β = 0.256), hedonic value (β = 0.232), relationship quality (β = 0.230), social commerce constructs (β = 0.226), performance expectancy (β = 0.224) and social support (β = 0.209) are found to exert a strong and significant influence on BI. Meta-analysis results show an overall non-significant influence of risk, informational support, social influence, perceived ease of use, effort expectancy and social presence on BI where the p values found greater than 0.05.

Table 1. Behavioural intention as a dependent variable

IV	DV	#	Sample size	Average β	95% low β	95% high β	Z-value	p effect size
Attitude	BI	4	1093	0.492	0.188	0.710	3.025	0.002
Web quality	BI	2	401	0.434	0.350	0.510	9.227	0.000
Flow	BI	2	401	0.342	0.252	0.426	7.082	0.000
Trust	BI	17	5,918	0.315	0.217	0.407	6.055	0.000
Subjective norm	BI	5	1771	0.260	0.030	0.464	2.210	0.027
Perceived usefulness	BI	8	2203	0.256	0.159	0.348	5.077	0.000
Hedonic value	BI	2	587	0.232	0.154	0.307	5.690	0.000
Relationship quality	BI	2	452	0.230	0.140	0.316	4.945	0.000
Social commerce constructs	BI	7	2195	0.226	0.101	0.345	3.489	0.000
Performance expectancy	BI	2	541	0.224	0.023	0.407	2.181	0.029
Social support	BI	5	1487	0.209	0.094	0.317	3.546	0.000

(continued)

Table 1. (*continued*)

IV	DV	#	Sample size	Average β	95% low β	95% high β	Z-value	p effect size
Social influence	BI	2	541	0.206	−0.028	0.418	1.729	0.084
Enjoyment	BI	2	394	0.185	0.087	0.279	3.678	0.000
Emotional support	BI	3	563	0.172	0.090	0.251	4.087	0.000
Social presence	BI	3	601	0.158	−0.248	0.517	0.758	0.448
Perceived ease of use	BI	8	2220	0.146	−0.156	0.424	0.947	0.344
Risk	BI	5	1830	−0.136	−0.274	0.007	−1.859	0.063
Facilitating conditions	BI	2	541	0.129	0.044	0.211	2.990	0.003
Effort expectancy	BI	2	541	0.100	−0.116	0.307	0.905	0.366
Information l support	BI	3	528	0.079	−0.007	0.164	1.811	0.070

[Legend: SCC-Social commerce constructs; IV-Individual variable; DV-Dependent variable; BI-Behavioural intention; β = Beta value; # - Number of studies]

3.2   Trust as a Dependent Variable

Within social commerce studies, trust (as an independent variable) has been examined in 17 individual studies. Also, its role as a dependent variable has been examined in five studies. The results from meta-analysis reveal that informational support has a significant influence on trust in all eight studies [e.g. 3, 5]. Further, emotional support and trust were also found to have positive and significant relationship in all seven studies [e.g. 16, 17]. Social commerce constructs (Rating and reviews; Forums and communities; Recommendation and referral) had a significant and positive influence on trust in all three studies [3, 18]. Finally, effects of familiarity and perceived usefulness on trust have been examined by four studies each [19, 20]. The meta-analysis of social commerce revealed that familiarity as an independent predictor has a strongest influence on trust and emotional support was found to have the least but also the most significant influence (see Table 2).

Table 2. Trust as a dependent variable

IV	DV	#	Sample size	Average (β)	95% low (β)	95% high (β)	Z-value	p (effect size)
Familiarity	Trust	2	734	0.527	0.087	0.795	2.302	0.021
Perceived usefulness	Trust	2	625	0.362	0.146	0.546	3.199	0.001
Social commerce constructs	Trust	3	1130	0.348	0.234	0.452	5.719	0.000
Informational support	Trust	8	2854	0.308	0.214	0.396	6.200	0.000
Emotional support	Trust	7	2669	0.201	0.080	0.315	3.245	0.001

3.3 Perceived Usefulness as a Dependent Variable

Perceived usefulness (PU) is one of the significant variables of the TAM model [21]. The analysis found that perceived ease of use significantly influences perceived usefulness in five studies. The significant relationship between perceived ease of use and perceived usefulness is also shown by the original TAM model. Amongst five studies, one study [6] has found the negative effects of perceived ease of use on perceived usefulness. Subjective norm has also been found to influence perceived usefulness in five studies and all relationships are found to have significant and positive values. On the contrary, risk negatively influences perceived usefulness in three studies. However, in the social commerce studies, risk has been used in different forms such as social, psychological, financial, time and privacy that influence perceived risk and subsequently impacts perceived usefulness [22].

The outcome of the meta-analysis highlights that subjective norms and risk are stronger predictors than perceived ease of use. The relationship with subjective norm is significant whereas the effects of perceived ease of use and risk on PU were found to be non-significant (see Table 3).

Table 3. Perceived usefulness as a dependent variable

IV	DV	#	Total sample size	Average (β)	95% low (β)	95% high (β)	Z-value	p (effect size)
Subjective norm	PU	5	1661	0.118	0.066	0.169	4.447	0.000
Perceived ease of use	PU	6	1991	0.093	−0.065	0.247	1.155	0.248
Risk	PU	3	1374	−0.128	−0.475	0.253	−0.651	0.515

3.4 Social Support (Informational and Emotional Support) as a Dependent Variable

Social support is another relevant outcome variable utilised in social commerce studies. Several social commerce studies have identified that social support has two significant dimensions, namely informational support and emotional support that influences user to adopt social commerce [23, 24]. Table 4 shows that social commerce constructs (i.e. rating and reviews; forums and communities; recommendation and referral) had significant positive influence on informational support in four studies ($\beta = 0.683$) and emotional support in three studies (β = 0.576). The influence of reputation and enjoyment on informational support have also been examined by two studies each. The results presented in Table 4 suggest a positive and significant influence of reputation on informational support (β = 0.163) while enjoyment had an overall non-significant (p = 0.310) influence.

Table 4. Social support (informational and emotional support) as a dependent variable

IV	DV	#	Total sample size	Average (β)	95% low (β)	95% high (β)	Z-value	p (effect size)
SCC	Informational Support	4	1414	0.683	0.444	0.831	4.583	0.000
SCC	Emotional Support	3	1200	0.576	0.297	0.764	3.674	0.000
Enjoyment	Informational support	2	2090	0.181	−0.169	0.491	1.015	0.310
Reputation	Informational support	2	2090	0.163	0.041	0.279	2.616	0.009

3.5 Use Behaviour, Urge to Buy Impulsively, Social Sharing Intention, Relationship Quality, Attitude and WOM Intention as Dependent Variables

The meta-analysis also revealed other dependent variables namely use behaviour, urge to buy impulsively, social sharing intention, relationship quality, attitude and WOM intention (see Table 5) each with only one antecedent associated with them. For example, three studies found significant influence (β = 0.480) of purchase intention on use behavior [25–27]). Urge to buy impulsively as a DV is significantly influenced by impulsiveness with the average β value of 0.441. Social sharing intention as a DV is significantly influenced by trust (β = 0.286). The relationship amongst social support and relationship quality also found to be significant. Similarly, the influence of perceived usefulness on attitude found to be significant. Finally, informational support had a nonsignificant effect on WOM intention in social commerce studies (see Table 5).

Table 5. Use behaviour, urge to buy impulsively, social sharing intention, relationship quality, attitude and WOM intention as dependent variables

IV	DV	#	Sampl e size	Average β	95% low β	95% high β	Z-value	Effect size (p)
Purchase Intention	Use Behaviour	3	870	0.480	0.144	0.717	2.713	0.007
Impulsiveness	Urge to buy impulsively	3	996	0.441	0.107	0.686	2.538	0.011
Trust	Social sharing intention	3	952	0.286	0.162	0.401	4.424	0.000
Social support	relationship quality	2	452	0.274	0.057	0.466	2.463	0.014
Perceived usefulness	Attitude	2	598	0.208	0.013	0.388	2.091	0.037
Informational support	WOM intention	2	293	0.003	−0.196	0.202	0.031	0.976

4 Discussion

The main purpose of this paper was to integrate and synthesis results from social commerce studies by employing the meta-analysis technique. The study integrated the findings associated with relationships that have been examined in at least two or more times in social commerce research. The results of the review of existing constructs revealed that BI, trust, perceived usefulness, social support, use behaviour, urge to buy impulsively, social sharing intention, relationship quality, attitude and WOM-intention, are the major dependent variables examined in social commerce studies. Various antecedents of the dependent variables related to social commerce literature have been identified for estimating their cumulative effect and size. TAM, TRA, and SOR models and social support theory are frequently used in social commerce research [11]. The variables related to these models (such as perceived ease of use, perceived usefulness, subjective norms, performance expectancy and BI) have been tested in existing studies with significant results. However, this study shows that variables such as trust, risk, information and emotional support relationship quality have been integrated with the theories [as identified by 11] as additional (external) constructs demonstrating theoretical advances. The importance and role of integrating external variables (such as trust and risk) have previously been discussed in existing social commerce studies [22–29].

The meta-analysis of social commerce revealed important independent variables that have been shown to strongly influence the dependents variables. This study has highlighted the significant and non-significant relationships of each pair of constructs. The results highlight that website quality, flow, trust, hedonic value, perceived usefulness, relationship quality, emotional support, enjoyment, social support, social commerce constructs, attitude, facilitating condition subjective norm and performance expectancy have significant influence on Behavioural intention. These variables have directly and indirectly influenced consumers to adopt social commerce. For example, trust and social support on social commerce platform and community motivate consumer to adopt this technology. After the evaluation of online shopping technology, different factors were originated to create a comfortable, easy to use platform for consumers. The analysis also revealed that attitude, website quality and trust have a strong positive influence on consumers' behavioural intention where risk inhibits consumers intention to adopt social commerce platforms.

Additionally, informational support, social commerce construct, emotional support, perceived usefulness and familiarity, significantly affect trust in social commerce research. Impulsiveness towards the urge to buy impulsively, trust towards social sharing intention, social support towards relationship quality, subjective norm towards perceived usefulness, reputation and social commerce constructs towards informational support and perceived usefulness towards attitude found to be significant. However, the meta-analysis results also identified several non-significant relationships. For example, risk, informational support, social influence, perceived ease of use, effort expectancy and social presence are found to have non-significant relationships with BI. Additionally, enjoyment with information, risk with perceived usefulness and informational support with WOM intention also found to have non-significant relationships. The meta-analysis also revealed that social commerce constructs (forums and communities, rating and reviews, referrals and recommendations) are the variables that strongly influence both informational support and emotional support. Additionally, emotional and informational support was found to have a strong influence on BI. Attitude, trust, website quality, perceived usefulness and subjective norms are utilised by more than one study as independent variables that strongly influenced consumer BI. A number of prior studies from the adoption and diffusion of various technologies [e.g. 30–41] and consumer behaviour [e.g. 42] have already shown relationships of attitude [e.g. 39, 42–51], trust [e.g. 30, 52–60], perceived usefulness or performance expectancy [e.g. 13, 48, 53–55, 62–67] and website quality [e.g. 33–41, 47–51, 63] trends suggest that such factors are relevant and important across various studies focusing on differing technologies. Although the hypotheses amongst purchase intention towards use behaviour appeared in three studies, the average coefficient (β) value of 0.480 indicates a strong impact of BI on use behaviour. The results also shown a negative influence of risk construct on both BI and perceived usefulness.

This study is contributing by highlighting different antecedents that have been used in social commerce studies. This study has found that researchers repeatedly examined similar kind of constructs and models in the various context of social commerce. However, this research identifies different antecedents using meta-analysis and summarises the effect of those antecedents in the examination of social commerce. Thus, the antecedents such as cost, price value, hedonic motivation have been used in limited studies. Moreover, some of the antecedents such as anxiety, innovativeness, grievance redressal have not been used in the social commerce context. Hence, those antecedents found to be significant in various technology acceptance studies [57, 58]. Therefore, future researchers should examine theories and variables in a different context of social commerce [47, 67].

5 Conclusion

The meta-analysis accomplished the aim by underlining important variables and significant relationship. 65 empirical journal articles have been identified to collect relevant data (e.g. sample size and path coefficient value) for conducting meta-analysis. Through analysis of results reported in existing studies identified a total of ten dependent variables namely BI, trust, perceived usefulness, social support, use behaviour, urge to buy impulsively, social sharing intention, relationship quality, attitude and WOM-intention. These dependent variables were reported in two or more studies related to social commerce. The meta-analysis has resulted in the identification of variables such as attitude, web site quality, flow that although examined by fewer studies but they have a strong impact on BI. However, variables such as trust, perceived ease of use, perceived usefulness and social support were more frequently used to determine their influence on BI. Meta-analysis also shows that only three studies have examined effects of BI on actual behaviour. Given that understanding actual behaviour is critical for promoting consumer adoption of social commerce. Unlike any other research, this study also has some limitation. Firstly, this study did not consider conference papers due to lack of space and limited empirical research. However, conference papers may consider in future studies. Several studies of social commerce used behavioural intention as a proxy of actual behaviour. This is important that behavioural intention to use social commerce is not equal to actual behaviour. Therefore, future research should focus on identifying and examining the influence of relevant antecedents (including BI) on adoption and usage of social commerce.

References

1. Baabdullah, A., Alalwan, A., Rana, N.P.: Examining the impact of social commerce dimensions on customers' value co-creation: the mediating effect of social trust. J. Consum. Behav. 18(6), 431–446 (2019)
2. Liang, T.P., Ho, Y.T., Li, Y.W., Turban, E.: What drives social commerce: the role of social support and relationship quality. Int. J. Electron. Commer. 16(2), 69–90 (2011)
3. Ullah, L., Kousar, R., Saba, I., Khan, A.B.: Use of social commerce to develop intentions to buy with mediating role of social support. J. Bus. Soc. Rev. Emerg. Econ. 5(1), 63–78 (2019)
4. Zeng, F., Huang, L., Dou, W.: Social factors in user perceptions and responses to advertising in online social networking communities. J. Interact. Advert. 10(1), 1–13 (2009)
5. Chen, J., Shen, X.L.: Consumers' decisions in social commerce context: an empirical investigation. Decis. Support Syst. 79(1), 55–64 (2015)
6. Featherman, M.S., Hajli, N.: Self-service technologies and e-services risks in social commerce era. J. Bus. Ethics 139(2), 251–269 (2016)
7. Han, H., Xu, H., Chen, H.: Social commerce: a systematic review and data synthesis. Electron. Commer. Res. Appl. 30(1), 38–50 (2018)
8. Altınışık, S., Yıldırım, S.Ö.: Consumers 'adoption of social commerce: a systematic literature review. Mugla J. Sci. Technol. 3(2), 131–137
9. Zhou, L., Zhang, P., Zimmermann, H.D.: Social commerce research: an integrated view. Electron. Commer. Res. Appl. 12(2), 61–68 (2013)

10. Busalim, A.H.: Understanding social commerce: a systematic literature review and directions for further research. Int. J. Inf. Manage. **36**(6), 1075–1088 (2016)
11. Sarker, P., Kizgin, H., Rana, N.P., Dwivedi, Y.K.: Review of theoretical models and limitations of social commerce adoption literature. In: Pappas, I.O., Mikalef, P., Dwivedi, Y.K., Jaccheri, L., Krogstie, J., Mäntymäki, M. (eds.) I3E 2019. LNCS, vol. 11701, pp. 3–12. Springer, Cham (2019). https://doi.org/10.1007/978-3-030-29374-1_1
12. Stone, D.L., Rosopa, P.J.: The advantages and limitations of using meta-analysis in human resource management research. Hum. Resour. Manage. Rev. **27**(1), 1–7 (2017)
13. Tamilmani, K., Rana, N.P., Dwivedi, Y., Sahu, G.P., Roderick, S.: Exploring the role of' price value for understanding consumer adoption of technology: a review and meta-analysis of UTAUT2 based empirical studies. In: Pacific Asia Conference on Information Systems, p. 64 (2018)
14. Hidayatulloh, A.: The role of social commerce constructs, social support, and trust in community on social commerce activities. Muhammadiyah Int. J. Econ. Bus. **1**(2), 74–83 (2018)
15. Fu, S., Xu, Y., Yan, Q.: Enhancing the parasocial interaction relationship between consumers through similarity effects in the context of social commerce: evidence from social commerce platforms in China. J. Strategic Mark. **27**(2), 100–118 (2017)
16. Li, C.Y.: How social commerce constructs influence customers' social shopping intention? An empirical study of a social commerce website. Technol. Forecast. Soc. Chang. **45**(2), 342–345 (2017)
17. Zhao, J.D., Huang, J.S., Su, S.: The effects of trust on consumers' continuous purchase intentions in C2C social commerce: a trust transfer perspective. J. Retail. Consum. Serv. **50**(2), 42–49 (2019)
18. Hajli, N.: Social commerce constructs and consumer's intention to buy. Int. J. Inf. Manage. **35**(2), 183–191 (2015)
19. Cheng, X., Gu, Y., Shen, J.: An integrated view of particularized trust in social commerce: an empirical investigation. Int. J. Inf. Manage. **45**(3), 1–12 (2019)
20. Gibreel, O., AlOtaibi, D.A., Altmann, J.: Social commerce development in emerging markets. Electron. Commer. Res. Appl. **27**(2), 152–162 (2018)
21. Davis, F.D.: Perceived usefulness, perceived ease of use, and user acceptance of information technology. MIS Q. 319–340 (1989)
22. Biucky, S.T., Harandi, S.R.: The effects of perceived risk on social commerce adoption based on TAM model. Int. J. Electron. Commer. Stud. **8**(2), 173–196 (2017)
23. Tajvidi, M., Richard, M. O., Wang, Y., Hajli, N.: Brand co-creation through social commerce information sharing: the role of social media. J. Bus. Res. (2018)
24. Hajli, M.N.: The role of social support on relationship quality and social commerce. Technol. Forecast. Soc. Chang. **87**, 17–27 (2014)
25. Akman, I., Mishra, A.: Factors influencing consumer intention in social commerce adoption. Inf. Technol. People **30**(2), 356–370 (2017)
26. Al-Adwan, A.S.: Revealing the influential factors driving social commerce adoption. Interdisc. J. Inf. Knowl. Manage. **14**, 295–324 (2019)
27. Sheikh, Z., Islam, T., Rana, S., Hameed, Z., Saeed, U.: Acceptance of social commerce framework in Saudi Arabia. Telemat. Inf. **34**(8), 1693–1708 (2017)
28. Sarker, P., Hughe, L., Dwivedi, Y.K., Rana, N.P.: Social commerce adoption predictors: a review and weight analysis. In: Hattingh, M., Matthee, M., Smuts, H., Pappas, I., Dwivedi, Y.K., Mäntymäki, M. (eds.) I3E 2020. LNCS, vol. 12066, pp. 176–191. Springer, Cham (2020). https://doi.org/10.1007/978-3-030-44999-5_15

29. Sarker, P., Hughes, D.L., Dwivedi, Yogesh K.: Extension of META-UTAUT for examining consumer adoption of social commerce: towards a conceptual model. In: Martínez-López, F.J., D'Alessandro, S. (eds.) Advances in Digital Marketing and eCommerce. SPBE, pp. 122–129. Springer, Cham (2020). https://doi.org/10.1007/978-3-030-47595-6_16

30. Baabdullah, A., Alalwan, A., Rana, N.P., Kizgin, H., Patil, P.: Consumer use of mobile banking (M-Banking) in Saudi Arabia: towards an integrated model. Int. J. Inf. Manage. **44**, 38–52 (2019)

31. Baabdullah, A.M., Alalwan, A.A., Rana, N.P., Patil, P., Dwivedi, Y.K.: An integrated model for m-banking adoption in Saudi Arabia. Int. J. Bank Mark. **37**(2), 452–478 (2019)

32. Baabdullah, A., Rana, N.P., Alalwan, A., Islam, R., Patil, P., Dwivedi, Y.K.: Consumer adoption of self-service technologies in the context of Jordanian banking industry: examining moderating role of channel types. Inf. Syst. Manage. **36**(4), 286–305 (2019)

33. Rana, N.P., Williams, M.D., Dwivedi, Y.K., Williams, J.: Reflection on e-government research: toward a taxonomy of theories and theoretical constructs. Int. J. Electron. Govern. Res. **7**(4), 64–88 (2011)

34. Rana, N.P., Williams, M.D., Dwivedi, Y.K., Williams, J.: Theories and theoretical models for examining the adoption of e-government services. e-Serv. J.: J. Electron. Serv. Public Priv. Sect. **8**(2), 26–56 (2012)

35. Rana, N.P., Dwivedi, Y.K., Williams, M.D.: Evaluating alternative theoretical models for examining citizen centric adoption of e-government. Transf. Govern.: People Process Policy **7**(1), 27–49 (2013)

36. Rana, N.P., Williams, M.D., Dwivedi, Y.K.: Analysing challenges, barriers and CSFs of e-government adoption research. Transf. Govern.: People Process Policy **7**(2), 177–198 (2013)

37. Rana, N.P., Dwivedi, Y.K., Williams, M.D.: e-government adoption research: an analysis of the employee's perspective. Int. J. Bus. Inf. Syst. **14**(4), 414–428 (2013)

38. Rana, N.P., Dwivedi, Y.K., Williams, M.D.: Evaluating the validity of is success models for e-government research: an empirical test and integrated model. Int. J. Electron. Govern. Res. **9**(3), 1–22 (2013)

39. Rana, N.P., Dwivedi, Y.K., Williams, M.D.: A review and weight analysis of the predictors and linkages in electronic government adoption research. Int. J. Indian Cult. Bus. Manage. **8**(2), 139–158 (2014)

40. Rana, N.P., Dwivedi, Y.K., Williams, M.D., Lal, B.: Examining the success of the online public grievance redressal systems: an extension of the is success model. Inf. Syst. Manage. **32**(1), 39–59 (2015)

41. Rana, N.P., Dwivedi, Y.K., Williams, M.D.: A meta-analysis application for synthesizing findings of existing research on citizen adoption of e-government. Inf. Syst. Front. **17**(3), 547–563 (2015)

42. Ismagilova, E., Dwivedi, Y.K., Rana, N.P.: Weight analysis of the factors affecting eWOM providing behavior. I3E2020, South Africa. J. Bank Mark. **37**(2), 452–478 (2020)

43. Dwivedi, Y.K., Khan, N., Papazafeiropoulou, A.: Consumer adoption and usage of broadband in Bangladesh. Electron. Govern. Int. J. **4**(3), 299–313 (2007)

44. Dwivedi, Y.K., Rana, N.P., Jeyaraj, A., Clement, M., Williams, M.D.: Re-examining the unified theory of acceptance and use of technology (UTAUT): towards a revised theoretical model. Inf. Syst. Front. **21**(3), 719–734 (2017). https://doi.org/10.1007/s10796-017-9774-y

45. Dwivedi, Y.K., Rana, N.P., Jeyaraj, A., Clement, M., Williams, M.D.: Re-examining the unified theory of acceptance and use of technology (UTAUT): towards a revised theoretical model. Inf. Syst. Front. **21**(3), 719–734 (2019)

46. Dwivedi, Y.K., Rana, N.P., Tamilmani, K., Raman, R.: A meta-analysis based modified unified theory of acceptance and use of technology (meta- UTAUT): a review of emerging literature. Curr. Opin. Psychol. **36**, 13–18 (2020)
47. Rana, N.P., Dwivedi, Y.K., Williams, M.D., Weerakkody, V.: Adoption of online public grievance redressal system in india: toward developing a unified view. Comput. Hum. Behav. **59**, 265–282 (2016)
48. Rana, N.P., Dwivedi, Y.K., Lal, B., Williams, M.D., Clement, M.: Citizens' adoption of an electronic government system: toward a unified view. Inf. Syst. Front. **19**(3), 549–568 (2017)
49. Rana, N.P., Dwivedi, Y.K., Williams, M.D., Lal, B.: Examining the success of the online public grievance redressal systems: an extension of the IS success model. Inf. Syst. Manag. **32**(1), 39–59 (2015)
50. Rana, N.P., Dwivedi, Y.K., Williams, M.D., Piercy, N.C.: An extended DeLone and McLean's information system (IS) model for examining success of online public grievance redressal system in indian context. Int. J. Indian Cult. Bus. Manage. **10**(3), 267–290 (2015)
51. Rana, N.P., Dwivedi, Y.K., Williams, M.D., Weerakkody, V.: Investigating success of an e-government initiative: validation of an integrated IS success model. Inf. Syst. Front. **17** (1), 127–142 (2015)
52. Alalwan, A., Baabdullah, A., Rana, N.P., Tamilmani, K., Dwivedi, Y.K.: Examining adoption of mobile internet in Saudi Arabia: extending TAM with perceived enjoyment, innovativeness and trust. Technol. Soc. **55**, 100–110 (2018)
53. Alalwan, A.A., Dwivedi, Y.K., Rana, N.P., Algharabat, R.S.: Examining factors influencing Jordanian customers' intentions and adoption of internet banking: extending UTAUT2 with risk. J. Retail. Consum. Serv. **40**, 125–138 (2018)
54. Alalwan, A.A., Dwivedi, Y.K., Rana, N.P., Simintiras, A.C.: Jordanian consumers' adoption of telebanking: influence of perceived usefulness, trust and self-efficacy. Int. J. Bank Mark. **34**(5), 690–709 (2016)
55. Alalwan, A.A., Dwivedi, Y.K., Rana, N.P., Williams, M.D.: Consumer adoption of mobile banking in Jordan: examining the role of usefulness, ease of use, perceived risk and self-efficacy. J. Enterp. Inf. Manage. **29**(1), 118–139 (2016)
56. Alalwan, A.A., Dwivedi, Y.K., Rana, N.P., Lal, B., Williams, M.D.: Consumer adoption of internet banking in Jordan: examining the role of hedonic motivation, habit, self-efficacy and trust. J. Financ. Serv. Manage. **20**(2), 145–157 (2015)
57. Patil, P., Tamilmani, K., Rana, N.P., Raghavan, V.: Understanding consumer adoption of mobile payment in India: extending Meta-UTAUT model with personal innovativeness, anxiety, trust, and grievance redressal. Int. J. Inf. Manage. **54**, 102144 (2020)
58. Slade, E.L., Dwivedi, Y.K., Piercy, N.C., Williams, M.D.: Modeling consumers' adoption intentions of remote mobile payments in the United Kingdom: extending UTAUT with innovativeness, risk, and trust. Psychol. Mark. **32**(8), 860–873 (2015)
59. Slade, E.L., Williams, M.D., Dwivedi, Y.K.: Devising a research model to examine adoption of mobile payments: an extension of UTAUT2. Mark. Rev. **14**(3), 310–335 (2014)
60. Slade, E.L., Williams, M.D., Dwivedi, Y.K.: Extending UTAUT2 To explore consumer adoption of mobile payments. UK Acad. Inf. Syst. **36** (2013)
61. Alryalat, M., Rana, N.P., Dwivedi, Y.K.: Citizen's adoption of an e-government system: validating the extended theory of reasoned action (TRA). Int. J. Electron. Govern. Res. **11** (4), 1–23 (2015)
62. Kapoor, K.K., Dwivedi, Y.K., Williams, M.D.: Innovation adoption attributes: a review and synthesis of research findings. Eur. J. Innov. Manage. **17**(3), 327 (2014)
63. Rana, N.P., Dwivedi, Y.K.: Using clickers in a large business class: examining use behavior and satisfaction. J. Mark. Educ. **38**(1), 47–64 (2016)

64. Tamilmani, K., Rana, N.P., Dwivedi, Y.K.: Consumer acceptance and use of information technology: a meta-analytic evaluation of UTAUT2. Inf. Syst. Front. (2020). https://doi.org/10.1007/s10796-020-10007-6

65. Tamilmani, K., Rana, N.P., Prakasam, N., Dwivedi, Y.K.: The battle of brain vs. heart: a literature review and meta-analysis of "hedonic motivation" use in UTAUT2. Int. J. Inf. Manage. **46**, 222–235 (2019)

66. Williams, M.D., Rana, N.P., Dwivedi, Y.K.: The unified theory of acceptance and use of technology: a systematic review. J. Enterp. Inf. Manage. **28**(3), 443–488 (2015)

67. Saumya, S., Singh, J.P., Baabdullah, A.M., Rana, N.P., Dwivedi, Y.K.: Ranking online consumer reviews. Electron. Commer. Res. Appl. **29**, 78–89 (2018)

68. Al-Adwan, A.S., Kokash, H.: The driving forces of Facebook social commerce. J. Theor. Appl. Electron. Commer. Res. **14**(2), 15–32 (2019)

69. Bhat, I.H., Singh, S.: Intention to participate on social commerce platform: a study on e-commerce websites. Acad. Mark. Stud. J. **22**(4), 1–10 (2018)

70. Cheng, X., Gu, Yu., Mou, J.: Interpersonal relationship building in social commerce communities: considering both swift guanxi and relationship commitment. Electron. Commer. Res. **20**(1), 53–80 (2019). https://doi.org/10.1007/s10660-019-09375-2

71. Cho, E., Son, J.: The effect of social connectedness on consumer adoption of social commerce in apparel shopping. Fashion Text. **6**(1), 1–17 (2019). https://doi.org/10.1186/s40691-019-0171-7

72. Chung, N., Song, H.G., Lee, H.: Consumers' impulsive buying behaviour of restaurant products in social commerce. Int. J. Contemp. Hospit. Manage. **29**(2), 709–731 (2017)

73. Dalvi-Esfahani, M., Shahbazi, H., Nilashi, M., Samad, S., Mardani, A., Streimikiene, D.: Factors influencing beliefs formation towards the adoption of social commerce in SME travel agencies. Econ. Sociol. **11**(3), 207–225 (2018)

74. Escobar-Rodríguez, T., Bonsón-Fernández, R.: Analysing online purchase intention in Spain: fashion e-commerce. IseB **15**(3), 599–622 (2016). https://doi.org/10.1007/s10257-016-0319-6

75. Gan, C., Wang, W.: The influence of perceived value on purchase intention in social commerce context. Internet Res. **27**(4), 772–785 (2017)

76. Gatautis, R., Medziausiene, A.: Factors affecting social commerce acceptance in Lithuania. Proc.-Soc. Behav. Sci. **110**(2014), 1235–1242 (2014)

77. Hajli, M.: An integrated model for e-commerce adoption at the customer level with the impact of social commerce. Int. J. Inf. Sci. Manage. **22**(1), 77–97 (2012)

78. Hajli, M.: A research framework for social commerce adoption. Inf. Manage. Comput. Security. **21**(3), 144–154 (2013)

79. Hajli, N., Sims, J.: Social commerce: the transfer of power from sellers to buyers. Technol. Forecast. Soc. Chang. **94**(1), 350–358 (2015)

80. Hajli, N., Shanmugam, M., Powell, P., Love, P.E.: A study on the continuance participation in on-line communities with social commerce perspective. Technol. Forecast. Soc. Chang. **96**(2), 232–241 (2015)

81. Hajli, N., Sims, J., Zadeh, A.H., Richard, M.O.: A social commerce investigation of the role of trust in a social networking site on purchase intentions. J. Bus. Res. **71**(1), 133–141 (2017)

82. Hajli, N., Wang, Y., Tajvidi, M., Hajli, M.S.: People, technologies, and organizations interactions in a social commerce era. IEEE Trans. Eng. Manage. **64**(4), 594–604 (2017)

83. Hassan, M., Iqbal, Z., Khanum, B.: The role of trust and social presence in social commerce purchase intention. Pak. J. Commer. Soc. Sci. **12**(1), 111–135 (2018)

84. Hettiarachchi, H.A.H., Wickramasinghe, C.N., Ranathunga, S.: The influence of social commerce on consumer decisions. Int. Technol. Manage. Rev. **7**(1), 47–58 (2018)

85. Hung, S.Y., Yu, A.P.I., Chiu, Y.C.: Investigating the factors influencing small online vendors' intention to continue engaging in social commerce. J. Organ. Comput. Electron. Commer. **28**(1), 9–30 (2018)

86. Kim, D.: Under what conditions will social commerce business models survive? Electron. Commer. Res. Appl. **12**(2), 69–77 (2013)

87. Lee, H., Choi, J.: Why do people visit social commerce sites but do not buy? The role of the scarcity heuristic as a momentary characteristic. KSII Trans. Internet Inf. Syst. **8**(7), 125–127 (2014)

88. Lin, J., Li, L., Yan, Y., Turel, O.: Understanding Chinese consumer engagement in social commerce: the roles of social support and swift guanxi. Internet Res. **28**(1), 2–22 (2018)

89. Lin, J., Yan, Y., Chen, S.: Understanding the impact of social commerce website technical features on repurchase intention: a Chinese guanxi perspective. J. Electron. Commer. Res. **18**(3), 225–226 (2017)

90. Lin, X., Li, Y., Wang, X.: Social commerce research: definition, research themes and the trends. Int. J. Inf. Manage. **37**(3), 190–201 (2017)

91. Liu, H., Chu, H., Huang, Q., Chen, X.: Enhancing the flow experience of consumers in China through interpersonal interaction in social commerce. Computers in Human Behaviour **58**(4), 306–314 (2016)

92. Liu, L., Cheung, C.M., Lee, M.K.: An empirical investigation of information sharing behaviour on social commerce sites. Int. J. Inf. Manage. **36**(5), 686–699 (2016)

93. Lu, B., Fan, W., Zhou, M.: Social presence, trust, and social commerce purchase intention: an empirical research. Comput. Hum. Behav. **56**(2), 225–237 (2016)

94. Lu, B., Zeng, Q., Fan, W.: Examining macro-sources of institution-based trust in social commerce marketplaces: an empirical study. Electron. Commer. Res. Appl. **20**(2), 116–131 (2016)

95. Mikalef, P., Giannakos, M.N., Pappas, I.O.: Designing social commerce platforms based on consumers' intentions. Behav. Inf. Technol. **36**(12), 1308–1327 (2017)

96. Molinillo, S., Liébana-Cabanillas, F., Anaya-Sánchez, R.: A social commerce intention model for traditional e-commerce sites. J. Theor. Appl. Electron. Commer. Res. **13**(2), 80–93 (2018)

97. Omwansa, T., Lule, I., Waema, T.: The Influence of trust and risk in behavioural intention to adopt mobile financial services among the poor. Int. Arab J. e-Technol. **4**(1), 8–15 (2015)

98. Ooi, K.B., Hew, J.J., Lin, B.: Unfolding the privacy paradox among mobile social commerce users: a multi-mediation approach. Behav. Inf. Technol. **37**(6), 575–595 (2018)

99. Samarasinghe, S., Silva, K.: Social commerce acceptance: integrated model with collaboration theories and technology acceptance model. Am. Sci. Res. J. Eng. Technol. Sci. (ASRJETS) **62**(1), 39–53 (2019)

100. Sharma, S., Crossler, R.E.: Disclosing too much? Situational factors affecting information disclosure in social commerce environment. Electron. Commer. Res. Appl. **13**(5), 305–319 (2014)

101. Sheikh, Z., Yezheng, L., Islam, T., Hameed, Z., Khan, I.U.: Impact of social commerce constructs and social support on social commerce intentions. Inf. Technol. People **32**(1), 68–93 (2019)

102. Shi, S., Chow, W.S.: Trust development and transfer in social commerce: prior experience as moderator. Ind. Manage. Data Syst. **115**(7), 1182–1203 (2015)

103. Shin, D.H.: User experience in social commerce: in friends we trust. Behav. Inf. Technol. **32**(1), 52–67 (2013)

104. Yang, J., Sia, C.L., Liu, L., Chen, H.: Sellers versus buyers: differences in user information sharing on social commerce sites. Inf. Technol. People **29**(2), 444–470 (2016)

Antecedences and Consequences of Customer Engagement in Online Brand Communities: Multi-national Perspective

Ali A. Alalwan[1], Abdullah M. Baabdullah[2(✉)], Yogesh K. Dwivedi[3],
Nripendra P. Rana[4], and Rand H. Al-Dmour[5]

[1] Amman College of Banking and Finance, Al-Balqa' Applied University,
Amman, Jordan
alwan.a.a.ali@gmail.com
[2] Department of Management Information Systems, Faculty of Economics
and Administration, King Abdulaziz University, Jeddah, Kingdom of Saudi Arabia
baabdullah@kau.edu.sa
[3] Emerging Markets Research Centre (EMaRC), School of Management,
Swansea University, Bay Campus, Swansea, Wales, UK
y.k.dwivedi@swansea.ac.uk
[4] Faculty of Business, Law and Social Sciences, University of Bradford,
Richmond Road, Bradford BD7 1DP, UK
n.p.rana@bradford.ac.uk
[5] School of Business, Department of Management Information Systems,
The University of Jordan, Amman, Jordan
rand.aldmour@ju.edu.jo

Abstract. This paper aims to look at the importance of online brand communities on the customer experience in terms of customer brand loyalty and information capital. Thus, the proposed conceptual model was based on the information exchange theory. The current model was also expanded by proposing for main factors (social trust, interactivity, hedonic motivation, and perceived involvement) as key drivers of customers' engagement with online brand communities. Two main consequences of customers' engagement were also proposed in the current study model, namely: information capital and brand loyalty. The empirical part of the current study will be conducted within two main countries: one developed (United Kingdom) and one developing (Jordan). This study will adopt online questionnaire survey to collect the required data. Structural equation modelling will be adopted as a statistical technique to test the current model and validate the main research hypotheses. This study will expand the theoretical understanding regarding very important phenomenon (online brand communities), which requests more exploration and examination. This is in light of the fact that, this phenomenon has not yet studied and examined over the Middle-East countries.

Keywords: Online brand communities · Brand loyalty · Information capital

© IFIP International Federation for Information Processing 2020
Published by Springer Nature Switzerland AG 2020
S. K. Sharma et al. (Eds.): TDIT 2020, IFIP AICT 618, pp. 419–427, 2020.
https://doi.org/10.1007/978-3-030-64861-9_36

1 Introduction

Increasingly, organisations worldwide have been looking forward to benefiting from social networking and Web 2.0 revaluation to enhance and sustain their associations with their targeted customers [3]. Indeed, social networking revolutions allow customers to construct and shape their virtual communities especially these related to commercial brands. Online brand communities are one of the most common examples about these communities in which customers could interact with many customers who have a common interest toward the targeted brands. Conceptually, online brand community could be defined as "a network of relationships between consumers and the brand, product, fellow consumers, and the marketer" [28].

One of the main positive outcomes of such communities is increasing the level of customer engagement and involvement with their brands and service providers as discussed by [38]. In this regard, it is important mentioning that online communities that are constructed by customers based on their emotional attachment with the brands and away from the organisations are more crucial and effective in predicting the customers' experience [29]. Online brand communities also help organisations to efficiently capture the required information from credible direct source (users and community members) [1, 13]. This is returned to the fact that such user generated information is a kind of main outcomes among interactions and conversions that take place in the community among the customers themselves [22]. Another reason supporting the importance of such digital communities and the quality of information generated is related to the fact that customers are fully free to join these platforms and provide their own contribution without any restrictions.

Members of online brand communities have increasingly effective role to be a value co-creator [12]. For example, customers are more able to provide their own assessment regarding new products, services, and ideas introduced by organisations, and therefore, helping organisations to have more comprehensive and accurate feedback and process of development adopted by brands [20]. By doing so, customers are more likely to feel their importance on the organisation side, and this will surely enrich their experience in terms of spreading word-of-mouth, satisfaction and loyalty [2, 11, 19]. Over the prior literature, several studies (i.e. [5]) that have supported the significance of online communities for marketing practices especially in terms of customer engagement, brand co-creation, and value co-creation.

However, there is still a necessity to capture an accurate and comprehensive view regarding the main antecedents of customers' intention and engaging with online brand communities. Further, there is an important question regarding how could the antecedents and consequences of online brand communities engagement behave differently from culture to another?. Accordingly, this study aims firstly to see and validate the main drivers that motivate customers to join online brand communities. As well as, this study intends to see and discover the main consequences of customer joining online brand communities on the customer experience and organisation marketing performance.

2   Literature Review

By looking carefully at the main studies that have tested the related issues of online communities, it has been noticed that this area needs further research and examination as well as most studies examining online brand community largely consider the positive side of such virtual communities and how could enhance the customers brand engagement and perception [12]. However, there is a need to discover the dark side of these communities from both customers and organisational perspectives. In this respect, [12] argued online brand communities as double edged sword as it could evoke negative outcomes for both perspectives i.e. customers and organisation. For example, customers, who are not pleased about their experience with the organisation, could see such virtual community as a place to spread their negative experiences and revenge against the company [12]. Another example of the dark side of online communities could be pertained customer misbehaviour and dysfunctional customer behaviour as named by [9], which could be resulted from the customer's feeling of dissatisfied or injustice. According to [9], such kind of misbehaviour taking place over online communities may have a disastrous impact on the organisation and its reputation and brand image, which in turn, will negatively impact the staff satisfaction and organisational sales and financial performance [6, 27].

According to [16], online communities could come in several forms (i.e. social media platforms, forums, blogs, webinar, and wikis). This, in turn, allows those customers, who are active members over these communities, to share their own experience, attitude, knowledge about the targeted brands with large number of members [4, 15, 32, 35]. To put it differently, online brand communities provides people with new mechanisms to have more synchronous and simple communication, and accordingly, facilitating the process of information exchange [11]. Therefore, such social interactions and collaboration among community will surely sustain the community membership feeling among the users as stated by [12].

As discussed in the introduction part, marketing researchers have always been attempting to figure out the most influential drivers of customers' engagement in online brand communities. As well as, closer look at the prior literature in this regard leads to a need to propose a conceptual model that could be able to address these drivers and provide a comprehensive picture from the customers' perceptive. The impact of culture also requires further examination especially when the vast majority of prior studies have tested online brands communities over the highly developed countries where only a few studies have been explored in the developing countries' context [8]. Furthermore, consequences of customers' interacting over such communities call for more research in this area. Accordingly, proposing a conceptual model capturing the most important antecedences and consequences of customer engagement in online brand communities from multinational perspectives.

3 Proposed Conceptual Model

By reviewing the key literature pertaining to online brand communities, it has been noticed that there are several drivers that could motivate customers to engage with online communities. According to [25], a number of factors (i.e. information, selfdiscovery, social integration, social enhancement, and entertainment) were suggested to have a direct impact on the customers' engagement with such communities. Recent study proposed by [30] adopted social capital model, and proposed a number of dimensions (i.e. sharing language, shared vision, norm of reciprocity, and social trust) as key derivers of both aspects related to customers' engagement with online brand communities: individual network ties and individual sense of belonging. In their qualitative study, [5] categorised these drivers over three groups: brand related (i.e. brand identification, brand satisfaction, and brand trust); social aspects (i.e. OBC identification); and community value (i.e. information, networking, entertainment, and monetary incentives). Moreover, the impact of online community kind, which could be created either by customers or marketers has been tested by [21]. Aspects related to OBC such as membership identification, influence and relatedness, involvement, and shared emotional connection were considered by [18]. [39] have validated the role of interactivity and trust as key determinants of the individuals' experience and flow of online travel communities.

In the light of the above reviews, it could be noticed that drivers of customers' engagement with online brand communities could be allocated within social drivers, personal drivers, informational and social media drivers. Therefore, proposing a strong model will request considering the most important of these drivers. Some of these factors such as hedonic motivation (entertainment) [5], social trust [30], perceived involvement [18], and interactivity [39]. All of these factors will be considered as a key driver of customers' engagement with online brand communities. The nature of online brand community if it is user's generated or marketing generated will be tested as a moderator factor could shape the relationships between the main independent and dependent factors. In this regard, it is important to indicate that three main dimensions (cognitive, emotional, and behavioural) that will be considered to measure the customer' engagement were highly suggested by [5].

For the purpose of the current study which also attempts to look at the main consequences of customers' engagement with online brand communities, information exchange theory proposed by [34] and [36] was adopted to address these consequences. According to [33], information exchange pertains to the size and the nature of the information sent and shared among community members. This could be attributed to the fact online brand community enabled social media networks is a place where members are more able to play an effective role in creating and exchanging their own content [16]. Such process of information creating and sharing will lead online community members to develop their resources in terms of information capital [16, 40]. Practically, in the line with Lu and Yang [24], information exchange (information capital) could be tested and categorised in two main dimensions quantity of information and quality of information. Customer brand loyalty will be also considered alongside with information capital as main consequences of the customer engagement with online brand community. This could be returned to the fact that customers are more likely to have more social and emotional bonds with the brand that they are able to have an effective role in sharing their experience around it. As discussed above, online brand communities enable their members to have such role of creating and sharing their experience, and accordingly, having a strong emotional and social attachment with such brand. All factors considered and research hypotheses are presented in Fig. 1. All proposed research hypotheses are presented below:

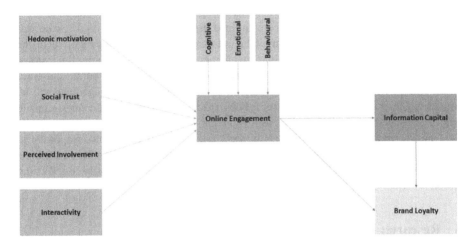

Fig. 1. Conceptual model - Adapted from [5, 18, 30, 33, 39]

H1: Hedonic motivation will positively influence customer engagement with online brand communities.

H2: Trust will positively influence customer engagement with online brand communities.

H3: perceived involvement will positively influence customer engagement with online brand communities.

H4: Interactivity will positively influence customer engagement with online brand communities.

H5: Customer engagement with online brand communities will positively influence information capital.

H6: Customer engagement with online brand communities will positively influence customer brand loyalty.

H76: Information capital will positively influence customer brand loyalty.

4   Proposed Research Methodology

The empirical part of the current study will be conducted in two main countries: Jordan and United Kingdome. In details, online questionnaire survey will be used to target the main participants in these selected countries [7]. The main constructs of the model will be tested based on scale items from their original studies. For example, information capital will tested using scale items extracted from [26]; items adapted from [39] will be used to measure Interactivity; hedonic motivation will be measured using items extracted from [37]; dimensions of customer enragement will be tested based on items derived from [14]; social trust will be examined using items from [23]; [10] scale was considered to test both perceived involvement and brand loyalty. As reported in the conceptual model part, customer online engagement will be tested as a unidimensional constructs, and therefore, the main sub-dimensions: cognitive, behavioural, and emotional will be treated as first order factors while customer online engagement will be considered as a second order construct. For participants in Jordan, the questionnaire will be translated to Arabic language as it is the native language over this country while the English version will be used as is in the United Kingdom. It is also important to mention that cross cultural comparison study will be conducted between Jordan and the Western culture country selected. The data collected will be statistically tested using structural equation modelling by facilitating AMOS.

5   Research Contributions

This study will expand the theoretical understanding regarding very important phenomenon (online brand communities), which requests more exploration and examination. This phenomenon has not yet studied and examined over the MiddleEast countries. Further, the vast majority of prior studies have tested such phenomenon over highly developed and Western countries. As these online communities could be predicted and shaped by the common culture and value system, there is always a need to see and discover the impact of cultural differences between developed countries (i.e. UK) and developing (i.e. Jordan) [8, 17]. Indeed, there is a quite a few studies that have addressed the issues of online community from different cultural aspects particularly between developed and developing countries. Therefore, a considerable contribution could be captured for this project for being the first attempt that will examine the related issues of online brand communities over two sittings: Jordan and one Western European country (i.e. UK). The current study model also provides a new mechanism (social trust, interactivity, hedonic motivation, and perceived involvement) that could shape the customers experiences over digital economy. This study will go further by considering the main consequences of customer engagement with online communities. The vast majority of prior studies have addressed traditional consequences like customer's satisfaction, loyalty, and word of mouth while the current study attempts to see other types of these consequences, which addressed in terms of information capital in the current study. Furthermore, based on empirical results which will be captured, this paper will provide practical guidelines that will help organisations and brands to manage their marketing activities over online communities. Accordingly, such project will not only help brands to guarantee positive outcomes via online communities but also brands will be capable enough to mitigate the negative and misbehaviours over such platforms.

6 Limitations and Future Research Directions

As the nature of the current study seems to be more conceptual theoretical paper, it is restricted to provide a deep understanding about the actual customer's behaviour and perception. Accordingly, future study could provide a closer and accurate picture regarding this phenomenon. Such empirical study will also introduce a sufficient statistical evidence that will help in validating the current study model as well as to see which the most important and influential factors. This study has considered the information exchange theory as a theoretical foundation to propose the conceptual model; yet, the theoretical horizon could be expanded by examining other important models over the related area such as social capital theory and uses and gratification theory [31]. As discussed in the literature part, there are several mechanisms that could predict the customer's engagement with online brand communities. However, only four factors that have be conceptualised in the current model as derivers of the customer's engagement. Thus, future studies could look carefully at other factors that could cover different aspects of the consumers' motivations and drivers of joining online brand communities. Another limitation raised in the current study is ignoring the negative consequences (i.e. negative word of mouth, online customer revenge, and customer misbehaviour) of online communities. Hence, future studies are suggested to look at both kinds of positive and negative consequences of online brand communities.

References

1. Adler, P.S., Kwon, S.W.: Social capital: prospects for a new concept. Acad. Manag. Rev. 27 (1), 17–40 (2002)
2. Alalwan, A.A.: Investigating the impact of social media advertising features on customer purchase intention. Int. J. Inf. Manage. 42, 65–77 (2018)
3. Alalwan, A.A., Rana, N.P., Dwivedi, Y.K., Algharabat, R.: Social media in marketing: a review and analysis of the existing literature. Telemat. Inf. 34(7), 1177–1190 (2017)
4. Bi, Q., Vogel, D.R.: Influences of e-retailer sponsored virtual community on consumer loyalty: an exploration of underlying mechanisms. Influences of ERetailer sponsored virtual community on consumer loyalty: an exploration of underlying mechanisms. In: PACIS, p. 83 (2013)
5. Dessart, L., Veloutsou, C., Morgan-Thomas, A.: Consumer engagement in online brand communities: a social media perspective. J. Prod. Brand Manage. 24(1), 28–42 (2015)
6. Dholakia, U.M., Blazevic, V., Wiertz, C., Algesheimer, R.: Communal service delivery: how customers benefit from participation in firm-hosted virtual P3 communities. J. Serv. Res. 12 (2), 208–226 (2009)
7. Dwivedi, Y.K., Choudrie, J., Brinkman, W.P.: Development of a survey instrument to examine consumer adoption of broadband. Ind. Manage. Data Syst. 106(5), 700–718 (2006)

8. Dwivedi, Y.K., Shareef, M.A., Simintiras, A.C., Lal, B., Weerakkody, V.: A generalised adoption model for services: a cross-country comparison of mobile health (m-health). Govern. Inf. Quart. **33**(1), 174–187 (2016)

9. Fisk, R., et al.: Customers behaving badly: a state of the art review, research agenda and implications for practitioners. J. Serv. Mark. **4**(6), 417–429 (2010)

10. France, C., Merrilees, B., Miller, D.: An integrated model of customer-brand engagement: drivers and consequences. J. Brand Manage. **23**(2), 119136 (2016)

11. Füller, J.: Refining virtual co-creation from a consumer perspective. Calif. Manag. Rev. **52** (2), 98–122 (2010)

12. Gebauer, J., Füller, J., Pezzei, R.: The dark and the bright side of co-creation: triggers of member behavior in online innovation communities. J. Bus. Res. **66**(9), 1516–1527 (2013)

13. Gutierrez, A., O'Leary, S., Rana, N.P., Dwivedi, Y.K., Calle, T.: Using privacy calculus theory to explore entrepreneurial directions in mobile location-based advertising: identifying intrusiveness as the critical risk factor. Comput. Hum. Behav. **95**, 295–306 (2018)

14. Harrigan, P., Evers, U., Miles, M., Daly, T.: Customer engagement with tourism social media brands. Tour. Manag. **59**, 597–609 (2017)

15. Hossain, M.A., Dwivedi, Y.K., Chan, C., Standing, C., Olanrewaju, A.S.: Sharing political content in online social media: a planned and unplanned behaviour approach. Inf. Syst. Front. **20**(3), 485–501 (2018)

16. Kaplan, A.M., Haenlein, M.: Users of the world, unite! The challenges and opportunities of Social Media. Bus. Horiz. **53**(1), 59–68 (2010)

17. Kapoor, K.K., Tamilmani, K., Rana, N.P., Patil, P., Dwivedi, Y.K., Nerur, S.: Advances in social media research: Past, present and future. Inf. Syst. Front. **20**(3), 531–558 (2018)

18. Kim, W.G., Lee, C., Hiemstra, S.J.: Effects of an online virtual community on customer loyalty and travel product purchases. Tour. Manag. **25**(3), 343–355 (2004)

19. Kozinets, R.V., De Valck, K., Wojnicki, A.C., Wilner, S.J.: Networked narratives: understanding word-of-mouth marketing in online communities. J. Mark. **74**(2), 71–89 (2010)

20. Kozinets, R.V., Hemetsberger, A., Schau, H.J.: The wisdom of consumer crowds: collective innovation in the age of networked marketing. J. Macromark. **28**(4), 339–354 (2008)

21. Lee, D., Kim, H.S., Kim, J.K.: The impact of online brand community type on consumer's community engagement behaviors: consumer-created vs marketer-created online brand community in online social-networking web sites. Cyberpsychol. Behav. Soc. Netw. **14**(1–2), 59–63 (2011)

22. Li, S., Clark, L., Wheeler, C.: Unlocking the marketing potential of social capital: a study to identify the dimensions of social capital considered represented within online brand communities. In: 2013 IEEE 10th International Conference on eBusiness Engineering, pp. 138–141. IEEE (2013)

23. Liao, S., Chou, E.: Intention to adopt knowledge through virtual communities: posters vs lurkers. Online Inf. Rev. **36**, 442–461 (2012)

24. Lu, Y., Yang, D.: Information exchange in virtual communities under extreme disaster conditions. Decis. Support Syst. **50**(2), 529–538 (2011)

25. Madupu, V., Cooley, D.O.: Antecedents and consequences of online brand community participation: a conceptual framework. J. Internet Commer. **9**(2), 127–147 (2010)

26. Malhotra, A., Gosain, S., El Sawy, O.A.: Leveraging standard electronic business interfaces to enable adaptive supply chain partnerships. Inf. Syst. Res. **18**(3), 260–279 (2007)

27. Manchanda, P., Packard, G., Pattabhiramaiah, A.: Social dollars: the economic impact of customer participation in a firm-sponsored online customer community. Mark. Sci. **34**(3), 367–387 (2015)

28. McAlexander, J.H., Schouten, J.W., Koenig, H.F.: Building brand community. J. Mark. **66**(1), 38–54 (2002)
29. McWilliam, G.: Building stronger brands through online communities. Sloan Manag. Rev. **41**(3), 43 (2000)
30. Meek, S., Ryan, M., Lambert, C., Ogilvie, M.: A multidimensional scale for measuring online brand community social capital (OBCSC). J. Bus. Res. **100**, 234–244 (2019)
31. Ruggiero, T.E.: Uses and gratifications theory in the 21st century. Mass Commun. Soc. **3**(1), 3–37 (2000)
32. Shaari, H., Ahmad, I.S.: Brand evangelism among online brand community members. Int. Rev. Manag. Bus. Res. **5**(1), 80 (2016)
33. Silver, S.D., Cohen, B.P., Crutchfield, J.H.: Status differentiation and information exchange in face-to-face and computer-mediated idea generation. Soc. Psychol. Quart. **57**(2), 108–123 (1994)
34. Silver, S.D., Cohen, B.P., Rainwater, J.: Group structure and information exchange in innovative problem solving. In: Lawler, E.J., Markowsky, B. (eds.) Advances in Group Processes, vol. 5, pp. 169–194. JAI Press, Greenwich (1988)
35. Sloan, S., Bodey, K., Gyrd-Jones, R.: Knowledge sharing in online brand communities. Qual. Mark. Res.: Int. J. **18**(3), 320–345 (2015)
36. Troyer, L., Watkins, G., Silver, S.D.: Time dependence in micro social interaction: an elaboration of information exchange theory and initial empirical test. Sociol. Focus **40**(2), 161–181 (2007)
37. Venkatesh, V., Thong, J.Y., Xu, X.: Consumer acceptance and use of information technology: extending the unified theory of acceptance and use of technology. MIS Q. **36**(1), 157–178 (2012)
38. Wirtz, J., et al.: Managing brands and customer engagement in online brand communities. J. Serv. Manag. **24**(3), 223–244 (2013)
39. Wu, J.J., Chang, Y.S.: Toward understanding members' interactivity, trust, and flow in online travel community. Ind. Manag. Data Syst. **105**(7), 937–954 (2005)
40. Wu, Y.L., Li, E.Y., Chang, W.L.: Nurturing user creative performance in social media networks. Internet Res. **26**(4), 869–900 (2016)

Social Media Uses Among Youths and Matured Person

Shubhendra S. Parihar[(✉)] and Puneet Rai

Jaipuria Institute of Management, Vineet Khand, Gomti Nagar, Lucknow, India
{Shubhendra.parihar,Puneet.rai}@jaipuria.ac.in

Abstract. Social media usage is ubiquitous among all age groups. The purpose and needs may vary with age and environment. It is general observations that youngsters use Snapchat and Instagram more frequently and working professionals use LinkedIn or Twitter. The theory of user and gratification defines the uses of different media and reasons for consumption. Individuals now tilted more towards hedonic activities like enjoyment and relaxation and find digital platform more convenient to satisfy their psychological and social needs. The usage of inbound and outbound active platforms like Facebook, WhatsApp, Instagram and Twitter is increasing as compared to passive media like television and radio.

This study is an attempt to identify the uses and gratifications found by youngsters and others by using social networking sites? A preliminary review of the literature was done to understand the usage pattern of social media and identifying why individuals spend reasonable time on social media platforms. Well, ahead a questionnaire is formed to collect data on the usage pattern of individuals.

The analysis discloses that age does not have any significant role in the usage pattern of various social media platforms. It means all individuals use social media platforms for similar purposes. Even there is no association between age and influence of social media on the purchase decision. Although age influences preference of combination of social media platforms. This study shall be useful for online marketers to design their online promotion strategy. This will also be useful for digital marketing agencies to target the right social media platform for specific brand-related activities.

Keywords: Social media · User gratification · Social networking sites

1 Introduction

The worldwide users of social media platforms are 2.95 billion. The total social media users in India are 680 million. The Facebook users are 280 million, Instagram users are 88 million, LinkedIn users are 65 million and Snapchat users are also growing very fast. The most preferred platforms among Indian are Facebook, WhatsApp and You-Tube. India has hugged the internet with open arms, and its digital population has been swiftly mounting in the past decade with active internet users (Diwanji Sanika 2020).

After Reliance Jio introduction in 2007, the internet user base has increased fast. Reliance Jio offered very attractive schemes which were affordable irrespective of the

© IFIP International Federation for Information Processing 2020
Published by Springer Nature Switzerland AG 2020
S. K. Sharma et al. (Eds.): TDIT 2020, IFIP AICT 618, pp. 428–437, 2020.
https://doi.org/10.1007/978-3-030-64861-9_37

income levels and socio-economic classes. The impact was significant as over 60% of the mobile data traffic coming from Jio services in less than ten years of its introduction in the market.

An individual with a smartphone is using either one or many social media sites. The gender, age and socioeconomic status is not a boundary. The individuals are using social media platforms according to their choice and likings subject to fulfil their drives. According to age and working status, their usages may differ. There is some common usage which applies to every user like stay connected to friends and family, networked with people and entertainment.

According to a survey conducted by Ipsos on the state of happiness, about 43% of Indians thought that the time they spend on social media was a source of some happiness for them, while 29% of respondents stated that it did not or could not give them happiness. Globally only 42% of respondents viewed their time on social media as a source of happiness.

Young adults (ages 18 to 29) are the most likely to use social media – fully 90% do. Still, the usage among those 65 and older has more than tripled since 2010 when 11% used social media. Today, 35% of all those 65 and older report using social media, compared with just 2% in 2005.

Women were more likely than men to use social networking sites for some years, although since2014 these differences have been modest. Today, 68% of all women use social media, compared with 62% of all men. (Perrin 2015) Social networking site users can be categorized based on usage. It depends on user interest and purpose. Facebook and WhatsApp are the most common among other social media platforms usage in India. The use of twitter and LinkedIn is more inclined to professionals, organizations and for socio-economic-political interest. Snapchat and Instagram is common among youngsters because this gives a privacy feature and they can send text and photos privately which is difficult to monitor by anyone else (Table 1).

If we study why individuals use social media? The theory of Uses and gratification (Blumler and McQuail 1969) explained why individuals use media and reasons for consumption? Does the UG theory explain why individuals use various media platforms to satisfy their social and psychological needs? The UG perspective has led to a new understanding of audiences as active media users who chosen media based upon a variety of needs. Since both the production and consumption of social media are fundamentally user-driven (Shao 2009). Social media users can be broadly classified according to active users and the activities performed on various social media platforms. These activities can be contribution (post) or consumption like Loitering and Witnessing (Schlosser 2005; Shao 2009). They suggested that consumption is more than a contribution.

There are various theories and models used by many kinds of research in social media practice and individual's behaviour towards social media in social media research, Colliander and Dahlen (2011) used PSI to study user behaviour concerning brand attitudes and purchase intentions. Uses and Gratification (UGT) is another theory of mass communication (Eighmey and McCord 1998) which is appreciated well in social media research to understand consumer need and behaviour.

A communication tool that allows users to create a network with a public or private profile and interact with people in that network (Boyd and Ellison 2008). Social media

Table 1. SNS and their purpose

SNS	Purpose
Facebook	Facebook supports communicating online chat and the gift to comment on your friend's profile pages to keep in touch, share information or to say "something". Facebook supports group pages, fan pages, and business pages that let businesses use Facebook as a vehicle for social media marketing
WhatsApp	Connectivity - Sending messages, and making calls have a new destination, WhatsApp. So even without a balance, we can reach our loved ones. Sharing: It has a fitness to share wide range of media, be it photos, audio, video, and even documents
LinkedIn	Professionals, professional bodies and organizations uses it for showcasing their capabilities, achievements and for any professional activities
Instagram	Use of visual marketing features on this platform. It build up user generated content
Snapchat	Snapchat is a mobile messaging application used to share photos, videos, text, and drawings. It's free to download the app and free to send messages using it. It has become hugely popular in a very short space of time, especially with young people because of its privacy

sites fulfil many wants and needs via virtual communication. It is what social media sites do college students use most? Social media is a convenient method of communication which provides the ability to stay connected with friends and family at the discretion of the users' rate and time (Urista et al. 2009). Social media are highly efficient because they are one of the many methods of communication that allow users too quickly and widely disseminate information. According to Duggan and Brenner (2012), 83% of 18–29-year-olds disseminate information via social networking sites. Social media are increasing student engagement outside of the classroom and they are creating new and innovative ways to learn Knight-McCord et al. (2016).

Uses and gratifications theory applies to social media because of its roots in the communications literature. Social media is a communication mechanism that allows users to communicate with thousands, and perhaps billions, of individuals all over the world (Williams et al. 2012). The basic evidence of uses and gratifications theory is that people will seek out media among participants that fulfill their needs and chiefs to ultimate gratifications (Lariscy et al. 2011).

Dolan et al. (2016) reconnoitered relationship between social media and engagement behaviour. This paper examined the Facebook users' gratification and the relationship between users' gratification and their political participation offline. A factor analysis revealed four primary needs for participation which are socializing, entertainment, self-status seeking and information. Valenzuela et al. (2009) explained the uses and gratification of social media. Their study test and quantifies the reciprocal causal relationship between needs, social media use and gratification as well as their self-sustaining endogenous (feedback) effect. Social media use is significantly driven by all four categories of needs examined (emotional, cognitive, social and habitual) but only gratify some of them. Ungratified needs accumulate over time drive subsequent social media use. Interpersonal social environment also affects social media use. Brooks (2015) explained the adverse effect of social media usage that leads to negative effects, both on efficiency and well-being. Specifically, social media usage is associated with lower task performance, increased technostress, and lower happiness. Social media will remain and grow in the future. As more and more people spend increased amounts of time with the technologies, the potential for these negative effects may grow. Whiting and Williams (2013) study identifies ten uses and gratifications for using social media. The ten uses and gratifications found in their study are social interaction, information seeking, pass time, entertainment, relaxation, communicatory utility, expression of opinions, convenience utility, information sharing, and surveillance and watching of others.

Social media usage is increasing at a rapid rate due to better availability of smartphones and data. The previous research work talked about uses and gratification of social media by individuals but how uses vary with age factor is not explained. How the social media uses and preference of using a particular social network changes along with age is important to learn from a marketer viewpoint to design their social media marketing strategy. Henceforth our proposed conceptual framework outlining the antecedents and consequences of Youths and mature individuals.

2 Review of Literature

Xie et al. (2012) explained in their study that the adoption of social media among elderly individuals is inhibited by the concern of privacy, technology use and negative perception. But the education to them helps to improve the adoption of social media among them. Haddon (2015) expressed in his study that youth are a continuous learner and learn technology very fast. They are also malleable to understand the issues and practices. Dhaha et al. (2013) explained in their study that youth in Somalia use Facebook to portray the positive image of their country and help the word to know what is happening in the country. Barker (2012) stated that Regardless of age, participants reporting high collective self-esteem and group identity were more likely to use social networking sites for peer communication and social identity gratifications, while those reporting negative collective self-esteem were more likely to use social networking sites for social compensation.

Berger et al. (2012) researched about the relationship between social media use and the overall impact social media marketing has on purchase behaviour.

Malik (2016) identified six different gratifications which are affection, attention-seeking, disclosure, habit, information sharing and social influence behind sharing digital photos on Face book. It was found that age has a positive correlation with disclosure and social influence gratifications. Frequency of posting on Facebook is negatively correlated with habit and information sharing gratifications.

3 Methodology

This study has been designed to understand the need of individuals for social media usage in a structured manner and classifying them based on demographic variables. This study tried to measure social media as a habit among users like how many hours they spend on social media? What is the level of satisfaction when they get a like or comment on their posted content? How do they feel about social media Good or Bad and how they are addicted to social media.

The uses and gratification framework available in the literature, this study focus on basic two frameworks which are: Papacharissi and Rubin's (2000) and Ko et al. (2005). The Palmgreen and Rubin's scale is selected because it looks at both uses and gratification together and it has been applied in television viewing studies which is similar to social media engagement. The Palmgreen and Rubin (2000) and the Ko et al. (2005) framework were selected because it looks at uses and gratification concerning the internet. Considering the above two frameworks there are seven themes along with one component from the PSI framework to study the influence of social media endorsement on buying behaviour of its users that will cover in this study.

(1) Social interaction;
(2) Education and awareness
(3) Entertainment;
(4) Relaxation;
(5) Communicatory utility;
(6) Convenience utility and
(7) Influence of Social media endorsement on the purchasing behaviour of its users.

A questionnaire was developed to interview users of various age group individuals. It was promised with each respondent not to disclose the identity and their responses. To collect the responses a list was prepared according to the age group to collect the responses. The age groups were like individuals up to 25 years age and the second age group of the mature one above 25 years of age. The sample size was taken 200. The weightage was given more to youths less than 25 years of age in data collection.

The questionnaire was sent to respondents either via a link on their email IDs or through personal interview. The collected responses were tabulated according to demography for analysis and interpretation. The data were analyzed using descriptive statistics and non-parametric chi-square test method.

4 Findings and Discussion

A chi-square test of independence was performed to examine the relation between age and influence of social media in purchase decision. The relation between these variables was not found to be statistically significant, $X2$ (2, N = 400) = 2.505, p = .286. This indicates that there is no association between age and influence of social media on the purchase decision (Tables 2 and 3).

A chi-square test of independence was performed to examine the relation between age and purpose of use of social media. The purpose of use considered included are:

Table 2. Relationship between age and influence of Social media in purchase decisions

Chi-square tests

	Value	df	Asymp. Sig. (2-sided)
Pearson chi-Square	2.505[a]	2	.286
Likelihood ratio	2.513	2	.285
Linear-by-linear association	1.289	1	.256
N of valid cases	400		

a. 0 cells (0.0%) have expected count less than 5. The minimum expected count is 35.24.

Table 3. Relationship between age and influence of Social media in purchase decisions

Chi-square tests

	Value	df	Asymp. Sig. (2-sided)
Pearson chi-square	1.882[a]	4	.757
Likelihood ratio	1.869	4	.760
Linear-by-linear association	.329	1	.566
N of valid cases	400		

a. 3 cells (30.0%) have expected count less than 5. The minimum expected count is 1.91.

entertainment and work, enlarge social network, to create new useful content, image management and making new friends. The relation between these variables was not found to be statistically significant, X2 (4, N = 400) = 1.882, p = .757. This indicates that there is no association between age and purpose of use of social media. This indicates that the usages of social media does not differ for those who are below 25 years and those who are above 25 years (Table 4).

Table 4. Age vs. uses of Social media

Chi-square tests

	Value	df	Asymp. Sig. (2-sided)
Pearson chi-square	3.834[a]	2	.147
Likelihood ratio	3.649	2	.161
Linear-by-linear association	1.897	1	.168
N of valid cases	400		

a. 0 cells (0.0%) have expected count less than 5. The minimum expected count is 5.08.

A chi-square test of independence was performed to examine the relation between age and purpose for which social media is used. In this analysis purpose for which

Table 5. Age vs. major purpose of using social networking sites

Chi-square tests

	Value	df	Asymp. Sig. (2-sided)
Pearson chi-square	27.966[a]	4	.000
Likelihood ratio	28.812	4	.000
Linear-by-linear association	3.011	1	.083
N of valid cases	400		

a. 2 cells (20.0%) have expected count less than 5. The minimum expected count is .32.

Table 6. Age vs. preferred choice of social media

Count

		Average_time_spending			Total
		1.00	2.00	3.00	
Age	1.00	64	115	94	273
	2.00	31	64	32	127
Total		95	179	126	400

Table 7. Age vs. preferred choice of social media

Chi-square tests

	Value	df	Asymp. Sig. (2-sided)
Pearson chi-square	3.705[a]	2	.157
Likelihood ratio	3.775	2	.151
Linear-by-linear association	1.647	1	.199
N of valid cases	400		

a. 0 cells (0.0%) have expected count less than 5. The minimum expected count is 30.16.

social media is used included: mixed use, professional use and personal use. The relation between these variables was not found to be statistically significant, $X2$ (2, $N = 400$) = 3.834, $p = .147$. This indicates that there is no association between age and purpose of use of social media. This indicates that the usages of social media does not differ for those who are below 25 years and those who are above 25 years (Table 5).

A chi-square test of independence was performed to examine the relation between age and preference for combination of social media platforms. The relation between these variables was found to be statistically significant, $X2$ (4, $N = 400$) = 3.834, $p = .147$. This indicates that there is an association between age and preference for combination of social media platforms. This indicates that the preference for combination of social media platforms differ for those who are below 25 years and those who are above 25 years. Less than 25 years customer show more preference for Face book/WhatsApp/Instagram combination, while the preference for WhatsApp/Facebook/LinkedIn is similar across the two age groups (Tables 6 and 7).

The two age groups (below 25 years and those who are above 25 years) do not differ in the time spent on the social media (Tables 8 and 9).

Table 8. Age vs. time spend on social media

Age * reaction exit Cross tabulation							
Count							
		Reaction exit					Total
		1.00	2.00	3.00	4.00	5.00	
Age	1.00	121	126	15	9	2	273
	2.00	38	74	5	4	6	127
Total		159	200	20	13	8	400

Table 9. Age vs. time spend on social media

Chi-square tests			
	Value	df	Asymp. Sig. (2-sided)
Pearson chi-square	14.398[a]	4	.006
Likelihood ratio	13.982	4	.007
Linear-by-linear association	7.345	1	.007
N of valid cases	400		

a. 2 cells (20.0%) have expected count less than 5. The minimum expected count is 2.54.

A chi-square test of independence was performed to examine the relation between age and reaction on exit of social media platform. The relation between these variables was found to be statistically significant, $X2$ (4, N = 400) = 14.398, p = .006. This indicates that there is an association between age and reaction on exit of social media platform (Tables 10 and 11).

Table 10. Social Media Good vs. Bad

Social media is good or bad	
Mean	1.14
Standard Error	0.020050063
Median	1
Mode	1
Standard Deviation	0.401001253
Sample Variance	0.160802005

Almost all age group social media network users see value in using it because the most of them confirmed that social media is good (Median −1).

Table 11. Age vs Average time spending on social media

Average spending time	
Mean	2.0775
Standard error	0.037008898
Median	2
Mode	2
Standard deviation	0.740177957
Sample variance	0.547863409

The average spending time by social media users per day is 2 h which is significant if used during working hours.

5   Conclusion

It is found in the data analysis that age is not a barrier in using social media networks. Even there is no significant difference in social media in buying behaviour of individuals due to the age group. The study also indicates that there is no association between age and purpose of the use of social media. It means the usages of social media does not differ for those who are below 25 years and those who are above 25 years. The preference for a combination of social media platforms differs for those who are below 25 years and those who are above 25 years. Less than 25 years customer show more preference for Face book/WhatsApp/Instagram combination, while the preference for WhatsApp/Facebook/LinkedIn is similar across the two age groups. Although the affinity towards social media is more in youngsters as compared to mature individuals. It means marketers have to look at the use of social media platform while designing their digital brand communication strategy according to age groups. The limitation of this study is that data collection for the study is majorly from northern India and college-going individuals.

References

Barker, V.: A generational comparison of social networking site use: the influence of age and social identity. Int. J. Aging Hum. Dev. **74**(2), 163–187 (2012)

Berger, P.D., Pooja, M., Black Jennifer, E., Jiangmei, C., Weinberg Bruce, D.: The Impact of Social Media Usage on Consumer Buying Behavior. Adv. Manage **5**(1) (2012)

Xie, B., Watkins, I., Golbeck, J., Huang, M.: Understanding and changing older adults' perceptions and learning of social media. Educ. Gerontol. **38**(4), 282–296 (2012). https://doi.org/10.1080/03601277.2010.544580

Bolton, R., et al.: Understanding generation Y and their use of social media: a review and research agenda. J. Serv. Manage. **24**(3), 245–267 (2013)

Boyd, D.M., Ellison, N.B.: Social network sites: definition, history, and scholarship. J. Comput.-Mediat. Commun. **13**(1), 210–230 (2007)

Brooks, S.: Does personal social media usage affect efficiency and well-being? Comput. Hum. Behav. **46**, 26–37 (2015)

Colliander, J., Dahlén, M.: Following the fashionable friend: the power of social media: weighing publicity effectiveness of blogs versus online magazines. J. Advert. Res. **51**(1), 313–320 (2011)

Dhaha, I.S.Y., Igale, A.B.: Facebook usage among Somali youth: a test of uses and gratifications approach. Int. J. Hum. Soc. Sci. **3**(3), 299–313 (2013)

Diwanji sanika (2020). https://www.statista.com/topics/5113/social-media-usage-in-india/

Dolan, R., Conduit, J., Fahy, J., Goodman, S.: Social media engagement behaviour: a uses and gratifications perspective. J. Strategic Mark. **24**(3–4), 261–277 (2016). https://doi.org/10.1080/0965254X.2015.1095222

Duggan, M., Brenner, J.: The demographics of social media users, 2012, vol. 14. Pew Research Center's Internet & American Life Project, Washington, DC (2013)

Eighmey, J., McCord, L.: Adding value in the information age: uses and gratifications of sites on the World Wide Web. J. Bus. Res. **41**(3), 187–194 (1998)

Haddon, L.: Social media and youth. In: The International Encyclopedia of Digital Communication and Society, pp. 1–9 (2015)

Knight-McCord, J., et al.: What social media sites do college students use most. J. Undergr. Ethnic Minor. Psychol. **2**(21), 21–26 (2016)

Ko, H., Cho, C.H., Roberts, M.S.: Internet uses and gratifications: a structural equation model of interactive advertising. J. Advert. **34**(2), 57–70 (2005)

Malik, A., Dhir, A., Nieminen, M.: Uses and Gratifications of digital photo sharing on Facebook. Telemat. Inf. **33**(1), 129–138 (2016). https://doi.org/10.1016/j.tele.2015.06.009

Papacharissi, Z., Rubin, A.M.: Predictors of internet use. J. Broadcast. Electron. Media **44**(2), 175–196 (2000)

Perrin, A.: Social media usage, pp. 52–68. Pew Research Center (2015)

Weaver Lariscy, R., Tinkham, S.F., Sweetser, K.D.: Kids these days: examining differences in political uses and gratifications, Internet political participation, political information efficacy, and cynicism on the basis of age. Am. Behav. Sci. **55**(6), 749–764 (2011)

Whiting, A., Williams, D.: Why people use social media: a uses and gratifications approach. Qual. Mark. Res.: Int. J. **16**(4), 362–369 (2013). https://doi.org/10.1108/qmr-06-2013-0041

Urista, M.A., Dong, Q., Day, K.D.: Explaining why young adults use MySpace and Facebook through uses and gratifications theory. Hum. Commun. **12**(2), 215–229 (2009)

Valenzuela, S., Park, N., Kee, K.F.: Is there social capital in a social network site?: Facebook use and college students' life satisfaction, trust, and participation. J. Comput.-Mediat. Commun. **14**(4), 875–901 (2009)

How Do Consumers Perceive Brand Campaigns on Twitter?

Muskan Jain[(✉)], Angeline Gautami Fernando[iD], and K. Rajeshwari

Great Lakes Institute of Management, Dr. Bala V. Balachandar Campus,
East Coast Road, Manamai Village, Thirukazhukundram Taluk,
Manamai 603102, Tamil Nadu, India
muskan.dm21246@greatlakes.edu.in

Abstract. Brands use microblogs like Twitter to launch hashtag campaigns. The efficacy of using this medium (Twitter) for crisis communication is well established, while little is known about its influence on brand engagement. In this exploratory study, we use medium theory and medium richness theory to highlight the fact that cultural differences and the medium of communication play a huge role in information diffusion. Comparing hashtag campaigns created during POST-COVID using text mining methods, we find that an international campaign had more brand related discussions when compared to Indian brands. Future research needs to delineate the constructs that influence these differences.

Keywords: Hashtag campaigns · COVID · Topic models

1 Introduction

Twitter is a American social networking service that brands use to connect to consumers through tweets (messages). The platform is highly suitable for rapid information dissemination. Therefore, it is very useful in crisis communication. The platform is also highly suitable for generating conversations on topical or cause related issues [1].

Consequently, brands usually create "hashtag campaigns" to increase brand buzz. For example, Amazon Prime used "#Comicstaan" leveraged the platform for creating awareness of the launch of their stand-up comedy competitive series. Uber India "#LoveMovesForward" to celebrate the Supreme Court's judgement that was of interest to the LGBTQ + community. Despite its popularity, there are very studies that examine the effect of Twitter hashtag campaigns on generating brand engagement. Based on medium theory and previous research we believe that Twitter is not a suitable platform for engaging with consumers. Culturally, Indians prefer rich media and therefore prefer platforms like Instagram or Facebook.

In this study, we conduct an exploratory study to compare consumer responses to hashtag campaigns created on Twitter by Indian and international brands during COVID (Coronavirus disease 2019). Specifically, we address the following research question:

RQ1: Does consumer buzz differ for Indian and international hashtag brand campaigns related to COVID?

© IFIP International Federation for Information Processing 2020
Published by Springer Nature Switzerland AG 2020
S. K. Sharma et al. (Eds.): TDIT 2020, IFIP AICT 618, pp. 438–443, 2020.
https://doi.org/10.1007/978-3-030-64861-9_38

We believe that answering this question would foster further research 'what is the utility of Twitter to create brand buzz?'.

2 Literature Review

2.1 Medium, Culture and Twitter

"The medium is the message" is the cornerstone of medium theory [2]. This theory posits that the nature of the medium plays a key role in the subsequent engagement with the message transmitted [3]. Stakeholders respond in different ways based on the nature of the medium chosen for communication. The nature of Twitter is extremely suitable for crisis communication as it facilitates instantaneous reactions and responses from organization [4]. Brands use Twitter for viral marketing and invest in content diffusion. Influencers and opinion leaders who are on Twitter help in achieving this goal [5].

Cultural differences are also important in the usage of a medium. Users from collectivistic cultures use social media for social relationships [6]. They also differ in the way they react to messages on social media. For example, a user in a low context culture may feel comfortable responding to a political leader on Twitter vis-à-vis the one in a high context culture [7]. While tweets are restricted to 280 characters for most languages, audio and video tweets are limited to 140 s for most users. Twitter is therefore more suitable for short text communication and is inadequate for handling rich media (image, video) content [8]. Users in collectivistic, high context culture based countries typically prefer rich medium [9]. Thus, they may not exhibit a preference to engage on Twitter.

In this study, we add to these investigations by exploring the suitability of using Twitter for topical brand related campaigns.

2.2 Twitter Hashtag Campaigns

Twitter hashtags allow users to identify topics that are of personal interest. They are also help in creating ad hoc topics when they want to focus on specific issues [10]. These tags are followed by a group of people who seek information on trending topics in politics (e.g. Arab Spring), or movements like "Black Lives Matter" [11]. There are very few studies that examine the effect of brand related hashtag campaigns. Recent studies show that users tend to react to influencers' tweets about a cause related brand campaign rather than to the actual issue [12]. Users can also form brand communities that have unique interests relating to the brand [13]. We believe that this study will add to this growing body of literature.

3   Research Methodology

3.1   Data

The sampling technique used was purposive sampling. Hashtag campaigns associated with COVID were chosen for analysis. Three Indian and one international brand were chosen. Details are as follows:

> HUL & UNICEF's #BreakTheChain: This campaign was launched to inform and empower the general public about Covid-19 and its preventive measures like social distancing and hand washing.
> Savlon's #ChainOfProtection: Savlon rolled out this initiative on World hand hygiene day to increase adherence to hand hygiene amid Covid-19.
> Nike's #PlayInside and #PlayForTheWorld were released by Nike to increase awareness about social distancing and still play inside your home during Covid-19.
> Tata tea's #JaagoRe #BadonKeLiye: This is an initiative by Tata Tea for specific social causes, and recently it has been aimed for elderly by partnering with HelpAge India.

> The tweets were collected for 3 weeks post the launch-date of the campaign.

3.2   Data Analysis

Keyword plots and word clouds were used to display the top keywords. We used Latent Dirichlet Allocation (LDA) technique to identify the underlying keywords grouped as a random set of topics in a collection. Latent Dirichlet allocation (LDA) is a particularly popular method for fitting a topic model. The words in the dataset were cleaned and pre-processed by removing the stop words, links and punctuations.

4   Results and Discussion

4.1   Key Words Plot

This refers to the top 15 unique words which are most frequently used in the tweets. This is also done to see if all the keywords are relevant to the marketing campaigns or whether the hashtag was used for different reasons.

4.2   Word Cloud

As a next step, a word cloud was created (Fig. 2), which is a visual representation of the data using the unique words. Nike's campaign comparatively has more brand coherent words when compared to the other campaigns.

4.3   Topic Modelling by LDA

The topics found by LDA were identified and named according to the common characteristics of the words present under that particular topic (Fig. 3). All the Indian campaigns contained around two topics. HUL's campaign was related to UNICEF (as intended) and the associated words that were generic to COVID. Similarly, Tata tea's topic were connected to the elderly and medical aid for them. However, Savlon's campaign did not contain distinct topics. The international nature of Nike's campaign was showcased in the variety of the topics generated. Football clubs(BARCA/USLM), National Athletic association (National Collegiate Athletic Association were associated with the #playinside campaign (FIg. 1).

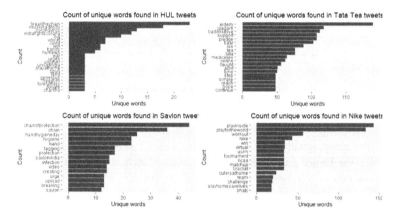

Fig. 1. Keyword plots

Fig. 2. Word cloud of campaigns

The campaign run by HUL and UNICEF, #Breakthechain is also used by Kerala's state government and also randomly by people to address the breaking of covid-19's chain in their tweets. Thus, most of the tweets with this hashtag, are not relevant to the

Fig. 3. Topic models for the data

specific brand campaign. Savlon's competitor brand Dettol was one of the most used words of the campaign. No other competitor's name was seen in keywords which suggests that the Dettol and Savlon are often viewed as similar brands by consumers. Tweet key words were related to Tata's brand, its product like Tata tea, tata tea gold etc., which means that the users value its brand and connect to it. Some key words were also related to the target audience like "age", "elderly", "senior" etc., which means it was clear among the users that the campaign is targeted at senior citizens.

Unlike the Indian campaigns, Nike's campaign had many keywords related to the community spirit, like "teamnike", "club" etc. which shows that Nike has done a great job creating a community of its own. Tweets also had the famous tagline of the brand "just do it" which suggests how consumers are well aware of the brand's tagline and its values. The campaign also had keywords related to exercises and workouts, particularly running, which means that the consumers see Nike as a fitness brand and relate to it running and other exercises. The theme of playing indoors was also adopted by a number of football clubs and athletics associations indicating that it was well received.

5   Conclusion

Our study shows that medium is an important component that decides audience engagement. We find that topical brand hashtag campaigns from Indian brands relating to COVID did not foster engagement or diffusion when compared to International brand campaign. Our findings highlight the fact that brand managers should consider cultural differences and the nature of the medium before launching a campaign on social media. Future studies can extend this exploratory work and investigate specific effects in detail.

References

1. Voorveld, H.A.M., van Noort, G., Muntinga, D.G., Bronner, F.: Engagement with social media and social media advertising: the differentiating role of platform type. J. Advert. **47**, 38–54 (2018). https://doi.org/10.1080/00913367.2017.1405754
2. Levine, S., McLuhan, M.: Understanding media: the extensions of man. Am. Q. (1964). https://doi.org/10.2307/2711172
3. Meyrowitz, J.: Medium theory. In: The International Encyclopedia of Communication. Wiley, Chichester (2008). https://doi.org/10.1002/9781405186407.wbiecm064
4. Schultz, F., Utz, S., Göritz, A.: Is the medium the message? Perceptions of and reactions to crisis communication via Twitter, blogs and traditional media. Public Relat. Rev. **37**, 20–27 (2011). https://doi.org/10.1016/j.pubrev.2010.12.001
5. Araujo, T., Neijens, P., Vliegenthart, R.: Getting the word out on Twitter: the role of influentials, information brokers and strong ties in building word-of-mouth for brands. Int. J. Advert. **36**, 496–513 (2017). https://doi.org/10.1080/02650487.2016.1173765
6. Kim, Y., Sohn, D., Choi, S.M.: Cultural difference in motivations for using social network sites: a comparative study of American and Korean college students. Comput. Hum. Behav. **27**, 365–372 (2011). https://doi.org/10.1016/j.chb.2010.08.015
7. Al-saggaf, Y., Chutikulrungsee, T.T.: Twitter usage in Australia and Saudi Arabia and influence of culture : an exploratory cross-country comparison. In: Refereed proceedings of the Australian and New Zealand Communication Association Conference: Rethinking communication, space and identity, pp. 1–12 (2015)
8. Ott, B.L.: The age of Twitter: Donald J. Trump and the politics of debasement. Crit. Stud. Media Commun. **34**, 59–68 (2017). https://doi.org/10.1080/15295036.2016.1266686
9. Setlock, L.D., Quinones, P.A., Fussell, S.R.: Does culture interact with media richness? The effects of audio vs. video conferencing on Chinese and American dyads. In: Proceedings of the Annual Hawaii International Conference on System Sciences (2007). https://doi.org/10.1109/HICSS.2007.182
10. Bruns, A., Burgess, J.: The use of twitter hashtags in the formation of ad hoc publics. In: European Consortium for Political Research conference, Reykjavík, 25–27 August 2011 (2011)
11. Bruns, A., Moon, B., Paul, A., Münch, F.: Towards a typology of hashtag publics: a large-scale comparative study of user engagement across trending topics. Commun. Res. Pract. **2**, 20–46 (2016). https://doi.org/10.1080/22041451.2016.1155328
12. Xu, S., Zhou, A.: Hashtag homophily in twitter network: examining a controversial cause-related marketing campaign. Comput. Hum. Behav. **102**, 87–96 (2020). https://doi.org/10.1016/j.chb.2019.08.006
13. Naraine, M.L., Pegoraro, A., Wear, H.: #WeTheNorth: examining an online brand community through a professional sport organization's hashtag marketing campaign. Commun. Sport. (2019). https://doi.org/10.1177/2167479519878676

A Conceptual Framework of Social Media Influence on Mobile Banking Usage Among Young Indian Consumers

Manisha Sharma$^{(\boxtimes)}$ and Subhojit Banerjee

School of Management, Gautam Buddha University, Greater Noida, India
smanisha13@gmail.com

Abstract. With the advances in technology, consumers have equally shown positive inclination towards the adoption of the same on the premise of their saved time and energy and more so they have identified these technological advancements as a precursor to enhanced quality of life as a whole. Mobile banking is one such technology which has gained immense acceptance amongst its consumers. However, there is a need to gain an insight of mobile users' attitude towards mobile banking if it has to replace the traditional ways of banking in eternity. There is no denying to the fact that Social Media has played the role of an immensely powerful arbitrator in orienting consumers towards mobile banking. This conceptual paper thereby attempts to seek the role of Social Media towards various stages of consumers' attitude in accepting such technologies such as mobile banking in India. Through this paper we intend to build a framework which identifies the role of social media in the transition of mobile banking consumers from one stage of cognitive process to the other. The work primarily addresses young consumers for their being the early influencers of social media. The paper is expected to contribute towards decision making of the government agencies, mobile operators, financial institutions and researchers.

Keywords: Mobile banking · Attitude · Social media · Young consumers · India

1 Introduction

Mobile phones have witnessed an exponential pattern of usage during the last decade and one of the distinctive and prominent usages of Mobile phones that has completely revolutionised the nature of transaction is Mobile banking (MB) owing to the technological innovations and the user-friendly software packages developed over the years. It is therefore precedented and desired that the government, the banks and the mobile operators work in alignment towards enabling mobile banking services for their customers and give way to mobile banking which can emerge more dynamically as one of the breakthrough revolution technologies in banking to provide a complete digital environment to the consumers.

Changing consumer behaviour always takes a reasonable amount of time and there are instances when consumers are attracted to such technologies however refrain from actual usage. Thereby, it is imperative that the mobile operators understand the

© IFIP International Federation for Information Processing 2020
Published by Springer Nature Switzerland AG 2020
S. K. Sharma et al. (Eds.): TDIT 2020, IFIP AICT 618, pp. 444–450, 2020.
https://doi.org/10.1007/978-3-030-64861-9_39

acceptability and usability pattern among consumers in order to sustain the continuous usage of mobile banking. There have been many studies which have tried to explore behavioural intention and intention to use mobile banking through various technology acceptance models (Sharma 2017; Liebana-Cabanillas and Lara-Rubio 2017; Riffai et al. 2012; Lee and Chung 2009). Researchers have also focused on the continuous usage of the mobile payment and banking services once adopted (Sharma and Sharma 2019; Zhou 2013) in order to examine users' post-adoption behaviour. The adoption behaviour transits many factors such as trust and satisfaction apart from the factors identified in various technological acceptance models such as the Unified Theory of Acceptance and Use of Technology (UTAUT: Venkatesh et al. 2003), D&M IS success model (Delone and Mclean 1992) Technology Acceptance Model (TAM: Davis 1989), the Theory of Planned Behaviour (TPB: Fishbein and Ajzen 1975). Post-adoption behaviour also depends on certain influencers such as attitudinal beliefs, normative beliefs along with perceived behavioural control (Hong et al. 2008), relationship quality and switching barrier (Liu et al. 2011), trust and quality dimensions (Sharma and Sharma 2019). However, with the increasing influence of social media (SM), it is imperative to identify its role in mobile banking as well which has already been proposed by several researchers. It is important to bring to notice that despite various studies on social media influence on bank marketing and internet banking (Godey et al. 2016; Vinerean et al. 2013; Mitic and Kapoulas 2012), there has not been any study which focuses on the role of various cognitive attitudinal stages of the consumers towards their acceptance of mobile banking. There are scant studies which broadly express the influence of social media as a promotional tool for promotion of banking services.

St. Elmo. Lewis in (1898) propounded the idea of cognitive stages of consumer adoption and thus suggested the widely accepted theory of 'Hierarchy of Effects' (HOE). Early hierarchy of effects models such as AIDA which is an acronym for Attention, Interest, Desire and Action, posit the gradual transition of consumers from the Attention stage to the final Action stage. This study is aimed at charting this transition in context of mobile banking and also to develop a framework for its adoption amongst young consumers under the influence of social media. Social media communication has also been the top communication media for banks (Shankar et al. 2020; Tam and Oliveira 2017; Sahoo and Pillai 2017). A major reason for this has been the convenience on the side of Banks to give personalised promotions to their clients (Santini et al. 2020; Madan and Yadav 2018). Based on the classification given by Banerjee (2009) of sales promotion; cash discounts in terms of money-back, and coupons are most popular with young consumers (Santini et al. 2020).

This paper thereby makes an original contribution in identifying the role of social media on various cognitive stages of mobile banking consumers. The paper, thereby, uniquely develops a framework by integrating the Hierarchy of Effects Model with Social Media Influence for the Indian mobile banking consumers. The work solely focuses on young consumers for their being the substantial influencers of social media and early adopters. This research builds upon the theory of Lavidge and Steiner (1961) by explaining the reason for movement of consumers in the hierarchy of effect.

2 Theoretical Framework and Development of Hypotheses

Adoption of Mobile Banking services is similar to adoption or purchase of a new product or service. The consumer passes through distinctive phases and finally adopts MB services. There is extant research on the influence of social media on purchase behaviour. However, through this paper we intend to see the influence of social media in the transition of consumers from one stage of cognitive process to the other as laid out in the Hierarchy of Effects model. The hierarchy of effects in this case is being observed through the AIDA model. Consumers adopting the Mobile Banking move through distinctive stages of Awareness, Interest, Desire and Action. These stages are distinct as the consumer's attitude towards mobile banking changes favourably and as the consumer climbs up each stage his/her motivation for the adoption of the mobile banking service also increases. This finally culminates in to the adoption of MB services. The distinctiveness of each of these stages can be observed by the information requirement of the individual in each stage.

Zaikovisky (1985) way back identified involvement as one of the parameters of consumer purchase. On the same line, degree of involvement with social media can be observed from the usage pattern. It has been argued by many researchers of social media that the influence of social media is a conglomeration of different aspects that social media tends to address e.g. individuals who are highly involved with social media tend to have high usage pattern.

Similarly, Yadav and Rahman (2017) and Shankar et al. (2020) have defined informativeness as "the strength or plausibility of persuasive argumentation" to be the construct for social media influence. Thus, more informative social media interaction would have higher degree of influence. The influence of SM also increases if the information that can be obtained from these SM interactions are useful in addressing to the problems or contextual issues of the user (Kaur et al. 2018; Hollebeek et al. 2014). Therefore, users who seek information for solving problems through social media are more likely to be influenced than people who do not seek such information.

2.1 The Proposed Theoretical Model

(See Fig. 1)

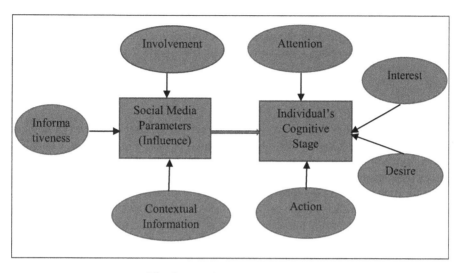

Fig. 1. The theoretical framework

2.2 Hypothesis Formulation

The conceptual framework given above clearly defines the Dependent and the Independent variable in the study. As stated, and also represented in the Fig. 1, Social Media parameters which combine together to form the impetus of the Independent Variable is made up majorly of three constructs viz; Involvement, Informativeness and Contextual Information. These together affect the dependent variable representing the cognitive stage of the consumer as given by the Hierarchy of Effects. Thus, the following hypothesis can be constructed for the dependent variable:

H_1: Higher the influence of social media on an individual higher will be his cognitive stage in MB adoption.

As information requirement varies in each stage, the degree of influence that social media has as a whole in each cognitive stage taken separately varies. Thus the influence that SM will have in attention stage may not be the same as in the action stage. This leads us to the next hypothesis as:

H_2: Social Media influence varies in each stage and increases as individual climbs higher in cognitive stages.

3 Research Design and Measurements

The Research can be designed as a pre-post experimental as well as a post-test only non-experimental design. In a pre-post experimental design, the identified test groups can be exposed to varying degrees of social media campaigns and their progress can be recorded on a cognitive adoption scale.

In a post-test only type of scenario, random subjects who are in varying stages of adoption will be measured for the social media influence as well as the cognitive stage of mobile banking adoption, and the results are one-to-one mapped. Analysis of this map is to be tested for hypothesis validation.

3.1 Measurement

Independent Variable is constructed of three determinants, a set of statements defining each construct. These statements will be measured against a Likert scale. Composite scores from all the items can be used to show the degree of social media influence. These constructs of social media being widely accepted in research, hence standardized scales for each of these constructs exist which can be customised to suit this study.

The dependent variable is the cognitive stage of the individual. Any measure of this variable should be able to (a) clearly identify the stage in which an individual is (b) validate the ordinal position of all individuals in a sample. Thus, the statements chosen to measure each stage should be such that, for each part the first question is the leading question followed by three corroborative statements. The leading statement would be framed such that not only would it identify the cognitive stage in which the individual respondent was in, but would also be able to distinguish one cognitive stage from the other.

4 Discussions

Social Media is rapidly becoming a favourite marketing communication media. The best thing about SM is its versatility and wide acceptance. Thereby, more and more service providers are using it to influence and target their customers. Banks are also using this platform to aggressively increase their customer base of Mobile Banking Service Users. Experts in the industry strongly recommend that Banks who will be able to harness digital platforms will rapidly gain market share and eventually be profitable.

Banks are aggressively targeting young consumers through social media for adoption of their MB services. Amongst young consumers the role of peer group environment is well established (Banerjee 2016), hence social media which has active peer-group members becomes highly influential. Although by now it has been shown through a large number of studies that social media is highly influential, however this study has further pointed in the direction of assessing the effectiveness of social media. This study also shows that the informational requirements in each cognitive stage varies, and social media which is most effective in disbursing functional information (Dholakia 2009) has greater influence on information intensive stages such as interest and action.

An important outcome of this study is to be the use of social media amongst young consumers. Higher usage and involvement will increase the acceptance of Mobile Banking Services. Mobile Banking Services are also high-involvement services in themselves, implying that users consciously seek out relevant information about the service. Banks who develop a personal rapport with their customers through social media and dispense information that is relevant and useful will surely increase the overall mobile baking acceptance.

5   Concluding Remarks

Mobile banking is becoming the preferred banking medium day by day and is all set to bring about the complete technological revolution in the way we do banking. It has been realized that Social Media has been a key influencer in mobile banking adoption. It is thereby required that mobile operators exploit the social media platforms to its maximum potential to reach out the mobile banking consumers. The first and foremost way to create mobile banking consumers is to understand the young consumers at the outset as they remain the key users of mobile banking due to their easy adaptability towards digital technology and this is also the segment which has the largest user base of social media.

The big task for mobile operators to identify is not only to attract consumers towards mobile banking but retain them as continuous users in order to replace the traditional method of banking and hence it is important that the operators understand the various stages of consumers' mindset towards such technological adoption. Though there have been studies related to social media influence on internet banking however there is no substantial study which identifies the role of social media on the various cognitive attitudinal stages of mobile banking consumers. With this premise, the main objective of the paper was to develop a theoretical model that can integrate the social media parameters with various cognitive stages of the mobile banking consumers through Hierarchy of Effects (HOE) model. The other main objective was to develop the framework for the young consumers in the context of India which can further be extended to the entire user base. The theoretical framework aims to contribute significantly in the decision making of government agencies, mobile operators, banking institutions and researchers.

References

Banerjee, S.: Effect of product category on promotional choice: comparative study of discounts and freebies. Manage. Res. News. **32**(2), 120–131 (2009)

Banerjee, S.: Moderating effect of peer group environment on consumer predisposition towards premium promotions: a study on young urban consumers in India. IIMB Manage. Rev. **28**(4), 225–234 (2016)

Davis, F.: Perceived usefulness, perceived ease of use, and user acceptance of information technology. MIS Q. **13**(3), 319–340 (1989)

DeLone, W.H., McLean, E.R.: Information systems success: the quest for the dependent variable. Inf. Syst. Res. **3**(1), 60–95 (1992)

Dholakia, U.M., Blazevic, V., Wiertz, C., Algesheimer, R.: Communal service delivery. J. Serv. Res. **12**(2), 208–226 (2009)

Fishbein, M., Ajzen, I.: Belief, Attitude, Intention, and Behavior: An Introduction to Theory and Research. Addison-Wesley, Reading (1975)

Godey, B., et al.: Social media marketing efforts of luxury brands: influence on brand equity and consumer behavior. J. Bus. Res. **69**(12), 5833–5841 (2016)

Hollebeek, L.D., Glynn, M.S., Brodie, R.J.: Consumer brand engagement in social media: conceptualization, scale development and validation. J. Interact. Mark. **28**(2), 149–165 (2014)

Hong, S.-J., Thong, J.Y.L., Moon, J.-Y., Tam, K.Y.: Understanding the behavior of mobile data services consumers. Inf. Syst. Front. **10**(4), 431–445 (2008)

Kaur, P., Dhir, A., Rajala, R., Dwivedi, Y.: Why people use online social media brand communities. Online Inf. Rev. **42**(2), 205–221 (2018)

Lavidge, R.C., Steiner, G.A.: A model for predictive measurements of advertising effectiveness. J. Mark. **25**, 59–62 (1961)

Lee, K.C., Chung, N.: Understanding factors affecting trust in and satisfaction with mobile banking in Korea: a modified DeLone and McLean's model perspective. Interact. Comput. **21** (5), 385–392 (2009)

Lewis, E.S.: AIDA sales funnel. Obtenido de Proven Models (1898). http://www.provenmodels. com/547/aidasales-funnel/elias-st.-elmo-lewis. Accessed 18 Feb 2020

Liébana-Cabanillasa, F., Lara-Rubio, J.: Predictive and explanatory modeling regarding adoption of mobile payment systems. Technol. Forecast. Soc. Chang. **120**, 32–40 (2017)

Liu, C.T., Guo, Y.M., Lee, C.H.: The effects of relationship quality and switching barriers on customer loyalty. Int. J. Inf. Manage. **31**(1), 71–79 (2011)

Madan, K., Yadav, R.: Understanding and predicting antecedents of mobile shopping adoption. Asia Pac. J. Mark. Logist. **30**(1), 139–162 (2018)

Mitic, M., Kapoulas, A.: Understanding the role of social media in bank marketing. Mark. Intell. Plann. **30**(7), 668–686 (2012)

Riffai, M.M.M.A., Grant, K., Edgar, D.: Big TAM in Oman: exploring the promise of on-line banking, its adoption by customers and the challenges of banking in Oman. Int. J. Inf. Manage. **32**(3), 239–250 (2012)

Sahoo, D., Pillai, S.: Role of mobile banking servicescape on customer attitude and engagement: an empirical investigation in India. Int. J. Bank Mark. **35**(7), 1115–1132 (2017)

Santini, F.D.O., Ladeira, W.J., Sampaio, C.H., Boeira, J.P.: The effects of sales promotions on mobile banking a cross-cultural study. J. Promot. Manage. **26**(3), 350–371 (2020)

Shankar, A., Jebarajakirthy, C., Ashaduzzaman, M.: How do electronic word of mouth practices contribute to mobile banking adoption? J. Retail. Consum. Serv. **52**, 101920 (2020)

Sharma, S.K.: Integrating cognitive antecedents into TAM to explain mobile banking behavioral intention: a SEM-neural network modeling. Inf. Syst. Front. **1**, 1–13 (2017)

Sharma, S., Sharma, M.: Examining the role of trust and quality dimensions in the actual usage of mobile banking services: an empirical investigation. Int. J. Inf. Manage. **44**, 65–75 (2019)

Tam, C., Oliveira, T.: Literature review of mobile banking and individual performance. Int. J. Bank Mark. **35**(7), 1042–1065 (2017)

Venkatesh, V., Morris, M.G., Davis, G.B., Davis, F.D.: User acceptance of information technology: toward a unified view. MIS Q. **27**(3), 425–478 (2003)

Vinerean, S., Cetina, I., Dumitrescu, L., Tichindelean, M.: The effects of social media marketing on online consumer behavior. Int. J. Bus. Manage. **8**(14), 66–79 (2013)

Yadav, M., Rahman, Z.: Measuring consumer perception of social media marketing activities in e-commerce industry: scale development & validation. Telemat. Inf. **34**(7), 1294–1307 (2017)

Zaichkowsky, J.L.: Measuring the involvement construct. J. Consum. Res. **12**(3), 341–352 (1985)

Zhou, T.: An empirical examination of continuance intention of mobile payment services. Decis. Support Syst. **54**, 1085–1091 (2013)

Fans' Attachment to Players in the Indian Premier League: Insights from Twitter Analytics

Giridhar B. Kamath[1,2(✉)], Shirshendu Ganguli[2], Simon George[2], and Vibha[1]

[1] Manipal Institute of Technology, Manipal Academy of Higher Education, Manipal 576104, India
giridhar.kamath@manipal.edu
[2] T A Pai Management Institute, Manipal 576104, India

Abstract. Sports in India are gradually gaining traction, and people are more and more inclined towards various other sports apart from cricket. Even though several sporting leagues are currently running in India, the attention and viewership that the Indian Premier League (IPL) enjoys are unmatchable. Social media posts and the growing viewership on TV and Over the Top (OTT) platforms are evidence of this. This research investigates the level of attachment of the fans with the players of their favorite team. We study the opinions of fans through the tweets extracted during the IPL players auctions held in the preseason of the thirteenth edition of the IPL. The fans were very active on social media, airing their views about the various players available in the auction for their team to buy, indicating high team identification. In total, 15,374 tweets that were extracted and processed confirmed the same. Further, using System Dynamics (SD) methodology, we develop a causal loop linking the various parameters of importance in the IPL ecosystem that could help the league and the team managers to understand the importance of player attachment among the fans better. This study is the first in the context of IPL that uses the System Dynamics methodology to justify the findings of twitter analytics.

Keywords: Opinion mining · Twitter analytics · Indian Premier League · Player auctions · Causal loop diagram · System dynamics

1 Introduction

Social media has emerged as a medium to express the feelings of the users without any hesitation. Such impulsive postings that people make on social media regarding various events/topics/issues have many implications to various interested parties. Researchers have been studying the social media posts of people and have successfully drawn conclusions about specific topics under concern. E.g., Brand marketers have successfully captured the sentiments/opinions of the people towards their brands based on social media posts. Likewise, social media posts about specific issues help the stakeholders to gauge the sentiments of people like positive, negative, neutral, fear, agony, etc.

© IFIP International Federation for Information Processing 2020
Published by Springer Nature Switzerland AG 2020
S. K. Sharma et al. (Eds.): TDIT 2020, IFIP AICT 618, pp. 451–462, 2020.
https://doi.org/10.1007/978-3-030-64861-9_40

In sports, especially in Western countries, the user-generated content on social media has been a prevalent concept. Fans with high attachment to their favorite teams and favorite players have been generating much content on social media, and such contents have gained millions of views and have helped the team or players to maintain their popularity and has garnered much interest from the sponsor and other stakeholders alike.

In India, cricket is watched more than any other sport. With the penetration of the internet happening at a never seen before pace, the viewership of all other sports is on the rise, but cricket stills stand much ahead. The current study deals with the auctions of players in the Indian Premier League (IPL). IPL is a T20 cricket league based in India with a viewership of over 400 million both on TV and over the top (OTT) platforms. IPL is the second most popular sporting league in the world. The first season of IPL was played in 2008 in India, and in 2019 it completed its 12 years. Even though there were several player auctions held from time to time, this research deals with the player auctions held in December 2019 before the 13th season of the IPL. The auctions were live on TV, and also live streaming was available on OTT platforms.

The purpose of this study is to look into the social media posts of the fans during the auctions and assess the involvement of the fans through their posts and their sentiments displayed during the auction process. Fans who were following the auctions have expressed their opinions on social media sites like Facebook and Twitter. Our study deals with posts on Twitter. The tweets were extracted, and then through opinion mining using the software R, we tried to gauge the attachment the fans have towards the various players, both national and international. The word cloud of the frequently used words helped in visualizing the words clearly and helped in highlighting the underlying pattern of the content of the tweets.

Further, we try to highlight the effect of fans' attachment to the players in IPL on the other parameters in and around the IPL ecosystem using a causal loop diagram based on the available literature and highlight the possible linkages between the points of attachment and the fans' attachment to their favorite teams. In this pursuit, we consider the bigger picture with several direct and indirect factors influencing the entire IPL ecosystem.

The rest of the paper is designed as follows: First, we discuss the importance of attachment points in sports. Next, we look at social media analytics literature in the context of sports. Subsequently, we discuss the methodology of this study, followed by the results and discussions leading to the contribution of this study.

2   Literature Review

2.1   Attachment Points

Attachment theory says that human beings tend to maintain psychological ties with particular objects. Attachment points influence indirect sports consumption. Kwon et al. (2005) define attachment points as "a consumer's psychological ties with various aspects associated with his or her favorite sport team." Funk et al. (2016) define attachment as the emotional, functional, and symbolic meaning assigned by a fan to a sports team. Heere and James (2007) argue that the American sports team usually carries the name of the city or state in their team name because, according to them, the attachment with a team happens because of several external factors like geographical, ethnic, or several other factors surrounding the team. In the IPL, all the eight teams have their city names included in their team name like Chennai Super Kings (CSK), Delhi Capitals (DC), Kings XI Punjab (KXI Punjab), Kolkata Knight Riders(KKR), Mumbai Indians (MI), Rajasthan Royals (RR), Royal Challengers Bangalore (RCB), and, SunRisers Hyderabad (SRH).

Yoshida et al. (2015) studied attachment points in Japan professional League and established a link between the attachment points and team identification. According to Katz and Heere (2013), attachment points play a role in influencing how the sport is consumed (direct or indirect).

Shapiro et al. (2013) highlighted that multiple attachment points could influence the way the sport is consumed and how the fans would react to the sponsors. Heere et al. (2011) highlighted the importance of attachment towards players in a sport and argued that including players in the marketing plans can be fruitful for the sponsors. Lock et al. (2011) say that attachment towards the sport itself can be a vital factor that influences the formation of team identification in the case of a new team.

Overall, the literature on attachment points indicates that there are three main attachment points with respect to any sport. They are sport attachment, player attachment, and the city attachment. In this research, since we study the sentiments of fans during the pre-season players' auction, we confine our scope to the players' attachment with an assumption that fans who are tweeting already have higher sport attachment.

2.2   Social Media Analytics

According to Pang and Lee (2008) and Liu (2012), Opinion Mining has become an active area of research, and there are various applications such as competitive intelligence (Xu et al. 2011), and market prediction (Liu et al. 2007; Zhang and Skiena 2010), product pricing Zhang and Skiena (2010), Jin et al. (2019), and nation relationship analysis (Chambers et al. 2015). There is a significant growth in user-generated content on the internet. Extracting useful information from the user-generated content is interesting and challenging (Pang and Lee 2008).

Several prior studies, like Derczynski et al. (2013), Pak and Parouubek (2010), have researched twitter and sentiment analysis. According to Liu (2012) the word opinion can be represented as a quintuple (ei, aij, sijkℓ, hk, tℓ), in which ei is the ith entity, aij is the jth aspect of the ith entity, hk is the kth opinion holder, tℓ is the time when the opinion is expressed, sijkℓ is the opinion or sentiment towards the ith aspect of the jth entity from opinion holder hk at time tℓ. As per the definition, for opinion mining, for the given text, the quintuple is determined. The third component is enough for document-level opinion mining instead of the full quintuple. However, for the fine-grained level, more components are required.

The growth of social media platforms, e-commerce, and review sites such as Twitter, Reddit, Yelp, and Amazon provides a sufficient amount of resources as corpora for academic research. Mining the useful information from social media will be valuable and benefits the different applications. Hence social media data can be used as a representative tool of real-time experiences such as for sports events. During these events, people post a large number of posts, thus revealing their expressions, opinions, and suggestions according to the circumstances occurring during the events. Stojanovski et al. (2015) analyzed the views conveyed in the users' posts during football games and could intimate the concerned authorities of possible riots after the match. Fan and Gordon (2014) investigated the differences and similarities between the Chinese NBA fans and western NBA fans with a global presence in terms of their social media usage and points of attachment to a team.

The Social Media Analytics Process (Fan and Gordon 2014) is mainly a three-stage process that involves capturing relevant data from social media sites by carefully monitoring various social media resources and extracting the required details from those sources. The data extracted is generally in an unstructured format. The second stage involves an understanding of the data and converting the extracted unstructured data in a structured format. This stage is crucial because it involves selecting relevant data for modeling, removing noisy and low-quality data. This process consists of various advanced data analytic strategies to analyze the retained data and gain insights from it. The third stage is the presentation, which becomes a representational way to visualize the relevant information extracted. There are many easy to use built-in analytic tools available in the market for research and academic purposes for Facebook, Twitter, etc. The problem with these tools is that these are "black-box" where a researcher does not know how the data model is built and the methodology is not transparent. The use of programming languages such as Python or R with their associated packages for data science analytics to analyze social media data makes a fully transparent methodology (Yun et al. 2019).

3   Methodology

This research combined two methods. First, opinion mining was done using social media analytics. Next, the importance of attachment points was highlighted using the system dynamics methodology. A causal loop was developed to study the interrelationships between the various constructs and parameters within the scope of this study.

3.1   Twitter Analytics Using R

The IPL players' auction was held on 19th December 2019 in Kolkata, India. The tweets were extracted for the following period: one week before the auction date and one week after the auction ended. This research is limited to opinion mining of the tweets during and after the IPL player auction. Fifteen thousand three hundred seventy-four tweets were extracted concerning all the eight teams in the tournament. This study is limited to developing a word cloud using the software R. The word cloud would enable one to understand the frequently used words in the tweets and analyze the opinions of fans visually, regarding the auctioning and buying of their choicest players by the team management.

3.2   Data Mining

We have collected data from the popularly used social media platform Twitter. Twitter data is actively used for many purposes like to make recommendations, gather insights, and lodge public complaints. The tweets posted by the users are in the form of hashtags, and the extent that users find valuable information shows its validity. Hence appropriate hashtags used by the concerned eight IPL teams were used to extract the tweets posted. To ingest the social media data from Twitter, Twitter API is used, which requires consumer key, consumer secret key, request token URL, access token URL, and authorize URL. The function called searchTwitter defined in twitter package will pull the tweets associated with the hashtags defined in the function. Data is mined for all eight teams using the teams' hashtags and stored in separate files.

The data thus mined is not well structured and hence requires some preliminary processing. Preliminary processing involves converting all words to lowercase, removing all punctuation, and dropping the stopwords. The pre-processing mainly consists of imposing some structure on the text data and converting it into a document-term matrix (dtm). The necessity of the Document-term matrix is the easiness of analyzing the terms and finding the unique, common, and repeated words from the collection of documents called corpus. Further from this matrix, we can explore the data and find the correlation in the document-term matrix between the term it references and the specific word in the corpus using the term association (i.e., using a function called findAssocs). Data visualization provides an easy way to view and analyze the data. In this paper, from the obtained document-term matrix (dtm), a word cloud is formed, and this is used to visualize the term frequency. Only the top 250 terms were used in this wordcloud. The process used for data mining is depicted in Fig. 1.

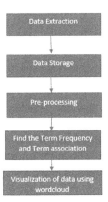

Fig. 1. Process of data collection and processing.

3.3   System Dynamics Methodology

The main objective of using this methodology is to develop a cause and effect relationship between the player attachment and other selected parameters in and around the event. If we consider only the player attachment, it will not be clear how the attachment fits in with the system. When we look at the bigger picture of the league with player attachment points as one of the parameters, we can see how the whole cause and effect relationship unfolds within the given boundary. The current study takes some links among the variables from the research conducted by Choi et al. (2017), Crescitelli and Figueiredo (2009), Hsiao et al. (2010), and Levine and Call (2003). Hsiao et al. (2010), in their study on a professional baseball game in Taiwan, developed a system dynamics simulation model to understand the system structure and simulate the developing trend. Using System Dynamics methodology (Sterman 2000), we attempt to model the IPL ecosystem by focussing on the following clusters: attachment points, player attachment, sport attachment, city attachment, event attachment, team identification, number of fans, team income, and the event income. SD methodology follows the steps as shown in Fig. 2.

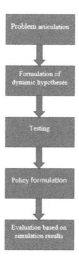

Fig. 2. System Dynamics methodology (Source: Sterman 2000).

As seen in Fig. 3, we relate the city attachment, player attachment, and sport attachment to the event attachment. The other attachment points drive the attachment towards the event. The players' attachment is also dependent on player performances and the players' popularity. Players who enjoy immense popularity because of their on-field performances and off-field conduct are the most sought after by the teams and the team fans.

Fig. 3. Factors affecting event attachment.

Fans wish that their team buys such popular players who can contribute to the team performances. This is evident from the tweets during the auction period. Fans were either hoping their teams bought certain players or were seen tweeting positive tweets after their favorite teams bought the anticipated players.

Fig. 4. Factors affecting event image.

Figure 4 shows the links assumed in this study to relate specific parameters with the event image. The market shares of the event sponsors and the team sponsors determine their decision to continue with the sponsorship deals, respectively. This decision could have an impact on the event image. Also, the attitude towards the event that the fans' have influences the event image.

Fig. 5. Factors affecting event income.

The number of fans and the image of the team influences fan attendance. The event image and the popularity of the players influence sponsorship. The income that the event generates depends on the factors such as the fan attendance at the games in the stadium, the sponsorship deals with the sponsors, and the television broadcast licensing fees, as shown in Fig. 5.

Fig. 6. Factors leading to team identification.

Figure 6 depicts the connection between the parameters that explain the team identification. As seen in the previous research work, we have equated the attachment points as predictors of team identification. Also, event attitude and fan attendance at the games strengthen team identification. Event attitude is influenced by the event attachment and the perceived fit between the event and the sponsoring brand of the event. We further assume that the link or the strength of the relationship between the event and the sponsor influences the attitude the fans hold towards the event, which in turn affects the team identification.

4   Results and Discussions

The tweets were structured in the pre-processing stage to estimate the word frequency. From these structured tweeted data, we found the term frequency of each term present in the corpus and found the associativity of these terms. From the obtained term frequency matrix, wordcloud was created for data visualization purposes. The wordcloud of the selected three active teams in the auctions are as follows. We can see that the fans have tweeted about the players already existing in their favorite team and also are welcoming the new buys their team management has made. The word cloud helps us visualize the word frequencies as shown in Fig. 7.

Fig. 7. Wordcloud for Delhi Capitals.

Fig. 8. Wordcloud for Rajasthan Royals.

Fig. 9. Wordcloud for Mumbai Indians.

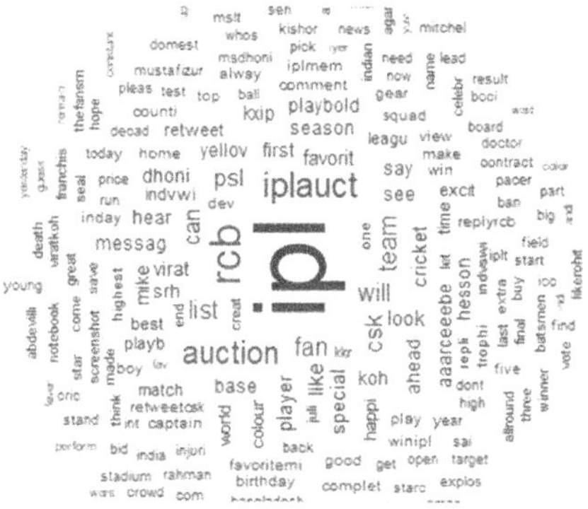

Fig. 10. Wordcloud for the entire auctioning event.

The wordcloud of the next two teams is shown in Fig. 8 and 9, respectively. It is very evident that the fans were very concerned about the players of their teams and had a strong attachment, which leads to higher team identification. A clear link between the players' attachment and team identification can be seen here. Figure 10 depicts the wordcloud after considering the overall tweets of the auction. Here it is visible that apart from the player names, fans have been tweeting about their favorite teams and, in general, positively about the event and the sport as such in excitement.

This overall involvement of the fans is an indication that the event is held in high regard by the fans and the sponsors of the event, and the teams can make use of the fans' attachment to communicate with their target audiences strategically.

In the next step, we model the IPL ecosystem with key emphasis on the attachment points leading to team identification and study its causal impact on other associated parameters. By considering the wordclouds as the base, a causal loop is developed, as shown in Fig. 11.

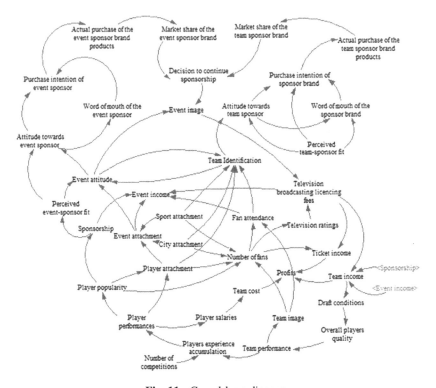

Fig. 11. Causal loop diagram.

Figure 11 shows the bigger picture of how the attachment points are related to the various parameters of the system. The primary constructs considered are the attachment points, team identification, the number of fans, event income, and team income. The causal loop shows how the attachment points influence the team identification, which then affects the attitude towards the team sponsors, thus affecting the purchase intention and word of mouth about the sponsor brand. Similarly, the link between the event attitude and the purchase intention of the event sponsor brand is explored.

The causal loop highlights the benefits of fans' attachment to players in a sporting league. If seen in isolation, the fans' attachment to players may not seem to be of much importance to the sponsors. But when modeled and focused on the interrelations, one can see how strong the attachment to the players is. Attachment to specific players is dependent on the player's past performance and experience too. Hence, teams can target to get players based on their experience in the sport. This could add stability and balance to the side, and a balanced team can always be backed for better performance in the league, thereby satisfying the fans' anticipation.

5   Conclusions

Through opinion mining of the 15374 tweets during the players' auction in the IPL, this study highlights the importance of the fans' attachment to players. The context here was the IPL players auctions held in December 2019. The resulting word frequency tables and the wordclouds generated thereby, using the software R indicates that the fans were actively involved in the auctions celebrating the bids won by their respective teams, of their anticipated players. It was clear that the attachment points like sport attachment and city attachment were the driving factors along with the attachment to players that strengthened the team identification of the fans.

Further, a causal loop was developed using the attachment points as the epicentre to model the interrelationship among the various parameters influencing the event income and the team income. The causal loop can help the event organizers to understand the underlying structure of the IPL ecosystem. Further, the respective team management can target the right players to buy for their team so that the fans' team identification caused because of the attachment to players remains intact and favorable to the stakeholders involved, especially the sponsors.

6   Limitations and Future Work

This study has some limitations. Firstly, this study only considered opinion mining of the tweets extracted based on one-off auction in the IPL. Future studies can compare the tweets of two or more auctions and try to draw conclusions about the fluctuating attachment points. Secondly, the current study is limited to drawing the causal loop diagram. Future studies can simulate the model by drawing the stock and flow diagram whereby the system can be simulated using the mathematical equations governing the inter-relationships. The graphs that can be generated as the simulation outputs can highlight the importance of the various causal links. Further, future studies can attempt to model the players' auctions by modeling all the parameters that influence the fans and the team's decision to go for a particular player in the auction.

References

Chambers, N., et al.: Identifying political sentiment between nation states with social media. In: Proceedings of the 2015 Conference on Empirical Methods in Natural Language Processing, pp. 65–75, September 2015

Choi, M., Park, M., Lee, H.S., Hwang, S.: Dynamic modeling for apartment brand management in the housing market. Int. J. Strateg. Property Manag. **21**(4), 357–370 (2017)

Crescitelli, E., Figueiredo, J.B.: Brand equity evolution: a system dynamics model. BAR-Braz. Adm. Rev. **6**(2), 101–117 (2009)

Derczynski, L., Ritter, A., Clark, S., Bontcheva, K.: Twitter part-of-speech tagging for all: overcoming sparse and noisy data. In: Proceedings of the International Conference Recent Advances in Natural Language Processing RANLP 2013, pp. 198–206, September 2013

Fan, W., Gordon, M.D.: The power of social media analytics. Commun. ACM **57**(6), 74–81 (2014)

Funk, D.C., Alexandris, K., McDonald, H.: Sport Consumer Behaviour: Marketing Strategies. Routledge (2016)

Heere, B., James, J.D.: Sports teams and their communities: examining the influence of external group identities on team identity. J. Sport Manag. **21**(3), 319–337 (2007)

Heere, B., James, J., Yoshida, M., Scremin, G.: The effect of associated group identities on team identity. J. Sport Manag. **25**(6), 606–621 (2011)

Hsiao, C.T., Peng, H.L., Huang, H.H.: Dynamic simulation for development of the professional baseball game in Taiwan. Int. J. Electron. Bus. Manag. **8**(3), 173 (2010)

Jin, J., Liu, Y., Ji, P., Kwong, C.K.: Review on recent advances in information mining from big consumer opinion data for product design. J. Comput. Inf. Sci. Eng. **19**(1) (2019)

Katz, M., Heere, B.: Leaders and followers: an exploration of the notion of scale-free networks within a new brand community. J. Sport Manag. **27**(4), 271–287 (2013)

Kwon, H.H., Trail, G.T., Anderson, D.S.: Are multiple points of attachment necessary to predict cognitive, affective, conative, or behavioral loyalty? Sport Manag. Rev. **8**(3), 255–270 (2005)

Levine, R.L., Call, O.: Models of attitude and belief change from the perspective of system dynamics. In: Proceedings of the 21st International Conference of the System Dynamics Society, New York City, USA. The System Dynamics Society (2003)

Liu, B.: Sentiment analysis and opinion mining. Synth. Lect. Hum. Lang. Technol. **5**(1), 1–167 (2012)

Liu, Y., Huang, X., An, A., Yu, X.: ARSA: a sentiment-aware model for predicting sales performance using blogs. In: Proceedings of the 30th Annual International ACM SIGIR Conference on Research and Development in Information Retrieval, pp. 607–614, July 2007

Lock, D., Taylor, T., Darcy, S.: In the absence of achievement: the formation of new team identification. Eur. Sport Manag. Q. **11**(2), 171–192 (2011)

Pak, A., Paroubek, P.: Twitter as a corpus for sentiment analysis and opinion mining. In: LREc, vol. 10, no. 2010, pp. 1320–1326, May 2010

Pang, B., Lee, L.: Opinion mining and sentiment analysis. Found. Trends® Inf. Retrieval **2**(1–2), 1–135 (2008)

Shapiro, S.L., Ridinger, L.L., Trail, G.T.: An analysis of multiple spectator consumption behaviors, identification, and future behavioral intentions within the context of a new college football program. J. Sport Manag. **27**(2), 130–145 (2013)

Sterman, J.D.: Business dynamics: systems thinking and modeling for a complex (2000)

Stojanovski, D., Strezoski, G., Madjarov, G., Dimitrovski, I.: Emotion identification in FIFA world cup tweets using convolutional neural network. In: 2015 11th International Conference on Innovations in Information Technology (IIT), pp. 52–57. IEEE.world (No. HD30. 2 S7835 2000, November 2015

Xu, K., Liao, S.S., Li, J., Song, Y.: Mining comparative opinions from customer reviews for competitive intelligence. Decis. Support Syst. **50**(4), 743–754 (2011)

Yoshida, M., Heere, B., Gordon, B.: Predicting behavioral loyalty through community: why other fans are more important than our own intentions, our satisfaction, and the team itself. J. Sport Manag. **29**(3), 318–333 (2015)

Yun, J.T., et al.: The social media macroscope: a science gateway for research using social media data. Future Gener. Comput. Syst. **111**, 819–828 (2019)

Zhang, W., Skiena, S.: Trading strategies to exploit blog and news sentiment. In: Fourth International AAAI Conference on Weblogs and Social Media, May 2010

Trusting Social Media News: Role of Social Influence and Emotions Using EEG as a Brain Imaging Tool

Gaurav Dixit[(⊠)] and Shristi Bose

Department of Management Studies, Indian Institute of Technology Roorkee, Roorkee, India
gaurav.dixit@ms.iitr.ac.in

Abstract. Social Networking Sites have been all-pervasive in our lives. With a staggering 296 billion social media users in India itself, social networking sites have a considerable impact in shaping the views and opinions of people. These platforms provide people to not only lend voices to the cause they care for but also enable them to remain regularly updated with the latest news stories related to the cause. However, how social media affect a user's perception of a particular news feed item lacks clarity. In this paper, we analyze the trustworthiness of the widely circulated news feed items. Specifically, we examine the role of social influence and emotions in deciding social media users' trustworthiness of feed items by conducting EEG experiments. By demonstrating how the perceived trustworthiness of social media feed items is affected by our neurobiology, our study has significant implications for both information systems research and management. The study also has implications for policymakers and society.

Keywords: Social media · EEG · NeuroIS · Trust · Influence

1 Introduction

Humans are social beings. They seek relationships with others, usually forming social networks based on friendships on common professional or personal interests or some other interdependencies (Wasserman and Faust 1994). What is different now is that these social networks have increasingly become computer-mediated. With the increasing prevalence of social networking sites (SNSs) like Twitter, Whatsapp, Facebook, Linkedin, etc., people are connecting over these SNSs more than ever before. These SNSs have become a popular source for sharing information, exchanging ideas about various topics, political canvassing, and dissemination of new information (Haythornthwaite 2005). The omnipresence of SNSs has increased its utility and appeal among the masses, with millions of users using it as a source of news (Holton and Lewis 2011). Previous researches indicate that SNSs allow the rapid proliferation of news through individual sharing of stories (Diakopoulos and Naaman 2011). Thus, every individual can become a potential news source, raising concerns about the authenticity of the information shared and the spread of fake news feed items.

© IFIP International Federation for Information Processing 2020
Published by Springer Nature Switzerland AG 2020
S. K. Sharma et al. (Eds.): TDIT 2020, IFIP AICT 618, pp. 463–474, 2020.
https://doi.org/10.1007/978-3-030-64861-9_41

Recent researches suggest that people these days are mainly relying on social media sites for getting news, with SNS platforms like Facebook, WhatsApp, and Twitter slowly replacing the print media for the same (Aneez et al. 2019). In SNSs like Twitter, Facebook, and Linkedin, users are exposed to a wide array of articles in their news feed, which are an amalgam of posts from family, friends and influencers, sponsored articles, and articles from sources that the users subscribe to (Moravac et al. 2018). Also, social media is emerging as a non-conventional source of providing information, where users do not consciously pick the source of all the news feed items. Instead, selective information (with little to no transparency) gets disseminated to users through proprietary algorithms. The news feed items and can be intentionally or unintentionally true or false, with some of them overtly created to influence netizens (Shane 2017).

In an era where information, facts, and news are so widely prevalent and comes at a zero marginal cost, it becomes vital to understand how the varied exposure of information influences the judgments, opinions, and perceptions of the social media users. It is in this perspective that we seek to understand how users in social networking sites get influenced in trusting information, facts, and news shared in their SNS feed. What emotions do they carry towards certain news feed items? These research questions will provide us a way forward in preventing the infodemic where information can be used as a potential weapon to polarise the views and opinions of the masses.

We aim to carry out our research in the context of the user's cognitive response towards the news feed items on Twitter. Given the fact that Social Networking Sites offer a reflection of user's sentiments and perspectives, it underlies the basic behavioral traits that go behind the information that users of social networking sites choose to like, dislike, or share. Developing an understanding of what factors induce trustworthiness or emotional response towards a content will enable a better understanding of how misinformation in social media can be eliminated and information that triggers a positive change can be promulgated. We chose Twitter for this research study because of its popularity and its distinctive features. Twitter being a microblogging site, the content generated is bite-sized and requires less attention span, as a result of which the user consumes more content in a relatively short period. Additionally, the retweet, hashtag, and trending features available on twitter, provide a holistic view about group behavior of users and the impact a certain content has on developing the mindset of users.

2   Theoretical Background and Hypotheses Development

2.1   Social Media and Trust

Trust plays a very pivotal role in social interactions. A high level of trust helps in facilitating democratic and efficient institutions, socio-economic developments, and reduced violence. In this backdrop, social networking sites have proved to be an effective mechanism in nurturing social connections, even though the contribution of social media in fostering trust formation remains indefinite (Witmer and Håkansson 2015). According to Robert Putnam, trust gets created due to reciprocity, which gets developed during coordination with others. Putnam is doubtful about the positive relationship between trustworthiness and digitalized social media. He reasoned that user interactions over social media, unlike live face to face interactions, are time-consuming and limit the interactions to people one already knows (Putnam 2000). In support of this view is the fact that some individuals exist in the online domain using false identities to persuade unsuspecting and unguarded individuals into relationships that can have dangerous consequences (Rheingold 2000). In counterargument of this, it can be stated that social media has a positive impact on the user's trustworthiness. Social media enables faster dissemination of information as compared to information sharing in a live interaction. Also, information proliferates at a relatively lower cost through social media. Since information sharing becomes an essential part of the trust-building mechanism, faster information transmission through social media has a positive impact on the user's trust formation (Witmer and Håkansson 2015). Uslaner, on the other hand, attributes trust as a moral issue, which gets entrenched by family relationships in the formative years of life and thus supports the fact that social media has no impact on trust creation (Uslaner 2002).

Social Networking Sites have a marked influence on strengthening social connections and augmenting existing social networks (Ellison et al. 2007). A considerable amount of content generated by social networking sites gets consumed and shared daily by a large chunk of the audience, who rely upon it and occasionally acts upon it. Assimilating such information can sometimes pose a high degree of risk and uncertainty for the users, particularly when they choose to act upon the information obtained. This information needs a certain degree of verification, which can help in risk evaluation, before the users place their trust in it and act upon it (Moturu and Liu 2011). An objective assessment of risk factors is needed, which can be obtained by backing up the information with knowledge of real facts. It becomes a time consuming and cumbersome process.

Individuals use social media for hedonic purposes (Chauhan and Pillai 2013) rather than for gaining utility (Johnson and Kaye 2013). This difference in the user's mindset alters the way they perceive information, making the user's consumption of news in social media different from his consumption of news from elsewhere on the internet. The hedonic mindset makes users in social media avoid activities involving arduous thought processes but choose articles and information, which makes them feel good and confirms their existing beliefs. Additionally, the source of the news feed items appearing in the social networking sites is not entirely decided by the users. These news feed items are an intermixture of articles: either chosen by social media algorithms, or feeds subscribed by users, or sponsored advertisements, or the news shared by family and friends, or other items with the unclear source (Moravec et al. 2018). Given the enormous volume of content exchanged in social media platforms daily, the task of separating truth from fiction becomes highly challenging and effortful, making the users in the hedonic mindset not feel motivated enough to invest time and energy to find and understand the source (Kim and Dennis 2019). Thus the users are more likely to trust facts that align with their opinions, whereas information that challenges their views and beliefs receives little cognitive attention (Moravec et al. 2018).

In the current scenario, fake news and posts have become widely prevalent in social networking sites. Common users, as well as many of the prominent news media houses, famous personalities, and social media influencers (individuals having a high number of follower base on SNS), get affected by it. This scenario makes fake posts and news appear more authentic, making unsuspecting people easily fall for it and reshare it without fact-checking or verifying the authenticity of the information collected over the SNS. The escalation of misinformation in SNS gives a subtle indication that people are gullible to the information that appears on social networking sites. A news feed content can be considered trustworthy by people if it gathers a more number of likes, dislikes, retweets, and shares. These parameters make the visibility of the post more prominent among the masses. Thus based on the theoretical literature of trust and the present trend that the users of social media exhibit, we hypothesize that:

H1: SNS news feed item having a high number of likes, shares, and retweets has a positive effect on trustworthiness toward the social media feed item.

H2: SNS news feed item shared by a social media influencer has a positive effect on trustworthiness toward the social media feed item.

2.2   Social Media and Emotions

Emotions are pervasive. They can either induce positive feelings (a pleased or relaxed state) or negative (a nervous, annoyed, or sad state) feelings in a person (Lee et al. 2009). Emotions have a significant impact on human behavior with their effects, at times overshadowing the rationality of humans (Hudson, Roth, Madden, & Hudson). Often, human actions are guided by feelings from the heart or a hunch, which is independent of conscious control, indicating high emotional and intuitive behavioral traits of individuals. Shedding some light on how emotions are processed, Damasio theorized that activities involving emotions and feelings (which forms in 'proto-self') precede the activities involving thought process (which forms in 'core consciousness'). Therefore, the creation of emotions and feelings happens pre-cognitively and pre-attentively. However, the potency of a non consciously processed emotional content gets weakened when it is processed consciously (Bornstein 1989). This suggests that less aware social media users project greater emotional vulnerability to the content that gets circulated on social networking sites.

Emotions are contagious (Fowler and Christakis 2008) and play a vital role in the way people interact with each other online. It gets reflected in the form of excitement before an event (Wakefield and Wakefield 2016), a retweeting decision (Gruzd 2013), or discerned utility of an online review (Salehan and Kim 2016). Emotions in the social media environment also result in rumor-mongering behavior (Oh et al. 2013). Emotions influence what we see, what we hear, what we learn, and how we behave, making it a useful tool to trigger user response through general sentimentalism. Previous research suggests that, when it comes to written communication, the emotional composition of messages, and emotional sentence framing, kindles cognitive responses, and accentuates user attention. In the context of information sharing, higher cognitive response, and increased attention span, increase the probability of generating behavioral responses to the emotional stimuli.

Emotions influence what we see, what we hear, what we learn, and how we behave, making it an effective tool to trigger user response through general sentimentalism (Forgas 2012). Previous researches suggest that, when it comes to written communication, the emotional composition of messages, and emotional sentence framing, kindles cognitive responses, and accentuates user attention (Bayer et al. 2012). In the context of information sharing, higher cognitive response, and increased attention span, increase the probability of generating behavioral responses to the emotional stimuli (Heath 1996; Luminet et al. 2000). Attention capturing information has an impact on emotional contagion. Emotional contagion is a phenomenon where one person's emotions or mood trigger similar emotional responses from other people by simple exposure (Hatfield et al. 1994). Emotional contagion can happen across different kinds of social networks in various contexts. More prevalently between people in frequent contacts such as families (Larson and Almeida 1999) or during workplace interactions (Barsade 2002), and directly affect individual and group level communication, in terms of information sharing (Sy et al. 2005). Besides this, specific kind of emotions triggers high cognitive and physiological arousal, which is characterized by activity, whereas low physiological arousal is characterized by relaxation or inactivity (Berger 2011). Physiological arousal is linked to information sharing, wherein content-generating high arousal through positive emotions (happiness or awe) or negative emotions (anger or anxiety) tends to get more viral. In contrast, the content which elicits low arousal or deactivates emotional response (such as sadness) is less viral (Berger and Milkman 2012; Stieglitz and Dang-Xuan 2013).

The communication over the computer has a considerable influence on the receiver's processing and interpretation of the message (Riordan and Kreuz 2010). The receivers of the message can identify with the sender's emotions through the verbal and non-verbal cues used in framing the messages. The verbal cues in messages are the emotional words or linguistic markers used in its composition, while the non-verbal cues are in the form of paralinguistic cues or emoticons. The use of emoticons in the messages attract more feedbacks than those which do not use emoticons (Harris and Paradice 2007). A previous study found that the positive effect of messages augmented community sense and increase in user engagement, whereas the negative effect of messages attracted belligerent and offensive user responses (Joyce and Kraut 2006).

Emotions have a huge potential to generate public interest for a topic that may or may not be relevant in terms of the impact it has on individual lives. Time and again, we find instances where social media has been used as a weapon to generate sympathy, acknowledgment, praise, and, to polarize views and thought process, to garner public support. The positive and negative feedback received in the comments, the number of likes and dislikes, and the emoticons used to show the feelings towards the content posted in the SNS, indicate the user's sentiments towards a post. Sometimes individuals develop their emotions towards a certain content posted online by taking cues from others' reactions to the post. If this is true, then SNS can be used as a medium to promote social campaigns, which can significantly improve people's participation in facilitating positive social changes and eliminate societal prejudices and biases. Thus on the basis of this, we hypothesize that:

H3: SNS news feed item having information about the number of likes, retweets, and comments generate a high emotional response in social media users.

H4: SNS news feed item shared by a social media influencer generates a high emotional response in social media users.

2.3   EEG for Measuring Trustworthiness and Emotions

The concept of NeuroIS is a new and emerging field in the Information Systems (IS) research domain. NeuroIS research will prove to be path-breaking in the evolution of new theories backed by a high degree of accuracy in measuring the behavioral interaction of users in a computer-mediated environment. In the field of NeuroIS research, the earliest research involved in exploring research questions based on trust in the online environment using functional magnetic resonance imaging (fMRI) came in the year 2010 (Dimoka 2010; Riedl et al. 2010). Prior research in this field indicates that EEG is a dominant neuroscience research tool due to its relative benefits in researching as compared to other neuroscience tools. EEG, as a neuroscience research tool, offers many benefits. Not only it has an exceptional temporal resolution, but also it is relatively cheaper and less intrusive (Müller-Putz et al. 2015).

EEG, as a neuroscience tool, has been used in the study of the human neural response of trust and emotions in varied situations before. In one such behavioral experiment conducted on social media users to understand their truth judgments of articles circulated in social networking sites, it was found that confirmation bias is prevalent among users. While the fake news flag generated increased cognitive activity and an increased attention span, the flag did not alter the user's beliefs about the information's veracity. The users are more likely to consider news information and facts which support their opinion than the one which challenges it (Moravec et al. 2018). In another experiment carried out by Dong to assess the trustworthiness of humans on the machine, it was found that humanlike cues are vital in generating trust in the partner's technical capability during the theory of mind game (Dong et al. 2015).

Furtherance in neuroscience allows us to leverage the opportunity of delving deeper into the emotional aspects of consumer and user sentiment in the social media environment. EEG gives an insight into this with much relative ease and offers a high degree of accuracy (Takahashi 2004). An experiment carried out for understanding the subjective experience of social media users in both PC and mobile settings indicated increased physiological arousal, valence, apprehension during Facebook navigation, with the effects in mobile being far more prominent than in the PC setting (Cipresso et al. 2015). Kuan, in another controlled experiment, measured the effects of group buying information on the opinions and emotions of users of social networking sites. He found that positive and negative buy information had a disproportionate impact on the user's attitude and intention (Kuan et al. 2014).

EEG gauges cognitive activities using brain waves as sound waves, measured in hertz. It makes use of electrodes, which act as sensors and are placed across the scalp covering different regions of the brain. These sensors catch the electrical signals from the brain and region of cognitive activity. These brain waves fall into five categories based on the frequency band, which are as follows:

- Delta: 1–4 Hz
- Theta: 4–8 Hz
- Alpha: 8–12 Hz
- Beta: 12–30 Hz
- Gamma: 30–100 Hz

The above categories have different mental states associated with them. The delta represents deep sleep or coma, and theta represents drowsiness or meditative state. The alpha represents readiness or relaxed state, and beta represents active concentration or focussed attention. The gamma represents arousal or peak performance state. Thus alpha and beta hold relevance in decision making and is a useful measure to evaluate user trustworthiness and emotions in response to the visual stimuli (Kuan et al. 2014; Müller-Putz et al. 2015). Alpha bands are of two types: low alpha band (8–10 Hz) and high alpha band (10–12 Hz). The high alpha band represents emotional processing, whereas the low alpha band represents awareness and attention. In addition to this, positive emotions and negative emotions get reflected in different regions of the brain. Positive emotions trigger the left frontal hemisphere, whereas negative emotions trigger the right frontal hemisphere (Kuan et al. 2014). On the other hand, previous researches suggest that some parts of the medial frontal cortex (MFC) are pivotal in tracking neural responses for trust measurement. Hence, our focus of attention will be alpha and beta activity in the medial frontal cortex region and the brain's right and left hemispheres.

3 Experiment

We plan to examine the influence of Social Media newsfeed items on the trust and emotions of the subjects using a controlled experiment. The experiment will consist of two sessions per subject and will take an average of 40 min per session. In these two sessions, the mental response of the subjects will be captured for neural correlates of two variables, trust, and emotion, using separate stimuli for each variable. The change in trust and emotions due to social influence on the subjects will be measured using EEG. Newsfeed items from a popular social networking site Twitter, will be used as stimuli for the experiment.

3.1 Procedure

Each variable will be measured using 30 stimuli grouped into two sets with 15 stimuli in each set. It will comprise tweets from social media influencers (individuals having a large number of followers on twitter who are well-known public personalities in the country). The first set of stimuli will contain tweets in baseline format (described in the succeeding section) containing information only about the number of likes, retweets, and comments in the tweet. The second set will have an enhanced format with added information about the number of likes on the tweet by other social media influencers.

In the first session, the subjects will be shown 30 stimuli randomly taken from each set. The stimuli in the first session will be manipulated to trigger trust inducing mental responses in the subjects. The second session will be undertaken half an hour after the first session. In this session, the subjects will be shown 30 stimuli randomly chosen from either of the two sets, inducing emotional responses from the subjects (Fig. 1).

3.2   Stimulus Material

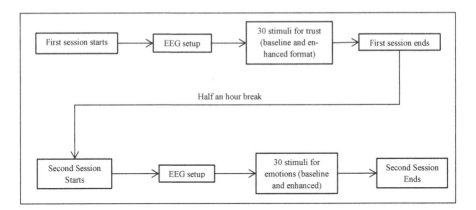

Fig. 1. Experiment design

Stimulus material for this research will be identified from newsfeed items taken from Twitter. The decision to prefer Twitter over other SNS is that Twitter has a large user base attracting opinions and views of prominent people and well-known personalities across different domains. Opinions from such prominent people mold the thinking of their followers and people in general. The advantage of using tweets from Social Media influencers as a potential stimulus is that social influencers enjoy a huge follower base. Their tweets can thus have a direct impact on their follower's trustworthiness about the information being shared through their tweets. This information can have both positive and negative implications for society.

Each session will involve 30 chosen stimuli, which are likely to trigger changes in the level of trust and emotions about the information disseminated by the tweet. The stimuli will be grouped into two sets: Set A and Set B. The stimuli from set A will be manipulated to include tweets from Social media influencers, in baseline format. Figure 2 shows a sample stimulus in baseline format. In this format, we shall include details of the tweet along with information about the number of people who liked the tweet, number of views, and the number of retweets garnered by the tweet. Set B will include stimuli in an enhanced format. As shown in Fig. 3, the enhanced format will include additional information about other social media influencers who like the tweet.

3.3   Measurements

We will capture EEG measures during the experiment. We may also add a pre or post-experiment questionnaire, which will provide us with additional information about the subjects. This can include information like the subjects' interests on social media, frequency of social media usage, and opinions regarding the stimuli shown. We will be using a 128 channel EEG machine, similar to a clinical-grade EEG. More number of channels will allow us to capture a significant amount of neural responses, thus

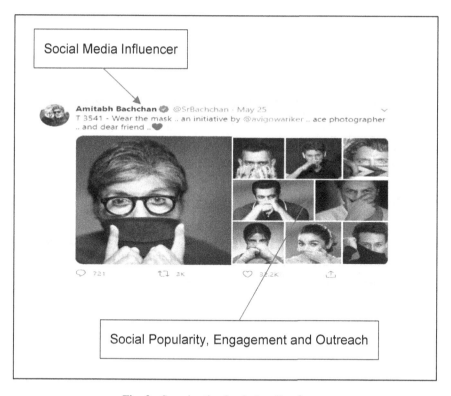

Fig. 2. Sample stimulus in baseline format

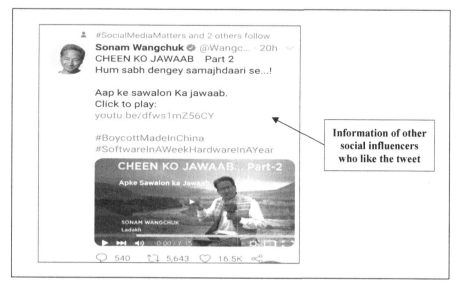

Fig. 3. Sample stimulus in the enhanced format

increasing the research validity. Measurement variables like trust and emotion are adapted based on previous research (Kuan et al. 2014; Riedl et al. 2014).

EEG is highly effective in picking up brain activities induced by a stimulus. It measures brain wave patterns in the form of sound waves measured in Hertz (Kevin et al. 2014). In line with the prior research in this area, our study will specifically focus on tracking brainwaves in the range of 8–12 Hz and 13–25 Hz. Brain waves in the range of 8–12 Hz are called alpha waves and are characterized by medium frequency activity. It indicates a state of relaxed wakefulness. Brain waves in the range of 13–25 Hz constitute beta waves and include high-frequency activities such as active concentration, task engagement, or attention (Müller-Putz et al. 2015).

3.4   Participants

The experiment will be undertaken with 50 undergraduate, postgraduate, or Ph.D. students from a major university in India. Subjects shall be asked to give details on their familiarity with social networking sites, particularly Twitter, and their social media experience in years. The data collection will be undertaken in the EEG lab of the university. All the subjects will be provided with refreshments and snacks during their participation. We shall obtain subjects' consent before allowing their participation. They will be provided with an adequate briefing about the whole process so that they feel relaxed during the entire process of experimentation. This is to keep our study data free from any biases or errors.

Acknowledgment. Funding for this research work was provided by ICSSR's IMPRESS Scheme for a Project titled "A Study on Trust, Social Influence, and Emotion in Social Media Context: Using EEG as a brain imaging tool". Grant no.: IMPRESS/P2140/586/2018-19/ICSSR.

References

Aneez, Z., Neyazi, T.A., Kalogeropoulos, A., Nielsen, R.K.: Reuters Institute India digital news report. Reuters Institute for the Study of Journalism/India Digital News Report (2019). https://reutersinstitute.politics.ox.ac.uk/sites/default/files/2019-03/India_DNR_FINAL.pdf

Barsade, S.G.: The ripple effect: emotional contagion and its influence on group behavior. Adm. Sci. Q. **47**(4), 644–675 (2002)

Bayer, M., Sommer, W., Schacht, A.: Font size matters—emotion and attention in cortical responses to written words. PLoS ONE **7**(5), e36042 (2012)

Berger, J.: Arousal increases social transmission of information. Psychol. Sci. **22**(7), 891–893 (2011)

Berger, J., Milkman, K.L.: What makes online content viral? J. Mark. Res. **49**(2), 192–205 (2012)

Bornstein, R.F.: Exposure and affect: over-view and meta-analysis of research, 1968-1987. Psychol. Bull. **106**(2), 265–289 (1989)

Chauhan, K., Pillai, A.: Role of content strategy in social media brand communities: a case of higher education institutes in India. J. Prod. Brand Manag. **22**(1), 40–51 (2013)

Cipresso, P., Serino, S., Gaggioli, A., Albani, G., Mauro, A., Riva, G.: Psychometric modeling of the pervasive use of Facebook through psychophysiological measures: stress or optimal experience? Comput. Hum. Behav. **49**, 576–587 (2015)

Diakopoulos, N., Naaman, M.: Towards quality discourse in online news comments. In: Proceedings of the ACM 2011 Conference on Computer Supported Cooperative Work, pp. 133–142, March 2011

Dimoka, A.: What does the brain tell us about trust and distrust? Evidence from a functional neuroimaging study. MIS Q., 373–396 (2010)

Dong, S.Y., Kim, B.K., Lee, K., Lee, S.Y.: A preliminary study on human trust measurements by EEG for human-machine interactions. In: Proceedings of the 3rd International Conference on Human-Agent Interaction, pp. 265–268 (2015)

Ellison, N.B., Steinfield, C., Lampe, C.: The benefits of Facebook "friends:" social capital and college students' use of online social network sites. J. Comput.-Mediated Commun. **12**(4), 1143–1168 (2007)

Forgas, J.P. (ed.): Affect in Social Thinking and Behavior. Psychology Press (2012)

Fowler, J.H., Christakis, N.A.: Dynamic spread of happiness in a large social network: longitudinal analysis over 20 years in the Framingham Heart Study. BMJ **337** (2008)

Gruzd, A.: Emotions in the twitterverse and implications for user interface design. AIS Trans. Hum.-Comput. Interact. **5**(1), 42–56 (2013)

Harris, R.B., Paradice, D.: An investigation of the computer-mediated communication of emotions. J. Appl. Sci. Res. **3**(12), 2081–2090 (2007)

Hatfield, E., Cacioppo, J.T., Rapson, R.L.: Mechanisms of emotional contagion: I. Emotional mimicry/synchrony (1994)

Haythornthwaite, C.: Social networks and Internet connectivity effects. Inf. Commun. Soc. **8**(2), 125–147 (2005)

Heath, C.: Do people prefer to pass along good or bad news? Valence and relevance of news as predictors of transmission propensity. Organ. Behav. Hum. Decis. Process. **68**(2), 79–94 (1996)

Holton, A.E., Lewis, S.C.: Journalists, social media, and the use of humor on Twitter. Electron. J. Commun. **21**(1/2), 1–22 (2011)

Johnson, T.J., Kaye, B.K.: The dark side of the boon? Credibility, selective exposure and the proliferation of online sources of political information. Comput. Hum. Behav. **29**(4), 1862–1871 (2013)

Joyce, E., Kraut, R.E.: Predicting continued participation in newsgroups. J. Comput.-Mediated Commun. **11**(3), 723–747 (2006)

Kuan, K.K.Y., Zhong, Y., Chau, P.Y.K.: Informational and normative social influence in group-buying: evidence from self-reported and EEG data. J. Manag. Inf. Syst. **30**(4), 151–178 (2014)

Kim, A., Dennis, A.R.: Says who? The effects of presentation format and source rating on fake news in social media. MIS Q. **43**(3), 1025–1039 (2019)

Larson, R.W., Almeida, D.M.: Emotional transmission in the daily lives of families: a new paradigm for studying family process. J. Marriage Fam. **61**(1), 5–20 (1999)

Lee, Y.K., Back, K.J., Kim, J.Y.: Family restaurant brand personality and its impact on customer's emotion, satisfaction, and brand loyalty. J. Hosp. Tourism Res. **33**(3), 305–328 (2009)

Luminet IV, O., Bouts, P., Delie, F., Manstead, A.S., Rimé, B.: Social sharing of emotion following exposure to a negatively valenced situation. Cogn. Emot. **14**(5), 661–688 (2000)

Moravec, P., Minas, R., Dennis, A.R.: Fake News on Social Media: People Believe What They Want to Believe When it Makes No Sense at All. Kelley School of Business Research Paper, pp. 18–87 (2018)

Moturu, S.T., Liu, H.: Quantifying the trustworthiness of social media content. Distrib. Parallel Databases **29**(3), 239–260 (2011)

Müller-Putz, G.R., Riedl, R., Wriessnegger, S.C.: Electroencephalography (EEG) as a research tool in the information systems discipline: foundations, measurement, and applications. Commun. Assoc. Inf. Syst. **37**(1), 46 (2015)

Oh, O., Agrawal, M., Rao, H.R.: Community intelligence and social media services: a rumor theoretic analysis of tweets during social crises. MIS Q. 407–426 (2013)

Putnam, R.D.: Bowling Alone: The Collapse and Revival of American Community. Simon and Schuster (2000)

Rheingold, H.: The Virtual Community: Homesteading on the Electronic Frontier. MIT Press (2000)

Riedl, R., Hubert, M., Kenning, P.: Are there neural gender differences in online trust? An fMRI study on the perceived trustworthiness of eBay offers. MIS Q. **34**(2), 397–428 (2010)

Riedl, R., Mohr, P.N., Kenning, P.H., Davis, F.D., Heekeren, H.R.: Trusting humans and avatars: a brain imaging study based on evolution theory. J. Manag. Inf. Syst. **30**(4), 83–114 (2014)

Riordan, M.A., Kreuz, R.J.: Emotion encoding and interpretation in computer-mediated communication: reasons for use. Comput. Hum. Behav. **26**(6), 1667–1673 (2010)

Salehan, M., Kim, D.J.: Predicting the performance of online consumer reviews: a sentiment mining approach to big data analytics. Decis. Support Syst. **81**, 30–40 (2016)

Shane, S.: The fake Americans Russia created to influence the election. N. Y. Times Polit. Sect. (2017). https://www.nytimes.com/2017/09/07/us/politics/russiafacebook-twitter-election.html

Stieglitz, S., Dang-Xuan, L.: Emotions and information diffusion in social media—sentiment of microblogs and sharing behavior. J. Manag. Inf. Syst. **29**(4), 217–248 (2013)

Sy, T., Côté, S., Saavedra, R.: The contagious leader: impact of the leader's mood on the mood of group members, group affective tone, and group processes. J. Appl. Psychol. **90**(2), 295 (2005)

Takahashi, K.: Remarks on emotion recognition from bio-potential signals. In: 2nd International Conference on Autonomous Robots and Agents, pp. 186–191, December 2004

Uslaner, E.M.: The Moral Foundations of Trust. Cambridge University Press (2002)

Wakefield, R., Wakefield, K.: Social media network behavior: a study of user passion and affect. J. Strateg. Inf. Syst. **25**(2), 140–156 (2016)

Wasserman, S., Faust, K.: Social Network Analysis: Methods and Applications, vol. 8. Cambridge University Press (1994)

Witmer, H., Håkansson, P.: Social media and trust: a systematic literature review. J. Bus. Econ. **3**, 6 (2015)

Value Creation Through Social Media Marketing: A Threat to Sustainability Performance?

Adwoa Yeboaa Owusu Yeboah[1,2(✉)] [ID], Michael Adu Kwarteng[1] [ID], and Petr Novak[1] [ID]

[1] Faculty of Management and Economics, Tomas Bata University in Zlin, Zlin, Czech Republic
{owusu_yeboah,kwarteng,pnovak}@utb.cz
adwoa.yeboah@ucc.edu.gh
[2] School of Business, University of Cape Coast, Cape Coast, Ghana

Abstract. This paper contributes to the discussion on value creation. Using the literature review approach, it explains why co-creation cannot be the sole consequence of the value creation process between producers and customers. The paper shows through some empirical studies how value co-destruction sometimes occurs; depending on how the collaborative process between producers and customers is handled. The authors further discuss how sustainability performance may be affected by value creation. The review exposes the lack of both empirical and conceptual work in the area. Based on this, the authors suggest a framework that incorporates sustainability performance and value co-destruction and also offer propositions for further studies.

Keywords: Value creation · Value co-creation · Value co-destruction · Sustainability · Indicators of value co-destruction · Social media marketing

1 Introduction

Value co-creation has become an important business strategy due to changing market dynamics. The market has become a proactive stakeholder with customers having options and demanding them. Far from the early 20th century customers who had to go along with the desires of producers, as they experimented with marketing management approaches such as; product, production, and selling concepts, modern customers take active roles in the production activity. Current marketing views insist that customers should be made an integral part of the value creation goals of producers (Jaworski and Kohli 1996; Kotler 1992; Fang et al. 2008), a position that makes business sense since customers end up judging and determining the value of outputs (Anderson and Narus 1998; Parasuraman 1997).

One avenue that has made this collaboration possible is Web 2.0 via social media. Equipped with this platform, customers have participated in co-production leading to value creation (Hamilton et al. 2016; Suseno et al. 2018). Several studies have explored this route (Buzeta et al. 2020; Tuan et al. 2019; Tajvidi et al. 2017; Yu et al. 2020;

© IFIP International Federation for Information Processing 2020
Published by Springer Nature Switzerland AG 2020
S. K. Sharma et al. (Eds.): TDIT 2020, IFIP AICT 618, pp. 475–486, 2020.
https://doi.org/10.1007/978-3-030-64861-9_42

Hamilton et al. 2016) and reported positive outcomes. Others have questioned the perfect role played by social media in value co-creation, suggesting that this is not always the situation (Echeverri and Skålén 2011; Plé and Cáceres 2010). The current work shares this view and aims to contribute to the value creation literature in this respect.

Additionally, this work aims to look at an important area which has been neglected in the value creation discourse. Studies on value creation (co-creation) usually, focus on limited marketing (firm) outcomes like loyalty, brand awareness, brand image, and consumer brand engagement (Luo et al. 2015; Cheung et al. 2020). Considering that most firms are working towards sustainability performance, it must be also examined. These gaps identified in the literature are what the current work purposes to fill. The objectives of this paper are 1. Propose indicators on value co-destruction from existing literature. 2. To connect value creation with sustainability performance. 3. Suggest a framework that incorporates sustainability along with the relevant value creation indicators and to achieve a more complete model. 4. To make propositions for empirical works that may be considered by other researchers in this subject area.

The rest of the paper covers a discussion of key constructs and their indicators, the relationship between value creation and sustainability performance, and the development of a conceptual framework and propositions.

2   Literature Review

2.1   Value and Value Co-creation

Businesses no doubt appreciate the need to create value for their market. Value is viewed as an antecedent to customer loyalty (Luo et al. 2015; Singaraju et al. 2016). Based on this assertion, value plays a major role in determining whether businesses operate under optimum conditions, whether they merely survive or whether they exit from the market. To be able to properly situate the construct within the context of this paper, it must be properly defined. This is significant because the construct has different "faces" and has been described as having a "kaleidoscopic" character (Dolan et al. 2019). The current work refers to two definitions from two different time frames.

The first definition is one of the earliest definitions proposed at the outset of the study of the construct. It was defined as: "a customer's perceived preference for and evaluation of those product attributes performances, and consequences arising from use that facilitate (or block) achieving the customer's goals and purpose in use situations. (Woodruff (1997) in Parasuraman (1997), p. 156). The definition highlights, the purpose or use of the product and whether it results in positive or negative consequences. Even though Parasuraman (1997) observes a measure of ambiguity in the definition and questions "*whether it readily translates into an effective operational definition*", the definition will suffice for this paper, since the purpose of this paper is not to contribute to the operationalization of the construct.

Another definition of value which immerged a decade later states that: "value is embedded in the products or services that focal organizations produce; is added during the production process, which is separated from the customer; and equals the price that the customer pays for product and services - value is objectively measured in terms of money" (Echeverri and Skålén 2011, p. 353) This definition projects value from a monetary perspective as had been done by Anderson and Narus (1998) when discussing the construct in relation to business markets. The definition limits value creation to the firm whilst giving the customer a minimal role which is only activated by monetary payments made for goods and services provided by the business.

The two definitions that have been provided give evidence of the differences in how the construct has been used. Whilst one author focuses on the use and benefits associated with the offering of a business, the other looks at the amount of money consumers are willing to exchange for the product. The authors of this work merge the two perspectives into a form that gives credence to the benefits (or otherwise) that accrue from the usage of the product and also, the monetary measure paid for the product. This position is to give a more complete picture of the construct to readers and to provide a general position on how value could be viewed as has been used in this work.

Because value is ultimately relevant to the success of the business, firms have over the years adopted numerous strategies to create value for their customers. The value chain analysis as well as the resource-based view of the firm are notable frameworks that have guided in developing value creation strategies. The traditional stance of these frameworks and other researchers in the field was that the responsibility of creating value solely rested on the producer (Porter 1985; Hart 1995). Organizations were deemed to have the responsibility and the knowledge needed to create value for customers by primarily following the G-D logic. Investing and supplying innovative products was thus a good place to start earning customers' loyalty.

The 21st century ushered in a contrary thought about value creation. Prahalad and Ramaswamy (2000) hinted at the need to change the existing value creation model replacing it with the concept of co-creation. This thought placed the customer in active mode in the value creation model. They argued that evolving circumstances had changed customers' roles. According to them, customers are now sources of competence because they have access to market information, are forming customer communities, are becoming diverse, and finally, customers are looking for opportunities for co-creating personalized experiences. Vargo and Lush (2004, 2008) built on this by introducing the S-D logic, which emphasized the concept of co-creation. The conclusion was that businesses were required to include customers in value creation. Doing this would produce better results in terms of customer satisfaction.

Producers must assess the benefits of value co-creation. To do this, relevant measures needed to be applied. From a pool of literature, Ranjan and Read (2016) identified and subsequently, validated some dimensions of value co-creation. These they broadly categorized into two main dimensions, co-production and Vin (value in use). These broad dimensions are related to the common definitions and descriptions that have been suggested for value (Parasuraman 1997). Following this, they identified sub-dimensions for each of them. These are; interaction, equity, and knowledge (sharing) for co-production and experience, personalization, and relationship for Vin.

2.2   Value Co-destruction

Contrary to the assertions by co-creation and S-D logic that value is always created when producers and consumers (customers) interact (Prahalad and Ramaswamy 2000;

Vargo and Lush 2004); some few researchers have proposed an additional outcome. Value co-destruction is a concept that some researchers have opined that it should be included in the value creation model (Echeverri and Skålén 2011; Plé and Cáceres 2010). The literature on value co-destruction is still evolving after a decade of its introduction. It is expected that with time, researchers and practitioners alike would come to fully appreciate it. However, it has been defined as: "an interactional process between service systems that results in a decline in at least one of the systems' well-being (which given the nature of a service system, can be individual or organizational), (Plé and Cáceres 2010, p. 431). The definition claims that value could be destroyed as a result of the interaction process between producers and customers, herein, referred to as systems. The authors of this work take a similar position and further deepen the argument by stating that when value co-destruction occurs, it affects both parties in the system at least in the long run.

Echeverri and Skålén (2011) argue for this position by providing two reasons why the co-creation and S-D logic position is skewed. They insist that: 1. The foundation for a perfect interaction model for value creation is conceptual studies and hence shaky. 2. Such a conclusion is inconsistent with real-life experiences that we all encounter. Based on these they explicitly insist that producer-consumer interactions do not only result in value co-creation but could potentially destroy value. Using the practice theory, they were able to evidence co-destruction through empirical work. Their study showed that the producer-consumer interaction resulted in both co-creation (in some instances) and co-destruction (in other instances).

A study by Daunt and Harris (2017) also connected customer show rooming to value co-destruction. According to the authors, when customers collect information from a producer and use it in their purchase decisions whilst purchasing from another producer, then value is destroyed for the source of the information. They argue that showrooming has a simultaneous effect by creating value for the producer that was chosen but destroying value for the producer that was rejected since the purchase decision was based on information from the rejected producer. They also used their work to prove the possibility of co-destruction through such interactions.

Finally, Dolan et al. (2019) contribute to the argument on co-destruction by conducting a study in the airline industry where they analyzed customer complaints and airline representative responses into either value co-creation or value co-destruction. The work identified three complaining practices for customers on social media platforms as falling into any of these categories; solution-seeking, support seeking, and social engagement. They concluded from the findings that for each of the categories, depending on how the representatives handled the complaints, it resulted in either cocreation or co-destruction.

As have been indicated, value co-destruction is still evolving and it is still at the concept stage yet to be fully conceptualized and measured by researchers in the area. This gap has resulted in very few empirical works with the majority conducted qualitatively probably due to unavailable measures. The current work fills this gap by proposing some measures that have been identified in the existing literature. The authors approach this exercise by arguing that any attempt at conceptualizing co-destruction should be done from a balanced perspective; focusing on the loss of value arising from the interaction between producers and consumers. The authors, therefore, create a taxonomy which puts the measures into producer-related measures and consumer related measure. This path is consistent with the central theme of the concept (Camilleri and Neuhofer 2017).

Existing literature on the subject provides insight into how it can be measured.

For example, consumer exploitation (Cova et al. 2011), miscommunication (Echeverri and Skålén 2011), power insecurity (shifting control in favor of consumers) (Fisher and Smith 2011), misuse of customers' resources (Smith 2013), misuse of firms' resources (Daunt and Harris 2017) and unfair customer complaints. A more organized, precise, and detailed way of looking at this is presented in Table 1.

Table 1. Dimensions of value co-destruction

Customer-related measures (dimensions)	Producer-related measures (dimensions)
Customer exploitation: Cova et al. (2011); Arvidsson 2005; Bonsu and Darmody (2008); Humphreys and Grayson 2008	**Power insecurity:** Fisher and Smith (2011); Pongsakornrungsilp and Schroeder (2011)
Abuse of customers' resources: Daunt and Harris 2017; Smith 2013	**Abuse of producers' resources:** Daunt and Harris 2017
Miscommunication: Echeverri and Skålén (2011)	**Miscommunication:** Echeverri and Skålén (2011)
Abuse of customers: Echeverri and Skålén (2011)	**Customer complaints:** Xu et al. (2016)

Consumer exploitation describes the concept because, producers use consumers' labor for free during value creation and yet charge them premium prices for the value that has been created (Cova et al. 2011; Terranova 2000; Arvidsson 2005; Bonsu and Darmody 2008; Humphreys and Grayson 2008) thus resulting in value co-destruction. *Miscommunication* is another feature in value co-destruction. All the empirical works indicate that miscommunication between producers and customers leads to value breakdown. This ultimately results in; disagreement, misinterpretations, obstructive responses, keeping information, neglect, and a complete breakdown of communication (Echeverri and Skålén 2011). *Power insecurity* is also another situation that has been mentioned with co-destruction. Consumers feel empowered by the value creation process however, this has negative consequences for the producer since ceding power is not something they are comfortable with (Fisher and Smith 2011; Pongsakornrungsilp and Schroeder 2011). *Misuse of customers' resource* is also seen in coproduction (Smith 2013). Producers take advantage of consumers' knowledge, experiences, and desires without properly acknowledging these in their production. They end up taking credit for their innovative products when in reality, consumers played a major role in that endeavor. On the other hand, consumers have also been blamed for *misusing producers' resources* through showrooming (Daunt and Harris 2017). There could also be *unfair customer claims*. There are instances when customers make malicious complaints (Xu et al. 2016) and exaggerate situations to their advantage to court sympathy from other customers. Finally, there are also instances where customers are abused during the value creation process by producers and their representatives a situation that is all too common.

2.3 Social Media Marketing

Social media has been defined as: "…a group of internet-based applications that build on the ideological and technological foundations of Web 2.0, and that allow the creation and exchange of User Generated Content" (Kaplan and Haelein (2010) in Yadav and Rahman 2017, p. 1295). Yadav and Rahman (2017) further point out that social media comes in several forms such as social networking sites, blogs, wikis, and microblogging. When firms manage aspects of their marketing activities especially those relating to their brand and customer relationships on social media platforms (such as WhatsApp, Facebook, Instagram, Twitter, and YouTube) they are practicing social media marketing (Cheung et al. 2020; Hinson et al. 2019). Yadav and Rahman (2017) attempted to provide a comprehensive definition of social media marketing after reviewing eight definitions (Taubenheim et al. 2008; Chan and Guillet 2011; Chi 2011; Chang et al. 2015; Pham and Gammoh 2015; Choi et al. 2016; Tuten and Solomon 2017; Felix et al. 2017). Though insightful, they produced a superfluous and unbalanced definition which like the others touched on value creation (by firms) instead of value co-creation (firms and customers). Other future attempts at creating a definition, should focus on both firms and their customers.

Social media marketing has become an avenue through which firms reach a large segment of their market and provide them with information about their brands and firm activities. It is reported that over 65 million businesses have taken advantage of this platform to reach their markets (Cheung et al. 2020; Hinson et al. 2019). Customers and potential customers are also able to contact firms through these platforms on issues about their brands for specific personalized information to help them in their brand choices and purchase decisions. These platforms provide firms and customers the opportunity to co-create value (Yu et al. 2020).

Extant literature on social media marketing conceptualizes it as a multi-dimensional construct consisting of five dimensions. These are entertainment, customization, interaction, EWOM, and trendiness. *Entertainment* in social media represents the fun aspect of a marketers' content. Studies show that a positive relationship exists between entertaining content on social media and behavioral loyalty (Yoshida et al. 2018). *Customization* deals with providing customers with personalized products and experiences (Cheung et al. 2020; Seo et al. 2018). *EWOM* are customers' opinions about the products expressed on-line (Cheung et al. 2019; Hennig-Thurau et al. 2004). These stories and experiences reflect customers' most intimate impressions about assessments since they have been gathered through use and exposure to the firm and their products. Interaction is the ability to communicate. Social media as a platform allows firms to interact and create some form of relationship with their market. Finally, *trendiness* according to Naaman et al. (2011) is a topic in its infant stage. Through social media, producers can provide current information about their firms and their offerings.

The nature of social media puts it in the right spot for value co-creation as producers and customers can easily collaborate to create value. But it is perhaps these qualities that make it vulnerable and a route to co-destruction. Currently, very few works have been done on how social media marketing is a source of co-destruction. To better understand this, researchers must build on the conceptual works and test these empirically since very limited studies exist in this regard.

2.4 Sustainability Performance and Value Creation

Sustainability performance has become a laudable goal that most businesses work towards. Sustainability performance requires that businesses balance their economic interests with social and environmental considerations (O'Neil and Ucbasaran 2016). Their stakeholders expect that in addition to their financial growth, they support them and the environment. This is how value is created for both the business and its stakeholders. This rather broad measure for business success (in terms of value) makes it quite challenging, yet, much of the studies that have been conducted in sustainability claim that it is a strategic tool for value creation (Zaman et al. 2012; Lesk et al. 2016).

Sustainability performance provides a good opportunity for value co-creation as firms can invite their customers (stakeholders) to collaborate with them and thus mutually achieve value. For example, when social media marketing facilitates the prompt handling of customers' complaints then social goals are being achieved. As businesses entertain, interact, and customize their offerings for their customers, they are using social media for value co-creation and working towards their social sustainability goals. Environmental sustainability goals can equally be achieved as producers and their customers (stakeholders) work within the social media marketing space. When these parties collaborate using social media, they take off some pressure from the physical environment. Online engagements are a good way of minimizing waste and protecting the environment (Sharma and Iyer 2012) thus achieving environmental goals. They can also collectively work to design programs that can support the environment especially in situations where the firm is not a specialist in such environmental issues and stakeholders are willing to provide their expertise. Finally, economic goals are achieved even as these businesses take advantage of social media marketing. This significantly reduces the marketing budget as traditional marketing strategies are exorbitant (Zhao and Zhu 2010; Weber 2002). Additionally, this allows them to build stronger brands and reap the financial benefits associated with them.

Consistent with the arguments put forward, sustainability could result in value co-destruction. This can happen when the parties do not achieve their goals. Sustainability presents businesses with the challenge of dealing with diverse stakeholders who have competing interests (Mena et al. 2019). It must be noted that unlike shareholders who usually seek out economic goals. Other stakeholders focus on social and environmental goals and are usually keen on demanding them from firms. The effect of this situation is worst especially when they have an online relationship. Value co-destruction ultimately results in the firms' inability to achieve their economic goals. Further research must be conducted in this research area so that the mechanism by which value creation is achieved by sustainable businesses can be fully appreciated.

3 Methodology

The literature review method was used for the work. The authors searched the Scopus and Google scholar databases and selected over 50 scientific articles. The selection of the papers was based on search terms such as value creation, value co-creation, value co-destruction, dimensions of value creation, dimensions of value co-creation, sustainability performance. The selected papers formed the basis for the current work.

4 Discussion of Findings

4.1 Conceptual Framework

The literature review, in addition to the S-D logic, stakeholder theory, and resource-based theory form the basis for the sustainability value creation model. Firms can use social media tools to achieve competitive advantage and hence, create value for their stakeholders through sustainability goals i.e. social, economic, and environmental. Further as indicated in the framework, the value creation process could result in either co-creation or co-destruction. This framework could form the basis for future empirical works. This is shown in Fig. 1: Sustainability Value Creation Model through Social Media Marketing.

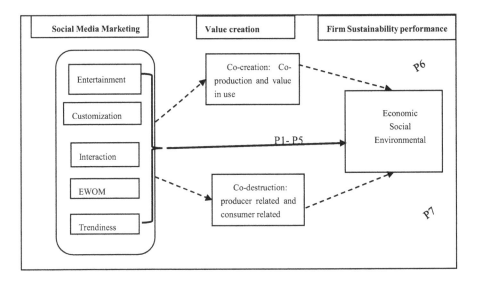

Source: Author's Construct
Hypothesized effect ⎯⎯⎯⎯⎯→
Non-hypothesized effect - - - - - - →

Fig. 1. Conceptual framework

4.2 Propositions Based on Literature Review

P_1–P_5: Social media marketing tools have a direct relationship with firm sustainability performance.

P_6: It is proposed that value co-creation has a mediating influence on social media marketing and firm sustainability performance.

P_7: It is proposed that value co-destruction has a mediating influence on social media marketing and firm sustainability performance.

4.3 Theoretical and Practical Implications of the Paper

The work has explored current ideas on value creation and found that in addition to value co-creation, value co-destruction also occurs. This implies that authors in this research field would need to accommodate value co-destruction in their future works and work at developing the concept just as it has been done for value co-creation. The arguments put forward indicate that any discussion on value creation that ignores value co-destruction and its consequences would be deficient.

The authors have further expanded and enriched the theory on value creation by suggesting appropriate dimensions useful in ascertaining value co-destruction. These dimensions focus on both consumers and producers, therefore, giving researchers who may be interested in a study of this nature a complete perspective. This contribution to the existing is no means exhaustive, rather, it forms a sound basis for exploring further dimensions.

This paper has also deepened the understanding of value creation within the context of sustainability by drawing attention to the connection between social media and firms' sustainability performance. With the aid of the S-D logic, resource-based theory, and stakeholder theory, a conceptual framework has been developed with testable hypotheses that researchers can explore. This analysis provides a good foundation for future related studies.

Practically, firms have been provided insights into how they can use social media marketing to create value whilst achieving their sustainability goals. It is expected that firms take lessons from the argument on value co-destruction so that they manage the value creation process well to avoid destroying value.

4.4 Limitations of the Paper

Even though the literature review was extensive, it was still limited to papers that could be accessed by the authors. There may be other scientific papers that could have influenced the direction of the discussion. Also, the concept of value co-destruction though interesting and relevant has not received the attention it deserves. Because of that, there were only a handful of papers that were useful and relevant to the discussion. Finally, this work is only a conceptual paper it is possible that even with the evidence that has been provided, empirical findings may suggest otherwise.

5   Conclusions

The authors set out to contribute to value creation by highlighting value co-destruction as a possible outcome of producer-consumer interaction. They also introduced a model that connects sustainability performance with social media value creation. It is anticipated that others may build upon the work.

Acknowledgment. The authors are grateful to the anonymous reviewers for their comments.

References

Anderson, J.C., Narus, J.A.: Business marketing: understand what customers value. Harvard Bus. Rev. **76**, 53–67 (1998)

Arvidsson, A.: Brands: a critical perspective. J. Consum. Cult. **5**(2), 235–258 (2005)

Bonsu, S.K., Darmody, A.: Co-creating second life: market-consumer cooperation in contemporary economy. J. Macro Mark. **28**(4), 355–368 (2008)

Buzeta, C., De Pelsmacker, P., Dens, N.: Motivations to use different social media types and their impact on consumers' online brand-related activities (COBRAs). J. Interact. Mark. **52**, 79–98 (2020)

Camilleri, J., Neuhofer, B.: Value co-creation and co-destruction in the Airbnb sharing economy. Int. J. Contemp. Hosp. Manag., 2322–2340 (2017)

Chan, N.L., Guillet, B.D.: Investigation of social media marketing: how does the hotel industry in Hong Kong perform in marketing on social media websites? J. Travel Tour. Mark. **28**(4), 345–368 (2011)

Chang, Y.T., Yu, H., Lu, H.P.: Persuasive messages, popularity cohesion, and message diffusion in social media marketing. J. Bus. Res. **68**(4), 777–782 (2015)

Cheung, M.L., Pires, G.D., Rosenberger III, P.J., Leung, W.K., Ting, H.: Investigating the role of social media marketing on value co-creation and engagement: an empirical study in China and Hong Kong. Australas. Mark. J. (AMJ), 1–13 (2020)

Cheung, M.L., Pires, G.D., Rosenberger III, P.J.: Developing a conceptual model for examining social media marketing effects on brand awareness and brand image. Int. J. Econ. Bus. Res. **17**(3), 243–261 (2019)

Chi, H.H.: Interactive digital advertising vs. virtual brand community: exploratory study of user motivation and social media marketing responses in Taiwan. J. Interact. Advert. **12**(1), 44–61 (2011)

Choi, E.K., Fowler, D., Goh, B., Yuan, J.: Social media marketing: applying the uses and gratifications theory in the hotel industry. J. Hosp. Mark. Manag. **25**(7), 771–796 (2016)

Cova, B., Dalli, D., Zwick, D.: Critical perspectives on consumers' role as 'producers': broadening the debate on value co-creation in marketing processes. Mark. Theory **11**(3), 231–241 (2011)

Daunt, K.L., Harris, L.C.: Consumer showrooming: value co-destruction. J. Retail. Consum. Serv. **38**, 166–176 (2017)

Dolan, R., Seo, Y., Kemper, J.: Complaining practices on social media in tourism: a value co-creation and co-destruction perspective. Tour. Manag. **73**, 35–45 (2019)

Echeverri, P., Skålén, P.: Co-creation and co-destruction: a practice-theory based study of interactive value formation. Mark. Theory **11**(3), 351–373 (2011)

Fang, E., Palmatier, R.W., Evans, K.R.: Influence of customer participation on creating and sharing of new product value. J. Acad. Mark. Sci. **36**(3), 322–336 (2008)

Felix, R., Rauschnabel, P.A., Hinsch, C.: Elements of strategic social media marketing: a holistic framework. J. Bus. Res. **70**, 118–126 (2017)

Fisher, D., Smith, S.: Cocreation is chaotic: what it means for marketing when no one has control. Mark. Theory **11**(3), 325–350 (2011)

Hamilton, M., Kaltcheva, V.D., Rohm, A.J.: Social media and value creation: the role of interaction satisfaction and interaction immersion. J. Interact. Mark. **36**, 121–133 (2016)

Hart, S.L.: A natural-resource-based view of the firm. Acad. Manag. Rev. **20**(4), 986–1014 (1995)

Hennig-Thurau, T., Gwinner, K.P., Walsh, G., Gremler, D.D.: Electronic word-of-mouth via consumer-opinion platforms: what motivates consumers to articulate themselves on the internet? J. Interact. Mark. **18**(1), 38–52 (2004)

Hinson, R., Boateng, H., Renner, A., Kosiba, J.P.B.: Antecedents and consequences of customer engagement on Facebook. J. Res. Interact. Mark., 204–226 (2019)

Humphreys, A., Grayson, K.: The intersecting roles of consumer and producer: a critical perspective on co-production, co-creation and prosumption. Sociol. Compass **2**(3), 963–980 (2008)

Jaworski, B.J., Kohli, A.K.: Market orientation: review, refinement, and roadmap. J. Market-Focused Manag. **1**(2), 119–135 (1996)

Kaplan, A.M., Haenlein, M.: Users of the world, unite! The challenges and opportunities of Social Media. Bus. Horiz. **53**(1), 59–68 (2010)

Kotler, P.: Marketing's new paradigms: what's really happening out there. Plan. Rev., 50–52 (1992)

Lesk, C., Rowhani, P., Ramankutty, N.: Influence of extreme weather disasters on global crop production. Nature **529**(7584), 84–87 (2016)

Luo, N., Zhang, M., Liu, W.: The effects of value co-creation practices on building harmonious brand community and achieving brand loyalty on social media in China. Comput. Hum. Behav. **48**, 492–499 (2015)

Mena, J.A., Hult, G.T.M., Ferrell, O.C., Zhang, Y.: Competing assessments of market-driven, sustainability-centered, and stakeholder-focused approaches to the customer-brand relationships and performance. J. Bus. Res. **95**, 531–543 (2019)

Naaman, M., Becker, H., Gravano, L.: Hip and trendy: characterizing emerging trends on Twitter. J. Am. Soc. Inf. Sci. Technol. **62**(5), 902–918 (2011)

O'Neil, I., Ucbasaran, D.: Balancing "what matters to me" with "what matters to them": exploring the legitimation process of environmental entrepreneurs. J. Bus. Ventur. **31**(2), 133–152 (2016)

Parasuraman, A.: Reflections on gaining competitive advantage through customer value. J. Acad. Mark. Sci. **25**(2), 154 (1997)

Pham, P.H., Gammoh, B.S.: Characteristics of social media marketing strategy and customer-based brand equity outcomes: a conceptual model. Int. J. Internet Mark. Advert. **9**(4), 321–337 (2015)

Plé, L., Cáceres, R.C.: Not always co-creation: introducing interactional co-destruction of value in service - dominant logic. J. Mark. Serv., 430–437 (2010)

Pongsakornrungsilp, S., Schroeder, J.E.: Understanding value co-creation in a co-consuming brand community. Mark. Theory **11**(3), 303–324 (2011)

Porter, M.E.: Value chain. The Value Chain and Competitive advantage: creating and sustaining superior performance (1985)

Prahalad, C.K., Ramaswamy, V.: Co-opting customer competence. Harvard Bus. Rev. **78**(1), 79–90 (2000)

Ranjan, K.R., Read, S.: Value co-creation: concept and measurement. J. Acad. Mark. Sci. **44**(3), 290–315 (2016)

Seo, E.J., Park, J.W.: A study on the effects of social media marketing activities on brand equity and customer response in the airline industry. J. Air Transp. Manag. **66**, 36–41 (2018)

Sharma, A., Iyer, G.R.: Resource-constrained product development: Implications for green marketing and green supply chains. Ind. Mark. Manag. **41**(4), 599–608 (2012)

Singaraju, S.P., Nguyen, Q.A., Niininen, O., Sullivan-Mort, G.: Social media and value co-creation in multi-stakeholder systems: a resource integration approach. Ind. Mark. Manag. **54**, 44–55 (2016)

Smith, A.M.: The value co-destruction process: a customer resource perspective. Eur. J. Mark., 1889–1909 (2013)

Suseno, Y., Laurell, C., Sick, N.: Assessing value creation in digital innovation ecosystems: a social media analytics approach. J. Strateg. Inf. Syst. **27**(4), 335–349 (2018)

Tajvidi, M., Wang, Y., Hajli, N., Love, P.E.: Brand value co-creation in social commerce: the role of interactivity, social support, and relationship quality. Comput. Hum. Behav. 105238 (2017)

Taubenheim, A.M., Long, T., Smith, E.C., Jeffers, D., Wayman, J., Temple, S.: Using social media and internet marketing to reach women with the heart truth. Soc. Mark. Q. **14**(3), 58–67 (2008)

Terranova, T.: Free labor: producing culture for the digital economy. Soc. Text **18**(2), 33–58 (2000)

Tuan, L.T., Rajendran, D., Rowley, C., Khai, D.C.: Customer value co-creation in the business-to-business tourism context: the roles of corporate social responsibility and customer empowering behaviors. J. Hosp. Tour. Manag. **39**, 137–149 (2019)

Tuten, T.L., Solomon, M.R.: Social Media Marketing. Sage (2017)

Vargo, S.L., Lusch, R.F.: Evolving to a new dominant logic for marketing. J. Market. **68**(1), 1–17 (2004)

Vargo, S.L., Lusch, R.F.: Service-dominant logic: continuing the evolution. J. Acad. Mark. Sci. **36**(1), 1–10 (2008)

Weber, J.A.: Managing the marketing budget in a cost-constrained environment. Ind. Mark. Manag. **31**(8), 705–717 (2002)

Xu, Y., Yap, S.F.C., Hyde, K.F., Alejandro, T.B.: Who is talking, who is listening? Service recovery through online customer-to-customer interactions. Mark. Intell. Plan., 1–47 (2016)

Yadav, M., Rahman, Z.: Measuring consumer perception of social media marketing activities in e-commerce industry: scale development & validation. Telemat. Inform. **34**(7), 1294–1307 (2017)

Yoshida, M., Gordon, B.S., Nakazawa, M., Shibuya, S., Fujiwara, N.: Bridging the gap between social media and behavioral brand loyalty. Electron. Commer. Res. Appl. **28**, 208–218 (2018)

Yu, C.H., Tsai, C.C., Wang, Y., Lai, K.K., Tajvidi, M.: Towards building a value co-creation circle in social commerce. Comput. Hum. Behav. **108**, 105476 (2020)

Zaman, G., Vasile, V., Cristea, A.: Outstanding aspects of sustainable development and competitiveness challenges for entrepreneurship in Romania. Econ. Finan. Proced. **3**, 12–17 (2012)

Zhao, L., Zhu, J.: Internet marketing budget allocation: from practitioner's perspective. Int. J. Inf. Technol. Decis. Mak. **9**(05), 779–797 (2010)

An Exploratory Study of Twitter Sentiment Analysis During COVID-19: #TravelTomorrow and #UNWTO

V. Senthil$^{(\boxtimes)}$ and Susobhan Goswami

Thiagarajar School of Management, Madurai, India
{senthil,goswami}@tsm.ac.in

Abstract. Purpose: The COVID-19 has impacted travel and tourism like no other event before in history and Tourism is the hardest hit of all economic sectors. As of now, 96% of all worldwide destinations have introduced travel restrictions in response to the pandemic. Analyzing the impact of COVID-19 sentiments throws some light on the overall situation and provides insights and guidance for recovery measures.

Design: The research focuses on the collection of tweets referring to #TravelTomorrow online campaign and tweets from #UNWTO subsequently evaluated through a sentiment analysis using NViVo.

Findings: We analyzed the twitter sentiments in a systematic way and investigate the insights of twitter sentiments in COVID-19 situation. Our research result shows the valence of sentiments such as positive, moderately positive, very positive, negative, moderately negative and very negative sentiments which are helpful to the tourism stakeholders for their decision making.

Research Implications: The key insights, themes, subthemes and sentiments which are useful to the policy makers for their strategic decision making and the implications of this research is helpful for the academic and tourism practitioners in tourism industry.

Originality: The insights of this research are helpful to Destination Marketing Organizations of developing countries to popularize their destinations and helpful for the faster recovery measures from the pandemic situations.

Keywords: Electronic word of mouth · Twitter data analysis · COVID-19 sentiments · Destination marketing organization · Strategy

1 Introduction

Information sharing platforms on the internet have shifted from being relatively static websites, to become dynamic with socio-cultural exchanges between a sender and a receiver. In addition to the rise of users, technology has enabled the number of options for near synchronous distribution of digital data characterized by mobility and wearability (Kotsakos et al. 2015). These fusions of technological developments have boosted up the number of potential participants and the volume of synchronously shared destination eWOM (Wang et al. 2014). This has permitted direct studies of technology influences on any event or a social cause. Here we take the fecundity of

© IFIP International Federation for Information Processing 2020
Published by Springer Nature Switzerland AG 2020
S. K. Sharma et al. (Eds.): TDIT 2020, IFIP AICT 618, pp. 487–498, 2020.
https://doi.org/10.1007/978-3-030-64861-9_43

pandemic Covid 19. The effects are phenomenal and changing lives of millions. All facets of human life have been struck, not the least of which is a basic intention of human beings to see the unknown, and to visit places not seen hitherto. In the absence of visits or in the event of curtailed visits, like cutaneous pigmentation occurring, tourists take to sharing their experiences, opinions, moods, emotions and other sentiments in digital channels such as YouTube, Twitter, FaceBook, and others. Marketing has fructified more on packaging existing resources and assets of a tourist destination, and onward sales to new markets (McCabe et al. 2015), basing on opinions and sentiments vented out. Liu et al. (2018) presents the idea of 'social envy' that emanates from social posts of visiting luxurious vacation spots. In a way then, Twitter handles incite millennials to visit such places. Financial capacity though determines travel, but the intention remains.

In this research we used Twitter sentiments as an e-WOM; Twitter is a social networking service in which users post and interact with messages known as "tweets". Registered users can post, like, and retweets, but unregistered users can only read them. Twitter interaction enriches the value exchange between consumers and marketers. Twitter as a crowd sourced messaging service. The United Nations World Trade Organization (UNWTO) is a leading global organization promoting tourism for sustainable development. In this paper we researched the #TravelTomorrow an online campaign promoted by UNWTO with the tagline "by staying home today, we can travel tomorrow". The main objective of this paper is to explore the twitter sentiments with macroscopic (#UNWTO) and microscopic (#TravelTomorrow) data analysis. The flow of this paper is as follows; Sect. 2 discusses the literature review on how the tourist sentiments are captured, modelled, and analyzed in e-WOM. Section 3 discusses the conceptual framework proposed in our research. The Sect. 4 shows the research methodology and the findings are discussed in Sect. 5 and the final section discusses the theoretical and practical implications with conclusion.

2   Literature Review

This study draws upon a resource and capabilities-based perspective (Trainor 2012) as the theoretical basis. According to this perspective, a firm is properly viewed as a collection of resources, such as brand names, reputation, in-house IT knowledge, skilled employees and capital (Wernerfelt 1984). Organizational capabilities (or competences) can be generated from such resources and, as a result, lead to competitive advantage. Organizational capabilities are shown in different forms, including business processes (Teece et al. 1998), routines (Grant 1999) and IT deployment and use (Bharadwaj 2000). Resources allow sentiments to develop if used and delivered properly to consumers. Accordingly, moods of people are positive or negative and have been found to make more optimistic or pessimistic in travel decisions (Dragouni et al. 2016). According to Grant (1999), a capability is 'a regular and predictable patterns of activity' (p. 122), such as customer service, new product development, advertising and technology adoption and use. In technology contexts, Bharadwaj (2000) noted that IT capability is a firm's ability to leverage IT for organizational benefit. The adoption and use of organizational technologies, which varies among companies, largely rely on firms' resources (Caldeira and Ward 2002). This resource and capability perspective has been adopted in social media contexts (Trainor 2012).

Within this framework, Tweets are an important resource, being a reservoir of information. Destinations and sentiments too are a vital resource that are amenable for competitive advantage. A Twitter user profile includes a description of the user, his or her profile age, number of followers (both individuals and groups) and other user information. Twitter portrays public destination and eWOM at the time it is generated. Twitter members take recourse to it for public conversations, information-sharing (including eWOM) disseminating news and self-promotion (Balachander et al. 2008).

While other social media platforms have significantly larger audiences (for example, Facebook), Twitter postings are public by default, enabling participation without prior social (Facebook) or professional (LinkedIn) ties (Zhang et al. 2011). Though Twitter is a mass platform albeit with a difference of concise comments, a destination eWOM participant may use it for cogent reasons. Overall, it makes up an index of public online activity that can encapsulate empirical scale, structure and geographic distribution of information (Takhteyev et al. 2012). On a Twitter platform, anyone can post views, due to low barriers for participation; tweets can be shared via email, dedicated applications (apps) or SMS (Waters and Jamal 2011). The medium is also a flexible communications mode that can support multiple nodes of communication from one-to-one and many-to-many (D'heer and Verdegem 2014). Not only that, Twitter also throws insights into online communications while activities are happening.

A low time lag for updates (Zhao and Rosson 2009) spurs reporting of events or festivals while activities are occurring. Unlike other platforms, Twitter metadata (user profile, location, time and interaction data) are widely available to provide detail about the characteristics of users sharing eWOM (Kwak et al. 2010). In addition, organisations archive Twitter data accessible at later date (Proferes 2016). These ingredients (public posts, low barriers, timely, archiving) make it a fertile ground for research in challenging times like Covid. A limitation here exists, however, is that Twitter users tend to be younger and are located in urban areas.

Coming to COVID-19, this pandemic is a witness to fierce competition. Industry contours are changing and so also sentiments. Exploring and deciphering the trends and sentiments of the industry can provide a clue to face competition. Only creative and innovative destinations can survive in this competition from the post Covid-19 macroeconomic situation. Innovations are continually implemented in Social Media (stories, lives, stickers) which makes tasks interestingly creative for DMO employees (Wacker and Groth 2020). In this context, Lien et al. (2018) examines the functional and symbolic value linkages between positive moods and WOM. Not to be left out is the visuals. Dnhopl and Gretzal (2016) discusses the practice of selfie taking in specific to the visual culture of the self. Even the colour compositions of visual UGC count for consumer response as per Jalali and Papatla (2016)'s study.

The newly discovered twitter sentiments on tourist destination are quite actionable similar to e-WOM and can potentially lead to higher level of credibility as widely studied by Lugosi (2016). Coming to content, Ingawale et al. (2013) examines whether high and low quality of User Generated Content differs in their connectivity structures in Wikipedia. High quality content will make room for dense connectivity which in turn, will make for quality e-WOM. Mood is also a determining factor. Dragouni et al.

(2016) analyses why the moods of people is positive or negative and have been found to make more optimistic or pessimistic in travel decisions. Both cognitive and affective values influence travel tweets and so the intention to travel. Where than DMOs can take refuge? DMOs can plan downstream activity that was scarcely touched in literature before. Past research concentrated on reviews. Potential visitors observing the destination via social media reviews might have been confused by the dizzying array of updates. To clear this confusion, marketers or DMOs have to find the area of intersection between credibility of reviews and genuine consumers' interests. Only then, a suitable sharp marketing strategy can be devised. However, reviews or comments may be sporadic or a gush of feeling or a haphazard observation. As such, it needs more scrutiny. What is apparent however is that consumers' tweets of comments and implementing firm's suggestions jointly can make the purchase decision.

In the event of Twitter sharing, writers may adopt simple heuristics (i.e. mental rules) that focus attention on updates shared from the point of the experience (Aladhadh et al. 2014). In this scenario, hubs play a critical role in the cohesion of local and global destination e-WOM networks. Due to their high visibility, they reduce the confusion community participants may face in their search for useful information. Celebrities, media or institutions, whose identity is independently verifiable and therefore have source credibility, can act as hubs. A dynamic flow results.

Based on the review of literature, the Stimulus-Organism-Response (SOR) theory is an appropriate thematic foundation for analyzing the Twitter sentiments. This proposed theory foundation also helps to diagnose COVID-19 scenario with a Model laid down in discussion. The moot research question is Does #TravelTomorrow and #UNWTO twitter sentiments are positive or negative in Covid-19 scenario?.

3 Research Model and Methodology

The online campaign of #TravelTomorrow by the #UNWTO tweets are taken for our research analysis in specific to COVID-19 situations. Why? Because the Twitter sentiments of #TravelTomorrow and #UNWTO have a massive impact on social networks and is being embraced by a growing number of countries, destinations and companies linked to tourism, cities, media outlets and individuals from all over the world. We used sentiment analysis on tweeter comments to systematically extract, quantify, and study the affective states and subjective information of twitters. The Fig. 1 depicts the conceptual framework of our proposed research work. The number of followers, number of following, number of tweets in the twitter channels (#TravelTomorrow and #UNWTO) are act as stimulus, users of twitter act as Organism and their comments manifest as a response. The data for these stimulus, organism and response variables are collected automatically almost in real time which is cheaper than the traditional techniques using Ncapture.

Cantallops et al. (2018) and Van Noort and Willemsen (2012), highlighted that people with high self-esteem are more likely to share and discuss their experiences online. We assume that the tweeter comments are trustworthy and are generated by the self-esteem public. The exchange of tweets has an effect on perception and likelihood to visit or increase the attractiveness of the destination. Opinions are in the garb of

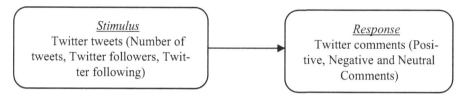

Fig. 1. Conceptual framework of Twitter Sentiment Analysis

comments. It is classified as positive sentiments, negative sentiments, moderately positive sentiments, moderately negative sentiments, very positive sentiments and very negative sentiments and is analyzed qualitatively using NVivo.

Information from secondary sources is very useful as it exists for almost any theme and can give pointers to current trends and issues. Secondary data are collected from the publicly available sources on Twitter channel. It refers to the information collected through direct observation of actual online behavior. Users may create an account for free while the tweets are freely accessible online and this online observed secondary data is helpful in controlling the common method variance with reduced measurement error. The samples are collected using Ncapture and qualitatively analyzed using NVivo. By dint of this qualitative nature, sentiment analysis has started acquiring top attention of researchers. One can investigate the polarity of the twitter sentiments on selected twitter tags #TravelTomorrow and #UNWTO. The number of followers, number of following, number of tweets, high frequency of words and sentiments of comments in these tweets throw up interesting insights which are helpful to the DMOs for better understanding of their destinations.

4 Data Analysis and Findings

4.1 Microscopic Twitter Sentiment Analysis

The NVivo software is used for qualitative data analysis for #TravelTomorrow, it has number of followers 48, number of following 111 and the number of tweets 102. The bar-graph in Fig. 2 depicts the frequency of references for #TravelTomorrow, most of the conversations occurred in the month of April 2020, and it was the starting period of Covid-19 pandemic, where most of countries are announced their lockdown and many travellers rescheduled or cancelled their trips. The Table 1 shows the different hashtags such as #stayhome, #staysafestayhome, #staycation, #travelpodcast, #newepisode, #socialdistancing and #TravelTomorrow are actively participated in online campaign by UNWTO. The bar-graph in Fig. 3 shows the coding percentages of sentiments, positive (13.07), negative (9.96), moderately positive (9.70), moderately negative (6.90), very positive (3.38) and very negative (3.05) in #TravelTomorrow. The total percentage of positive sentiments (26.15) is higher than the negative sentiments (19.91) that indicates more number of positive efforts are taken by the DMO's during the COVID-19 pandemic.

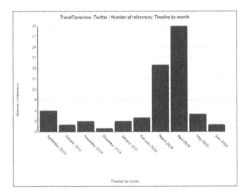

Fig. 2. Month-wise frequency of #TravelTomorrow sentiments

Table 1. Weighted percentage of hashtags

Word	Length	Count	Percentage
#traveltomorrow	15	17	1.70
#stayhome	9	16	1.60
#staysafestayhome	17	11	1.10
#staycation	11	10	1.00
#travelpodcast	14	8	0.80
#newepisode	11	5	0.50
#socialdistancing	17	5	0.50

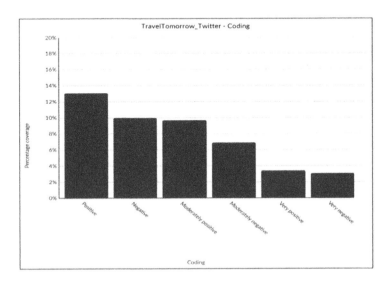

Fig. 3. Sentiment analysis of #TravelTomorrow

4.2   Macroscopic Twitter Sentiment Analysis

The twitter data analysis of #UNWTO has number of followers (108431), number of following (3977) and the number of tweets of a week duration (3821) is used in this research. These twitter sentiments are captured from all over the world. The percentage of #UNWTO sentiments is, positive (14.22), negative (10.35), moderately positive (9.88), moderately negative (5.56), very negative (4.80) and very positive (4.34). The percentage of very negative sentiments is higher (0.46) than the percentage of very positive sentiments. We infer that this higher negative value may be the negative emotions of COVID-19 pandemic or bad quality of services from the tourism industry or negative emotions of twitter users. DMOs should carefully read these very negative sentiments to take appropriate actions or strategies to improve their destinations. The different themes and sub-themes of #UNWTO tweets are tabulated in Table 2 and the major themes of conversations are centered around Efforts, Future, Guides, Sector, Services, Tourism sector, Tourist, Travel, Travel restrictions. The major sub-themes are centered around COVID-19 is, Future: future crisis, future generations, future holidays, future trips, next future, resilient future, sustainable future, Sector: Covid19 travel sector, Tourism: recovery accessible tourism, getting emergency tourism, promoting peace through tourism, supporting tourism recovery, tourism destination recovery, tourism recovery, Tourist: million tourist arrivals, safety tourists, tourist confidence, travel restrictions, Travel: Covid19 travel sector, easing travel restrictions, responsible traveller, safe travel, travelling tomorrow, world travel19, travel restrictions, Travel restrictions: easing travel restrictions, lifting restrictions, travel restrictions and others. DMOs should spend quality time to read all these details of themes and sub-themes to explore the insights that are relevant to their business and devise appropriate strategies to keep their destinations tourist friendly.

5   Discussion and Conclusion

5.1   Discussion of Results

Table 2 above shows themes and a panoply of sub-themes. Various types of 'tourist' can be termed marketing segments, 'services' are value added, and travel banner includes all value-chain activities. 'Sector' theme is the focus of all marketing efforts. Future connotes strategy. A plethora of 'Tourism' sub-themes are adding to the fanfare. The traditional approach to strategy is sequential: 1) Strategies are formulated, DMOs set goals, 2) strategies are implemented, and 3) performance is measured against the predetermined goal set. Such traditional control systems are termed 'single-loop learning' by Argyris (1994). This model is more appropriate when the environment is stable and relatively simple.

As opposed to this model, we have a contemporary approach first given by Quinn (1992). Carefully integrated plans seldom work according to Quinn. Most strategic change process occurs incrementally-one step at a time. Mintzberg visualizes strategic change as crafting change like a potter. Leaders should introduce a sense of direction, some logic in incremental steps. So fixed ideas become dysfunctional in crisis times like Covid. Uncertainty looms large and nothing can be predicted. Strategies need to

Table 2. The themes and sub-themes of #UNWTO sentiments

Themes	Sub-themes
Efforts	Gradual efforts, illustrating efforts, joint efforts, tireless efforts
Future	Future crisis, future generations, future holidays, future trips, next future, resilient future, sustainable future
Guides	District level tourist guides, fledged guide, freelance guide, guide jobs, guides status, knowledgeable guide, level guides, little guide, qualified guides, regional guides, tour guide, word guide, affected sectors
Services	Inbound logistic services, service qualities, standard services
Tourism sector	Abusive tourism, accelerating tourism, recovery accessible tourism, allowing tourism, boosting tourism, business tourism, coastal tourism, planning controlled tourism, cross-border tourism, cultural tourism, direct tourism, policies discussing tourism, domestic tourism, eco-tourism, european tourism, fun tourism, gastronomy tourism, getting emergency tourism, funding global leisure tourism, global tourism, family global tourism industry, heritage tourism, inbound tourism, inbound tourism policies, inclusive tourism, independent tourism, indian tourism, indian tourism industry, international tourism, international tourism receipts, kerala tourism, leading tourism, leading tourism destinations, love tourism, making tourism, performing quality tourism, promoting peace thru tourism, responsible tourism, restarting tourism, spanish tourism, package deal spanish tourism, package support tourism, supporting tourism recovery, sustainable tourism, tourism board, tourism bureaucrats, tourism committee, tourism companies, tourism destination recovery, tourism development, tourism government, tourism industry, tourism minister, tourism ministry, tourism professions, tourism recovery, tourism returns, tourism sector, tourism stakeholders, tourism supply chain, tourism worker, tourism workforce cultural tourism sector
Tourist	Foreign tourist, foreign tourist arrivals, global tourist destinations, global tourist receipts, global tourists arrivals, inbound tourist, international tourist, international tourist arrivals, million tourist arrivals, tourist attractions, safety tourists, tourist arrivals, tourist confidence, tourist facilitators, tourist industry, tourist numbers, tourist protection, tourist traffic, travel restrictions
Travel	Travel experts, accessible travel, covid19 travel sector, easing travel restrictions, must-see travel destination, outbound travellers, responsible traveller, safe travel, seamless travels, travel agencies, travel businesses, travel corridors, travel division, travel experiences, travel industry, travel insights, travel pros, travel sector, travellers, travelling tomorrow, world travel 19, travel restrictions
Travel restrictions	Easing travel restrictions, lifting restrictions, travel restrictions

change frequently and opportunistically. Predetermined goals and milestones can prevent adaptability that is required of a functional clear strategy. As we see in Table 2, all the themes are highly interrelated and interactive. Adapting to and anticipating both internal and external environmental change is crucial in Covid time. So information gleaned from tweets need to be controlled suiting whether or not a firm, or DMO is doing the right job. Another control is required here what is called 'behavior control'. It asks whether an organization is doing things right by listening to twitter sentiments.

In such double-loop learning, a firm's assumptions, premises, goals, and strategies are continuously monitored, tested, and reviewed. Benefits are that time lags are shortened, changes in environment are detected early, and DMO's ability to respond with speed and flexibility is enhanced.

Tweets display experiences, moods, emotions and other sentiments which are classified as very positive, positive, moderately positive, moderately negative, negative and very negative. The exchange of these sentiments between tourist and potential tourists have a positive effect on the perception of destination and increase the attractiveness of the destinations. The loyal tourist is one whose experiences with the destination exceed their expectations and who provide very positive sentiments about the destination to others. The defectors feel neutral or moderately positive satisfied with the destination and are likely to switch to another destination for lower prices. DMOs should take adequate efforts to raise the satisfaction levels of defectors and turn them into loyalists. Even in the crisis situations such as COVID-19 pandemic, DMO's efforts if positive, are having positive effect on tourism and should carefully discern the very negative sentiments and grope on the details of themes and sub-themes to extract insights.

5.2 Practical Implications

Any Strategy chosen must address information always on flows. Focus is of strategic importance as even in Covid-19 times, new flows and frontiers are coming like iconic tourism, marine tourism. If DMOs have the ability to properly manage the large amount of these sentiments, they can design tailor-made services to the specific needs of tourists' requirements. Frivolous comments can be filtered out lest it can be pernicious for business results. DMOs can optimize their resources by targeting potential tourists instead of large audiences.

The locus of finding potential tourists lies within agencies, Govt departments, hoteliers, travel assistants and the ecosystem. Not only informed downstream activities like communications can tide over the crisis now but also upstream activities like product development on destinations can hike the score. Well designed tweets will achieve good reach and have the capability to positively influence the destination image. An image booster marketing plan together with associated activities can add sentiments which can act as 'psychological overhaul'. The positive and negative sentiments will reveal critical information to drive marketing managers to demarcate marketable segments, notwithstanding pricing and positioning tasks. Not all the negative comments are rumors; so the DMOs should take effective steps to reduce the undesirable impact of negative comments. In case of crisis situations like COVID-19, the guidelines by the DMOs can help both employees and customers. Not only words, but some form of pictography, symbols, caution, rejoinders can alleviate to an extent the anxiety of nonormal situation now. Based on the theoretical and practical implications and dearth of such studies on Twitter, its comments broach up for further study and findings. Specifically, how traumas can be avoided or negotiated for tourism intentions can be dealt with in future studies.

5.3 Limitations

There are two limitations found in this study, first, this study is restricted to only on #TravelTomorrow and #UNWTO; it limits the generalization of our findings. The second limitation is short duration of uploaded tweets that are taken in this research. Longitudinal data analysis will be considered for future research work. Many text-based features in tweets, such as the average rating of tweets and the length of the tweets can be the denominators for onward research analysis. These limitations may inspire future undertakings in this area.

5.4 Conclusion

Recent researchers have shifted from an interrogatory research framework to more listening based and interactive research. If the DMOs think of viral tweets, either they are funny or surprising that makes no sense to share. There are contagious tweets like awe or elevation or aha moments which people like to pass it to others. Different types of tweets by tourists lead to different impacts on destinations but identifying and leveraging them effectively is a challenging task. Several strong emerging markets have powerful implications for the future shape of tourism demand. In any case tourism demand should be made inelastic. DMOs should regularly post quality tweets on various newly created themes, such as cuisine, sporting activities, adventure, fishing trips, marine tourism, underwater restaurants overlooking marine life already opened in Norway. New vectors of inputs and outputs can emerge in the domain of tourism, may be giving Twitter the top slot for eliciting consumer opinion. Animators can inject new life into static attractions within destinations, which would be a cultural capital in Tweets (Getz and Page 2016). Large-scale events can be perceived as part of a destination's offering of products, services and experiences, rendering them indistinguishable from the location in which they are staged.

References

Wacker, A., Groth, A.: Projected and perceived destination image of tyrol on Instagram. In: Neidhardt, J., Wörndl, W. (eds.) Information and Communication Technologies in Tourism 2020, pp. 103–114. Springer, Cham (2020). https://doi.org/10.1007/978-3-030-36737-4_9

Aladhadh, S., Zhang, X., Sanderson, M.: Tweet author location impacts on tweet credibility. Presented at the Proceedings of the 2014 Australasian Document Computing Symposium, p. 73. ACM (2014)

Bharadwaj, A.S.: A resource-based perspective on information technology capability and firm performance: an empirical investigation. MIS Q. **24**(1), 169–196 (2000). https://doi.org/10.2307/3250983

Dnhopl, A., Gretzal, U.: Selfie-taking as touristic looking. Ann. Tour. Res. **57**, 126–139 (2016)

Cantallops, A.S., Cadona, J.R., Salvi, F.: The impact of positive emotional experiences on e-WOM generation and loyalty. Span. J. Mark. ESIC **22**(2), 142–162 (2018)

Wernerfelt, B.: A resource-based view of the firm. Strateg. Manag. J. (1984). https://doi.org/10.1002/smj.4250050207

Lien, C.-H., Wu, J.-J., Hsu, M.K., Wang, S.W.: Positive moods and wordof-mouth in the banking industry: a moderated mediation model of perceived value and relational benefits. Int. J. Bank Mark. **36**(1) (2018). https://doi.org/10.1108/IJBM-05-2017-0097

Argyris, C.: Good communication that blocks learning. HBR **72**, 77–85 (1994)

Wang, D., Xiang, Z., Fesenmaier, D.R.: Smartphone use in everyday life and travel. J. Travel Res. **55**(1), 52–63 (2014)

Teece, D.J., Pisano, G., Shuen, A.: Dynamic capabilities and strategic management (1998). https://doi.org/10.1002/(SICI)1097-0266(199708)18

Kotsakos, D., Sakkos, P., Katakis, I., Gunopulos, D.: Language agnostic meme-filtering for hashtag-based social network analysis. Soc. Netw. Anal. Min. **5**(1), 1–14 (2015). https://doi.org/10.1007/s13278-015-0271-3

Getz, D., Page, S.J.: Event Studies: Theory, Research and Policy for Planned Events. Routledge Publications (2016)

Pantano, E., Giglio, S., Dennis, C.: Making sense of consumers' tweets: sentiment outcomes for fast fashion retailers through Big Data analytics. Int. J. Retail Distrib. Manag. **47**(9), 915–927 (2019)

D'heer, E., Verdegem, P.: Conversations about the elections on Twitter: towards a structural understanding of Twitter's relation with the political and the media field. Eur. J. Commun. **29**(6), 720–734 (2014)

Liu, H., Wu, L., Li, X.: Social media envy: how experience sharing on social networking sites drives millennials' aspirational tourism consumption. J. Travel Res. **58**(3), 355–369 (2018)

Quinn, J.B.: Intelligent Enterprise: A Knowledge and Service Based Paradigm for Industry (1992)

Trainor, K.J.: Relating social media technologies to performance: a capabilities-based perspective. J. Pers. Selling Sales Manag. **32**(3), 317–331 (2012)

Balachander, K., Gill, P., Arlitt, M.: A few chirps about Twitter (2008)

Kwak, H., Lee, C., Park, H., Moon, S.: What is Twitter, a social network or a news media?. In: Proceedings of the 19th International Conference on World Wide Web, WWW 2010 (2010). https://doi.org/10.1145/1772690.1772751

Quinn, L., Dibb, S., Symkin, L., Canhoto, A., Analogbei, M.: Troubled Waters: the transformation of marketing in a digital world. Eur. J. Mark. (12), 21032133 (2016)

Caldeira, M., Ward, J.: Understanding the successful adoption and use of IS/IT in SMEs: an explanation from portuguese manufacturing industries. Inf. Syst. J. **12**(2), 121152 (2002). https://doi.org/10.1046/j.1365-2575.2002.00119.x

Dragouni, M., Filis, G., Gavriilidis, K., Santamaria, D.: Sentiment, mood, and outbound Tourism demand. Ann. Tour. Res. **60**, 80–96 (2016)

Ingawale, M., Dutta, A., Roy, R.K., Seetharaman, P.: Network analysis of user generated content quality in Wikipedia. Online Inf. Rev. **37**(4), 602–619 (2013). https://doi.org/10.1108/OIR-03-2011-0182

Jalali, N.Y., Papatla, P.: The palette that stands out: color compositions of online curated visual UGC that attracts higher consumer interaction. Quant. Mark. Econ. **14**(4), 353–384 (2016). https://doi.org/10.1007/s11129-016-9178-1

Lugosi, P.: Socio-technological authentication. Ann. Tour. Res. **58**, 100–113 (2016)

Proferes, N.: Web 2.0 user knowledge and the limits of individual and collective power. First Monday **21** (2016). https://doi.org/10.5210/fm.v21i6.6793

Grant, R.M.: The resource-based theory of competitive advantage: implications for strategy formulation. Calif. Manag. Rev. **33**(3), 3–23 (1999)

McCabe, S., Li, C., Chen, Z.: Time for a radical reappraisal of tourist decision making? Toward a new conceptual model. **55**(1), 3–15 (2015). https://doi.org/10.1177/0047287515592973

Takhteyev, Y., Gruzd, A., Wellman, B.: Geography of Twitter networks. Soc. Netw. Spec. Issue Space Netw. **34** (2012). https://doi.org/10.1016/j.socnet.2011.05.006

Van Noort, G., Willemsen, L.M.: Online damage control: the effects of proactive versus reactive webcare interventions in consumer-generated and brand-generated platforms. J. Interact. Mark. **26**, 131–140 (2012)

Waters, R., Jamal, J.: Tweet, Tweet, Tweet: a content analysis of nonprofit organizations' Twitter updates. Public Relat. Rev. **37**, 321–324 (2011)

Zhang, M., Jansen, J., Chowdhury, A.: Business engagement on Twitter: a path analysis. Electron. Mark. **21**, 161–175 (2011). https://doi.org/10.1007/s12525-011-0065-z

Zhao, D., Rosson, M.B.: How and why people Twitter: the role that micro-blogging plays in informal communication at work. In: Proceedings of the 2009 ACM SIGCHI International Conference on Supporting Group Work, GROUP 2009 (2009)

Preliminary Insights into Social Commerce in the Fitness Industry of Ghana

Eric Klutse Adevu[1], Joseph Budu[1($\boxtimes$)] (iD), Walter Dzimey[2],
and Edward Entee[3]

[1] Department of Information Systems and Innovation, School of Technology,
Ghana Institute of Management and Public Administration, Accra, Ghana
`josbudu@gimpa.edu.gh`
[2] Ghana Technology University, Accra, Ghana
[3] University of Ghana Business School, Accra, Ghana

Abstract. The purpose of this study is to explore how value is created for customers in the fitness industry using social commerce. The study employed a single case study by which data was obtained through a one on one structured interview. Data gathered was analyzed by employing an explanation-building analysis approach. The findings of the study revealed that the fitness instructor leverage on the affordances and features of social media tools he is familiar with to create value for his customers, by using Facebook live for training sessions, uploaded videos of customers and work-outs on Instagram, and WhatsApp status together with WhatsApp video call. The strategy deduced was proposed to be an ideal one for the fitness industry to use to create value for customers, in conformity to the critical case sampling technique.

Keywords: Social commerce · Value creation · Case study

1 Introduction

Social commerce is a form of commerce engaged on the platform of social media networking sites. In other words, the existence of social media created an opportunity for buying and selling. 'social commerce,' this term mainly refers to the provision and implementation of activities and transactions related to electronic commerce in social media, and particularly social networks (Esmaeili and Hashemi 2019). Social commerce as defined by (Zhou et al. 2013) includes the use of online-based media that enables individuals to engage in commercial activities like selling, buying, marketing, curating, and sharing of products and services. Social commerce has become increasingly dominant on social media platforms (Alalwan et al. 2019) Social commerce has been on the rise since its inception in 2005 (Esmaeili and Hashemi 2019), this is because of the numerous benefits it provides to both retailers and consumers who engage in it. The term social commerce is a combination of electronic commerce and social media.

The term social commerce is a combination of electronic commerce and social media. E-commerce is the use of information technology to mediate the buying and selling of goods and services over the internet. On the other hand, social media is an

© IFIP International Federation for Information Processing 2020
Published by Springer Nature Switzerland AG 2020
S. K. Sharma et al. (Eds.): TDIT 2020, IFIP AICT 618, pp. 499–507, 2020.
https://doi.org/10.1007/978-3-030-64861-9_44

online environment that allows vast users to interact with each other, share media contents, and build relationships. Bringing these two elements together makes social commerce a potent tool as far as businesses are concerned.

Businesses have adopted social commerce to become a part of their business operations to increase revenue and sales, as well as customer retention. According to (Wang et al. 2016) Organizations are progressively using social media in business to enhance their customer engagement, collaborate with external stakeholders, and promote internal cooperation and communication. Social commerce has been the subject of many researchers for the past few years. Researchers have studied how businesses in various industries adopt social commerce as part of their business model. It can be seen from previous research that a lot of studies have been done in the area of social commerce. However, the value creation of social commerce that fitness instructors get from their implementation of social media into their business model has been overlooked. This paper is an appropriate response to the research gap observed. Hence, the purpose of this paper is to explore how value is created in the fitness industry by the application of social commerce in business activities.

2   Literature and Theoretical Foundation

2.1   Previous Literature

Research on social commerce is enriched with multiple studies that seek to understand or explain the phenomenon from different perspectives (Entee et al. 2018). Such research can be divided into empirical and analytical research. Still, they cover themes such as user behaviour, business models, adoption strategy, social commerce website design, the study of social process channels, and firm performance (Busalim and Hussin 2016). Previous research has studied social commerce features (Friedrich et al. 2016; Tajvidi et al. 2018); and explain the influence social commerce features might have on buying behaviour. Also, Tajvidi et al. (2018) conducted an empirical study to examine how social interaction, social support, relationship quality, and consumers' intention are related to co-create brand value. The study revealed that social commerce interaction, particularly, marketer perspective and user perspective, have a positive effect on social support and as a result, intention to create brand value.

Second, Factors affecting consumers' engagement and purchase intention in social commerce, The purpose was to examine how word-of-mouth influences purchase intentions in the social commerce domain, by using trust and value co-creation theories, (Mikalef et al. 2017) established in a survey that word-of-mouth has both direct and indirect impact on purchase intentions. This investigation was conducted in the context of users of social commerce. (Maia et al. 2018) also surveyed to analyze the determining factors that influence consumers to engage in social commerce activities. The findings of this study showed that information quality and perceived usefulness are key factors why consumers engage in social commerce activities. According to Qin and Kong (2015), this paper explores the factors that drive the intention of users to pursue shopping recommendations on s-commerce sites. The results of this paper established that the perceived trustworthiness and perceived helpfulness of a particular social commerce user are the key drivers behind the influence of other users' intention to go after shopping recommendations on social commerce sites.

In explaining social commerce capabilities, Entee et al. (2018), talked about the examination of how small entrepreneurs develop, deploy, and manage their social media platforms to form social commerce capabilities to maximize benefits. The findings of this paper were presented in three dimensions. First, the combination of technical and non-technical in the development of social commerce is needed. Second, no personal social capital is readily available for use in the development of s-commerce capabilities.

Third, the affordances of the current social media platform determine the level of scommerce capabilities be developed. Another paper was constructed a social commerce adoption model (SCAM) to tackle the adoption of social commerce. This paper provided in its finding that the variable "trust" was shown to have a significant influence on the reason why people venture into social commerce activities. Hence, the importance of the position of trust in the SCAM model (Hajli 2012). Other themes under social commerce concerns, social media use (Wang et al. 2016; He and Yan 2013), quality of service (Polyakova and Mirza 2016), review and evolution of social commerce (Wang and Zhang 2012; Esmaeili and Hashemi 2019), and Technology and value creation (Criado and Gil-Garcia 2019; Ormiston and Seymour 2011; Chiu et al. 2019; Stephen and Toubia 2010).

The reviewed articles in this paper shown clearly how social commerce is still a growing trend with vast issues that can be researched. In response, these issues would have to be tackled to broaden knowledge in the social commerce discipline and make it more effective. However, these studies neglect strategic issues such as the application of social commerce to create value for the customer. This issue is a significant research gap because social commerce is an information technology resource that needs to be built to meet business objectives. This gap is further reflected in the existing conceptual approaches to the study of social commerce. For instance, many businesses don't know how to assess or evaluate their customer co-creation efforts on social media. As a result, they have difficulty deciding if their social media usage and investments pay off or not. A new evaluation system would have to be built to solve this issue.

2.2 Research Framework

This study conforms to induction as a reasoning mode and argues for what informs the use of social commerce by fitness instructors. Induction includes generalizations of an object using observations of the particular instances of the object. This mode of reasoning contrasts with deduction in which one has to postulate a particular theory or theories which can be tested to produce results that will show a fit between the theory and the facts observed. This study does not postulate a priori theory because of the critiques of existing theories, as already presented (Fig. 1).

This study examined existing knowledge from previous research, which was under the literature review section, to guide how to look for real-life observations. The results section will include the real-life findings describing a corresponding set of theoretical contributions and generalizations. We would then draw a general conclusion describing the links between real-life observations and informing future forecasts in other cases

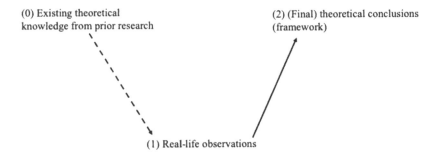

Fig. 1. The inductive approach framework

(Entee et al. 2018). It is not arbitrary but justifiable to choose the induction for various reasons.

Firstly, a shift from deductions from the theory to the inference based on real beliefs is taking place (Evans and Over 2013). This change may be due to the growing awareness that while theories are useful for understanding certain circumstances, the researcher works with little room for serendipity in a near corner. She has to prove or refute a certain theory.

Secondly, there is also a growing interest in the field in information system about studying its context influence (Wiredu 2007; Durkin et al. 2015; Avgerou 2008). For example, previous work demonstrates how contextual information system implementation processes can influence the implementing organization (Avgerou 2001). If the context is so significant, observations must be made before generalizations are drawn rather than generalization before the study.

Induction affords us to make the observations first before drawing such general conclusions (Budu 2020). Therefore, it is empirical to choose induction approach for this study, considering it allows observations to be made before making generalizations.

3   Methodology

Data was collected through interviews. An interview is a vital data collection technique encompassing verbal interaction between the researcher and the subject (Xie and Zhang 2005). We formulated a case study protocol which included a data collection and data collection procedures instrument, to make my case study more reliable. Data collected comprises structured interviews, observation, and private documentary material, and Including public sources. We interviewed our respondent over a telephone call. All research questions were asked, and the interviewee took the time to answer them accordingly. The whole session lasted for one hour and twenty-three minutes. However, the method used in collecting the data does not affect the reliability of the data collected. For the analysis of this case study, explanation-building approach. The approach consists of developing a case description, which would provide an organizational framework for the case study.

4   Case Findings

Jay Fitness Club is an indigenous fitness training centre, popularly known as JFC. It has been in existence for about four years now. It started when a young entrepreneur known as "Jay Ice" discovered his passion for staying fit and healthy at all times. He understood how relevant it was to keep up with regular training to keep the body in shape and still maintain a healthy life, for this reason, he started personal training which he called "one-on-one" training with friends and people in his neighbourhood. Not only limited to body training, but Jay is also a swimming pro. So, he combined the swimming lessons with the physical training and offered free service to his friends and people who needed his help in training. Jay worked with MTN gym, pipers, and many other local gym centres in Accra. Jay, with his over 20 years' experience in swimming and Body training, decided to venture into his own business in the fitness industry. He began with a small group of customers who stayed committed to what they sought to achieve.

As of now, Jay has a membership of about 140 customers who are consistent with their daily training sessions. The group meets at the forecourt of Trade fair centre- La, Accra. Every morning, members of Jay Fitness Club meet at exactly 5:00 am for their daily training session with their coach, Jay. The training duration is exactly 1 h, which means they close at 6:00 am. Members are happy with the training duration because there are both government and private workers who are a part of the membership, and these people go to work after their daily training session with Jay. During this one-hour training session, daily work-out tasks are accomplished. Aside from the group training sessions, Jay trains customers at personal levels at their various homes. He has about 11 customers; he engages them in training at their homes. Outside the borders of Ghana, Jay has three customers he trains over the internet, using WhatsApp video call. These are customers who cannot be with Jay physically for the training session. Jay uses social commerce in his business for several reasons. He currently has accounts on three social media platforms, where he shares videos of himself training and also the team workout daily. He has been consistent with it ever since he started using these social media tools. Although this strategy helps him market his business, he also shares the video on his platform to create value for his customers, in the sense that the videos and pictures he shares on his social media platforms help customers to have self-training using the videos as their guide. So, Jay's use of social commerce enables continuity in terms of customers working out daily, even if they couldn't be with him physically. Questions were asked to find out how the interviewee as a fitness instructor uses social media tools in his business.

To set the grounds, it was essential to know from the interviewee about his business.

Hence the question;

How did your business start and what the business entails?

"I started training people for free with the aim of getting customers too. I train people for fitness and swimming, everything about fitness and wellness. I was able to reach out to several people, and those people referred me to other people who needed

to train for weight-loss and swimming lessons also. "What type of customers do you serve?

"I train people from all walks of life, both children and adults. Once they are ready to commit to the health goals they have set."

Why did you start using social media for your business, and how did it start? *"I began with taking videos and pictures of myself; this happened when I recorded a video of my first client while he was taking his swimming lessons and I shared it my on my Facebook page, this got the attention of my Facebook friends and other people. I was excited about the feedback I got from my first post; then, I was motivated by the swimming posts. The first social media Started with Facebook, Instagram, and now WhatsApp."*

What social media tools do you use? And how do you use them?

"Currently, I have business accounts on three social media platforms. I started with Facebook and later progressed to Instagram and WhatsApp. I share my pictures and videos of our daily work-out and swimming lessons with friends and the public across Facebook and Instagram. I run a paid advertisement page on Facebook. And on WhatsApp, I share daily videos and pictures on my WhatsApp status."

5   Case Findings

Nature of S-commerce Use in the Fitness Industry
The response from the trainer found two features of social commerce in the fitness company, i.e. marketing and training video.

First, the response from Jay Ice shows that his fitness club as a business started marketing when he took a picture of himself and his first client and uploading it on Facebook. He later got feedback from people who had the intention of exercising. Social media platform helps to manage social media solution and services. The platform helps to advertise primarily with a specific person or broadcast to all. This presents continuous content that is visible and persistence to target people. The primary purpose of using social media for his fitness club was to let his training video get a vast number of people. The application used to share and advertise at the beginning stage was Facebook. Mostly, the WhatsApp platform helps him to get in touch with his customers by sharing videos.

Fitness Industry Use of Social Commerce to Create Value
In this section, the response from the trainer shows that motivation happens to be the value created for customers to be engaged in training activities. Customers are motivated anytime they see their pictures and videos being shared on the trainer's pages. This motivation has been effectual on their urge to continue with their daily training.

The Motive of Using Social Commerce in Their Business Activity
The response from the trainer found Four reasons why the trainer uses social media to engage and get new customers. These are convenience, accessibility, cost, and motivation. First, the trainer uses social media to interact with his old customers by sending

them himself training videos, which they can follow up to train on their own when they can't join us physically.

Second, accessibility refers to trainee finding it more accessible to have free access to training videos from his/her trainer that will help to practice for some time continuously. Old clients receive updates on all work-out they missed and can catch up. Through the videos and pictures, the trainers share on my page. He also reaches out to new customers who later join the fitness club.

Third, the means of transport from home to training centre is more expensive as compared to the use of social media to engage in training activities.

Four, trainees are given a reason for doing something, especially when they see themselves in video training. This motivates them to train more, and they also become excited and proud of seeing themselves being posted on the trainer's social media pages.

6   Conclusions

Having dealt with the objectives set out in this research, the study revealed how value is created for customers in the fitness industry using social commerce. Through the gathered data, the case of Jay fitness club explained how fitness instructors use social media tools to create value for their customers, and also the perception of customers on how value is created for them by the presence of the fitness club on social media. From the trainer's point of view, the responses found four reasons why the trainer uses social media to engage and get new customers. These are convenience, accessibility, cost, and motivation.

First, the trainer uses social media to interact with his old customers by sending them himself training videos, which they can follow up to train on their own when they can't join us physically.

Second, accessibility refers to trainee finding it more accessible to have free access to training videos from his/her trainer that will help to practice for some time continuously. Old clients receive updates on all work-out they missed and can catch up. Through the videos and pictures, the trainers share on my page. He also reaches out to new customers who later join the fitness club.

Third, the means of transport from home to training centre is more expensive as compared to the use of social media to engage in training activities. Four, trainees are given a reason for doing something, especially when they see themselves in video training. This motivates them to train more.

Also, the response from the trainer shows that motivation happens to be the value created for customers to be engaged in training activities. Customers are motivated anytime they see their pictures and videos being shared on the trainer's pages. This motivation has been effectual on their urge to continue with their daily training.

From the perspective of the customers, the following responses were gathered concerning the social media use of Jay fitness club. These responses were essential to understanding how value is created for them. A trainee finds it more comfortable to engage in either live training activity or follow the instruction of already made video just to save him/her from travelling from a far distance to a taring centre. Accessibility was revealed as another factor - most of the time, trainees will find it easier to have free access to training videos from his/her trainer that will help to practice for some time continuously. Jay fitness club's social media presence provides accessibility means to customers who won't continue with their daily work-out. The accessibility has to do with how they can get to train easily when it is inconvenient for them. Also, Costeffectiveness has to do with the means of transport from home to training centre is more expensive as compared to the use of social media to engage in training activities. Trainees are given a reason to do more, especially when they see themselves in a video training. This motivates them to train more.

This study now recommends that for fitness instructors to create value for their customers, they have to adopt the strategies and framework of Jay fitness club. Customers' perception of the fitness club's online/social media presence has a significant effect on how fitness instructors create value for them. For instance, how customers comment and share feedback on their videos posted on social media encourages the fitness instructor to keep on posting and sharing those videos. Consistency is also revealed by the case and analysis of Jay fitness club as another factor to create value for customers. This study is an attempt that has dealt with the problem identified in this discipline. These issues have been tackled to broaden knowledge in the social commerce discipline and make it more effective. However, there is still more to be done in this topic area. For instance, many businesses don't know how to assess or evaluate their customer cocreation efforts on social media. As a result, they have difficulty deciding if their social media usage and investments pay off. Hence, a new evaluation system will have to be built to solve this issue. Future research can also focus on adopting multiple case studies to validate the framework proposed in this study.

References

Alalwan, A.A., et al.: Examining the impact of social commerce dimensions on customers' value co-creation: the mediating effect of social trust. J. Consum. Behav. **18**(6), 431–446 (2019). https://doi.org/10.1002/cb.1782

Budu, J.: Disruptive technology adoption in developing countries, pp. 51–69 (2020). https://doi.org/10.4018/978-1-7998-2610-1.ch003

Caldwell, N.D., Roehrich, J.K., George, G.: Social value creation and relational coordination in public-private collaborations. J. Manag. Stud. **54**(6), 906–928 (2017). https://doi.org/10.1111/joms.12268

Chiu, W., Won, D., Bae, J.: Customer value co-creation behaviour in fitness centres: how does it influence customers' value, satisfaction, and patronage intention? Manag. Sport Leisure **24**(1–3), 32–44 (2019). https://doi.org/10.1080/23750472.2019.1579666

Criado, J.I., Gil-Garcia, J.R.: Creating public value through smart technologies and strategies. Int. J. Public Sector Manag. ahead-of-p(ahead-ofprint) (2019). https://doi.org/10.1108/ijpsm-07-2019-0178

Entee, E., Budu, J., Boateng, R.: Preliminary insights into social commerce capability development. In: MWAIS 2018 Proceedings (2018)

Esmaeili, L., Hashemi, G.S.A.: A systematic review of social commerce. J. Strategic Mark. **27**(4), 317–355 (2019). https://doi.org/10.1080/0965254X.2017.1408672

Evans, J.S.B.T., Over, D.E.: Reasoning to and from belief: deduction and induction are still distinct. Think. Reason. **19**(3–4), 267–283 (2013). https://doi.org/10.1080/13546783.2012.745450

Friedrich, T., Overhage, S., Schlauderer, S.: The more, the better? Exploring the relationship between social commerce feature intensity, social factors, and consumers' buying behaviour. In: 2016 International Conference on Information Systems, ICIS 2016, pp. 1–21 (2016)

Hajli, M.: Social commerce: the role of trust. In: 18th Americas Conference on Information Systems 2012, AMCIS 2012, vol. 1, pp. 201–211 (2012)

He, W., Yan, G.: Examining the use of social media in customer co-creation: a blog mining study. In: 19th Americas Conference on Information Systems, AMCIS 2013 - Hyperconnected World: Anything, Anywhere, Anytime, vol. 2, pp. 1537–1546 (2013)

Ketonen-Oksi, S., Jussila, J.J., Kärkkäinen, H.: Social "media-based" value creation and business models. Ind. Manag. Data Syst. **116**(8), 1820–1838 (2016). https://doi.org/10.1108/IMDS-05-2015-0199

Li, H., Liu, Y., Tukkinen, P.: Social commerce in retailing why you use it? In: 27th Bled conference: EEcosystems – Proceedings (2014)

Maia, C., Lunardi, G., Longaray, A., Munhoz, P.: Factors and characteristics that influence consumers' participation in social commerce. Revista de Gestão **25**(2), 194–211 (2018). https://doi.org/10.1108/rege-03-2018-031

Matthews, D., et al.: Value Creation - Background Paper for Integrated Reporting. EY (United States) Benjamin Miller (2013). http://integratedreporting.org/wp-content/uploads/2013/07/IR-Background-Paper-Value.pdf

Mikalef, P., Pappas, I.O., Giannakos, M.N.: Value co-creation and purchase intention in social commerce: the enabling role of word-of-mouth and trust. In: America's Conference on Information Systems: A Tradition of Innovation, AMCIS 2017, August, pp. 1–10 (2017)

Ormiston, J., Seymour, R.: Understanding value creation in social entrepreneurship: the importance of aligning mission, strategy, and impact measurement. J. Soc. Entrep. **2**(2), 125–150 (2011). https://doi.org/10.1080/19420676.2011.606331

Polyakova, O., Mirza, M.T.: Service quality models in the context of the fitness industry. Sport Bus. Manag. Int. J. **6**(3), 360–382 (2016). https://doi.org/10.1108/SBM-04-2014-0015

Qin, L., Kong, S.: Perceived helpfulness, perceived trustworthiness, and their impact upon social commerce users' intention to seek shopping recommendations. J. Internet Commer. **14**(4), 492–508 (2015). https://doi.org/10.1080/15332861.2015.1103634

Shin, D.H.: User experience in social commerce: in friends we trust. Behav. Inf. Technol. **32**(1), 52–67 (2013). https://doi.org/10.1080/0144929X.2012.692167

Stephen, A.T., Toubia, O.: Deriving value from social commerce networks. J. Mark. Res. **47**(2), 215–228 (2010). https://doi.org/10.1509/jmkr.47.2.215

Tajvidi, M., Wang, Y.C., Hajli, N.: Technological advancement in marketing: cocreation of value with customers. In: Americas Conference on Information Systems 2018: Digital Disruption, AMCIS 2018, pp. 1–10 (2018)

Wang, C., Zhang, P.: The evolution of social commerce: the people, management, technology, and information dimensions. Commun. Assoc. Inf. Syst. **31**(1), 105–127 (2012). https://doi.org/10.17705/1CAIS.03105

Wang, P., Li, H., Suomi, R.: Value co-creation in business via social media: a technology affordance approach. In: Pacific Asia Conference on Information Systems, PACIS 2016 – Proceedings (2016)

Xie, J., Zhang, W.: Optimal sensor placement for damage detection in smart composite material based on genetic algorithms and neural networks. Yi Qi Yi Biao Xue Bao/Chin. J. Sci. Instrum. **26**(11), 1184–1187 (2005)

Zhou, L., et al.: Social Commerce: An Integrated View The Determinants of Continuous Use of Social Networking Sites Hsiu-Chia Ko 6. Improving Trust Modeling through the Limit of Advisor Network Size and Use of Referrals (2013)

Diffusion of Information Technology and Systems (Conference Theme)

Digital Transformation of Organizations – Defining an Emergent Construct

Ashis Kumar Pani[1] and Himadri Sikhar Pramanik[1,2(✉)]

[1] XLRI - Xavier School of Management, Jamshedpur, Jharkhand, India
akpani@xlri.ac.in, rl2010@astra.xlri.ac.in
[2] Tata Consultancy Services (TCS) Limited, Kolkata, West Bengal, India

Abstract. Focus on digital technology led transformation of institutions revolves around multiple areas including customer experience, operational process and business model. It encompasses varied discussions from smart cities to future of work. This research driven conceptual point of view explores the essence of transformation based on evidences across large global institutions. The paper proposes a clear definition of *what is digital transformation*? Digital transformation is viewed as a complex process, under-taken by institutions – manifested through multiple technology and business initiatives, to capitalize differential benefits. Based on descriptions from existing literature, public narratives from institutions, news, discussions with expert technology practitioners, qualified by grounded theoretical understanding of technology-led transformations, the research identifies specific institutional focus areas. The definition highlights a process perspective around digital transformation. Transforming organizations are at transient maturities based on continued focus over a period of time. A clear definition, elaborates on the key components of transformation. This helps form a relatable common understanding of the digital transformation construct.

Keywords: Digital · Transformation · Technology · Strategy · Process · Innovation · Definition

1 Introduction

Technology will increasingly become a prime enabler as our world emerges out of the prevailing pandemic crisis. It will determine newer ways of working for individuals and organizations. Paradigms of business, customer connect, conceptualizations of value chain will increasingly depend on technology. Institutions will adopt digital technologies as default to transform and as a strategic imperative for growth.

There has been significant discussion on 'digital transformation' already. It is likely to become prime consideration for institutions, as means to be resilient and generate opportunities. Leading global academics are attempting to understand and define digital transformation. While most operate on some common premise related with the construct of digital transformation there is no established definition yet. Existing descriptions cover varied concepts including smart living, future of work, automation, industry convergence, and technology. These are sometimes fairly all encompassing,

© IFIP International Federation for Information Processing 2020
Published by Springer Nature Switzerland AG 2020
S. K. Sharma et al. (Eds.): TDIT 2020, IFIP AICT 618, pp. 511–523, 2020.
https://doi.org/10.1007/978-3-030-64861-9_45

inconsistent and incomparable as a point of reference. Interestingly, major consulting firms, technology promoters, independent influencers and analysts have developed digital transformation solutions, each with own models, descriptions and views.

In this paper, we attempt to develop a definition based on relevant descriptions from existing literature and discussions with expert practitioners qualified by a grounded theoretical understanding of the context in which institutions transform through adoption of digital technologies. *The definition also factors in how the essence of digital transformation itself is transient with scope and opportunities available with new technology innovations and transient environment.* Multiple existing definitions as captured in Table 1 were analyzed to establish a pattern to structure our definition. While there are some similar practices followed in earlier definition conceptualizations in academic literature [1, 2] the definition proposed here presents a process-centric perspective. Moreover, the definition is built factoring academic and practitioner perspective and studying public narratives from large global institutions.

Table 1. Digital Transformation - Comparing Key Relevant and Recent Definitions.

Authors	Definition
Liu et al. (2011)	"Integration of digital technologies into business processes"
Bharadwaj et al. (2013)	"An organizational strategy formulated and executed by leveraging digital resources to create differential value"
Fitzgerald et al. (2013)	"The use of digital technologies to enable major business improvements"
Lucas et al. (2013)	"Altering traditional ways of doing business by redefining business capabilities, process and relationships"
Mithas et al. (2013)	"The extent to which an organization engages in any activity of IT"
Westerman et al. (2014)	"The use of technology to radically improve performance or reach of enterprise"
Henriette et al. (2015)	"A business model driven by changes associated with application of digital technology in all aspects of society"
Piccinini et al. (2015)	"Characterized by the use of new digital technologies to enable significant business improvements"
Schuchmann and Seufert (2015)	"Realignment of technology and new business models to more effectively engage digital customers at every touch-point in the customer experience life cycle"
Chanias and Hess (2016)	"Reflect the pervasiveness of changes induced by digital technologies throughout an organization"
Hess et al. (2016)	"Concerned with the changes digital technologies can bring about in a company's business model, which result in changed products or organizational structures or in the automation processes"
Morakanyane et al. (2017)	"Digital technologies to enable business models, operational processes and customer experience to create value"
Ziyadin1, S (2020)	"Organizations digitally change and outlines organizations inspirations, and additionally their triggers"

Based on literature key relevant themes and concepts were identified. Further, in consultation with experts from practice and academia, a more encompassing definition is conceptualized. The process of conceptualization was iterative, and utilized different keywords and components to ensure rigor and relevance. The definition is further refined based on narratives from large global organizations. The narrative evidences helped to build greater context and applicability to understand how large global organizations digitally transform. Based on assessment of findings from multiple sources we propose the following definition of digital transformation: **"Digital transformation is a complex process, consciously under-taken by institutions in response to their eco-system imperatives, which involves application and exploitation of digital technologies, to capitalize differential benefits for the institutions as well as key stakeholders."**

It is important to have a clear definition of the construct and its boundaries as the definition guides future research and subsequent scale definitions from an academic perspective. Divergent and varied construct definitions will lead to different sets of items and confusion. 'The boundaries of the phenomenon must be recognized so that the content of the scale does not inadvertently drift into unintended domains' [3] Moreover, an ambiguous definition creates difficulty to decide on inclusion and exclusion of specific items, properties and manifestation of the construct. A challenge in relation to defining the construct of digital transformation is how to differentiate it from other related constructs in information sciences and other studies. This differentiation is important for future scale developments and subsequent tests for convergent and discriminant validity of the construct. Therefore while defining the digital transformation, even at a conceptual level; it is important to consider how the construct demonstrates relationship to other relevant constructs [4, 5] The proposed definition is further scoped into boundary and context through our subsequent discussions based on association among related constructs. Figure 1 helps understand definition in context to relevant and associated constructs.

While most prevailing discussion on digital transformation focuses on larger organizations, even smaller institutions can undertake digital transformation. In fact the level of complexity would be more manageable for them. Further the ability of getting the entire organization to adopt and adapt to the ensuing technology-enabled transformations would be easier. Additionally, the eco-system itself being small would aid in the transformation further. Perhaps a constraint in digital transformation of smaller organizations vis-a-vis larger organizations may be availability of resources including investments in technology and people capability.

The process of selection, adoption and subsequent transformation (if any), we believe, is moderated by multiple internal to organization and external factors [6]. Factors like digital business strategy, institutional ability (readiness), ecosystem, available technology are relevant for transformation. Subsequent discussions in this paper **elaborate the key components of the proposed definition** with relatable instances. **There are four components of the proposed definition: (A)** Digital Transformation is a complex process; **(B)** Digital transformation is under-taken by institutions in response to eco-system imperatives; **(C)** It involves application and exploitation of digital technologies; **(D)** Digital transformation helps capitalize differential benefits.

(A) Digital Transformation is a complex process: There exist established theories to explain institutional maturity towards technology in terms of selection, adoption and exploitation of technologies for enabling functions, networks, and the organization as an integrated whole [7]. *Studies on technology enabled transformations indicate somewhat staged progression of what institutions can do with technology from localized exploitation, internal integration, business process and network redesign to business scope redefinition* [8]. References of IT-enabled transformation is longitudinal, there is sustained beneficial impact, institutions experience through continuous learning and strategic focus on technology. Institutions undergoing digital transformation in phased manner are best able to realize benefits by continuous selection, adoption, exploitation of digital technology ensuring overall strategic fitment.

Institution's ability to exploit digital technology moderates how new-age technologies are selected, adopted for conceptualized applications. *The ability to exploit technology towards value generation largely differentiates transforming organizations and demonstrates heterogeneity in performance.* Ability to exploit digital technology is dependent on nature, levels of readiness and core capabilities of an organization including its leadership. Chief Digital Officers (CDOs) are increasingly positioned for digital transformation of organizations [9]. Roger's Diffusion of Innovation Theory at firm/institution level discussed how technology adoption and innovativeness are related to independent variables as individual (leader) characteristics, internal organizational structural characteristics of the institution. Such internal capabilities develop over time and continuous learning to become more mature and normative across organization. Ability to exploit technology resources, an acquired competency, is difficult to emulate, may eventually become a core-competency, and a key differentiator.

The complex process of digital transformation is not pre-defined and structured in most institutions. The process can be rather random and unique for institutions as they select, adopt and exploit digital technologies pertaining to functions, their networks and towards integrations. *Large organizations can co-exist in various stages of the process of digital transformation – not representative of a single identity. In other words large institutions may live through various phases of digital transformation not appearing as if they are parts of the same entity.* Plurality of stakeholders, priorities and distribution of resources including budget allocations across institutional functions may lead to intra-institution variances [10]. Large institutions demonstrate instances of systemic, disruptive and somewhat ad-hoc developments like changes in organization and leadership, performance impact by competition, preparation for new regulations etc. *These developments may either accelerate or even impede digital transformation process. It is evident; the process of digital transformation is influenced by internal and external change drivers impacting large organizations.*

Despite the complexity and diversity, in digital transformation of large institutions, some commonalities are identifiable. A prime emergent factor is the **prominence of digital business strategy at institutional level**. As a benchmark, institutions are focusing on development of a strategic perspective around how to leverage digital technologies? Instances across institutions in multiple industries demonstrate a somewhat fuzzy interpretation of what digital business strategy is? How can digital business strategy impact digital transformation?

While at one end there are instances of mature integrative practices towards digital transformation through re-thinking and redesigning of business model taking advantages of technology opportunities and resources; there are also many examples of institutions merely leveraging digital channels as ad-hoc measures to automate, improve and enhance efficiency or customer experience. The behaviors of large institutions are largely impacted by innovations and technologies available. Technology follows a trajectory of development, typically categorized by technology lifecycle; based on how they emerge, evolve and become obsolete. Large organizations applying digital technology demonstrate imagination, ingenuity while improving business efficiency simultaneously. Driving this at one end of the transformation continuum is digital automation and at the other end there is machine intelligence and autonomous behavior with established necessary conditions for connections and collaborations between humans and machines and among machines. Such trajectories of technology-enabled transformation are key outcomes of organizational digital business strategy.

Digital Business Strategy [11], we believe, moderates the process of digital transformation as indicated in Fig. 1. *The presence, absence or maturity of an institution's digital business strategy impacts the digital transformation process, orientation towards efficiency or imagination and value generated.* There is a fair amount of indicative literature establishing how IT enables business and how important it is to ensure IT and Business alignment. Conventionally in information sciences literature the premise of IT strategy is predominantly function-level aligned to that of institution's overall business strategy. There are multiple studies [12] indicating how business strategy directs IT strategy and alignment. *The essence of digital transformation is not about mere IT enablement or alignment. On the contrary, it stems from assessments indicating that, benefits from technology deployment are marginal if superimposed on existing organizational conditions (like strategy, structure, process, culture...) – real advantages of technology are derivatives of institutional transformations [13–15]. In such instances technology is being leveraged as a key resource to differentiate, compete and generate value. Observations indicate large institutions are increasingly focusing towards technology-centric strategic planning.*

Digital business strategy is defined as *'organizational strategy formulated and executed by leveraging digital technology resources to create differential value'.* Perspectives on digital business strategy includes (**1**) the scope of digital business strategy, (**2**) the scale of digital business strategy, (3) the execution of digital business strategy, and (**4**) the sources of business value creation [11]. Another theoretical perspective of digital business strategy describes it as *'a set of strategic responses to the collective choices of industry competitors that is shaped by industry conditions, motivates the construct of digital strategic posture'* [16] Digital strategic posture indicates digital technology focus relative to the industry norm. The term strategic posture refers *'crucial strengths and weaknesses from a strategic standpoint'.* The concept of digital strategic posture focuses on an institution's stance with respect to digital activities of peers in its operating environment. *Digital strategic posture complements others like entrepreneurial posture, market orientation, consumer orientation, competitor orientation, innovation orientation, and technology orientation.* Recent research of large organizations [17] adopting digital business strategies indicate

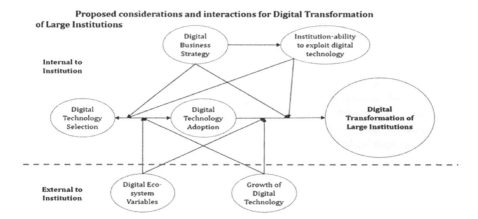

Fig. 1. A Conceptual Model - Indicating Interactions among Constructs Related to Digital Transformation of Large Organizations

how mature practices focus on integrating across digital technologies, and business functions towards transformation of business models. *Technology as a strategic resource enables institutions to re-imagine and re-think business focus. Digital technologies render capabilities and resources beyond solving discrete problems. It enables institutions to use technology to develop core–competencies and competitive advantage.*

(B) Digital transformation is under-taken by institutions in response to eco-system imperatives: While there is significant discussion on preferences and adoption of technology at an individual level, our focus here is on the digital transformation at an organizational/institutional level. These institutions may be public, private, profit-making, philanthropic, government etc. These organizations intend to deploy digital technologies aspiring for beneficial social, economic and technology impacts. *At this point, it is important to clearly distinguish between conventional large organizations, where technology enables strategy, and the relatively newer institutions, which are devising strategies focused upon digital technology as the key resource. Digital transformation is more suited to explain technology selection, adoption and exploitation in the conventional institutions vis-à-vis the digital institutions (some of them digital unicorns). A distinction between large traditional organizations embarking on digital transformation vis-à-vis digital technology startups and market disrupters are necessary. This is so, because the large conventional institutions demonstrate the essence of transformation in legacy processes, practices and technology by embracing newer digital technologies. On the other hand the disruptive emergent digital institutions/start-ups (digital unicorns or otherwise) are emerging into prominence by exploiting digital technologies as a prime resource. It is observed in many instances large institutions are collaborating with emergent technology start-ups and other established technology providers to infuse agility in innovative transformations.* The transforming institutions experience challenges such as institutional inertia along with imperatives (economic, social, technological, regulatory, competitive, political, legal, and others) from immediate and wider eco-systems. Large organizations are also influenced by collective choices of industry competitors that may be further shaped by industry conditions; and other opportunities that influence the digital strategic posture. *These imperatives and multiple actors constitute the* **Digital Ecosystem Variables** *for the large global organizations and influence the choice of technology and institutional dispositions (shown in* Fig. 1*). Innovations and associated technologies are stimuli for transforming large institutions achieve beneficial outcomes. The large institutions demonstrate varied levels of technology adoption and diffusion. This heterogeneity in adoption under similar eco-system conditions and the associated results may be attributed to multiple factors. The nature of influence of such factors is subtle and may not be known perfectly.*

Factors influencing adoption of digital technologies can be somewhat explained by the technology adoption models relevant at an institutional level in information systems literature. The *three most popular models are Roger's Diffusion of Innovation (DOI)* [18]*; Technology, Organization, and Environment (TOE)* [19] *framework by Tornatzky and Fleischer (1990) and Iacovou's Model* [20] *studying the influence of Inter-organizational Systems.* These models help understand the institutional imperatives, the digital eco-system variables. The TOE framework identifies three aspects of an organization's context as (1) Technological context, (2) Organizational context, and (3) Environmental context. The TOE framework enables Rogers' innovation diffusion theory better explain intra-firm innovation diffusion [21]. *Institutional Theory* [22, 23] *emphasizes how the institutional environments are crucial in shaping organizational structure and actions, where decisions are not driven purely by rational goals of efficiency, but also by social and cultural factors and concerns for legitimacy. In many cases institutional decisions to adopt technology are not purely internal and driven by rational motives only. Institutions are likely to be induced to adopt and use technology by external isomorphic pressures* [24]. *These drivers may arise from peers and competitor actions, trading partner influences, collaboration with technology start-ups, customer expectations, advocacies, regulations and government incentives among others – considering most of the dominant actors and imperatives of the institution's eco-system. Mimetic* [25] *coercive and normative pressures influence disposition towards technology* [26]. *The institutional theory further adds to the environmental context of the TOE framework including three factors: perceived benefits, organizational readiness, and external pressure.* It is interesting to note, that digital technology as a resource for imagination or re-thinking business strategy, towards extension of institutional boundaries, cross-industry leverage, convergence, customization, re-design of product-services offering does not feature explicitly as determinants of technology adoption in the prevalent IS literature. Based on understanding of existing literature and perspectives across large organizations (based on public narratives) Fig. 2 is an indicative non-exhaustive representation of key considerations explored from an eco-system perspective. These have been derived through study of extant literature and views from experts, practitioners and academics. These are particularly relevant for calibrating and scaling digital transformation maturity.

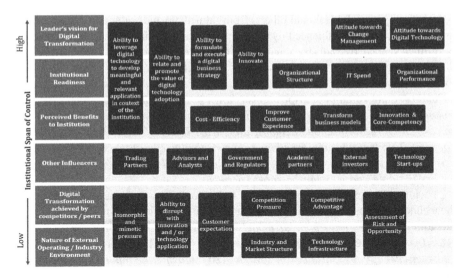

Fig. 2. Key Considerations for Organizations - Representations from multiple perspectives

(C) Digital transformation involves application and exploitation of digital technologies: The new and emergent digital technologies demonstrate considerable complementary capabilities. *The ability to derive greater value from adopting these technologies in conjunction, rather than individually, leading to digital technology convergence is one of the most important considerations that go into formulation of digital business strategy.* The individual to individual, individual to institution and institution to institution transactions are presently influenced by level of technology adoption both by individuals and institutions.

Proliferations of digital technology is ushering in multiple opportunities, manifesting in varied forms for considerations at societal and institutional levels – multichannel, interactivity, virtualization, eco-system networks, sharing resources, internet of services and things, automation, future of jobs, artificial intelligence, convergence, cyber-physical systems, autonomous machines among others. This is changing the rules of generating value and deriving competitive advantage across industries. Technology enabled business models in many ways are resulting in the emergence of complex, overlapping and dynamic ecosystem [27]. Increasingly it is being observed that institutions are breaking the distinctions between products and services rendering them as activity-based 'offerings' for customers to create value independently or collectively. The role of large institutions along-side digital revolution translates into reconfiguration and integration of core-competencies, eco-system actors and customers where value creation and capture is happening by coalition of different economic agents [28]. *A majority of the respondents across a survey of 4,800 executives across 27 industries indicate digital technologies are disruptive in nature* [17]. *Other researches indicate many digitally enabled institutions focused on business strategy, process, and quality* [29] *while demonstrating transformation life-cycles* [30]. *The institutions adopting new-age digital technologies play a critical role in diffusion of innovations integrating social, mobile, analytics, cloud, internet of things, artificial intelligence, 3D printing, blockchain and augmented/virtual reality.* Our experience

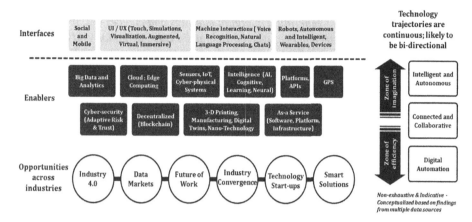

Fig. 3. Digital technology led transformation trajectories drive value; improve experience aligned to industry opportunities

indicates a broad-based categorization of these emergent digital technologies into interface technologies and underlying enablers as shown in Fig. 3 indicating how transformation trajectories drive value; improve experience aligned to industry opportunities.

Social and mobile interfaces are transforming user interfaces and experiences. Increasingly humans will be interacting with intelligent and autonomous machines empowered by natural language processing, voice recognition and robotic chat technologies. Wearables, sensors and other devices will become interfaces in consumption of many products and services and for interaction with institutions. Such technology proliferations generate large amount of unstructured data that will be further used, analyzed to personalize and improve experiences. To enable these interfaces to be even more relevant, ubiquitous and contextual – delivering value; we see the growth of multiple enabling components. These include analytics, cloud and as a service models, edge computing, a truly connected and collaborative cyber-physical system, artificial intelligence and distributed models along with disruptions in manufacturing. Data and security are at the center of most interface and enabling components. Technology providers are improving protocols, methods of standardization, inter-operability in pursuit of truly open, secure, connective and collaborative technologies.

(D) Digital transformation is to capitalize differential benefits for institutions as well as key stakeholders: With the advent and growth of new-age digital technology consumers are being empowered leading to greater power parity between individuals and institutions. These technologies have created a state of somewhat perfect information by reducing information asymmetries between institutions and individuals [31].

These technologies are increasingly rendering boundaries between hardware and software somewhat fuzzy. Embedded hardware is increasingly intelligent executing contextual and cognitive functions based on underlying codes and decision systems. *Value generation is not only dependent on products and services alone (where IT can be an enabler) but also on generation of digital offerings and choices* [32] *propositions and platforms enabling customers to also participate in value definition and creation to varying extent. Embedding technology within the products and services* [33] *leading to an integrated customizable and configurable offering. Technology transformations extend organizations into newer industry eco-systems. This is leading to convergence, new set of customers, partners generating in value shift. Competitive forces likely to rise as existing and emergent players will target key parts of value chain, bypass incumbents and seize customer relationship opportunities* [28].

Technological developments and their manifestations, applications by individuals and institutions are leading to development of digital consumers (may extend beyond customers to include employees, partners and others). The demands of digital consumers are unconventional and institutions need to factor that into the products, services and offerings. *For many of the digital consumers the new-age digital technologies render bundled experiences. As an instance it can be discussed how high-speed internet, ubiquitous computing, mobility, digital connectivity on smart devices all seems as a bundled technology experience enabling digital consumers. Similarly from a specific customer perspective - for digital consumer interactions with a retailer, or a bank, or a healthcare provider over digital channels all create spill-over effects of expectations and demands across disparate industries. For example, customers who regularly receive retail deliveries at home expect that as an institution a bank or a hospital also needs to be offering at home services.* This is evidenced in multiple instances as well, banks are adopting video-engagement initiatives, healthcare providers are conceptualizing digital homecare/ubiquitous solutions by capturing data from wearables and other sensors and will become increasingly relevant post pandemic. *There will be increased instance of vertical and horizontal consolidations within the value stream ensuring greater degree of overlap among suppliers, aggregators, manufacturers and service providers. Within this changing value network, profits and competitive advantages reside dynamically at control points that are the positions of greatest leverage* [34]. Digital business strategy needs to factor these considerations. Innovative transformations increasingly shift value networks from static, vertically integrated within industry to more loosely coupled cross-industry networks - shift towards multi-sided market models are likely.

Evidences across multiple large organizations and their public narratives on benefits indicate non-exhaustive benefit articulations across a few broad categories. The narrative analysis of the institutions revealed benefits that may be broadly classified into **business benefits, operational benefits, growth through digital technology, better marketing and brand positioning through awards and accolades received by institutions achieving digital technology leadership and ability to deliver greater social good** through use of digital technology [35]. *Key business benefits include ability to improve customer acquisition, satisfaction, efficiency, agility through digital technology towards better brand recognition leading to better market share. Ability to realize savings and growth by streamlining, optimizing workflows and* *overall simplification with digital technology is also viewed as key business benefits. Ability to achieve benefits like simplification and agility of processes, reduction of errors, enhancing customer and employee experience – addressing convenience and other value-add technology enablers promoting self-service, virtual and lower manual interventions for processes are evident operational improvements. Ability to reach newer markets and including newer customer segments is possible including suppliers and partners. Adoption of technology towards transformation promotes organizations to digital technology leadership position helps to demonstrate capabilities, to earn trust and respect from customers and investor community.*

Conclusion: A clear construct definition is important for academics and practitioners. Amidst lack of unified perspectives this point of view paper provides a comprehensive definition of digital transformation. A clear definition of digital transformation in the context and consideration of large conventional organizations operating globally is discussed. While extending on existing point of views it clearly establishes digital transformation as a process undertaken by organizations. The process centric perspective is important for continuous improvement and maturity. It further discusses how the essence of transformation is more relevant to large conventional institutions vis-à-vis emergent technology start-ups. This definition will help establish a common point of reference; understanding key consideration including digital business strategy. It helps understand associations among related constructs - will enable large institutions focus accordingly. In doing so it clearly indicates variance in performance and benefits realized by institutions undergoing transformation. The definition has been deconstructed to elaborate with relatable context and key insights, which provide contextual relevance, guiding institutions towards digital transformation. A construct definition can be taken further into scale development helping organizations calibrate progression and maturity on technology enabled transformation.

References

1. Morakanyane, R., Grace, A., O'Reilly, P.: Conceptualization of digital transformation in business organizations: a systematic review of literature. In: 30th Bled eConference (2017)
2. Ziyadin, S., Suieubayeva, S., Utegenova, A.: Digital transformation in business. In: Ashmarina, S.I., Vochozka, M., Mantulenko, V.V. (eds.) ISCDTE 2019. LNNS, vol. 84, pp. 408–415. Springer, Cham (2020). https://doi.org/10.1007/978-3-030-27015-5_49
3. Devellis, R.: Scale Development: Theory and Applications - Applied Social Research Methods Series, vol. 26. Sage Publications, Newbury Park (1991)
4. Campbell, D.T., Fiske, D.W.: Convergent and discriminant validation by the multitrait-multimethod matrix. Psychol. Bull. **56**(2), 81–105 (1959). [PubMed: 13634291]
5. Cronbach, L.J., Meehl, P.E.: Construct validity in psychological tests. Psychol. Bull. **52**(4), 281–302 (1955). [PubMed: 13245896]
6. Loonam, J., Eaves, S., Kumar, V., Parry, G.: Towards digital transformation: lessons learned from traditional organizations. Strateg. Change **27**(2), 101–109 (2018)
7. Heberle, A., Löwe, W., Gustafsson, A., Vorrei, Ö.: Digitalization canvas – towards identifying digitalization use cases and projects. J. Univ. Comput. Sci. **23**(11), 1070–1097 (2017)

8. Venkataraman, N.: IT-enabled business transformation: from automation to business scope redefinition. Sloan Manag. Rev. **35**(2), ABI/INFORM Globalpg. 73 (1994)

9. Singh, A., Klarner, P., Hess, T.: How do chief digital officers pursue digital transformation activities? The role of organization design parameters. Long Range Plan. **53**(3), 101890 (2020)

10. Kretschmer, T., Khashabi, P.: Digital transformation and organization design: an integrated approach. Calif. Manag. Rev. **62**, 1–19 (2020)

11. Bharadwaj, A., El Sawy, O.A., Pavlou, P.A., Venkatraman, N.: Digital business strategy: toward a next generation of insights. MIS Q. **37**(2), 471–482 (2013)

12. Henderson, J.C., Venkatraman, N.: Strategic alignment: leveraging information technology for transforming organizations. IBM Syst. J. **32**(1), 4–16 (1993)

13. Keen, P.W.: Shaping the Future: Business Design Through Information Technology. Harvard Business School Press (1991)

14. McFarlan, F.W.: Information Technology Changes the Way You Compete, pp 98–103. Harvard Business School (1984)

15. Benjamin, R.I., Rockart, J.F., Scott Morton, M.S., Wyman, J.: Information technology: a strategic opportunity. Sloan Manag. Rev. **25**(3) (1984)

16. Mithas, S., Tafti, A., Mitchell, W.: How a firm's competitive environment and digital strategic posture influence digital business strategy. MIS Q. **37**(2), 511–536 (2013)

17. Kane, G.C., Palmer, D., Phillips, A.N., Kiron, D., Buckley, N.: Strategy, not technology, drives digital transformation. IT SMR and Deloitte University Press (2015)

18. Rogers, E.: Diffusion of Innovations, 5th edn. Simon & Schuster (2003). ISBN 9780743258234

19. Tornatzky, L., Fleischer, M.: The Process of Technology Innovation. Lexington Books, Lexington (1990)

20. Iacovou, C.L., Benbasat, I., Dexter, A.S.: Electronic data interchange and small organizations: adoption and impact of technology. MIS Q. **19**(4), 465–485 (1995)

21. Hsu, P.F., Kraemer, K.L., Dunkle, D.: Determinants of e-business use in U.S. firms. Int. J. Electron. Commer. **10**(4), 9–45 (2006)

22. Scott, W.R.: Institutions and Organizations, 2nd edn. Sage, Thousand Oaks (2001)

23. Scott, W.R., Christensen, S.: The Institutional Construction of Organizations: International and Longitudinal Studies. Sage Publications, Thousand Oaks (1995)

24. DiMaggio, P.J., Powell, W.W.: The iron cage revisited - institutional isomorphism and collective rationality in organizational fields. Am. Sociol. Rev. **48**(2), 147–160 (1983)

25. Soares-Aguiar, A., Palma-Dos-Reis, A.: Why do firms adopt e-procurement systems? Using logistic regression to empirically test a conceptual model. IEEE Trans. Eng. Manag. **55**(1), 120–133 (2008)

26. Teo, H.H., Wei, K.K., Benbasat, I.: Predicting intention to adopt inter-organizational linkages: an institutional perspective. MIS Q. **27**(1), 19–49 (2003)

27. Iansiti, M., Levien, R.: The Keystone Advantage: What the New Dynamics of Business Ecosystems Mean for Strategy, Innovation, and Sustainability. Harvard Business School Press (2004)

28. Margherita, P.: Digital business strategy and value creation: framing the dynamic cycle of control points. MIS Q. **37**(2), 617–632 (2013)

29. Ponsignon, F., Kleinhans, S., Bressolles, G.: The contribution of quality management to an organisation's digital transformation: a qualitative study. Total Qual. Manag. Bus. Excell. **30** (sup1), S17–S34 (2019)

30. von Rosing, M., Etzel, G.: Introduction to the digital transformation lifecycle. In: CEUR Workshop Proceedings, vol. 2574, no. 2018, pp. 92–99 (2020)

31. Granados, N., Gupta, A.: Transparency strategy: competing with information in a digital world. MIS Q. **37**(2), 637–641 (2013)
32. Keen, P., Williams, R.: Value architectures for digital business beyond the business model. MIS Q. **37**(2), 643–647 (2013)
33. El Sawy, O.A.: The IS Core IX: The 3 faces of information systems identity: connection, immersion, and fusion. Commun. AIS (12), Article 39, pp. 588–598 (2003)
34. IBMCxOSurvey IBM Offering Information (2016). http://www-01.ibm.com/common/ssi/cgi-bin/ssialias?subtype=XB&infotype=PM&htmlfid=GBE03695USEN&attachment
35. Pramanik, H.S., Kirtania, M., Pani, A.K.: Essence of digital transformation—manifestations at large financial institutions from North America. Future Gener. Comput. Syst. **95**, 323–343 (2019)

Opposite Outcomes of Social Media Use: A Proposed Model

Rita Rocha-Penedo$^{(\boxtimes)}$, Frederico Cruz-Jesus$^{(\boxtimes)}$ (iD),
and Tiago Oliveira$^{(\boxtimes)}$ (iD)

NOVA Information Management School (NOVA IMS),
Universidade Nova de Lisboa, Campus de Campolide,
1070-312 Lisbon, Portugal
{m2018635, fjesus, toliveira}@novaims.unl.pt

Abstract. Social media are probably one of the most influential and disruptive technology of the present times. It is ubiquitous and has the capability to influence virtually every aspect of one's life while, at the same time, also influence the way firms and public organizations operate and communicate with individuals. Although there is a plethora of studies in the IS literature focused on SM adoption and outcomes, studies hypothesizing positive and negative outcomes together are scarce. We propose a comprehensive research model to shed light on SM positive and negative outcomes, and how these affect one's happiness. We also explore how personality traits can influence these relationships.

Keywords: Social media · Outcomes · Happiness · Personality traits

1 Introduction

Social media (SM) are ubiquitous. They are increasingly important as mean of communication and information access [1]. SM already changed the way individuals, organizations, and governments, interact, produce, and consume information. These platforms enable people to chat through real-time instant message, create and share content, read news, build online relationships, gamming, post photos, videos and thoughts, under social, emotional and educational intentions [2]. SM use represent an opportunity for users to fulfil their social interaction needs and find solutions for their problems and daily tasks. However, they also entail several possible threats to its users. A decade ago, the presence of SM as we know nowadays, was unthinkable. According to the European Union, in 2010, less than one billion people were using SM platforms and in 2018 the number passed the three billion users. This growth of users is due to the increase in the time that people spend online [3].

In the information systems (IS) literature, research on SM have mainly focused on its adoption drivers and/or some specific outcomes. However, this fact entails a big caveat: SM are ubiquitous and multipurpose technologies, and can therefore affect, in a positive or negative way, virtually every dimension of one's life. When virtually every study focuses on one specific outcome, only a partial view of the picture is shown, thus hiding other opposite outcomes these technologies may yield in one's life. To fill this

© IFIP International Federation for Information Processing 2020
Published by Springer Nature Switzerland AG 2020
S. K. Sharma et al. (Eds.): TDIT 2020, IFIP AICT 618, pp. 524–537, 2020.
https://doi.org/10.1007/978-3-030-64861-9_46

gap, the present research aims to develop a research model to shed light on how SM can yield different (positive and negative) outcomes and how these can ultimately affect one's happiness. We also assess the role that personality traits have on these relationships. In doing so, this paper is organized as follows: Section two presents the literature review for SM and SM outcomes; Sect. 3 introduces the model and the propositions; Sect. 4 its perspective implications; whereas Sect. 5 the conclusions and future work.

2 Literature Review

2.1 Social Media

Before the 1990's, mobile phones and Internet were only available to a non-significant part of world population [4]. The appearance of Information and Communication Technologies (ICT) made a revolution on contemporary society, emerging as new ways for individuals and businesses to perform daily tasks [5]. ICT diffusion around the world, had impact on economic growth on areas where access to communication and information were essential for a successful development [6]. From the way people communicate and spend free time, to the way people search and share information, the appearance of Internet came to change individuals' daily realities, "becoming one of the most dominant tools for social interaction". Internet enabled the creation of new technological environments like "blogs, social networking sites, virtual social worlds, collaborative projects, content communities and virtual game worlds", representing a new channel for authentic behaviour. Social sharing applications allowed Internet usage to skip from a read-only phase, Web 1.0, in the early 90 s', to a read-write phase, Web 2.0, in the beginning of 21st century, enabling users to present and participate on content creation [7].

The concepts and technical basis of Web 2.0, qualified the creation of SM as online platforms, with origin on a "group of Internet-based applications" [8], where users can create and share content in a way to maintain online relationships with their family and friends and also to stablish new social connections [9]. The fact that each user can generate and share personal content in a public way, is the key factor that separate SM from other ways of traditional media [10]. This activities allow individuals to build social laces, with people with similar interests, based on opinions, knowledge and information sharing [11], constructed under social, emotional and educational intentions [2]. The connection between the offline persona and the online profile is kept by "the use of one's real name, recognizable pictures that make a user visually identifiable, and the presence of real-world acquaintances such as friends and family in the user's friends list" [12].

Myspace was the first social network site to reach a huge amount of popularity among Internet users but ultimately lost this position to Facebook. New SM sites intend now to reach users' time and attention, focusing on niches of individuals, instead of trying to replace the existing social networks [13]. Nowadays, users have a variety of choices according to their use objectives. An individual can use Facebook to share personal interests and keep in touch with family and friends [14]. Instagram provides fun and entertainment through creative content [15]. If users pretend to find a new job opportunity, share professional experiences or keep in touch with former colleagues, they can use LinkedIn [16].

SM represents a tool where users can satisfy their needs of entertainment, information, free time [17] or "to improve their performance to find solutions to problems for their daily or difficult tasks" [18]. Motivations to use SM, vary among social platforms and for different types of individuals, as people chose the one/ones to adopt basing on their personal needs and under influence of their social and psychological characteristics [15, 19]. The applicability of SM is present in several areas: political, education, health, etc. For instance, SM platforms allow brands to collaborate in a new consumer experience, creating fan pages to develop and advertise their products [20]. In the health field, [21] showed that, the more an individual uses SM, more likely he is to access online health information (nutrition, tobacco use or general health maintenance). In 2004, blogs became a part of US election campaigns. However, the Obama's 2008 US presidential elections were remarkable using SM like Facebook, YouTube, Myspace, and Flickr, as a source of news and marketing tool, representing the first 'SM election'. This example of success, was followed, not only in 2016 US presidential elections, by Hilary Clinton and Donald Trump, but as well as, Norway and U.K. parties [22]. In the last years however, as a result of the Cambridge Analytica scandal, much attention has been given to the potential negative impacts SM may have in electoral processes [23]. The use of SM during disaster management, also revels to be very helpful, once that these platforms represent a way of fast information diffusion. During hurricane Sandy (2012) and Louisiana floods (2016), a big amount of information, regarding emergency shelters and medical services, was spread through Facebook and Twitter profiles and after Haiti earthquake (2010) SM channels, were used to gather donations [24, 25].

2.2   Social Media Outcomes

SM outcomes have been studied thoroughly during these past years. However, the research question is often postulated in terms of a specific outcome (positive or negative) can be achieved through SM use: some researchers have an optimistic approach, i.e., test beneficial effects that SM bring to people's lives, whereas others hold the idea that these platforms have a major negative impact for its users. People's skills and what they do online influence the benefits and arms they will obtain upon SM use. However, to feel completely satisfied with the outcomes achieved, Internet skills are more important [26]. It is noticeable by screening the literature that few, to say the least, empirically show that SM can yield both. For a review of studies focused on SM outcomes, please see Table 1.

Table 1. Literature review on social media outcomes.

Broad outcome	Specific Outcomes	Findings	Ref.
Psychological	Psychological Dependence	Internet experiences revealed to develop an addiction behaviour; The habit created by the maximization of media use, drives to dependence.	[27]
	Social Media Fatigue	SM users that think that is helpful to use SM platforms consequently experience higher levels of SM fatigue.	[30]
		Compulsive use of SM and fear of missing out conduct to SM fatigue, that consequently leads to anxiety and depression.	[28]
	Technostress	Higher levels of SM use, are associated with higher technostress.	[10]
	Positive and Negative Affect	Authenticity in using SM platforms have a positive longitudinal effect on positive affect and a negative longitudinal effect on negative affect.	[12]
	Psychological Well-Being	There is evidence to defend that SM use may have a positive effect on well-being, if the intention is to participate in social connections.	[31]
	Strain	Psychological strain is lower in employees' that have a higher SM use for information-sharing.	[32]
	Loneliness	Instagram addiction is positively related with loneliness.	[36]
	Shyness	There is a positive relation between Instagram addiction and shyness.	[36]
Productivity	Task/Job Performance	The use of SM is negatively associated with task performance.	[10]
		SM usage is related with a better work performance.	[17]
		There is a positive association between SM use at work and job performance; SM usage can create favourable conditions for a better performance on job-related tasks.	[9]
		The excessive use of SM, especially for social and entertainment purposes, have a negative impact on work demand.	[32]
	Professional Informational Benefits	LinkedIn and Twitter users revealed higher informational benefits than non-users; SM users that have a professional knowledge sharing intention, report the highest informational benefits.	[16]

(continued)

Table 1. (*continued*)

Broad outcome	Specific Outcomes	Findings	Ref.
	Job Satisfaction	There is a positive relation between SM use at work and job satisfaction.	[9]
	Cognitive Absorption	The direct relationship between SM use and cognitive absorption is not significant.	
	Technology-Work Conflict	Excessive social and hedonic causes are positively related with technology-work conflict.	[32]
Social	Performance	A compulsive use of SM leads to lower levels of social performance.	[37]
	Connection	SM use is positively associated with social connection.	[31]
	Support	Active users of SM benefit from social support.	[33]
	Capital	Social capital is one of the benefits that SM users gain from SM activities.	[33]
Overall Happiness	Happiness	Higher levels of SM use drive to lower levels of happiness.	[38]
		Image-based SM are positively associated with happiness.	[10]
	Satisfaction With Life	Image-based SM cultivates satisfaction with life.	[38]
		Authenticity in using SM platforms contributes to well-being and have a positive relationship with satisfaction with life.	[12]
		There is an impact of Instagram addiction on life satisfaction through the negative relation between Instagram addiction and academic performance and the positive impact on loneliness and shyness.	[36]

Most studies involve the impact on well-being and psychological levels. Some researchers argue that Internet experiences have a key role in addiction behaviour development [27]. Compulsive SM use has been found to be related with higher levels of technostress, SM fatigue, which is a sentiment of mental exhaustion after experiencing an overload of information, and fear of missing out, described as the pervasive apprehension that an individual is absent from an rewarding experience that others might be having. These behaviors might generate anxiety, depression, lower-levels of happiness and individual performance, later bedtimes and shorter sleep duration, especially in adolescents and young adults [10, 28–30]. Although, fear of missing out is largely indicated as a negative driver, in some cases can be a good predictor to enhance social connection [31].

Potential opposite outcomes are also noticeable in terms of individuals' productivity (i.e., job performance, satisfaction, or academic achievement). Some researchers posit that the hedonic motivation, a driver of socialization and entertainment, associated with personal purposes, can affect work demand and job performance [32]. On the other hand, there is evidence that use SM at work, allow employees to connect with their family and friends, keeping a balance between work and personal life, reflecting in a larger concentration at work and revealing a positive association between job satisfaction and job performance [9]. This positive idea is supported by other studies, which find another import conclusions regarding the use of these platforms in professional domain, like, the influence of SM in increasing social capital or the opportunity to use SM as a tool to watch market competitors [16, 17].

Positive benefits regarding individual's social relations, well-being and lifestyle are also found in previous research. SM use contributes to several positive social outcomes like increased contact with family and friends, creation of online relations that may continue offline, sharing and getting new life experiences (travels, hotels, restaurants, brands, etc.) or information and knowledge trade off among social group communities [33–35].

3   Research Model

There is a plethora of studies in the IS literature concluding that SM can impact one's life in many different (and opposite) ways (please see Table 1). However, there is no evidence about how SM can yield simultaneous outcomes at the same time. From a psychological perspective, we can see that SM can lead people to experience SM fatigue [30], but at the job level, it can also be associated with higher job satisfaction [9]. From a social standpoint, people can feel more connected [31] or as they get addicted, they can feel lonely [36]. But can this take place in one individual concurrently? And if so, what is the overall outcome in the ultimate one, i.e., happiness? These questions remain to be answered, and our paper aims to provide a theoretical lens for them for subsequent empirical testing. Thus, in our model (please see Fig. 1), we consider three specifics outcomes from the psychological, productivity and social dimensions and one general outcome related with overall life happiness.

The psychological effects of SM are contradictory. However, we believe that the more an individual uses SM, the more difficult will be for him/her organize and follow a structured daily routine, in which he/she will not include the regular presence of these platforms. There is evidence that frequent use of SM platforms can result in addiction [27]. In terms of productivity, Some authors observed that there is a positive relation between social and hedonic motives to use SM and technology-work conflict [32]. Although, it seems that people can lose on psychological stability and work performance, in a social way, individuals can gain on capital and support [33]. Probably, the ultimate goal of a human being is to be happy. In fact, "people are repulsed by unhappiness" [10]. We believe that psychological, professional, and social stabilities are main drives to achieve that state.

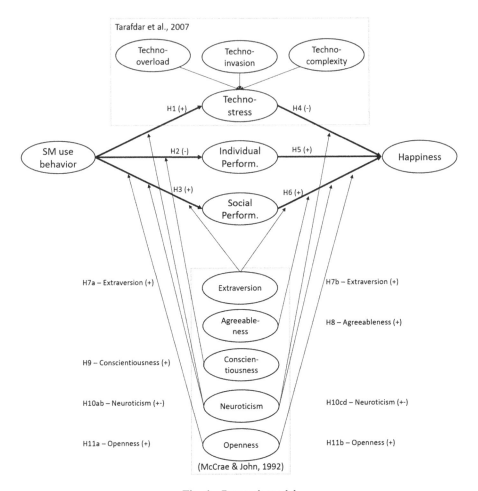

Fig. 1. Research model

To capture the potential negative effects of social media in one's psychological wellbeing, we resort to the concept of technostress, operated as a second-order reflectiveformative construct (see Fig. 1). Technostress can be defined as "any negative impact on attitudes, thoughts, behaviors, or body physiology that is caused either directly or indirectly by technology" [10]. Virtually every feature of every SM can drive individuals to be constantly alert to what it is happening with their connections, interfering with their current tasks. From here, it is easy to feel divide between the need of keep attention to the real world and the intention to just check on what others are virtually doing. Dhir et al. [28] concluded that, users that reveal an excessive use of SM and also be afraid of missing something on these platforms, can feel fatigued and consequently may experience anxiety or depression, which will subsequentially affect one's happiness. An illustrative example is the fact that many SM users claim they see their SM pages during the night, and it is the first thing they do in the morning. Hence, we hypothesize:

H1:Social media use is positively associated with technostress.
H2:Technostress is negatively associated with happiness.

Another important impact SM may have on individuals is in their performance, either professional or academic. Thus, we resort to the concept of individual performance to capture this effect. Individual performance is the degree to which an individual is successful in achieving a goal related with a task he/she is engaged with [17]. It shows the consequent impact of the technology, in this case SM platforms, on individuals' tasks [10, 39] concluded that task performance was negatively influenced by the use of SM. Cao and Yu [32] demonstrate that people who overly use SM, especially for hedonic reasons, reveal a negative effect on their work demand. Thereby, we believe that SM use will have a negative impact on one's performance, which will subsequentially negatively impact one's happiness. Consequently, we hypothesize:

H3:   *Social media use is negatively associated with individual performance.*
H4:   *Individual performance is positively associated with happiness.*

As for the social dimension, we set social performance as being the way SM users "invoke different patterns of socialization beliefs and behaviors". More specifically, is the way individuals use SM to communicate and interact in a way to achieve social capital [26]. These platforms allow its users not only to keep in touch with their close friends and family, anyway anytime, but also to create social ties with other people that they first know online. SM set a new level on loving and friendly relationships. SM use is positively associated with social connection [31]. Hsu and Lin [33] showed that by engaging on SM activities, users benefit from social capital and support. Thus, we believe that the use of SM leads people to perform better regarding social relations, which in its turn will be positively associated with overall happiness. Therefore, we argue that:

H5:   *Social media use is positively associated with social performance.*
H6:   *Social relations use is positively associated with happiness.*

It is reasonable to assume that the previously hypothesized relations can vary from individual to individual, i.e., with one's personality. In fact, it is even possible that some of the hypothesis in our research model can be reverted in individuals with some specific and highly distinctive personality traits. To comprise this important aspect in our research model, we use the Five Factor Model (FFM), arguably the most relevant model to capture one's personality and idiosyncrasy [40]. It comprises five main personality traits - extraversion, agreeableness, conscientiousness, neuroticism, and openness. In the IS literature, there is a growing interest of how these traits affect one's relation with technology, although past studies usually consider this aspect in the pre-adoption stage of a technology, whereas we argue it will also play a role in post-adoption [1, 5, 41, 42].

Extraverts are relaxed in the way they socially connect with others, they have positive emotions, are moved by new stimulus, are audacious, friendly, and loquacious, whereas introverts are typically silent and cautious [40]. Those who score high in extraversion tend to pay more attention to their image, relate with more people, and like to new more people. Thus, they are more likely to use ICT, including SM [41]. We argue extraverts are more prone than introverts to use SM in a more intensive and extensive way. As one of SM main functionalities is connecting (known and new) people, the stronger extraversion trait is, the more likely can SM use yield new and/or reinforced social relations. Extraverts value social relations more than introverts do. Thus, it is reasonable to assume that for an extrovert, social relations are more relevant to happiness than for an introvert person, meaning that as extraversion increases so does the importance of social relations on one's happiness. Note that SM provide or demand new ways of communication such as emails, instant messaging, video sharing, video-broadcast, among others. In the IS literature, extraversion has been proved to be positively associated with ICT [41] and SM [43] use. For all the above, we hypothesize:

H7a: *Extraversion will moderate the effect of SM use on social performance, such that the relationship will be stronger among people with higher extraversion.*

H7b: *Extraversion will moderate the effect of social performance on happiness, such that the relationship will be stronger among people with higher extraversion*

Agreeableness refers to the level of one's understanding, compassion, clemency, and kindness [40], which echoes one's orientation to others [43]. Agreeableness is therefore related with having positive feelings in the relationships with others [44]. Those who score high on agreeableness also reveal a lower level of technology-related anxiety [45]. Moreover, it also seems plausible that those who are less agreeable may be more likely to have difficulties in relating with others in traditional (offline) ways. One of the most known aspects of SM is that in it, people are less constrained to behave in ways that outside the SM environment would never do as they are morally unacceptable. News companies all over the world were forced to disable the comments sections because of the aggressiveness people showed in it. SM comments (e.g., in Facebook) are abundantly filled of offenses and arguments despite the original content of the post. For this reason, we argue that those who tend to face others with a positive perspective, i.e., with compassion, are more exposed to the influence that social performance has on their SWL/happiness. Consequently, those who show low levels of compassion and clemency will not see its SWL/happiness influenced by social performance, as they will see others, especially who do not fit their views, as despicable. Thus, we believe:

H8:   *Agreeableness will moderate the effect of social performance on happiness, such that the relationship will be stronger among people with higher agreeableness.*

Highly conscientious people are generally systematic, efficient and organized [40]. They are self-disciplined and self-driven; goal- and task-oriented (Barrick, 2001). Conscientiousness is often pointed as the strongest of the five personality trait, as it is associated with one's ability to define and achieve long-term objectives by being able to adapt their behavior to a multiple plethora of environments [44]. Hence, conscientiousness is important in the context of achieving outcomes one desires. We argue that conscientiousness is particularly important in the (negative) effect SM has on individual performance. It is well known that SM (excessive) use can lead to procrastination of non-hedonic tasks, whether job- or school-related. However, we believe, that this negative effect of SM will become weaker as conscientiousness increases. Highly conscientiousness individuals are more likely to cope with SM distraction effects. In fact, we believe it is possible that for very high conscientiousness people, SM can even improve individual performance. Thus, we hypothesize:

H9: *Conscientiousness will moderate the effect of SM use on individual perfor-mance, such that the relationship will be weaker among people with higher conscientiousness.*

Individuals who score high on neuroticism are typically more delicate and anxious, with a tendency to be concerned easily [40]. People who score high on neuroticism more prone to give in to impulses, deal poorly with stressful events, and deal emo-tionally to situation where most people would deal rationally [40]. Therefore, neurotic people are prone to undergo negative emotions in situations that they perceive to be hostile [44]. Research has shown that those who score high on neuroticism are more prone to show higher levels of computer anxiety [45]. Those with higher levels of neuroticism "are likely to view technological advances in their work as threatening and stressful, and to have generally negative thought processes when considering it" [46]. These authors have shown that those who score high on neuroticism are less likely to perceived usefulness in a collaborative system, like SM. Neurotic individuals are more prone to find a technology useless and therefore tend to think that SM can represent a threat. Thus:

H10a:Neuroticism will moderate the effect of SM use on technostress, such that the relationship will be stronger among people with higher neuroticism.
H10b:Neuroticism will moderate the effect of SM use on social relations, such that the relationship will be weaker among people with higher neuroticism.

It seems reasonable to assume that the more neurotic one individual is, the more important technostress' (negative) influence in overall happiness will be, as the first two dimensions will feed each other in a snow-ball effect. Moreover, the potentially good impact of social relations in one's happiness will also be attenuated as neuroticism grow because more social relations will be perceived as more potential threats. Thus:

H10c:Neuroticism will moderate the effect of technostress on happiness, such that the relationship will be stronger among people with higher neuroticism.
H10d:Neuroticism will moderate the effect of social relations on happiness, such that the relationship will be weaker among people with higher neuroticism.

Finally, openness is one of the big five personality traits and represents one's receptivity to new ideas and experiences [40]. It is associated with broad interests, novelty seeking, creativity, curiousness, flexibility, and non-conformist [47], opposing with those who prefer stability [48]. Thus, openness is positively associated with SM adoption. Openness yields lower levels of computer anxiety [49], which work as a catalyst for users to take the most of SM potential to meet new people and find new interests. Open individuals are non-conformists and experimentalist in nature. It seems then natural that for open individuals, the social dimension also has a higher importance in overall happiness, Accordingly:

H11a:*Openness will moderate the effect of SM use on social relations, such that the relationship will be stronger among people with higher openness.*
H11b:*Openness will moderate the effect of social relations on happiness, such that the relationship will be stronger among people with higher openness.*

Social media use behavior will be measured through a reflective construct adapted from [50], which is considered to be the most successful model for technology adoption. We will also use a formative construct considering the intensity of use of the SM with more than 1 billion active users in 2019 according with Statista. Happiness will be measured using the Oxford Happiness Survey [51]. The research model can be seen in Fig. 1.

4   Perspective Implications of the Proposed Model

Understanding SM outcomes is an issue of special importance considering that in the last decade SM has emerged as a critical part of individuals', firms', and public organizations lives. This increasing widespread is related to the potential of SM to yield a plethora of (positive and negative) outcomes. To cope with these opportunities and threats SM comprise, we propose a research model to shed some light on this issue.

Our proposed model intends to help researchers and policymakers to better understand SM outcomes, to mitigate its negative and, at the same time, improve the positive outcomes. From the empirical validation of our model, and its hypotheses, we expect researchers, policymakers, and other stakeholders, to better understand how SM can be helpful and how it can be harmful. If we can do so, then a smoother and most effective SM influence in our lives may take place. For researchers, the perspective implications of our work lie in shed some light on what the most influential technology of our times is arguably.

5   Conclusions and Future Work

We developed a research model that sheds light on how SM use yields different hypothesized outcomes and how these affect one's happiness. Moreover, we propose that personality traits can play a significant role in these relations. We believe that our model is tailor-made to SM in the sense that it will not be as effective if it is applied to other technological innovations. Overall, we developed 16 hypotheses. Six are directly between SM use and outcomes, whereas 10 are moderating effects. The model will be empirically tested using partial least squares structure equation modelling (PLS-SEM) using data collected in the European context.

References

1. Hughes, D.J., Rowe, M., Batey, M., Lee, A.: A tale of two sites: Twitter vs. Facebook and the personality predictors of social media usage. Comput. Human Behav. **28**(2), 561–569 (2012)
2. Sobaih, A.E.E., Moustafa, M.A., Ghandforoush, P., Khan, M.: To use or not to use? Social media in higher education in developing countries. Comput. Human Behav. **58**, 296–305 (2016)
3. Patel, L.: The rise of social media, T and D (2010)s
4. Jorgenson, D.W., Vu, K.M.: The ICT revolution, world economic growth, and policy issues. Telecomm. Policy **40**(5), 383–397 (2016)
5. Goncalves, G., Oliveira, T., Cruz-Jesus, F.: Understanding individual-level digital divide: Evidence of an African country. Comput. Human Behav. **87**(March), 276–291 (2018)
6. Rsnen, P.: The aftermath of the ICT revolution? Media and communication technology preferences in Finland in 1999 and 2004. New Media Soc. **10**(2), 225–245 (2008)
7. Rosen, D., Nelson, C.: Web 2.0: A new generation of learners and education. Comput. Sch. **25**(3–4), 211–225 (2008)
8. Ngai, E.W.T., Tao, S.S.C., Moon, K.K.L.: Social media research: theories, constructs, and conceptual frameworks. Int. J. Inf. Manag. **35**(1), 33–44 (2015)
9. Charoensukmongkol, P.: Effects of support and job demands on social media use and work outcomes. Comput. Human Behav. **36**, 340–349 (2014)
10. Brooks, S.: Does personal social media usage affect efficiency and well-being? Comput. Human Behav. **46**, 26–37 (2015)
11. Lee, C.S., Ma, L.: News sharing in social media: the effect of gratifications and prior experience. Comput. Human Behav. **28**(2), 331–339 (2012)
12. Reinecke, L., Trepte, S.: Authenticity and well-being on social network sites: a twowave longitudinal study on the effects of online authenticity and the positivity bias in SNS communication. Comput. Human Behav. **30**, 95–102 (2014)
13. Mcintyre, K.: The Evolution of Social media from 1969 to 2013. J. Soc. Media Soc. **3**(2), 5–24 (2014)
14. Dumas, T.M., Maxwell-Smith, M., Davis, J.P., Giulietti, P.A.: Lying or longing for likes? Narcissism, peer belonging, loneliness and normative versus deceptive likeseeking on Instagram in emerging adulthood. Comput. Human Behav. **71**, 1–10 (2017)
15. Sheldon, P., Bryant, K.: Instagram: Motives for its use and relationship to narcissism and contextual age. Comput. Human Behav. **58**, 89–97 (2016)
16. Utz, S.: Is LinkedIn making you more successful? The informational benefits derived from public social media. New Media Soc. **18**(11), 2685–2702 (2016)
17. Leftheriotis, I., Giannakos, M.N.: Using social media for work: losing your time or improving your work? Comput. Human Behav. **31**(1), 134–142 (2014)
18. Idemudia, E.C., Raisinghani, M.S., Samuel-Ojo, O.: The contributing factors of continuance usage of social media: an empirical analysis. Inform. Syst. Front. **20**(6), 1267–1280 (2016). https://doi.org/10.1007/s10796-016-9721-3
19. Sheldon, P., Rauschnabel, P.A., Antony, M.G., Car, S.: A cross-cultural comparison of Croatian and American social network sites: exploring cultural differences in motives for Instagram use. Comput. Human Behav. **75**, 643–651 (2017)
20. Chen, S.C., Lin, C.P.: Understanding the effect of social media marketing activities: the mediation of social identification, perceived value, and satisfaction. Technol. Forecast. Soc. Change **140**(2018), 22–32 (2019)

21. Mano, R.S.: Social media and online health services: A health empowerment perspective to online health information. Comput. Human Behav. **39**, 404–412 (2014)
22. Enli, G.: Twitter as arena for the authentic outsider: exploring the social media campaigns of Trump and Clinton in the 2016 US presidential election. Eur. J. Commun. **32**(1), 50–61 (2017)
23. Isaak, J., Hanna, M.J.: User data privacy: Facebook, Cambridge analytica, and privacy protection. Computer (Long. Beach. Calif.) **51**(8), 56–59 (2018)
24. Roy, K.C., Hasan, S., Sadri, A.M., Cebrian, M.: Understanding the efficiency of social media based crisis communication during hurricane Sandy. Int. J. Inf. Manage. **52**(August 2018), 2020 (2018)
25. Kim, J., Hastak, M.: Social network analysis: characteristics of online social networks after a disaster. Int. J. Inf. Manage. **38**(1), 86–96 (2018)
26. Van Deursen, A.J.A.M., Helsper, E.J.: Collateral benefits of Internet use: explaining the diverse outcomes of engaging with the Internet. New Media Soc. **20**(7), 2333–2351 (2018)
27. Wang, C., Lee, M.K.O., Hua, Z.: A theory of social media dependence: Evidence from microblog users. Decis. Support Syst. **69**, 40–49 (2015)
28. Dhir, A., Yossatorn, Y., Kaur, P., Chen, S.: Online social media fatigue and psychological wellbeing—A study of compulsive use, fear of missing out, fatigue, anxiety and depression. Int. J. Inf. Manag. **40**(December 2017), 141–152 (2018)
29. Scott, H., Woods, H.C.: Fear of missing out and sleep: cognitive behavioural factors in adolescents' nighttime social media use. J. Adolesc. **68**(July), 61–65 (2018)
30. Bright, L.F., Kleiser, S.B., Grau, S.L.: Too much Facebook? an exploratory examination of social media fatigue. Comput. Human Behav. **44**, 148–155 (2015)
31. Roberts, J.A., David, M.E.: The social media party: Fear of Missing Out (FoMO), social media intensity, connection, and well-being. Int. J. Hum. Comput. Interact. **36**(4), 386–392 (2020)
32. Cao, X., Yu, L.: Exploring the influence of excessive social media use at work: a three-dimension usage perspective. Int. J. Inf. Manag. **46**(July 2018), 83–92 (2019)
33. Hsu, C.L., Lin, J.C.C.: Antecedents and gains of user participation in social media in Taiwan. Technol. Soc., **61**(February) (2020)
34. van Deursen, A.J.A.M., Helsper, E.J.: The third-level digital divide: who benefits most from being online? Commun. Inf. Technol. Ann, pp. 29–52 (2015)
35. Workman, M.: New media and the changing face of information technology use: The importance of task pursuit, social influence, and experience. Comput. Human Behav. **31**(1), 111–117 (2014)
36. Ponnusamy, S., Iranmanesh, M., Foroughi, B., Hyun, S.S.: Drivers and outcomes of instagram addiction: psychological well-being as moderator. Comput. Human Behav. **107** (May), 2020 (2019)
37. Benson, V., Hand, C., Hartshorne, R.: How compulsive use of social media affects performance: insights from the UK by purpose of use. Behav. Inf. Technol. **38**(6), 549–563 (2019)
38. Pittman, M., Reich, B.: Social media and loneliness: why an instagram picture may be worth more than a thousand twitter words. Comput. Human Behav. **62**, 155–167 (2016)
39. Tam, C., Oliveira, T.: Does culture influence m-banking use and individual performance? Inf. Manag. **56**(3), 356–363 (2019)
40. McCrae, R.R., John, O.P.: An introduction to the five-factor model and its applications. J. Pers. **60**(2), 175–215 (1992)
41. Chipeva, P., Cruz-Jesus, F., Oliveira, T., Irani, Z.: Digital divide at individual level: evidence for eastern and western european countries. Gov. Inf. Q. **35**(3), 460–479 (2018)

42. Amichai-Hamburger, Y., et al.: Psychological factors behind the lack of participation in online discussions. Comput. Human Behav. **55**, 268–277 (2016)
43. Liu, D., Campbell, W.K.: The Big Five personality traits, big two metatraits and social media: a meta-analysis. J. Res. Pers. **70**, 229–240 (2017)
44. DeYoung, C.G.: Cybernetic big five theory. J. Res. Pers. **56**, 33–58 (2015)
45. Korukonda, A.R.: Personality, individual characteristics, and predisposition to technophobia: Some answers, questions, and points to ponder about. Inf. Sci. (Ny) **170**(2–4), 309–328 (2005)
46. Devaraj, U.S., Easley, R.F., Michael Crant, J.: How does personality matter? Relating the five-factor model to technology acceptance and use. Inf. Syst. Res. **19**(1), 93–105 (2008)
47. Li, Y., Tan, C.H., Teo, H.H., Tan, B.C.Y.: Innovative usage of information technology in Singapore Organizations: Do CIO characteristics make a difference? IEEE Trans. Eng. Manag. **53**(2), 177–190 (2006)
48. Yoon, H.S., Steege, B.L.M.: Development of a quantitative model of the impact of customers' personality and perceptions on Internet banking use. Comput. Human Behav. **29**(3), 1133–1141 (2013)
49. Korukonda, A.R.: Differences that do matter: A dialectic analysis of individual characteristics and personality dimensions contributing to computer anxiety. Comput. Human Behav. **23**(4), 1921–1942 (2007)
50. Venkatesh, V., Thong, J.Y.L., Xu, X.: Consumer acceptance and use of information technology: extending the unified theory of acceptance and use of technology. MIS Q. Manag. Inf. Syst. **36**(1), 157–178 (2012)
51. Hills, P., Argyle, M.: The oxford happiness questionnaire: a compact scale for the measurement of psychological well-being. Pers. Individ. Dif. **33**(7), 1073–1082 (2002)

The Effect of Technostressers on Universities Teaching Staff Work Performance During COVID19 Pandemic Lockdown

Zainah Qasem[1](✉), Ali Abdallah Alalwan[2],
Zaid Mohammad Obeidat[3], and Raeda AlQutob[4]

[1] The School of Business, Department of Marketing, The University of Jordan,
Amman, Jordan
z.qasem@ju.edu.jo
[2] Amman College of Banking and Finance, Al-Balqa' Applied University,
Amman, Jordan
Jordanalwan.a.a.ali@gmail.com
[3] Marketing Department, University of Jordan, Amman, Jordan
z.obeidat@ju.edu.jo
[4] Department of Family and Community Medicine, School of Medicine,
University of Jordan, Amman, Jordan
ralqutob@ju.edu.jo

Abstract. The World Health Organization declared the COVID19 pandemic in March 2020 as one of the most rapid outbreaks in known human history (Gros et al., 2020). To adapt to the new situation, universities around the world have activated online learning plans using information communication technology (ICT). The teaching staff had to adapt to using ICT rapidly and to turn their homes into a working station. Being bombarded with all the changes it is believed that like all workers using ICT teaching staff is suffering technostress coming from different techno stressors associated with the use of ICT during the complete lockdown. This paper is a call to start studying the effect of techno stressors on university teaching staff work performance. In this paper, we are suggesting a transactional model of stress as a theoretical background to understand the way teaching.

Keywords: Technostress · COVID19 · Work performance · Transactional model of stress

1 Introduction

The World Health Organization declared the COVID19 pandemic in March 2020 as one of the most rapid outbreaks in known human history (Gros et al., 2020). To face this pandemic governments and countries around the world began to implement strict measures that amounted to complete lockdown. For example, Jordan was one of the first countries to impose a countrywide round-the-clock curfew which started in March 2020 with no exact duration (Alsharif, 2020).

© IFIP International Federation for Information Processing 2020
Published by Springer Nature Switzerland AG 2020
S. K. Sharma et al. (Eds.): TDIT 2020, IFIP AICT 618, pp. 538–543, 2020.
https://doi.org/10.1007/978-3-030-64861-9_47

Despite the complete lockdown of all sectors, universities had to continue delivering their service and have moved from full on-campus learning to fully online learning.

Through using information communication technology (ICT) universities have been able to solve a large part of the crisis and to deliver education to students in isolation (Q.S, 2020).

The massive move to online learning forced thousands of university educators (teaching staff) to work from home and to adapt to using different online platforms, and to conduct an interactive education in a very short period (Q.S, 2020).

Although Using online platforms is not new to university educators especially teaching staff, the new situation forced teaching staff to use online platforms to perform major activities such as giving live lectures and managing discussion forums in a very short period. The teaching staff was also forced to increase their existence on social media platforms.

Using different online platforms and being available through social media has created an unfamiliar situation for teaching staff. For example, Under the new circumstance teaching staff are frequently interrupted by students' instant messages on official platforms and social media during and out of working hours. These factors imitate frequent interruptions and technology intrusiveness (Ayyagari et al. 2011; Tarafdar et al. 2011) which represents technostress creators and will lead to technostress- a state of stress caused by the use of ICT (Gaudioso et al., 2017)

Technostress at the workplace has been shown to negatively affect employees psychologically and physiologically which adds financial burdens to the company (Macik-Frey et al. 2007). However, very little is known about what type of techno stressors occur while working from home in university teaching context, the effect of induced technostress on teaching staffs' performance, and how teaching staff deal with resulted technostress. Hence, this conceptual paper comes to propose some prepositions to address the effect of the rapid adoption of online platforms by university educators on their performance.

In this paper, we are proposing a research direction based on the transactional model of stress that explains how to identify the positive or negative effect of technostress while working from home on university educators.

The following parts of this paper are organized as the following. First, we will explain the concept of technostress and techno stressors based on the related literature. The second part of the paper will present the transactional model of stress as a theoretical background followed by an introduction to the proposed conceptual model. Finally, we will suggest a methodology plan.

2 Literature Review

2.1 Technostress

Research on technostress and related topics such as technostress creators, inhibitors, and outcomes arise to look at the other side of technology, the dark side. Contrary to the prevailing research which views ICT as full of benefits, this part of the literature places most of its focus on the negative effect of ICT on individuals' mental and physical health (Tarafdar et al., 2010).

Lazarus defined Stress as a vast spectrum of problems that "stimuli producing stress reactions, the reactions themselves, and the various intervening processes" (Lazarus, 1966 p. 27). Technostress is one form of stress (Hudiburg, 1989) that was introduced by Craig Brod and defined as "a modern disease of adaptation caused by an inability to cope with the new computer technologies in a healthy manner" (Brod, 1984, p. 16). Weil and Rosen (1997) has also introduced technostress as a direct or indirect effect of dealing with ICT on users' cognition, emotions, and thoughts.

With the development of technology and its penetration into the life of modern man, there was a need to further study technostress causes and impact in different fields such as organizations and working environment (Bradshaw and Zelano, 2013).

While Brod's definition of technostress implies negativity a more neutral definition was suggested by (Lei and Nagi, 2014) where they defined technostress as "as the state of mental or physiological stimulation caused by the ICT usage for work purpose, which is usually attributed to increasing work overload, accelerated tempo, and erosion of personal time, among others" Lei and Nagi, 2014, p3). Being forced to work from home and to rapidly adopt different forms of ICT including the eLearning platform and social media for teaching is a new situation for university teaching staff. The effect of the latter is still unclear on the university educator's satisfaction and commitment. Hence, in this conceptual paper, we will adopt a Lei and Nagi (2004) definition of technostress.

2.2 Techno Stressors

In this paper, we will focus on understanding the effect of technostress creators (techno stressors) associated with the rapid adoption of online learning ICT during the lockdown on university educator's (teaching staff) performance.

Techno stressors are the causes of technostress (Ayyagari et al., 2011) which presence and intensity form technostress (Gaudioso et al., 2017). There are some known techno stressors that are found in the workplace. For example, lack of experience with technology and lack of training were marked as the top caused by technostress (Ahmad and Amin, 2012). Tarafdar et al. (2019) suggested that some technologies are invasive in nature (e.g. instant messaging technologies), overloading (e.g. smartphones which allows work to overwhelm individuals through continuously communicating demands), described as fast-changing and insecure. Technologies with such characteristics were described as techno stressors.

Being forced to move to full online learning within a very short period is a new situation for university educators. Hence, we will assume that there is a possibility that university educators are facing all types of stressors.

2.3 Technostress in Education

The topic of technostress and the effect of techno stressors on variables such as workers' performance and satisfaction, is a fairly recent topic in the literature. Although most studies focused mainly on the effect of techno stressors on workers in private and government organizations educators (Wang and Li, 2019), there is an urgent need to understand the impact of technology in the university education sector.

The large investments made by universities and higher education institutions in ICT and online learning platforms brings many benefits for universities and higher education institutions. These benefits include higher reachability and convenience. For example, students from all around the world can join these universities without the need to travel (Wang and Li, 2019). However, and similar to any other job where ICT is introduced to the working system, university educators are facing new challenges related to ICT at their workplace and are prone to technostress. Hence, there is a need to understand the effect of using ICT and online learning on the university teaching staff.

Previous studies on techno stressors' effect on university educators mainly revolved around two topics. first is the effect of techno stressors on the non-teaching staff of universities such as librarians. Secondly the effect of using ICT inside classrooms on the university teaching staff. Ahmad and Amin (2012) have examined the level of technostress among academic librarians in Malaysian public universities. In their study, Ahmad and Amin (2012) measured the level of existence of techno stressors among academic librarians. The results of their study showed that only techno-uncertainty was at a high level. This indicates that not all techno stressors will lead to negative outcomes. In a second study, Jena (2015) studied the effect of techno stressors job satisfaction among Pakistani university librarians. In his study, Jena (2015) reported a positive significant relationship between three techno stressors and job satisfaction among Pakistani university librarians.

Lin and wang (2020) explored the relationship between specific technostress inhibitors, techno stressors, and strains on university teachers' work performance in higher education. The main focus of this study was on the ICT used in classrooms. The results of this study showed that some techno stressors (work performance, techno-complexity, and techno-insecurity) had a negative significant influence on performance while other techno stressors (techno-overload) have a significant positive effect on performance. The empirical results of these studies indicate that techno stressors have both positive and negative effects on work performance.

The lack of studies that clarify the potential type of techno stressors, and the effect of each techno stressor on teaching staff work performance in the time of lockdown, brings a gap in the literature that we will try to bridge in this study.

3 Theoretical Background and Propositions

The way techno stressors are processed differs from one person to another. Hence, the outcome of techno stressors varies among individuals, while it might bring positive outcomes to some individuals it might bring negative outcomes among others (Newton and McIntosh, 2010).

To explain this variation in outcomes we will use the transactional model of stress. The transactional model of stress assumes that stress is a result of an imbalance between demands and resources (Lazarus and Folkman, 1984). When a person is faced with a stressor that surpasses his or her abilities or resources, the individual will appraise the nature of the stress and determine his or her interactions with the identified stressors (Lei and Ngai, 2014).

The transactional model of stress consists of two stages of the appraisal. The first stage is assessed by the level of which the stressor will bring harm to the individual and cause stress. If the individual believes that the stressor will potentially cause harm a secondary appraisal will take place (Lazarus and Folkman, 1984). In this stage, the individual will compare the stressor against his ability to cope with it. Hence, we propose the following propositions

Proposition 1: effect of various techno stressors on university teaching staff work performance is mediated by perceived technostress

Proposition 2: unmanageable technostress will weaken the relationship between techno stressors and teaching staff performance

Proposition 3: manageable technostress will strengthen the relationship between techno stressors and teaching staff performance

4 Proposed Research Methodology

This research aims to study the effect of techno stressors on the work performance of university educators during the time of compulsory online learning shift and delivering a full curriculum from home. Therefore, the sample of this study will be the university teaching staff who participated in the shift to online teaching during the time of the COVID 19 pandemic. A mixed-method strategy is recommended for this research. The first part of this study will aim at understanding what types of techno stressors university educators are exposed to. To collect this data, we are proposing qualitative research. A one to one interview will be conducted with an adequate number of university teaching staff to collect different techno stressors. The second part of this research will be qualitative survey-based research. This research aim is to measure the effect and to determine the direction of the relationship between the proposed techno stressors and work performance among university educators.

5 Research Outcome

This research is coming at the time of COVID 19, which continues to affect university education dramatically. As online learning might continue until the pandemic is contained it is becoming more important to understand its effect on teaching staff. Similar to any job that relays on ITC it is expected that teaching staff will be faced with techno stressors and will suffer from technostress. Therefore, it is very important to understand the effect of developed technostress on teaching staff performance. This research is expected to enrich the literature of technostress by investigating new types of techno stressors and technostress in university education domain, and to provide universities' management with an insight to what type of techno stressors teaching staff will face, and how they are coping with it. The outcomes of this research is expected to help universities' management in creating training and support plan to overcome the effect of techno stressors.

References

Ahmad, U.N.U., Amin, S.M.: The dimensions of technostress among academic librarians. Proc. Soc. Behav. Sci. **65**, 266–271 (2012)

Alsharif, O.: Al-Monitor. Jordan eases lockdown, focuses on opening economy (12.5.2020). https://www.almonitor.com/pulse/originals/2020/04/jorda-coronavirus-easelockdown-econom y-aqaba-html

Ayyagari, R., Grover, V., Purvis, R.: Technostress: technological antecedents and implications. MIS Q **35**(4), 831–858 (2011)

Bradshaw, R., Zelano, J.A.: Exploring themes of technostress for end users working with hardware and software technology (2013). Accessed July

Brod, C.: Technostress: The Human Cost of the Computer Revolution. Addison-Wesley, Reading (1984)

Gaudioso, F., Turel, O., Galimberti, C.: The mediating roles of strain facets and coping strategies in translating techno-stressors into adverse job outcomes. Comput. Hum. Behav. **69**, 189–196 (2017)

Gros, C., Valenti, R., Valenti, K., Gros, D.: Strategies for controlling the medical and socio-economic costs of the Corona pandemic (2020). arXiv:2004.00493

Hudiburg, R.A.: Psychology of computer use: VII. Measuring technostress: computer-related stress. Psychol. Rep. **64**(3), 767–772 (1989)

Jena, R.K.: Technostress in ICT enabled collaborative learning environment: an empirical study among Indian academician. Comput. Hum. Behav. **51**, 1116–1123 (2015)

Lazarus, R.S., Folkman, S.: Stress, Appraisal, and Coping. Springer, New York (1984)

Lei, C.F., Ngai, E.W.: The double-edged nature of technostress on work performance: A research model and research agenda (2014)

Lazarus, R.S.: Psychological Stress and The Coping Process. McGraw-Hill, New York (1966). Lee, R.: Social attitudes and the computer revolution. Publ. Opin. Q. **34**, 53- cn JY (1970)

Li, L., Wang, X.: Technostress inhibitors and creators and their impacts on university teachers' work performance in higher education. Cognit. Technol. Work, pp. 1–16 (2020)

Macik-Frey, M., Quick, J.C., Nelson, D.L.: Advances in occupational health: From a stressful beginning to a positive future. J. Manag. **33**, 809–840 (2007)

Newton, A.T., McIntosh, D.N.: Specific religious beliefs in a cognitive appraisal model of stress and coping. Int. J. Psychol. Relig. **20**(1), 39–58 (2010)

Q.S 2020 How Universities are Embracing Online Learning During the Coronavirus Outbreak (online) (12.5.2020). https://www.qs.com/how-universities-areembracing-online-learning-during-the-coronavirus-outbreak/

Tarafdar, M., Tu, Q., Ragu-Nathan, T.S.: Impact of technostress on end user satisfaction and performance. J. Manag. Inform. Syst. **27**, 303–334 (2010). https://doi.org/10.2753/MIS0742-1222270311

Tarafdar, M., Tu, Q., Ragu-Nathan, T.S., Ragu-Nathan, B.S.: Crossing to the dark side: examining creators, outcomes, and inhibitors of technostress. Commun. ACM **54**(9), 113–120 (2011)

Tarafdar, M., Cooper, C.L., Stich, J.F.: The technostress trifecta-techno eustress, techno distress and design: Theoretical directions and an agenda for research. Inform. Syst. J. **29**(1), 6–42 (2019)

Wang, X., Li, B.: Technostress among teachers in higher education: an investigation from multidimensional person-environment misfit. Front. Psychol. **10**, 1 (2019)

Weil, M.M., Rosen, L.D.: TechnoStress: Coping with Technology @WORK @HOME @PLAY. Wiley, New York (1997)

Role of Intrinsic and Extrinsic Factors Affecting Continuance Intentions of Digital Payment Services

Anup Kumar[1]([⊠]) [iD], Parijat Upadhyay[1], Sujeet K. Sharma[2],
and Prashant Gupta[2]

[1] IMT Nagpur, Nagpur, India
anunwin@gmail.com
[2] IIM Tiruchirappalli, Tiruchirappalli, India

Abstract. This paper examines the continual usage intentions of digital payments. It investigates the effects of perceived risk, quality of service, and grievance redressal structure on the Digital Payment Service continuation through the integration of the Expectation-Confirmation Model (ECM) with some of the most researched technology adoption models. The survey was conducted at two different time line, pre and post demonetization in India. The results of the study were compared to the model (pre demonetization in India), suggest that there is a control effect of ease of usage in experience, gender, and age. The effect of hedonic motivation on the desire to use is moderated by age, gender, and experience to a higher degree among young people in the early phases of digital payments also the effect of grievance redressal as a moderator variable was significant.

Keywords: Digital payment services · Continuance intentions behavior · Expectation-confirmation model · Demonetization

1 Introduction

The digital payment service is a financial service that has reported gaining popularity in emerging economies. It is essential to study digital service quality, perceived usefulness (PU) of the service, and perceived security of the financial service to explore the loyalty and retention attributes for digital payment services, This study attempts to investigate young consumers' perception of the continual usage of digital Payment services. The study is focused on young and mature end-users. The effects of perceived security, quality of service, and grievance redressal structure on the continuation intention of digital Payment services in emerging markets (Chemingui and Iallouna 2013; Chen 2013; Vlachos and Vrechopoulos 2008) has been explored in this study. This paper has attempted a longitudinal study to identify the factor(s) affecting continual usage intention of services like digital Payments (M Payment), which has not been reported before by any researcher. Also, the moderating effects of age, gender, and experience on usage intention have been investigated in this study, which is not available in published literature.

© IFIP International Federation for Information Processing 2020
Published by Springer Nature Switzerland AG 2020
S. K. Sharma et al. (Eds.): TDIT 2020, IFIP AICT 618, pp. 544–555, 2020.
https://doi.org/10.1007/978-3-030-64861-9_48

The adoption of platform-based (mainly digital) services is expected to witness exponential growth in the near future, particularly in countries where the government intervention has been inadequate. The rate of adoption has been encouraging, and so many new-age start-up companies have built their business models based on digital Payments. It is also projected that young consumers (in the 18–30 age group) would primarily fuel this growth through increased adoption. Though there has been considerable research done to study the adoption issues (Gan and Li 2015; Gao and Bai 2014), there is a dearth of significant published literature on the study of continual usage intention amongst young consumers in developing countries.

The study of continuation intention depends on the multidimensional consumer's expectations and is studied by structural equation models (Gallarza, Arteaga-Moreno, Del Chiappa, and Gil-Saura 2016). The research on the linkages among intrinsic variables such as value, loyalty, spirituality, and aesthetics and their effect on the satisfaction of service is imperative to predict the continuation of a service. The use of an expectation-confirmation model in predicting the continuation intention has been widely extended in various service conditions (Cheng 2014; Hamer 2006; Joo and Choi 2016; Zhang, Lu, Gupta, and Gao 2015). The research questions concerning the linkages of the demographic and socioeconomic conditions of a region with intrinsic variables are also important to predict the continuance intention of the services (Walker and Baker 2000). The perceived risk (PR) of structural reliability affects the quality of service, and hence continuation intention (Hamer 2006), the effect of PR, should be investigated to predict the usage intention.

2   The Theory Underlying Predictive Research Model Framework

The theoretical foundation of this research is based on the Expectation-Confirmation Model ECM is prominently used for investigation of consumers' post usage behaviors (Bhattacharjee 2001c). Oliver (1993) opines that Expectation-Confirmation theory (ECT) is instrumental in the promotion of cutting edge goods. Business organizations must comprehend the factors of users' satisfaction. It should be viewed as an "overall evaluation of technology, which reflects an emotion-based response about the target technology".

ECM was developed from two fundamental psychological theories; the first is the Theory of Planned Behavior (TPB) and the second is the Technology Acceptance Model (TAM). There have been several applications in which the six versions of ECM have been thoroughly studied and discussed (Brown, Venkatesh, and Goyal 2014). The past decade has seen a substantial surge in experiential research into implementation problems in products and services based on technology. The studies on the use of emerging technologies are primarily focused on Technology Adoption Model (TAM) (Davis, Bagozzi, and Warshaw 1989), TPB, and Innovation Diffusion Theory (IDT). The concept behind the use and expansion of the ECM model for this work is largely attributable to the capacity to investigate the pre and post-product interaction, which contributes to an improvement in the model's predictive ability.

TAM suggests that when new technology is introduced to consumers, certain factors affect their decision about the pattern and time of their use. The model has been continually researched and extended, the leading updates being TAM 2 and Unified Technology Acceptance and Use Theory or UTAUT. A TAM 3 was also suggested in the context of e-commerce, including trust effects and perceived system usage risk.

Digital payment has become the most common and obvious forms of payment in most of the countries. Zhou (2013) highlighted problems of system quality related to the continued use of digital payment services by users. As digital transactions are expected to increase in India in the near future dramatically, issues concerning the acceptance and the ongoing usage intentions of Indian consumers need to be investigated. We have extended the seminal work of Kumar et al. (2018) to study the effect of demonetization on the continuation intention of digital payments. The paper seeks to examine the factors influencing the continuity of Digital Payment services by examining the hybrid model (Fig. 1). We also explored the impact of age, gender, experience, and grievance redressal (GR) as the variables moderator and mediator. For the study, the proposed models (Fig. 1) have been compared to the model of pre demonetization.

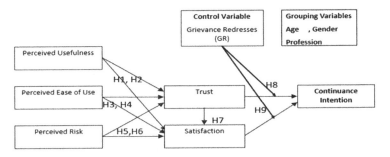

Fig. 1. Proposed model post demonetization.

This paper is organized as follows. The theoretical foundation of the paper has been attempted through the literature review in the next section. Section 4 outlines the research model and hypotheses. Section 5 reports instrument development and data collection. The results of the data analysis are detailed in Sect. 6, along with the subsequent discussion and implications for business managers. The possible limitations of this study, along with future scope for research, are presented in the conclusion section (Sect. 7).

3   Literature Review and Hypotheses Development

User behaviors have been distinguished from first-hand application of technologies and the desire of consumers before and after adoption (Bhattacharjee 2001a). A few hypotheses and models have been used as an interpretation and prediction of technology adoption and diffusion, using TPB, TAM, IDT, and ECM. The prediction of confirmation of the continual usage model (of ECM) extends the principle of TPB and TAM (Bhattacharjee 2001a). In different contexts, for example, ECM was introduced and extended to research variables that affect continued social network usage. Customers' value was added as a new construct to accentuate the ECM model. As this research focuses on the prediction of the continuation intention of the Digital Payment Services, it is also essential to address the variables and constructs employed by different researchers for the study of technology in several circumstances.

Since this research uses a new framework that encompasses PR, so the impact of risk on customer satisfaction needs to be considered. The effect on users' continuity of perceived benefit is less than that of PR. By developing a relationship model, multiple behavioral factors that have an emotional impact were discussed. The EC model has been improved by adding specific variables under different demographic conditions.

The easy use of e-learning tools plays an important role. Zhou (2011b) has found in their study that there is a significant association among perceived advantage, endorsement, and gratification whereas, Zhao and Lu (2012) reports that there is a positive relationship between trust and loyalty to user's satisfaction. The study has undertaken, seven latent constructs for the investigation and are listed in Table 1. Five constructs have been taken from the previous studies of these seven constructs, and two latent variables have been developed according to the Indian scenario.

3.1   Perceived Usefulness

It can be described as users' awareness of the expected advantages of digital Payment usage (Bhattacharjee 2001c). Post consumption expectations are revealed as ex-post observed usefulness. In this study of M-Payment, following hypothesis have been proposed:

H1:   The PU of Digital Payment use is attributed positively to satisfaction.
H2:   The PU of Digital Payment use is attributed positively to trust.

3.2   Perceived Ease of Use

It is defined as the extent to which physical and mental activities are excluded from a specific system. Perceived ease of use (PEU) represents the user-friendly nature of the technology that a customer might have perceived. Hence it can be hypothesized as follows:

H3:   PEU of Digital Payment is attributed positively to satisfaction.
H4:   PEU of Digital Payment is attributed positively to trust.

3.3   Perceived Risk

While a user makes a financial transaction user always worried about security-related concerns like a steal of login credentials, loss payment, and multiple deductions of money from the account during and after use of Digital Payment (Widodo et al. 2019). Therefore, we hypothesize:

Table 1. Constructs and observed items for the research.

Construct	Adapted from	Questionnaire items
Perceived Usefulness (PU)	(Davis 1989)	PU1,PU2,PU3, PU4,PU5
Perceived Ease of Use (PEU)	(Davis 1989)	PE1,PE2,PE3, PE4
Perceived Risk (PR)	Self-derived from the literature	PR1,PR2,PR3
Grievance Redressal (GR)	Kumar et al. (2018)	GR1,GR2,GR3, GR4
Trust (T)	(Zhou 2013)	T1,T2,T3
Satisfaction (SAT)	(Oghuma et al. 2015; Oghuma et al. 2016), (Bhattacherjee 2001a, 2001c)	SAT1,SAT2, SAT3
Continuance Intension (CI)	(Bhattacherjee 2001a, 2001c)	CI1,CI2,CI3

H5:   PR of Digital Payment use is attributed negatively to the Trust of Digital payment usage

H6:   PR of Digital Payment use is attributed negatively to the Satisfaction.

3.4   Trust

It is also an indicator of behavioral intention. Trust for the service primarily for e-commerce and e-banking services plays a vital role in the use of the services (Zhou 2011a). Trust can be described as the desire to be faithful to a technology provider based on optimistic anticipation of future behavior. Trust has the three dimensions: ability, honesty, and goodwill; Several studies have found that trust is a crucial component in the continuance of a service or product. Hence, the study proposes the following hypothesis:

H7:   Trust in Digital Payment service providers is attributed positively to Satisfaction.

3.5   Grievance Redressal

It is a form of management framework structured to resolve conflicts between consumer and service providers. The construct was selected from a focus group analysis where consumers are asked a well-structured question about the proper process of the failed transaction. It is not related to perceived security. In a few cases, even if consumers feel that the system is secure, they prefer those services that assure failed transactions. Such a management system in India is very active and has a constructive impact on the intention of a service's use by consumers. If the user believes that the use of a particular service is secure and straightforward, then the service can continue. Thus, it can be hypothesized as follows.

3.6   Association Among GR, Trust, and Satisfaction

it offers a legal and social guarantee that users have access to some appellate authority in case of fraudulent transactions. The presence of such authority generates trust. The trust offers a subjective promise that users would receive excellent service. Furthermore, the trust may affect users' satisfaction and adoption and continuance intention. Thus, trust in the service provider of a Digital Payment has a positive impact on continual usage intention. Therefore, we hypothesize:

H8:   GR of Digital Payment moderates the effect of trust on CT.

3.7   Satisfaction

Post usage satisfaction always has a high impact on consumer intention to reuse the service. Satisfaction, in turn, leads to behavioral intention towards the technology (Venkatesh et al. 2012). Satisfaction represents the cumulative emotions gathered during the use of a product or service. If the customers are not happy with technology, their use can refrain. Several published studies have shown that satisfaction is a critical element in continuity. Thus we hypothesize,

H9:   GR moderates the effect of User satisfaction of Digital Payment to digital Payment continuance intention.

3.8   Grouping Variables

As indicated earlier in the introduction section, the effect of age, gender, and experience of use have been investigated, establishing them as grouping variables. The effect of these variables had been theoretically verified in UTAUT2 model (Venkatesh et al. 2012). In this research, the controllability of the variables described above is investigated.

4   Research Methodology

4.1   Design of the Questionnaire

Relevant constructs were taken from the related literature for the research. The ECM and TAM items were assessed in compliance with Bhattacherjee (2001c). All products were measured on a five-point scale with reliability greater than 0.8 (Table 2). Specifically for Digital payments, a new latent construction (PR) has been derived, which affects the continuation of the user and is measured by a self-derived scale, with reliability greater than .83.

Table 2. Goodness of fit indices and explanatory power of the model.

Fit indices	Chi^2/df	TLI	CFI	RMSEA
Recommended value	<3	>0.90	>0.90	<.08
Proposed model	1.386	0.928	0.937	0.061
Integrated model of (Kumar et al., 2018)	1.53	0.866	0.966	0.052

Note: *chi2/df = ratio between Chi-square and degrees of freedom, CFI = Comparative Fit Index, NFI = TLI = Tucker-Lewis Index and RMSEA is the Root Mean Square Error.*

4.2 Data Collection

A pilot analysis to test the reliability of the initial items in the questionnaire was performed. Thirty questionnaires from telecom service providers and academic experts were sent to the company managers. Since several improvements proposed by them had been introduced, the readability of the items increased and reduced the chance of common method bias and endogeneity. Modified items have been given to postgraduate students of business administration. Data were collected using self-administered questionnaire items from mobile Internet users (in the 18–45 age group) across several Indian States. Convenience sampling was used to get responses. A Google Form for the questionnaire was planned to promote data collection. The Google web form has been submitted to about 1000 users of the online service.

The results were pre-processed by deleting incomplete responses and outliers; two hundred and fifty credible responses were eventually included in this sample for analysis. The sample size was calculated according to Little and Rubin (1989) norms. For this research, a minimum of 170 samples was needed, as the research has 34 objects. The final sample of 250 used in this analysis; therefore, it can be considered as adequate.

The demographic data on respondents are as follows: 150 males (60 percent) and 100 females (40%) were among the total number of respondents. Majority of the respondents were in the 18–45 age group (91%). A majority of respondents were graduates (65%), followed by postgraduates (35%). The annual income of respondents' categorization (in Indian Rupee, INR) was as follows: 0–3 (15.7%), 3–6 (18.9%), 6–9 (22%), 9–12 (17.7%) and above 12 (25.6%).

5   Results

5.1 Measurement Model: Reliability and Validity

To gain information concerning latent factors, exploratory factor analysis (EFA) was initially applied to the items observed. EFA reveals that the EFA fit index value reflects appropriate factor loads with seven latent factors (see Fig. 2). The above information was used to establish a theoretical research framework (see Fig. 2). A Confirmatory Factor Analysis (CFA) was conducted to reconfirm the adequacy and fit indices of the latent constructs measured.

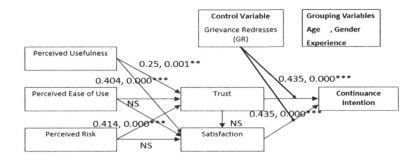

Notes: 2. $^*P < 0.05$, $^{**}P < 0.001$, $^{***}P < 0.000$

Fig. 2. Proposed model results.

Cronbach Alpha has been tested for consistency and reliability of the measurement scale. The analysis is accurate enough as values vary from 0.80 to .83. Construct reliability has been calculated by the use of composite reliability. The value is between .80 and .854, indicating that both values meet the acceptable range of 0.6 and above. Convergent and discriminant validity have also been evaluated. Convergent validity of factor loading, AVE, was assessed. Both items were loaded over normal cut-off 0.6 (ranges from 0.63 to 0.84) as suggested by Bowen and Guo (2012) and Hu and Bentler (1999).

A comparison was made of the AVE (Average Variance Extracted) square root and factor-correlation coefficients, as described in Table 3, to examine the discrimination validity. The correlation of factor below 0.8 indicates ample discriminant validity. The construct's square root of AVE was found to be higher than its correlation value, which also ensures discriminant validity. Table 3 depicts the construct association, while the diagonal values show the square root of AVE.

Table 3. Results of hypothesis

Hypothesis	Estimated Beta	P value	Remark	
H1	0.25	0.001	Significant	Supported
H2	0.404	0.000	Significant	Supported
H3	0.073	0.353	Not significant	Not supported
H4	0.061	0.459	Not significant	Not supported
H5	0.414	0.000	Significant	Supported
H6	−0.006	0.964	Not significant	Not supported
H7	0.079	0.581	Not significant	Not supported
H8	0.435	0.000	Significant	Supported
H9	0.435	0.000	Significant	Supported

5.2 Proposed Model: Goodness of Fit Statistic, Modeling Comparisons, and Hypotheses Testing

Continuing with the measurement model, the suggested theoretical model fulfills the reliability and validity requirements. In addition, the goodness of fit was evaluated using a structural analysis; the fitness index of the model indicated also above the proposed criteria (Table 2). The model fit was higher than Kumar et al. (2018), and the findings demonstrate that the suggested theoretical models have better fit indices (CFI = 0.95, GFI = 0.96, TLI = 0.98, IFI = 0.97, chisq/df = 1.043, RMSEA = 0.016). The results show that the use of GR and perceived security is a better predictor of the continued intention ($R2 = .377$ adjusted) than the Zhou model (2013) ($R2 = .371$ adjusted). In addition to the above, the fitness indices of the suggested model are higher (RMSEA = .061, $\chi2/df$ = 1.386) than Kumar et al.,(2018) and Zhou (2013) (RMSEA = .052, $\chi2/df$ = 1.53). In the case of Digital Payment, the findings accentuated the inclusion of GR as a mediator component and perceived safety in the ECM. The fitness indices are shown in Table 4. The proposed model fit metrics even surpass Bhattacharjee's original ECM (2001a).

Table 4. Moderation Effect and comparison of Pre Demonetization Model with Post Demonetization

Decision variable: continuation intention	Pre Demonetization Model		Post Demonetization Model	
	Estimated Beta	P value	Estimated Beta	P value
H1	NS	NS	0.25	0.001
H2	0.271	0.000	0.404	0.000
H3	0.342	0.000	NS	NS
H4	0.115	0.000	NS	NS
H5	0.225	0.053	0.414	0.000
H6	NS	NS	NS	NS
H7	0.358	0.000	NS	NS
H8	NA	NA	0.435	0.000
H9	NA	NA	0.435	0.000

Notes: 1. Table indicates SEM results.
2. $^{*}P < 0.05$, $^{**}P < 0.01$, $^{***}P < 0.001$, NS (Not significant).

6   Discussion and Conclusion

The objective of this study was to examine the influence of PR and GR on the continuance intention of young subscribers of digital Payment users in India while taking the PU, satisfaction, and user-friendliness. As shown in Fig. 1A and B, excluding hypotheses H2 and H9, the other hypotheses are accepted.

PEU and PR have significant impacts on trust and satisfaction. PR and utility have a significant impact on GR and trust. The findings also show that PR does not affect satisfaction. The continuance intention can be predicted by GR, trust, and satisfaction. The PEU is the factor among the factors which have the most significant effect ($\beta = 0.342$), and these findings are following Zhou (2013) and Bhattacharjee (2001c) results. The results tend to corroborate, to some degree, the results of previous research on developing economies. This research has also provided new ideas in theoretical terms, which appear to resolve the perception of the continuous usage of services such as M-Payment. The original model (Output of R Lavaan) is presented in Fig. 2. Test results are tabulated in Table 3. The comparison of the strength of the relationship amongst variable (Pre and Post Demonetisation) are tabulated in Table 4.

Figure 2 indicates that GR, moderates the effect of satisfaction, and trust on the continuation intention of digital payments. In their research, McKnight et al. (2002b) stated that structural safety in the form of an institutional security framework has a major impact on consumer intention. GR mechanism in the case of failed and fraudulent transactions and their time-bound settlement are necessary to instill trust and confidence in subscribers.

There is a control effect of ease of usage in experience, gender, and age. Such results are more dominant in older age women at the initial experience of digital payments. The effect of hedonic motivation on the desire to use is moderated by experience, gender, and age to a higher degree among young people in the early phases of digital payments. These findings are consistent with Venkatesh et al. (2002) and indicate that experience, gender, and age should moderate the impact of habit on behavioral intent and the use of technology. Table 4 findings also reveal that the model (Pre) predictive ability ranges from 0.46 to 0.71 of post demonetisation.

6.1 Theoretical and Managerial Implications

From a managerial perspective, the findings are significant for business as over the last few years, costs of smartphones and data have come down significantly. Reduction of costs has attracted more users from tier 2 and tier 3 cities to avail digital-based value-added services like M-Payment. This has presented a big opportunity for businesses to offer more products and services to subscribers in tier 2 and tier 3 cities. Now the digital Payment service provider target low-income group people in tier 2 and tier 3 cities. Digital Payment service providers must have adequate security for a precise grievance redress mechanism. Therefore, digital Payment providers in emerging economies like India will concentrate on showing prospective customers how such a technology-based service would easily handle their transfer payment job but also without risk. Few published studies have reported the significance of the risk factor.

7 Conclusion

The study presented in this paper has attempted to investigate young consumers' Continuation intention of digital payment services. The effects of perceived security, quality of service, and GR structure on the continuation intention of digital Payment services in emerging markets have been undertaken in this study. The moderating effects of age, gender, and experience on continual usage intention have been investigated and reported for the first time in this study. Future researchers may get some valuable insights from the findings of this paper and may examine the usage intentions for other age groups as well. It will be equally interesting to learn about the usage intentions in context to developed economies as well.

References

Bhattacherjee, A.: An empirical analysis of the antecedents of electronic commerce service continuance. Decis. Support Syst. **32**(2), 201–214 (2001a)

Bhattacherjee, A.: Understanding information systems continuance: an expectation-confirmation model. MIS Q. **25**, 351–370 (2001b)

Bhattacherjee, A.: Understanding information systems continuance: an expectation-confirmation model. MIS Q. **25**(3), 351–370 (2001c)

Bhattacherjee, A., Perols, J., Sanford, C.: Information technology continuance: a theoretic extension and empirical test. J. Comput. Inf. Syst. **49**(1), 17–26 (2008)

Brown, S.A., Venkatesh, V., Goyal, S.: Expectation confirmation in information systems research: a test of six competing models. MIS Q. **38**(3), 729–756 (2014)

Chang, A.: UTAUT and UTAUT 2: a review and agenda for future research. The Winners (2012). https://doi.org/10.21512/tw.v13i2.656

Chemingui, H., Iallouna, H.B.: Resistance, motivations, trust and intention to use mobile financial services. Int. J. Bank Market. **31**(7), 574–592 (2013)

Chen, C.: Perceived risk, usage frequency of mobile banking services. Manag. Serv. Qual. Int. J. **23**(5), 410–436 (2013). https://doi.org/10.1108/MSQ-10-2012-0137

Cheng, Y.-M.: Extending the expectation-confirmation model with quality and flow to explore nurses' continued blended e-learning intention. Inf. Technol. People **27**(3), 230–258 (2014). https://doi.org/10.1108/ITP-01-2013-0024

Davis, F.D.: Perceived usefulness, perceived ease of use, and user acceptance of information technology. MIS Q. **13**, 319–340 (1989)

Davis, F.D., Bagozzi, R.P., Warshaw, P.R.: User acceptance of computer technology: a comparison of two theoretical models. Manage. Sci. **35**(8), 982–1003 (1989)

Deng, Z., Lu, Y., Wei, K.K., Zhang, J.: Understanding customer satisfaction and loyalty: an empirical study of mobile instant messages in China. Int. J. Inf. Manage. **30**(4), 289–300 (2010)

Gallarza, M.G., Arteaga-Moreno, F., Del Chiappa, G., Gil-Saura, I.: Intrinsic value dimensions and the value-satisfaction-loyalty chain: a causal model for services. J. Serv. Mark. **30**(2), 165–185 (2016)

Gan, C., Li, H.: Understanding continuance intention of mobile instant messaging: motivators and inhibitors. Ind. Manage. Data Syst. **115**(4), 646–660 (2015)

Gao, L., Bai, X.: An empirical study on continuance intention of mobile social networking services: integrating the IS success model, network externalities and flow theory. Asia Pac. J. Mark. Logist. **26**(2), 168–189 (2014)

Gao, L., Waechter, K.A., Bai, X.: Understanding consumers' continuance intention towards mobile purchase: a theoretical framework and empirical study–a case of China. Comput. Hum. Behav. **53**, 249–262 (2015)

Hamer, L.O.: A confirmation perspective on perceived service quality. J. Serv. Mark. **20**(4), 219–232 (2006)

Joo, S., Choi, N.: Understanding users' continuance intention to use online library resources based on an extended expectation-confirmation model. Electron. Libr. **34**(4), 554–571 (2016)

Venkatesh, V., Thong, J.Y., Xu, X.: Consumer acceptance and use of information technology: extending the unified theory of acceptance and use of technology. MIS Q. **36**, 157–178 (2012)

Vlachos, P.A., Vrechopoulos, A.P.: Determinants of behavioral intentions in the mobile internet services market. J. Serv. Mark. **22**(4), 280–291 (2008)

Walker, J., Baker, J.: An exploratory study of a multi-expectation framework for services. J. Serv. Mark. **14**(5), 411–431 (2000)

Widodo, M., Irawan, M.I., Sukmono, R.A.: Extending UTAUT2 to explore digital Payment adoption in Indonesia. In: 2019 International Conference on Information and Communications Technology, ICOIACT 2019 (2019). https://doi.org/10.1109/ICOIACT46704.2019.8938415

Zhang, H., Lu, Y., Gupta, S., Gao, P.: Understanding group-buying websites continuance: an extension of expectation confirmation model. Internet Res. **25**(5), 767–793 (2015)

Zhao, L., Lu, Y.: Enhancing perceived interactivity through network externalities: an empirical study on micro-blogging service satisfaction and continuance intention. Decis. Support Syst. **53**(4), 825–834 (2012)

Zhou, T.: An empirical examination of initial trust in mobile banking. Internet Res. **21**(5), 527–540 (2011a)

Zhou, T.: An empirical examination of users' post-adoption behaviour of mobile services. Behav. Inf. Technol. **30**(2), 241–250 (2011b)

Zhou, T.: An empirical examination of continuance intention of mobile payment services. Decis. Support Syst. **54**(2), 1085–1091 (2013)

Zhou, T., Lu, Y.: Examining mobile instant messaging user loyalty from the perspectives of network externalities and flow experience. Comput. Hum. Behav. **27**(2), 883–889 (2011)

Revisiting the Trust–Commitment and Export Performance Link: A Qualitative Comparative Analysis (QCA) Approach

AFM Jalal Ahamed[1(✉)] and Ilias O. Pappas[2]

[1] School of Business, University of Skövde, Högskolevägen 8,
541 28 Skövde, Sweden
jalal.ahamed@his.se
[2] Department of Information Systems, University of Agder (UiA),
Universitetsveien 25, Kristiansand, Norway
ilias.pappas@uia.no

Abstract. This research revisits the role of different foci of trust (interpersonal and inter-organizational), commitment (affective and calculative) and relationship lengths (inter-organizational and interpersonal) then on export relationship performance. 142 Ecuadorian non-oil exporters completed a self-administered questionnaire. This study applies fuzzy-set qualitative comparative analysis (fsQCA) and the findings help to re-establish the need for both trust dimensions and affective commitment in exporter–importer relationships. This research found three possible configurations of achieving high export relationship performance. The managerial implications noted that export managers should nurture trust and affective commitment to ensure improved relationship performance. This research is one of the very few studies to investigate the role of commitment and trust by taking a complexity theoretical turn. Exploring the causation of the relationship lengths on relationship performance also represents a novel contribution.

Keywords: Relationship marketing · Calculative commitment · Affective commitment · Interpersonal trust · Inter-organizational trust · FsQCA

1 Introduction

Relationship marketing literature extensively predicts the links of trust and commitment with other performance measures [8, 29, 42] often indicating that trust, whether inter-personal or inter-organizational, leads to commitment between a firm and its overseas customers, which enhances firm performance, including export performance [1, 8]. However, there are some apparent ambiguities and short comings in the pertaining literature: First, the dimensionality of trust, Zaheer and colleagues [48], argued that inter-personal trust and organizational trust are closely linked, such that interpersonal inter-actions of managers of partnering firms are critical to the success of the partnership [27]. However, if we view two trust dimensions as different yet closely liked constructs, then how they would affect the export performance is not explicitly sought in the literature. Further, is one type of trust sufficient to predict the relationship

© IFIP International Federation for Information Processing 2020
Published by Springer Nature Switzerland AG 2020
S. K. Sharma et al. (Eds.): TDIT 2020, IFIP AICT 618, pp. 556–568, 2020.
https://doi.org/10.1007/978-3-030-64861-9_49

export performance? Or both forms of trust are necessary? We have not found any conclusive findings to the question. The second area is the different dimensions of commitment. Treating commitment as a universal construct risk creating an over-simplified view [20] and thereby prevents an in-depth perspective on how trust-commitment contributes to export performance. The last area is the relational performance outcome of the commitment-trust configuration. Research shows that firms achieve enhanced interactions with committed customers before being able to establish a relationship with them [30].

To enrich the literature in the areas mentioned above, we theoretically develop and empirically test a model that grounded on the conjunctional causation, implying that combinations of various causal conditions (trust, commitment in this case) rather than one alone condition cause the outcome (relationship export performance) [45]. We subsequently propose the research question as, to explore which configurations of trust (interpersonal and inter-organizational), commitment (calculative and affective), the size of the organization, and the length of the relationships (personal and organizational) lead to relationship export performance? We used complexity theory as a theoretical underpinning of the proposed conceptual model and addressed this question with a fuzzy-set qualitative comparative analysis (fsQCA). Complexity theory posits that the investigation of the net effects of predictive variables does not provide accurate results that are capable of predicting the causal models that lead to expected outcome conditions. It also postulates that the prediction of behavioral outcomes is a complex process, a set of complex interactions between antecedents (i.e., conjunctional causation) must be considered as a causal model capable of predicting the conditions leading to the desired outcome [40]. Qualitative Comparative Analysis (QCA) a method mostly used in political science and sociology [21] is now deemed to be an exciting method in business and management studies [39, 40]. The fundamental attribute of this method is causal asymmetry and capability to deal with smaller sample sizes because causal conditions or their combinations, which can lead to an equifinal outcome are observed [36]. This method is deemed suitable for this research as it can accommodate a high degree of complexity that can be captured through testing theory-based conditions and contextual influences instead of focusing on the single effects of individual variables.

The key contribution of this research is to provide a fine-grained view on the mechanism of the commitment and trust by uncovering the non-linear and asymmetric effect of trust and commitment dimensions on export relationship performance. Further, the use of QCA will facilitate a different perspective of the trust-commitment based relationship marketing as we are using asymmetric analysis instead of the symmetric analysis and null hypothesis significance tests, which are to date is dominating in export marketing research.

2 Literature Review

2.1 Commitment-Trust Theory of Relationship Marketing

Relationship marketing is a dominant paradigm in marketing literature, and commitment-trust theory [29] is central to relationship marketing; it postulates that commitment and trust are essential determinants of long-term relationships. Originating from social exchange theory [7], this theory predicts how businesses organize their activities to establish, develop, and maintain successful relations. It suggests that trust and commitment facilitate relational exchanges by creating a compliant environment, such that they enhance interfirm relationships [29]. In this research we use Mayer and colleagues [24] definition of trust – "trust is the willingness of a party to be vulnerable to the actions of another party based on the expectation that the other will perform a particular action important to the trustor, irrespective of the ability to monitor or control that other party" (p. 712).Trust directly influences relationship commitment by reducing the vulnerability that two parties perceive when they commit to an exchange relationship. Trust, and commitment also are key factors in exporter–importer relationships and are the most frequently cited antecedents of export performance [42].

In international marketing literature, there are two traditions of viewing trust andcommitment. The first one is to view them as mediating variables [29, 42] and the other is to view them as energizing forces [8]. Despite being of the most researched concept in international marketing, most of the research in this research stream is heavily focused on the symmetric approach and the 'null-hypothesis' testing; which can be criticized by not capturing the full spectrum of complexities in the relationships [46]. The critics advocating of 'seeing both the trees and the forest' and argued that the symmetric analysis could be potentially a mismatch in testing case-based identification models, whereas, in behavioral and management science most theory constructions are case-based proposals [12, 13, 46]. In the subsequent sections of this research, we will discuss the complex association of trust commitment then will move to the conceptual model of this research.

2.2   Association Among Different Dimensions of Trust and Commitment

Commitment, a multifaceted construct, is defined as an enduring desire to maintain a valued relationship [28]. Of the various types of commitment cited in marketing and organizational science literature [26], affective and calculative commitment appear most frequently and seem to be the most relevant for inter-organizational relationships [16]. Although both types of commitment reflect relatively stable attitudes and beliefs, their motives differ, and they evoke different psychological states about a relationship [16]. Affective commitment implies a desire to maintain the relationship due to positive feelings; calculative commitment reflects a need to maintain the relationship, due to pragmatic considerations [5]. In this research conceptualize affective commitment as the exporter's understanding, belief, and willingness to exert effort to maintain a relationship with an importing organization. This willingness to continue the relationship results from positive sentiment and attitudes toward the trading partner [43] which creates a sense of unity between the exporter and overseas importer. The calculative dimension of organizational commitment instead relates to extrinsic rewards, such as pay, status, promotions, and other benefits that encourage an employee to commit to the organization because these benefits would be lost were this employee to leave [6].

A typical conceptualization of commitment in the literature indicates that the two forms of commitment are independent; affective commitment does not determine the degree of calculative commitment, and vice versa [16]. Following the conceptualization of Zaheer and colleagues [48], we define inter-organizational trust as the extent to which members of one *organization* hold a collective *trust* orientation toward another *organization*. Research also has sought to establish a link between trust and commitment [15, 28, 29, 43]. To avoid any potential bias associated with using unidimensional trust and commitment constructs, we include different dimensions [20]. Accordingly, we leverage previous research to view that exporters' trusts and commitments are intertwined and extract a combined effect on the relationship performance.

2.3 Association of Trust and Commitment to Relationship Performance

Commitment is related to export performance outcomes, as is well established by prior research [11]. We also seek to test the effect of commitment and trust on exporter–importer relationship performance. Relationship performance defined as the perceived economic performance of the jointly acting relationship parties, relative to expectations in that network [25] can be instrumental for sales growth, superior market positions, better marketing support, or qualified services for the parties involved. Successful inter-organizational relationships are critical to firms' financial performance because most firms must leverage partners' capabilities and resources to compete effectively. Not only do strong interfirm relationships directly enhance sales and profits [30], but because they encourage increased cooperation and reduced conflict, they also can benefit innovation efforts, expand markets and reduce costs [9, 38]. Marketers' and researchers' efforts to uncover the drivers of inter-organizational relationship performance are necessary because managers can develop suitable strategies to leverage these causal drivers only if they understand the precursors of performance. Thus, the critical question is, what are the key drivers of inter-organizational relationship performance? To answer this question, researchers usually employ four theoretical perspectives: (1) commitment–trust, (2) dependence, (3) transaction cost economics, and (4) relational norms [19, 29]. We conceptualize commitment and trust as key drivers of organizational relationship performance. In short, our basic premise is that if trading partners commit to each other, they invest more in the relationship to gain more mutual benefits and thus achieve better relationship performance [31].

2.4 Relationship Lengths and Performance

Social exchange theory viewed the development of a cooperative relationship is analogous to a marriage relationship, and a stable relationship is closely related to the development of trust [22], and the tendency to remain in the same relationship over time is an important component of commitment [41]. In the organizational context, Cao and Lumineau [10] defined relationship length as "the number of years firms have been dealing with each other" (p. 21). The length of the export relationship is always considered crucial for export performance literature. Usually, in marketing literature, relationship length is being used as a control variable [10]. However, some studies also call for more research on the moderating effects of relationship length [10]. Although prior researches have been prioritized the linkage between the long-term relationship and the affective quality of a relationship and that may foster mutual interest, trust, and good partnership [2]. However, when talking about the length of the relationship, researchers took the opportunity to talk about the inter-organizational relationship length; the inter-personal relationship length mainly between two boundary spanners is vastly ignored. In this research, we wanted to tap both the personal relationship length and inter-organizational relationship length as a causal condition for predicting export relationship performance.

2.5   Size of the Organization and Performance

Previous researches [44] articulate that firm size is has a direct positive influence on export performance. However, the findings are mixed; hence, to have a better understanding, we conceptualize the firm size as a causal condition to have higher export relationship performance.

2.6   The Conceptual Model

Based on the above discussions, we explain relationship export performance by identifying configurations of causally related sets of factors, and posit that a synergy exists among different dimensions of trust, commitment, organization's size and the length of the relationships (personal and organizational) in explaining relationship export performance. The conceptual model is developed as, the outcome of interest is relationship export performance, and the three sets of causal conditions are trust (i.e., interpersonal and inter-organizational trust), commitment (affective and calculative), relationship length (personal and organizational relationships) & size. The intersections represent factor configurations, which are higher-level interactions.

3   Methodology

3.1   Sample and Data Collection Procedure

142 responses were collected from active, Ecuadorian, non–oil exporting companies. We checked for nonresponse bias by following the guidelines suggested by Armstrong and Overton [3] and tested for any significant differences between early and late responses. Harman's one-factor test [34] in SPSS shows, with exploratory factor analysis, that the first factor represents only 39% of the total variance. Thus, we found little threat of common method bias. Their average exporting experience was about 18 years (SD = 11.38), with an average of 191 employees (minimum 4, maximum 1500). The average length of the focal organizational relationship was more than ten years, and for interpersonal relationships, the average was higher than eight years. Among the respondents, 43% are presidents, 16% are chief financial officers, and 18% are export managers or executives. Similar to other exporters in the region [34], the United States was the most targeted export destination (37%) for the Ecuadorian exporters, followed by Colombia (22%), while, the European Union (12.6%) was the third attractive destination and followed by Russia (9.2%).

3.2 Measurement Instruments

The construct operationalization were based on established scales. Relationship performance uses four items derived from Luo and colleagues [23]. To measure inter-organizational trust and interpersonal trust, we used ten and five items, respectively, from Zaheer and colleagues [48]. Affective commitment was measured with a five-item scale [18], and calculative commitment *was* measured by a three-item scale [17]. All items, but the length and size variables measured on a 7-point Likert-type scale ranging from 7 = *strongly agree* to 1 = *strongly disagree*.

3.3 Fuzzy-Set Qualitative Comparative Analysis (fsQCA)

Qualitative Comparative Analysis (QCA) is an innovative approach suitable in situations with multilevel explanations and influences [45]. QCA facilities a detailed analysis of how causal conditions contribute to a particular result and draws on a configurational understanding of how a combination of causes leads to the same series of results. Fuzzy set qualitative comparative analysis (fsQCA), which integrates fuzzy set and fuzzy logic with QCA will be used in this research [35]. FsQCA uses analyzing combinations of conditions (i.e., configurations) in a systematized manner [35]. Two main benefits of the fsQCA sought as i) suitability to work with medium-sized samples, ii) suitable for analyzing high levels of causal complexity [37, 47]. In this research, we used the statistical software package fsQCA 3.0 for its analysis [31]. FsQCA expresses causality in terms of necessity and sufficiency. A condition will be considered as necessary if an outcome cannot be produced without it. A condition is sufficient if its presence always produces the outcome (but the outcome may also occur without the condition). These conditions can combine in various ways. Thus, causality in fsQCA is configurational (combinations of conditions produce the outcome), equifinal (different combinations may produce the outcome), and multifinal (a condition can play a different role in different configurations) [31].

4 Analysis and Results

4.1 Measurement Model Evaluation

Confirmatory factor analyses (CFA) using AMOS 23, performed on all multi-item scales, produce results with sufficient overall model fit all fit indexes meet the conventional cut-off values. The overall chi-square for the model is 420.73 ($p < .001$) and the CMIN/DF is 1.91, comparative fit index (CFI) = .91, Tucker-Lewis index (TLI) = .90, incremental fit index (IFI) = .91, and root mean square error of approximation (RMSEA) = .08. We note strong convergent validity, with four exceptions (three inter-organizational trust items and one interpersonal trust item) (all other loadings $\geq$ .50), and those items are excluded from further analysis. We establish discriminant validity by observing the construct inter-factor correlations that differ significantly from 1. The average variance extracted (AVE) for each construct exceeds the square of its largest inter-factor correlation [14]. Table 1 contains the correlation matrix and further confirms discriminant validity because, for all constructs, the diagonal elements are greater than the off-diagonal elements. With regard to reliability, all the constructs achieve desirable levels of composite reliability (CR) and exceed the .60 minimum recommended by previous researches [4]. Regarding the AVE, all constructs achieved scores above .50. Therefore, we conclude that the indicators are sufficient and adequate for specifying the measurement model (Table 2).

Table 1. Summary data for the conditions and outcome

Statistics	relationship	calcomit	affcommit	orgtrust	pertrust	orgrel	perrel
N	142	142	142	142	142	142	142
Mean	5.14	4.15	5.9	5.7	5.52	10.57	8.13
SEM	0.12	0.13	0.08	0.09	0.09	0.52	0.48
Median	5.5	4.33	6	6	5.75	10	6
SD	1.38	1.58	0.94	1.01	1.04	6.2	5.68
Minimum	1	1	3	1	1	1 year	1 year
Maximum	7	7	7	7	7	30 years	30 years
Calibration value at							
95%	6	6	6	6	6	25	25
50%	4	4	4	4	4	15	15
5%	2	2	2	2	2	5	5

Note: *relationship* = Relationship performance, *calcommit* = Calculative commitment, *affcommit* = Affective commitment, *orgtrust* = Inter-organizational trust, *pertrust* = Interpersonal trust, *orgrel* = Length of inter-organizational relationships, *perrel* = Length of interpersonal relationships. SD = Standard deviation, SEM = Standard error of mean.

In this research, the outcome is 'export relationship performance' (*fz_relationship*). The antecedents examined, following the calibration procedure, are a series of characteristics of interfirm relationships: 'calculative commitment' (*fz_calcommit*), 'affective commitment' (*fz_affcommit*), 'inter-organizational trust' (*fz_orgtrust*), 'interpersonal trust' (*fz_pertrust*), 'length of the inter-organizational relationship' (*fz_orgrel*) and 'length of the interpersonal relationship' (*fz_perrel*). The analysis process first requires a calibration to transform the raw data into fuzzy categories or conditions [48]. Calibration assigns the variables a value between 0.0 and 1.0, depending on their degree of membership [47]. We employed the same procedure for converting Likert scales into fuzz sets, as followed by previous researches [31–33]. First, the three thresholds are based on the questionnaire scale (7-point Likert scale) as such - the full membership threshold is set at the value of 6; the full non-membership is set at value 2, and the crossover point is set at value 4. All values are calibrated on a logistic function to fit into the three thresholds. In fsQCA, cases exactly on 0.5 are dropped from the analysis which makes it difficult to analyze the conditions that are set exactly on 0.05 (i.e., intermediate-set membership) [35]. To overcome this issue, Fiss [13] suggests adding a constant of 0.001 to the causal conditions below full membership scores of 1. To do this, we have added 0.001 in all conditions after the calibration has been done.

Table 2. Construct reliability and validity

	CR	AVE	MSV	MaxR(H)	1	2	3	4	5
1. Calcomit	0.89	0.73	0.05	0.89	**0.85**				
2. Relationship	0.87	0.63	0.28	0.88	0.16	**0.80**			
3. Orgtrust	0.90	0.58	0.54	0.94	0.07	0.31	**0.76**		
4. Pertrust	0.87	0.63	0.33	0.88	0.23	0.46	0.44	**0.79**	
5. Affcommit	0.92	0.71	0.54	0.94	0.20	0.53	0.73	0.58	**0.84**

Then, in the next step, we performed the analysis of necessity, which intended to identify if any of the causal conditions is a necessary (i.e., indispensable) condition for the presence of relationship export performance. For a condition to be necessary, its consistency should exceed the threshold of 0.9 [31, 39]. Consistency is the degree to which the cases in the sample that share a causal condition or configuration agree in displaying the focal outcome [35]. To examine necessity, the dedicated function in fsQCA software is used, which calculates the consistency and coverage scores for every causal condition and their negation. As the following Table 3, depicts – affective commitment, inter-organizational trust, and interpersonal trust are the necessary conditions for achieving high relationship export performance, while inter-organizational trust, absence of the length of interpersonal and inter-organizational relationships are the necessary condition for having low/medium relationship performance.

The software then produces a truth table, consisting of 2k logically possible configurations, where k represents the number of conditions that are included in the analysis [35], where each of the combinations is assessed as to whether it is sufficient for the outcome to occur or not. We looked at the consistency statistics to determine whether configuration is necessary and/or sufficiency in terms of set-theoretic relations [31, 32]. We also consider the coverage of the configurations as they are the way in which cases are distributed over these configurations [37]. From Table 3, we found that there are three configurations for achieving high export relationship performance; and three configurations for having low/medium relationship performance. However, the overall solution consistency for having low/medium relationship export performance is too low to accept; hence, we will not discuss these condition. Finally, we have the following configuration for achieving export relationship performance, as follows, where C1 = consistency and C2 = raw coverage:

Outcome: High export relationship performance (*fz_relationship*)

i) fz_calcomit*fz_affcommit*fz_orgt*fz_pert*fz_orgrel (1a, C1 = 0.94, C2 = 0.25): A combination of calculative commitment, affective commitment, inter-organizational trust, interpersonal trust and organizational relation length is a sufficient condition for achieving high export relationship performance (Table 4).

ii) fz_affcommit*fz_orgt*fz_pert*fz_perrel*fz_orgrel (1b, C1 = 0.99, C2 = 0.21): A combination of affective commitment, inter-organizational trust, interpersonal trust, personal relationship length and organizational relation length is a sufficient condition for achieving high export relationship performance.

Table 3. Analysis of the necessary conditions

Condition	Outcome			
	High relationship performance		~Low/medium relationship performance	
	Consistency	Coverage	Consistency	Coverage
Calculative commitment	0.64	0.87	0.67	0.30
~Calculative commitment	0.49	0.82	0.70	0.39
Affective commitment	0.98[a]	0.83	0.89	0.25
~Affective commitment	0.11	0.75	0.38	0.86
Inter-organizational trust	0.95[a]	0.82	0.90[a]	0.26
~Inter-organizational trust	0.15	0.82	0.39	0.72
Interpersonal trust	0.95[a]	0.84	0.87	0.26
~Interpersonal trust	0.16	0.80	0.46	0.73
Organizational relation length	0.35	0.92	0.42	0.36
~Organizational relation length	0.76	0.80	0.91[a]	0.32
Personal relationship length	0.24	0.96	0.28	0.38
~Personal relationship length	0.85	0.78	0.97[a]	0.30

Note: ~ indicates the absence of a condition.
[a] meets 0.90 consistency benchmark for necessary conditions.

Table 4. Results of the intermediate solution

Condition	Relationship performance					
	fz_relationship			~fz_relationship		
	1a	1b	1c	2a	2b	2c
Calculative commitment	●		●	●		●
Affective commitment	●	●	●	●	●	●
Inter-organizational trust	●	●	○	●	●	○
Interpersonal trust	●	●	●	●	●	●
Organizational relation length	●	●	○		●	○
Personal relationship length		●	○		●	○
Consistency	0.94	0.99	0.91	0.75	0.38	0.42
Raw coverage	0.25	0.21	0.11	0.28	0.25	0.34
Unique coverage	0.07	0.05	0.03	0.07	0.02	0.06
Solution coverage	0.34			0.43		
Solution consistency	0.93			0.39		
Frequency cutoff	3			3		
Consistency cutoff	0.90			0.90		

Note: Black circles indicate the presence of a condition; empty circles indicate the absence.

iii)   fz_calcomit*fz_affcommit* ~ fz_orgt*fz_pert* ~ fz_perrel* ~ fz_orgrel   (1c, C1 = 0.91, C2 = 0.11): A combination of calculative commitment, affective commitment, interpersonal trust and Low/medium inter-organizational trust, with low/medium length inter-organizational relationships, low/medium length interpersonal relationship is a sufficient condition for achieving high export relationship performance.

5   Discussion

In this research, we analyzed seven conditions as – calculative commitment, affective commitment, inter-organizational trust, interpersonal trust, organization size, length of inter-organizational relationship and length of interpersonal relationships; and set them to explore the necessary conditions and configurations that may lead to export relationship performance. By using FsQCA to analyze the data, this research examines the underlining mechanism of trust and commitments, causing export relationship performance. By doing so, we extend the previous researches on trust, commitment, and export performance, which were predominately focused on a hypothesis based symmetric relationships.

We found three configurations to cause export relationship performance. As it was expected, we identify that a combination of high calculative commitment, high affective commitment, high inter-organizational, and interpersonal trust, and large size organization is a necessary condition for achieving export relationship performance. This finding attests the previous researches and recognizes that both the trust and commitment dimensions are necessary for achieving higher relationship performance. In this connection, this research further reestablished the importance of relational considerations in export marketing. The inclusion of the organizational size is also a significant finding of this research. Worthy of remembering that here, the larger firms are defined with an annual sales of 5 million USD. Our explanation is for a smaller sized exporting firm from a smaller economy like Ecuador might not have enough capability to invest in inter-organizational and interpersonal trust increasing activities; hence, the bigger sized firms might be in a better condition here. The second configuration we identified tells that - a combination of high affective commitment, high inter-organizational trust, high personal trust, larger organizations, less length of inter-organizational and inter-personal relationship is a necessary condition for achieving export relationship performance. This finding also deserves some attention, the inclusion of affective commitment, and both dimensions of trust and the size of the organization is in congruence with the literature. However, the negation of the length of the relationships (inter-organizational and interpersonal) tells us that relationships are good but how long. This finding points essential aspects of relationships and posits the question of how long the relationships are good in the export-import relationship? The final configuration indicates that a combination of high affective commitment, high inter-organizational trust, high personal trust, larger organizations, high length of inter-organizational and inter-personal relationships is a necessary condition for achieving export relationship performance, which is again in line with the theoretical arguments of previous literature. However, if we look at the three configurations at the same time, we will see that affective commitment, interpersonal trust, inter-organizational trust, and the size of the organization is very crucial for achieving the relationship performance. Attesting the importance of affective commitment and the trust dimensions is one of the significant contributions of this research.

We also explored the combinations that may cause not having higher relationship export performance, and found that a low affective commitment is a sufficient condition for not having export relationship performance. Which, we consider as a significant contribution of this research. In Latin America, in general, the importance of affective commitment is very much crucial. Hence, a foreign company that wants to have a successful business relationship with a Latin American firm must and invest in affective commitment. The second configuration is also important, as it says - a combination of low calculative commitment, low affective commitment, high inter-organizational trust, high interpersonal trust, smaller organizations, longer inter-organizational relationships, and shorter interpersonal relationship is a necessary condition for not achieving higher export relationship performances. It implies that the low level of commitments, the shorter interpersonal relationships can also cause low relationship performance for the smaller firms even if they have high trusts and longer inter-organizational relationships. This finding disposes of a closer look at the commitment-trust theory of [30] as it suggests that in the case of the export-import relationship, inter-organizational trust and affective commitment are the key mediating variables.

References

1. Alteren, G., Tudoran, A.A.: Enhancing export performance: betting on customer orientation, behavioral commitment, and communication. Int. Bus. Rev. **25**, 370–381 (2016)
2. Anderson, E., Weitz, B.: Determinants of continuity in conventional industrial channel dyads. Mark. Sci. **8**, 310–323 (1989)
3. Armstrong, J.S., Overton, T.S.: Estimating nonresponse bias in mail surveys. J. Mark. Res. **14**, 396–402 (1977)
4. Bagozzi, R.P., Yi, Y.: On the evaluation of structural equation models. J. Acad. Mark. Sci. **16**, 74–94 (1988)
5. Bansal, H.S., Irving, P.G., Taylor, S.F.: A three-component model of customer to service providers. J. Acad. Mark. Sci. **32**, 234–250 (2004)
6. Becker, H.S.: Notes on the concept of commitment. Am. J. Sociol. **66**, 32–40 (1960)
7. Blau, P.: Power and Exchange in Social Life, p. 352. Wiley, New York (1964)
8. Bloemer, J., Pluymaekers, M., Odekerken, A.: Trust and affective commitment as energizing forces for export performance. Int. Bus. Rev. **22**, 363–380 (2013)
9. Cannon, J.P., Homburg, C.: Buyer-supplier relationships and customer firm costs. J. Mark. **65**, 29–43 (2001)
10. Cao, Z., Lumineau, F.: Revisiting the interplay between contractual and relational governance: a qualitative and meta-analytic investigation. J. Oper. Manage. **33**, 15–42 (2015)
11. Dowell, D., Morrison, M., Heffernan, T.: The changing importance of affective trust and cognitive trust across the relationship lifecycle: a study of business-to-business relationships. Ind. Mark. Manage. **44**, 119–130 (2015)

12. Fiss, P.C.: A set-theoretic approach to organizational configurations. Acad. Manag. Rev. **32**, 1180–1198 (2007)
13. Fiss, P.C.: Building better causal theories: a fuzzy set approach to typologies in organization research. Acad. Manag. J. **54**, 393–420 (2011)
14. Fornell, C., Larcker, D.F.: Evaluating structural equation models with unobservable variables and measurement error. J. Mark. Res. **18**, 39–50 (1981)
15. Ganesan, S.: Determinants of long-term orientation in buyer-seller relationships. J. Mark. **58**, 1–19 (1994)
16. Geyskens, I., Steenkamp, J.-B.E., Scheer, L.K., Kumar, N.: The effects of trust and interdependence on relationship commitment: a trans-Atlantic study. Int. J. Res. Mark. **13**, 303–317 (1996)
17. Gilliland, D.I., Bello, D.C.: Two sides to attitudinal commitment: the effect of calculative and loyalty commitment on enforcement mechanisms in distribution channels. J. Acad. Mark. Sci. **30**, 24–43 (2002)
18. Gounaris, S.P.: Trust and commitment influences on customer retention: insights from business-to-business services. J. Bus. Res. **58**, 126–140 (2005)
19. Hibbard, J.D., Kumar, N., Stern, L.W.: Examining the impact of destructive acts in marketing channel relationships. J. Mark. Res. **38**, 45–61 (2001)
20. Jain, M., Khalil, S., Johnston, W.J., Cheng, J.M.-S.: The performance implications of power–trust relationship: the moderating role of commitment in the supplier–retailer relationship. Ind. Mark. Manage. **43**, 312–321 (2014)
21. Kraus, S., Ribeiro-Soriano, D., Schüssler, M.: Fuzzy-set qualitative comparative analysis (fsQCA) in entrepreneurship and innovation research–the rise of a method. Int. Entrep. Manage. J. **14**, 15–33 (2018)
22. Liu, Y., Li, Y., Tao, L., Wang, Y.: Relationship stability, trust and relational risk in marketing channels: evidence from China. Ind. Mark. Manage. **37**, 432–446 (2008)
23. Luo, Y., Liu, Y., Yang, Q., Maksimov, V., Hou, J.: Improving performance and reducing cost in buyer–supplier relationships: the role of justice in curtailing opportunism. J. Bus. Res. **68**, 607–615 (2015)
24. Mayer, R.C., Davis, J.H., Schoorman, F.D.: An integrative model of organizational trust. Acad. Manag. Rev. **20**, 709–734 (1995)
25. Medlin, C.J.: Relationship performance: a relationship level construct. In: IMP Conference Proceedings (2003)
26. Meyer, J.P., Allen, N.J.: A three-component conceptualization of organizational commitment. Hum. Resour. Manage. Rev. **1**, 61–89 (1991)
27. Mohr, J., Spekman, R.: Characteristics of partnership success: partnership attributes, communication behavior, and conflict resolution techniques. Strateg. Manag. J. **15**, 135–152 (1994)
28. Moorman, C., Zaltman, G., Deshpande, R.: Relationships between providers and users of market research: the dynamics of trust within and between organizations. J. Mark. Res. **29**, 314–328 (1992)
29. Morgan, R.M., Hunt, S.D.: The commitment-trust theory of relationship marketing. J. Mark. **58**, 20–38 (1994)
30. Palmatier, R.W., Dant, R.P., Grewal, D.: A comparative longitudinal analysis of theoretical perspectives of inter-organizational relationship performance. J. Mark. **71**, 172–194 (2007)
31. Pappas, I.O., Giannakos, M.N., Sampson, D.G.: Fuzzy set analysis as a means to understand users of 21st-century learning systems: the case of mobile learning and reflections on learning analytics research. Comput. Hum. Behav. **92**, 646–659 (2017)

32. Pappas, I.O., Kourouthanassis, P.E., Giannakos, M.N., Chrissikopoulos, V.: Explaining online shopping behavior with fsQCA: the role of cognitive and affective perceptions. J. Bus. Res. **69**, 794–803 (2016)

33. Pappas, I.O.: User experience in personalized online shopping: a fuzzy-set analysis. Eur. J. Mark. **52**(7/8), 1679–1703 (2018). https://doi.org/10.1108/EJM-10-2017-0707

34. Podsakoff, P.M., Organ, D.W.: Self-reports in organizational research: problems and prospects. J. Manag. **12**, 531–544 (1986)

35. Ragin, C.C.: Redesigning Social Inquiry: Fuzzy Sets and Beyond. University of Chicago Press, Chicago (2009)

36. Rihoux, B., Álamos-Concha, P., Bol, D., Marx, A., Rezsöhazy, I.: From niche to mainstream method? A comprehensive mapping of QCA applications in journal articles from 1984 to 2011. Polit. Res. Q. **66**, 175–184 (2013)

37. Rihoux, B., Ragin, C.C.: Configurational Comparative Methods: Qualitative Comparative Analysis (QCA) and Related Techniques. Sage Publications, Thousand Oaks (2008)

38. Rindfleisch, A., Moorman, C.: The acquisition and utilization of information in new product alliances: a strength-of-ties perspective. J. Mark. **65**, 1–18 (2001)

39. Schneider, C.Q., Wagemann, C.: Set-Theoretic Methods for the Social Sciences: A Guide to Qualitative Comparative Analysis. Cambridge University Press, Cambridge (2012)

40. Sehring, J., Korhonen-kurki, K., Brockhaus, M.: Qualitative comparative analysis (QCA): an application to compare national REDD+ policy processes. CIFOR, Bogor (2013)

41. Simpson, J.A.: The dissolution of romantic relationships: factors involved in relationship stability and emotional distress. J. Pers. Soc. Psychol. **53**, 683 (1987)

42. Styles, C., Patterson, P.G., Ahmed, F.: A relational model of export performance. J. Int. Bus. Stud. **39**, 880–900 (2008)

43. Talay, M.B., Akdeniz, M.B.: In time we trust?: the effects of duration on the dynamics of trust-building processes in inter-organizational relationships. Strateg. Manage. Rev. **8**, 77–90 (2014)

44. Williams, D.A.: Impact of firm size and age on the export behaviour of small locally owned firms: fresh insights. J. Int. Entrep. **9**, 152 (2011)

45. Woodside, A.G.: Moving beyond multiple regression analysis to algorithms: calling for adoption of a paradigm shift from symmetric to asymmetric thinking in data analysis and crafting theory. J. Bus. Res. **66**, 463–472 (2013)

46. Woodside, A.G.: Releasing the death-grip of null hypothesis statistical testing (p < .05): applying complexity theory and somewhat precise outcome testing (SPOT). J. Glob. Scholars Mark. Sci. **27**, 1–15 (2017)

47. Xie, X., Fang, L., Zeng, S.: Collaborative innovation network and knowledge transfer performance: a fsQCA approach. J. Bus. Res. **69**, 5210–5215 (2016)

48. Zaheer, A., McEvily, B., Perrone, V.: Does trust matter? Exploring the effects of inter-organizational and interpersonal trust on performance. Organ. Sci. **9**, 141–159 (1998)

The Influence of Public Service Experience on Adopting Digital Government Innovations in Ethiopia

Debas Senshaw[1,2]([⊠]) [iD] and Hossana Twinomurinzi[1,3] [iD]

[1] Sudan University of Science and Technology, Khartoum, Sudan
debassenshaw@gmail.com, twinoh@gmail.com
[2] Bahir Dar Institute of Technology, Bahir Dar University,
Bahir Dar, Ethiopia
[3] Department of Applied Information Systems, University of Johannesburg,
Johannesburg, South Africa

Abstract. This research explored the moderating effect of public service experience on the adoption of digital government innovations in Ethiopia. The results from the structural equation modeling (SEM) reveal that public service experience positively moderates the relationship between effort expectancy and behavioral intention to adopt digital government innovations. Unlike previous studies which found that experience positively moderates the relationship between effort expectancy and behavioral intention of less experienced ICT users, this study finds that the longer the time spent in the public service, the higher the perception of government employees regarding the ease of use (effort expectancy) of the digital innovation. The findings might be attributable to the lack of training for government staff. The paper makes recommendations for IS research, government policy and practice in similar low-income countries.

Keywords: Digital government · Digital innovation · WoredaNet · UTAUT

1 Introduction

Governments have been using information and communication technology (ICTs) to provide services to their citizen effectively and efficiently [1, 2]. Governments implement digital government to enhance the quality of services as well as to save time and resources needed to provide services. Digital government significantly improves the conveniences and availability of services to citizens to fulfill their demands [3, 4]. Governments also aim to implement digital government to improve the quality of government services and facilitate political processes [4, 5].

However, most governments in low-income countries fail to implement digital government though they invest a significant amount of capital [6, 7]. Previous studies suggest that one of the factors for the failures are low acceptance and use of digital innovations [8, 9]. Most digital government innovations such as government web-based applications are developed by the ICT staff without including the active participation of government employees who would indicate their needs and perceptions

© IFIP International Federation for Information Processing 2020
Published by Springer Nature Switzerland AG 2020
S. K. Sharma et al. (Eds.): TDIT 2020, IFIP AICT 618, pp. 569–580, 2020.
https://doi.org/10.1007/978-3-030-64861-9_50

towards the digital innovation [9]. Consequently, this results in low user acceptance of digital government services.

In many low-income countries, digital government has not been designed based on the local context but has mainly been adopted from elsewhere [10]. Digital innovations in low-income countries that are based on the local context such as m-pesa [11, 12] have been shown to enjoy rapid adoption compared to innovations that have been adopted from other contexts.

The use of local digital government innovations that can provide accurate, useful, and context-based information for government employees is important especially during difficult times such as the current COVID-19, considering access is now required when working from home [13].

This study focused on evaluating the influence of public service experience (time spent working in government) on adopting locally designed digital government innovations. In this research, government service experience is hypothesized to have a moderating influence as seen in other studies [14, 15] which have shown that prior experience significantly influences the acceptance and usage of digital innovations [15–17].

Experience is different to age in that older users of ICT have been shown to have lower computer self-efficacy as they are driven by ease of use of ICTs as opposed to younger users. The opposite is true in the case of experience. Experienced users of ICT have higher computer self-efficacy as compared to the inexperienced ones [14, 18].

This study assesses the influence of experience on the adoption of a digital government innovation that identifies opportunities for public service innovation within the local context in Ethiopia [19]. Specifically, the study investigated the moderating influence of experience in the public service on the adoption of the digital government innovation using the Unified Theory of Acceptance and Use of Technology (UTAUT) [20, 21].

The remainder of the paper is organized as follows: The next section gives the theoretical background of digital government and digital government innovation. It is followed by the Unified Theory of Acceptance and Use of Technology (UTAUT). The research design is followed by the results and analysis section. Then, discussion of findings is presented. Finally, the paper draws conclusions and identifies limitations and future research.

2   Theoretical Background

2.1   Digital Government

Digital government has, in some contexts, been defined as a digital platform that aims to achieve improved governance in government [22]. Digital government is also defined as the use of ICTs that can transform government initiatives and services by enhancing their quality [23]. Digital government plays a significant role in achieving better efficiency of government by changing citizens' behavior [4, 23]. However, the advantage of digital government can only be achieved if the technologies are accepted by the users [9]. The next section describes a digital government platform in Ethiopia and a digital innovation targeted at the digital platform.

2.2   Overview of the Adaptive Capability Digital Innovation

The WoredaNet is a digital government platform using fiber and satellite infrastructure across Ethiopia that was implemented by the government of Ethiopia with the intention to provide government services to the lowest administrative regions (Woredas). The name WoredaNet comes from "Woreda" which is Amharic for an administrative region with a population of about 100,000. It has the equivalent meaning of a district.

The WoredaNet provides various digital government services to Woredas. Among the services provided are video-conferencing, internet, electronic messaging, and voice over IP between federal, regional, and Woreda sites.

There are 1,050 Woredas in Ethiopia, 976 of which (93%) have access to the WoredaNet. Despite the access, only a few Woredas actively use the WoredaNet [24]. Considering this, a digital government adaptive capability web-based app was created based on the findings of the adaptive capabilities of Woredas that innovatively use the WoredaNet. Adaptive capabilities are capabilities that seek to introduce a new service or a new way of performing a service [25, 26]. A case study with a qualitative-interpretive approach was adopted to identify the adaptive capabilities of three *innovative* Woredas. Elaborated Action Design Research (EADR) [27] was followed to create the digital government web-based app (Fig. 1).

Fig. 1. Digital government adaptive capability web-based app

2.3   Unified Theory of Acceptance and Use of Technology (UTAUT)

The Unified Theory of Acceptance and Use of Technology (UTAUT) [15] examines the intention of users to adopt and use information systems [20, 21]. UTAUT integrates the key features of previous adoption models. UTAUT was preferred to the newer UTAUT2 as it explicates the achievement of learning tasks in the work place [28]. UTAUT has four important constructs; performance expectancy (PE), effort expectancy (EE), social influence (SI), and Facilitating conditions (FC); that are determinants of the behavioral intention (BI) and usage [15, 29]. Moreover, UTAUT also uses four variables (experience, gender, age, and voluntariness of use) as moderators.

The UTAUT model was adopted in this study to explain the moderating effect of public service experience on the acceptance and adoption of the web-based app.

Performance Expectancy (PE). Performance expectancy refers to the extent to which a user believes that using ICT enhances the job performance [30]. It plays a significant role in validating intention to use [31]. When users expect that the ICT improves their job performance, they tend to accept the technology [32–34]. Moreover, experience affects the influence of performance expectancy on the intention to use ICTs [9]. Therefore, the following hypothesis is tested:

H1:   *Performance expectancy positively influences behavioral intentions of government employees to use the app, moderated by experience.*

Effort Expectancy (EE). Effort expectancy refers to the extent of ease related to the use of ICTs [15, 35, 36]. The amount of effort the user puts in affects the behavioral intention of users to accept or adopt ICTs. Moreover, experience affects the influence of effort expectancy on the intention to use ICTs [15]. Therefore, the following hypothesis was tested:

H2:   *Effort expectancy positively influences the behavioral intentions of government employees to use the app, moderated by experience.*

Social Influence (SI). Social influence refers to the extent to which an individual thinks the boss or colleagues believe he or she should use the new ICT [15]. Social communication affects users' intention to use ICTs [37]. Moreover, experience influences the effect of social influence on behavioral intentions to use ICTs [15, 17]. Therefore, the following hypothesis was tested:

H3:   *Social influence positively influences the behavioral intentions of government employees to use the app, moderated by experience.*

Facilitating Conditions (FC). Facilitating conditions refer to the availability of resources to use the ICT [15]. Unpredictable support of resources results in lower use behavior, whereas predictable support of resources positively influences use behavior [30]. Moreover, experience influences the effect of facilitating conditions on use behavior [15]. Therefore, the following hypothesis is tested:

H4:   *Facilitating condition positively influences government employee's use behavior of the app, moderated by experience.*

3   Research Design

3.1   Data Collection and Evaluation

Non-probability sampling was used to select ten Woredas that have access to the WoredaNet. The Amhara Regional State Science, Technology, and Information Communication Commission (STICC) supported the principal researcher in distributing the questionnaire online and assigning the WoredaNet exerts in each Woreda to facilitate the evaluation of the app. The process owners (those who manage similar tasks or processes in the public agency) and experts, Woreda administrators/representatives in the Woredas participated.

The questionnaire consisted of a 5-point Likert-scale from strongly disagree to strongly agree and demographic questions. Following the suggestions by Owoseni and Twinomurinzi [38], the twenty items were modified from previous literature to ascertain scale validity. From a survey of 400 questionnaires administered, only 270 complete responses were obtained in 25 days between Dec. 3 to 27, 2019.

SPSS 26 and AMOS 26 were used to capture and process the data [38–40]. The normality of the data was checked for compliance with the assumption of the general linear regression model. The skewness and kurtosis of the constructs (for each item) were identified. Most of the items were within the acceptable range of -2 and $+2$ [41, 42], except for a few items where kurtosis was greater than 2.0. The results showed acceptable skewness and kurtosis values.

There were fewer women than men. This might be attributed to the unequal representation of women in Ethiopia's education, training, and employment sectors despite the recent significant actions [43]. Table 1 presents demographics.

Table 1. Respondents' demographic data

	Variable	Frequency	Percent
Gender	Male	185	68.5
	Female	85	31.5
Experience	5 years and below	29	10.7
	6–10	123	45.6
	11–15	101	37.4
	16–20	17	6.3
Age	30 and below	43	16
	31–35	121	44.8
	36–40	86	31.9
	41 and above	20	7.3
Education	Diploma	35	13
	Bachelor	186	68.9
	Masters	49	18.1

4 Result and Analysis

4.1 Measurement Model

Confirmatory Factor Analysis (CFA) was used to evaluate the data, while covariance-based SEM was implemented to create the model and test the hypotheses [38]. Covariance-based SEM is fitting for model measurement, where the latent variables could drive meaning from the measured variables [39, 40].

The CFA model examines the influence of constructs on the responses. CFA verifies the arrangement of constructs that are considered. The model was also accessed for its reliability and validity. The final refined model ($\chi2$ = 234.850, df = 154, p-value = 0.000), had acceptable fit indices: $\chi2$/df = 1.530, GFI = 0.920, TLI = 0.956, CFI = 0.964, NFI = 0.904, RMSEA = 0.044.

The acceptable reliability and validity measurements revealed that items shown in the model were supposed to be relevant. Due to the acceptable results by CFA, it enabled to build the structural model.

4.2 Structural Model

Maximum likelihood estimates, using AMOS26 were applied to measure the structural model. As a result, acceptable fit indices ($\chi2$/df = 1.848, GFI = 0.902, TLI = 0.928, CFI = 0.940, NFI = 0.880, RMSEA = 0.056) were displayed. Results of regression weights as indicated in the structural model are represented in Table 2. The structural model with a chi-square ($\chi2$) value of 293.786, df value of 159, and p-value of 0.000 was displayed. This revealed that the model fitted the data adequately. As a result, it is possible to conclude the research hypotheses using the structural model (shown in Fig. 2). The numbers following the UTAUT constructs in the SEM signifies the items in the construct.

Table 2. Regression weights (Groupnumber1-default model)

Independent variable	Relation	Dependent variable	Estimate (β-values)	P-value	Hypothesis conclusion
Performance expectancy	$\rightarrow$	Behavioral intention	−0.151	0.256	Rejected
Social influence	$\rightarrow$	Behavioral intention	0.184	0.033	Accepted
Effort expectancy	$\rightarrow$	Behavioral intention	0.213	0.105	Rejected
Behavioral intention	$\rightarrow$	Use behavior	0.360	0.000	Accepted
Facilitating condition	$\rightarrow$	Use behavior	0.301	0.000	Accepted

Performance expectancy (β = −0.151, p-value > 0.05) and effort expectancy (β = 0.213, p-value > 0.05) do not influence the behavioral intention of government employees to use and accept the new government digital innovation. This may be attributed to 89.6% of the respondents with more than 5 years of experience using the government digital platform the WoredaNet as a tool. This helped them to adjust their perception to use new ICTs based on the accumulated knowledge [16, 18, 37, 44–47].

On the other hand, social influence has a positive impact on the intention to use the app (β = 0.184, p-value < 0.05).This means that when employees are encouraged by their leaders or colleagues, they will more likely use the app. Moreover, the behavioral

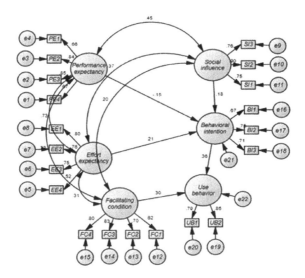

Fig. 2. The structural model results

intention (β = 0.360, p-value < 0.05) indicates a significant positive impact on the use behavior of government employees. This demonstrates that when employees have a greater intention of using the app, they will use it more frequently. Facilitating conditions (β = 0.301, p-value < 0.05) demonstrate the importance of accompanying resources to use the app. In other words, when government employees are supported with the appropriate resources to use the app, they will frequently use it.

4.3 Moderating Effect

To assess the effect of public service experience on the key constructs, a bootstrap technique with 200 iterations was run to ensure stability [48]. The results (Table 3) revealed not all hypotheses are supported. The relationship between effort expectancy and behavioral intention (β = 0.310, p-value = 0.042) was positively moderated by public service experience with t-value = 2.031. In other words, a positive beta value suggests a positive moderating influence.

Table 3. Moderator analysis results

Hypothesis	Relationship	Std. Beta	t-value	p-value	Decision
H1	PE x Experience → BI	−0.117	−0.858	0.391	Rejected
H2	EE x Experience → BI	0.310	2.031*	0.042	Accepted
H3	SI x Experience → BI	−0.030	−0.323	0.747	Rejected
H4	FC x Experience → UB	0.102	1.354	0.176	Rejected

Notes: * Significance at 0.05 levels

On the other hand, all other hypotheses except H2 are rejected indicating public service experience does not affect the relationship between performance expectancy and behavioral intention, social influence and behavioral intention, and facilitating condition and use behavior.

5 Discussion of Findings

These results are partially consistent with the UTAUT model in that experience has a positive impact on the relationship between effort expectancy and the intention to use and adopt digital government innovations; and that experience does not have a moderating effect on the relationship between performance expectancy and intention behavior [15, 16].

Although works [15, 16, 18, 37] indicate that experience significantly moderates the relationship between effort expectancy and intention to use behavior, particularly in the case of lower experienced users, the study shows a different outcome. 89.6% of the respondents (government employees) have more than 5 years of public service experience using the digital government platform, WoredaNet, as a tool to provide government services. The results nonetheless indicate that experience still significantly influences the relationship between effort expectancy and intention behavior ($\beta = 0.310$, p-value < 0.05) of government employees to accept and use the new government digital innovation. In other words, the greater the service experience, the higher the perception of employees regarding the ease of use to use the new government digital innovations.

One of the reasons attributed to these results, as indicated in the response of the evaluation, was government employees are rarely provided with a start-up training program that facilitates usage (effort expectancy) of new government digital innovations. For example, WoredaNet experts were assigned by the STICC to merely facilitate the evaluation response rate and assist evaluators when they needed help during evaluation. This implies that government organizations should set up a start-up training program on how to use a new digital government innovation in order to enhance the perception of ease of use (effort expectancy) of employees to accept and use a new government digital innovation. Previous research indicated that setting up a start-up appropriate training and adequate support to the users of ICT considerably influences the ease of use (effort expectancy) of ICTs [16, 18, 37, 44–47].

On the other hand, the research showed that public service experience does not have a moderating effect on the relationship between performance expectancy and behavioral intention ($\beta = -0.117$, p-value > 0.05), nor does it have a moderating effect between social influence and behavioral intention ($\beta = -0.030$, p-value > 0.05). It also does not have a moderating effect on the relationship between facilitating condition and use behavior ($\beta = 0.102$, p-value > 0.05) of government employees.

As indicated above respondents have enough experience in using the government digital platform, WoredaNet as a tool. This means that the usefulness of the new digital government innovation is not a significant issue as their previous experience helps them improve the perception to use the new digital innovation [16, 18].

Similarly, these experienced government employees may not be significantly influenced by their social relations to use the new government digital innovation as they have enough experience in using the government digital platform, the WoredaNet [15, 16, 18, 49].

Moreover, these employees may not also be significantly influenced by facilitating conditions such as organizational support to use the new digital government innovation since they have long experience in using the WoredaNet digital platform [37, 49, 50].

6 Conclusion

The study aimed to explore the moderating effect of public service experience on the acceptance and adoption of a new digital government innovation, in the form of a web-based app. UTAUT model was adopted in this research. Moreover, structural equation modeling (SEM) was used to examine the moderating effect of public service experience on acceptance and adoption of the government digital innovation. The research revealed that public service experience only has a positive moderating effect on the relationship between effort expectancy and the behavioral intention ($\beta = 0.310$, p-value < 0.05) of government employees to accept and use digital innovation.

Although the respondents were experienced in using the WoredaNet digital platform as a tool to provide government services, it still has a positive impact on the perception of ease of use of the new digital government innovation. This implies that having public service experience alone is not sufficient to enhance the perception of ease of use (effort expectancy) of new digital government innovation. Therefore, government organizations should design appropriate start-up training strategies before they implement any new digital innovation.

6.1 Limitation and Feature Research

The research was limited to using only public service experience as a moderating factor. Future studies should also consider other moderating factors such as age and gender (which was imbalanced) to examine their effects on the relationship between the independent and dependent variables of the UTAUT model.

References

1. Flórez-Aristizábal, L., Cano, S., Collazos, C.A., Moreira, F.: Digital transformation to support literacy teaching to deaf Children: from storytelling to digital interactive storytelling. Telematics Inform. **38**, 87–99 (2018)
2. Janssen, M., Estevez, E.: Lean government and platform-based governance-doing more with less. Gov. Inf. Q. **30**, S1–S8 (2013)
3. Montarnal, A., Delgado, A., Astudillo, H.: Introduction to the Minitrack on Digital Government and Business Process Management (BPM). In: Proceedings of the 53rd Hawaii International Conference on System Sciences, pp. 2007–2008 (2020)
4. Norris, D.F., Reddick, C.G.: Local e-government in the United States: transformation or incremental change? Public Adm. Rev. **73**, 165–175 (2013)

5. Chatzoglou, P., Chatzoudes, D., Symeonidis, S.: Factors affecting the intention to use e-Government services. In: Proceedings of the Federated Conference on Computer Science and Information Systems, pp. 1489–1498 (2015)

6. Anthopoulos, L., Reddick, C.G., Giannakidou, I., Mavridis, N.: Why e-government projects fail? An analysis of the Healthcare.gov website. Gov. Inf. Q. **33**, 161–173 (2016)

7. Aladwani, A.M.: Corruption as a source of e-Government projects failure in developing countries: a theoretical exposition. Int. J. Inf. Manage. **36**, 105–112 (2016)

8. Abu-Shanab, E.A.: E-government familiarity influence on Jordanians' perceptions. Telematics Inform. **34**, 103–113 (2017)

9. Alshehri, M., Drew, S., Alhussain, T., Alghamdi, R.: The effects of website quality on adoption of e-government service: an empirical study applying UTAUT model using SEM. In: Proceedings of the 23rd Australasian Conference on Information Systems, ACIS 2012 , pp. 1–13 (2012)

10. Senshaw, D., Twinomurinzi, H.: Reflecting on the role of dynamic capabilities in digital government with a focus on developing countries. In: Proceedings of the 11th Annual Pre-ICIS SIG GlobDev Workshop, p. 5. AIS eLibrary, San Francisco, USA (2018)

11. Wamuyu, P.K.: Bridging the digital divide among low income urban communities. Leveraging use of community technology centers. Telematics Inform. **34**, 1709–1720 (2017)

12. Kim, M., Zoo, H., Lee, H., Kang, J.: Mobile, financial inclusion and development: a critical review of academic literature. In: 10th Annual Pre-ICIS SIG Global Development Workshop, p. 28. Association for Information Systems eLibrary, Seoul (2017)

13. Ahn, N., Park, J.E., Lee, D.H., Hong, P.C.: Balancing personal privacy and public safety in COVID-19: case of Korea and France. IEEE Access **8**, 171325–171333 (2020)

14. Suki, N.M., Suki, N.M.: Determining students' behavioural intention to use animation and storytelling applying the UTAUT model: the moderating roles of gender and experience level. Int. J. Manag. Educ. **15**, 528–538 (2017)

15. Venkatesh, V., Morris, M.G., Davis, G.B., Davis, F.D.: User acceptance of information technology: toward a unified view. MIS Q. **27**, 425–478 (2003)

16. Liébana-Cabanillas, F., Sánchez-Fernández, J., Muñoz-Leiva, F.: The moderating effect of experience in the adoption of mobile payment tools in virtual social networks: the M-Payment Acceptance Model in Virtual Social Networks (MPAM-VSN). Int. J. Inf. Manage. **34**, 151–166 (2014)

17. Venkatesh, V., Davis, F.D.: Theoretical extension of the technology acceptance model: four longitudinal field studies. Manage. Sci. **46**, 186–204 (2000)

18. Tarhini, A., Hone, K., Liu, X.: The effects of individual differences on e-learning users' behaviour in developing countries: a structural equation model. Comput. Hum. Behav. **41**, 153–163 (2014)

19. Senshaw, D., Twinomurinzi, H.: Designing for digital government innovation in resource constrained countries: the case of Woredas in Ethiopia. In: 15th International Conference on Design Science Research in Information Systems and Technology. Springer, Kristiansand, Norway (2020)

20. Raman, A., Don, Y., Khalid, R., Hussin, F., Omar, M.S., Ghani, M.: Technology acceptance on smart board among teachers in Terengganu using UTAUT model. Asian Soc. Sci. **10**, 84 (2014)

21. Tai, Y., Ku, Y.-C.: Will stock investors use mobile stock trading? A benefit-risk assessment based on a modified UTAUT model. J. Electron. Commer. Res. **14**, 67–84 (2013)

22. Mettler, T.: The road to digital and smart government in Switzerland. In: Ladner, A., Soguel, N., Emery, Y., Weerts, S., Nahrath, S. (eds.) Swiss Public Administration. GPM, pp. 175–186. Springer, Cham (2019). https://doi.org/10.1007/978-3-319-92381-9_10

23. Misuraca, G., Pasi, G.: Landscaping digital social innovation in the EU: structuring the evidence and nurturing the science and policy debate towards a renewed agenda for social change. Gov. Inf. Q. **36**, 592–600 (2019)

24. Miruts, G., Asfaw, M.: The implementation of civil service reforms in Ethiopia: the Woreda-Net as a sole promoter to implement civil service reform of Tigray National Regional State. Civ. Environ. Res. **6**, 96–103 (2014)

25. Olufemi, A.: Adaptive capabilities as predictors of sustainable competitive advantage among selected banks in Nigeria. Int. J. Oper. Res. Manag. Soc. Sci. Educ. **4**, 53–62 (2018)

26. Wilden, R., Gudergan, S.P.: The impact of dynamic capabilities on operational marketing and technological capabilities: investigating the role of environmental turbulence. J. Acad. Mark. Sci. **43**, 181–199 (2015)

27. Mullarkey, M.T., Hevner, A.R.: An elaborated action design research process model. Eur. J. Inf. Syst. **28**, 1–15 (2018)

28. Ramírez-Correa, P., Rondán-Cataluña, F.J., Arenas-Gaitán, J., Martín-Velicia, F.: Analysing the acceptation of online games in mobile devices: an application of UTAUT2. J. Retail. Consum. Serv. **50**, 85–93 (2019)

29. Yang, K.C., Shih, P.H.: Cognitive age in technology acceptance: at what age are people ready to adopt and continuously use fashionable products? Telematics Inf. **51**, 101400 (2020)

30. Attuquayefio, S.N.: Using the UTAUT model to analyze students' ICT adoption. Int. J. Educ. Dev. Using Inf. Commun. Technol. **10**, 75–86 (2014)

31. Agarwal, R., Prasad, J.: The antecedents and consequents of user perceptions in information technology adoption. Decis. Support Syst. **22**, 15–29 (1998)

32. Bhatiasevi, V.: An extended UTAUT model to explain the adoption of mobile banking. Inf. Dev. **32**, 799–814 (2016)

33. Chiu, J.L., Bool, N.C., Chiu, C.L.: Challenges and factors influencing initial trust and behavioral intention to use mobile banking services in the Philippines. Asia Pac. J. Innov. Entrep. **11**(2), 246–278 (2017)

34. Khasawneh, M.: AI: an empirical examination of consumer adoption of mobile banking (m-banking) in Jordan. J. Internet Commer. **14**, 341–362 (2015)

35. Davis, F.D., Bagozzi, R.P., Warshaw, P.R.: User acceptance of computer technology: a comparison of two theoretical models. Manage. Sci. **35**, 982 (1989)

36. Lim, W.M., Su, C., Phang, C.: Toward a conceptual framework for social media adoption by non-urban communities for non-profit activities: insights from an integration of grand theories of technology acceptance. Australas. J. Inf. Syst. **23**, 1–11 (2019)

37. Hung, W.H., Hsieh, P.H., Huang, Y.De: Critical factors of the adoption of e-textbooks: a comparison between experienced and inexperienced users. Int. Rev. Res. Open Distance Learn. **19**, 171–190 (2018)

38. Owoseni, A., Twinomurinzi, H.: Mobile apps usage and dynamic capabilities: a structural equation model of SMEs in Lagos, Nigeria. Telematics Inform. **35**, 2067–2081 (2018)

39. Adil, M.S., Owais, M., Qamar, A.: Impact of occupational stress, interpersonal trust, and organizational commitment on valence, OCB and job satisfaction: a variance-based SEM analysis. J. Manag. Sci. **5**(1), 38–61 (2018)

40. Fan, Y., Chen, J., Shirkey, G., John, R., Wu, S.R., Park, H., Shao, C.: Applications of structural equation modeling (SEM) in ecological studies: an updated review. Ecol. Process. **5**, 19 (2016). https://doi.org/10.1186/s13717-016-0063-3

41. Abdullah, N.A., Chong, M., Widjaja, W., Shahrill, M.: Utilizing lesson study in improving year 12 students' learning and performance in mathematics. Math. Educ. Trends Res. **2017**, 24–31 (2017)

42. Jamie, L., et al.: Development of risk maps to minimize uranium exposures in the Navajo Churchrock mining district. Environ. Heal. **8**, 1–15 (2009)
43. Kassa, S.: Challenges and opportunities of women political participation in Ethiopia. J. Glob. Econ. **3**, 1–7 (2015)
44. Alshare, K.A., Lane, P.L.: Predicting student-perceived learning outcomes and satisfaction in ERP courses: an empirical investigation. Commun. Assoc. Inf. Syst. **28**, 571–584 (2011)
45. Magsamen-Conrad, K., Upadhyaya, S., Joa, C.Y., Dowd, J.: Bridging the divide: using UTAUT to predict multigenerational tablet adoption practices. Comput. Hum. Behav. **50**, 186–196 (2015)
46. Marshall, B., Mills, R., Olsen, D.: The role of end-user training in technology acceptance. Rev. Bus. Inf. Syst. **12**, 1–8 (2008)
47. Pynoo, B., Devolder, P., Duyck, W., van Braak, J., Sijnave, B., Duyck, P.: Do hospital physicians' attitudes change during PACS implementation? A cross-sectional acceptance study. Int. J. Med. Inform. **81**, 88–97 (2012)
48. Riskinanto, A., Kelana, B., Hilmawan, D.R.: The moderation effect of age on adopting e-payment technology. In: 4th Information Systems International Conference 2017, ISICO 2017, pp. 536–543. Elsevier B.V. (2017)
49. El Ouirdi, M., El Ouirdi, A., Segers, J., Pais, I.: Technology adoption in employee recruitment: the case of social media in Central and Eastern Europe. Comput. Hum. Behav. **57**, 240–249 (2016)
50. Jewer, J.: Patients' intention to use online postings of ED wait times: a modified UTAUT model. Int. J. Med. Inform. **112**, 34–39 (2018)

Accessibility Issues in Indonesian E-Commerce Portals: Issues and Recommendations for Business Improvement and Growth

Raghuram Balaga[(✉)]

Indian Institute of Technology (IIT)-Tirupati, Tirupati, Andra Pradesh, India
`hs20d001@iittp.ac.in`

Abstract. E-commerce is the fastest and most profitable business that has a global presence. E-commerce companies can attain more profits by creating an accessible environment so that visually challenged consumers can access the website hassle-free. This research work focuses on the identification of accessibility issues in Indonesian E-commerce portals and certain recommendations have been suggested. E-commerce companies in Indonesia can use these recommendations to correct accessibility issues. All the Homepages of three top E-commerce portals have been analyzed using TVT (Total Validator Test) accessibility checking software and few accessibility issues have been identified. Ecommerce companies can identify the accessibility issues and use these recommendations to increase their userbase and finally they can reach the targeted goals and attain more profits.

Keywords: Accessibility · E-commerce companies · Profitable business · Issues · Growth

1 Introduction

Indonesia is the fourth largest country in terms of population, and Indonesia has more than 17000 islands making it one of the most island-clustered country. Due to this, the Indonesian government facing many problems in providing quality health care or eye care services to the people who are living in remote locations. According to the report provided by WHO, there are around 3% of the people who are suffering from visual impairments and in Indonesia, most of the eye care centers are maintained by Government or NGOs or Defence organizations [2]. Cataract has been considered as one of the most prevalent visual impairment among the Indonesian population and other impairments include glaucoma. Since many visually challenged people in Indonesia want to use online services to purchase daily necessities or any other requirements, it is of utmost importance to make the E-business services compatible to visually challenged so that they can use those services hassle-free [3].

The Internet is everywhere, and in every house, there is a computer and Nowadays many people in Indonesia are using smartphones with internet connectivity. A lot of technological advancements such as screen readers and display readers came into existence to fulfill the requirements of visually challenged people. With the advent of

© IFIP International Federation for Information Processing 2020
Published by Springer Nature Switzerland AG 2020
S. K. Sharma et al. (Eds.): TDIT 2020, IFIP AICT 618, pp. 581–591, 2020.
https://doi.org/10.1007/978-3-030-64861-9_51

Information and communication technology in Indonesia, the growth of the online retail business has reached astronomically [4, 5, 8]. The main objective of this research work is to suggest commendable changes in the existing E-business chain in Indonesia and make it accessible to visually challenged people. On implementing these changes companies can increase their user base and can gain goodwill for making their valuable services accessible to all Indonesians.

Indonesian E-commerce is growing rapidly these days. The market potential of the E-commerce sector is growing exponentially. Since there is a huge scope of E-commerce sector companies often try to engage more consumers by portraying creative and innovative offers, In such a competitive environment, companies fail to address the issues of core and potential consumers. In this paper, such type of potential consumer problems has been addressed. Possible suggestions have been mentioned for the enlightenment of the business and increasing the accessibility levels. The ultimate aim of any E-commerce is to increase the business potential in the form of increasing consumers and increasing conversion [7]. To any E-commerce company, these are the two important and essential parameters for growth and existence. Increasing accessibility will suffice these two aspects, the Conversion rate of visually challenged consumers will increase to a significant percentage if and only if the accessibility issues are rectified. The entire evaluation has been done manually using an accessibility tool called TVT, using that tool, all the three E-commerce portals have been examined thoroughly.

1.1 Reason for Examining the Accessibility of E-Commerce Portals

Since E-commerce websites are more dynamic, it is evident that there could be some issues in accessibilities that are ignored by the companies. In several cases, the accessibility levels are not up to the guidelines. Consumer visits the web portal in several stages such as product listing, purchasing, and billing section. The problem with website accessibility is the web developers who designed the portal are not disabled, hence they cannot exactly understand the problems of visually challenged people or people with disabilities. When visually challenged consumers try to interpret the information using the screen reader, they tend to get misfocused because of the complexity and misrepresentation of the portal elements. In simple terms, accessibility means making the portal more user friendly to all types of people. Disabled people should feel comfortable in accessing the portal, increasing perceived impression, Understandable text and context will enable the user to more interact with the portal for longer durations. Robustness of the content is another key aspect because the content must be exactly interpreted by assistive technologies. E-commerce portal consists of text and non-text elements. Images are widely present in all most all the E-commerce portals, decoding the images and content present on the images will be a problem for visually challenged consumers, hence examining the webpage thoroughly is very important and essential these days.

1.2   Problem Statement

Ecommerce portals ignoring the persons with disabilities, despite advanced web portal technology, still there exists certain accessibility issues in these E-commerce portals. Visually challenged people are facing a lot of problems in interpreting the contents on the website. This can impact the revenue because the visually challenged consumer is also a potential buyer. Ecommerce portals should resolve these issues periodically and systematically.

1.3   Objectives of This Research Work

1. To identify the accessibility issues (related to visually challenged people) in the Existing Indonesian E-commerce portals.
2. To design a research model to find accessibility issues.
3. To determine the accessibility issues using TVT software.
4. To suggest the necessary corrections for better accessibility of the portal.

1.4   Impact of Accessibility on Business Growth

Increases the Innovation
The increasing accessibility level of the website always helps in standing ahead from competitors in innovation perspective, because in the field of E-commerce competitors always create unique propositions by creating innovative page layouts, discount coupons, and attractive images. Increasing accessibility is the best strategy. Accessibility innovation can be done at various stages. Auto screen magnifiers and adjustable screen font will help visually impaired consumers who have low vision.

Legal Compliance
According to W3C guidelines, an E-commerce website should be accessible to all, so maintaining the portal to better accessibility conditions is also a favorable aspect from a legal perspective because law enforcement guidelines must be followed [11].

Increasing the Market Size
There will a huge visitor growth for the E-commerce portals because visually challenged persons will visit the portal more frequently, perhaps there will more returning consumers than previous. [10, 11], Price competition always exists as a competitive element in digital commerce, competitors tend to lower the price more frequently. So, it is very difficult to survive in the E-commerce market if the market size is limited.

2   Literature Review

Indonesian E-commerce sector is growing at a rapid rate, a lot of foreign investors are considering Indonesia as one of the most profitable and advantageous countries for E-commerce. People are more compelled towards online purchasing because of the time and price aspect. Consumers can also choose over a wide range of products through the portal [3]. Generally, E-commerce portals mention the product specifications in the form of images, and descriptions or brief specifications of the products. Using screen readers, visually challenged persons can understand the product specification but speech synthesizer cannot decode the image of the product. This is one of the major problems encountered by visually challenged people while shopping online using an E-commerce portal [4]. WCAG gave certain regulations regarding website design standards and E-commerce companies must consider those guidelines while designing the portal. The E-commerce market in Indonesia has grown rapidly in the last few years and many people in Indonesia are opting to purchase online because they have an option to choose a wide range of products and they can also choose their favorite product from billions of available products. The total revenue generated from E-commerce is around 8 billion dollars annually.

According to a survey report, there are around 77 million active Internet users in Indonesia, compared to other countries, Internet users in Indonesia are growing rapidly. Mobile users are also growing rapidly because of the advent of mobile technology [1]. This scenario gave a chance to many companies to enter into the B2C market. Apart from the rapid technological advancement, the Indonesian economy has shown significant growth in these years. Because of economic growth and advancement, people in Indonesia are more interested in spending their disposable income. Online consumers are from a middle-class background [6]. Another noticeable fact is 'convenience' since online shopping is more convenient. Visually challenged consumers often use screen reader software to access the E-commerce portal for shopping, but the unfavorable aspect of screen reader software is it cannot decode the images on the portal. Hence certain elemental text must be included. JAWS is the major software, almost used by 82% of visually challenged consumers to purchase the products online.

2.1 Accessibility Guidelines

According to the rules and regulations provided by the web content accessibility (W3C), the websites must follow these rules and regulations [2], Descriptive titles are to be mentioned in every page, Labels must be mentioned in all pages, In case of images and other graphical elements, necessary site description should be provided, so that speech synthesizer can decode the information to visually challenged consumers [9]. There should be a universal webpage that can be accessed by all the people irrespective of their disabilities, the most common problems that are observed during accessing the portal is broken tags, Image positioning is not available According to the web content accessibility guidelines, there are 4 important principles that must be considered before developing a web portal. The first principle is perceptiveness, as the name itself indicates that the website should be easy to read and interpret fast. The content should not be limited to only a certain class of people, it should be universal and more relevant to all the people. In case, if there is any form of graphical elements, corresponding should be mentioned clearly. Information should not be complex; it should be clear and neat. It needs continuous modification and updating. The second most important principle is the ease of operation. The consumer should be able to access the information on the portal using keyboard strokes and also mouse buttons, both actions should yield similar results. Sometimes, for the skip notification section, mouse operation can be used as an alternative to keyboard strokes. User navigation should be simple and deterministic. Understandability and Robustness are two important principles, the content present on the website should be easy to read and the website should run on all types of browsers.

2.2 Websites Chosen for the Study

Bukalpak is one of the fastest-growing E-commerce companies in Indonesia, Apart from E-Commerce, Bukalpak has expanded its business to flight and train ticket booking services. This implies that the company is keen on business expansion through diversified strategies. According to the survey report, the percentage of mobile traffic is high compared to other digital access systems. Lazada, Another E-commerce company that has a huge presence in Indonesia. Started as a small online platform for goods, with continuous growth it has reached to 2nd largest E-commerce portal in Indonesia. It has got showering investments from many giants such as Alibaba. The business model of Lazada is similar to other E-commerce portals, Elevenia is started with a motto price, convenience, and trust. Now it has become word of mouth for its speed of delivery and competitive pricing strategies.

2.3 W3C Guidelines for Accessibility of Web Portal

Ecommerce companies must follow these additional guidelines to improvise the scale of Business. Updating the portal with ample software assistive technologies such as screen reading addon and magnifier addon for consumers with low or minimal vision. Checking the accessibility aspect, time to time to gauge the level of performance of accessibility tools. Considering the feedback from visually challenged consumers, through speech messages or using chatbots, talking chatbots must be established on the Homepage of these Ecommerce portals. While displaying the discounts or offers, Heavy Red-colored font must not be used, because consumers who are suffering from color blindness cannot access the portal freely. All the product-related information must be recorded, so that visually challenged consumers can immediately access the information by clicking the speech navigation button. Product description must be short and lengthy, complicated sentences shall be avoided. It is very important to add ALT text to Text (HTML format) because screen readers often find difficulty in decoding the text without ALT. The web design team must implement commercial applications such as Dream weaver because they have inbuilt accessibility guidelines.

2.4 Accessibility Testing Using TVT Software

Using TVT software multiple aspects can be tested and reports can be generated in seconds, this software has predominant importance in designing the web portals and considering the level of accessibility in all these aspects. Different errors such as HTML errors, CSS errors, broken links errors can be identified using this software. TVT can also check for spellings in the webpage, that may cause misrepresentation and disturbance because text readers don't have autocorrection feature. Hence all the text present on the portal must be checked thoroughly. Using TVT we can test the portal offline and we can ensure that the page is free from all types of errors and then the page can be uploaded. TVT can be used in all platforms, Windows, Mac, Linux, etc.

3   Research Methodology

Accessibility checking tools have been used to check the accessibility of E-commerce portals in Indonesia. A four-step model has been used in this methodology, Identification, selection, Analysis, Evaluation of the reports (Fig. 1).

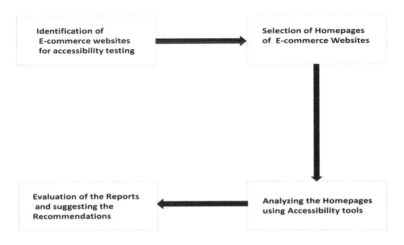

Fig. 1. Research model representing four sequential steps

Step 1: Identification of Ecommerce websites
Three top E-commerce websites have been chosen for this study; the websites are selected based on the annual number of visitors. Website statistics have been collected using online information sources. All the websites, more or less have equal characteristics and they offer similar product catalog. But each Ecommerce portal has its unique strategy for business growth. Certain key information such as information processing, security aspect, and several landing pages has been collected from the online sources to identify the foresaid Ecommerce companies. B2C category E-commerce portals offers a wide range of products to the consumers and consumers can select the products and they can buy those products using debit or credit card numbers or using internet banking. Since the focus area of this study is related to the accessibility issues of visually challenged consumers, only viewing and clicking aspects have been considered. Accessibility issues in order and payment have not been discussed in this paper.

Step 2: Selection of Homepages of These Websites

Homepages are only considered for analyzing the accessibility because it is very difficult to analyze all the pages of E-commerce portals and it is evident that people visit Homepages and navigate through the entire portal using navigation buttons. Only home pages are selected in this study because it is very difficult to perform accessibility tests on all the pages of a particular E-commerce website. The following parameters have been considered while selecting the Homepages of these websites.

Step 3: Analyzing Homepage Using TVT Accessibility Testing Software

TVT tool has been used to check the accessibility in all aspects such as HTML pages, color contrast levels, buttons, navigation, mobile compatibility, Text to speech, size of the font, and WCAG guidelines. All these accessibility tools are designed according to international guidelines issued by WCAG. Total validator test software has been considered as one of the best software to test the accessibility levels of the portal, this software has many advantages compared to other software, Before uploading the webpage to the server, the developer can subject the webpage to test the accessibility levels, TVT software can determine HTML errors, webpage accessibility warning, and other minor and neglected issues. In this software, the URL of the E-commerce portal must be entered, it automatically verifies the URL and its analysis of the page and reports the errors. The best part of this software, apart from analyzing the portal it also segregates the errors into various categories and it assigns the codes for interpretation of those warnings. Further details regarding the interpretation of those have been explained in the results section. The warning is mentioned in numbers preceded by codes.

Step 4: Evaluating the Report and Suggestion of Recommendations

After analyzing all the 3 E-Commerce portals, the generated reports have been studied and compiled in tabular form, after finding the pertaining issues, recommendations have been suggested to increase the accessibility levels of all these E-commerce portals. Apart from the specified suggestions certain other suggestions also mentioned for Business development and engagement of visually impaired consumers. Business improvement recommendations are provided in specific to Indonesian E-commerce because E-commerce business potential varies from one country to another. However, these mentioned business recommendations can be very helpful for the improvement of the portal and creating more impact than the present.

Among these five E-commerce portals, three of them have been chosen for this study, the following table represents the specific details of these portals and categorization (Business to Business, Business to Consumer, Consumer to Consumer) (Table 1).

Table 1. Details of Ecommerce companies offering their services in Indonesia

Ecommerce portal	Type	Annual visitors	Product
Lazada	Category Business to consumer	50 million+	Retail goods
Tokopedia Bukalpak	Consumer to consumer and Business to Consumer	45 million+	Retail goods
	Consumer to consumer and Business to consumer	28 million+	Retail goods
Elevenia	Consumer to consumer	30 million+	Retail goods
Blibli	Business to consumer	25 million+	General and electronic goods

4   Results and Interpretation

After analyzing the website homepages, these are the issues that have been identified and necessary recommendations have been suggested to mitigate these issues and these recommendations must be followed to make the website accessible to visually challenged.

4.1   Interpretation of TVT Accessibility Analysis Report

W001 warning is related to attribute, white spaces shall not be added to the attributes. W001 issue is the most neglected and ignored issue, there are 13 issues related to attribute errors that might cause difficulty in accessing the portal more frequently. W619 is a warning related to the missing name attribute in the element, 2 W619 warnings have been found in the Home page of Lazada portal. W860 warning is related to compliance of W3C guidelines, it states that ALT test is left empty, it may result in difficulty in accessing the portal in some situations where the consumer uses screen recorder software to decode the information on the portal. W868 error is related to the multiple links that may cause confusion for visually impaired consumers, Links that are not essential shall be removed and utmost care must be taken to avoid the combination of multiple links. W874 is related to skip navigation, this warning highlights that skip navigation is missing on the Homepage of Lazada. W884 discusses mouse and keyboard equivalent, for some actions, consumers rely on the mouse pointer. To provide more comfort all the keyboard actions shall be provided with equivalent mouse pointers (Fig. 2).

4.2   Interpretation of the TVT Accessibility Analysis Report (Bukalpak)

W001 indicates the warning related to the presence of whitespace before an attribute value. W618 is related to an obsolete attribute value, web browsers such as google chrome, Internet explorer and firefox will not consider the obsolete attributes. So, while designing the webpage, the CSS should be managed properly, so that W618 can be avoided. W619 is common in both the portals: Lazada and Bukalpak. W860 warning is related to decoding of image attributes, Text reading software cannot perfectly decode the image attributes. White spaces must be avoided. W874 is common in both the portals, this warning is related to skip navigation option (Fig. 3).

Accessibility analysis report – Total validator test software

Start page: **https://www.lazada.co.id**
Started at: 2020/06/21 05:37:30 IST
Time taken: 8 seconds
Validator Version: 15.0.2
Total pages checked: 1
Total pages with issues: 1
✚ Total errors found: 592
➖ Total warnings found: 45
                 Parsing [13]: **W001 [13]**
                 HTML [2]: **W619 [2]**

Fig. 2. Homepage of Lazada and TVT accessibility test results.

Accessibility Analysis report – TVT software

Start page: **https://www.bukalapak.com**
Started at: 2020/06/24 10:08:24 IST
Time taken: 1 seconds
Validator Version: 15.0.2
Total pages checked: 1
Total pages with issues: 1
✚ Total errors found: 51
➖ Total warnings found: 7
                 Parsing [2]: **W001 [2]**
                 HTML [3]: **W618 [2], W619 [1]**
             WCAG21 A [2]: **W860 [1], W874 [1]**

Fig. 3. Homepage of Lazada and TVT accessibility test results.

4.3   Interpretation of TVT Accessibility Analysis Report (Elevania)

Elevania has the highest number of accessibility warnings compared to Lazada and Bukalpak. Attribute error exists common in all the three E-commerce portals. W860 is also common in all these E-commerce portals. W872 is a warning related to changing with keyboard strokes. Warning related to mouse and keyboard equivalents W884 is also present in Elevania. W895 warning identifies that the submit button is missing on the Homepage of the E-commerce portal and it causes several misinterpretations while accessing the portal (Fig. 4).

Start page:	https://www.elevenia.co.id
Started at:	2020/06/25 03:18:09 IST
Time taken:	2 seconds
Validator Version:	15.0.2
Total pages checked:	1
Total pages with issues:	1
⊡ Total errors found:	178
⊟ Total warnings found:	109
Parsing [22]:	W001 [22]
HTML [5]:	W614 [1], W618 [4]
WCAG21 A [82]:	W860 [2], W863 [1], W867 [67], W872 [2], W874 [1], W884 [1], W892 [1], W895 [7]

Fig. 4. Homepage of Elevenia and TVT accessibility test results.

5   Discussion and Recommendations

These issues identified using TVT total accessibility testing software. These results represent the overview of no. of accessibility issues in these E-commerce portals. One important aspect is visually challenged consumers use the mouse instead of the keyboard since the keyboard has a lot of complicated keys, they often feel that using a mouse can be an option to better access the portals. The navigation menu should be made more accessible to the visually impaired consumers, To do that Navigation menu shall be equipped more mouse oriented rather than complex keyboard navigations. All the navigation menus consist of submenus, that provide more information related to categorical product listing. So, while navigating, visually challenged consumers often get confused due to multiple submenus, and multiple landing pages with complex hyperlinks. High graphical content and complex sentences should be avoided in navigation menus and submenus. Tags must be added so that the screen reader can read the main page first and the remaining pages next. Screen readers cannot decode the buttons, text present on the buttons should be readable and short and more informative. The time factor is also an important aspect, Nowadays, many E-commerce companies are focusing on this aspect. The process of viewing, purchasing should not be time-consuming. For Normal consumers, this wouldn't be a big deal but for visually challenged consumers, time is the most important aspect when it comes to accessing the E-commerce portal because whatever the screen reader says they should memorize it first and they should proceed to the next step accordingly. Heterogeneity of the content often disturbs the visually challenged consumers and it creates more entropy. Information should be limited and ample. It also helps the portal to load much faster compared to high content portals. Adding shorter text, shorter images helps the visually challenged consumers to access the portal at a better speed. One menu is sufficient and through that menu using hyperlinks, other submenus shall be made accessible, because while operating the screen reader visually challenged consumers to need to listen to all the elements that are present on the main menu, this creates a little stress in remaining connected to the content flow. Before selecting the favorite product, visually challenged consumers want to listen to the product description, Hence product description should be shorter in length and it should be meaningful and convective. If the consumer has a product of his own choice, Consumers will enter the product name using speech software or braille enabled keyboard. In such situations, search results should be minimum. To reduce the number of items, sorting can be used as the technique to reduce the item count. A small sort option must be provided so that visually challenged consumers can access it using a mouse click.

References

1. Aribawa, D.: International journal of economics and financial issues e-commerce strategic business environment analysis in Indonesia. Int. J. Econ. Financ. Issues **6**(S6), 130–134 (2016). https://doi.org/10.1890/130324
2. Bai, A., Stray, V., Mork, H.: What methods software teams prefer when testing web accessibility. In: Advances in Human-Computer Interaction (2019). https://doi.org/10.1155/2019/3271475
3. Checker, W.A., It, C., Review, A.: IDI Web Accessibility Checker : Web Accessibility Checker IDI Web Accessibility Checker : Web Accessibility Checker. 3–5 (2020)
4. Damuri, Y.R., Negara, S.D., Azali, K.: Indonesia's E-Commerce : a new engine of growth ? In: Symposium on E-Commerce, ASEAN Economic Integration, and Competition Policy & Law, March, 1–24 (2017)
5. Ismail, A., Kuppusamy, K.S.: Web accessibility investigation and identification of major issues of higher education websites with statistical measures: a case study of college websites. J. King Saud Univ.-Comput. Inf. Sci. (2019). https://doi.org/10.1016/j.jksuci.2019
6. Kang, K., Sohaib, O.: Individualists vs. collectivists in B2C E-business purchase intention. J. Internet e-Bus. Stud., 1–11 (2016). https://doi.org/10.5171/2016.948644
7. Kartiwi, M.: Case studies of E-commerce adoption in Indonesian SMEs: the evaluation of strategic use. Australasian J. Inf. Syst. **14**(1). https://doi.org/10.3127/ajis.v14i1.8
8. Pandey, A.: Web application accessibility testing. Int. J. Sci. Res. Publ. **5**(9), 461–472. http://citeseerx.ist.psu.edu/viewdoc/download?doi=10.1.1.736.4248&rep=rep1&type=pdf#page=473
9. Permatasari, A., Kuswadi, E.: The impact of social media on consumers' purchase intention: a study of ecommerce sites in Jakarta, Indonesia. Rev. Integr. Bus. Econ. Res. **6**(1), 321–335 (2017)
10. Pramono, C., Wahyono, T., Agnes, M., Qadri, U.L.: Anal. Finan. Perform. Comp. Emerg. E-Commerce Indonesian Retail Company **7**(1), 182–186 (2020)
11. Rahayu, R., Day, J.: E-commerce adoption by SMEs in developing countries: evidence from Indonesia. Eurasian Bus. Rev. **7**(1), 25–41 (2016). https://doi.org/10.1007/s40821-016-0044-6

Proposed Model for Effective Implementation of IS Megaproject in an Emerging Economy

Sharad Sharma[✉], Rekha Jain, and Vishal Gupta

IIM Ahmedabad, Ahmedabad, India
phd16sharads@iima.acin

Abstract. Like other megaprojects, IS megaprojects are also large-scale, complex ventures having long duration that involve multiple stakeholders from diverse interests, are transformational in nature, and impact large population. The challenges and complexities are accentuated in the case of IS megaproject, and significantly more so in an emerging economy. In the latter case, the national context of low technology and infrastructure, institutional voids, poor governance, and higher user resistance to technology adoption are often contributory factors.

The study aims at developing a conceptual model that links governance mechanisms and their influence on performance, usage, and success of IS megaproject. This is exploratory, qualitative research based on empirical evidence and uses the institutional theory framework. We have conducted 36 semi-structured interviews of the stakeholders of an IS megaproject in an emerging economy.

Through the analysis of the interview transcripts and the help of relevant literature, we identified seven antecedents to the IS megaproject performance, and a conceptual model of seventeen propositions among those eight constructs, and a total of 119 scale items for the measurement of those constructs. The conceptual model explains how norms and work practices governing the project get established, and influence IS megaproject performance. This study contributes both to the empirical and the theoretical body of knowledge.

Keywords: IS megaproject · Performance · Institutional theory · Conceptual model · Scale development

1 Introduction

The increasing complexity in public service delivery, greater demands, and higher expectations from the citizens and enhanced technological capabilities have led to the expansion of areas, scope, and scale, of megaprojects over time. Recognizing the potential impact of the ICTs on the economy and society, active participation of government and public, IS megaprojects (ISMPs) have been receiving increased attention from the policymakers globally [13], and recently in the emerging economies [26].

ISMPs, while having all the characteristics of a megaproject, such as long duration, multiple stakeholders, complex, large-scale, high cost, and new technology [21, 29], also have additional characteristics typically associated with IS projects. These include

© IFIP International Federation for Information Processing 2020
Published by Springer Nature Switzerland AG 2020
S. K. Sharma et al. (Eds.): TDIT 2020, IFIP AICT 618, pp. 592–607, 2020.
https://doi.org/10.1007/978-3-030-64861-9_52

time and/or cost overrun, inadequate utilization of potential benefits, and fast pace of technological change [21, 29]. Such characteristics lead to additional challenges, modest success rates, and low adoption rates for ISMPs. Further, impediments in the design, implementation, and acceptance of ISMPs arise due to inertia and resistance from the users, which are the typical characteristics of any government organization [7]. As a result, challenges are accentuated in the case of ISMP, and often, the underlying challenges can neither be comprehended nor anticipated.

Over and above these factors, ISMPs in an emerging economy face significant challenges because the national context may lag in technology and infrastructure, be plagued with institutional voids, and the users may have higher resistance and inertia in adopting newer technologies [26].

2 Research Gaps

There are very limited studies on ISMPs, especially in the context of emerging economies. In relation to organizations or projects, ISMPs are subject to changing institutional dynamics and organizational forms that serve as the main determinant of project performance, usage, and, eventually, success [5]. As per our knowledge and review of the literature, there are no scale items available for the measurement of antecedents and the performance, usage, and success of ISMPs.

3 Aim of the Study

Recognizing this gap in the existing literature, the study aims at developing scale items that measure the governance mechanisms and their influence on performance, usage, and success of ISMP. We recognize that in the context of the network form of ISMPs, governance of the same emerges from the formal and informal rules of participating organizations, and interactions of the various stakeholders and organizations operating for the cause of the megaproject [8]. Adopting this perspective allows us to examine ISMPs as complex and embedded in institutional frames.

4 Methodology

This is exploratory research in which we conducted 36 semi-structured interviews of the stakeholders of an ISMP in an emerging economy. We developed the scale items based on the analysis of these interview transcripts and review of the academic literature on megaprojects, IS projects, and other related research.

5 Project Background

Indian Railways (IR) is considered as the lifeline of the nation responsible for the socio-economic growth of the country through the transportation of passengers and freight across the length and breadth of the country [19]. Freight transportation is more important to IR's operation as it generates around 65% of its revenue. This segment generates profit for IR, which cross subsidizes the loss-making passenger services [19, 32].

Freight transportation through railways is more efficient, less expensive, and more environment-friendly than road transportation. Despite this, IR's share of freight transportation has come down close to 30% today, which used to stand at 90% in the post-independence era[1]. This falling share in freight traffic has been a cause of major concern on IR, and numerous initiatives and actions have been taken to improve upon the delivery of freight services. One of the plausible ways to control this downward trend involves the efficient utilization of freight assets, which includes technological innovations as well as the deployment of appropriate decision support systems and management information systems [6]. FOIS is one such initiative in this regard, and it has an inherent potential to improve the ease of doing business with railways. FOIS was initially conceived as an application to monitor the movement of freight trains on IR and track the wagons, locomotives. Today it has evolved as a complete freight operations management application, including the on-line freight calculation and generating & processing the billing. IR claims it to have played a major role in the increased efficiency of wagon utilization. The objective of the project is to fulfil the needs of the emerging Indian economy through efficient utilization & improved productivity of the assets and better customer services[2].

6 Theoretical Background

Kipp et al. [21], compared the characteristics and literature of megaprojects with that of ISMPs. They found that there is a commonality in the characteristics and issues involved with megaprojects and ISMPs. Therefore, they suggest that existing knowledge and literature from the domain of megaprojects may be drawn to the field of ISMP. Omar and Elhaddadeh [28], have examined the role of actors and structures in the institutionalization process in ISMPs. They proposed conceptual framework based on institutional and structuration theory, which is focused on the institutionalization of changes in public sector organizations through IS.

The institutional logics influence transformations in the governance mechanisms and the established work practices of stakeholders. Understanding an ISMP is possible only through its examination from the institutional theory perspective by considering the influence of regulatory, normative, and cultural-cognitive factors [8]. The

---

[1] Source: https://www.financialexpress.com/economy/railway-traffic-increases-revenue-falls-in-2016-17/628801/, last accessed 2020/07/30.

[2] Source: http://fois.indianrail.gov.in/FOISWebPortal/pages/FWP_AboutFOIS.jsp, last accessed 2020/07/30.

institutional theory views an organization from an "open systems" perspective; this is what the temporary organization implementing the ISMP is. In such temporary organizations, the environment does influence the organization, as is the usual case. Besides, atypically, the organization influences the environment [5]. This environment is a social construction having strong historical underpinnings [5]. The social exchanges of individuals and organizations under such an environment are governed by the rules determined by institutions [5]. Megaprojects are such temporary organizations that experience the paradox of embedded agency [25]. Although the agents are embedded in an institutional context, they can still manage to influence the context rather than their agency being influenced by the context [35]. The institutional theory explains how organizations interact with their environment to survive and thrive amidst all the competition and challenges thrown at them [9]. Because of these reasons, examining the megaprojects from an institutional theory perspective is an emerging research area. This includes the broader environment of the project, sponsorship, and governance [5, 35]. Because of these reasons, we used the institutional theory framework for the development of the conceptual model for ISMP.

7 Data Collection

We conducted semi-structured interviews of the 36 stakeholders of the FOIS project. These stakeholders belonged to Top Management, Developer, Implementor, User (internal as well as external) and one Expert, who was a senior railway officer and a Ph. D. on complex projects and had a vast experience of executing and leading complex project. The majority of the respondents were government officials, with a large number of them occupying senior positions. Therefore, prior permissions from the competent authorities were obtained to safeguard the interests of the respondents and also demonstrate the same to them. The respondents were briefed about the research and assured about the confidentiality and anonymity of the data collected from them [15, 27]. All the respondents willingly participated in the study and accordingly, the consent forms were signed by them. Institutional Review Board's approval was obtained to ensure that unethical means and practices were not adopted during the research study. All the interviews were audio-recorded with the permission of the respondents, and the average duration of the interviews was 33 min. The transcriptions were shared with the respondents, and they were asked to suggest any modifications if they wished to add or remove something from the transcriptions. This was done with the view of enhancing the validity of the data and to give an opportunity to the respondent to rephrase their statements [14].

8 Construct Identification

8.1 Environment

A number of respondents reported that ISMPs are influenced due to the environment, i.e., factors outside the implementing organization. Some of the environmental factors include evolving technological capabilities, growing expectations of the users, competition in the market, political influence and financial support from the government [5, 16, 20, 21, 23, 30, 41].

Coercive pressure from the government side was reflected in the statement of the project manager from the vendor side when she mentioned that "there were time pressure because the project was being monitored at the Ministry level." Normative pressure operating from the environment was visible in the statement of the project manager from the implementing organization through, "any transporter not having a global picture, which is accurate, is no transporter." The project manager from the vendor side also mentioned that "they were losing their market share. So, that is why people realize; top management was involved." The project manager tried to convey that IR was losing its market share to road transport. Therefore, the top management of IR decided to go for FOIS. Our respondents also reported that ISMP for a transporter becomes necessary to have a global view of its operations and the assets, as this is the trend internationally. IS researchers have termed this environmental influence on the ISMP as institutional isomorphism [8].

8.2 Top Management Support

The issue that most prominently emerged out of the analysis of the transcripts was that the top management support played a vital role in the ISMP. Top management refers to the key decision-makers, and their support to the ISMP is the crucial determinant for the initiative, implementation, and adoption. The top management was responsible for taking appropriate decisions that determine how the ISMP evolves and takes shape [1, 24].

The Director of the implementing organization mentioned during the interview that "the mandate is there from the top management only; then only it gets translated straight into the field." There were a large number of statements that repeatedly highlighted the role and importance of the top management support, and all class of stakeholders made such statements.

8.3 Core Team

The interview respondents brought out that top management constituted the core team for the project with the deployment of the project leader at the helm. The project leader was a domain expert of the railway operations as well as having enough knowledge and experience of the IT systems. The project leader was given full freedom for the team selection, and there was no interference from the top management in the project and team-related matters. The project leader was acceptable to almost all the stakeholders, and he was able to take everyone along. The analysis of the interview transcripts brings forth that the core team should be competent and cohesive. And also, the core team members should be provided with a reasonably long tenure [34]. The respondents mentioned that the core team members should not be governed strictly by the norms of usual terms of tenure. Instead, they should be informed beforehand that they are responsible till the development of a specific module or submodule of the ISMP. The cohesiveness of the core team was also reflected in the statement of one of the implementors, "The way this project was launched by the team, it was like no other teams have done before. There was, no hierarchy barriers. There was, no seniority barriers. Everybody was sharing with everyone. So, team was very cohesive."

8.4   IS/IT Governance

The respondents brought out during the discussions that the ISMP gave rise to the creation of new organizations, departments, and positions for the design, development, planning, and execution of the ISMP [5, 21]. The government and the implementing organization formulate various policies which are implemented through the ISMP. The implementing organization also comes up with policy initiatives that facilitate and overcome various impediments in the ISMP. The ISMPs also generate various capabilities that enable evidence-based policymaking in the implementing organization [16, 20, 40]. The General Manager of the implementing organization mentioned that "Whatever policy changes are taking place or, or, the type of improvement that railway wants to bring in, to improve the user-friendliness, the policy have to be aligned towards the requirement of the customers that is actually an ongoing process, depending on the changes in the environment and the requirement of the customers." One of the respondents, a FOIS user, mentioned about the project that "it has provided the evidence-based policymaking and thereby reducing any post facto scrutiny, etc."

8.5   Contractual Governance

Our respondents reported that multiple stakeholders operating in the ISMP have well-defined roles and responsibilities. The formal rules provide an overarching contractual framework for day-to-day functioning and collaboration among stakeholders [33]. This framework of formal rules is termed as contractual governance [4, 22]. Based on formal rules and regulations, contractual governance explicitly defines the responsibilities of various stakeholders [39]. Contractual governance thus serves as a reference point for various transactions and interactions taking place [17]. One of the end-users mentioned during the interview that, "We have directly access because we have contract between CRIS and NTPC and whatever information we want, we approach to these people and if something new is required, for which, we can pay, and we can seek the information."

8.6   Relational Norms

Megaprojects are network organizations involving multiple stakeholders from diverse organizations [37]. Coming together of these multiple stakeholders gives rise to new organizational norms, which are often different from the underlying organizations to which they originally belong. Due to the long-term association and regular interaction, combined with complex interrelationships and interdependencies among multiple stakeholders, informal rules tend to develop in the megaprojects [37]. These informal rules termed as relational norms are driven by shared beliefs, cultural practices, and social values [4]. Our respondents revealed that many times they resort to such practices that expedite the processes, e.g., one respondent mentioned that, "most of the cases, I've given my personal email also. If you are not able to reach to SBI email, okay, you send me on my gmail id and I used to take care of that."

8.7   Project Management

The respondents highlighted the importance of project management for megaprojects. Project management is defined as "the application of knowledge, skills, tools, and techniques to project activities to meet the project requirements" [31]. It was brought out by the respondents that project management plays a key role in ensuring that the ISMP does not suffer from the time and cost over-run [11]. One respondent, who was the Member of the Railway Board, while talking about the role of project management mentioned that, "the project management now becomes a very important thing particularly for the railways because a lot of investments are coming up and mega investments are there." Effective project management of ISMPs builds around employing a professional approach and promoting economic and social development [2, 10]. Project management is responsible for deploying the necessary resources and skill sets to the ISMP, managing the risk, uncertainty and complexity, engaging the suitable vendors & contractors, and adhering to the delivery schedule [2, 11].

8.8   Project Performance

Based upon the interviews with the participants, we found that the traditional definition of the fulfillment of laid down goals & objectives and achieving the time, cost, and quality requirements of the project are the desirable criteria for defining the success of an ISMP [2]. The reason being that evolving technological capabilities and changing business needs, increase the expectations of the organizations as well as users [10, 13]. Ultimately, the user wants to have more and more control over the outcomes through the use of technology [3]. Additionally, ISMPs tend to bring more and more users to its fold. They lead to changes in the usage profile of the users. E.g., the traffic accounts branch and the statistics branch of IR were originally meant for registering and updating the freight revenue and the statistics of the freight operation. After the implementation of FOIS, all this information is readily available from the system. Now, their role has become more of an auditor to see and report if any malpractices are taking place in those areas.

Therefore, the goals and objectives of the ISMPs are not fixed. Because of the changing goals and objectives, the initial time, cost, and quality requirements do not remain relevant throughout the entire life cycle of the project. Though they are important, it is not plausible to monitor them rigidly because of the newer time, cost, and quality requirements that arise. Because of these changing goals & objectives and shifting time, cost, and quality requirements, user satisfaction is seldom achieved. As a result, user satisfaction in an ISMP may be strived for, but usually, it is never attained [36]. From this discussion, we concluded that the goals & objectives, time, cost and quality requirements, and user satisfaction are the desirable criteria for an ISMP. Though, these are important but not the necessary conditions.

Some of the implementors and users suggested that a successful system is one, which is indispensable, i.e., the user cannot work without the system or the total dependence on the system. However, the closer examination of the ISMPs reveals that every successful system is indispensable, but every indispensable system may not be necessarily successful. Due to the scale and magnitude of the operations, it may not be practically possible to carry out the functions without the help of the system, as is the case with FOIS. Without entering into the debate of FOIS being a successful project or not, today, it is unimaginable for any user to work without the FOIS.

Some of the participants suggested that the acceptance of the system by the users is one of the dimensions to evaluate the success of the ISMP. However, if the system is not acceptable to a large number of users, they would reject the system. And the developers would be forced to make suitable and relevant changes in the system [3]. Therefore, user acceptance is the fundamental criteria to evaluate ISMPs. The customer-centric approach and benefits to the users as well as organizations are the two dimensions that almost all the participants have agreed as the key criteria for evaluating an ISMP. Implementors and users have highlighted that usefulness and ease of use are also vital dimensions to evaluate ISMP.

Continuous evolution and up-gradation of the system is a dimension which only a few of the participants have recognized as a criterion to evaluate the ISMP. However, we realized that this is an area that is very important for the ISMP. Otherwise, it would become irrelevant and obsolete in no time. Therefore, a successful ISMP is one that is regularly updated in terms of the software as well as hardware with the reasonably latest technologies [2].

From the above discussions, we realized that the evaluation of the success of an ISMP is a subjective continuum that has user acceptance at the one end and the satisfaction at the other end. In between, there are objective criteria like achieving the goals and objectives, fulfilling the time, cost and quality requirement, and the sub-jective criteria like indispensability, usefulness, ease of use, benefit, and up-gradation.

9 Development of Propositions

The analysis of interview transcripts revealed that the external environment operates on the ISMP through the top management, formulation, and implementation of various policies influencing ISMP. The respondents reported that monitoring of the ISMP by the government exerts pressure on the top management and leads to their greater involvement and participation in the project [16, 23, 41]. The analysis of the interview transcripts also revealed that ISMPs serve the means of IT initiatives implementation of the government [20, 28, 41]. The respondents brought out that the environment influences IS/IT Governance through the formulation and implementation of the policies, which give rise to the increase in the goals and scope of the ISMP [16, 20, 40]. The above arguments lead us to formulate the following propositions.

P1. *Environment influences top management support,*
P2. *Environment influences the core team, and*
P3. *Environment influences IS/IT Governance.*

According to our respondents, the top management support is responsible for the deployment of the core team for the ISMP, formulation of the necessary structures, processes and policies, and the conflict resolution [16, 24, 34, 41]. The constitution of the core team also depends upon the environmental factors. At the same time, top management keeps coming with various policy initiatives that aim at facilitating the

ISMP through the creation of various organizations, departments, positions, and processes [1, 18, 41]. From the above discussion, we arrive at following propositions:

P4. Top management support influences the core team, and
P5. Top management support influences IS/IT Governance.

The relational norms serve as an informal control mechanism in the ISMPs and help the top management, core team, and the project management to exert control during their interaction with the ISMP stakeholders [24]. Cohesion, commitment, and the long-term association of the core team influence these relational norms [12]. At different hierarchical levels, top management support and project management also resort to informal practices and processes during their interaction with the stakeholders [12]. Therefore, we propose:

P6. Core team influences relational norms
P7. Top management support influences relational norms, and
P8. Project management practices influence relational norms.

During the interview, the project managers mentioned that they can achieve and perform because of the top management support [1, 10]. The respondents indicated that a committed, competent and a cohesive team helps the project management in decision-making, risk apportionment, complexity handling, and stakeholder management [30, 34]. Based on this discussion, we have the following propositions:

P9. Top management support influences project management practices, and
P10. The core team influences project management practices.

Project management is directly responsible for the award and execution of various tenders and contracts, and the top management is involved in finalizing the MOU's with other ministries and state governments [24]. Therefore, we propose the following:

P11. Project management practices influence contractual governance, and
P12. Top management support influences contractual governance.

New policies are formulated and implemented to tap the potentials generated through the ISMPs, which give rise to new contracts, e.g. e-Payment module of FOIS has given rise to tripartite contracts between banks, freight customers and IR. Therefore, we propose:

P13. IS/IT Governance influences contractual governance.

ISMPs usually have long term association with the vendors, contractors, and other stakeholders, and their interactions are not necessarily driven by the contract conditions or the formal rules itself. The respondents revealed during the interview that vendors try to prove their credentials, through their association with the ISMP [13, 16]. Therefore, we propose:

P14. Relational Norms influence contractual governance.

Project management, contractual governance and relational norms influence the project performance [4, 11, 12, 38]. Therefore, we propose:

P15. Project management practices influence ISMP performance,
P16. Contractual governance influences ISMP performance, and
P17. Relational Norms influence ISMP performance.

Based on the above discussion and combining all the 17 propositions, we propose the conceptual model, as shown in Fig. 1, for ISMP in an emerging economy.

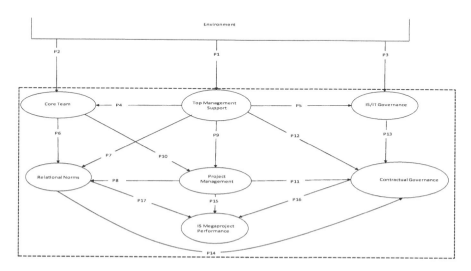

Fig. 1. Conceptual model of IS megaproject

10   Scale Items

For the measurement of eight constructs as discussed above, a total of 119 scale items were developed. These scale items are given separately in Appendix-I. The scale items were adapted to our context by modifying the original scale items based on the analysis of interview transcripts.

11   Contribution

Through the analysis of the interview transcripts and the support of related literature, we have developed a conceptual model for ISMP in an emerging economy. The model embedded in the institutional theory framework explains how the environmental factors influence ISMP, what is the significance of the top management support, how the policies, structures, and processes are formulated and implemented that influence the ISMPs. What are the formal and informal control mechanisms in an ISMP, and how do they interact?

As per our knowledge and the review of available literature, these aspects have not been studied before in the context of ISMP. Therefore, our study makes a unique contribution to the field of ISMP.

12   Limitation and Future Research

The conceptual model has been developed primarily based on the analysis of the interview transcripts of ISMP stakeholders. Therefore, it's validity and generalizability is limited to a similar context [42]. This is an exploratory study, and the findings need to be confirmed through empirical and confirmatory studies.

As the next step to this research, we intend to collect survey responses from the ISMP stakeholders and test the proposed relationships delineated in the model.

Appendix

Sr. no.	Item
A	**Environment**
1	The Government of India (GoI) is determined for digitalization in the service delivery
2	Freight customers need Indian Railways (IR) to develop FOIS
3	The competitive environment in the transport sector compels IR to develop FOIS.
4	The GoI has supported the FOIS project
5	The government plays a significant role in building a harmonious relationship among stakeholders of the FOIS project
6	The GoI implements policies that promote coordination among multiple stakeholders of the FOIS project
7	The freight customers are making extensive use of IT
8	IR aspires for improvement in service delivery through FOIS
9	IR aspires for improvement in operational efficiency through FOIS
10	GoI's promotion of IT influences IR's decision to develop FOIS
11	Transporters use IT to compete against each other
12	Successful transporters are making good use of IT
13	It is common for large organizations to use IT increasingly
B	**Top Management Support**
14	Railway Board actively implements policies that push for the use of FOIS
15	Railway Board has a firm belief in FOIS that it will be significantly beneficial
16	Railway Board is committed to provide the necessary resources for FOIS
17	Railway Board has clear cut plans to enhance the capabilities of FOIS
18	Railway Board has clear cut plans to increase the usage of FOIS
19	The FOIS project has never experienced funding constraints
C	**Core Team**

(continued)

(continued)

Sr. no.	Item
20	The core team is competent to accomplish the FOIS project tasks
21	The core team has acquired the necessary skills required for the FOIS project
22	The core team is competent to handle various challenges of the FOIS project
23	The core team does not believe in hierarchy
24	The core team does not follow bureaucratic processes
25	The core team members are integrated as one team
26	The core team members are focused on the project
27	The core team members are committed to the success of the FOIS project
28	The core team members are dedicated to ensure that the FOIS project achieves its objectives
29	The core team members work hard to take along all the project stakeholders
D	**IS/IT Governance**
30	There is a process in place for planning the IT initiatives in IR
31	There is a process in place to monitor the IT implementation in IR
32	There is a process in place to monitor the performance of IT implementation in IR
33	Necessary organization has been created for the IT implementation in IR
34	Necessary department has been created specifically for the implementation of IT on IR
35	Necessary posts have been created specifically for the implementation of IT on IR
36	There is a regular structure in place for the audit of IT implementation in IR
37	IR's IT implementation decisions are in line to achieve organizational goals
38	IR's IT implementation decisions have helped the organization to deliver better services to freight customers
39	IR's IT implementation decisions have helped to reduce the cost of operations
E	**Contractual Governance**
40	Past association with the vendors/contractors helps the smooth execution of the project related contracts
41	The vendors/contractors are committed to the success of FOIS
42	There exists mutual trust among the stakeholders belonging to CRIS, IR, and vendors/contractors
43	FOIS related contracts are well defined
44	FOIS related MOU's are well defined
45	There is clarity about the project scope
46	There is clarity about the goals of the project
47	The contract conditions attempt at minimizing the uncertainties in the FOIS Project
48	The contract conditions attempt at minimizing the risks in the FOIS Project
F	**Relational Norms**
49	The stakeholders are committed to improvement in the FOIS
50	The stakeholders are eager to help each other whenever the need arises
51	The vendors/contractors feel that CRIS is reliable and trustworthy
52	The vendors/contractors are committed to the success of FOIS
53	Concerned stakeholders participate in decision-making
54	CRIS regularly asks feedback from users for improvement in FOIS

(continued)

(*continued*)

Sr. no.	Item
55	The stakeholders are contributing to improve FOIS in accordance with their specific potential
56	Project related urgent information exchange across the stakeholders takes place informally
57	Information exchange across the stakeholders takes place frequently
58	Concerned stakeholders are informed about the event or changes that may affect them
G	**Project Management**
59	Project management is concerned about the business requirements of IR
60	Project management regularly interacts with users
61	Project management is considerate about the business requirements of freight customers
62	Project management is aware of the technological changes taking place in the environment
63	Project management explores various technological options before arriving at a technology decision
64	Project management continuously looks for new opportunities for the improvement in FOIS
65	Project management is concerned about the smooth implementation of the FOIS modules
66	Project management has successfully managed the changes in the project scope
67	Project management has successfully delivered FOIS that satisfies new and changing demands
68	Project management is responsible for deploying suitable persons on the project
69	Project management is responsible for engaging suitable vendors/contractors for the project
70	Project management is responsible for upgrading the skills of project persons
71	Project management is responsible for the breakdown of the project complexity into the manageable chunks
72	Project management is responsible for updating FOIS architecture
73	Project management is responsible for evaluating user requirements
74	Project management regularly interacts with vendors/contractors
75	Project management continually monitors the progress of the project
76	Project management establishes a schedule of various project activities
H	**Project Performance**
77	The FOIS project is beneficial to IR
78	The FOIS project is beneficial to freight customers
79	FOIS has led to an improvement in IR's capability
80	The outcomes of the FOIS project are aligned with the expectations
81	The FOIS project has been delivered with minimum disruptions to the freight operations of IR
82	It is not possible to carry out freight operations without FOIS

(*continued*)

(continued)

Sr. no.	Item
83	The users are dependent on FOIS
84	Freight operations managers are dependent on FOIS
85	Freight customers are dependent on FOIS
86	When I can do a task using FOIS, I will sometimes choose to use other ways to complete the task
87	When given a choice between using or not using FOIS for a task, I usually choose not to use it
88	FOIS is useful for its users
89	FOIS has made it easier for users to perform their job
90	FOIS is useful for freight customers
91	FOIS is easy to use
92	Learning to use FOIS is easy
93	It is easy to become a skillful user of FOIS
94	The FOIS hardware is regularly upgraded
95	The FOIS software is regularly upgraded
96	The FOIS system architecture is regularly upgraded
97	Technological evolutions are suitably adopted in FOIS
98	Technological capabilities of FOIS are continuously enhanced
99	FOIS architecture permits information filtering
100	FOIS architecture permits on-demand information delivery
101	FOIS provides personalized services to freight customers
102	FOIS attempts to fulfill the expectations of freight customers
103	FOIS provides customized information to freight customers
104	FOIS is acceptable to freight customers
105	FOIS is acceptable to freight operations manager
106	FOIS is acceptable to the top management of IR
107	FOIS project satisfies the need of the users
108	FOIS provides reliable information
109	FOIS provides accurate information
110	FOIS provides relevant information
111	CRIS employees have a positive attitude towards users' grievances
112	Users readily grab new additions to FOIS
113	Users often suggest modifications in the existing FOIS
114	FOIS provides sufficient information
115	FOIS provides adequate information
116	Users have confidence in FOIS
117	FOIS has achieved its goals
118	FOIS has achieved its short-term objectives
119	FOIS long-term objectives are being strived for

References

1. Ashja, M., Moghadam, A.H., Bidram, H.: Comparative study of large information systems' CSFs during their life cycle. Inf. Syst. Front. **17**(3), 619–628 (2015)
2. Barclay, C.: Towards an integrated measurement of IS project performance: the project performance scorecard. Inf. Syst. Front. **10**(3), 331 (2008)
3. Barki, H., Paré, G., Sicotte, C.: Linking IT implementation and acceptance via the construct of psychological ownership of information technology. J. Inf. Technol. **23**(4), 269–280 (2008)
4. Benítez-Ávila, C., Hartmann, A., Dewulf, G., Henseler, J.: Interplay of relational and contractual governance in public-privatepartnerships: the mediating role of relational norms, trust and partners' contribution. Int. J. Project Manag. **36**(3), 429–443 (2018)
5. Biesenthal, C., Clegg, S., Mahalingam, A., Sankaran, S.: Applying institutional theories to managing megaprojects. Int. J. Project Manag. **36**(1), 43–54 (2018)
6. Boysen, N., Fliedner, M., Jaehn, F., Pesch, E.: A survey on container processing in railway yards. Transp. Sci. **47**(3), 312–329 (2013)
7. Clegg, C., Shepherd, C.: The biggest computer programme in the world… ever!': time for a change in mindset? J. Inf. Technol. **22**(3), 212–221 (2007)
8. Currie, W.L., Guah, M.W.: Conflicting institutional logics: a national programme for IT in the organisational field of healthcare. J. Inf. Technol. **22**(3), 235–247 (2007)
9. DiMaggio, P.J., Powell, W.W.: The iron cage revisited: institutional isomorphism and collective rationality in organizational fields. Am. Sociol. Rev. 147–160 (1983)
10. Eom, M.T., Wu, W.W., Preston, D.S., Luftman, J.N.: Effective IT project leadership. MIS Q. Exec. **19**(2), 6 (2020)
11. Eriksson, P.E., Larsson, J., Pesämaa, O.: Managing complex projects in the infrastructure sector—a structural equation model for flexibility-focused project management. Int. J. Project Manag. **35**(8), 1512–1523 (2017)
12. Eskerod, P., Vaagaasar, A.L.: Stakeholder management strategies and practices during a project course. Project Manag. J. **45**(5), 71–85 (2014)
13. Flyvbjerg, B.: What you should know about megaprojects and why: an overview. Project Manag. J. **45**(2), 6–19 (2014)
14. Forbat, L., Henderson, J.: Theoretical and practical reflections on sharing transcripts with participants. Qual. Health Res. **15**(8), 1114–1128 (2005)
15. Gill, P., Stewart, K., Treasure, E., Chadwick, B.: Methods of data collection in qualitative research: interviews and focus groups. Br. Dent. J. **204**(6), 291–295 (2008)
16. Goo, J., Kishore, R., Rao, H.R., Nam, K.: The role of service level agreements in relational management of information technology outsourcing: an empirical study. MIS Q. 119–145 (2009)
17. Hart, O., Moore, J.: Contracts as reference points. Q. J. Econ. **123**(1), 1–48 (2008)
18. Jewer, J., McKay, K.N.: Antecedents and consequences of board IT governance: institutional and strategic choice perspectives. J. Assoc. Inf. Syst. **13**(7), 1 (2012)
19. Jha, U.S.: Indian railways contribution to Indian Economy. Sankalpa **8**(1), 122–130 (2018)
20. King, A., Crewe, I.: The Blunders of Our Governments. Simon and Schuster, New York (2014)
21. Kipp, A., Riemer, K., Wiemann, S.: IT mega projects: what they are and why they are special (2008)
22. Krishnan, R., Geyskens, I., Steenkamp, J.B.E.: The effectiveness of contractual and trust-based governance in strategic alliances under behavioral and environmental uncertainty. Strateg. Manag. J. **37**(12), 2521–2542 (2016)

23. Liang, H., Saraf, N., Hu, Q., Xue, Y.: Assimilation of enterprise systems: the effect of institutional pressures and the mediating role of top management. MIS Q. 59–87 (2007)
24. Liu, G.H., Wang, E.T., Chua, C.E.H.: Leveraging social capital to obtain top management support in complex, cross-functional IT projects (2015)
25. Lundin, R.A., Arvidsson, N., Brady, T., Ekstedt, E., Midler, C., Sydow, J.: Managing and Working in Project Society. Cambridge University Press, Cambridge (2015)
26. Miller, R., Lessard, D.R.: Evolving strategy: risk Management and the Shaping of Mega-Projects, pp. 145–72. Edward Elgar, Cheltenham (2008)
27. Newcomer, K.E., Hatry, H.P., Wholey, J.S.: Conducting semi-structured interviews. In: Handbook of Practical Program Evaluation, p. 492 (2015)
28. Omar, A., Elhaddadeh, R.: Structuring institutionalization of digitally-enabled service transformation in public sector: does actor or structure matters? (2016)
29. Patanakul, P.: Managing large-scale IS/IT projects in the public sector: problems and causes leading to poor performance. J. High Technol. Manag. Res. 25(1), 21–35 (2014)
30. Patanakul, P., Kwak, Y.H., Zwikael, O., Liu, M.: What impacts the performance of large-scale government projects? Int. J. Project Manag. 34(3), 452–466 (2016)
31. Pmi, A.: Guide to the project management body of knowledge. In: Project Management Institute, vol. 130 (2004)
32. Pucher, J., Korattyswaroopam, N., Ittyerah, N.: The crisis of public transport in India: overwhelming needs but limited resources. J. Publ. Transp. 7(4), 1 (2004)
33. Qiu, Y., Chen, H., Sheng, Z., Cheng, S.: Governance of institutional complexity in megaproject organizations. Int. J. Project Manag. 37(3), 425–443 (2019)
34. Scott-Young, C., Samson, D.: Project success and project team management: evidence from capital projects in the process industries. J. Oper. Manag. 26(6), 749–766 (2008)
35. Söderlund, J., Sydow, J.: Projects and institutions: towards understanding their mutual constitution and dynamics. Int. J. Project Manag. 37(2), 259–268 (2019)
36. Tesch, D., Miller, R., Jiang, J.J., Klein, G.: Perception and expectation gaps of information systems provider skills: the impact on user satisfaction. Inf. Syst. J. 15(4), 343–355 (2005)
37. Van Marrewijk, A., Clegg, S.R., Pitsis, T.S., Veenswijk, M.: Managing public–private megaprojects: paradoxes, complexity, and project design. Int. J. Project Manag. 26(6), 591–600 (2008)
38. Wang, D., Fang, S., Li, K.: Dynamic changes of governance mechanisms in mega construction projects in China. Eng. Const. Arch. Manag. (2019)
39. Williamson, O.E.: The Economic Institutions of Capitalism. Free Press, New York (1985)
40. Winch, G.: Megaproject stakeholder management. In: The Oxford Handbook of Megaproject Management, pp. 339–361 (2017)
41. Xue, Y., Liang, H., Boulton, W.R.: Information technology governance in information technology investment decision processes: the impact of investment characteristics, external environment, and internal context. MIS Q. 67–96 (2008)
42. Yin, R.K.: Validity and generalization in future case study evaluations. Evaluation 19(3), 321–332 (2013)

Antecedents of the Barriers Toward the Adoption of Unified Payment Interface

Sayantan Khanra[1,2(✉)] 🆔, Rojers P. Joseph[2] 🆔, Amandeep Dhir[3,4] 🆔,
and Puneet Kaur[5]

[1] Woxsen University, Hyderabad 502345, Telangana, India
sayantan.khanra@iimrohtak.ac.in
[2] Indian Institute of Management Rohtak, Rohtak 124010, Haryana, India
[3] University of Agder, Kristiansand 4630, Norway
[4] Lappeenranta University of Technology, Lappeenranta 53850, Finland
[5] University of Bergen, Bergen 5007, Norway

Abstract. This study examines the influence of factors related to consumer resistance on the intention to continue using the Unified Payment Interface (UPI) for electronic payments. UPI facilitates advanced, peer-to-peer, immediate payment with seamless interoperability among banks in India. The study extends the innovation resistance theory by including two behavioral measures - privacy concerns and visibility - and two moderators - security concerns and word of mouth (WOM). It used cross-sectional data collected from 714 UPI users aged between 16 and 55 years to test the proposed research model. The findings suggest that privacy concerns and usage barrier are the two crucial factors to be addressed for breaking down consumer resistance towards continuing usage of UPI. The other significant factors are image barrier and visibility. In addition, security concerns and WOM are found to partially moderate the influences on the associations between the key variables and continuing usage of UPI.

Keywords: Consumer resistance · Digital financial service · Innovation resistance theory · Mobile payment · Online payment · Unified payment interface (UPI)

1 Introduction

Consumer preference for performing routine tasks is gradually shifting towards innovative services driven by the advancement of information and communication technologies [1]. Recognizing the potential of innovative mobile-based financial services, the National Payments Corporation of India (NPCI), an umbrella organization promoted by the Reserve Bank of India (RBI) and Indian Banks' Association for retail payments, launched a mobile-based service named the "Unified Payment Interface (UPI)" to facilitate an advanced level of interoperability among different banks in India [2]. Simply put, UPI facilitates a smartphone-based secure services that can instantly transfer money directly from one bank to another with few clicks [3]. The only instant payment service that offers a comparable level of simplicity and interoperability as UPI

© IFIP International Federation for Information Processing 2020
Published by Springer Nature Switzerland AG 2020
S. K. Sharma et al. (Eds.): TDIT 2020, IFIP AICT 618, pp. 608–625, 2020.
https://doi.org/10.1007/978-3-030-64861-9_53

does is named 'Swish,' available in Sweden [4]. Following the trend, several countries, especially developed economies, are now in the process of launching instant payment services similar to UPI [4, 5].

Since the launch of UPI in 2016, the government as well as the banks in India have undertaken several initiatives to introduce and popularize UPI among the citizens [3, 6]. These initiatives include incentives for referring new customers, promotional cashbacks on transactions over a certain value and volume, and even discounts at certain marketplaces [7, 8]. According to the recent data released by RBI [2], it is evident that these initiatives have boosted the use of UPI in terms of the number of transactions as well as the total value of transactions to some extent. The growth in number of UPI-based transactions led to an increase in the total number of electronic transactions in India, especially in the second half of the financial year 2017–2018 [2]. However, the Real Time Gross Settlement and National Electronic Funds Transfer, two modes of electronic payment systems offered as a part of the online banking services provided by the full-service banks, accounted for more than 91% of the value of all electronic transactions [2]. Within the remaining value of about 9%, the total value of UPI-based transactions is found to be minuscule [2].

Though UPI was expected to provide the much-needed push for digital transactions in the country, its adoption has been quite low so far [9, 10]. Several media reports also confirmed that UPI faces resistance from a large majority of consumers who are not innovators or early adopters [11, 12]. A major reason for this resistance may be attributed to the ineffective knowledge transmission about the use of UPI to many consumers who prefer to pay in cash over using online payment methods [12, 13]. According to some of the trusted media houses for financial news in India, UPI has grossly underachieved the desired target of the government [13, 14]. Therefore, we felt it important to investigate the possible causes of consumer resistance to UPI, as an awareness of the causes might help the appropriate bodies work towards achieving better adoption of the payment interface [15].

There is a vast body of literature on the adoption of various digital financial services. However, the majority of these studies are centered around understanding the factors behind the adoption of various digital banking solutions. In contrast, empirical studies examining the reasons for resistance towards the usage of digital financial services are rare. Woodside's seminal work on technology adoption argues that even superior innovations may often be unsuccessful because of a high degree of consumer resistance [15]. Hence, the objective of this study is to identify and examine the factors related to consumer resistance, which affect the intention to continue the usage of UPI. We draw from the Innovation Resistance Theory (IRT) [16], a theoretical framework best suited to examine user resistance associated with the intention to continue UPI usage.

This study extends the original IRT framework through the inclusion of important behavioral measures, namely privacy concerns and visibility. The two main justifications for this model extension by including these specific variables are as follows: First, this study aims to complement the existing list of consumer barriers provided by IRT with other relevant and important variables. Second, relatively recent studies have suggested that variables like privacy-related concerns [17–19] and visibility [16, 20] play an important role in the successful adoption of digital payment solutions. In addition, previous research hints that security concerns may moderate the associations between different barriers and the adoption of digital payment services [21, 22]. Furthermore, we also recognize the possibility of word of mouth (WOM) [23–25] moderating the associations investigated in this study. Hence, the study also examines the moderating influence of security concerns and WOM on the relationship between the different barriers and the users' intention to continue using UPI. Thus, the proposed research model includes seven independent variables associated with the intention to continue using UPI and two interaction variables that may moderate these associations. The study used a cross-sectional data set collected from 714 UPI users aged between 16 and 55 years to test the research model.

The remainder of the article is organized as follows. The Sect. 2 of the paper is dedicated to developing the hypotheses of this study. In the Sect. 3, we report the data that is analyzed to test the different hypotheses. The findings from the analysis are discussed in the Sect. 4. Section 5 concludes the paper with a brief assessment of the limitations of this study and recommendations for future research.

2   Background Literature

Over the years, research on this topic began to polarize into two broad dimensions, namely adoption and resistance. Pioneered by Rogers [26], the first dimension explains how potential users adopt an innovation, whereas the other dimension brings resistance to innovation into focus. However, these two dimensions are not mutually exclusive, as the theory of adoption was later linked to the theory of innovation resistance by Ram and Sheth [16]. Gradually, it was established that the resistance to innovation may determine the popularity of new products and services [16].

2.1   Innovation Resistance Theory (IRT)

IRT is a pioneering theoretical framework for studying consumer resistance toward newer innovations [16]. IRT suggests two main components of innovation resistance, namely functional barriers and psychological barriers. Functional barriers originate in the consumers' perception about the changes from adopting an innovation; whereas psychological barriers arise because of the perceived contradictions with the consumers' prior beliefs while adopting an innovation. While extending the concept introduced by Ram and Sheth [16], many researchers, including Woodside [15], reinforced the argument that superior innovations may fail to achieve commercial success because of consumer resistance. Three recent studies on the digital payment ecosystem in India also support this argument. The first study [27] suggests that although users of mobile banking recognize its benefits, most of them prefer to use cash because of privacy and security concerns. Upadhyay and Jahanyan [28] studied the adoption of mobile-based money transfers and found that value barrier and risk barrier do not hinder the adoption of this technology as much as usage barrier and insufficient technological infrastructure. In the third study, Sivathanu [29] examined the barriers to adoption of digital payment systems and found that innovation resistance creates a barrier toward the usage of digital payment systems in India.

Functional Barriers. There are three types of functional barriers: (a) usage barrier, (b) value barrier, and (c) risk barrier. A usage barrier is observed when a new innovation conflicts with the existing workflows, practices, or habits of the consumers who consequently tend to resist the innovation [16]. This IRT component is similar to 'perceived ease-of-use', an important parameter in the Technology Acceptance Model (TAM) [30]. Furthermore, it is also closely related to complexity, that is, the degree of perceived difficulty by a consumer in understanding and using an innovation as defined by Rogers [26]. Therefore, the importance of usage barrier is recognized in different theories, in different forms, to measure the practical usability of an innovation. Value barrier develops when consumers perceive an innovation to be incapable of delivering better functionalities than the alternative options, for the same economic resources. In such cases, the consumers are less likely to change their present practices and habits [16]. Risk barrier is important because innovations are perceived to come with some inherent risks and the degree of risk determines the risk barrier toward the innovation [16].

Laukkanen and Cruz [31] argue that the usage barrier is probably the strongest among the three aforementioned barriers in the case of resistance to digital banking. Laukkanen and Kiviniemi [32] report that the association of value barrier is important in the case of resistance to mobile banking. Perceived risks related to an innovation are often inherent in its nature and in the case of mobile banking, users generally perceive risk from limited battery life and poor strength of wireless connection [33]. Risk barrier reportedly plays an important role in developing resistance to mobile banking [32]. Many users perceive risks in making mistakes in performing online banking, as they may not be familiar with the processes [34]. Martins, Oliveira, and Popovič [35] report that the association of risk barrier is found to be important in the context of Internet banking. Therefore, we hypothesize that

H1:   *Low usage barrier is positively associated with users' intention to continue the usage of UPI.*

H2:   *Low value barrier is positively associated with users' intention to continue the usage of UPI.*

H3:   *Low risk barrier is positively associated with users' intention to continue the usage of UPI.*

Psychological Barriers. There are two types of psychological barriers: (a) tradition barrier and (b) image barrier. A tradition barrier reflects resistance to the change that an innovation may cause to the daily routines of a consumer [16]. In the case of Internet banking, the tradition barrier may occur if consumers prefer to interact with the banks or to perform banking operations such as payments through traditional means instead of adapting to new technologies [36]. An image barrier arises because of stereotypes about an innovation, which may relate to factors like the country of origin or the associated brand [16]. Over time, it was found that image barrier in the digital banking ecosystem is developed through non-availability of information for the common people [37], frequently failed transactions [32], high adoption costs and lack of demand from the merchant perspective [38].

In the context of our study, both tradition barrier and image barrier may be considered important because UPI intends to reduce dependence on cash – challenging the existing routines for payments and combating prior beliefs that technology use is complicated or "something wrong could happen." In the early days of digital banking, users reportedly preferred to interact with banks to perform banking operations in traditional ways [36]. Later, an exploratory study in four countries with advanced wireless infrastructure revealed that tradition barrier still acts as an important inhibitor in delaying the diffusion of mobile banking services [39]. Laukkanen [33] identified tradition barrier as a key factor for driving the rejection of Internet banking in Finland. A recent study by Park, Jun, and Park [40] reported the importance of habit in using traditional payment methods over mobile payment services in South Korea. Similar findings by Low [41] reinforced the role of tradition barrier in causing user resistance to mobile payment adoption among youths in Malaysia. Laukkanen [33] also reported that image barrier is primarily responsible for driving the rejection of mobile banking. Therefore, we formulate the following hypotheses.

H4: *Low tradition barrier is positively associated with users' intention to continue the usage of UPI.*

H5: *Low image barrier is positively associated with users' intention to continue the usage of UPI.*

2.2 Barriers Emerging from Privacy Concerns and Visibility

According to the extant literature in the domain of digital banking ecosystem, information privacy risk is associated with the concern about the potential compromise of sensitive user information - both personal and financial - that is not meant for unauthorized access [1]. In the context of online banking, users may be concerned about privacy, as personal information such as identity of the user is also exchanged at the time of monetary transactions [42]. Perceived privacy risk is often studied to expand the established theoretical frameworks to understand the issues related to user acceptance of digital payment services [17]. Privacy risk plays a role in creating barriers to the adoption of different modes of digital payment. For instance, in-store mobile payments in France [43], people-to-people (P2P) mobile wallet services in South Africa [18], tap-and-go payments among university students in the US [44], and mobile payments in China [19], all face barriers because of privacy concerns. Even mobile payment services made available worldwide by high-profile technology companies such as Apple, Google, and PayPal are not spared from such concerns [17]. Therefore, we hypothesize that

H6: *Privacy concerns are negatively associated with users' intention to continue the usage of UPI.*

The theory of diffusion of innovation proposes that adoption of an innovation can be better understood as an uncertainty reduction process, where potential adopters accumulate and synthesize information regarding the innovation [26]. Eventually, the rate of adoption of an innovation among the potential adopters is influenced by five perceived characteristics of the innovation. Two such characteristics, namely relative advantage and trialability, pertains to value barrier. Another two characteristics, namely compatibility and complexity are captured in the discussions related to tradition barrier and usage barrier, respectively. The fifth perceived characteristic of innovation is observability that refers to the visibility of usage of an innovation in a society, without changing the measures [26]. The extant literature suggests that more visibility leads to more awareness and results in a higher intention to use technological innovations [45]. Also, a group of adopters may be influenced to adopt mobile internet when they see that many are already using the technology [46, 47]. From the perspective of merchants, higher visibility of mobile payments indicates a steady stream of revenue, which motivates them to allocate resources required for receiving mobile payments [20]. Thus, we formulate the hypothesis:

H7:   *High visibility of UPI is positively associated with users' intention to continue the usage of UPI.*

2.3   Moderating Role of Security Concerns and Word of Mouth (WOM)

Information security is primarily concerned with the extent to which sensitive information such as financial details are perceived as safe to transmit online [1]. Security threats appear when data, either stolen from a hacked device or retrieved from a lost or stolen device, may cost the user financial and non-financial losses [48]. Security-related concerns often raise barriers to the adoption of mobile payment services [17, 48, 49]. Prior literature suggests that security concerns moderate the association between factors influencing the user intentions and the adoption intentions in the context of online banking [21] and mobile banking [22] respectively. Therefore, this study intends to examine whether security concerns exhibit a moderating role in the context of UPI, with the following hypothesis.

H8:   *Security concerns moderate the relationships reported in hypotheses H1 to H7.*

Word-of-Mouth (WOM) refers to peer-to-peer exchange of opinion and information via an informal medium within a society influencing the future intention to use and continue the usage of concerned services in the society [47, 50]. This may be because of a tendency among users to look for experiences derived from personal recommendations, which also influence their usage pattern [51, 52]. Therefore, it is not surprising that a wide range of studies often report that WOM has a moderating influence on various decisions in the context of service economy, such as purchase and re-purchase intention on e-commerce [23, 24], brand trust [53], destination selection and travel intentions [54, 55], and tickets re-purchase intention [25]. Based on these findings, we formulate the following hypothesis to examine if WOM exhibits a moderating role in the context of this study.

H9:   *WOM moderates the relationships reported in hypotheses H1 to H7.*

3 Study Design and Results

3.1 Data Collection

We designed a closed-ended questionnaire with the help of the extant literature. Our study used instruments that most appropriately measured the constructs of our study. Next, we consulted with an expert in the domain to refine the questionnaire. Finally, the respondents were required to choose an option from a five-item Likert scale for a total of 34 statements. The questionnaire also contained eight questions to capture the demographics of our sample (see Table 1). The data were collected during April to July of 2018 from several field studies at the Common Service Centers (CSCs) in different parts of the country. The CSCs are ICT-enabled, government-authorized service delivery points for government services [52]. We reached out to the dedicated departments responsible for providing e-government services in all 29 states in India. With permission from the appropriate authorities, we arranged our visits to several CSCs in five big states, namely Bihar, Haryana, Telangana, Uttar Pradesh, and West Bengal. During the field studies, only those visitors to the CSCs familiar with the usage of UPI were asked to complete a questionnaire. However, 18 completed questionnaires, out of a total of 732, were discarded, as they failed the consistency check. Therefore, our sample is made up of 714 valid responses.

3.2 Data Analysis

We used SPSS 23, AMOS 23, and PROCESS macro in SPSS to perform the required tests. Throughout the analysis, demographic variables, namely age, gender, education, and economic condition were controlled to better understand the relationships under examination [56]. Any change in control variables would skew the results and invalidate the correlation among the constructs involved in the hypotheses. The results suggest that the study measures possessed sufficient convergent validity because the factor loading for the measurement items were above the threshold limit of 0.50 (see Table 2), the average variance extracted (AVE) was above 0.50, and composite reliability (CR) for all the measures was above 0.70 (see Table 3) [57]. The study results also confirmed the presence of sufficient discriminant validity because the correlation between any two variables did not exceed the threshold limit of 0.70, and the square root of AVE was higher than the correlations across constructs [58]. Also, AVE surpassed average shared variance (ASV) as well as maximum shared variance (MSV). The construct reliability was investigated by examining the CR value for the different study measures. The study variables possess sufficient construct reliability because the CR for all study measures was found to be comfortably above 0.70 [57].

It is important to note that two constructs of the study - value barrier and risk barrier - yielded low factor loadings and failed to meet the criteria of validity and reliability for measuring the structural model [57]. Therefore, following the extant literature on theoretical and methodological suggestions for SEM [57, 59], both of these measures were eliminated from the later stages of analysis. However, exclusion of value barrier is not surprising in the context of this study because UPI provides more convenience, benefits, and control to the users than digital banking alternatives. Also, the low cost of

Table 1. Demographic characteristics of the study sample (N = 714)

Demographic measures	Category	Percentage (Frequency)
Age	18 or less	2.2 (16)
	19 – 25	32.4 (231)
	26 – 32	36.4 (260)
	33 – 40	22.8 (163)
	41 – 50	5.5 (39)
	50 or more	0.7 (5)
Gender	Female	34 (243)
	Male	66 (471)
Economic background	Difficult	11 (79)
	So-So	31 (221)
	Middle-Class	45.5 (325)
	Rich	12.5 (89)
Educational background	Higher Secondary or less	20.3 (145)
	Pursuing / completed Under Graduation	51.3 (366)
	Pursuing / completed Post Graduation	23.9 (171)
	Pursuing / completed Doctorate	4.5 (32)
Prior experience of using Mobile banking	Yes	76.8 (548)
	No	23.2 (166)
Prior experience of using Debit / Credit card	Yes	96.4 (688)
	No	3.6 (26)
Prior experience of using Mobile wallets	Yes	71.1 (508)
	No	28.9 (206)
Duration of UPI usage experience	Less than 3 months	13.6 (97)
	3 – 6 months	26.1 (186)
	6 – 12 months	32.6 (233)
	More than 12 months	27.7 (198)

Internet further diminishes any chance of developing value barrier in our context, as low financial cost to access Internet is expected to increase the adoption of Internet-based services. Besides, considering that a UPI-based transaction attracts zero fee, there is limited ability of a value barrier to act as a significant barrier toward the adoption of UPI. For the same reason, there are limited opportunities for economic and functional risks in the context of this study. Besides, in the case of using a smartphone-based app, the significance of physical and social risks is nominal, if not non-existent. Thus, no aspect of the risk barrier was significant in the context of our study and therefore, its exclusion seems justified.

Table 2. Study measures and measurement items

Study Measures (Reference)	Measurement items	Standardized regression weights	
		Measurement Model	Structural Model
Usage Barrier [33]	The use of UPI is clear and understandable.	0.96	0.96
	Using UPI isn't mentally challenging.	0.95	0.95
	It was easy for me to become skillful at using the UPI.	0.96	0.96
Tradition Barrier [33]	I find it difficult to contact customer service at UPI.	0.93	0.93
	I find it difficult to get my problem resolved from UPI.	0.89	0.89
	I find customer service at UPI is not pleasant.	0.92	0.92
	UPI customer service is not good.	0.93	0.93
Image Barrier [33]	In my opinion, UPI is often too complicated to be useful.	0.88	0.88
	I have such an image that UPI is difficult to use.	0.95	0.95
Privacy [17]	I would not feel safe providing personal private information over UPI.	0.95	0.95
	I am worried about other people gaining access to my account if I use UPI.	0.96	0.96
	Using UPI would reveal important financial information.	0.84	0.84
Visibility [46-47]	I have seen others to use UPI.	0.89	0.89
	It is easy to observe UPI being used.	0.81	0.81
	I have often seen others using UPI.	0.85	0.85
Intention to use [33]	I expect my use of UPI to increase in the future.	0.94	0.94
	I intend to continue using UPI in the future.	0.90	0.90
	I shall try to use UPI whenever possible.	0.92	0.92

3.3   Measurement Model

With a $\chi 2$ value of 1451.37 for 369 degrees of freedom, the value of this normed chi-square ratio (C_{min}/df or χ^2/df) stood at 3.93. The ratio represents a satisfactory fit when less than five, considering that the $\chi 2$ statistic is sensitive to sample size, model size, and distribution of data. Hence, we checked other absolute fit indices such as goodness of fit and error of approximation for this model. High values of goodness of fit indices (GFI = 0.87 and AGFI = 0.84) with a presence of low root mean square residual (RMR = 0.04) indicated that the data fits our measurement model well. The value of Root Mean Square Error of Approximation (RMSEA = 0.06 at $p < 0.001$), within a range of 0.061 and 0.068 at 90% confidence interval, is close to the value of perfect fit.

Table 3. Convergent and discriminant validity and measurement reliability

	CR	AVE	MSV	ASV	UPI	UB	TB	IB	PRV	VIS
UPI	0.95	0.85	0.79	0.60	0.92					
UB	0.97	0.91	0.82	0.66	0.89	0.96				
TB	0.96	0.84	0.46	0.35	-0.56	-0.60	0.92			
IB	0.91	0.84	0.82	0.60	-0.78	-0.90	0.64	0.92		
PRV	0.94	0.84	0.82	0.65	-0.88	-0.91	0.68	0.89	0.92	
VIS	0.89	0.72	0.52	0.40	0.70	0.72	-0.45	-0.60	-0.64	0.85

Note: CR = Composite reliability; AVE = Average Variance Extracted; MSV = Maximum Shared Squared Variance; ASV = Average Shared Squared Variance.

Additionally, our model reported satisfactory scores of relative fit indices with respect to a baseline model where all measured variables are uncorrelated. Our model scored comfortably above the cut-off score of 0.90 in Bentler-Bonett Normed Fit Index (NFI = 0.96), Bollen's Incremental Fit Index (IFI = 0.97), and the Tucker-Lewis Index (TLI = 0.96). Also, Bentler's Comparative Fit Index (CFI = 0.97) confirms that our model is not subject to any significant threat posed by the non-centrality problem. Finally, the parsimony adjusted fit indices for our model (PGFI = 0.69, PNFI = 0.81, PCFI = 0.82) signify that it is not too complex.

3.4 Structural Model

The structural model provided satisfactory model fit with a χ^2/df = 4.35; GFI = 0.92; AGFI = 0.89; RMR = 0.05 and RMSEA = 0.07. Baseline fit indices of this model are CFI = 0.98; TLI = 0.97; IFI = 0.98; NFI = 0.97. From the results, we may confirm that usage barrier, image barrier, privacy concerns, and visibility are significantly associated with users' intention to continue the usage of UPI. Thus, hypotheses H1, H5, H7, and H8 are supported. However, as there was no significant association found between tradition barrier and users' intention to continue the usage of UPI, H4 was not supported. In the context of our study, privacy concerns (ß = −0.62) and usage barrier (ß = 0.54) emerged as the strongest variables that correlated with users' intention to continue the usage of UPI, followed by image barrier (ß = 0.31), and visibility (ß = 0.10). In this study, we also examined the role of two moderators in the relationships among the constructs. The results of this analysis are presented in Table 4. The results of the hypotheses testing are presented in Fig. 1. From the results we confirm that security concerns reasonably moderate the association between usage barrier, image barrier, privacy, and visibility and users' intentions to continue the usage of UPI. WOM moderated the association between usage barrier and visibility and users' intention to continue using the UPI. However, we found an insignificant moderating role of security concerns in the association between the tradition barrier and users' intention to continue using the UPI. Also, we found no significant moderating role of WOM in the associations between tradition barrier, image barrier, and privacy concerns, and users' intention to continue the usage of UPI.

Table 4. Moderation results

	β	t	p	LLCI	ULCI	Moderation?
H8: Moderation Results for Security concerns						
UB → UPI	-.04	-3.35	.001	-.0697	-.0182	Yes
TB → UPI	-.02	-1.65	.10	-.0541	.0048	No
IB → UPI	.05	4.17	.000	.0271	.0754	Yes
PRV → UPI	.03	2.19	.029	.0033	.0620	Yes
VIS → UPI	-.06	-3.86	.000	-.0894	-.0291	Yes
H9: Moderation Results for WOM						
UB → UPI	-.001	-.11	.91	-.0253	.0226	No
TB → UPI	-.01	-.43	.67	-.0310	.0198	No
IB → UPI	.02	1.76	.04	-.0023	.0416	Yes
PRV → UPI	.01	.94	.35	-.0140	.0396	No
VIS → UPI	-.03	-1.83	.03	-.0545	.0019	Yes

4   Discussion and Study Implications

The literature on technology use and continuance largely comprises studies focused on understanding the factors contributing toward acceptance, adoption, and use. Scholars have applied different technology acceptance models such as TAM, UTAUT, and UTAUT2 in previous studies. This approach has two main drawbacks. First, these acceptance models are more suitable for analyzing the initial intention to adopt a technology than understanding the intention to continue using the same. Second, prior research on technology acceptance focused on positive contributing factors and ignored reasons behind consumer resistance. This study draws from the innovation resistance theory (IRT) to enrich the prior literature related to continued technology usage. Also, the investigation has extended the original framework of IRT by incorporating two relevant measures, namely privacy concerns and visibility. Besides this, the study used two important moderating variables – security concerns and word of mouth- that may provide valuable insights to the scholars interested in addressing similar research objectives. Thus, this is one of the earliest empirical studies on the intention to continue the usage of UPI and similar new age interface payment services. Consumer resistance toward newer innovations is a major cause of concern for businesses and governments alike. Thus, the current examination of user resistance toward UPI is timely and addresses a growing need of the present times. Consequently, the research model

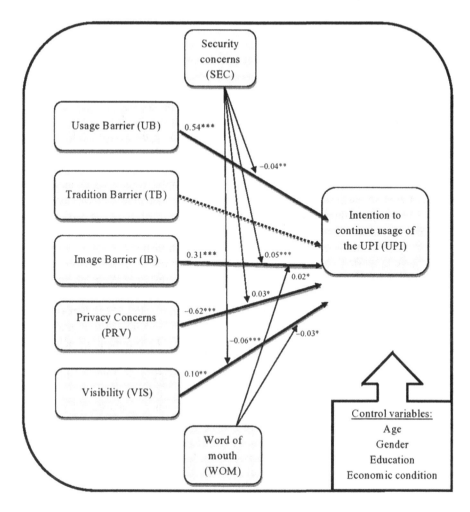

Fig. 1. Results of Structural model

Note: *** p<0.001; ** p<0.01; * p<0.05.
Thick arrows, thin arrows and the dotted arrow represent supported hypotheses, moderation and unsupported hypotheses, respectively.
Hypotheses H2 and H3 were not examined since both value and risk barriers did not satisfy the minimum thresholds set for ensuring construct validity and reliability.

proposed in this paper significantly contributes to the literature related to e-governance and digital payments.

The strong support for H1 that examined if a low usage barrier is positively associated with users' intention to continue the usage of UPI is consistent with the majority of the prior literature available in the context of digital banking [31], mobile commerce [60], and mobile payment services [38]. Furthermore, prior literature also supports the significant role of usage barriers in developing countries [61, 62]. To lower the existing usage barriers, mass awareness should be increased and the citizens need to be educated about how to use UPI. It is important that citizens of all socio-economic divisions come to realize that UPI is easy to use and can replace several inconvenient aspects of physical transactions. Hypotheses H2 and H3 were not examined in this study, as value barrier and risk barrier did not satisfy the minimum thresholds set for ensuring construct validity and reliability.

The study findings did not support H4, which proposed that low tradition barrier is positively associated with a users' intention to continue the usage of UPI. This is inconsistent with most of the prior literature available in the context of digital banking and payment systems [33, 39–41]. A possible reason for this could be that the over-whelming majority of the UPI users in the data sample were already familiar with various forms of cashless payments. Hence, they may perceive that UPI brought no significant change to their daily routines and habits. Therefore, tradition barrier may not influence the users' intention to continue the usage of UPI. We interpret this as a positive sign for the overall digital payment ecosystem in India.

H5 was supported, which suggests that low image barrier is positively associated with users' intention to continue using UPI. This suggests the need for diminishing negative stereotypes about UPI. As discussed previously, non-availability of infor-mation for the common people [37], frequently failed transactions [32], lack of demand from the merchant's perspective [38], and security concerns related to digital services [35, 38] are the major causes that build image barriers. Government agencies should focus on resolving issues regarding transaction failures and security concerns, encourage merchants to improve acceptability, and ensure availability of information about UPI to reduce the possible image barriers.

H6, which suggested that privacy concerns are negatively associated with users' intention to continue the usage of UPI, was supported. This finding is largely consistent with the extant literature that indicates that privacy concerns negatively influence the adoption-related decisions [17–19, 43, 44]. Government agencies need to reassure the citizens about privacy protection when it comes to the usage of UPI. The policymakers may implement systematic solutions like regulation of machine-to-machine data transfer, supervision of data release to unauthorized organizations, and protection of financial details and personal information [63]. Additionally, the cyber laws need to be periodically upgraded to match the demands of the fast-changing information-processing environment.

H7 was supported, which suggested that the high visibility of UPI in the society is positively associated with users' intention to continue the usage of UPI. This is con-sistent with prior literature that suggests a positive association between visibility and technology adoption [20, 46]. To improve the visibility of UPI usage among peers, the government may launch community-based activities. Higher educational institutes, or public and private organizations may be encouraged to arrange similar activities. If the merchants, especially those in unorganized retail, are incentivized to accept UPI-based payments, visibility among the peers may be highly improved, even in rural areas.

H8, which indicated that security partially moderates the association between dif-ferent predictor variables and users' intention to continue the usage of UPI, was par-tially supported. To be specific, security concerns exert a moderating impact on the associations involving usage barrier, image barrier, privacy concerns, and visibility with users' intention to continue the usage of UPI. The finding is consistent with prior literature on digital payment services [17, 21, 22, 48, 49]. NPCI has promised strong end-to-end security and high level of data protection by the government, especially in digital payments [64, 65]. Besides, neither the sender nor the receiver needs to reveal much sensitive data while using UPI, if both parties have VPAs. Additionally, to protect the users against unethical hacking and phishing, UPI requires two-factor authentication from the user's side—one to start a transaction session and the other to authenticate after confirming a transaction. Therefore, government agencies have to communicate in clear terms that security need not be a major concern for UPI users, while dedicated cyber security teams should relentlessly work on ensuring protection against data theft and misuse of stolen data.

H9 proposed that WOM partially moderates the association of different barriers, privacy, and visibility with users' intention to continue the usage of UPI. This hypothesis was partially supported. Specifically, the results suggest that WOM moderated the association between usage barrier and visibility and users' intention to continue using UPI. Our finding is in partial agreement with previous research that suggested a significant moderating role of WOM [23–25]. The findings indicate that government agencies should advertise the various benefits of UPI to create positive WOM. Furthermore, they should incentivize community leaders to spread positive WOM and discuss UPI from verified accounts on various social media platforms to spread good electronic WOM.

5   Limitations and Future Scope

This study includes only the constructs that are relevant to continuous usage of UPI and, hence, some of the findings of this research may be limited to the context of India. It is important that future studies test our model in other contexts to validate our study results. In the case of other innovations similar to UPI, there may exist more relevant constructs, which can possibly explain the usage behavior of those innovations. For example, different forms of trust such as trust on a technology and trust on government agencies providing the technology. Future research may also borrow measures from other theories to extend our research model, which is developed using IRT as a baseline theory. The study design may aid scholars interested in conducting empirical studies on user barriers toward continuous usage of UPI or similar financial services in other countries. Furthermore, the study design can guide scholars interested in understanding consumer resistance toward different e-government issues, especially those involving digital financial services. Therefore, this study may interest researchers who investigate whether innovative payment methods influence purchasing behavior. Besides, this paper potentially provides valuable insights to the scholars examining online businesses, as different forms of electronic banking may play an important role in the development of those businesses.

We acknowledge the possibility of potential bias in our data collection method that relied on a cross-sectional design. Future research may use other techniques such as qualitative data, and experimental or longitudinal design to overcome such biases and deploy resources accordingly. For example, a longitudinal study to analyze the behavioral intention over time, would overcome the inherent limitation of a cross-sectional study. Also, this paper has validated a conceptual model for analyzing users' intention to continue the usage of UPI. Future research may analyze actual usage behavior instead of expressed intention to do that. Alternatively, a qualitative research or an experimental design-oriented study would help comprehend the enrollment and detachment processes among the users. Our study focuses on the individual users. Researchers may examine group level respondents such as UPI users within a university where peers may play much stronger role. It may also be interesting to explore the perspectives about UPI from individuals with low or no experience of using digital payments. Research can also be conducted to understand the merchants' perspective. UPI is fairly new as a method of payment and the behavioral intention of users is expected to evolve as the ecosystem surrounding this method matures. Therefore, similar empirical studies may be conducted in future to capture this evolution.

References

1. Khanra, S., Dhir, A., Mäntymäki, M.: Big data analytics and enterprises: a bibliometric synthesis of the literature. Enterp. Inf. Syst. **14**(6), 737–768 (2020). https://doi.org/10.1080/17517575.2020.1734241
2. National Payments Corporation of India. https://www.npci.org.in/product-overview/upi-product-overview. Accessed 10 Oct 2020
3. Business Standards Report. http://tiny.cc/Asthana. Accessed 10 Oct 2020
4. FIS Flavours of fast Report. http://tiny.cc/FIS2015. Accessed 10 Oct 10 Oct 2020
5. Deloitte Report. http://tiny.cc/deloittepayment. Accessed 10 Oct 2020
6. Harvard Business Review Note. http://tiny.cc/HBRspl. Accessed 10 Oct 2020
7. Inc 42 Report. http://tiny.cc/inc42. Accessed 10 Oct 2020
8. Livemint Repor. http://tiny.cc/bhimreferral. Accessed 10 Oct 2020
9. The Economic Times Report. http://tiny.cc/demonitization. Accessed 10 Oct 2020
10. Livemint Report. http://tiny.cc/nilekani. Accessed 10 Oct 2020
11. The Economic Times Report. http://tiny.cc/bhakta. Accessed 10 Oct 2020
12. The Wire Report. http://tiny.cc/thewire. Accessed 10 Oct 2020
13. The Economic Times Report. http://tiny.cc/25bn. Accessed 10 Oct 2020
14. Financial Express Report. http://tiny.cc/finxp. Accessed 10 Oct 2020
15. Woodside, A.G.: Theory of rejecting superior, new technologies. J. Bus. Ind. Mark. **11**(3/4), 25–43 (1996). https://doi.org/10.1108/08858629610125450
16. Ram, S., Sheth, J.N.: Consumer resistance to innovations: the marketing problem and its solutions. J. Consum. Mark. **6**(2), 5–14 (1989). https://doi.org/10.1108/eum0000000002542
17. Johnson, V.L., Kiser, A., Washington, R., Torres, R.: Limitations to the rapid adoption of M-payment services: understanding the impact of privacy risk on M-Payment services. Comput. Hum. Behav. **79**, 111–122 (2018). https://doi.org/10.1016/j.chb.2017.10.035
18. Matemba, E.D., Li, G.: Consumers' willingness to adopt and use WeChat wallet: an empirical study in South Africa. Technol. Soc. **53**, 55–68 (2017). https://doi.org/10.1016/j.techsoc.2017.12.001
19. Su, P., Wang, L., Yan, J.: How users' Internet experience affects the adoption of mobile payment: a mediation model. Technol. Anal. Strateg. Manag. **30**(2), 186–197 (2018). https://doi.org/10.1080/09537325.2017.1297788

20. Carton, F., Hedman, J., Damsgaard, J., Tan, K.T., McCarthy, J.B.: Framework for mobile payments integration. Electron. J. Inf. Syst. Eval. **15**(1), 14–25 (2012). http://cora.ucc.ie/handle/10468/2910

21. Mangin, J.P.L.: The moderating role of risk, security and trust applied to the TAM model in the offer of banking financial services in Canada. J. Internet Bank. Commerc. **19**(2) (2014)

22. Yoon, H.S., Occeña, L.U.I.S.: Impacts of customers' perceptions on internet banking use with a smart phone. J. Comput. Inf. Syst. **54**(3), 1–9 (2014). https://doi.org/10.1080/08874417.2014.11645699

23. Khare, A., Labrecque, L.I., Asare, A.K.: The assimilative and contrastive effects of word-of-mouth volume: an experimental examination of online consumer ratings. J. Retail. **87**(1), 111–126 (2011).https://doi.org/10.1016/j.jretai.2011.01.005

24. Kuo, Y.F., Hu, T.L., Yang, S.C.: Effects of inertia and satisfaction in female online shoppers on repeat-purchase intention: the moderating roles of word-of-mouth and alternative attraction. Manag. Serv. Qual. Int. J. **23**(3), 168–187 (2013). https://doi.org/10.1108/09604521311312219

25. Saleem, M.A., Zahra, S., Yaseen, A.: Impact of service quality and trust on repurchase intentions–the case of Pakistan airline industry. Asia Pac. J. Mark. Logist. **29**(5), 1136–1159 (2017). https://doi.org/10.1108/apjml-10-2016-0192

26. Rogers, E.M.: Diffusion of innovations: an overview. In: Anderson, J.G., Jay, S.J. (eds.) Use and Impact of Computers in Clinical Medicine, pp. 113–131. Springer, New York (1981). https://doi.org/10.1007/978-1-4613-8674-2_9

27. Bhatt, A., Bhatt, S.: Factors affecting customers adoption of mobile banking services. J. Internet Bank. Commerc. **21**(1) (2016)

28. Upadhyay, P., Jahanyan, S.: Analyzing user perspective on the factors affecting use intention of mobile based transfer payment. Internet Res. **26**(1), 38–56 (2016). https://doi.org/10.1108/intr-05-2014-0143

29. Sivathanu, B.: Adoption of digital payment systems in the era of demonetization in India: an empirical study. J. Sci. Technol. Policy Manag. **10**(1), 143–171 (2018). https://doi.org/10.1108/JSTPM-07-2017-0033

30. Davis, F.D., Bagozzi, R.P., Warshaw, P.R.: User acceptance of computer technology: a comparison of two theoretical models. Manag. Sci. **35**(8), 982–1003 (1989). https://doi.org/10.1287/mnsc.35.8.982

31. Laukkanen, T., Cruz, P.: What determines mobile banking non-adoption? In: Proceedings of Australian and New Zealand Marketing Academy Conference 2010. ANZMAC, Christchurch (2010)

32. Laukkanen, T., Kiviniemi, V.: The role of information in mobile banking resistance. Int. J. Bank Mark. **28**(5), 372–388 (2010). https://doi.org/10.1108/02652321011064890

33. Laukkanen, T.: Consumer adoption versus rejection decisions in seemingly similar service innovations: the case of the Internet and mobile banking. J. Bus. Res. **69**(7), 2432–2439 (2016). https://doi.org/10.1016/j.jbusres.2016.01.013

34. Kuisma, T., Laukkanen, T., Hiltunen, M.: Mapping the reasons for resistance to Internet banking: a means-end approach. Int. J. Inf. Manag. **27**(2), 75–85 (2007). https://doi.org/10.1016/j.ijinfomgt.2006.08.006

35. Martins, C., Oliveira, T., Popovič, A.: Understanding the Internet banking adoption: a unified theory of acceptance and use of technology and perceived risk application. Int. J. Inf. Manag. **34**(1), 1–13 (2014). https://doi.org/10.1016/j.ijinfomgt.2013.06.002

36. Heinonen, K.: Reconceptualizing customer perceived value: the value of time and place. Manag. Serv. Qual. Int. J. (2004). https://doi.org/10.1108/09604520410528626

37. Laukkanen, T., Sinkkonen, S., Laukkanen, P.: Communication strategies to overcome functional and psychological resistance to Internet banking. Int. J. Inf. Manag. **29**(2), 111–118 (2009). https://doi.org/10.1016/j.ijinfomgt.2008.05.008

38. Liébana-Cabanillas, F., Lara-Rubio, J.: Predictive and explanatory modeling regarding adoption of mobile payment systems. Technol. Forecast. Soc. Change **120**, 32–40 (2017). https://doi.org/10.1016/j.techfore.2017.04.002

39. Luo, X., Lee, C.P., Mattila, M., Liu, L.: An exploratory study of mobile banking services resistance. Int. J. Mob. Commun. **10**(4), 366–385 (2012). https://doi.org/10.1504/ijmc.2012.048136

40. Park, M., Jun, J., Park, H.: Understanding mobile payment service continuous use intention: an expectation-confirmation model and inertia. Qual. Innov. Prosperity **21**(3), 78 (2017). https://doi.org/10.12776/qip.v21i3.983

41. Low, K.H.: Factor affecting consumer resistance to Paypal mobile payment adoption: a study of generation X consumers. Doctoral dissertation, Universiti Tunku Abdul Rahman (2017). http://eprints.utar.edu.my/2427/1/Thesis_(PayPal).pdf

42. Chang, Y., Wong, S.F., Libaque-Saenz, C.F., Lee, H.: The role of privacy policy on consumers' perceived privacy. Gov. Inf. Q. **35**(3), 445–459 (2018). https://doi.org/10.1016/j.giq.2018.04.002

43. De Kerviler, G., Demoulin, N.T., Zidda, P.: Adoption of in-store mobile payment: are perceived risk and convenience the only drivers? J. Retail. Consum. Serv. **31**, 334–344 (2016). https://doi.org/10.1016/j.jretconser.2016.04.011

44. Bailey, A.A., Pentina, I., Mishra, A.S., Ben Mimoun, M.S.: Mobile payments adoption by US consumers: an extended TAM. Int. J. Retail Distrib. Manag. **45**(6), 626–640 (2017). https://doi.org/10.1108/ijrdm-08-2016-0144

45. Cruz, P., Barretto Filgueiras Neto, L., Munoz-Gallego, P., Laukkanen, T.: Mobile banking rollout in emerging markets: evidence from Brazil. Int. J. Bank Mark. **28**(5), 342–371 (2010). https://doi.org/10.1108/02652321011064881

46. Hsu, C.L., Lu, H.P., Hsu, H.H.: Adoption of the mobile internet: an empirical study of multimedia message service (MMS). Omega **35**(6), 715–726 (2007). https://doi.org/10.1016/j.omega.2006.03.005

47. Khanra, S., Joseph, R.P., Ruparel, N.: Dynamism of an e-government network in delivering public services. In: Academy of Management Global Proceedings Slovenia 2019, p. 376. Academy of Management, New York (2019)

48. Liu, Y.: Consumer protection in mobile payments in China: a critical analysis of Alipay's service agreement. Comput. Law Secur. Rev. **31**(5), 1–10 (2015). https://doi.org/10.1016/j.clsr.2015.05.009

49. Oliveira, T., Thomas, M., Baptista, G., Campos, F.: Mobile payment: understanding the determinants of customer adoption and intention to recommend the technology. Comput. Hum. Behav. **61**, 404–414 (2016). https://doi.org/10.1016/j.chb.2016.03.030

50. Arndt, J.: Word-of-mouth advertising and of informal communication. In: Cox, F. (ed.) Risk Taking and Information Handling in Consumer Behaviour, pp. 188–239. Harvard University Press, Cambridge (1967)

51. Anderson, E.W.: Customer satisfaction and word of mouth. J. Serv. Res. **1**(1), 5–17 (1998). https://doi.org/10.1177/109467059800100102

52. Khanra, S., Joseph, R.P.: Adoption of e-governance: the mediating role of language proficiency and digital divide in an emerging market context. Transforming Gov. People Process Policy **13**(2), 122–142 (2019). https://doi.org/10.1108/tg-12-2018-0076

53. Lock, A.C.: Impact of brand knowledge on brand trust in private higher education institutions: how do word of mouth sources intervene'. Sarjana **31**(2), 13–32 (2016)

54. Ishida, K., Slevitch, L., Siamionava, K.: The effects of traditional and electronic word-of-mouth on destination image: a case of vacation tourists visiting Branson, Missouri. Adm. Sci. **6**(4), 12 (2016). https://doi.org/10.3390/admsci6040012

55. Jalilvand, M.R., Samiei, N., Dini, B., Manzari, P.Y.: Examining the structural relationships of electronic word of mouth, destination image, tourist attitude toward destination and travel intention: an integrated approach. J. Destination Mark. Manag. **1**(1), 134–143 (2012). https://doi.org/10.1016/j.jdmm.2012

56. Khanra, S., Joseph, R.P.: Adoption and diffusion of e-government services: the impact of demography and service quality. In: De Baguma, R., Janowski, T. (eds.) The 10th International Conference on Theory and Practice of Electronic Governance 2017, pp. 602–605. Association for Computing Machinery, New York (2017). https://doi.org/10.1145/3047273.3047301

57. Hair, J., Black, W., Babin, B., Anderson, R.: Multivariate Data Analysis a Global Perspective, 7th edn. Prentice Hall, Upper Saddle River (2010)

58. Fornell, C., Larcker, D.F.: Evaluating structural equation models with unobservable variables and measurement error. J. Mark. Res. **18**(1), 39–50 (1981). https://doi.org/10.1177/002224378101800104

59. Farrell, A.M.: Insufficient discriminant validity: a comment on Bove, Pervan, Beatty, and Shiu (2009). J. Bus. Res. **63**(3), 324–327 (2010). https://doi.org/10.1016/j.jbusres.2009.05.003

60. Bouwman, H., Carlsson, C., Molina-Castillo, F.J., Walden, P.: Barriers and drivers in the adoption of current and future mobile services in Finland. Telemat. Inform. **24**(2), 145–160 (2007). https://doi.org/10.1016/j.tele.2006.08.001

61. Rahman, M.M.: Barriers to M-commerce adoption in developing countries-a qualitative study among the stakeholders of Bangladesh. Int. Technol. Manag. Rev. **3**(2), 80–91 (2013). https://doi.org/10.2991/itmr.2013.3.2.2

62. Suki, N.M.: Factors affecting third generation (3G) mobile service acceptance: evidence from Malaysia. J. Internet Bank. Commerc. **16**(1), 1–12 (2011)

63. Khanra, S., Joseph, R.P.: E-governance maturity models: a meta-ethnographic study. Int. Technol. Manag. Rev. **8**(1), 1–9 (2019). https://doi.org/10.2991/itmr.b.190417.001

64. The Quint Report. http://tiny.cc/thequint. Accessed 10 Oct 2020

65. Firstpost Report. http://tiny.cc/madanapalle. Accessed 10 Oct 2020

Understanding the Challenges of Mandatory Telework Adoption and Its Effect on Employee Engagement

Harshit Kumar Singh[✉] and Sanjay Verma

Indian Institute of Management Ahmedabad, Ahmedabad, India
{phdl6harshits,sverma}@iima.ac.in

Abstract. Telework is increasingly becoming more prevalent over the last few decades. Mandatory teleworking is an unforeseeable side-effect of the recent pandemic. Managers and employees are inexperienced in handing large scale adoption of telework. The challenges of these implementations need to be explored in detail to develop counter-strategies. The study collected data from 231 managers across industries on these challenges and their effects through an online survey. These managers are part of active teleworking teams. We find that the challenges present by the large-scale mandatory telework affect employees' perceived autonomy, which subsequently increases the work monotonicity. This has an adverse effect on the work engagement of employees in organizations. A framework detailing the challenges and its outcomes has been presented and empirically tested as part of this research initiative.

Keywords: Telework · Autonomy · Employee engagement

1 Introduction

Telework, also referred to as telecommuting, or commonly known as work-fromhome, has been adopted by organizations worldwide due to the recent pandemic. It is a work practice where employees of an organization do not physically travel to the work location but use technology as a medium to work remotely with virtual presence (Nilles 1991). Although the last two decades have seen a plethora of research on telework, its implementation on this scale has not been analyzed in the extant literature. Further, the abrupt and mandatory nature of the adoption further differentiates the current implementations of telework from earlier.

Well-functioning organizations are often constrained in their ability to adapt to a change in work practices. The adoption of telework on a bigger scale has traditionally been a challenge (Silva 2019). The outlook of non-adopters towards telework has been non-aspirational, which acted as a barrier to the introduction of the process itself (Illegems and Verbeke 2004). Such organizations are inexperienced in handling the sudden shift towards telework, which presents a new set of challenges for them. Even for organizations that were able to adopt teleworking on some scale, the research has found a mixture of positive and negative outcomes of telework in organizations (Chung and Van der Horst 2018; Martin and MacDonnell 2012; Steward 2000; de Vries et al. 2019).

© IFIP International Federation for Information Processing 2020
Published by Springer Nature Switzerland AG 2020
S. K. Sharma et al. (Eds.): TDIT 2020, IFIP AICT 618, pp. 626–637, 2020.
https://doi.org/10.1007/978-3-030-64861-9_54

In this paper, we explore how this sudden shift towards telework on a large scale has affected employees' engagement levels. There are three aspects in which the current research contributes to the literature on telework. First, we explore the challenges that teleworkers face while experiencing a large scale implementation of the practice. Although present in the literature, these challenges have not been explored on this scale of telework. Second, the abrupt nature of the telework implementation across organizations helps in understanding the psychological and behavioral effects of these challenges on the employees in its raw form. Third, the mandatory nature of the telework in this context provides us the opportunity to study these effects across industries. We call this telework implementation mandatory as the organizations across the world have no other option than implementing telework if they are to continue operating in this scenario.

To understand the effect of telework on engagement, we analyze the change in employees' autonomy support due to telework implementations. Autonomy is considered to be one of the primary psychological needs that affect employees' motivation at the workplace (Deci and Ryan 2010). It is defined as the perception of having control over one's actions. A lack of autonomy can have a detrimental effect on the engagement levels of employees in the workplace. We further argue that an increase in work monotonicity mediates this decrease in engagement levels. A lack of autonomy is expected to result in work monotonicity (Loukidou et al. 2009). Telework can have an indirect relation with work monotonicity through stress and anxiety (Tavares 2017).

To conclude, we explore the challenges that employees face while teleworking and the effect of these challenges on employee engagement through the changes in autonomy support, and monotonicity. We present a framework that details the relationship between these challenges to understand them better and to prepare countermeasures.

2 Literature Review and Hypotheses Formation

2.1 Employee Engagement and Telework

Employee engagement is a crucial part of any organization. Some of the direct benefits of an engaged employee include job satisfaction, organizational commitment, employee retention, and an increase in organizational citizenship behaviour (Saks 2006). These factors directly affect the employees' productivity and efficiency, which in turn affect the business output of any organization (Harter et al. 2002).

Telework has seen mixed results in terms of its effect on employee engagement. Studies have shown negative (Sardeshmukh et al. 2012), positive (Demerouti et al. 2014), and no effect (de Vries et al. 2019) of telework on employee engagement. We explore how the psychological outcome of the lack of autonomy in the form of workmonotonicity transfers to behavioural outcomes through engagement. We believe that exploring these mediating variables will shed a better light on the effect of telework on employee engagement.

2.2 Challenges of Teleworking

Telework has been an area of active research, but it has not seen a very active adoption in organizations, as shown by research initiatives periodically (Atkin and Lau 2007; Martin and MacDonnell 2012; Silva 2019). The primary barriers that inhibit the adoption of the practice are discussed in the section.

Availability of Time as a Resource. Lack of time as a resource and its management is one of the primary challenges of telework. The employees are often expected to work beyond the official working hours (Abendroth and Reimann 2018). A common outcome of this is overwork and long work hours while teleworking (Pinsonneault and Boisvert 2001). This leads to stress, fatigue, sleeping problems, anxiety, and a reduction in the number of work-breaks, which affects the functioning of employees (Tavares 2017). Often, the time saved from traveling while teleworking goes into the work-hours, increasing the work-load further (Quoquab and Malik 2013). Time-planning becomes an essential skill, and lack of freedom of time-planning directly affects the autonomy of workers (Nakrošienė et al. 2019). We hypothesize that this lack of availability time and loss of control over work induces a sense of autonomy loss for the employees, which gives us our first hypothesis:

H1:   Availability of time resource will be positively related to the perceived autonomy of employees.

Communication Satisfaction. Another major challenge while teleworking is the lack of face-to-face communication (Greer and Payne 2014), which presents its own set of challenges in terms of communications and collaborations.

First, team managers' direct supervision becomes difficult while teleworking (Quoquab and Malik 2013), which induces a loss of control for teams whose functioning depends on collaborations. Second, lack of physical cues and in-person interaction while communicating virtually causes increased misunderstandings between team members and can also lead to depletion of trust over time (Nandhakumar and Baskerville 2006). Third, communication itself becomes less efficient while teleworking, and it has been reported to be failing when extensive meetings are required as part of work tasks (Sharit and Czaja 2009). Fourth, unreliable internet connections can hinder communication efficiency. As telework is heavily dependent on technology, slow network connections add overhead to the communication process (Lewis 2013). Further, as organizations worldwide shift to telework, more congestion in the network can be expected, which will make effective communication more difficult.

All the factors discussed here are expected to directly affect employees' autonomy as communication inefficiency can affect the perceived autonomy of employees at the workplace (Brunetto and Farr-Wharton 2004). Hence our second hypothesis is as follows:

H2:   Communication satisfaction will be positively related to the perceived autonomy of employees.

Perceived Web Security. Accessibility to confidential data and concerns over sharing organizational information over the internet is another challenge of telework. Secure access to proprietary technology is not available, and security is always a concern even when it is available. (Pinsonneault and Boisvert 2001). Access to specific resources or data sources is often location-based, which is difficult to acquire over telework. Even when secure channels are available, a failure in these channels is always possible, limiting the employees' control over access to resources, which forms the basis of our third hypothesis:

H3:   *Perceived web security will be positively related to the perceived autonomy of employees.*

2.3   Autonomy Support and Work Monotonicity

An employee functions in a very different environment from their usual workspace while teleworking. We posit that this change in the environment affects the employee's motivation towards the work, and we use autonomy to analyze the effect of this change. Autonomy is one of the basic needs at the workplace and has been found to affect employee productivity, creativity, and engagement levels (Naotunna and Zhou 2018; Johannsen and Zak 2020; Malinowska et al. 2018). Organizations perceive a loss of control over employees who are teleworking (Quoquab and Malik 2013) and try to regain this control through additional monitoring and reporting mechanisms, which further reduces autonomy support.

Traditionally, telework is expected to increase employee's autonomy as the teleworkers are not in the direct supervision of their managers and supervisors, and are expected to gain a sense of increased freedom over their work tasks (Nakrošienė et al. 2019). However, other research initiatives have shown that this is not always the case. As argued by Sewell and Taskin (2015), even when managers are not present physically with teleworkers, they leverage technology to maintain the control and monitoring of employees on the same level as when the employees are under direct supervision. Also, employees who have a well-developed sense of self-determination at work are likely to perceive telework as a loss of autonomy. The context of this study is expected to have a similar effect on employees. As the change towards the telework was sudden and on a much larger scale, many employees will experience this loss of autonomy as a result of the challenges discussed earlier.

A lack of autonomy can cause workers to experience monotonicity and routineness (Loukidou et al. 2009). Employees tend to become passive and less creative as autonomy in the workplace decreases.

H4:   *Perceived fulfilment of autonomy will have a negative relation with work monotonicity.*

2.4 Work Monotonicity and Employee Engagement

Work monotonicity has been indirectly associated with telework in the literature. Telework results in social isolation, lack of career opportunities, and depression, leading to work monotonicity (Tavares 2017). As the employees are away from the workplace, their inability to control and affect work content and practices often limit their engagement with work. Loneliness and worry are side-effects of separation from workspace, which can further add to the routineness of the work (Mann and Holdsworth 2003).

Activated employees are engaged more towards work than employees who find their work monotonous or boring (Schaufeli and Salanova 2007). Soane et al. (2012) list three types of engagements at workplace - intellectual, social, and affective engagement. Authors defined intellectual engagement as 'the extent to which one is intellectually absorbed in work', social engagement as 'the extent to which one is socially connected with the working environment and shares common values with colleagues,' and affective engagement as 'the extent to which one experiences a state of positive affect relating to one's work role.' Each type reflects a different aspect of engagement, and work monotonicity can affect each one differently. We explore the effect of work monotonicity on all three types of engagement (Fig. 1).

H5a: Work monotonicity will have a negative relation with intellectual engagement.
H5b: Work monotonicity will have a negative relation with social engagement.
H5c: Work monotonicity will have a negative relation with affective engagement.

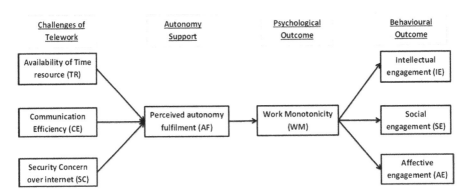

Fig. 1. Research model

3 Research Methods

3.1 Sample and Data Collection

To collect data for our study, we emailed our survey to a total of 800 managers across several industries. The email detailed the purpose of the study and the participants had the option to remain anonymous or provide their email ID for further correspondence to discuss the topic if necessary. We received 269 responses, of which 231 were usable, which provides an effective return rate of 28.97%. All the respondents are currently managing teleworking teams. A total of 92 participants choose to remain anonymous, while 139 participants provided their email for further correspondence. The participants consisted of 202 males and 29 females. The age of 13 participants was in the range of 20–30 years, 140 were in the range of 30–40 years, 76 were in the range of 40–50 years, and 2 were above 50 years. The number of people that they interacted with via telework daily was in the range 5–10 for 69 participants, 10–20 for 94 participants, 20–50 for 64 participants, and more than 50 for 4 participants. The functional areas that the participants worked in covered marketing, sales, support, research and development, information technology, business management, product management, human resources, and operations. Most of the participants were leading employees from multiple functional areas. The industries covered included software and IT, ecommerce, healthcare, education, banking, telecommunications, retail, FMCG, and media organizations.

The questionnaires were prepared to measure the perceived challenges that emerged due to the sudden large scale implantation of teleworking practice and their psychological and behavioral effects on five-point scales (1 = 'strongly disagree' to 5 = 'strongly agree'). These questionnaires were prepared from previous studies, which have been detailed in the next sections.

3.2 Variable Measurement

Here we discuss in brief the instruments used to measure the latent constructs in our study.

Employee Engagement. Employee engagement is the dependent variable in our study and is measured through the ISA Engagement scale developed by Soane et al. (2012). The ISA engagement scale measures the intellectual (IE), social (SE), and affective (AE) engagement of employees. The scale consists of nine items, where three items represent each of the sub-constructs.

Time Resource (TR). Time resource is used as an independent variable in our study. To measure the availability of time as a resource, we use the scale provided by Rowland et al. (1985). This scale is used to measure the 'perceived adequacy of time resources' as mentioned by the authors and contains three items.

Security Concerns Over Internet (SC). Perceived security concerns over the internet while teleworking is another independent variable that we used to measure the perceived challenges of telework. We adapted from the scale presented by Salisbury et al. (2001). The scale measured the perceived comfort of using the internet to communicate and exchange work-related information.

Communication Efficiency (CE). To measure the perceived challenges in communication, scales have been adapted from Yen and Tu (2008) and Steele and Plenty (2015). The questions used in the scale measure the efficiency of virtual communication with colleagues and supervisors while teleworking.

Perceived Autonomy Fulfilment (AF). We adapted the scale to measure the autonomy from Jang et al. (2009) and Sheldon et al. (2001). The scale measures the basic need satisfaction for autonomy in employees.

Work Monotonicity (WM). To measure the psychological outcome in our framework, we measure the subjective monotonicity of the work. We adapt form the scale used by Melamed et al. (1995).

Control Variables. For control variables, we measure age, gender, total work experience. We also control for the prior experience for telework experience as this can affect the perceived effect of the challenges faced by telework. Any previous knowledge in handling the effects of the challenges is controlled through this items. Further, we controlled for the number of people that the participants interact with daily. The effect of challenges on employees that telework present may differ depending on the number of people that the employees interact with as the communications will get more complicated. This can also affect the time management of employees. We control for these effects through this item.

3.3   Validity and Reliability of Measures

To measure the internal consistency of the constructs, we calculated the Cronbach's alpha for each of the constructs, which are listed in Table 1. As we can see from the table, all the constructs have accepted reliability levels, donated by Cronbach's alpha of more than 0.70 (Nunnally 1994). We use R to calculate the Cronbach's alpha of the constructs.

Table 1. Squared correlations, average variance explained, composite reliability and Cronbach's alpha

	CR	AVE	SC	WM	IE	SE	AE	TR	CE	AF	α
SC	0.85	0.65	0.81								0.84
WE	0.74	0.50	−0.20	0.71							0.77
IE	0.86	0.67	0.27	−0.37	0.82						0.86
SE	0.88	0.71	0.30	−0.52	0.85	0.84					0.88
AE	0.82	0.60	0.28	−0.24	0.53	0.50	0.78				0.82
TR	0.77	0.53	0.09	−0.25	0.33	0.42	0.23	0.73			0.77
CE	0.75	0.50	0.74	−0.42	0.52	0.55	0.38	0.26	0.71		0.75
AF	0.74	0.50	0.25	−0.35	0.52	0.51	0.37	0.48	0.46	0.71	0.72

To measure the validity of the constructs, we used confirmatory factor analysis (CFA) technique using AMOS software. After the initial analysis, some of the items were dropped as they were loading poorly to the underlying constructs. The new model with dropped items was analyzed again, and the resulting model had an acceptable fit. The $\chi2$/d.f. value of the used model is 1.430; CFI is 0.96; IFI is 0.96; GFI is 0.90; and

RMSEA is 0.04, which represents good model fit indices. Next, the convergent validity and discriminant validity of the model was tested, and the resulting model indices are listed in Table 1. Convergent validity of all the variables is within the acceptable range, while divergent validity for intellectual engagement and social engagement lies on the boundary acceptable range. This is presumably due to the measurement of engagement by both the variables.

4   Results and Discussion

4.1   Test of Hypotheses

To test the hypotheses, we again used the AMOS software to carry out the path analysis. The base model was tested using the independent variables, mediators, and the control variables. Figure 2 describes the result of the analysis with the effect sizes of the path analysis. The fit indices for the analysis are χ^2/d.f. = 1.62; CFI = 0.94; TLI = 0.93; IFI = 0.94; RMSEA = 0.05.

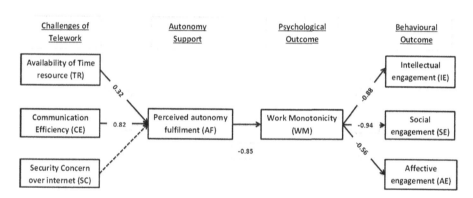

Fig. 2. Path analysis results (significant at 0.001 level) - standardized coefficients

The results prove our hypothesis H2, H3, H4, H5a, H5b, and H5c at significance level $p < 0.001$. H1 is found to be insignificant in our analysis. The effect size for the effect of communication issues on autonomy is 0.82, and the availability of time resources on autonomy is 0.32. The coefficient of the effect of autonomy on work monotonicity is −0.85. For engagement, work monotonicity effects intellectual, social, and affective engagement at −0.88, −0.94, and −0.56 level of magnitudes. For control variables, only Age has a positive coefficient at $p < 0.05$ level of significance for intellectual engagement and affective engagement.

4.2   Discussion

The result obtained in the path analysis provides several important points for discussions. First, we find that the time availability of resources and communication efficiency has a direct effect on employees' autonomy. When the time as a resource is not available to teleworkers or communication becomes challenging, the perceived autonomy of the teleworkers decreases. Greer and Payne (2014) use the boundary theory to explain the effect of telework on time-related challenges. They argue that employees have a psychological separation between time spent working and at home which they cross while traveling between work and home. However, while teleworking, these boundaries overlap and are broken down into parts throughout the day, affecting work coordination. The official working hours are not clearly defined while teleworking, and employees increasingly start working in the evenings or on the weekends (Steward 2000).

Second, the effect of communication efficiency is very significant in the fulfillment of autonomy for employees as seen from the results. This can help resolve the conflict in the literature, wherein the autonomy of teleworkers was found to be increased in some cases, while negative in others. We can postulate further from here, that when communication is efficient between teleworkers, the autonomy is positively supported. Communication issues force organizations to introduce initiatives that promote the exchange of information between coworkers and supervisors as lack of communication can lead to isolation and decreased organizational commitment (de Vries et al. 2019). These involve steps like more reports and more calls with mangers. The attempt to gain more control by the organization creates a loss of autonomy for the teleworkers. More reporting emails and tracking introduced by firms to track employee productivity further fuels this loss of autonomy (Gagné and Deci 2005).

Third, as hypothesized, a decrease in the perceived autonomy of teleworkers will significantly impact work attitude. Work monotonicity increases as autonomy decreases. Lack of perceived control by the organizations and the lack of autonomy by the employees create a sense of organizational distrust (van Hoorn 2018). A similar pattern can be observed in the results obtained by this study. Employees with a higher need for autonomy feel frustrated when subjected to this loss of control (Mekler et al. 2017). Negative Psychological outcome is a result of these phenomena (Deci and Ryan 2014), which was measured in the form of work monotonicity in our study. Increasing flexibility and freedom from superiors through less micromanagement can help the employee's need for autonomy fulfillment. One of the strategies to regain autonomy is to reinforce routines by employees. This lessens their loss of control over the scenario and reinforces their sense of autonomy. Additionally, increasing their perceived competence can also reinforce autonomy (Radel et al. 2013). Finally, work monotonicity has a significant impact on all types of work engagement – intellectual, social, and affective.

5 Conclusion and Implications

Telework is expected to be more prevalent in future workplace designs. The effectiveness of teleworking is dependent on the current technologies and needs to be revisited periodically. Certain events (such as the recent pandemic outbreak) forced organizations to implement mandatory teleworking policies. Challenges that emerged from these implementations and there effects on employee engagement have been studied in this article. We believe that the insights that the paper provides have implications for the future design of telework.

In this paper, we have explored the challenges faced by teleworkers under mandatory organizational policies. The results not only bring out some of the traditional teleworking challenges, such as inefficient communication and collaboration issues, but also shed light on its effect on employee engagement. Further, we investigated the mediating effect of change in autonomy support and the psychological challenges that emerge from this shift.

Managerial and Policy Implications. The results have implications for designing organizational policies and transformations to move towards a large-scale implementation of teleworking. It provides the focus areas for managing employee engagement in terms of the challenges explored in the study.

Further, the results presented here have implications for understanding the interplay of autonomy while teleworking. Efficient communication management can help organizations provide the necessary fulfillment of autonomy for employees, which form one of the basic needs of the workplace.

Limitations and Future Research. While the study provides relevant and interesting findings for understanding the effect of large scale telework on employees, more research is needed to understand the complete picture. As the next step in this research initiative, we plan to interview the participants of our study and dive deeper into the issues that have been reported in our study. This will help us understand the relation between them in more depth.

References

Abendroth, A.K., Reimann, M.: Telework and work-family conflict across workplaces: Investigating the implications of work-family-supportive and high-demand workplace cultures. In: Blair, S.L., Obradovic, J. (eds.) The Work-Family Interface: Spillover, Complications, and Challenges. Contemporary Perspectives in Family Research, vol. 15, pp. 323–348. Emerald Publishing, Bingley (2018)

Atkin, D.J., Lau, T.Y.: Information technology and organizational telework. In: Lin, C.A., Atkin, D.J. (eds.) Communication Technology and Social Change: Theory and Implications, p. 79. LEA, Mahwah (2007)

Brunetto, Y., Farr-Wharton, R.: A case study examining the impact of publicsector nurses' perception of workplace autonomy on their job satisfaction: Lessons for management. Int. J. Org. Behav. **8**(5), 521–539 (2004)

Chung, H., Van der Horst, M.: Women's employment patterns after childbirth and the perceived access to and use of flexitime and teleworking. Hum. Relat. **71**(1), 47–72 (2018)

de Vries, H., Tummers, L., Bekkers, V.: The benefits of teleworking in the public sector: Reality or rhetoric? Rev. Pub. Pers. Adm. **39**(4), 570–593 (2019)

Deci, E.L., Ryan, R.M.: Autonomy and need satisfaction in close relationships: Relationships motivation theory. In: Weinstein, N. (ed.) Human Motivation and Interpersonal Relationships, pp. 53–73. Springer, Dordrecht (2014). https://doi.org/10.1007/978-94-017-8542-6_3

Deci, E.L., Ryan, R.M.: Self-determination. In: Weiner, I.B., Craighead, W.E. (eds.) The Corsini Encyclopedia of Psychology. Wiley, Hoboken, NJ (2010)

Demerouti, E., Derks, D., ten Brummelhuis, L.L., Bakker, A.B.: New ways of working: Impact on working conditions, work–family balance, and well-being. In: Korunka, C., Hoonakker, P. (eds.) The Impact of ICT on Quality of Working Life, pp. 123–141. Springer, Dordrecht (2014). https://doi.org/10.1007/978-94-017-8854-0_8

Elliot, A.J., Thrash, T.M.: Achievement goals and the hierarchical model of achievement motivation. Educ. Psychol. Rev. **13**(2), 139–156 (2001)

Elliot, A.J., McGregor, H.A., Thrash, T.M.: 16: The need for competence. In: Deci, E.L., Ryan, R.M. (eds.) Handbook of Self-Determination Research, pp. 361–388. University Rochester Press, New York, NY (2002)

Fernet, C., Austin, S., Trépanier, S.G., Dussault, M.: How do job characteristics contribute to burnout? Exploring the distinct mediating roles of perceived autonomy, competence, and relatedness. Eur. J. Work Organ. Psychol. **22**(2), 123–137 (2013)

Frenkel, S.: The week in tech: Welcome to the age of mandatory videoconferencing. New York Times. https://www.nytimes.com/ (2020). Accessed 6 Mar 2020

Greer, T.W., Payne, S.C.: Overcoming telework challenges: Outcomes of successful telework strategies. Psychol.-Manag. J. **17**(2), 87 (2014)

Gagné, M., Deci, E.L.: Self-determination theory and work motivation. J. Organ. Behav. **26**(4), 331–362 (2005)

Harter, J.K., Schmidt, F.L., Hayes, T.L.: Business-unit-level relationship between employee satisfaction, employee engagement, and business outcomes: A metaanalysis. J. Appl. Psychol. **87**(2), 268 (2002)

Illegems, V., Verbeke, A.: Telework: What does it mean for management? Long Range Plan. **37**(4), 319–334 (2004)

Jang, H., Reeve, J., Ryan, R.M., Kim, A.: Can self-determination theory explain what underlies the productive, satisfying learning experiences of collectivistically oriented Korean students? J. Educ. Psychol. **101**(3), 644 (2009)

Johannsen, R., Zak, P.J.: Autonomy raises productivity: An experiment measuring neurophysiology. Front. Psychol. **11**, 963 (2020)

Lewis, R.A.: The influence of information technology on telework: The experiences of teleworkers and their non-teleworking colleagues in a French public administration. Int. J. Inf. Educ. Technol. **3**(1), 32 (2013)

Loukidou, L., Loan-Clarke, J., Daniels, K.: Boredom in the workplace: More than monotonous tasks. Int. J. Manag. Rev. **11**(4), 381–405 (2009)

Malinowska, D., Tokarz, A., Wardzichowska, A.: Job autonomy in relation to work engagement and workaholism: Mediation of autonomous and controlled work motivation. Int. J. Occup. Med. Environ. Health **31**(4) (2018)

Martin, B.H., MacDonnell, R.: Is telework effective for organizations? Manag. Res. Rev. (2012)

Mann, S., Holdsworth, L.: The psychological impact of teleworking: Stress, emotions and health. New Technol. Work Employ. **18**(3), 21–196 (2003)

Mekler, E.D., Brühlmann, F., Tuch, A.N., Opwis, K.: Towards understanding the effects of individual gamification elements on intrinsic motivation and performance. Comput. Hum. Behav. **71**, 525–534 (2017)

Melamed, S., Ben-Avi, I., Luz, J., Green, M.S.: Objective and subjective work monotony: Effects on job satisfaction, psychological distress, and absenteeism in bluecollar workers. J. Appl. Psychol. **80**(1), 29 (1995)

Naotunna, S., Zhou, E.: Autonomy and creativity of professional teleworkers: The mediating role of creative self-efficacy. Int. J. Organ. Innov. (Online) **10**(3), 300–307 (2018)

Nakrošienė, A., Bučiūnienė, I., Goštautaitė, B.: Working from home: Characteristics and outcomes of telework. Int. J. Manpow. **40**, 87–101 (2019)

Nandhakumar, J., Baskerville, R.: Durability of online teamworking: Patterns of trust. Inf. Technol. People **19**(4), 371–389 (2006)

Nilles, J.M.: Telecommuting and urban sprawl: Mitigator or inciter? Transportation **18**(4), 411–432 (1991)

Nunnally, J.C.: Psychometric Theory 3E. Tata McGraw-Hill Education (1994)

Olson, M.H., Primps, S.B.: Working at home with computers: Work and nonwork issues. J. Soc. Issues **40**(3), 97–112 (1984)

Panteli, N., Duncan, E.: Trust and temporary virtual teams: Alternative explanations and dramaturgical relationships. Inf. Technol. People **17**, 423–441 (2004)

Pinsonneault, A., Boisvert, M.: The impacts of telecommuting on organizations and individuals: A review of the literature. In: Johnson, N. (ed.) Telecommuting and Virtual Offices: Issues and Opportunities, pp. 163–185. IGI Global, Hershey, PA (2001)

Quoquab, F., Lim, C.S., Malik, H.A.: Malaysian employees perception pertaining to telework. Bus. Manag. Q. Rev. (BMQR) **3**(1), 63–76 (2013)

Radel, R., Pelletier, L., Sarrazin, P.: Restoration processes after need thwarting: When autonomy depends on competence. Motiv. Emot. **37**(2), 234–244 (2013)

Rowland, V.T., Dodder, R.A., Nickols, S.Y.: Perceived adequacy of resources: Development of a scale. Home Econ. Res. J. **14**(2), 218–225 (1985)

Salisbury, W.D., Pearson, R.A., Pearson, A.W., Miller, D.W.: Perceived security and World Wide Web purchase intention. Ind. Manag. Data Syst. **101**, 165–177 (2001)

Sardeshmukh, S.R., Sharma, D., Golden, T.D.: Impact of telework on exhaustion and job engagement: A job demands and job resources model. New Technol. Work Employ. **27**(3), 193–207 (2012)

Saks, A.M.: Antecedents and consequences of employee engagement. J. Manag. Psychol. **21**(7), 600–619 (2006)

Schaufeli, W., Salanova, M.: Work engagement. Manag. Soc. Eth. Issues Organ. **135**, 177 (2007)

Sharit, J., Czaja, S.J.: Telework and Older Workers (2009)

Sheldon, K.M., Elliot, A.J., Kim, Y., Kasser, T.: What is satisfying about satisfying events? Testing 10 candidate psychological needs. J. Pers. Soc. Psychol. **80**(2), 325 (2001)

Silva-C, A.: The attitude of managers toward telework, why is it so difficult to adopt it in organizations? Technol. Soc. **59**, 101–133 (2019)

Soane, E., Truss, C., Alfes, K., Shantz, A., Rees, C., Gatenby, M.: Development and application of a new measure of employee engagement: The ISA Engagement Scale. Hum. Res. Dev. Int. **15**(5), 529–547 (2012)

Steele, G.A., Plenty, D.: Supervisor–subordinate communication competence and job and communication satisfaction. Int. J. Bus. Commun. **52**(3), 294–318 (2015)

Steward, B.: Changing times: The meaning, measurement and use of time in teleworking. Time Soc. **9**(1), 57–74 (2000)

Sewell, G., Taskin, L.: Out of sight, out of mind in a new world of work? Autonomy, control, and spatiotemporal scaling in telework. Organ. Stud. **36**(11), 1507–1529 (2015)

Tavares, A.I.: Telework and health effects review. Int. J. Healthc. **3**(2), 30 (2017)

van Hoorn, A.: Trust and signals in workplace organization: evidence from job autonomy differentials between immigrant groups. Oxf. Econ. Pap. **70**(3), 591–612 (2018)

Yen, C.J., Tu, C.H.: Online social presence: A study of score validity of the computer-mediated communication questionnaire. Q. Rev. Distance Educ. **9**(3) (2008)

Competitiveness, Change Readiness, and ICT Development: An Empirical Investigation of TOE Framework for Poverty Alleviation

Mukesh Narmetta[(✉)] and Satish Krishnan

Indian Institute of Management Kozhikode, Kozhikode, Kerala, India
{mukeshnl2fpm, satishk}@iimk.ac.in

Abstract. The Sustainable Development Goal (SDG) 1 – 'No Poverty' is one of the ambitious goals of all nations across the globe. Multiple factors lead to poverty in a nation. Hence, the alleviation of poverty requires governments to address these multiple factors at various levels of society. This study is an attempt to understand a few factors that can help poverty alleviation. Many theoretical studies provide different frameworks for poverty alleviation but a dearth of studies that empirically shows that poverty alleviation is possible. This study is an empirical investigation that looks into the macro-level factors that could help alleviate poverty through the lens of the Technology-Organization-Environment (TOE) framework. It underscores the mediating role of ICT development of the nations that change-ready and are competitive enough to address poverty at the grass-root level and thus strive for achieving the SDG goal 1. The results strengthen our argument that nations that are competitive and change-ready using ICT development measures could address the problem of poverty.

Keywords: Competitiveness index · Change readiness index · ICT development · Poverty alleviation · TOE framework · SDGs

1 Introduction

"ICTs alone cannot improve peoples' lives; the use of ICTs needs to occur within broader strategies that are tailored to make the most use of these tools and techniques to reap their potential benefits for human development" [1]

Since the use of Information Communication Technologies (ICTs), the societal and economic structures have undergone drastic changes [2]. The unique strengths of ICTs have drawn great attention to overcome the drawbacks of conventional systems thus becoming the fundamental pillar of the knowledge economy [3]. This engendered ICTs to take on a predominant role in shaping the economies of the nations around the globe, providing a vital source for competitiveness thus leading to great attention in management Literature [4].

Informatization of the society and level of ICT knowledge are the two main drivers of improvement in human activities that lead to economic growth [5] and thus helping nations in poverty alleviation [6]. Though the role of ICTs in poverty alleviation is a

© IFIP International Federation for Information Processing 2020
Published by Springer Nature Switzerland AG 2020
S. K. Sharma et al. (Eds.): TDIT 2020, IFIP AICT 618, pp. 638–649, 2020.
https://doi.org/10.1007/978-3-030-64861-9_55

much debatable topic, its role as a fundamental pillar of knowledge economy empowers people that creates a spirit of competition. ICTs can help reduce poverty by improving poor people's access to education, healthcare, and various governments' financial initiatives [7]. Though low-cost ICT infrastructure is a necessary condition for the successful use of ICT by the poor, it is not sufficient. The implementation of ICT projects plays a prominent role in defining the success of poverty alleviation. Thus, nations promoting ICT development in poverty alleviation should consider various critical success factors [7].

Multiple studies looked into the SDG 1 i.e., poverty alleviation (no poverty), through various lens such as policy changes [8–10]; labor migration and poverty alleviation [11]; micro-financial services [12]; micro-enterprises [13]; technology and poverty [14]; integrated information ecosystems [15]. These studies provided useful insights on poverty alleviation and the contribution of various factors to the alleviate problem of poverty.

This study employs the TOE framework to propose factors that help achieve the Sustainable Development Goal 1 – No Poverty (Poverty Alleviation) and thus claim to make the following contributions. The study employs the TOE framework that underscores the importance of ICT development of a nation to alleviate poverty. It also empirically tests the mediating role of ICT development in alleviating poverty through competitiveness and change readiness. It adds rigor and robustness to the TOE framework by testing it empirically. Thus the research questions of this study addresses are as follows:

RQ1: What are a few factors that help a nation in poverty alleviation? RQ2: Does ICT Development of a nation help in poverty alleviation?

2   Literature and Theoretical Framework

2.1   Literature

There is no universal definition for *poverty* although most scholars consider income as a proxy for poverty. As per this definition, any person whose income is below the poverty line is considered as poor [16]. Most recent studies have argued that poverty is a multidimensional concept that includes the dimensions of social, economic, political, and cultural as well. Castro [17] defines poverty as "a multidimensional phenomenon and it refers to a pronounced deprivation in one or more facets of the wellbeing of a person." Along with the non-availability of abundant natural resources, proper infrastructure, and income opportunities, there are many other reasons for poverty to exist. Of them stand out the unequal access to basic amenities such as healthcare, education, sanitation facilities, clean drinking water, justice, and political protection. This results from poorly developed strategies and government policies [12]. Sachs [18] points out that an absolute resolute effort is required by both developing as well as developed nations to achieve ending global poverty by 2025 with a global compact that designated the shared equal responsibilities by both parties. He suggests a differential diagnosis that stresses to abandon a 'one size fit all' approach usually followed by internationally renowned agencies like of World Bank and IMF and formulate strategies that tailor the economies of the nations as per their own need and pace. On these grounds, the United Nations with its Sustainable Development Goals (SDGs) has created a framework that helps countries across the globe to put efforts to attain development in all aspects.

The SDGs agenda for 2030 is to take up multiple challenges that the countries face such as extreme poverty, access to education, poor healthcare, unemployment and ensure them of economic prosperity, social well-being, and environmental protection [8]. They provide nations with a multidimensional and holistic vista on development in contrast to the conventional development agendas that drive basis on a limited set of dimensions [12]. Among the 17 SDGs *"Ending Poverty and expanding social protection coverage"* is the number one goal that is of importance [19]. Dugarova [20] argues that the SDGs are of great importance to developing nations when compared developed as there has been a lot of progress achieved in terms of eradicating poverty, increase life-expectancy, and near-universal access to primary education in developed nations. Hence, the SDGs present them with a substantial opportunity to scale up what has been worked so far and address existing and emerging challenges [20].

It was during the late seventies where the concept of "information society" has been introduced with the advent of the latest technologies that were widely used for communications called as information and communication technologies (ICTs). Since then many scholars have acknowledged the close relationship between access to information and poverty. These are the main propositions that were proposed by [14]:

- "information leads to resources;
- information leads to opportunities that generate resources;
- access to information leads to access to resources; and
- access to information leads to access to opportunities that generate resources."

Flor [14] further explored the relationship between poverty and ICTs which posits that a person who is 'information-poor' is also 'resource-poor'. In a report prepared by Batchelor et al. [21] it's being argued that ICTs provide a platform to share information across different barriers and bridge the gap between stakeholders that gives voice to many underprivileged people that enhances their lives in economic, health and educational activities. ICTs potential to deal with the challenges related to information, communication, and knowledge dimensions caused a high degree of excitement during the past two decades [22].

Sen [23] and Adera et al. [24] opines that mere access to and deployment [25] of ICTs is not enough but how people are using it to reduce poverty is important. The World Bank [26] had proposed a strategy consisting of three ways to attack poverty using ICTs: *"promoting opportunity, facilitating empowerment, and enhancing security"*. Although the results of this strategy are yet to come to the light [7]. Two approaches have been identified when considering the use of ICTs for poverty reduction. They are the demand side and the supply side driven approaches. In demand-driven approaches, the poor stands at the center whereas in supply-driven approaches the focus is on the technology supply, access, and connectivity [16]. Many factors are linked to the benefits of ICTs in poverty alleviation such as ICTs integration at the policy to achieve goals at an individual, community, and societal level. It is equally important to have support mechanisms in place to encourage and motivate poor people who are using ICTs to overcome the fear of technology.

2.2   Theoretical Framework

Technology Organization Environment (TOE) Framework

The authors have used the TOE [27] framework as a theoretical lens to understand the impact of these factors on Poverty Alleviation. It is a well-marked theory that has strong theoretical and empirical support with a robust theoretical base [28]. The TOE framework has been used in multiple studies with the organizational context of innovative technologies adoption [29, 30]. But to the best of the knowledge of authors, this study is the first of its kind to apply an organizational level theory to a country-level context. The TOE framework has three elements that influence a firm's adoption decisions [29]. They are the technology context, organizational context, and the environmental context. The detailed explanation of these three contexts along with the operationalization of the factors to this study has been provided below. The authors posit that the factors determining the alleviation of poverty can be divided into three contextual categories, broadly, although the framework does not provide any additional information about what these factors are [31].

Technology Context

At an organization level, technology refers to all the technologies that are pertinent to the organization – both in use and are available in the marketplace that is not used [29]. The authors have used the dimensions ICT Access, ICT Use & ICT Skills from the ICT Development Index (IDI). IDI is a report that is published based on internationally agreed information and communication technologies (ICT) indicators annually by the United Nations International Telecommunication Union (ITU). The use of ICT Access, Use, and Skill seemed appropriate in the context of a nation with the studies done by [28, 32, 33]. IDI is a complex measure with 11 indicators that measure: the evolution and level of ICT development in countries; the digital divide; progress in ICT development in both developing and developed nations; and the potential of ICTs to the extent countries can benefit to complement development and growth [34]. A country's evolution process to become an 'information society' can be achieved in three stages: ICT readiness (ICT access); ICT intensity (ICT Use); and ICT impact (ICT Skills).

Organization Context

Baker [29] defines organization context as the resources and the characteristics of the firm that include the intra-firm communication process, linking structures between employees, firm size, and the number of resources. The authors have used the dimensions from the Global Competitive Index (GCI). GCI reports are published annually by [35]. Echoing with resources and characteristics of a firm, a nation's resources and characteristics resembles the dimensions of GCI. The dimensions used for this study are Enabling Environment, Human Capital, Markets, and Innovation Ecosystem. The dimensions used for this study in the context of a nation are in line with the factors of organizational context by the studies done by [33, 36, 37].

The GCI measures these four dimensions of a nation using 12 pillars with 98 indicators [35]. We live in a world that is experiencing the 4th Industrial Revolution (4IR) and technologies are shaping and changing every aspect of human life. With this background, the governments of every nation have a burning question that needs to be answered with integrity – How to sustain the growth with the growing technological advancements? This is where the GCI would provide an answer to the nations. It provides a holistic view of the nations on the pillars that are sustaining growth.

H1a: Enabling Environment of a nation is positively associated with the Poverty Alleviation of the nation.

H1b: Enabling Environment of a nation is positively associated with the ICT Development of the nation.

H2a: Human Capital of a nation is positively associated with the Poverty Alleviation of the nation.

H2b: Human Capital of a nation is positively associated with the ICT Development of the nation.

H3a: Markets of a nation is positively associated with the Poverty Alleviation of the nation.

H3b: Markets of a nation is positively associated with the ICT Development of the nation.

H4a: Innovative Environment of a nation is positively associated with the Poverty Alleviation of the nation.

H4b: Innovative Environment of a nation is positively associated with the ICT Development of the nation.

Environment Context

The environment context comprises the presence or absence of the technology providers, the structure of the industry, and the regulatory environment [29]. The authors have made use of the dimensions from the Change Readiness Index (CRI) published once in two years by [38]. The dimensions used for this study are Enterprise Capability; Government Capability; and People & Civil Society. The three dimensions adopted from the CRI used for this study seemed appropriate with the factors that were found in the studies conducted by [32, 33]. Hence, the authors have employed them as proxies for environment providers of a nation.

The Change Readiness Index comprises three dimensions measured using 30 indicators that represent regulatory environment controlled by nations' governments, enterprise capabilities that consist of labor markets, economic diversification & openness, etc., and finally people and civil society dimension that includes demographic variables.

H5a: Change Readiness of a nation is positively associated with Poverty alleviation of the nation

H5b: Change Readiness of a nation is positively associated with the ICT Development of the nation.

Poverty Alleviation: Definition

The dependent variable of the study is Poverty Alleviation which is being operationalized using measures adapted from the Global Multidimensional Poverty Index (GMPI) [39]. The GMPI report is published by the United Nations Development Programme and the Oxford Poverty and Human Development Initiative (OPHI) annually, with the cumulative poverty measurements. This is a much comprehensive Index when compared to Human Development Index (HDI) that replaced HDI from 2010. The GMPI comprises three main dimensions: Health; Education and Standard of Living as depicted in Fig. 1.

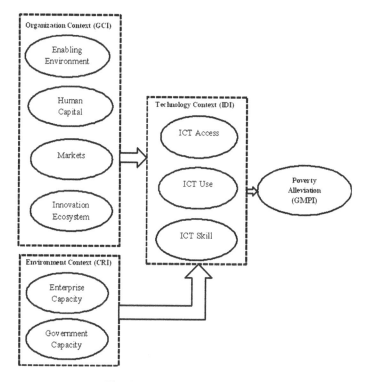

Fig. 1. Proposed research model

H6: ICT Development of a nation is positively associated with the Poverty Alleviation of the nation.

3 Methodology

3.1 Data

The study makes use of the secondary data available for 65 countries from the various indices like ICT Development Index (IDI) for the year 2018; Global Multidimensional Poverty Index (GMPI) for the year 2019; the Global Competitiveness Index (GCI for the year 2018 and the Change Readiness Index (CRI) for the year 2017. The study employs Structural Equation Modelling (SEM) to perform a cross-sectional analysis of the data. When compared to other multivariate techniques the use of SEM has several advantages in the current context. Its ability to allow correcting measurement errors gives the researcher the flexibility and freedom to explore different possible model outcomes. Also, in the current study, it is required to analyze the mediating role of IDI on Poverty alleviation which can be done using SEM that can assess direct and indirect effects [40]. The dependent variable Poverty Alleviation's (GMPI) data is from the latest the year 2019 and the remaining follows the previous years' to account for a lag of one to two years for the effect of technology and other institutional changes to take place. The data for GCI and IDI dimesons is of the year 2018, and the data for CRI is of 2017. Though the data for CRI in the year 2019 is available, it is not considered for analysis since the dependent variable's data is of 2019. Since the data is published by reputed international organizations, it is assumed that the measures are reliable and are free from method biases.

3.2   Analysis

Measurement Model
The model fitness indices are presented in Table 1. The CMIN of the measurement model is 141.520 with df as 70. The CMIN/df ratio is 2.022 which is excellent well under the acceptable upper value 3 [41]. Both CFI = 0.918 and SRMR = 0.10 are in acceptable range [42]. However, the RMSEA measure is 0.126 which should be less than 0.06 [43]. One of the reasons could be the very low sample size [42]. Unlike working with primary data, formulating measurement models with secondary data could be tricky given the limitations on data availability.

Path Analysis: SEM (Reduced Model)
Through path analysis the direct effect of independent variables on the dependent variable is analyzed. Here the effect of GCI dimensions and Change Readiness index were analyzed on poverty alleviation. The results of the model are presented in Table 2.

Table 1. Model fit measures

Measure	Estimate	Threshold	Interpretation
CMIN	141.520	–	–
DF	70.000	–	–
CMIN/DF	2.022	Between 1 and 3	Excellent
CFI	0.918	>0.95	Acceptable
SRMR	0.100	<0.08	Acceptable
RMSEA	0.126	<0.06	Terrible
PClose	0.000	>0.05	Not Estimated

Table 2. Reduced model – hypotheses testing

	Estimate	S.E.	C.R.	P	Hypotheses
PA <– CRI (H5b)	0.068	0.059	1.157	0.247	Not supported
PA <– GC_HC (H2b)	0.016	0.163	0.1	0.921	Not supported
PA <– GC_EE (H1b)	0.821	0.144	5.696	***	Supported
PA <– GC_M (H3b)	−1.233	0.328	−3.754	***	Supported
PA <– GC_IE (H4b)	0.48	0.275	1.745	0.081	Not supported

Mediation Analysis

Table 3 presents the results of the mediation model. This tests the effect of IDI as a mediator for CRI and GCI dimensions.

Table 3. Mediation model – hypotheses testing

	Estimate	S.E.	C.R.	p-value	Hypotheses
IDI <– GC_HC	0.039	0.01	3.823	***	Supported
IDI <– GC_M	−0.057	0.019	−2.975	0.003	Supported
IDI <– GC_EE	0.09	0.009	10.124	***	Supported
IDI <– GC_IE	−0.021	0.016	−1.268	0.205	Not supported
IDI <– CRI	−0.007	0.004	−1.934	0.053	Not supported
PA <– IDI	5.258	1.214	4.331	***	Supported

4 Results and Discussion

Table 2 presents the hypotheses testing results from the path analysis SEM without any mediation effect of ICT development on Poverty Alleviation. The results show that only hypotheses Enabling Environment and Markets dimensions with Poverty alleviation are supported. This infers that there is not much direct relationship of other dimensions such as Human Capital, Innovative Environment, and CRI independently does not affect poverty alleviation. Thus, the mediation analysis with ICT Development is justified with these results. Table 3 presents the hypotheses testing results for the mediation analysis. Except for Innovation Environment and CRI, all other hypotheses were supported showing that there is a mediating effect of ICT Development to alleviate poverty.

Furthermore, Table 4 presents the standardized total, direct and indirect effects path coefficients. The results show a clear meditation effect by ICT Development that exists between Competitiveness, Change Readiness, and Poverty Alleviation.

Table 4. Standardized total, direct and indirect effects

Standardized total effects (group number 1 - default model)

	CRI	GC_IE	GC_M	GC_HC	GC_EE	IDI	PA
IDI	−0.125	−0.155	−0.229	0.336	0.824	0	0
PA	−0.061	−0.076	−0.112	0.164	0.403	0.489	0

Standardized direct effects (group number 1 - default model)

	CRI	GC_IE	GC_M	GC_HC	GC_EE	IDI	PA
IDI	−0.125	−0.155	−0.229	0.336	0.824	0	0
PA	0	0	0	0	0	0.489	0

Standardized indirect effects (group number 1 - default model)

	CRI	GC_IE	GC_M	GC_HC	GC_EE	IDI	PA
IDI	0	0	0	0	0	0	0
PA	−0.061	−0.076	−0.112	0.164	0.403	0	0

5 Conclusion, Limitations, and Future Research

The role of ICT Development in alleviating poverty has been studied with factors such as competitiveness and change readiness. ICT mediates the relationship between competitiveness – poverty alleviation and changes readiness – poverty alleviation. This is done using secondary data available from various indices for the years 2017 (CRI), 2018 (GCI and IDI), and 2019 (GMPI). A cross-sectional analysis was done using Structural Equation Modelling to understand the mediating role of ICT development of nations on poverty alleviation. ICT development has found to be playing a statistically significant role in alleviating poverty in the given sample of nations. Though there are some direct effects large part of them remain insignificant stressing the importance of ICT development.

The study makes a decent contribution to the literature by employing the TOE framework for understanding the role of ICT development. Though numerous studies used the TOE framework earlier, none of those looked into the aspect of Poverty alleviation.

It also provides an empirical test for the TOE framework that further strengthens the robustness of the framework. Further, it acts as a signpost to the policymakers and governments of nations to understand the importance of ICT development and also stress equally on other dimensions that emerged from this study.

Since no study is without limitations, certain aspects could have provided better insights into this study. First, the study used data for only 65 countries because of the unavailability of data. This would prove to be an important future research agenda to acquire data from as many countries as possible so that the message would become strong to the nations revealing the importance of ICT development. Second, due to the low sample size, few model fit measures (particularly RMSEA) did not fall within an acceptable range which questions the framework. This could be addressed again with more number of countries being included in the study. Future research could also take into account the innovation capabilities (GII) of a nation that might help alleviate poverty. Third, the study used cross-sectional data for analysis. Future research could use panel data on the proposed framework to test the hypotheses. Fourth, our study employed secondary data available for the factors of Technology, Organization, and Environment. Because of the data unavailability, we have missed out on the latest ICT' such as Block chain, AI, Machine Learning, etc., Future studies could incorporate data on these ICTs to understand their impact on development. Overall, the study attempted to understand a few factors that could help poverty alleviation. Though, not exhaustive, the nations can work on these factors rigorously to achieve the Sustainable Development goal of 'No Poverty' by 2030.

References

1. Hamel, J.Y.: ICT4D and the human development and capabilities approach: The potentials of information and communication technology. Human Development Research Paper 2010/37, UNDP (2010)
2. Vilaseca, J., Torrent, J., Lladós, J., Garay, L.: El impacto de las TIC en la empresa turística: el caso de Cataluña. UOC, Working Paper Series, WP06-003.210A. Ollo-López, M.E. Aramendía-Muneta/Telematics and Informatics 29, pp. 204–210 (2012)
3. Takahashi, K.I., Tatemichi, H., Tanaka, T., Nishi, S., Kunioka, T.: Environmental impact of information and communication technologies including rebound effects. In: International Symposium on Electronics and the Environment (ISEE'04), pp. 13–16 (2004)
4. Ollo-López, A., Aramendía-Muneta, M.E.: ICT impact on competitiveness, innovation, and environment. Telemat. Inform. **29**(2), 204–210 (2012)
5. Doucek, P.: Human capital in ICT–competitiveness and innovation potential in ICT. DOUCEK, P, Gerhard CHROUST a Václav OŠKRDAL. IDIMT-2011: interdisciplinarity in complex systems. Linz: Trauner, pp. 11–22 (2011)
6. Heeks, R.: Information and communication technologies, poverty and development. Development Informatics Working Paper no. 5, 30 Oct 1999. Available at SSRN: https://ssrn.com/abstract=3477770 or http://dx.doi.org/10.2139/ssrn.3477770
7. Cecchini, S., Scott, C.: Can information and communications technology applications contribute to poverty reduction? Lessons from rural India. Inf. Technol. Dev. **10**(2), 73–84 (2003)
8. Pradhan, P., Costa, L., Rybski, D., Lucht, W., Kropp, J.P.: A systematic study of Sustainable Development Goal (SDG) interactions. Earth's Futur. **5**(11), 1169–1179 (2017)
9. Lu, Y., Nakicenovic, N., Visbeck, M., Stevance, A.-S.: Policy: Five priorities for the UN sustainable development goals—comment. Nature **520**(7548), 432–433 (2015). https://doi.org/10.1038/520432a
10. Schmidt, H., Gostin, L., Emanuel, E.: Public health, universal health coverage, and sustainable development goals: Can theycoexist? Lancet **386**(9996), 928–930 (2015). https://doi.org/10.1016/S0140-6736(15)60244-6Sen,A.(1983)
11. Nicolai, S., Wales, J., Aiazzi, E.: Education, Migration and the 2030 Agenda for Sustainable Development (2016)
12. Hassanain, K., Saaid, A.E.: Zakah for poverty alleviation: Evidence from Sudan. Int. Res. J. Financ. Econ. **154**, 83–104 (2016)
13. Khanam, D., Mohiuddin, M., Hoque, A., Weber, O.: Financing micro-entrepreneurs for poverty alleviation: A performance analysis of microfinance services offered by BRAC, ASA, and Proshika from Bangladesh. J. Glob. Entrep. Res. **8**(1), 27 (2018)

14. Flor, A.G.: ICT and poverty: The indisputable link. In: SEARCA, Paper for the Third Asian Development Forum on "Regional Economic Cooperation in Asia and the Pacific", Asian Development Bank, pp. 11–14, June 2001

15. Corbett, J., Mellouli, S.: Winning the SDG battle in cities: How an integrated information ecosystem can contribute to the achievement of the 2030 sustainable development goals. Inf. Syst. Journal **27**(4), 427–461 (2017)

16. Mbuyisa, B., Leonard, A.: The role of ICT use in SMEs towards poverty reduction: A systematic literature review. J. Int. Dev. **29**(2), 159–197 (2017)

17. Castro, M.C.: Poverty in Northern Sudan, Estimates from the NBHS 2009 (2010)

18. Sachs, J.D.: The End of Poverty: Economic Possibilities for Our Time. Penguin, New York (2006)

19. Carter, D.J., Glaziou, P., Lönnroth, K., Siroka, A., Floyd, K., Weil, D., et al.: The impact of social protection and poverty elimination on global tuberculosis incidence: A statistical modelling analysis of Sustainable Development Goal 1. Lancet Glob. Health **6**(5), e514–e522 (2018)

20. Dugarova, E.: Implementing SDG 1: Poverty eradication through family support policies and social protection measures in transition countries. In Expert Group Meeting "Family policies and the (Vol. 2030)

21. Batchelor, S., Scott, N., Woolnough, D.: Good practice paper on ICTs for economic growth and poverty reduction. DAC J. **6**(3) (2005)

22. McNamara, K.S.: Information and communication technologies, poverty and development: Learning from experience. In: Paper Presented at infoDev Annual Symposium, Geneva, 9–10 Dec 2003. http://www-wds.worldbank.org/servlet/WDSContentServer/IW3P/IB/2004/10/04/000160016_20041004140523/Rendered/PDF/300760PAPER0ICT0Learning0from0Experience.pdf. Accessed 01 Feb 2016

23. Sen, A.: A sociological approach to the measurement of poverty: a reply to Professor Peter Townsend. Oxf. Econ. Pap. **37**(4), 669–676 (1985)

24. Adera, E.O., Waema, T.M., May, J., Mascarenhas, O., Diga, K.: ICT Pathways to poverty reduction: Empirical evidence from East and Southern Africa. Practical Action Publishing, United Kingdom (2014)

25. Soriano, C.R.: Exploring the ICT and rural poverty reduction link: Community telecenters and rural livelihoods in Wu'an, China. Electron. J. Inf. Syst. Dev. Ctries **32**(1), 1–15 (2007)

26. World Bank: World Development Report: Attacking Poverty, 2000/2001. http://www.wds.worldbank.org/external/default/WDSContentServer/WDSP/IB/2000/12/13/000094946_00092605361978/Rendered/PDF/multi_page.pdf (2000). Accessed 30 May 2013

27. Tornatzky, L.G., Fleischer, M.: The Processes of Technological Innovation. Lexington Books, Lexington, MA (1990)

28. Chandra, S., Kumar, K.N.: Exploring factors influencing organizational adoption of augmented reality in e-commerce: Empirical analysis using technology-organization-environment model. J. Electron. Commer. Res. **19**(3) (2018)

29. Baker, J.: The technology–organization–environment framework. In: Dwivedi, Y.K., Wade, M.R., Schneberger, S.L. (Eds.) Information Systems Theory, vol. 28, pp. 231–245. Springer, New York, NY (2012). https://doi.org/10.1007/978-1-4419-6108-2

30. Bhattacharya, M., Wamba, S.F.: A conceptual framework of RFID adoption in retail using TOE framework. In: Khosrow-Pour, M. (Ed.) Technology Adoption and Social Issues: Concepts, Methodologies, Tools, and Applications, pp. 69–102. IGI Global, Hershey, Pennsylvania (2018)

31. Jia, Q., Guo, Y., Barnes, S.J.: Enterprise 2.0 post-adoption: Extending the information system continuance model based on the technology-Organization-environment framework. Comput. Hum. Behav. **67**, 95–105 (2017)

32. Pudjianto, B., Zo, H., Ciganek, A.P., Rho, J.J.: Determinants of e-government assimilation in Indonesia: An empirical investigation using a TOE framework. Asia Pac. J. Inf. Syst. **21**(1), 49–80 (2011)
33. Awa, H.O., Ojiabo, O.U.: A model of adoption determinants of ERP within the TOE framework. Inf. Technol. People **29**, 901–930 (2016)
34. IDU Report. https://www.itu.int/en/ITUD/Statistics/Pages/IDI2019consultation/default.aspx (2019). Accessed 26 April 2020
35. World Economic Forum. http://www3.weforum.org/docs/GCR2018/05FullReport/TheGlobal CompetitivenessReport2018.pdf (2018). Accessed 26 April 2020
36. Ramdani, B., Chevers, D., Williams, D.A.: SMEs' adoption of enterprise applications: A technology-organisation-environment model. J. Small Bus. Enterp. Dev. **20**(4), 735–753 (2013)
37. Rosli, K., Yeow, P.H., Siew, E.G.: Factors influencing audit technology acceptance by audit firms: A new I-TOE adoption framework. J. Account. Audit. **2012**, 1 (2012)
38. KPMG International. https://assets.kpmg/content/dam/kpmg/xx/pdf/2017/07/change-readine ss-index-report-2017.pdf (2017). Accessed 26 April 2020
39. Global Multidimensional Poverty Index (GMPI). http://hdr.undp.org/en/2019-MPI (2019). Accessed 26 April 2020
40. Bollen, K.: Structural Equations with Latent Variables. Wiley, New York (1989)
41. Byrne, B.M.: Structural equation modeling with AMOS, EQS, and LISREL: Comparative approaches to testing for the factorial validity of a measuring instrument. Int. J. Test. **1**(1), 55–86 (2001)
42. Kenny, D.A., Kaniskan, B., McCoach, D.B.: The performance of RMSEA in models with small degrees of freedom. Sociol. Methods Res. **44**, 486–507 (2015)
43. Hu, L.T., Bentler, P.M.: Cutoff criteria for fit indexes in covariance structure analysis: Conventional criteria versus new alternatives. Struct. Equ. Model. **6**(1), 1–55 (1999)

Implementing ICT at School Level: Factors Affecting Teachers' Perceived Proficiency

Chandan Singhavi[✉] and Prema Basargekar

K J Somaiya Institute of Management, Mumbai, India
{chandans, prema}@somaiya.edu

Abstract. Implementation of Information and Communication Technology (ICT) at the school level has become a need of the hour during the pandemic period. The factor which plays important aspect for adopting ICT in the schools is lack of readiness of the teachers for adopting ICT in the classrooms. This is very closely related to the teachers' perceived proficiency for usage of ICT effectively in the classroom. The present study tries to identify the factors like access to ICT, ICT material etc. affecting the perceived proficiency of teachers related to using ICT. The perceived proficiency is affected by number of factors such as school culture, school leadership, access to ICT resources, availability of digital content as well as support received from colleagues and the administration. These factors also impact the perception about ICT as an effective tool of teaching learning activity.

The study uses the primary data collection of 515 school teachers located in Maharashtra. It uses SmartPLS3 software for theory building to see the relationship between exogenous variable affecting perception about ICT and perceived proficiency of the teachers to use ICT in the teaching learning process. The study concludes that positive perception about ICT as a teaching learning tool positively and significantly impacts teachers' perceived proficiency to use ICT. Similarly, many of the factors such as availability of computer equipment and resources and ICT related digital content contributes perceived proficiency positively. The paper also provides few policy measures for effective implementation of ICT at school level.

Keywords: ICT · School education · Teachers' perceived proficiency · E-learning

1 Introduction

The World Bank estimation says, school closures due to Coronavirus – COVID19 impacted more than 1.5 billion students accounting for 87.5% of the learners from 180 countries[1]. In India more than 250 million students suffered due to closure of the schools. Along with risk of higher school drop-outs, decline in confidence and self-esteem of the children and declining effectiveness of teaching and learning process, it also puts a major threat to future skill building and manpower development. This

---

[1] https://edtechhub.org/wp-content/uploads/2020/04/education-during-covid-19-crisis.pdf.

© IFIP International Federation for Information Processing 2020
Published by Springer Nature Switzerland AG 2020
S. K. Sharma et al. (Eds.): TDIT 2020, IFIP AICT 618, pp. 650–661, 2020.
https://doi.org/10.1007/978-3-030-64861-9_56

proves that use of Information and Communication Technology (ICT) is no more a luxury or a supplementary tool for the schools and it is now become the most vital instrument to bring the continuum of education. Implementing ICT has many challenges such as access to computer equipment and internet, availability of educational content in digital platform and the readiness of the schools, parents and children to adapt the new pedagogies. One of the major challenges is readiness of the teachers to use ICT in their classrooms which is impacted by their perceived proficiency and perception of using ICT for teaching and learning. This paper tries to find out the impact of various school level factors such as school leadership and administrative support, access to ICT resources, access to ICT teaching-learning material and support from colleagues help in creating a positive perception about the efficacy of using ICT in the classroom and that in turn impacts perceived proficiency of teachers' in using ICT positively.

2   Objective

The objective of the study is to assess the impact of various school level factors on perception about ICT as an effective teaching-learning tool which acts as a mediator variable in creating a positive perceived proficiency to implement ICT effectively in the classroom.

3   Review of Literature

Importance of ICT in school education in making education more learners centric, more inclusive and more democratic is well proven in the existing literature. One of the major challenges in its successful implementation is the attitude and perceptions of the teachers about its effectiveness and their own perceived proficiency in implementing ICT in the classroom. Various factors such as school leadership, school culture, role of ICT coordinator, training facilities made available to the teachers play an important role in it.

This review of literature covers the impact of four important characteristics at school level which impact perception and perceived proficiency of teachers' in implementing ICT in the classroom. They are School leadership and administrative support, Access to ICT equipment and infrastructure, Availability of ICT teaching learning material and, Support of the colleagues. The literature shows that these four factors have an impact on the teachers' perception about the efficacy of ICT as a teaching-learning tool as well as on their perceived proficiency in using ICT in the classroom.

3.1   School Leadership and Administrative Support

School leadership plays an important role in creating mission and vision supporting ICT integration in the school, creating encouraging environment and providing administrative support for implementing ICT at the classroom level. Integration of ICT in school's mission and vision enables long-term sustenance [17, 25] which in turn encourages professional development of the teachers required for successful implementation of ICT. School leaders' own competency and attitude towards ICT influences school culture and day to day policies [2, 20]. Porten et al. [31] also state that school principals play an important role in not only designing mission and vision but also in providing required support in terms of provision of budget and designing educational policies to articulate mission in action. Along with that the school leaders also have to create shared vision with teachers and staff to implement ICT, motivate them and build collaborative culture which is necessary for integrating ICT in the classroom [24, 32]. Teacher's attitudes are positively affected by the support provided by administration towards the use of computers [14]. Buabeng-Andoh and Yidana [16] and Albugarni and Ahmed [3] found that lack of good school leadership and administrative support can lead to teacher centric education and lack of confidence amongst teachers for fully integrating ICT in curriculum.

Sharija and Watters [35] mention the role of school leadership in successful implementation of ICT in a very clear way. They mention that the school leaders have to go beyond the change maker and have to adopt the role of learning leader by demonstrating the use of ICT, persuading old and reluctant teachers to adopt ICT and building communication between teachers and ICT technology specialists. Eickelmann [15] summarizes the role of school leadership by stating that strong school leadership having a sound understanding of the potential of ICT as an effective teaching- learning tool and able to link ICT integration in regular classrooms by involving all the teachers and associating it with pedagogical aims of the school will make ICT sustainable in the long-run.

3.2   Access to ICT Equipment and Infrastructure

Researchers have also studied the impact of access of ICT resources to the teachers such as computers, internet, software, suitable classrooms and the degree of accessibility on building their perception related to ICT as an effective tool and building the confidence to use it in the classroom. Aramide and Ladipo [6] found that accessibility to ICT resources and location of ICT resource (i.e. whether it is in the classroom, computer lab, building, etc.) can impact the use of ICT and teachers' perception towards it. Teachers perceived access to ICT resources, perceived administrative support and their perceived confidence can lead to higher use of ICT in the classroom [8, 9]. Thunman and Persson [39] mention that unequal access of ICT resources at different schools such as public and private or independent schools can potentially cause significant differences in learning abilities for the children.

3.3   Availability of ICT Teaching Learning Material

Many authors have concluded that sheer provision of hardware and software will not increase the readiness of teachers to integrate ICT in the classroom. Availability of ICT teaching material and access to it is a key factor for ICT integration. Usage of ICT material positively affects teaching learning process. Inability of teacher for searching right content on internet is limiting factor for ICT adoption in the class [1]. Ekberg and Gao [16] also mention lack of digital content and time consuming process to find the right kind of content as major challenges in adoption of ICT at the school level. The lack of time available to master the software or adopting the ICT in the teaching learning process are the barrier for teachers to adopt ICT in the classroom [4, 17].

Onofrei [30] observes that many schools are using ICT at basic levels such as for finding information on internet, organizing activities and so on. But very few schools are using ICT by taking collaborative approach and making use of digital processing materials and various specialized software which will improve the learning outcomes. It is very important to build techno-pedagogical literacy of the teachers. Slabeycius and Polčin [37] describe the EDULAB project from Slovania of how it systematically created 30,000 projects by using digital technologies to teach mathematics and physics. Interface easiness and website interface displays are also important in making the learning process enjoyable and enriching [33].

3.4 Support of the Colleagues

ICT requires higher level of collaborations amongst teachers. The platform for teachers to share technology practices and experience is likely to help in increasing perceived proficiency of teachers. If schools provide opportunities to the teachers to observe the teachers who use technology effectively will help other teachers to try and adopt ICT in the classroom [18]. Ming et al. [26] report about the project 'e-CPDelT Model 2020' which will act as a catalyst to serve as a nucleus to all teachers of research, materials, pedagogical skills and will be a support system to bring out attitudinal change in teachers.

3.5 Relationship Between Perception Toward ICT as an Effective Teaching-Learning Tool and Perceived Proficiency of Teachers

The existing research throws a light on teachers' perception about ICT and their perceived proficiency. It shows that there is a positive relationship between teachers' attitude towards ICT and its successful implementation in the classroom. Lack of acceptance and enthusiasm of teachers to use ICT is cited as one of the principle reason for low penetration of ICT in education [27, 34].

Building teachers' proficiency for using ICT in the classroom requires multidimensional approach such as bringing attitudinal changes, changing organizational culture and providing scope for professional development for building competencies [36]. Mynaríková and Novotný [28] support this argument and state that efforts should be made to reduce the distrust of the teachers on ICT as a useful technology and reduce the level of anxiety to use it.

Buabeng-Andoh [7] found that teachers' competence and perception related to efficacy of ICT as a tool positively gets affected by their access to the instructional material which is learner centric. Amenyedzi et al. [5] report that willpower of the teachers to learn ICT tools and appropriate training programs to help them reflect on existing education practices and encourage them to adopt new technologies will go a long way to develop positive perceptions about ICT.

To sum up the existing literature speaks about the factors affecting the teachers' attitude towards implementation of ICT. It also proves how teachers' attitude plays an important role in its effective utilization of ICT in the classroom. The present study focuses on bridging two gaps in the existing literature – i) this type of study is not made in the Indian context – specifically covering its diverse range under school education system of various boards and different languages of delivery ii) the path analysis between the school related factors affecting teachers' perceptions which in turn affect their perceived proficiency of using ICT in the classroom is not attempted.

4   Research Methodology

The study uses the primary data collection method. The 515 respondents surveyed for the study were teachers teaching to grade 5th to 10th grades. The schools selected for the survey were located in Mumbai Metropolitan region, Suburban region of Mumbai and Navi Mumbai, Maharashtra, India. The study used stratified random sampling. The teachers selected were from different schools belong to different board of education, government & private school and medium of instruction as English and Regional (Marathi). The adoption of ICT, ICT enabled curriculum, ICT policies of these boards are different.

The questionnaire was designed with the help of three pretested questionnaires from the existing literature. First questionnaire used was taken from the questionnaire used by the survey which was funded by European Commission and the questionnaire was administered in 31 countries. The second questionnaire used for the study was designed by 'Professional Development Service by Teacher (PDST)', Dublin, Ireland. The third questionnaire was about the factors affecting teachers teaching with technology (SFA-T3) Copyright of Charoula Angeli, Department of Education, University of Cyprus ETC. These three questionnaires were used to prepare the teacher's questionnaire for the study. The face and content validity were administered on the scale. The Cronbach Alpha of the scale is found to **0.967**.

The sample characteristics showed that there were 76% female and 24% male respondents. They belonged to the age group between 21 to 50 years. The regional language (Marathi) schools were affiliated to only state board. The 72% teachers surveyed were from English medium school and only 28% were from regional (Marathi) medium school. 39% teachers were having more than 15 years of experience.

The study tries to find the relation of endogenous factors and perception of the teachers for the using ICT in the classroom and their perceived proficiency in using ICT in the classroom.

Objective 1: Measurement Model: Development of Model Fit to see the relationship between of factors related to ICT adoption and Perception of teachers related to ICT as a Teaching Learning tool and their perceived proficiency in using it in the classroom.

Objective 2: Structural Model Assessment: to measure the effect of factors related to ICT adoption on perceived proficiency and perception of teachers towards usage of ICT.

4.1 Hypothesis

- H1: Access to ICT will positively influence the perceived proficiency of teachers about ICT.
- H2: Administrative support for ICT will positively influence the perceived proficiency of teachers about ICT.
- H3: Support from Colleagues for ICT will positively influence the perceived proficiency of teachers about ICT.
- H4: ICT material and activities used will positively influence the perceived proficiency of teachers about ICT.
- H5: Access to ICT will positively influence the perception of teachers for adoption of ICT in the classroom
- H6: Administrative support for ICT will positively influence the perception of teachers for adoption of ICT in the classroom
- H7: Support from Colleagues for ICT will positively influence the perception of teachers for adoption of ICT in the classroom
- H8: ICT material and activities used will positively influence the perception of teachers for adoption of ICT in the classroom
- H9: Perception of teachers for adoption of ICT in the classroom influence positively the perceived proficiency of teachers about ICT.

5   Data Findings

5.1   PLS-SEM Model Assessment

Each latent variable in the model has 10 to 15 items. The model tries to find a complex relationship by using Partial Least Square structural equation model based on Principal Component Analysis. The study uses PLS-SEM model for theory building and complex structural model [23] (Fig. 1).

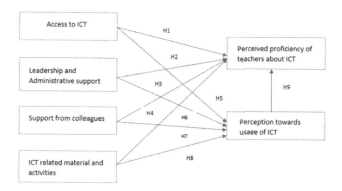

Fig. 1. The conceptual framework of the study is.

5.2   Measurement Model Assessment

The assessment of outer model of structural relation was done first with the composite reliability (assesses internal consistency), Outer loadings (Assesses indicator reliability) and average variance extracted (assesses convergent reliability).

Composite reliability coefficient assesses the internal consistency reliability. Composite reliability takes into consideration different outer loadings of indicator variables [23] (Table 1).

Table 1. Reliability and validity

Construct	CR #1	AVE #2	Access to ICT	Admin support	ICT material activities	Perceived proficiency	Perception towards ICT	Support colleagues
Access to ICT	0.893	0.626	**0.791**					
Admin support	0.937	0.679	0.441	**0.824**				
ICT material activities	0.930	0.595	0.535	0.388	**0.771**			
Perceived proficiency	0.957	0.648	0.381	0.423	0.386	**0.805**		
Perception towards ICT	0.953	0.718	0.388	0.507	0.372	0.692	**0.847**	
Support colleagues	0.951	0.796	0.205	0.510	0.282	0.383	0.451	**0.892**

The diagonal values represents square root of Average Variance Extracted and the off diagonal bold values are the correlations between the latent variables

CR #1 Composite reliability
AVE #2 Average Variance extracted

The above table shows composite reliability is found greater than 0.7 [22]. The average variance extracted (AVE) is greater than 0.5 [22].

The table also shows the square root of Average Variance Extracted (AVE) for all latent variable is higher than inter construct correlation [19]. It explains the discriminant validity.

The individual loading for all indicators were found higher than their respective cross loadings. This provides additional evidence of discriminant validity. The reliability of indicators was explained by outer loadings. The outer loadings ranged from 0.672 to 0.924. All the values of outer loadings were higher than the prescribed value 0.6 [29]. Some items had low values of outer loadings and hence those items were dropped. This resulted in improvement of composite reliability and validity of those latent variables.

5.3 Structural Model Assessment

The inner model was assessed to test the relationship between the variables. The path coefficients were attempted using Boot Strapping technique with 395 cases and 5000 samples for non-return model.

The R^2 value for proficiency of teachers for ICT was found 0.507 and the R^2 value for perception of teachers for ICT was found 0.351 (Table 2).

Table 2. Structural Relation

Hypothesis	Paths	Path coefficient	P-values	Decisions
H1	ACCESS -> PERCEIVED_PROF	0.079	0.050	Accepted
H5	ACCESS -> PERCEPTION	0.158	0.003	Accepted
H2	ADMIN_SUPP -> PERCEIVED_PROF	0.019	0.740	Not accepted
H6	ADMIN_SUPP -> PERCEPTION	0.266	0.001	Accepted
H4	ICT_MAT_ACT -> PERCEIVED_PROF	0.101	0.020	Accepted
H8	ICT_MAT_ACT -> PERCEPTION	0.113	0.015	Accepted
H3	SUPP_COLL -> PERCEIVED_PROF	0.065	0.183	Not accepted
H7	SUPP_COLL -> PERCEPTION	0.251	0.000	Accepted
H9	PERCEPTION -> PERCEIVED_PROF	0.585	0.000	Accepted

5.4 Findings

The above table shows that Support from colleagues and administrative support do not influence perceived proficiency of teachers. H2 and H3 are not accepted as p-values is greater than 0.05. Access to ICT equipment and ICT materials and activities used in class influence the perceived proficiency of teachers. H1 and H4 are accepted as p-values is less than 0.05. Access, Admin support, ICT materials and activities used in class and support from colleagues' influence perception of teachers towards ICT. H5, H6, H7 and H8 are accepted as p-value is less than 0.05. Perception of teachers towards ICT influences the perceived proficiency of teachers. H9 also accepted as p-value is less than 0.05 (Table 3).

Table 3. Effect size

Paths	Effect size (Cohen's f^2)
ACCESS -> PERCEIVED_PROF	**0.008**
ACCESS -> PERCEPTION	0.025
ADMIN_SUPP -> PERCEIVED_PROF	**0.000**
ADMIN_SUPP -> PERCEPTION	0.067
ICT_MAT_ACT -> PERCEIVED_PROF	**0.014**
ICT_MAT_ACT -> PERCEPTION	**0.013**
SUPP_COLL -> PERCEIVED_PROF	**0.006**
SUPP_COLL -> PERCEPTION	0.070
PERCEPTION -> PERCEIVED_PROF	**0.450**

Cohen's f^2 for all paths in the model to study effect size was attempted [13]. The stated values for f^2 are 0.02, 0.15, 0.35 Low, medium and large effect size [11]. It can be seen from above table the effect size of perception on perceived proficiency is large.

The blindfold technique helps to emphasize more the predictive relevance of structural model by using Stone-Geisser's Q^2 technique with omission distance 7. The Q^2 for perception of teachers towards ICT is 0.233 and The Q^2 for perceived proficiency of teachers is 0.298. These values are greater than zero. It indicates all endogenous variables are relevant in the model.

6   Conclusions

The study concludes that access to ICT equipment and resources contributes positively to the perception of the teachers related to efficacy of ICT as a teaching learning tool as well as their perceived proficiency in implementing it the classroom. Administrative support helps in improving the perception of the teachers towards ICT but may not help in improving their perceived proficiency to implement ICT in the classroom. Availability of ICT material and course content improves the perception of the teachers towards the ICT as well as their perceived proficiency in using the same. Support from the colleagues and experts in implementing ICT in the classroom improve the perception but may not improve the perceived proficiency of the teachers in implementing ICT in the classroom. Finally, positive perception of the teachers about efficacy of ICT as a teaching learning tool helps build their perceived proficiency in using it in the classroom.

7   Implications and Suggestions

- Timely and easy access to ICT equipment, resources and ICT material like digital content, activities, etc. to the teachers are of paramount importance for effective implementation of ICT in the schools. Many regional language schools do not have quality and adequate digital content to deliver. It may become a major hindrance in integrating e-learning in the mass education.

- The study shows that self-confidence of the teachers and their positive perception about ICT is important for building their perceived proficiency. It requires two interventions. Firstly teacher should be trained in soft-skills and communication skills along with the technical training in how to teach using ICT. Secondly the subject specific training is required to be given to the respective teachers so as to make ICT fully integrated in the course structure and make the teachers confident of its delivery in their own areas of expertise.
- Administrative support and support from the colleagues mainly play a supportive role in building positive perception related towards efficacy about ICT. But it cannot be ignored. Frequent training sessions of the administrative staff and organizing experts interactions with regular interventions will go a long way in building school culture positive for implementing ICT.

References

1. Adomi, E.E., Kpangban, E.: Application of ICTs in Nigerian Secondary schools. Library Philosophy and Practice 2010. ISSN 1522–0222. http://digitalcommons.unl.edu/libphilprac/345 (2010)
2. Afshari, M.: Transformational leadership role of principals in implementing information communication technology in schools. Life Sci. J. 9(1) (2012)
3. Albugarni, S., Ahmed, V.: Success factors for ICT implementation in saudi secondary schools: From the perspective of ICT directors, head teachers, teachers and students. Int. J. Educ. Dev. Inf. Commun. Technol. 11(1), 36–54 (2015)
4. Almekhlafi, A.G., Almeqdadi, F.A.: Teachers' perceptions of technology integration in the United Arab Emirates shool classrooms. Educ. Technol. Soc. 12, 165–175 (2010)
5. Amenyedzi, F.W.K., Lartey, M.N., Dzomeku, B.M.: The use of computers and internet as supplementary source of educational material: A case study of the senior high schools in the tema metropolis in ghana. Contemp. Educ. Technol. 2(2), 151–162 (2011)
6. Aramide, K.A., Ladipo, S.O., Adebayo, I.: Demographic variables and ICT access as predictors of information communication technologies' usage among science teachers in federal unity schools in Nigeria. Libr. Philos. Pract. 1–27 (2015)
7. Buabeng-Andoh, C.: An exploration of teachers' skills, perceptions and practices of ICT in teaching and learning in the ghanaian second-cycle schools. Contemp. Educ. Technol. 3(1), 36–49 (2012)
8. Buabeng-Andoh, C.: Teachers' ICT usage in second-cycle institutions in ghana: A qualitative study. Int. J. Educ. Dev. Inf. Commun. Technol. 11(2), 104–112 (2015)
9. Buabeng-Andoh, C.: ICT usage in ghanaian secondary schools: Teachers' perspectives. Int. J. Inf. Learn. Technol. 32(5), 300–312 (2015)
10. Andoh, Charles Buabeng-, Yidana, Issifu: Teachers' ICT usage in second-cycle institutions in Ghana: A qualitative study. Int. J. Educ. Dev. Inf. Commun. Technol. (IJEDICT) 2015 (11), 104–112 (2015)
11. Chin, W.W.: How to write up and report PLS analyses. Handbook of Partial Least Squares, pp. 655–690. Springer, Berlin Heidelberg (2010)

12. Chin, C., Todd, P.: On the use, usefulness and ease of use of structural equation modeling in MIS research: A note of caution. MIS Q. **19**(2) (1995)

13. Cohen, J.: Statistical Power Analysis for the Behavioral Sciences, pp. 20–26. Lawrence Earlbaum Associates, Hillsdale, NJ (1988)

14. Cox, M., Rhodes, V., Hall, J.: The use of computer assisted learning in primary schools: Some factors affecting the uptake. Comput. Educ. **12**(10), 173–178 (1988)

15. Eickelmann, B.: Supportive and hindering factors to a sustainable implementation of ICT in schools/förderliche und hemmende bedingungen der nachhaltigen implementierung von IKT in schulen. J. Educ. Res. Online **3**(1), 75–103 (2011)

16. Ekberg, S., Gao, S.: Understanding challenges of using ICT in secondary schools in sweden from teachers' perspective. Int. J. Inf. Learn. Technol. **35**(1), 43–55 (2018)

17. Francis, N.N., Ngugi, M., Kinzi, J.: Influence of selected factors on the implementation of information and communication technology policy in public secondary schools in naivasha sub-county, kenya. Int. J. Educ. Dev. Inf. Commun. Technol. **13**(2), 70–86 (2017)

18. Frederick, G.R., Schweizer, H., Lowe, R.: After the inservice course: Challenges of technology integration. Comput. Sch. **23**, 73–84 (2006)

19. Fornell, Claes, Larcker, David F.: Structural equation models with unobservable variables and measurement error: Algebra and statistics. J. Mark. Res. **18**(3), 382–388 (1981)

20. Gudmundsdottir, G.B.: From digital divide to digital equity: Learners' ICT competence in four primary schools in cape town, south africa. International Journal of Education and Dev. Inf. Commun. Technol. **6**(2), 22–1H,2H,3H,4H,5H,6H,7H,8H,9H,10H,11H,12H,13H,14H, 15H,16H,17H,18H,1 (2010)

21. Gurr, D.: The impact of information communication technology on the work of school principals. Learn. Manag. **6**(1), 63–67 (2010)

22. Hair, J.F., Black, W.C., Babin, B.J., Anderson, R.E., Tatham, R.L.: Multivariate Data Analysis, 6th edn. Pearson Prentice Hall, New Jersey (2006)

23. Hair Jr., J.F., Hult, G., Tomas, M., Ringle, C., Sarstedt, M.: A Primer on Partial Least Squares Structural Equation Modeling (PLS-SEM). SAGE Publications, Incorporated, Thousand Oaks, CA (2013)

24. Leithwood, K.A., Day, C., Sammons, P., Hopkins, D., Harris, A.: Successful school leadership: What it is and how it influences pupil learning. http://www.nysed.gov/common/nysed/files/principal-project-file-55-successful-school-leadership-what-it-is-and-how-it-influences-pupil-learning.pdf (2006). Accessed 21 Aug 2017

25. Levin, B., Schum, L.: Leading Technology-Rich Schools: Award Winning Models for Success. Teachers College Press, New York (2012)

26. Marshall, S.: Report on the 2000 UTDC Survey of Academic Staff Needs for Teaching Technology Support. Victoria University of Wellington, Wellington, New Zealand (2000)

27. Ming, T.S., Hall, C., Azman, H., Joyes, G.: Supporting smart school teachers' continuing professional development in and through ICT: A model for change. Int. J. Educ. Dev. Inf. Commun. Technol. **6**(2), 16–1B,2B,3B,4B,5B,6B,7B,8B,9B,10B,11B,12B,13B,14B,15B, 16B (2010)

28. Morales-Gomez, D., Melesse, M.: Utilizing information and communication technologies for development: The social dimension. Inf. Technol. Dev. **8**, 3–13 (1998)

29. Neyland, E.: Integrating online learning in NSW secondary schools: Three schools perspectives on ICT adoption. Aust. J. Educ. Technol. **27**(1), 152–173 (2011)

30. Nunnally, J.C.: Psychometric Theory, 2nd edn. McGraw-Hill, New York (1978)

31. Onofrei, S.G.: Access and use of new ICT resources in Romanian schools. Acta Didactica Napocensia **9**(4), 25–34 (2016)

32. Porten, B.S., Shen, J., Williams, R.C.: The changing principalship and its impact: Voices from principals. Natl. Assoc. Sch. Princ. Bull. **82**(602), 1–8 (1998)

33. Prain, V., Hand, B.: Using new technologies for learning: A case study of a whole-school approach. J. Res. Technol. Educ. **35**(4), 441–458 (2003)
34. Rahamat, R., Shah, P.M., Puteh, S., Din, R., Karim, A.: End-users' involvement in the development of web-based learning resources for english literature. 3L Lang. Linguist. Lit. **17** (2011)
35. Redmond, P., Albion, P.R., Maroulis, J.: Intentions v reality: Pre-service teachers' ICT integration during professional experience. Paper presented at the 16th International Conference of the Society for Information Technology & Teacher Education (SITE 2005), Phoenix, USA, Mar 2005
36. Sharija, M.A., Watters, J.J.: Innovative leadership by school principals: Embedding information communication and technology in Kuwaiti schools. J. Int. Educ. Res. **8**(4), 425 (2012)
37. Shin, W.S.: Individual and organizational factors influencing korean teachers' use of technology (Order No. 3424909). Available from Publicly Available Content Database. (756256003) (2010)
38. Slabeycius, J., Polčin, D.: How ICT can enhance the attractiveness of mathematics and physics in primary school. Probl. Educ. 21st Century **50**, 101–107 (2012)
39. Teo, T., Chai, C.S., Hung, D., Lee, C.B.: Beliefs about teaching and learning and uses of technology among pre-service teachers. Asia Pac. J. Educ. **36**(2), 165–176 (2008)

Child Online Safety Intervention Through Empowering Parents and Technical Experts: Indian Context

Dittin Andrews[1], Sreejith Alathur[2], and Naganna Chetty[2(✉)]

[1] Centre for Development of Advanced Computing, Thiruvananthapuram, India
dittin@cdac.in
[2] National Institute of Technology Karnataka, Surathkal, Mangalore, India
sreejith.nitk@gmail.com, nsc.chetty@gmail.com

Abstract. Child online safety is a state of being protected from online problematic content and environment. Purpose of this study is to examine the
stakeholders' empowered status influence on child online safety. Using questionnaires survey responses on relational aspects of stakeholder empowerment
and child online safety is collected from parents and technical experts who were
working with the Internet safety. The responses are analyzed with the help of
SPSS software and the results are examined for influencing factors of child
online safety. Restricting resources, blocking at different levels and parental
control are the different influencing factors of child online safety. As the parental
control influencing factor exists with both the models of parents and technical
experts initiated, it plays an important role in attaining child online safety. The
influencing factors which are observed from the study can be emphasized to
control child online threats and provide online safety.

Keywords: Child online safety · Parents and technical experts' initiatives ·
India · Online threats · Influencing factors

1 Introduction

In this digitized era, Internet is an essential part of life and its size is increasing with a
greater number of household connections. Evolution of computers and popularity of
Internet is allowing fast communication between people. World Wide Web, Peer to
Peer Networks, Emails, instant messaging applications and Social networking sites are
playing major role in information exchange (Thanuskodi 2019).

Child online safety is a state of being protected from online problematic content and
environment. Online Child Exploitation has been a concern across the globe. Safety is a
major concern of the children who use Internet since it is a medium to access different
types of information which could have positive and negative impacts on the children.
Children are more victimized from exploitation than older person (Kristensen and
Smith 2003). Online child exploitation or allied risks comes into picture only when
considering internet technologies as the use pattern. Though, the Internet technologies
have contributed towards the improvements of social, scientific or economic arena, its

© IFIP International Federation for Information Processing 2020
Published by Springer Nature Switzerland AG 2020
S. K. Sharma et al. (Eds.): TDIT 2020, IFIP AICT 618, pp. 662–673, 2020.
https://doi.org/10.1007/978-3-030-64861-9_57

adverse effects cannot be neglected. Understanding Internet technologies, its applications and allied vulnerable (virtual) world can be of paramount significance.

Acknowledging the dangers and hazards to children in the Internet depends on the blend of approaches which include self and co-regulatory, technical, legislative, educational awareness, not only positive content provision but also ensuring child safety zones. Every country has its own sets of policies to act against crimes related to child online safety. Different policy measures co-exist which address these risks and initiatives from different stakeholders which in turn create complex policies at national level and heterogeneous policies across different countries.

With these benefits and consequences of the Internet, this paper tries to identify different factors associated with child online safety and confirms some of the factors as influencers of child online safety. The current study involves testing of two different research models using the responses collected from parents and technical experts separately.

2   Theoretical Framework and Research Model

Increased growth of ICTs, high-speed connectivity and wider coverage of network made online activities easier and often harmful across the globe. In this digital era, the strong Internet governance practices are required to protect children's rights. The Internet governance organizations can incorporate multiple stake holders such as children, parents, teachers, Internet service providers, law enforcement agencies and governments for their better performance.

As the children online safety is a global issue, several countries have taken steps to act on it by introducing online child safety and protection related acts and various awareness programs (Livingstone and Smith 2014; Isaac et al. 2004; ITU 2015; UNICEF 2012). In this regard, the guidelines are prepared for children, parents, caretakers, policy makers and industry by international research organizations (O'Connell 2003; ITU 2015). The children online safety issues may be addressed within the categories such as governance, technology and social.

In this digitized era, attaining child online safety is a challenging task and demands a collective effort form the government, technical experts, parents and legal advisors. In the following subsections, the literature review is made on parents and technical experts-initiated child online safety.

2.1   Parents Initiated Child Online Safety

Digital Awareness. Awareness programs (NIST 1998) are identified as the mechanism to build a secure positive environment by alerting users on consequences of Internet use. Safety awareness can be made through traditional media, websites, specialized awareness content from experts and Internet service providers. For the protection of young Internet users, emphasis on policies is needed to raise awareness and back appropriate measures (Livingstone et al. 2012).

Hp1: Digital awareness is an influencing factor for parents-initiated child online safety.

Establishing Wanted Contact. Avoiding unwanted contact can reduce risk of cyber solicitation and allied crime (Madigan et al. 2018). Before establishing a contact with others online, it is essential to understand their background.

Hp2: Establishing wanted contact is an influencing factor for parents-initiated child online safety.

Limited Online Convenience. Social networking sites enable users to share their updates such as the status, content of cognition and any specific behavior or action to friends (Jones et al. 2008). Self-disclosure of personal information and status updates may be problematic because of the risks like identity theft, cyber-stalking and cyber bullying. Users are more concerned about privacy but self-disclosure is prevalent (Jones et al. 2008). The online presence can be made with the availability of technology and usage convenience. With limited online convenience, the online risks can be reduced.

Hp3: Limited online convenience is an influencing factor for parents-initiated child online safety.

Online Benefit. Children are spending more time with Internet and engaged in several online activities. The various concerns in this regard are cyber bullying, inappropriate content availability, addiction to Internet and issues of privacy (Livingstone et al. 2018). As the Internet is more personal and portable, it is hard to parents to monitor online activities of children (Shin 2015). Since the inception of Internet, Internet addiction is identified as one among some of the most preoccupation (Burnay et al. 2015). The more online presence may attract both benefits and risks.

Hp4: Online benefit is an influencing factor for parents-initiated child online safety.

Restricting Resources. Proliferation of Internet has significantly contributed to increased availability of pornographic or sexual content and changes in consumption of sexually explicit content by the children (Owens et al. 2012). It has enhanced the probability of children accidentally accessing such contents on the web. Restricting access to certain content and resources may reduce online risks.

Hp5: Restricting resources is an influencing factor for parents-initiated child online safety.

Educating on Online Risks. The online safety education is essential to reduce risks based on their usage pattern. The efforts on widely accepted preventive measures, awareness programmes and education are made by civil societies, industries, government initiatives and motivated individuals with a focus on online etiquette for children. The existing awareness programs for children are less appropriate to a system. System-wide awareness programmes needs to be implemented by accommodating in the high school and higher secondary curriculum. To provide training and workshops on online security, MEITY, a unit of the ministry of communications and information technology in India, has initiated a project on "information security education and awareness" for the duration 2015–2020 (ISEA 2014). A certification programme in online security is also conducted for interested children by the centre for development of advanced computing under this project.

Hp6: Educating on online risks is an influencing factor for parents-initiated child online safety.

Empowering Authorities. The national framework is a novel approach assigning responsibility to manpower to keep children safe. The framework establishes competencies and standards for people having direct/indirect contact with children to ensure that they are delivering a systematic and consistent standard of help to children and youngsters. A well-defined governance system for online grievance redressing with a mechanism to register online, investigate and respond within given time frame is developed. Empowering parents and concerned authorities may reduce online risks (Nawaila et al. 2018).

Hp7: Empowering authorities is an influencing factor for parents-initiated child online safety.

Parental Control. Cyber bullying is an encapsulation of all forms of harms or harassments that commonly occur with Internet, computers and mobiles such as sending threatening, harassing and harmful mails or messages, posting derogative comments, intimidating online, ignoring, disrespecting, spreading rumors, stalking and physical threatening (Hinduja and Patchin 2007). Therefore, identification of virtual harm may reduce the possibility of victimization. Video sharing sites are associated with age inappropriate content such as violent and pornographic content (Livingstone et al. 2013). Though, the parents are supportive to their children's Internet usage, setting limits on use, content types and time is a difficult task. Several tools are available to parents to limit the exposure of their children to age in-appropriate content. The parents can control online activities of their children to reduce online risks (McNally et al. 2018).

Hp8: Parental control is an influencing factor for parents-initiated child online safety.

2.2   Technical Experts-Initiated Child Online Safety

Establishing Wanted Contact. Avoiding unwanted contact can reduce risk of cyber solicitation and allied crime (Madigan et al. 2018). Before establishing a contact with others online, it is essential to understand their background.

HT1: Establishing wanted contact is an influencing factor for technical experts-initiated child online safety.

Content Filtering. Predators provoke children to participate in online sexual activities and broach the process through discussions on sexual nature by sending pornographic content based on the interest of children using chat rooms (Normand and Sallafranque-St- Louis 2016). Websites or applications with chatting blogs have been identified as sites with greater prevalence. By using content filtering strategy online risks can be reduced.

HT2: Content filtering is an influencing factor for technical experts-initiated child online safety.

Blocking at Different Levels. The mobile applications can be blocked at different levels for the safety of children (McNally et al. 2018). Similarly, the online content can be monitored and blocked at different levels over the Internet (Gosh et al. 2018; DeMarco et al. 2018).

HT3: Blocking at different levels is an influencing factor for technical experts-initiated child online safety.

Education on Online Behavior. Young Internet users should have the capability to identify online social networking fake account, sexual content and connection request from multiple accounts of same person (Boshmaf et al. 2011). Knowledge on the activity that children are performing online is important. Users accept friend requests to connect by unknown when there exist mutual friends (Boshmaf et al. 2011). Identification of strangers in the social networking profile and removing them from the friend list is essential to reduce online risks. Often, a password sharing among family members is a common practice.

HT4: Education on online behaviour is an influencing factor for technical experts-initiated child online safety.

Identification Systems. Parents and teachers may supervise children's activities at home and school. Often, the limited knowledge of parents to monitor children's activities online may lead to miss experiences of the victim and checking of predator actions. Identification of illegal content sources is important to control child online risks (DeMarco et al. 2018).

HT5: Identification systems is an influencing factor for technical experts-initiated child online safety.

ISP Level Effort. At the ISPs, the harmful content which originates from particular IP addresses can be blocked (Brennan et al. 2019). The blocking at ISP is a prevalent concept to mitigate risks.

HT6: ISP level effort is an influencing factor for technical experts-initiated child online safety.

Parental Control. Though, the parents are supportive to their children's Internet usage, setting limits on use, content types and time is a difficult task. Several tools are available to parents to limit the exposure of their children to age in-appropriate content. The parents can control online activities of their children to reduce online risks (McNally et al. 2018).

> HT7: Parental control is an influencing factor for technical experts-initiated child online safety

2.3   Research Model

Different variables related to child online safety are identified from literature review. The research model for parents-initiated child online safety is shown in Fig. 1. Digital awareness, establishing wanted contact, limited online convenience, online benefits, restricting resources, educating on online risks, empowering authorities and parental control are the different independent variables in the parent-initiated child online safety. Similarly, a research model for technical experts-initiated child online safety is shown in Fig. 2. The different independent variables in technical experts-initiated child online safety are establishing wanted contact, content filtering, blocking at different levels, education on online behavior, identification systems, ISP level efforts and parental control.

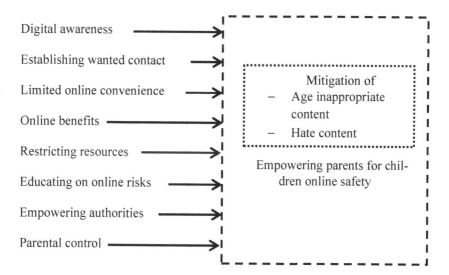

Fig. 1. Research model for parents-initiated child online safety

3   Methodology

The study uses a quantitative approach to determine the influence of online children safety. The data is collected through both online and offline modes by preparing questionnaires and requesting the different stakeholders who involved in Internet safety initiatives. The prepared questionnaire is shared through Google forms to identified

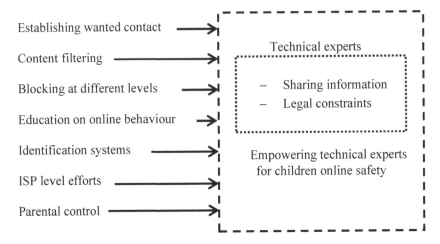

Fig. 2. Research model for technical experts-initiated child online safety

parents and experts by considering references from various incidents related to child online safety. To collect responses from the aforesaid stakeholders a convenient cum random sampling approach has been considered. The stakeholders have been requested through online media such as Skype, WhatsApp Video call and in person to assess respective concerns toward escalating cybercrime, online child exploitation, leaking of personal information and allied incidents.

Two different structured questionnaires have been constructed and administered to a sample of parents and technical experts belonging to different age groups and exposed to Internet safety incidents. The questionnaires are designed to retrieve significant information from the respondents pertaining to their respective views and perception towards online child exploitation and various mechanisms and parental control techniques involved to prevent online child abuse.

After collecting the data, both online and offline data are integrated to construct a dataset for research. The combined dataset is processed and analyzed using SPSS software. The outcome of the regression algorithm is interpreted and influencers of child online safety are identified.

4   Results and Discussion

The results obtained from two different models such as parents initiated and technical experts initiated on online children safety are represented in the following subsections.

4.1   Parent Initiated Online Children Safety

The Pearson's correlation between the different influencers of parent initiated online children safety along with the significant levels is shown in Table 1. The correlation between the child online safety (COS) dependent variable and restricting resources (RR) independent variable is 0.59 and is larger positive value than the other variables.

This correlations result will also serve as a mechanism for identifying multicollinearity among the influencers. As all the pairwise correlation values are below 0.9, there is no multicollinearity between the influencers (Field 2009).

Table 1. Correlation among different variables for parent-initiated model

	COS	DA	EWC	LOC	OB	RR	EOR	EA	PC
COS	1.00								
DA	0.30^{**}	1.00							
EWC	0.46^{***}	0.24^{*}	1.00						
LOC	0.33^{**}	0.23^{*}	0.27^{*}	1.00					
OB	0.26^{*}	0.30^{**}	0.34^{**}	0.37^{***}	1.00				
RR	0.59^{***}	0.27^{*}	0.51^{***}	0.17	0.43^{***}	1.00			
EOR	0.46^{***}	0.24^{*}	0.41^{***}	0.32^{**}	0.43^{***}	0.56^{***}	1.00		
EA	0.36^{**}	0.17	0.38^{***}	0.23^{*}	0.34^{**}	0.41^{***}	0.30^{**}	1.00	
PC	0.58^{***}	0.09	0.52^{***}	0.27^{*}	0.21^{*}	0.58^{***}	0.45^{***}	0.44^{***}	1.00

*$p < 0.05$; **$p < 0.01$; ***$p < 0.001$; COS: Child online safety; DA: Digital awareness; EWC: Establishing wanted contact; LOC: Limited online convenience; OB: Online behaviour; RR: Restricting resources; EOR: Educating on online risks; EA: Empowering authorities; PC: parental control.*

The result of regression analysis for parent initiated online children safety is shown in Table 2. R2 is a measure to know the variability resulting in dependent variable from independent variables. The model which is designed for predicting the parent initiated online children safety results 0.50 as R2 value. The effect size of the influencers on outcome variable is more. The F-Ratio for this model is 8.25 at highly significant level ($p < 0.001$). The F-Ratio represents the prediction ability of the model. The effect size R2 and F represents overall performance of the model, i.e. the combined performance of all the influencers. The collinearity among variables can be checked with variance inflation factor (VIF). As the VIF value of all measuring variables is less than 3, there is no collinearity among the variables. By referring to β values, the performance of individual predictor parameters can be measured.

From Table 2, a path from digital awareness to parent-initiated child online safety is not significant as its P value is greater than 0.05. Therefore, the hypothesis Hp1 is rejected. Similarly, paths from establishing wanted contact, limited online convenience, online benefits, educating on online risks and empowering authorities to parent initiated child online safety are not significant as their P values are greater than 0.05. Therefore, the hypotheses Hp2, Hp3, Hp4, Hp6 and Hp7 are not accepted.

The path form restricting resources to parent-initiated child online safety is significant as its P value is smaller the 0.05. This significance level made to accept the hypothesis Hp5. Hence, restricting resources is an influencing factor for parent-initiated child online safety. Similarly, the path from parental control to parent-initiated child online safety is also significant as its P value is smaller than the 0.05. Therefore, the hypothesis Hp8 is also accepted. Hence, parental control is an influencing factor for parent-initiated child online safety.

Table 2. Regression analysis result of parent-initiated model

Dept. Variable	R²	F	Ind. Variable	Beta	T	VIF
Parent	0.50	8.25	Digital awareness (DA)	0.15	1.56	1.18
			Establishing wanted contact (EWC)	0.07	0.62	1.63
			Limited online convenience (LOC)	0.15	1.51	1.30
			Online benefits (OB)	−0.10	−0.93	1.55
			Restricting resources (RR)	**0.31**	**2.45***	**2.14**
			Educating on online risks (EOR)	0.08	0.74	1.67
			Empowering authorities (EA)	0.04	0.34	1.38
			Parental control (PC)	**0.28**	**2.33***	**1.94**

*$p < 0.05$

4.2   Technical Experts Initiated Online Children Safety

The Pearson's correlation between the different variables of parent initiated online children safety along with the significant levels is shown in Table 3. The correlation between the identification systems and ISP level efforts is 0.65 and more than the other correlations. The regression analysis for technical experts initiated online children safety is shown in Table 4. As R2 is a measure to know variability, the model provides 0.63 as R2 value and results in large effect size of the influencers on outcome variable. F-Ratio with the value 5.36 represents prediction ability of the model at highly significant level ($p < 0.001$). There is no collinearity among variables as the VIF value of all measuring variables is less than 3.

A path from establishing wanted contacts to technical experts-initiated child online safety have P value more than 0.05 and is not significant. Therefore, the hypothesis HT1 is rejected. Similarly, paths from content filtering, education on online behavior, identification systems and ISP level efforts to technical experts-initiated child online safety are not significant as their P values are more than 0.05. Therefore, the hypotheses HT2, HT4, HT5 and HT6 are not accepted.

Table 3. Correlation among variables for technical experts-initiated model

	COS	EWC	CF	BDL	EOB	IS	ISPE	PC
COS	1.00							
EWC	0.33*	1.00						
CF	0.03	0.40*	1.00					
BDL	−0.19	0.31*	0.50**	1.00				
EOB	0.20	0.38*	0.23	0.38*	1.00			
IS	0.32*	0.47**	0.31*	0.57**	0.38*	1.00		
ISPE	0.16	0.50**	0.16	0.49**	0.45**	0.65***	1.00	
PC	0.59**	0.35*	0.38*	0.30	0.23	0.51**	0.43**	1.00

*$p < 0.05$; **$p < 0.01$; ***$p < 0.001$; *COS: Child online safety; EWC:* establishing wanted contact; *CF:* Content filtering; *BDL:* Blocking at different levels; *EOB:* Educating on online behavior; *IS:* Identification systems; *ISPE:* ISP level efforts; *PC:* Parental control.

Table 4. Regression analysis result of technical experts-initiated model

Dept. Variable	R^2	F	Ind. Variable	Beta	T	VIF
Technical Experts	0.63	5.36	Establishing wanted contact (EWC)	0.23	1.37	1.67
			Content filtering (CF)	−0.15	−0.86	1.78
			Blocking at different levels (BDL)	**−0.50**	**−2.72**[*]	**2.04**
			Education on online behaviour (EOB)	0.19	1.23	1.36
			Identification systems (IS)	0.30	1.54	2.29
			ISP level efforts (ISPE)	−0.23	−1.15	2.29
			Parental control (PC)	**0.62**	**3.84**[**]	**1.55**

*$p < 0.05$; **$p < 0.01$*

The path form blocking at different levels to technical experts-initiated child online safety is significant as its P value is less than the 0.05. Hence, the hypothesis HT3 is accepted and interpreted as blocking at different levels is an influencing factor for technical experts-initiated child online safety. Similarly, the path from parental control to technical experts-initiated child online safety is more significant as its P value is lesser than the 0.01. Therefore, the hypothesis HT7 is also accepted. Hence, parental control is also an influencing factor for technical experts-initiated child online safety. The set of determinants of contributors to child online safety are shown in Fig. 3.

The analysis shows that restricting resources influences child online safety. This indicates that facilitating children with limited resources such as Internet connection, Internet speed and connecting devices for online activities results in less online presence, which in turn may result in reduced exposure to online threats. Restricting web sites is also a part of restricting resources.

Parental control variable is influencing both parents and technical experts-initiated child online safety models. Therefore, the control of children online activities by the

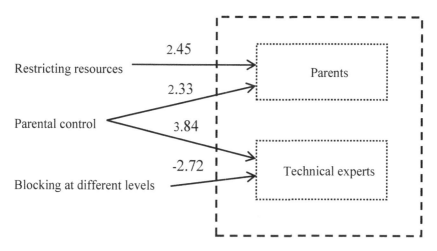

Fig. 3. Determinants of contributors to child online safety

parents plays an important role in attaining child online safety. This can be performed by maintain log records of online activities, installing supporting software and permitting the download of only genuine applications. Blocking at different levels is also an influencer of child online safety. This indicates that blocking some unwanted information at different levels, which may include blocking through the apps on the device to blocking at ISP.

5 Conclusion

Different dependent and independent variables are identified through the literature review. Based on these identified variables, the different hypotheses on prediction of parent and technical experts-initiated child online safety have been set. After collecting the responses using questionnaires, the data is analyzed with SPSS software package.

The analysis is made separately for two different models such as parents and technical experts-initiated child online safety. Parents initiated child online safety model identified two independent variables such as restricting resources and parental control as influencers of child online safety. Similarly, the technical experts-initiated child online safety model identified blocking at different levels and parental control as the influencers of the child online safety.

Even with the activeness of different international bodies to control online threats to children and attain child online safety, children are becoming online victims. Therefore, by emphasizing on the identified influencers the security measures can be improved to attain child online safety. As the parental control is observed form both the models, it can be strengthened by providing necessary assistance to parents for controlling the online activities of their children.

References

Boshmaf, Y., Muslukhov, I., Beznosov, K., Ripeanu, M.: The socialbot network: when bots socialize for fame and money. In: Proceedings of the 27th Annual Computer Security Applications Conference, pp. 93–102, ACM (2011)

Brennan, M., et al.: Best Practice in the Management of Online Sex Offending (2019)

Burnay, J., Billieux, J., Blairy, S., Larøi, F.: Which psychological factors influence Internet addiction? Evidence through an integrative model. Comput. Hum. Behav. **43**, 28–34 (2015)

DeMarco, J., Sharrock, S., Crowther, T., Barnard, M.: Behaviour and Characteristics of Perpetrators of Online-facilitated Child Sexual Abuse and Exploitation. NatCen Social Research Final Report, London (2018)

Ghosh, A.K., Badillo-Urquiola, K., Rosson, M.B., Xu, H., Carroll, J.M., Wisniewski, P.J.: A matter of control or safety?: examining parental use of technical monitoring apps on teens' mobile devices. In: Proceedings of the 2018 CHI Conference on Human Factors in Computing Systems, pp. 194. ACM (2018)

Hinduja, S., Patchin, J.W.: Offline consequences of online victimization: School violence and delinquency. J. Sch. Violence **6**(3), 89–112 (2007)

Isaac, D., Cusimano, M.D., Sherman, A., Chipman, M.: Child safety education and the world wide web: an evaluation of the content and quality of online resources. Inj. Prev. **10**(1), 59–61 (2004)

ISEA: Indulge with Information Security Education and Awareness. https://infosecawareness.in/ gallery/?typ=annual_magazines (2014). Accessed 12 Feb 2019

ITU.: Child Online Protection Initiative. www.itu.int/en/cop/Pages/default.aspx (2015). Accessed 15 March 2019

Jones, S., Millermaier, S., Goya-Martinez, M., Schuler, J.: Whose space is MySpace? a content analysis of MySpace profiles. First Monday, **13**(9) (2008)

Kristensen, S.M., Smith, P.K.: The use of coping strategies by Danish children classed as bullies, victims, bully/victims, and not involved, in response to different (hypothetical) types of bullying. Scand. J. Psychol. **44**(5), 479–488 (2003)

Livingstone, S., Leslie, H., Anke, G.: Children Risk and Safety on Internet: Research and Policy Challenges in Comparative Perspective. eprints.lse.ac.uk/44761/1/EUKidsOnlinebookExec Summary.pdf (2012). Accessed 10 March 2019

Livingstone, S., Kirwil, L., Ponte, C., Staksrud, E.: In their own words: what bothers children online? with the EU kids online network. EU Kids On-line, LSE London (2013)

Livingstone, S., Smith, P.K.: Annual research review: Harms experienced by child users of online and mobile technologies: The nature, prevalence and management of sexual and aggressive risks in the digital age. J. Child Psychol. Psychiatry **55**(6), 635–654 (2014)

Livingstone, S., Stoilova, M., Yu, S.H., Byrne, J., Kardefelt-Winther, D.: Using Mixed Methods to Research Children's Online Opportunities and Risks in A Global Context: The Approach of Global Kids Online. SAGE Publications Ltd, Thousand Oaks (2018)

Madigan, S., et al.: The prevalence of unwanted online sexual exposure and solicitation among youth: a meta-analysis. J. Adoles. Health **63**(2), 133–141 (2018)

McNally, B., et al.: Co-designing mobile online safety applications with children. In: Proceedings of the 2018 CHI Conference on Human Factors in Computing Systems, pp. 523. ACM (2018)

Nawaila, M.B., Kanbul, S., Ozdamli, F.: A review on the rights of children in the digital age. Child Youth Serv. Rev. **94**, 390–409 (2018)

NIST.: Information Technology Security Training Requirements: A Role and Performance Based Model, NIST-SP 800–16, USA. csrc.nist.gov/publications/nistpubs/800-16/800-16.pdf (1998). Accessed 15 Feb 2019

Normand, C.L., Sallafranque-St-Louis, F.: Cybervictimization of young people with an intellectual or developmental disability: Risks specific to sexual solicitation. J. Appl. Res. Intellect. Disabil. **29**(2), 99–110 (2016)

O'Connell, R.: A Typology of Child Cybersexploitation and Online Grooming Practices. University of Central Lancashire, Preston, UK (2003)

Owens, E.W., Behun, R.J., Manning, J.C., Reid, R.C.: The impact of Internet pornography on adolescents: a review of the research. Sex. Addict. Compulsivity **19**(1–2), 99–122 (2012)

Shin, W.: Parental socialization of children's Internet use: a qualitative approach. New Media Soc. **17**(5), 649–665 (2015)

Thanuskodi, S.: Usage of social media among LIS students in India. In: Literacy Skill Development for Library Science Professionals, pp. 1–24. IGI Global (2019)

UNICEF.: Child Safety Online, Global Challenges and Strategies, www.unicef-irc.org/ publications/pdf/ict_techreport3_eng.pdf (2012). Accessed 20 April 2019

Analysing ERP Implementations from Organizational Change Perspective: An Exploratory Study

S. L. N. Raja$^{(\boxtimes)}$ ⓘ, Nidheesh Joseph ⓘ, and Abhishek Totawar ⓘ

Indian Institute of Management Tiruchirappalli, Pudukkottai Main Road,
Chinna Sooriyur Village, Tiruchirappalli 620024, Tamil Nadu, India
raja.18322@iimtrichy.ac.in

Abstract. This study examines the impact of organisational change management on the outcome of digital transformation initiatives such as ERP implementation. The organisation's processes change to align with the best practices being brought on by the ERP system. The study examines the initiatives taken to manage such organisational changes during digital transformation and its impact on success of the project. A review of literature in the area of organisation change and digital transformation was conducted to explore the theoretical background. Further in-depth interviews of organisation leaders and industry practitioners involved in digital transformation were collected. Analysis of the data shows that organisations need to plan for continuous evaluation of the need for managing change for a successful digital transformation. A structured approach to the assessment of benefits before and after the change is essential. Implications for change practitioners and ERP implementation managers are discussed.

Keywords: ERP implementation · Digital transformation · Organizational change management · Project management

1 Introduction

Business organisations are transforming and improving their processes into digital formats to gain competitive advantage. The top companies in the industry frontier are at the forefront of their competition in their digital transformation journey.

Enterprise resource planning (ERP) deployment is the preliminary step for an organisation on their digital transformation journey. Digital transformations such as ERP implementation helps organisations automate the mundane manual tasks, improve the quality by avoiding human errors, reduce the cycle time and gain efficiencies to provide quick turnarounds and increase customer satisfaction level.

It is widely observed in ERP consulting that managing and driving organisational change as part of ERP implementation is the last area to be considered, and almost in every case it is a reactive measure rather than proactively planning and managing the manage. "People" aspects are left aside or assumed to be easily manageable, left to the client and line managers to handle them. The organisational change intervention

© IFIP International Federation for Information Processing 2020
Published by Springer Nature Switzerland AG 2020
S. K. Sharma et al. (Eds.): TDIT 2020, IFIP AICT 618, pp. 674–678, 2020.
https://doi.org/10.1007/978-3-030-64861-9_58

assumed as a natural outcome and is left to each function heads to figure out the impact on organisational changes in a reactive manner.

Organisation change management is one of the five categories in critical success factors contributing to the success of ERP implementations [3].

2 Literature Review

A keyword search was conducted based on the title by two primary search criteria, it must contain the keyword of "Organisation Change" and the keyword of "ERP".

2.1 Enterprise Resource Planning

ERP systems emerged in 1990s as an application integrating all functions in the organization starting from sales operations at the front end to manufacturing and planning operations at backend including the support functions of finance, accounts receivable and accounts payable [4]. ERP started out as a standalone island application, has now evolved into fully integrated solution touching all areas of Information Systems in the organisation.

ERP defined as "An ERP system is a set of business applications or modules, which links various business units of an organisation such as financial, accounting, manufacturing and human resources into a tightly integrated single system with a common platform for flow of information across the entire business" [8]. With the evolution of internet, ERP have now moved over to cloud. This has become more imminent with the current COVID19 situation, organisations are seriously considering moving all IT operations to cloud and this may entail moving to a cloud-based ERP. The important goal of ERP system is to provide current, accurate data. The cloud (internet) enables ERP systems to provide access to operational and financial data in hands of managers on demand for making strategic business decisions in a timely manner about their competitive position [8]. It is evident that an appropriate form of ERP system is a basic hygiene for organisation of all size and all types to be competitive in the market.

2.2 ERP Implementation Issues

It is observed that businesses started using digital transformation as a tool to drive strategic changes through business process re-engineering (BPR) [11]. The BPR school of thought did not consider the organisational change implications that lead to several failed ERP projects [11]. It is further important to note that studies have shown that business process re-engineering is not directly resulting in competitive advantage [10]. However, ERP empowers the organisation to achieve competitive advantage.

There is a significant change when we compare the relationships in an organisation before and after an ERP. New dotted and solid lines of relationships are established across various functions and even across continents [5]. This effect further compounds several times when combined with the prevalent internet technologies for communication, due to this team members are expected to decide, respond, coordinate with their colleagues across multiple functions and countries [5].

The improvements in technology raise organisational change a whole new level which reinforces the finding that organisational change the 2nd ranked challenge in cloud-based ERP implementation [9]. Organisation change continues to remain one of the top concerns for managers when it comes to successful implementation and utilisation of ERP [3]. Organisation change ranks 2nd in the challenges perceived in implementation of cloud ERP [9]. These observations were based on a study of several representatives from small and medium enterprises (SME's). These findings make logical sense considering that the SME's are the ones who do not have deep pockets to engage organisation change management consultants to run their change management programs.

2.3   ERP Implementation and Organizational Change

It is observed that the perception of a change and whether it is positive or negative plays a vital role in embracing the change. The understanding of the change varies between different levels of employees in an organisation. For example, senior executives may consider ERP as a positive change as the report is generated instantly or nowadays readily available on a dashboard. The operational manager and end-user may consider ERP as an additional overhead because now they must record the data in the software in addition to executing the job [1, 2].

3   Methodology

We adopted a qualitative methodology to understand the association between organisation change and digital transformation. We collected data through in-depth interviews of industry practitioners to gain knowledge from their experiences in digital transformation initiatives in their organisations. Interviewees are selected from multiple backgrounds to provide insights from multiple facets in ERP industry.

4   Discussion

4.1   Change Management Imperative

In our interview, a CIO cites change management as a necessity and is something beyond question. A principal and founder of ERP consulting firm explained the successful outcome of ERP implementation which had organization change management built into the ERP roll out strategy.

Lack of proactive change management leads to lack of ownership leading to losing the support of employees in making the ERP implementation successful. This is in line with the conclusion that the degree of resistance to change is inversely proportional to the level of involvement in change management activities [1].

4.2   Leadership Engagement

In our interview, a CIO cites a few critical factors for the success of ERP. (1) Strong Leadership to champion and lead, and (2) management of organisational change. A similar observation was explained by the principal and founder of ERP consulting firm.

4.3   Leadership Commitment

In addition to involvement, leadership commitment is more important. The leader should have faith and trust in the outcome of the implementation. The CIO expects undeterred trust from organisation leaders in the expected benefits of the implementation.

4.4   IT – Business Synergy

There is an increasing belief among analysts that human factors affect the success of an ERP project more than technical or economic factors [7]. It was found that users who are not motivated enough to use the ERP find innovative ways to circumvent the ERP [6]. These users were motivated through three groups in the organisation, the project lead, the power users and peers.

An ERP implementation must consider the inputs from all levels of employees to detect the need for managing a change.

5   Implications

We derive the following implications from our findings:

- Organisation leader's involvement in digital transformation is a critical factor.

Business leader should be part of the project. This is essential. The business leader needs to have clarity on what is being done, why.

- Change management must be implemented properly for a successful ERP implementation.

Organizational leaders need to be educated about the need for change management and its importance for digital transformation.

- Digital transformation is a corporate project.

Digital transformation projects impacting the entire organization such as an ERP implementation needs to be driven as a corporate project and not an IT project.

- Managing the cultural dynamics in an ERP implementation.

Managing the cultural dynamics of organization is important during an ERP implementation. This could have been avoided by managing the interpersonal dynamics arising out of the perceived cultural misfit.

- ERP implementation timeline is a key determinant.

Determining a realistic timeline to deploy the ERP is an important factor. It was identified that the outcome of ERP implementation was not up to the target level in several projects participated by the interviewees due to lack of adequate time.

6 Conclusion

Organization change management during digital transformation is a complex process and might be difficult to address through a textbook approach. Typically, there are unique challenges due to the involvement of human element in organizational change, so every digital transformation needs to be carefully analysed for such pertinent issues. There is scope for practitioners to further this study by applying these learnings in their next digital transformation projects.

References

1. Harley, B., Wright, C., Hall, R., Dery, K.: Management reactions to technological change the example of enterprise resource planning. J. Appl. Behav. Sci. **42**(1), 58–75 (2006)
2. Lin, F., Tapie Rohm, C.E.: Manager's and end-users' concerns on innovation implementation. Bus. Process Manage. J. **15**(4), 527–547 (2009). https://doi.org/10.1108/14637150910975525
3. Altamony, H., Tarhini, A., Al-Salti, Z., Gharaibeh, A., Elyas, T.: The Relationship between change management strategy and successful enterprise resource planning (ERP) implementations: a theoretical perspective. Int. J. Bus. Manage. Econ. Res. **7**(4), 690–703 (2016)
4. Klaus, H., Rosemann, M., Gable, G.G.: What is ERP? Inf. Syst. Front. **2**(2), 141–162 (2000). https://doi.org/10.1023/A:1026543906354
5. Taylor, J.C.: Participative design: linking BPR and SAP with an STS approach. J. Organ. Change Manage. **11**(3), 233–245 (1998)
6. Boudreau, M.-C., Robey, D.: Enacting integrated information technology: a human agency perspective. Organ. Sci. **16**(1), 3–18 (2005)
7. Sarker, S., Lee, A.S.: Using a case study to test the role of three key social enablers in ERP implementation. Inf. Manage. **40**, 813–829 (2003)
8. Beheshti, H.M.: What managers should know about ERP/ERP II. Manage. Res. News **29**(4), 184–193 (2006). https://doi.org/10.1108/01409170610665040
9. Gupta, S., Misra, S.C., Singh, A., Kumar, V., Kumar, U.: Identification of challenges and their ranking in the implementation of cloud ERP. Int. J. Qual. Reliab. Manage. **34**(7), 1056–1072 (2017)
10. Ram, J., Wu, M.-L., Tagg, R.: Competitive advantage from ERP projects: examining the role of key implementation drivers. Int. J. Project Manage. **32**(4), 663–675 (2014). https://doi.org/10.1016/j.ijproman.2013.08.004
11. Taylor, J.C.: Participative design: linking BPR and SAP with an STS approach. J. Organ. Change Manage. **11**(3), 233–245 (1998)

Employees' Acceptance of AI Integrated CRM System: Development of a Conceptual Model

Sheshadri Chatterjee[1], Kuttimani Tamilmani[2], Nripendra P. Rana[2(✉)], and Yogesh K. Dwivedi[3]

[1] Department of Computer Science and Engineering, Indian Institute of Technology Kharagpur, Kharagpur, India
sheshadri.academic@gmail.com
[2] International Business, Marketing and Branding Research Centre (IBMB), School of Management, University of Bradford, Richmond Road, Bradford BD7 1DP, UK
kuttimani.tamilmani@gmail.com, nrananp@gmail.com
[3] Emerging Markets Research Centre (EMaRC), School of Management, Swansea University Bay Campus, Swansea SA1 8EN, UK
ykdwivedi@gmail.com, y.k.dwivedi@swansea.ac.uk

Abstract. Artificial Intelligence (AI) integrated Customer Relationship Management (CRM) systems can maximize firms' value by identifying and retaining best customers. The success of such advanced technologies depends on employee's adoption. However, research on examining employee's acceptance of AI integrated CRM systems is scarce. Therefore, this study has taken an attempt to propose conceptual model to predict the use-behaviour of employees to use AI integrated CRM system in organizations. This study adapted meta-UTAUT model as theoretical lens and extended the model with constructs such as compatibility, CRM quality, and CRM satisfaction specific to the organizational context. Future researchers can empirically test the proposed model with data gathered from employees using AI integrated CRM system.

Keywords: AI- CRM · CRM quality · CRM satisfaction · User behaviour · UTAUT model

1 Introduction

Customer Relationship Management (CRM) is considered as an effective tool that can help organization's to understand the customers in a more systematic way by "identifying a company's best customers and maximizing the value from them by satisfying and retaining them" [1]. CRM can achieve customers' satisfaction and organizational performance [2, 3]. CRM ability is measured by the capability of this tool to analyse the customers' huge amount of data accurately and to proceed accordingly [4]. However, analysing such huge volume of customers' data by human endeavour is difficult and here comes the need of application of modern Information and Communication Technology (ICT) that calls for Artificial Intelligence (AI) application in CRM known as AI integrated CRM [5–7]. It is thus perceived that business organizations would emphasize to use AI integrated CRM to achieve best results. Report transpires

© IFIP International Federation for Information Processing 2020
Published by Springer Nature Switzerland AG 2020
S. K. Sharma et al. (Eds.): TDIT 2020, IFIP AICT 618, pp. 679–687, 2020.
https://doi.org/10.1007/978-3-030-64861-9_59

that AI integrated CRM system would ensure to earn a revenue of $1.1 trillion from 2017-2021 [8]. Moreover, with the help of AI integrated CRM system, Organizations can analyse huge volume of customers' data with less cost and ease [9]. Analysis of customers' data by the organizations provides effective inputs to the organizations to strengthen their CRM quality [10]. Since such data is huge in volume, accurate analysis is ensured quickly through AI as is observed in other studies [11, 12]. With the help of AI, it is possible for the organizations to arrive at an accurate decision by analysing huge volume of customers' data easily [13, 14].

Organization's successful AI integration with their CRM system depends on employee's motivation to use such systems. The employees responsible for analysing customers data using AI integrated CRM system need to be sincere. This will help the organizations to accurately realize the likings, habits, disliking of the customers [15, 16]. The users of AI integrated CRM system in organizations would exhibit their attitude and intention towards using the system if they feel the technology is compatible with existing technology and helps them to use the new system [17, 18]. However, there is limited understanding on various factors influencing employees use behaviour towards integration of AI with CRM systems in organization context. To this end, this research proposes a conceptual model based on review of dominant technology acceptance theories/models to provide holistic understanding on factors determining employee's acceptance of AI integrated CRM system.

The remaining parts of the paper are arranged as follows. Section 2 provides overview on dominant technology acceptance theories/models. After that, Sect. 3 provides background to meta-UTUAT model and how it is extended to propose the conceptual model. The subsequent Sect. 4 provides overview on the proposed research methodology and data analysis for empirical validation of the proposed model. The paper ends with conclusion in Sect. 5.

2   Overview of Technology Acceptance Theories and Models

Understanding individual acceptance of information technology (IT) is considered as one of the mature streams within the information systems(IS) research arena [19, 20]. Efficient implementation of any Information System principally depends on the acceptance of the users [21]. In recent times, in the domain of IS, psychology, and sociology, it is observed that a plethora of theoretical models have been developed for exploring and predicting users' acceptance of IS. Among these models, many researchers advocated in favour of Technology Acceptance Model (TAM) [22–25]. But on the contrary, some scholars observed that TAM has some specific drawbacks [26]. It does not provide sufficient insights towards individuals' perspective concerning a new system, it directly investigates the external variables like perceived usefulness and perceived ease of use neglecting the indicators, it is found to have ignored the linkage between use and attitude as well as use and intention [27, 28].

2.1   UTAUT Theories

In the quest to address the limitations of existing technology acceptance models such as TAM, many competing theories emerged towards the end of 20th century, such as diffusion of innovation (DoI) theory, Innovation Diffusion Theory (IDT), and model of personal computer utilization to explain individual adoption of IS/IT. This multitude of contexts and theories presented new challenge of plurality to IS researchers [29]. Venkatesh, Morris, Davis and Davis [17], developed comprehensive model - Unified Theory of Acceptance and Use of Technology (UTAUT) based on thorough review of eight dominant technology adoption models to overcome limitations of existing theories [see 17]. UTAUT model postulates performance expectancy, effort expectancy, and social influence as direct determinants of individuals behavioural intention towards using focal technology that together with facilitating conditions affects their use behaviour. The focal phenomenon of UTAUT was organizational users of technology primarily driven by their extrinsic motivation emphasizing on the utilitarian value. Since then, UTAUT model has been extensively used in different contexts including field communication technology [30], home-health services [22], mobile-health [31] and so on. The UTAUT model has effectively contributed the exploration towards technology acceptance and usage. Despite the comprehensiveness and popularity, many researchers were doubtful about UTAUT model ability to analyse the individuals' technology acceptance behaviour [18, 32]. It has been criticized by many scholars on different grounds [33, 34]. Recently, Li [35] observed that, for gaining high variance (R2), the UTAUT model considered four moderators which are impractical and not necessary and it was observed that good predicting power would have been achieved using simple model by applying appropriate initial scoring procedure. Besides, many researchers felt necessity to extend the UTAUT model by dropping some factors and including some other factors according to the contextualization [32, 36–39].

2.2   Meta-UTAUT Model

Researchers have acknowledged the inherent limitations of UTAUT both explicitly and implicitly during their empirical investigations. Dwivedi, Rana, Jeyaraj, Clement and Williams [18], re-examined the model using combination of meta-analysis and structural equation modelling (MASEM) techniques to address some of those limitations. Henceforth, this study will refer to the re-examined model as metaUTAUT. The findings revealed UTAUT model lacked individual differences variable attitude that could be influential in explaining their dispositions towards the use of focal technology. In meta-UTAUT model, attitude was found to partially mediate the effects of all four UTAUT exogenous variables (i.e. performance expectancy, effort expectancy, social influence, and facilitating conditions) to behavioural Intention and had direct effect on use behaviour. In addition, the study found significant association between facilitating conditions and behavioural intention that was not part of the original UTAUT model [see 18 for model]. Finally, meta-UTAUT excluded moderators as they are relevant only if significant variation exist among individuals examined in same context making the model more parsimonious and easier to use [39]. Meta-UTAUT model based on MASEM is a robust alternative to examine individual technology adoption and use as it addresses the shortcoming of UTAUT [18].

3 Proposed Extension to Meta-UTAUT

Attitude plays significant role on individual intentions towards performing underlying behaviour especially during early stages of technology adoption [40]. Employee's adoption of AI integrated CRM systems in organization's are still at the early stages. Therefore, this study deemed meta-UTAUT model as appropriate theoretical lens to evaluate antecedents in relation to employees use of AI integrated CRM system.

Table 1. Synopsys of the constructs

Construct	Explanation	Source(s)
Performance Expectancy (PE)	It is defined as the extent to which an individual would believe that use of a system would help to enhance one's job performance	Venkatesh, Morris, Davis and Davis [17]
Effort Expectancy (EE)	It is defined as the extent of easiness concerned with the usage of a new system	Venkatesh, Morris, Davis and Davis [17]
Facilitating Condition (FC)	It is conceptualized as the degree to which an individual would possess a belief that the existing available technological infrastructure would help and effectively support to use a new system	Venkatesh, Morris, Davis and Davis [17]
Behavioral Intention (BI)	Strength of an individual's intention in the context of performance of a specific behavior is construed to be the measure of Behavioral Intention	Fishbein and Ajzen [41]
Attitude (ATT)	It is associated with a conception that people can be ambivalent to an object through jointly exhibiting positive or negative feelings towards the same object	Wood [42]
Compatibility (COM)	It is defined as the extent to which an innovation is perceived to be consistent with the existing values and access with the help of previous experience	Rogers [43]; Wang, Cho and Denton [44]
CRM Quality (CRQ)	CRM quality refers to the employees as to how valuable information that the employees get from the CRM. AI CRM should help the decision-making process by automating the user recommendation field. To get the accurate and good quality CRM output, the data input to the AI CRM tool must be of good quality	Battor and Battor [45]; Chatterjee, Ghosh and Chaudhuri [12]; Nyadzayo and Khajehzadeh [46]
CRM Satisfaction (CRS)	CRM satisfaction refers to the employees' delight that they are expected to get once the employees start using AI integrated CRM system in their organization	Chatterjee, Ghosh, Chaudhuri and Nguyen [6]; Kalaignanam and Varadarajan [47]; Phan and Vogel [48]; Winer [49]

Prior research suggests researchers should focus on including attributes specific to the context rather than having the urge to replicate the entire baseline model [50]. It is argued that in the context of this study, since the organizations would adopt AI integrated CRM system, question of influencing the employees of the organizations by the society and question of voluntariness of the employees have become redundant. As such, it is thought cogent to drop social influence. Besides, this study added three new exogenous variables to meta-UTAUT model such as compatibility, CRM quality, and CRM satisfaction. This idea has been supplemented by another study where compatibility was included as a factor while dealing with UTAUT model [51]. The inclusion of other two exogenous contextual variables CRM quality and CRM satisfaction were based on the premise that they would better explain adoption and use behaviour. This is in consonance with the observation that the UTAUT based models can be extended from the light of other contextual constructs which may be deemed to explain better adoption and usage behaviour of individuals [18]. The synopsis of all the constructs is shown in a tabular form in Table 1. With all these information and discussions, the proposed conceptual to examine employee use behaviour towards AICRM in the organization is shown in Fig. 1.

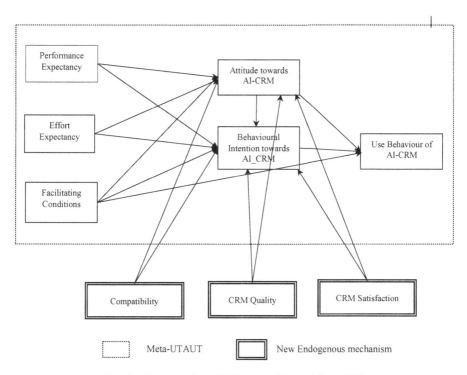

Fig. 1. Conceptual model (Source: Adapted from [18])

4   Research Methodology

Researchers can employ quantitative survey methodology to empirically validate the proposed conceptual model as validated scales are readily available to measure the latent constructs [52, 53]. Partial Least Square (PLS) – Structural Equation Modelling (SEM) can be employed for data analysis once the data is collected. PLS-SEM approach is helpful to analyse an exploratory study like this [54]. In addition, a complex model with comparatively small sample size (as it involves organizational users) can be best analysed by PLS-SEM approach [55]. Besides, PLS-SEM approach is known to have yielded better results for such studies that cover marketing issues [56, 57].

5   Conclusion

This study offers several inputs to the extant technology acceptance literature. The proposed model extended the meta-UTAUT model with context specific variables such as compatibility, CRM quality, and CRM satisfaction to analyse the use-behaviour of the employees of organizations to use AI integrated CRM system. Context effects can be broadly defined as the set of factors surrounding the focal phenomenon that exerts direct or indirect influence on it [58]. The proposed new endogenous mechanism which refers to new associations between external variables (compatibility, CRM quality, CRM satisfaction) and any of the three meta-UTAUT endogenous variables such as attitudes, intentions, and usage offers better adaptation of meta-UTAUT in the context of AI integrated CRM system [39]. The proposed model reveals that attitude could directly impacts intention as well as use behaviour of employees to use AI integrated CRM system in organizations. This implies that the managers of organizations have bounden duty to shape the attitude of the employees towards intention and use behaviour to use AI integrated CRM system. However, such assumptions require empirical validation of the proposed conceptual model. Therefore, future research in technology acceptance area can further examine meta-UTAUT alongside other variables to further contribute to employee's adoption of AI integrated CRM system. The proposed model could also be empirically validated to satisfy the conditions of generalisability of the model for varied samples [59–61].

References

1. Kennedy, A.: Electronic customer relationship management (eCRM): opportunities and challenges in a digital world. Irish Mark. Rev. **18**, 58 (2006)
2. Nguyen, B., Mutum, D.S.: A review of customer relationship management: successes, advances, pitfalls and futures. Bus. Process Manag. J. (2012)
3. Graca, S.S., Barry, J.M., Doney, P.M.: Performance outcomes of behavioural attributes in buyer-supplier relationships. J. Bus. Indust. Mark. (2015)
4. Li, M., Nguyen, B.: When will firms share information and collaborate to achieve innovation? The Bottom Line (2017)

5. Molinillo, S., Japutra, A.: Organizational adoption of digital information and technology: a theoretical review. The Bottom Line (2017)
6. Chatterjee, S., Ghosh, S.K., Chaudhuri, R., Nguyen, B.: Are CRM systems ready for AI integration? The Bottom Line (2019)
7. Laumer, S., Maier, C., Eckhardt, A., Weitzel, T.: Work routines as an object of resistance during information systems implementations: Theoretical foundation and empirical evidence. Eur. J. Inform. Syst. **25**, 317–343 (2016)
8. IDC https://www.import.io/wp-content/uploads/2017/04/Seagate-WP-DataAge2025-March-2017.pdf
9. Ferraris, A., Santoro, G., Bresciani, S.: Open innovation in multinational companies' subsidiaries: the role of internal and external knowledge. Eur. J. Int. Manag. **11**, 452–468 (2017)
10. Heide, J.B., Wathne, K.H., Rokkan, A.I.: Interfirm monitoring, social contracts, and relationship outcomes. J. Mark. Res. **44**, 425–433 (2007)
11. Verma, D., Verma, D.S.: Managing customer relationships through mobile CRM in organized retail outlets. Int. J. Eng. Trends Technol. **4**, 1696–1701 (2013)
12. Chatterjee, S., Ghosh, S.K., Chaudhuri, R.: Knowledge management in improving business process: an interpretative framework for successful implementation of AI–CRM–KM system in organizations. Bus. Process Manag. J. (2020)
13. Peters, L.D., Pressey, A.D., Greenberg, P.: The impact of CRM 2.0 on customer insight. J. Bus. Indust. Mark. (2010)
14. Maxwell, A.L., Jeffrey, S.A., Lévesque, M.: Business angel early stage decision making. J. Bus. Ventur. **26**, 212–225 (2011)
15. Vrontis, D., Thrassou, A., Santoro, G., Papa, A.: Ambidexterity, external knowledge and performance in knowledge-intensive firms. J. Technol. Transf. **42**(2), 374–388 (2016). https://doi.org/10.1007/s10961-016-9502-7
16. Chatterjee, D., Dandona, B., Mitra, A., Giri, M.: Airbnb in India: comparison with hotels, and factors affecting purchase intentions. Int. J. Cult. Tourism Hosp. Res. (2019)
17. Venkatesh, V., Morris, M.G., Davis, G.B., Davis, F.D.: User acceptance of information technology: toward a unified view. MIS Q. **27**, 425–478 (2003)
18. Dwivedi, Y.K., Rana, N.P., Jeyaraj, A., Clement, M., Williams, M.D.: Re-examining the unified theory of acceptance and use of technology (UTAUT): Towards a revised theoretical model. Inform. Syst. Front. **21**, 719–734 (2019)
19. Venkatesh, V., Davis, F.D., Morris, M.G.: Dead or alive? The development, trajectory and future of technology adoption research. J. Assoc. Inform. Syst. **8**, 267 (2007)
20. Tamilmani, K., Rana, N.P., Dwivedi, Y.K.: Mobile application adoption predictors: systematic review of UTAUT2 studies using weight analysis. In: Al-Sharhan, S.A., et al. (eds.) I3E 2018. LNCS, vol. 11195, pp. 1–12. Springer, Cham (2018). https://doi.org/10.1007/978-3-030-02131-3_1
21. Davis, F.D.: Perceived usefulness, perceived ease of use, and user acceptance of information technology. MIS Q. 319–340 (1989)
22. Cimperman, M., Brenčič, M.M., Trkman, P.: Analyzing older users' home telehealth services acceptance behaviour—applying an extended UTAUT model. Int. J. Med. Informatics **90**, 22–31 (2016)
23. Chauhan, S., Jaiswal, M.: Determinants of acceptance of ERP software training in business schools: empirical investigation using UTAUT model. Int. J. Manag. Educ. **14**, 248–262 (2016)
24. Šumak, B., Šorgo, A.: The acceptance and use of interactive whiteboards among teachers: differences in UTAUT determinants between pre-and post-adopters. Comput. Hum. Behav. **64**, 602–620 (2016)

25. Tamilmani, K., Rana, N.P., Alryalat, M.A.A., Al-Khowaiter, W.A., Dwivedi, Y.K.: Social media research in the context of emerging markets: an analysis of extant literature from information systems perspective. J. Adv. Manag. Res. **15**, 115–129 (2018)

26. Sánchez-Prieto, J.C., Olmos-Migueláñez, S., García-Peñalvo, F.J.: Informal tools in formal contexts: Development of a model to assess the acceptance of mobile technologies among teachers. Comput. Hum. Behav. **55**, 519–528 (2016)

27. Šumak, B., Pušnik, M., Heričko, M., Šorgo, A.: Differences between prospective, existing, and former users of interactive whiteboards on external factors affecting their adoption, usage and abandonment. Comput. Hum. Behav. **72**, 733–756 (2017)

28. Tsai, Y.-Y., Chao, C.-M., Lin, H.-M., Cheng, B.-W.: Nursing staff intentions to continuously use a blended e-learning system from an integrative perspective. Qual. Quant. **52**(6), 2495–2513 (2017). https://doi.org/10.1007/11135-017-0540-5

29. Tamilmani, K., Rana, N.P., Dwivedi, Y.K.: A systematic review of citations of UTAUT2 article and its usage trends. In: Kar, A.K., et al. (eds.) I3E 2017. LNCS, vol. 10595, pp. 38–49. Springer, Cham (2017). https://doi.org/10.1007/978-3-319-68557-1_5

30. Khalilzadeh, J., Ozturk, A.B., Bilgihan, A.: Security-related factors in extended UTAUT model for NFC based mobile payment in the restaurant industry. Comput. Hum. Behav. **70**, 460–474 (2017)

31. Hoque, R., Sorwar, G.: Understanding factors influencing the adoption of mHealth by the elderly: an extension of the UTAUT model. Int. J. Med. Inform. **101**, 75–84 (2017)

32. Chao, C.-M.: Factors determining the behavioural intention to use mobile learning: An application and extension of the UTAUT model. Front. Psychol. **10**, 1652 (2019)

33. Van Raaij, E.M., Schepers, J.J.: The acceptance and use of a virtual learning environment in China. Comput. Educ. **50**, 838–852 (2008)

34. Bagozzi, R.P.: The legacy of the technology acceptance model and a proposal for a paradigm shift. J. Assoc. Inform. Syst. **8**, 3 (2007)

35. Li, J.: Blockchain technology adoption: examining the fundamental drivers. In: Proceedings of the 2020 2nd International Conference on Management Science and Industrial Engineering, pp. 253–260 (2020)

36. Lin, C.-P., Anol, B.: Learning online social support: an investigation of network information technology based on UTAUT. CyberPsychol. Behav. **11**, 268–272 (2008)

37. Wang, Y.S., Wu, M.C., Wang, H.Y.: Investigating the determinants and age and gender differences in the acceptance of mobile learning. Br. J. Edu. Technol. **40**, 92–118 (2009)

38. Wang, H.-Y., Wang, S.-H.: User acceptance of mobile internet based on the unified theory of acceptance and use of technology: Investigating the determinants and gender differences. Soc. Behav. Pers. Int. J. **38**, 415–426 (2010)

39. Dwivedi, Y.K., Rana, N.P., Tamilmani, K., Raman, R.: A meta-analysis based modified unified theory of acceptance and use of technology (Meta-UTAUT): a review of emerging literature. Curr. Opin. Psychol. (2020)

40. Patil, P., Tamilmani, K., Rana, N.P., Raghavan, V.: Understanding consumer adoption of mobile payment in India: Extending Meta-UTAUT model with personal innovativeness, anxiety, trust, and grievance redressal. Int. J. Inf. Manage. **54**, 102144 (2020)

41. Fishbein, M., Ajzen, I.: Belief, attitude, intention and behaviour: an introduction to theory and research (1975)

42. Wood, W.: Attitude change: persuasion and social influence. Ann. Rev. Psychol. 51, (2000)

43. Rogers, E.: Diffusion of Innovations. Free Press, New York (1995)

44. Wang, M., Cho, S., Denton, T.: The impact of personalization and compatibility with past experience on e-banking usage. Int. J. Bank Mark. (2017)

45. Battor, M., Battor, M.: The impact of customer relationship management capability on innovation and performance advantages: testing a mediated model. J. Mark. Manag. **26**, 842–857 (2010)
46. Nyadzayo, M.W., Khajehzadeh, S.: The antecedents of customer loyalty: A moderated mediation model of customer relationship management quality and brand image. J. Retail. Consum. Serv. **30**, 262–270 (2016)
47. Kalaignanam, K., Varadarajan, R.: Offshore outsourcing of customer relationship management: conceptual model and propositions. J. Acad. Mark. Sci. **40**, 347–363 (2012)
48. Phan, D.D., Vogel, D.R.: A model of customer relationship management and business intelligence systems for catalogue and online retailers. Inf. Manag. **47**, 69–77 (2010)
49. Winer, R.S.: A framework for customer relationship management. Calif. Manag. Rev. **43**, 89–105 (2001)
50. Venkatesh, V., Thong, J.Y., Xu, X.: Unified theory of acceptance and use of technology: a synthesis and the road ahead. J. Assoc. Inform. Syst. **17**, 328–376 (2016)
51. Karahanna, E., Agarwal, R., Angst, C.M.: Reconceptualizing compatibility beliefs in technology acceptance research. MIS Q. 781–804 (2006)
52. Oliveira, T., Thomas, M., Baptista, G., Campos, F.: Mobile payment: Understanding the determinants of customer adoption and intention to recommend the technology. Comput. Hum. Behav. **61**, 404–414 (2016)
53. Slade, E.L., Dwivedi, Y.K., Piercy, N.C., Williams, M.D.: Modeling consumers' adoption intentions of remote mobile payments in the United Kingdom: extending UTAUT with innovativeness, risk, and trust. Psychol. Mark. **32**, 860–873 (2015)
54. Hair, J.F., Risher, J.J., Sarstedt, M., Ringle, C.M.: When to use and how to report the results of PLS-SEM. Eur. Bus. Rev. (2019)
55. Willaby, H.W., Costa, D.S., Burns, B.D., MacCann, C., Roberts, R.D.: Testing complex models with small sample sizes: A historical overview and empirical demonstration of what partial least squares (PLS) can offer differential psychology. Pers. Individ. Differ. **84**, 73–78 (2015)
56. Hair Jr., J.F., Hult, G.T.M., Ringle, C., Sarstedt, M.: A Primer on Partial Least Squares Structural Equation Modeling (PLS-SEM). Sage Publications, Thousand Oaks (2016)
57. Hair, J.F., Sarstedt, M., Ringle, C.M., Mena, J.A.: An assessment of the use of partial least squares structural equation modeling in marketing research. J. Acad. Mark. Sci. **40**, 414–433 (2012)
58. Whetten, D.A.: An examination of the interface between context and theory applied to the study of Chinese organizations. Manag. Organ. Rev. **5**, 29–56 (2009)
59. Saumya, S., Singh, J.P., Baabdullah, A., Rana, N.P., Dwivedi, Y.K.: Ranking online consumer reviews. Electron. Commer. Res. Appl. **29**, 78–89 (2018)
60. Kizgin, H., Jamal, A., Dey, B.L., Rana, N.P.: The impact of social media on consumers' acculturation and purchase intentions. Inform. Syst. Front. **20**(3), 503–514 (2017). https://doi.org/10.1007/s10796-017-9817-4
61. Rana, N.P., Dwivedi, Y.K.: Using clickers in a large business class: examining use behavior and satisfaction. J. Market. Educ. **38**(1), 47–64 (2016)

Modified UTAUT2 to Determine Intention and Use of E-Commerce Technology Among Micro & Small Women Entrepreneurs in Jharkhand, India

Sraboni Dutta[✉] and Shradha Shivani

Birla Institute of Technology, Mesra, Ranchi 835215, India
{sdutta,shraddhashivani}@bitmesra.ac.in

Abstract. E-commerce revolution is creating enormous growth opportunities for Indian SMEs. Yet, reports suggest that adoption of e-commerce remains low among women entrepreneurs in the micro and small sector. This research applies a technology acceptance perspective to examine the determinants which induce the behavioral intention to accept and use ecommerce among the women entrepreneurs of Jharkhand, a developing state of eastern India. The UTAUT2 model of technology acceptance was modified to measure the relative impact of performance expectancy, effort expectancy, social influence, facilitating conditions, hedonic motivation, price value, individual innovativeness and achievement motivation on their intention to adopt and use e-commerce under the influence of age and experience as moderators. Structural Equation Modeling was employed and the findings confirm the positive influence of all the core determinants except for hedonic motivation. This implies that in order to improve the weak penetration of e-commerce in the population, campaigns have to be designed and implemented to make the women entrepreneurs perceive that investment in ICT for e-commerce will be valuable for them and that they can easily use the technology.

Keywords: E-commerce · Modified UTAUT2 · Women micro & small entrepreneurs · Structural equation modelling

1 Introduction

One of the ICT applications which have gained immense usage is e-commerce (electronic commerce). India has been a witness to an e-commerce boom. With exponential growth in internet penetration in last few decades, the e-commerce sector in India is particularly lucrative for all. It is projected that by 2020 approximately 330 million people in India will be buying goods and services online. It is projected that between 2016 and 2021, retail e-commerce will grow from around 16 billion USD to over 45 billion USD and the CAGR for the sector is projected to reach 23% [23].

Given this scenario, it has become imperative for SMEs to embrace digitization and adopt ecommerce to accelerate their business growth. Moreover, with the onslaught of the Covid-19 pandemic, this is fast becoming a necessity for sustenance. Numerous

© IFIP International Federation for Information Processing 2020
Published by Springer Nature Switzerland AG 2020
S. K. Sharma et al. (Eds.): TDIT 2020, IFIP AICT 618, pp. 688–701, 2020.
https://doi.org/10.1007/978-3-030-64861-9_60

reports like the KPMG Snapdeal Report [26] highlighted the various benefits Indian SMEs using ecommerce have been reaping. Yet only 43% of SMEs are involved in online sales [52].

In India, where the economic contribution of women is approximately 17% of the GDP, the growth of women-run businesses could translate into a huge boost to the economy. Indian women entrepreneurs in the SME sector are increasingly coming to the forefront and are now confident and optimistic about the growth of their businesses [10].

ICT and e-commerce can help women entrepreneurs to reduce time and mobility constraints, increase market reach, upgrade skills and enable wider participation in business network [30]. Women entrepreneurs are increasingly prompted to use ICTs like mobile phones, SMS, e-mail, social network and internet based telephony (such as Skype) to reach their existing and potential customers and business partners, thereby increasing their confidence in conducting economic activities [3]. Big marketplaces like Amazon Mahila-e-Haat, e-Bay, Alibaba.com amongst others are continuously inspiring and encouraging Indian women entrepreneurs to adopt ecommerce [26, 34, 43]. The 'Digital India' campaign of the Government of India is also aimed at enabling wider section of businesses to adopt ICT. Despite this, the small and micro women entrepreneurs continue to encounter barriers in incorporating ICT for ecommerce into their business firms. It has been reported that only 20% of these women entrepreneurs in India use online platforms to sell [51]. This reflects the lack of infrastructure or awareness about the benefits of e-commerce platforms. Fear of security of payments and privacy of online transactions are issues plaguing women entrepreneurs. For women entrepreneurs, particularly at the bottom of the pyramid to make the most out of India's e-commerce boom, there is definitely need for mentorship, technical hand-holding and business advice [44].

An inherent reason for the above observations could be the gender digital divide, a characteristic of majority of the developing nations [18, 37–39]. It is stated that women in South Asia (including India) are 26% less likely to own a mobile phone than men and 70% less likely to use mobile internet [44]. The "Towards Gender Equity Online" study [15] and the India Internet 2019 report [19], also states that the female internet user population in India is only half of the 258 million male internet users, and 'the bias is more evident in rural India'. This digital divide possibly inhibits internet and ecommerce usage among women entrepreneurs as well.

In the above context arises the need for conducting a holistic study aimed at identifying and analyzing the determinants of ecommerce adoption by Indian small and micro women entrepreneurs. This research employs the extended Unified Theory of Acceptance and Use of Technology 2 (UTAUT2) Model [55] for empirical analysis to identify the key determinants affecting the behavioral intent and ensuing usage of ecommerce by these women entrepreneurs. This model is considered to have better explanatory power than the TAM (Technology Acceptance Model) and UTAUT models that have been used to explain users' behavioral intentions toward various information technologies [55]. Findings of this study may aid governments, international organizations, research institutions, NGOs, development banks and other stakeholders of women and entrepreneurial development in reviewing, designing and implementing gender-responsive trade and economic policies and programmes. This would also help in ensuring the success of the "Digital India" campaign of the Government of India and simultaneously enhance empowerment of women in the country.

2 Literature Review

E-commerce is an ICT application which has emerged as a catalyst for business growth. It is described as the "use of electronic means to conduct an organization's business internally and/or externally" [20]. Studies in recent years such as those by Barrosso et al. [7] Kartiwi et al. [22] Rahayu and Day [41] Garg and Choue [14] Yeh et al. [57], Klaiber et al. [25], investigate the determinants of e-commerce adoption by SMEs. The level of adoption of e-commerce technologies by SMEs bears some correlation with the level of development of the nation [16, 21] and its "E-readiness" [8].

Literature reveals a range of e-business adoption and usage challenges that women managed businesses specifically in the context of developing countries are confronted with [24, 40]. These include lack of human, social, financial and physical capital culminating in diminished entrepreneurial abilities. Moreover, institutional impediments that are manifested as socio-cultural expectations regarding their commitments to family and home, along with existence of gender-based discrimination within the business/organizational sphere also plagues these women entrepreneurs. In addition there are individual attitudinal issues and women centric perceptions towards adoption of technology [18, 29, 53]. However, limited number of studies focuses on the drivers inducing behavioral intention to adopt and use ecommerce from the technology adoption perspective, specifically amongst women entrepreneurs of developing nations and studies in India are scant. Thus, arises the rationale of this research.

The review of literature indicated that this research required a holistic and structured model that assumes an individual-level approach of technology acceptance to examine the determinants that influence behavioral intention of women entrepreneurs to adopt and use e-commerce technology in the Indian SME context. The theoretical framework for the study is presented in the next section.

2.1 Theoretical Framework

The Unified Theory of Acceptance and Use of Technology Model-2 (UTAUT2) originated in the theories of Technology Acceptance Model (TAM) and thereafter UTAUT developed by Venkatesh et al. in 2003 [54] to study the behavioral intention of people to accept and use technology. However Venkatesh et al. [55] extended the model to propose UTAUT2 in 2012, to study acceptance and use of technology in a consumer context. By introducing psychological and cognitive factors such as Hedonic Motivation (HM), Price Value (PV), and Habit (HT) in addition to the four core determinants, Performance Expectancy (PE), Effort Expectancy (EE), Social Influence (SI) and Facilitating Conditions (FC) which directly influence the user's behavioral intention to use new technologies. The Behavioral Intention (BI) then affects the Usage Behavior (UB). Three moderators of key relationships are Gender, Age and Experience which either amplify or constrain the influence of the core determinants, on Behavioral Intention and Usage Behavior.

It has been used by researchers to explain technology adoption in case of B2B/C2C e-marketplaces [4], mobile apps for restaurants [47], E-commerce payment systems [2, 9], food delivery apps [28], online shopping [49], mobile marketing [11], mobile wallet adoption [31], music e-commerce [56], cloud computing in organizations [6], social commerce [5] etc. Abushakra and Nikbin [1] extended the UTAUT2 Model to examine the factors guiding Acceptance and Adoption of the Internet of Things (IoT) by entrepreneurs in Oman. They posited that in addition to all the key constructs of the UTAUT 2 model, knowledge of information technology was an additional driver. Erumi-Esin and Heeks [12] used the UTAUT model to examine e-business adoption and use among African women owned SMEs and came to the conclusion that perceived usefulness (PE) had a greater influence than ease of use (EE) and facilitating conditions play a greater role than social influence in the adoption decision. Based on studies conducted on SMEs, few other researchers also concluded that performance expectancy is the strongest predictor of behavioral intention to use technology [35, 45].

It was concluded from the above review of literature explaining technology adoption that UTAUT 2 is a widely applicable theoretical model for an empirical study of intention and use of technology. Therefore, this was the model chosen for this research to analyze the drivers for adoption of ecommerce technology by Women Entrepreneurs in the state of Jharkhand. However, in this study an attempt has been made to modify the UTAUT 2 model to make it more relevant for the subject under consideration.

There were three modifications proposed in the UTAUT2 model. Habit as a determinant of behavioural intention was excluded and two psychological characteristics i.e. Innovativeness and Achievement Motivation were included. Finding from depth interviews conducted with few women entrepreneurs from the population of the study and with experts during the exploratory study suggested that majority of these women entrepreneurs are not habituated to use ecommerce repeatedly. Hence habit as a driver would be redundant for the study. The psychological traits of Innovativeness and achievement orientation included in the model have long been considered as drivers of entrepreneurial success. Many recent studies have also focused on these psychological traits as related with entrepreneurship [13, 33, 48, 50]. Since the population of this research consisted of women entrepreneurs and the focus of the research was adoption of new technology (ecommerce) of conducting business for achieving enterprise success, therefore these two entrepreneurial traits were included as drivers of BI. In line with the moderating impact of Age and Experience on the influence of the drivers of intention to use technology as depicted in UTAUT2 model, it is proposed in this study that these variables will moderate the influence of individual innovativeness and achievement motivation on behavioural intention of the entrepreneurs to use ecommerce. Table 1 provides a summary of each of the modified UTAUT2 determinants, (core constructs) and dependent variables alongwith its description. Figure 1 depicts the conceptual model of this study.

Table 1. Modified UTAUT2 (Venkatesh et al. 2012) variables

Construct	Definition
Core determinants	
Performance Expectancy (PE)	The degree to which an individual believes that using ecommerce will help him/her to attain gains in job performance
Effort Expectancy (EE)	The degree of ease associated with the use of ecommerce
Social Influence (SI)	The degree to which an individual perceives that important others believe that he/she should use ecommerce
Facilitating Conditions (FC)	The degree to which an individual believes that an organizational and technical infrastructure exists to support the use of ecommerce
Hedonic Motivation (HM)	The fun, pleasure (in context of status) derived from using ecommerce
Price Value (PV)	Entrepreneurs' cognitive tradeoff between the perceived benefits of ecommerce and the monetary cost involved
Individual Innovativeness (IN)	Extent to which entrepreneur is open to experiencing, and experimenting with, new technologies involved in ecommerce
Achievement Motivation (AM)	Degree to which the entrepreneur rates the positive or negative affect towards an achievement activity
Dependent variables	
Behavioural Intention (BI)	The intention of the individual to use the system
Usage Behaviour (UB)	The extent of usage of the system by the individual

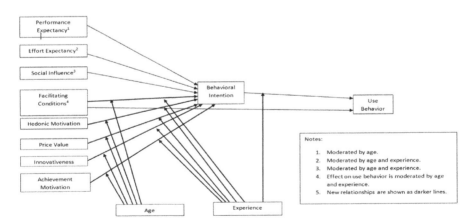

Fig. 1. Modified UTAUT2 model, (Venkatesh et al. 2012)

2.2   Research Hypotheses

Based on the modified UTAUT2 Model which forms the theoretical framework presented in the previous section the following hypothesis were formulated for the study:

H_1:   Performance expectancy positively influences intention to use e-commerce.

H_2:   Effort expectancy positively influences intention to use e-commerce.

H_3:   Social influence positively influences intention to use e-commerce.

H_4:   Facilitating conditions positively influences intention to use e-commerce.

H_5:   Hedonic motivation positively influences individual intention to use e-commerce.

H_6:   Price value positively influences individual intention to use e-commerce.

H_7:   Individual's innovativeness positively influences intention to use e-commerce.

H_8:   Individual's achievement motivation positively influences intention to use e-commerce.

H_9:   Facilitating conditions positively influence the individual's e-commerce usage behavior.

H_{10}:   Intention to use ecommerce positively influences the individual e-commerce usage behaviour.

H_{11}:   The influence of performance expectancy on behavioral intention is moderated by age.

H_{12}:   The influence of effort expectancy on behavioral intention is moderated by age.

H_{13}:   The influence of effort expectancy on behavioral intention is moderated by experience.

H_{14}:   The influence of social influence on behavioral intention is moderated by age.

H_{15}:   The influence of social influence on behavioral intention is moderated by experience.

H_{16}:   The influence of facilitating conditions on behavioral intention is moderated by age.

H_{17} The influence of facilitating conditions on behavioral intention is moderated by experience.

H_{18}:   The influence of hedonic motivation on behavioral intention is moderated by age.

H_{19}:   The influence of hedonic motivation on behavioral intention is moderated by experience.

H_{20} The influence of price value on behavioral intention is moderated by age.

H_{21}:   The influence of price value on behavioral intention is moderated by experience.

H_{22}:   The influence of individual's innovativeness on behavioral intention is moderated by age.

H_{23}:   The influence of individual's innovativeness on behavioral intention is moderated by experience.

H_{24}:   The influence of individual's achievement motivation on behavioral intention is moderated by age.

H_{25}:   The influence of individual's achievement motivation on behavioral intention is moderated by experience.

H_{26}:   The influence of facilitating conditions on use behavior is moderated by age.

H_{27}:   The influence of facilitating conditions on use behavior is moderated by experience.

H_{28}:   The influence of behavioural intention on use behavior is moderated by experience.

3   Research Methodology

The study is conducted amongst the small and micro women entrepreneurs in the state of Jharkhand in eastern India. The study has modified the UTAUT2 model of Venkatesh et al. [68], and theorizes that performance expectancy (PE), effort expectancy (EE), social influence (SI), and facilitating conditions (FC) hedonic motivation (HM), price value(PV), individual innovativeness (IN) and achievement motivation (AM) are the core determinants of women entrepreneurs' intention to adopt and use e-commerce moderators in the model being age and experience The purpose of this study was to determine the strength of these determinants (PE, EE, FC and SI, HM, PV, IN, AM) on behavioral intention to use ecommerce (BI) and usage behavior (UB) in light of the moderating effects of age and experience in using technology. The moderator, gender has been excluded in this study.

3.1   Data Collection and Data Analysis

The database on women entrepreneurs were collected from the District Industry Centres (DIC) of Bokaro, Ranchi and Jhamshedpur. A structured questionnaire was administered among a sample of 300 micro and small women entrepreneurs. Valid responses were received from 258 women- response rate of 86%. The first section of questionnaire captured the demographic profile of the respondents, their usage of various ICT tools and their extent of ecommerce adoption as per "hierarchical phases of e-commerce adoption" as indicated by Molla and Licker [32]. The second section captured their perceptions regarding the adoption of e-commerce on the basis of the modified UTAUT2 Model, using a 5-point Likert Scale (1-Strongly Disagree; 5-Strongly Agree). The items used by Venkatesh et al. [55] were replicated. For soliciting responses on individual innovativeness, a 3 item scale was adopted from Slade et al. [46] to assess the willingness of the women entrepreneur to try out e-commerce technologies. Responses on achievement motivation were collected via the 10 item Revised Achievement motivation Scale (AMS-R) designed by Lang & Fries [27] to gauge how these women rate their positive or negative affect towards an achievement activity like adopting ecommerce for business sustenance and growth. SPSS 22.0 and AMOS were the statistical packages used to analyze the data.

4   Analysis

The demographic profile of the respondents indicate that majority of these entrepreneurs is in the age group of 30–45 years and has graduated from college (55.7%). The predominant form of activity is manufacturing (70%) and sole proprietorship is the main form of ownership (81%) in these firms.

The study revealed that usage of ICT was prevalent amongst all the sampled women entrepreneurs in some form or the other. It varied from usage of smart phones, SMS, emails, social media and skype to employing financial accounting packages or hosting a website. With respect to adoption of ecommerce, approximately 28% utilized the Connected E-commerce phase in which the firms were using e-mail to support information and transactional processes with existing and potential trading partners, suppliers and customers. Merely 14% of them were hosting their own website for information sharing and even lesser percentage (10%) had adopted the phase of Interactive Ecommerce, thereby facilitating online interactions and queries between the firm and its customers. A very small fraction of these women entrepreneurs (5%) had adopted Transactive Ecommerce, allowing customers to purchase online, track orders, and manage their account information. None of these entrepreneurs had ventured into the scheme of Integrated Ecommerce in which the firm's website is integrated with suppliers, customers, and other back-office systems allowing most business transactions and processes to be conducted electronically. The descriptive statistics for the constructs used in this study reveal that except for Usage Behaviour, the mean values of all constructs exceed 3, indicating that most of the respondents agreed or strongly agreed with the statements in the questionnaire.

4.1 Analysis of Measurement Model

Structural equation modeling was undertaken to analyze the data. Hair et al. [17] suggests that factor loadings must be at least 0.5 and preferably greater than .7 for an acceptable measurement indicator. The construct reliability (CR) must be greater than 0.7 and average variance extracted (AVE) for each construct should be greater or equal to 0.5. There is evidence that the measurement model has adequate reliability and convergent validity because all factor loadings were greater than 0.7, the CRs exceeded acceptable criteria of 0.7, and the AVEs were greater than the threshold value of 0.5 in all cases

The results of different indices for structural model fit are RMSEA < 0394, GFI = .93, AGFI = .90, NFI = .95 and CFI = .94, all satisfying their respective threshold levels and hence implying that measurement model fits the data collected

5 Findings and Discussion

The results of this study are consistent with the original postulations of Venkatesh et al. [54] regarding influence of the four core determinants of intention and usage but they do not fully support the postulations regarding the effect of moderators.

As is evident from results presented in Table 2 the core determinants i.e. performance expectancy (PE), effort expectancy (EE), social influence (SI), facilitating conditions (FC), price value (PV), individual innovativeness (IN), achievement motivation (AM) have a significant positive influence on behavioral intention (BI). Among the determinant variables, PE is found to have the strongest influence of BI. The results further suggested that BI and improved facilitating conditions (FC) are significantly influencing usage behavior (UB) for ecommerce adoption by women entrepreneurs in a positive manner. Thus, the results support the H_1, H_2, H_3, H_4, H_6 H_7, H_8, H_9, and H_{10} hypotheses.

Table 2. Relationship between the core determinants and the dependent variables.

Path			Beta	t value	p	Decision
BI	←	PE	0.789	10.066 ***	0.000	Supported H1
BI	←	EE	0.696	10.266 ***	0.000	Supported H2
BI	←	SI	0.134	2.417 *	0.016	Supported H3
BI	←	FC	0.229	2.994 **	0.003	Supported H4
BI	←	HM	0.096	0.766	0.443	Rejected H5
BI	←	PV	0.25	3.45**	0.003	Supported H6
BI	←	IN	0.24	2.56*	0.031	Supported H7
BI	←	AM	0.530	9.788 ***	0.000	Supported H8
UB	←	FC	0.462	4.593***	0.000	Supported H9
UB	←	BI	0.212	2.136*	0.033	Supported H10

Note: $*p < 0.05$; $**p < 0.01$; $***p < 0.001$

The results from the moderator analysis indicate that the age of the entrepreneur does not moderate the effect of PE, EE, SI, FC, HM, PV, IN and AM on BI. Perception about effect of these core determinants on BI is similar across all age groups. Similarly, experience does not moderate the effect of EE, FC, HM, PV, IN and AM on BI. Experience also does not moderate the effect of FC and BI on UB. Hence H_{11}, H_{12}, H_{13}, H_{14}, H_{16}, H_{17}, H_{18}, H_{19}, H_{20}, H_{21}, H_{22}, H_{23}, H_{24}, H_{25} H_{26}, H_{27} and H_{28} are not supported. However, the results indicate that experience significantly moderates the effect of SI on BI, thus, supporting H_{15} hypothesis indicating that influence of peer members, associations, friends and business partners on intention to use technology will be stronger on women entrepreneurs who have the experience of using ICT in other walks of life.

Consistent with the results of moderator analysis, with respect to the direct influence of the moderators on the dependent variables it is observed that experience is significantly influencing the usage behavior in a positive manner. The direct effect of moderator age on the two dependent variables is found to be 'not significant'. From the results obtained we posit that age of the women entrepreneurs is no longer a relevant factor impacting technology acceptance by them. Although the overall penetration of ecommerce is low among the women entrepreneurs, the strength of intention to use ecommerce and extent of usage is spread evenly across women entrepreneurs of all age groups. It may be concluded that the impact of digitization awareness campaigns by various agencies has been uniform across women in all age groups.

6   Conclusion

The theoretical significance of this research is derived from the fact that it presents fresh empirical findings based on application of the widely used UTAUT2 model for predicting technology acceptance and use by a very specific target group of women entrepreneurs in a developing state in India. The results support the relationships between the core determinants of technology acceptance and the intention to use technology proposed in the model.

The findings of this study have many managerial and policy implications. Despite the thrust of the government and non-government agencies in India towards promotion of women entrepreneurs in the country, they do not seem to have reaped the benefits of the ecommerce boom in India. Only 20% of the women entrepreneurs in India use online platforms to sell [52]. Less than 30% of the women owning small and micro enterprises who were interviewed in this study were found to have adopted the rudimentary ecommerce processes. This highlights the need for interventions which can address the technology acceptance issues specific to such women enterprises in a developing nation context. This becomes all the more relevant in this Covid-19 pandemic situation where dependence on the virtual platform is imperative. Based on the empirical findings of this study various policy interventions can be forwarded

PE being the strongest predictor of ecommerce usage intention indicates that if interventions are directed towards inducing women entrepreneurs to perceive that using e-commerce applications would improve the performance of their businesses in terms of growth, efficiency and productivity, the intention to adopt such applications could be enhanced. The business benefits of ecommerce applications need to be highlighted amongst the women. This could be supplemented with success stories that they can relate to.

The statistically significant influence of EE suggests that the women entrepreneurs need to be convinced regarding the simplicity and ease of use of such technology. Workshops and training modules can be instrumental in building their confidence to handle ecommerce applications. The findings of this study also indicate SI via social networks of friends, family, customers, business partners, bankers is an important driver for the behavioral intent to adopt this technology. SI exerts a statistically significant influence on women entrepreneurs' intention to use e-commerce. Social awareness campaigns highlighting that investment in ICT for ecommerce is imperative for the success of women entrepreneurs can be utilized to strengthen the social influence.

FC too emerged as a strong driver for both intention to use and usage behavior, suggesting that agencies responsible for promoting women entrepreneurship need to stay focused on providing necessary resources and infrastructure for encouraging the women entrepreneurs to use e-commerce applications. Since, PV has a positive significant influence on behavioral intention to accept ecommerce, support agencies via campaigns can attempt to convince these women that long term business benefits of ecommerce adoption would outweigh the monetary costs. Entrepreneurship development programmes should continue to inculcate and enhance the entrepreneurial personality traits like innovativeness (IN) and achievement orientation (AM) amongst these women entrepreneurs so as to induce stronger intention to use ecommerce.

The interventions by institutions, both Government and private, need to reach a wider section of women owners of small and micro enterprises in the interiors of the country. Schemes which offer financial and technical assistance to new entrants to incorporate ecommerce and other technologies in their business firms, can be redesigned especially to target women owned small and micro enterprises so as to enable them to overcome the digital divide which still persists in various locations.

Information regarding availability of affordable ICT infrastructure and connectivity needs to be disseminated and highlighted in this target group. Widespread awareness building and motivational campaigns to reduce the attitudinal barriers to ecommerce usage can help to ensure large scale and effective adoption of these applications by the women entrepreneurs.

References

1. Abushakra, A., Nikbin, D.: Extending the UTAUT2 model to understand the entrepreneur acceptance and adopting internet of things (IoT). In: Uden, L., Ting, I.-H., Corchado, J.M. (eds.) KMO 2019. CCIS, vol. 1027, pp. 339–347. Springer, Cham (2019). https://doi.org/10.1007/978-3-030-21451-7_29
2. Acharya, V., Junare, S.O., Gadhavi, D.D.: E-payment: buzz word or reality. Int. J. Recent Technol. Eng. 8(3S2), 397–404 (2019)
3. Afrah, S.H., Fabiha, S.T.: Empowering women entrepreneurs through information and communication technology (ICT): a case study of Bangladesh. Management 7(1), 1–6 (2017)
4. Alazab, K., Dick, M., Malekifar, S.: Assessing the effect of UTAUT2 on adoption of B2B/C2C E-marketplaces. J. Internet e-Bus. Stud. (2020). https://doi.org/10.5171/2020.690228(2020)
5. Alotaibi, S.S.: The influence of information quality and gender on the social commerce adoption framework by Saudi Arabian Users using the UTAUT2 theory (2018). http://mars.gmu.edu/handle/1920/10955. Accessed 4 Aug 2020
6. Amponsah, R.A., Panford, J.K., Hayfron-Acquah, J.B.: Factors affecting cloud computing adoption in a developing country – Ghana: using extended unified theory of acceptance and use of technology (UTAUT2) model. Int. Res. J. Eng. Technol. 3(11), 59–76 (2016)
7. Barroso, R.M., Ferreira, F.A., Meidutė-Kavaliauskienė, I., Banaitienė, N., Falcão, P.F., Rosa, Á.A.: Analyzing the determinants of e-commerce in small and medium-sized enterprises: a cognition-driven framework. Technol. Econ. Dev. Econ. 25(3), 496–518 (2019)
8. Boateng, R.M.A., Heeks, R., Hinson, R.: Advancing e-commerce beyond readiness in a developing economy: experiences of Ghanaian firms. J. Electron. Commer. Org. 9(1), 1–16 (2011)
9. Chen, J.: Analyzing the factors influencing for third-party e-commerce payment with DEMATEL Based UTAUT2 model. In: Proceedings of 9th International on Education and Social Science (ICESS 2019), pp. 1342–1346. Francis Academic Press, UK (2019)
10. Dell: Dell Women's Global Entrepreneurship Study: India Key Findings. https://i.dell.com/sites/csdocuments/Business_smb_merchandizing_Documents/en/India-Research-Results-Fact-Sheet.pdf (2012). Accessed 3 Jan 2020
11. Eneizan, B., Mohammed, A.G., Alnoor, A., Alabboodi, A.S., Enaizan, O.: Customer acceptance of mobile marketing in Jordan: an extended UTAUT2 model with trust and risk factors. Int. J. Eng. Bus. Manag. 11, 1–10 (2019)
12. Erumi-Esin, R., Heeks, R.: E-business adoption and use among African women-owned SMEs: an analytical study in Nigeria. In: Proceedings of the Seventh International Conference on Information and Communication Technologies and Development, pp. 11–21. ACM (2015)
13. Frese, M., Gielnik, M.M.: The psychology of entrepreneurship. Annu. Rev. Org. Psychol. Org. Behav. 1(1), 413–438 (2014)

14. Garg, A.K., Choeu, T.: The adoption of electronic commerce by small and medium enterprises in Pretoria East. Electron. J. Inf. Syst. Dev. Countries **68**(1), 1–23 (2015)
15. Google: Toward Gender Equity Online (2019). http://services.google.com/fh/files/misc/toward_gender_equity_online.pdf. Accessed 10 Jan 2020
16. Gregorio, D.D., Kassicieh, S.K., Neto, R.D.G.: Drivers of e-business activity in developed and emerging markets. IEEE Trans. Eng. Manag. **52**(2), 155–166 (2005)
17. Hair, J.F., Black, W.C., Babin, B.J., Anderson, R.E.: Multivariate Data Analysis. Prentice Hall, Englewood Cliffs (2010)
18. Hilbert, M.: Digital gender divide or technologically empowered women in developing countries? A typical case of lies, damned lies, and statistics. Women's Stud. Int. Forum **34** (6), 479–489 (2011)
19. IAMAI: India Internet 2019 (2019). https://cms.iamai.in/Content/ResearchPapers/d3654bcc-002f-4fc7-ab39-e1fbeb00005d.pdf. Accessed 7 Jan 2020
20. Jelassi, T., Enders, A.: Strategies for e-Business: Creating Value Through Electronic and Mobile Commerce. Prentice Hall, London (2008)
21. Kartiwi, M., MacGregor, R.C.: Electronic commerce adoption barriers in small to medium-sized enterprises (SMEs) in developed and developing countries: a cross-Country comparison. J. Electron. Commer. Org. **5**(3), 35–51 (2008)
22. Kartiwi, M., Hussin, H., Suhaimi, M.A., Mohamed Jalaldeen, M.R., Amin, M.R.: Impact of external factors on determining e-commerce benefits among SMEs in Malaysia. J. Glob. Entrepreneurship Res. **8**(1), 1–12 (2018)
23. Keelery, S.: E-commerce in India (2019). https://www.statista.com/statistics/379167/e-commerce-share-of-retail-sales-in-india/. Accessed 7 Jan 2020
24. Kitching, B., Woldie, A.: Female entrepreneurs in transitional economies: a comparative study of businesswomen in Nigeria and China. In Proceedings of Hawaii International Conference on Business, Honolulu, Hawai (2004)
25. Klaiber, U., Hermanus, T., Mason, R.B.: E-business developments and skills requirements in the retail sector. Corp. Ownership Control **12**(4), 383–397 (2015)
26. KPMG Snapdeal Report: Impact of E-commerce on SMEs in India (2016). https://assets. kpmg/content/dam/kpmg/pdf/2015/10/Snapdeal-Report_-Impact-of-e-Commerce-on-Indian-SMEs.pdf. Accessed 7 Feb 2020
27. Lang, J.W.B., Fries, S.: A revised 10-item version of the achievement motives scale: psychometric properties in German-speaking samples. Eur. J. Psychol. Assess. **22**, 216–224 (2006)
28. Lee, S.W., Hye, J.S., Jeon, H.M.: Determinants of continuous intention on food delivery apps: extending UTAUT2 with information quality. Sustainability **11**(11), 1–15 (2019)
29. MacGregor, R.C., Vrazalic, L.: The role of gender in the perception of barriers to e-commerce adoption in SMEs: an Australian study. Commun. IBIMA **4**, 140–147 (2008)
30. Martinez, I., Nguyen, T.: Using Information and Communication Technology to Support Women's Entrepreneurship in Central and West Asia. ADB, Manila (2014)
31. Megadewandanu, S., Suyoto, Pranowo: Exploring mobile wallet adoption in Indonesia using UTAUT2 an approach from consumer perspective. In: Proceedings of 2nd International Conference on Science and Technology-Computer, ICST 2016, pp. 11–16 (2016)
32. Molla, A., Licker, P.S.: E-commerce adoption in developing countries: a model and instrument. Inf. Manag. **42**(6), 877–899 (2005)
33. Mueller, S.L., Thomas, A.S.: Culture and entrepreneurial potential: a nine country study of locus of control and innovativeness. J. Bus. Ventur. **16**(1), 51–75 (2001)
34. Nair, S.: The rising role of India's e-commerce women entrepreneurs (2015). https://yourstory.com/2015/07/ecommerce-women. Accessed 7 Feb 2020

35. Ndayizigamiye, P.A.: Unified approach towards e-commerce adoption by SMMES in South Africa. Int. J. Inf. Technol. Bus. Manag. **16**(1), 92–101 (2013)
36. Nejadirani, F., Behravesh, M., Rasouli, R.: Developing countries and electronic commerce the case of SMEs. World Appl. Sci. J. **15**(5), 756–764 (2011)
37. OECD: Bridging the Digital Gender Divide (2018). http://www.oecd.org/internet/bridging-the-digital-gender-divide.pdf. Accessed 7 Jan 2020
38. OECD: Empowering Women in the Digital Age: Where Do We Stand? (2018). www.oecd.org/going-digital/empowering-women-in-the-digital-age-brochure.pdf. Accessed 7 Jan 2020
39. OECD: The ABC of Gender Equality in Education: Aptitude, Behaviour, Confidence (2015). https://www.oecd.org/pisa/keyfindings/pisa-2012-results-gender-eng.pdf. Accessed 7 Jan 2020
40. Powers, J., Magnoni, B.: A Business To Call Her Own: Identifying, analyzing and overcoming constraints to women's small businesses in Latin America and the Caribbean. Multilateral Investment Fund, IDB, Washington, DC (2010)
41. Rahayu, R., Day, J.: Determinant factors of e-commerce adoption by SMEs in developing country: evidence from Indonesia. Procedia-Soc. Behav. Sci. **195**, 142–150 (2015)
42. Rufai, I.A.: The impact of communication technologies on the performance of SMEs in a developing economy: Nigeria as a case study. Electron. J. Inf. Syst. Dev. Countries **65**, 1–22 (2014)
43. Sabrina, A.: Role of e-Commerce in Women Empowerment (2014). https://www.academia.edu/6586964/Role_of_e_commerce_in_women_empowerment. Accessed 17 Jan 2020
44. Sachitanand, R.: How women are sidelined in India's e-commerce growth. The Economic Times (2019). https://economictimes.indiatimes.com/. Accessed 8 Mar 2020
45. Säntti, R.: Technology acceptance factors in ecommerce environment. Master's thesis, Aalto University, Espoo, Finland (2011)
46. Slade, E.L., Dwivedi, Y.K., Piercy, N.C., Williams, M.D.: Modeling consumers' adoption intentions of remote mobile payments in the United Kingdom: extending UTAUT with innovativeness, risk, and trust. Psychol. Mark. **32**, 860–873 (2015)
47. Saumell, R.P., Forgas-Coll, S., García, J.S., Robres, E.: User acceptance of mobile apps for restaurants: an expanded and extended UTAUT-2. Sustainability **11**(4), 1210–1234 (2019)
48. Sebora, T.C., Lee, S.M., Sukasame, N.: Critical success factors for e-commerce entrepreneurship: an empirical study of Thailand. Small Bus. Econ. **32**(3), 303–316 (2009)
49. Singh, M., Matsui, Y.: How long tail and trust affect online shopping behavior: an extension to UTAUT2 framework. Pac. Asia J. Assoc. Inf. Syst. **9**(4), 1–24 (2017)
50. Staniewski, M.W., Nowacki, R., Awruk, K.: Entrepreneurship and innovativeness of small and medium-sized construction enterprises. Int. Entrepreneurship Manag. J. **12**(3), 861–877 (2016)
51. Vagranti, S.: Skilling small and medium enterprises to conquer the world of online selling. The Economic Times (2019). https://economictimes.indiatimes.com/small-biz/marketing-branding/. Accessed 10 Mar 2020
52. Vagranti, S.: No place for women entrepreneurs? Can e-commerce reverse low share of women-led businesses in India Inc. The Financial Express (2020). https://www.financialexpress.com/industry/sme/cafe-sme/. Accessed 10 Mar 2020
53. Venkatesh, V., Davis, F.D.: A theoretical extension of the technology acceptance model: four longitudinal field studies. Manag. Sci. **46**(2), 186–204 (2000)
54. Venkatesh, V., Morris, M.G., Davis, D.F.: User acceptance of information technology: toward a unified view. MIS Q. **27**(3), 425–478 (2003)
55. Venkatesh, V., Thong, J.Y.L., Xu, X.: Consumer acceptance and use of information technology: extending the unified theory of acceptance and use of technology. MIS Q. **36**(1), 157–178 (2012)

56. Widodo, T., Setiadjie, P., Sary, F.P.: Analysis of the ecommerce use behavior on music products. In: Proceedings of 2017 International conference on Engineering Technology and Technopreneurship (ICE2T), pp. 1–6, IEEE (2017)
57. Yeh, C.H., Lee, G.G., Pai, J.C.: Using a technology-organization-environment framework to investigate the factors influencing e-business information technology capabilities. Inf. Dev. **31**(5), 435–450 (2015)

Author Index

Printed in the United States
by Baker & Taylor Publisher Services